Advancements in Distributed Computing and Internet Technologies:

Trends and Issues

Al-Sakib Khan Pathan
International Islamic University Malaysia, Malaysia

Mukaddim Pathan
Australian National University, Australia

Hae Young Lee
Electronics and Telecommunications Research Institute, South Korea

Senior Editorial Director:	Kristin Klinger
Director of Book Publications:	Julia Mosemann
Editorial Director:	Lindsay Johnston
Acquisitions Editor:	Erika Carter
Development Editor:	Mike Killian
Production Editor:	Sean Woznicki
Typesetters:	Christen Croley
Print Coordinator:	Jamie Snavely
Cover Design:	Nick Newcomer

Published in the United States of America by
Information Science Reference (an imprint of IGI Global)
701 E. Chocolate Avenue
Hershey PA 17033
Tel: 717-533-8845
Fax: 717-533-8661
E-mail: cust@igi-global.com
Web site: http://www.igi-global.com

Copyright © 2012 by IGI Global. All rights reserved. No part of this publication may be reproduced, stored or distributed in any form or by any means, electronic or mechanical, including photocopying, without written permission from the publisher. Product or company names used in this set are for identification purposes only. Inclusion of the names of the products or companies does not indicate a claim of ownership by IGI Global of the trademark or registered trademark.

Library of Congress Cataloging-in-Publication Data

Advancements in distributed computing and Internet technologies: trends and
issues / Al-Sakib Khan Pathan, Mukaddim Pathan and Hae Young Lee, editors.
       p. cm.
   Includes bibliographical references and index.
   Summary: "This book compiles recent research trends and practical issues in
the fields of distributed computing and Internet technologies, providing
advancements on emerging technologies that aim to support the effective design
and implementation of service-oriented networks, future Internet environments
and building management frameworks"-- Provided by publisher.
   ISBN 978-1-61350-110-8 (hardcover) -- ISBN 978-1-61350-111-5 (ebook) -- ISBN
978-1-61350-112-2 (print & perpetual access) 1. Electronic data processing--
Distributed processing. 2. Service-oriented architecture (Computer science)
3. Internet. I. Pathan, Al-Sakib Khan. II. Pathan, Mukaddim. III. Lee, Hae
Young, 1975-
   QA76.9.D5A3443 2012
   004.67'8--dc23
                         2011013015

British Cataloguing in Publication Data
A Cataloguing in Publication record for this book is available from the British Library.

All work contributed to this book is new, previously-unpublished material. The views expressed in this book are those of the authors, but not necessarily of the publisher.

Editorial Advisory Board

Ragib Hasan, *Johns Hopkins University, USA*
Riaz Ahmed Shaikh, *University of Quebec, Canada*
Victor Govindaswamy, *Texas A&M University, USA*
Christian Simone Vecchiola, *University of Melbourne, Australia*
George Pallis, *University of Cyprus, Cyprus*
Waleed W. Smari, *University of Dayton, USA*
Norihiko Yoshida, *Saitama University, Japan*
Tarem Ahmed, *BRAC University, Bangladesh*
Marcos Assuncao, *INRIA, France*

Table of Contents

Section 1
Internet-Based System Design

Section 2
Wireless Sensor Networks and Applications

Section 3
Next Generation Distributed Systems

Preface

The concept of the Internet has been a tremendous success by this time. Other than being a great source of fun and enjoyment, millions of people around the world rely on the Internet for various tasks related to their livelihoods. The overwhelming growth of the Internet and its users is now a reality, which has put new thoughts among the research community to devise new ideas for giving coverage to a huge number of people around the globe. Distributed computing is facilitating the growth and proper utilization of various internetworking technologies.

This book, entitled *"Advancements in Distributed Computing and Internet Technologies: Trends and Issues,"* compiles the recent research trends as well as common issues in the fields of distributed computing, and Internet technologies. The book aims to provide advancements on emerging technologies in these fields to support the effective design and implementation of distributed computing environments and Internet-based technologies. It is written mainly for graduate students, researchers, academics, and industry practitioners, working in the areas of Internet and distributed computing, who want to improve their understanding of the inter-related topics.

THE CONTENTS OF THIS BOOK

This book is comprised of 18 chapters, which are divided into three sections; Section I: Internet-Based Systems Design; Section II: Wireless Sensor Networks and Applications; and Section III: Next Generation Distributed Systems.

Section I of the book focuses on the issues and solutions related to the Internet-based technologies, such as VoIP, IPTV, and IP geolocation. In Chapter 1, Toral-Cruz *et al.* study the behavior of jitter and packet loss of VoIP traffic through the measurement and simulation-based measurements. As a result of this study, a detailed characterization of an accurate model of the QoS parameters is proposed. In Chapter 2, Yildirim and Kosar discuss the factors that affect the end-to-end application throughput in order to provide insight to the characteristics of the end-systems that cause the bottleneck for throughput. The authors then present a model to predict the optimal parallel stream number and show that the model gives very accurate results regardless of the type of the network. In Chapter 3, Zare and Rahbar review the challenges of IPTV in different contexts and present solutions and recommendations for each challenge. The methods to improve multicasting services in IPTV and the methods to improve QoS in DSL and wireless networks are also discussed in this chapter. In Chapter 4, Arif presents a systematic analysis of latency measurements between the Internet nodes and discusses the usages of latency for measurement-based Internet host geolocation. In Chapter 5, Bobelin gives a general overview of the process leading to topology reconstruction. The author also describes MINTCar that enables multiple sources, multiple destinations network tomography to measure available bandwidth. Chapter 6, by Kousaridas *et al.* presents an approach for service provisioning that incorporates cognitive features and promotes itself. In order to prove the viability and applicability of the proposed approach, the enhancement of the IP multimedia subsystem based on the proposed approach is also introduced.

Section II of the book deals with the WSN-related topics, including performance, energy saving, security, and localization issues. In Chapter 7, Lino *et al.* make a performance analysis of the IEEE 802.15.4 standard by using the author's routing protocol, the drain announcement-based routing scheme, in order to assess the effectiveness of the standard at supporting time-critical event monitoring applications. In Chapter 8, Lin *et al.* study multi-attribute data fusion in sensor networks and propose an energy equilibrium routing method, namely multi-attribute fusion tree, to balance and save energy. In Chapter 9, Zhang *et al.* address the security issues due to outliers and present an outlier detection and countermeasure scheme to identify outliers and consequently defend against their security attacks by using corresponding countermeasures. In Chapter 10, AbuHmed *et al.* describe the problem of public key authentication in context of sensor networks and propose a solution that uses collaboration among sensor nodes for public key authentication. In order to provide precise localization for indoor sensor networks, in Chapter 11, Han *et al.* improve the two-phase positioning algorithm and propose a reference node selection algorithm based on trilateration, which can provide real-time localization service. In Chapter 12, Guerrieri *et al.* define the specific requirements for applications of energy management in the building context and propose a framework for building management to support heterogeneous platforms, based on the requirements.

Section III of the book focuses on the future generation of distributed systems, such as pub/sub architecture, P2P, service oriented network (SON), Grid, and cloud systems. In Chapter 13, Pham and Tran provide a survey on the publish/subscribe techniques, which allows the nodes of a network to publish data and subscribe data interests efficiently, for P2P networks. In Chapter 14, Melchiors *et al.* propose a P2P-based architecture that supports polling network devices in a very flexible way, as required by real current Internet networks. In Chapter 15, Duan presents a new SON (Service-Oriented Networking) paradigm that applies the SOA (Service-Oriented Architecture) with network virtualization for integrating communication networks into distributed computing environments. In Chapter 16, He *et al.* discuss the major advances of the long-term evolution of a cellular network technology for mobile phone systems and its recent research efforts in improving its performance. The chapter is comprehensive, spanning from the physical layer, link layer, handover process, and even to security issues. In Chapter 17, Cardellini *et al.* analyze the problem of service level provisioning and the possible strategies that can be used to address the problem. The authors also propose an approach for the dynamic Quality of Service (QoS) provisioning of cloud-based applications, which takes into account that the provider has to fulfill the service level. In Chapter 18, Rahman *et al.* discuss the major challenges of designing and implementing decentralization in Grid and cloud systems. It also presents a survey of the existing decentralized distributed systems and technologies regarding how these systems have addressed the challenges.

WHAT NOT TO EXPECT FROM THE BOOK

This book is a not a tutorial that provides detailed introductory information on the basic topics in the fields of distributed computing and Internet technologies. Even though few chapters contain some introductory information, they should not be considered adequate for beginners. The readers need to have at least some basic knowledge about distributed computing and Internet technologies. Again, the book should not be considered as a detailed research report. Some chapters present specific problems and theirs solutions that might be helpful for graduate students, while some other chapters talk about elementary information that might be useful for general readers. As a whole, this could be a useful reference book that notes down the latest advancements in the related fields.

Al-Sakib Khan Pathan
International Islamic University Malaysia, Malaysia

Mukaddim Pathan
Australian National University, Australia

Hae Young Lee
Electronics and Telecommunications Research Institute, South Korea

Acknowledgment

We are very much thankful to the Almighty for giving us proper time and ability to accomplish this work. We thank the authors of different chapters from different locations of the globe (57 Authors from 16 different countries), who contributed in the making process of the book and responded to our requests whenever they were contacted. Without their amendments in the chapters and supply of the required items, it would have been impossible to get the work done. We are very thankful to the Editorial Assistant, Mr. Mike Killian, who helped us at each step of the publication process of the book. We also thank Kristin M. Klinger and Erika Carter for giving us this opportunity to work for the book. Also, special thanks to our family members whose continuous encouragements and support made the task easy for us, especially when we needed to work, even at late night.

Al-Sakib Khan Pathan
International Islamic University Malaysia, Malaysia

Mukaddim Pathan
Australian National University, Australia

Hae Young Lee
Electronics and Telecommunications Research Institute, South Korea

Section 1
Internet–Based System Design

Chapter 1
Analysis and Modeling of QoS Parameters in VoIP Traffic

Homero Toral-Cruz
University of Quintana Roo, Mexico

Deni Torres-Román
Center of Research and Advanced Studies, Mexico

Leopoldo Estrada-Vargas
Center of Research and Advanced Studies, Mexico

ABSTRACT

Several parameters influencing the voice quality on IP networks; in particular the one way delay (OWD), jitter and packet loss have an important impact on the quality of service (QoS) of voice over Internet protocol (VoIP). These parameters are intricately related to each other and can be used to configure other parameters to optimum values in order to afford good levels of QoS. Therefore, it is necessary to characterize the IP traffic nature, and implement adequate models of these QoS parameters in order to reliably evaluate the voice quality and design VoIP applications with reconfigurable parameters.

In this chapter, the jitter and packet loss behavior of VoIP traffic is analyzed by means of network measurements and simulations results. As result of these analyses, a detailed characterization and accurate modeling of these QoS parameters are provided.

Our studies have revealed that VoIP jitter can be modeled by self-similar processes, and through a decomposition based on Haar wavelet it is shown a possible reason of the presence of long range dependence (LRD) in VoIP jitter. On the other hand, we used a description of VoIP packet loss based on microscopic and macroscopic packet loss behaviors, where these behaviors can be modeled by 2-state and 4-state Markov chains, respectively. Besides, the distributions of the number of consecutive received and lost packets (namely gap and burst, respectively) are modeled from the transition probabilities of 2-state and 4-state Markov chains. Based on the above mentioned description, we presented a methodology for simulating packet loss and proposed a new model that allows to relate the Hurst parameter (H) with the packet loss rate (PLR). These models can be used by other researchers as input to problems related

DOI: 10.4018/978-1-61350-110-8.ch001

Copyright © 2012, IGI Global. Copying or distributing in print or electronic forms without written permission of IGI Global is prohibited.

to the design of VoIP applications, performance evaluation of IP networks, and the implementation of QoS mechanisms on convergent networks.

INTRODUCTION

In the last years, VoIP has became the most attractive and important application running over Internet, poised to replace the Public Switched Telephone Network (PSTN) in the future. There are several advantages in the case of voice transmission using VoIP technology: the reduced communication cost, the use of joined IP infrastructure, the use of multimedia applications, etc. However, the current Internet provides best-effort services and cannot guarantee the *QoS* of real-time multimedia applications, such as VoIP.

To achieve the satisfactory voice quality, the VoIP networks must be designed by using correct traffic models. In order to implement adequate traffic models it is necessary to study the traffic characteristics by means of network measurements of the main *QoS* parameters, such as One Way Delay (*OWD*), jitter and Packet Loss Rate (*PLR*).

Different models are used to describe different types of traffic. One of the models which have been widely applied in classical teletraffic modeling is the Poisson model. However, the IP networks traffic has different characteristics and the Poisson approximation will be acceptable only under particular conditions. Empirical studies showed that IP traffic exhibits self-similar and LRD (Lelan et al, 1994; Park & Willinger, 2000; Sheluhin et al, 2007), i.e., the autocorrelation function approaches zero very slowly in comparison with the exponential decay characterizing SRD traffic. Long range dependent traffic produces a wide range in traffic volume away from the average data rate. This great variation in the traffic volume leads to buffer overflow and network congestion that result in packet loss and jitter, which directly impact on the quality of VoIP applications.

Amongst the different quality parameters, packet loss is the main impairment which makes the VoIP perceptually most different from the PSTN. On Internet, packet losses occur due to temporary overloaded situations. Packet losses are bursty in nature and exhibit a finite temporal dependency (Yajnik et al, 1999) due to the multiplexing policy on the shared resources such as bandwidth and buffer through the transmission paths in the network. So, if packet *n* is lost then normally there is a higher probability that packet *n + 1* will also be lost. Consequently, there is a strong correlation between consecutive packet losses, resulting in a bursty packet loss behavior. The most generalized model to capture this temporal dependency is a finite Markov chain (ITU-T Recommendation G.1050, 2005). The objective of packet loss modeling is to characterize its probabilistic behavior, because an accurate model of the packet loss is required to design effective schemes for packet loss recovery.

Motivated by such concerns, we studied the jitter and packet loss behavior of VoIP traffic by means of networks performance measurements and simulations results. As result of these studies, it is shown that VoIP jitter can be modeled by self-similar processes with LRD or SRD (Toral et al, 2009). Through a decomposition based on Haar wavelet it is observed the components behavior of VoIP jitter as a function of packet loss and, by means of this decomposition it is shown a possible reason of the LRD presence in VoIP jitter.

Furthermore, we used a description of VoIP packet loss based on microscopic and macroscopic packet loss behaviors. The microscopic packet loss behavior can be represented by a *2*-state Markov chain in order to model the dependencies between packet losses. Correspondingly, the macroscopic packet loss behavior can be represented by *4*-state Markov chain. Here, substates represent phases of a given microscopic loss behavior. Ideally, an *n*-state model is required in order to capture the macroscopic packet loss behavior. However, for network planning, a trade off is desirable between very accurate modeling of data traces and a low number of model input parameters, in order to yield a model still usable for network planners with reasonable effort. On the other hand, the distributions of the number of consecutive received and lost packets, respectively named gap and burst, of a VoIP communication are modeled with discrete *2*-state and *4*-state Markov chains (Estrada et al, 2009-2).

Finally, we investigate the packet loss effects on the VoIP jitter, and present a methodology for simulating packet loss on VoIP jitter data traces. In order to generate the packet loss patterns, the *4*-state Markov model is used. We found a relationship between *H* and *PLR*; this relationship is based on voice traffic measurements and can be modeled by means of a power-law function with three fitted parameters (Toral et al, 2009). Simulations result shows the effectiveness of our models in terms of the Mean Squared Error (*MSE*).

The proposed models of the *QoS* parameters can be used by other researches as input to problems related to the design and evaluation of network and implementation of *QoS* mechanisms on VoIP applications.

QOS PARAMETERS AND IP TRAFFIC NATURE

This section introduces the basic concepts and mathematical background relating to *QoS* parameters and IP traffic nature.

QoS in VoIP

The QoS of VoIP applications depends on many parameters, including the OWD, jitter, packet loss rate, bandwidth, codec, voice data length, de-jitter buffer size, echo control, and the design of the network. In particular, OWD, jitter and packet loss have an important impact on voice quality.

The QoS is an important subject that takes a central place in the IP network technologies, it is a complex subject and its analysis involves mathematical disciplines such as: probability theory and stochastic processes. The QoS can be defined from three different points of view, QoS experienced by the end user, the QoS from the point of view of the application, and from the network.

From the end user's perspective, QoS is the end user's perception of the quality that he receives from the network provider for a service or a particular application, e.g., VoIP. The end user perception of the voice quality is determined by subjective/objective testing as a function of the QoS parameters such as: OWD, jitter, and *PLR*.

From the point of view of the application, the quality of service refers to the application's capabilities to reconfigure some parameters (voice data length, CODEC type, size of FEC redundancy, de-jitter buffer size) to values based on network conditions in order to meet good levels of voice quality.

From the network's perspective, the term QoS refers to the network's capabilities to provide the QoS perceived by the end user as defined above. A QoS mechanism has the capability to provide resource assurance and service differentiation in the IP network. Without a QoS mechanism, an IP network provides the best effort service. Two main QoS mechanisms are available for the IP networks: Integrated Services (IntServ), and the Differentiated Services (DiffServ).

In the best effort service, all packets are lumped into a single mass regardless of the source of the traffic. In IntServ, individual flows are distinguished end-to-end and the applications use the Resource reservation protocol (RSVP) to request and to reserve resources through a network. In DiffServ, individual flows are not identified end-to-end. Rather, they are aggregated into a smaller number of classes. Furthermore, these classes of traffic are given differential treatment per hop and there is no end-to-end treatment of these traffic classes.

Since, an IP network carries diverse traffic types with different performance requirements, one type of impairment can be important to a particular service or application and for other applications may not be as important and vice versa. Therefore, a QoS mechanism implemented in an IP network must consider various performance requirements and optimize the trade-off between the impairments.

The designing of VoIP applications with reconfigurable parameters and the implementation of QoS mechanisms in convergent networks, involves measurements, simulations, and modeling. In summary, this chapter is based on the studies of these topics.

QoS Parameters

One Way Delay

The delay experienced by a packet across a path consists of several components: propagation, processing, transmission, and queuing delays (Park, 2005). The Internet metric called one way delay (ITU-T Recommendation G.114, 2003) is the time needed for a packet to traverse the network from a source to a destination host. It is described analytically by Equation (1):

$$D^K\left(L\right)_{OWD} = \delta + \sigma + \sum_{h=1}^{s}\left(\frac{L}{C_h} + X_h^K\left(t\right)\right) \quad (1)$$

where $D^K\left(L\right)_{OWD}$ is the *OWD* of a packet K of size L, δ represents the propagation delay, σ the processing delay, s the number of hops, L/C_h the transmission delay and $X_h^K\left(t\right)$ the queuing delay of a packet K of size L at hop h $\left(h = 1,...,s\right)$ with capacity C_h. The *OWD* variation between two successive packets, K and $K-1$ is called "*OWD* jitter" and is given by the Equation (2):

$$J^K\left(L\right) = D^K\left(L\right)_{OWD} - D^{K-1}\left(L\right)_{OWD} \quad (2)$$

Jitter

When voice packets are transmitted from source to destination over IP networks, packets may experience variable delay, called delay jitter. The packet *IAT* on the receiver side is not constant even if the packet Inter-departure Time (*IDT*) on the sender side is constant. As a result, packets arrive at the destination with varying delays (between packets) referred to as jitter. We measure and calculate the difference between arrival times of successive voice packets that arrive on the receiver side, according to RFC 3550 (Schulzrinne et al, 2003).

Let S_K denote the RTP timestamp for the packet K of size L, and R_K the arrival time in RTP timestamp units for packet K of size L. Then for two packets K and $K-1$, $J^K\left(L\right)$ may be expressed as:

$$J^K\left(L\right) = (R_K - S_K) - (R_{K-1} - S_{K-1}) \quad (3)$$

$$IAT\left(K, K-1\right) = J^K\left(L\right) + IDT\left(K, K-1\right) \quad (4)$$

where $IDT\left(K, K-1\right) = (S_K - S_{K-1})$ is the *IDT* (in our experiments, *IDT*= {10ms, 20ms, 40ms, and 60ms}) and $IAT\left(K, K-1\right) = (R_K - R_{K-1})$ is the *IAT* for the packets K and $K-1$. In the current context, $IAT\left(K, K-1\right)$ is referred to as jitter. So, the Equation (4) describes the VoIP jitter between two successive packets, i.e., packets K and $K-1$.

Packet Loss

There are two main transport protocols used on IP networks, UDP and TCP. While UDP protocol does not allow any recovery of transmission errors, TCP include an error recovery process. However, the voice transmission over TCP connections is not very realistic. This is due to the requirement for real-time operations in most voice related applications. As a result, the choice is limited to the use of UDP which involves packet loss problems.

Amongst the different quality elements, packet loss is the main impairment which makes the VoIP perceptually most different from the public switched telephone network. Packet loss can occur in the network or at the receiver side, for example, due to excessive network delay in case of network congestion.

Owing to the dynamic, time varying behavior of packet networks, packet loss can show a variety of distributions. The packet loss distribution most often studied in speech quality tests is random or Bernoulli-like packet loss. Uniform random loss here means independent loss, implying that the loss of a particular packet is independent of whether or not previous packets were lost. However, uniform random loss does not represent the loss distributions typically encountered in real networks. For example, losses are often related to periods of network congestion. Hence, losses may extend over several packets, showing a dependency between individual loss events. In this work, dependent packet loss is often referred to as bursty. The packet loss is bursty in nature and exhibits temporal dependency (Yajnik et al, 1999). So, if packet n is lost then normally there is a higher probability that packet $n + 1$ will also be lost. Consequently, there is a strong correlation between consecutive packet losses, resulting in a bursty packet loss behavior. A generalized model to capture temporal dependency is a finite Markov chain (ITU-T Recommendation G.1050, 2005). In this work, the *2*-state and *4*-state Markov chains are used to simulate packet loss patterns.

In the *2*-state Markov chain, one of the states (S_1) represents a packet loss and the other state (S_2) represents the case where packets are correctly transmitted or received. The transition probabilities in this model, are represented by p_{21} and p_{12}. In other words, p_{21} is the probability of

going from S_2 to S_1, and p_{12} is the probability of going from S_1 to S_2. Different values of p_{21} and p_{12} define different packet loss conditions that can occur on the Internet.

The steady-state probability of the chain to be in the state S_1, namely the *PLR*, is given by Equation (5) (Lee et al, 2005):

$$S_1 = \frac{P_{21}}{P_{21} + P_{12}} \tag{5}$$

and clearly $S_2 = 1 - S_1$.

The distributions of the number of consecutive received or lost packets are called gap ($f_g(k)$) and burst ($f_b(k)$) respectively, and can be expressed in terms of p_{21} and p_{12}. The probability that the transition from S_2 to S_1 and S_1 to S_2 occurs after k steps can be expressed by Equations (6) and (7):

$$f_b(k) = P_{12}(1 - P_{12})^{k-1} \tag{6}$$

$$f_b(k) = P_{12}(1 - P_{12})^{k-1} \tag{7}$$

According to Equation (7), the number of steps k necessary to transit from S_1 to S_2, that is, the number of consecutively lost packets is a geometrically distributed random variable. This geometric distribution of consecutive loss events makes the *2*-state Markov chain (and higher order Markov chains) applicable to describing loss events observed in the Internet.

$$\bar{b} = E\{f_b(k)\} = \frac{1}{P_{12}} \tag{8}$$

$$\bar{g} = E\{f_g(k)\} = \frac{1}{P_{21}} \tag{9}$$

The average number of consecutively lost and received packets can be calculated by $\bar{b}$ and $\bar{g}$, respectively, as shown in Equations (8) and (9).

On the other hand, the collected data traces in real IP networks can be modeled accurately with a higher number of states, i.e., n-state Markov chains. However, for network planning, a trade off is desirable between very accurate modeling of data traces and a low number of model input parameters, in order to yield a model still usable for network planners with reasonable effort. Therefore, we used a simplification of an n-state chain, i.e., the *4*-state Markov chain.

Figure 1 shows the state diagram of this *4*-state Markov chain. In this model, a 'good' and a 'bad' state are distinguished, which represent periods of lower and higher packet loss, respectively. Both for the 'bad' and the 'good' state, an individual *2*-state Markov chain represents the dependency between consecutively lost or found packets. The two *2*-state chains can be described by four independent transition probabilities (two each one). Two further probabilities characterize the transitions between the two *2*-state chains, leading to a total of six independent parameters for this particular *4*-state Markov chain.

In the *4*-state Markov chain, states S_1 and S_3 represent packets lost, S_2 and S_4 packets found and six parameters (p_{21}, p_{12}, p_{43}, p_{34}, p_{23}, $p_{32} \in (0,1)$) are necessary to define all the transition probabilities. The four steady-state probabilities of this chain are:

$$S_1 = \frac{1}{1 + \dfrac{P_{12}}{P_{21}} + \dfrac{P_{12}P_{23}}{P_{21}P_{32}} + \dfrac{P_{12}P_{23}P_{34}}{P_{21}P_{32}P_{43}}} \tag{10}$$

$$S_2 = \frac{1}{1 + \dfrac{P_{21}}{P_{12}} + \dfrac{P_{23}}{P_{32}} + \dfrac{P_{23}P_{34}}{P_{32}P_{43}}} \tag{11}$$

$$S_3 = \frac{1}{1 + \dfrac{P_{34}}{P_{43}} + \dfrac{P_{32}}{P_{23}} + \dfrac{P_{21}P_{32}}{P_{12}P_{23}}} \tag{12}$$

$$S_4 = \frac{1}{1 + \dfrac{P_{43}}{P_{34}} + \dfrac{P_{32}P_{43}}{P_{23}P_{34}} + \dfrac{P_{21}P_{32}P_{43}}{P_{12}P_{23}P_{34}}} \tag{13}$$

The probability of the chain to be either in S_1 or in S_3, which corresponds to *PLR*, is then:

$$r = S_1 + S_3 \tag{14}$$

The average burst length ($\bar{b}$) is calculated as the quotient of the probability of loss and the probability of transition from a lossless state to a loss state, that is:

$$\bar{b} = \frac{S_1 + S_3}{S_2 \left(P_{21} + P_{23} \right) + S_4 \left(P_{43} \right)} \tag{15}$$

Similarly, the average gap length is:

$$\bar{g} = \frac{S_2 + S_4}{S_1 \left(P_{12} \right) + S_3 \left(P_{34} + P_{32} \right)} \tag{16}$$

The distribution of the burst length is given by:

$$f_b \left(k \right) = C_1 \left(1 \right) Q_1 \left(k \right) + C_3 \left(1 \right) Q_3 \left(k \right) \tag{17}$$

where $C_1 \left(1 \right) = \left(S_2 p_{21} \right) / \left[S_2 \left(P_{21} + P_{23} \right) + S_4 P_{43} \right]$, $C_3 \left(1 \right) = \left(S_2 p_{23} + S_4 p_{43} \right) / \left[S_2 \left(P_{21} + P_{23} \right) + S_4 P_{43} \right]$, $Q_1 \left(k \right) = p_{12} \left(1 - p_{12} \right)^{k-1}$ and $Q_3 \left(k \right) = \left(p_{34} + p_{32} \right) \left(1 - p_{34} - p_{32} \right)^{k-1}$.

As expressed by Equation (17), $f_b \left(k \right)$ is the sum of two geometric series with respective rates $1 - p_{12}$ and $1 - p_{34} - p_{32}$; this implies that $f_b \left(k \right)$

Figure 1. 4-state Markov chain

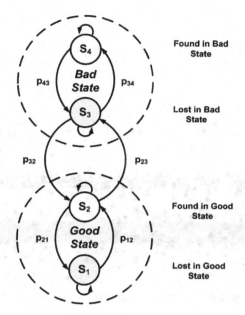

is a decreasing function of k, i.e., burst of greater length have lower probabilities than shorter ones.

Similarly, the gap length distribution is given by:

$$f_g(k) = C_2(1)Q_2(k) + C_4(1)Q_4(k) \qquad (18)$$

where:

$$C_2(1) = (S_1 p_{12} + S_3 p_{32})/[S_1 p_{12} + S_3(p_{32} + p_{34})],$$
$$C_4(1) = (S_3 p_{34})/[S_1 p_{12} + S_3(p_{32} + p_{34})],$$
$$Q_2(k) = (p_{21} + p_{23})(1 - p_{21} - p_{23})^{k-1} \text{ and }$$
$$Q_4(k) = p_{43}(1 - p_{43})^{k-1}$$

Packet Loss Effects on the VoIP Jitter

In this work, we used the voice data lengths of 10ms, 20ms, 40ms, and 60ms, and the successive voice packets are transmitted at a constant rate, i.e., 1 packet/10ms, 1 packet/20ms, 1 packet/40ms, and 1 packet/60ms, respectively. However, when voice packets are transported over IP networks, they may experience delay variations and packet loss.

On the other hand, these impairments are intricately related to each other. These relationships can be used to reveal the overall effects of these impairments and to implement accurate models in order to evaluate the QoS of VoIP applications.

Based on the above concerns, we investigated the packet loss effects on the VoIP jitter, and presented an analytical expression that describes the relationship between these two QoS parameters.

Let

$$IAT(K, K-1) = J^K(L) + IDT(K, K-1)$$

denote the *jitter* for two packets K and $K-1$, then:

If the packet $K-1$ is lost,

$$IAT(K, K-2) = J^K(L) + (2)IDT \qquad (19)$$

Therefore, if n consecutive packets are lost,

Figure 2. Packet loss effects on VoIP jitter

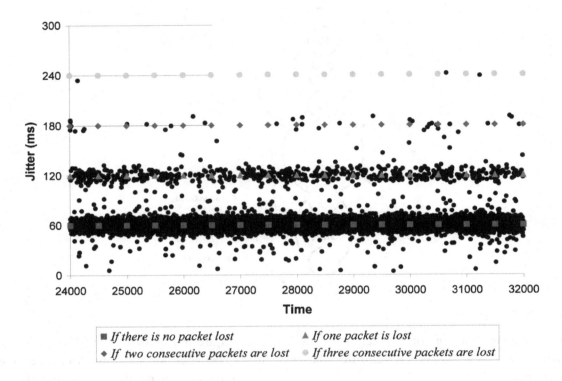

This behavior is illustrated in Figure 2, where a packet length of 60 ms for voice data is used. In this figure can be observed that: (a) if there is not packet lost, the mean values of the jitter are around of 60 ms, i.e. $IAT(K, K-1) = J^K(L) + 60$; (b) if one packet is lost, the mean values of the jitter are around of 120 ms, i.e. $IAT(K, K-2) = J^K(L) + 120$; (c) if two consecutive packets are lost, the mean values of the jitter are around of 180 ms, i.e. $IAT(K, K-3) = J^K(L) + 180$; and (d) if three consecutive packets are lost, the mean values of the jitter are around of 240 ms, i.e. $IAT(K, K-3) = J^K(L) + 240$.

$$IAT(K, K-n-1) = J^K(L) + (n+1)(IDT) \tag{20}$$

Therefore, the Equation (20) describes the packet loss effects on the VoIP jitter. The relationship expressed by this equation can be used for simulating packet loss on VoIP jitter data traces.

IP Traffic Nature

Many investigations of traffic measurements suggest that the IP traffic is self-similar and long range dependent (Leland et al, 1994; Park & Willinger, 2000; Sheluhin et al, 2007). The fact that IP traffic exhibits self-similarity characteristics means that it is bursty at a wide range of time scales. Practically speaking, the implication of this behavior for VoIP and other interactive multimedia applications is that receiver playout buffers may not be large enough to mask the jitter of LRD arrival processes.

Self-Similar Processes

Traffic processes are said to be self-similar if certain properties are preserved with respect to scaling in space or time. An attractive property of the self-similar processes for modeling a time series of IP traffic is the degree of self-similarity, which is expressed with a single parameter called Hurst parameter. This parameter expresses the speed of decay of the autocorrelation function of the time series.

In order to estimate this parameter there are several methods, for details see (Sheluhin et al, 2007). In this section, a brief overview of self-similar processes is given, based on (Sheluhin et al, 2007; Park & Willinger, 2000; Leland et al, 1994).

- *Continuous Self-similarity:* A real-valued continuous time series $\{X(t), t \in \Re\}$ is self-similar with the exponent $0 < H < 1$ if, for any $a > 0$ finite-dimensional distributions for $\{X(at), t \in \Re\}$ are identical to finite-dimensional distributions $\{a^H X(t), t \in \Re\}$; i.e.,

$$\{X(at), t \in \Re\} \overset{d}{=} \{a^H X(t), t \in \Re\} \quad ,$$

where $\overset{d}{=}$ denotes equality in distribution.

- *Discrete Self-similarity:* Let $X_t = (X_t; t \in N)$ denote a discrete time series with mean μ_X, variance σ_X^2, autocorrelation function $r(k)$ and Auto-covariance function (ACV) $\gamma(k)$, $k \geq 0$; where X_t can be interpreted as the VoIP jitter.

When considering discrete time series, the definition of self-similarity is given in terms of the aggregated processes, as following:

$$X_k^{(m)} = \left(X_k^{(m)}; k \in N \right) \tag{21}$$

where m represents the aggregation level and $X_k^{(m)}$ is obtained by averaging the original series X_t over non-overlapping blocks of size m, and each term $X_k^{(m)}$ is given by:

$$X_k^{(m)} = \frac{1}{m} \sum_{i=(k-1)m+1}^{km} X_i; \quad k = 1, 2, 3, \dots \tag{22}$$

Then it is said that X_t is self-similar $(H-ss)$ with self-similarity parameter $(0 < H < 1)$ if:

$$X_k^{(m)} \overset{d}{=} m^{H-1} X_t \tag{23}$$

- *Second-order Discrete Self-similarity:* X_t is called exactly second order self-similar with Hurst parameter H if the variance and ACV of the aggregated time series are defined by Equations (24) and (25), respectively:

$$\text{var}\left(X_k^{(m)}\right) = \sigma_X^2 \cdot m^{2H-2} \tag{24}$$

$$\gamma_X^m(k) = \frac{\sigma_X^2}{2}\left((k+1)^{2H} - 2k^{2H} + (k-1)^{2H}\right) \tag{25}$$

Second-order self-similarity has been a dominant framework for modeling IP traffic. So far role of second-order self-similarity has been discussed but not much has been mentioned about the role of H and limiting values.

Generally speaking, a self-similar time series with long-range dependence have a Hurst parameter $0.5 < H < 1$ and their ACV decays slowly, on the other hand, time series with short-range dependence have a Hurst parameter $0 < H < 0.5$ and their ACV decays quickly.

Haar Wavelet-Based Decomposition and Hurst Index Estimation

Let $X_t = \left(X_t; t \in \mathrm{N} \right)$ denote a discrete time series with finite variance σ_X^2. This time series can be represented by $X_t = \sum_i C_{X,t}^i$ and decomposed into a set of time series $C_{X,t}^i$ (Estrada et al, 2009-1), where:

$$C_{X,t}^i = X_t^{(2^{i-1}E)} - X_t^{(2^i E)} \qquad (26)$$

and $X_t^{(2^i E)}$ is the time series X_t after two operations, which are:

1. Aggregation at level 2^i, as defined by Equations (21) and (22). i.e., $m = 2^i$.
2. Expansion of level 2^i, which consists in 'repeat' each element of a time series 2^i times.

These zero mean components $C_{X,t}^i$ have an important property, if X_t is exactly self-similar, then the variance of the components comply:

$$\mathrm{var}(C_{X,t}^i) = 2^{2H-2} \cdot \mathrm{var}(C_{X,t}^{i-1}) \qquad (27)$$

The plot $\log_2[\mathrm{var}(C_{X,t}^i)]$ vs. i is equivalent to the wavelet-based diagram proposed in (Veitch et al, 1999), the Logscale Diagram (LD-Diagram); i.e., $\mathrm{var}(C_{X,t}^i) = \dfrac{E \mid d_X(j,\cdot) \mid^2}{2^j}$ when using the Haar family of wavelet basis functions $\psi_{j,k}(t) = 2^{-j/2} \psi_0(2^{-j} t - k)$ (Wickerhauser, 1994) where:

$$\psi_0(t) = \begin{cases} +1 & 0 \le t < \dfrac{1}{2} \\ -1 & \dfrac{1}{2} \le t < 1 \\ 0 & otherwise \end{cases} \qquad (28)$$

For a finite-length time series with "L" octaves, the number of octave (j) of the LD-Diagram is related to index i of Equation (26).

The LD-Diagram of an exactly self-similar time series is a straight line. Then a linear regression can be applied in order to estimate the Hurst index.

VOIP TRAFFIC MEASUREMENTS

In order to analysis the VoIP traffic characteristics and implement adequate traffic models, we monitored the QoS parameters by means of network measurements.

In this work, VoIP traffic was generated by establishing test calls with the VoIP application "Alliance foreign exchange station" (FXS) (Leyva, 2004).

The capture of VoIP traffic was accomplished by using Wireshark (Combs et al, 2010) to obtain a set of data traces. The subject of these measurements is to gather traffic patterns of voice packets such as jitter and packet loss for post-processing analysis.

The measurement scenario consists of two different local area networks (with different Internet service provider - ISP) interconnected by the Internet backbone:

1. LAN "A" - Local Cable ISP network (Link Speed-3MB).
2. LAN "B" - CINVESTAV GDL network (Link Speed-2MB).

The measurement scenario is based on a typical H.323 architecture (Sulkin, 2002; ITU-T Recommendation H.323, 2007), composed by two zones interconnected via Internet, as shown

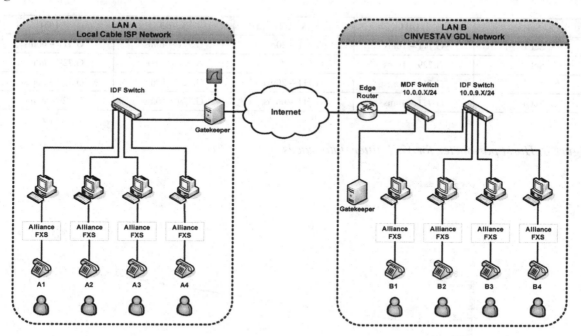

Figure 3. Measurement scenario

in Figure 3. Each zone consists of a single H.323 GK (Willamowius et al, 2009) which acts as the administrator of the zone, and a set of H.323 terminal endpoints (TEs), interconnected via a LAN. The zone "A" is composed by the endpoints A1, A2, A3, A4, and is administrated by the GK "A". In this zone, the network protocol analyzer Wireshark was installed for collecting the data traces. The zone "B" is composed of the endpoints B1, B2, B3, B4 and the GK "B".

In order to establish the test calls between any endpoints, each endpoint has installed an Alliance FXS peripheral component interconnect (PCI) card and a conventional cord phone. The parameters configuration employed in the test calls are shown in Table I.

The configuration shown in Table 1 and Figure 3, was selected because it is based on: a) the two coding schemes more used in speech processing (G.711 and G.729), b) different voice data lengths used for sending voice packets over IP networks (10ms, 20ms, 40ms and 60ms) and c) simultane-

ous test calls with different configuration (A1/B1, A2/B2, A3/B3 and A4/B4).

The measurements corresponding to the data sets described in Table I were collected in the following way:

1. The measurement periods were 60 minutes for each test call (call duration time).
2. For each measurement period (an hour), four jitter and packet loss data traces were obtained.
3. The four data sets contain 16.56 millions of RTP packets corresponding to 96 jitter and 96 packet loss data traces, measures in typical working hours.
4. Set 1: Friday 09/07/2007 from 10:00 hours until 16:00 hours.
5. Set 2: Monday 09/10/2007 from 10:00 hours until 16:00 hours.
6. Set 3: Tuesday 09/11/2007 from 10:00 hours until 16:00 hours.
7. Set 4: Wednesday 09/12/2007 from 10:00 hours until 16:00 hours.

Table 1. Parameters configurations employed in the test calls

Set	A1/B1	A2/B2	A3/B3	A4/B4
Set 1	G.711 – 10ms	G.711 – 20ms	G.711 – 40ms	G.711 – 60ms
Set 2	G.729 – 10ms	G.729 – 20ms	G.729 – 40ms	G.729 – 60ms
Set 3	G.711 – 10ms	G.711 – 20ms	G.729 – 10ms	G.729 – 20ms
Set 4	G.711 – 40ms	G.711 – 60ms	G.729 – 40ms	G.729 – 60ms

Figure 4. Hurst parameter for VoIP jitter data traces

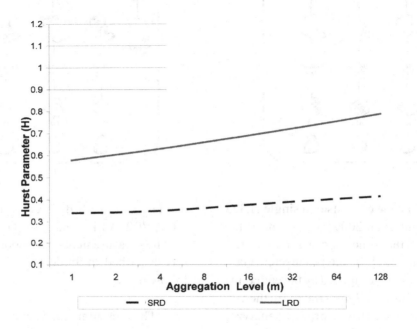

Our study is based on various data sets that provide valuable information into the behavior of test calls on IP networks. We selected these four data sets, because are representative of packet loss diversity present in all collected data traces.

ANALYSIS AND MODELING OF *QOS* PARAMETERS

This section presents an analysis of the jitter and packet loss behavior of VoIP traffic. As result of this analysis, it is provided a detailed characterization and accurate modeling of these QoS parameters.

Jitter Modeling

Jitter Modeling by Self-similar Processes

In this section it is realized a self-similar analysis on the jitter VoIP traffic. Several statistical methods are used for the estimation of the degree of self-similarity from the jitter data traces. The Hurst parameter was estimated at seven aggregation levels, ($m = \{2, 4, 8, 16, 32, 64, 128\}$) by means of six methods implemented in a tool called SelQoS (Ramírez & Torres, 2005) and a wavelet based method (Estrada et al, 2009-1). They are: Rescaled Adjusted Range (R/S), Absolute Moment (AM),

Figure 5. Auto-covariance function for VoIP jitter data traces: (a) SRD, and (b) LRD

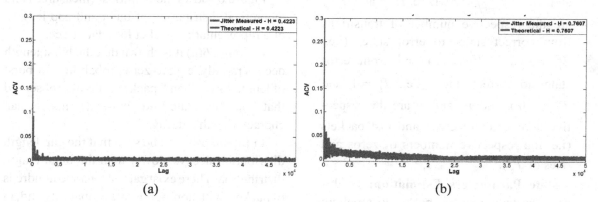

(a)   (b)

Variance Method (VAR), Modified Allan Variance (MAVAR), Periodogram (PER), Local Whittle (WHI), and a method based on Haar wavelet (HWAV). The result of this analysis it is shown in Figure 4, here the Hurst parameter of a representative set of jitter data traces were calculated for different aggregation levels (m).

In Figure 4, it is observed the phenomenon of scale invariance at different time scales when the H parameter took values of $0.35 < H < 0.41$, and $0.58 < H < 0.8$, these results indicate that the analyzed VoIP jitter data traces have self-similar characteristics with SRD or LRD, respectively. In this figure, each point of each curve represents the Hurst parameter of aggregation level m for a particular jitter data trace.

In order to complement the above discussion, a study of the ACV behavior of representatives jitter data traces is presented.

Figure 5 (a) shows the comparison between the ACV of a measured data trace with $H = 0.4223$ and the theoretical $\gamma(k)$ function defined by Equation (15). It can be observed that the ACV of the measured data trace behaves similarly to the ideal model and decay quickly to zero. This result confirms the presence of short range dependence or memoryless property in VoIP jitter data traces. In addition, it is compared the ACV

of a measured data trace with $H = 0.7607$ and the theoretical $\gamma(k)$ function, as shown in Figure 5 (b). In this figure it is observed a similar behavior between these ACV and a very slow decaying from them. This behavior indicates the presence of a high degree of long range dependence or long memory property.

These results show that VoIP jitter can be modeled by self-similar processes with short and long range dependence.

Packet Loss Modeling

Modeling Packet Loss Patterns

Let us define the packet loss patterns as a follows:

$$P_k = \begin{cases} 0 & \textit{if packet } k \textit{ is received} \\ 1 & \textit{if packet } k \textit{ is lost} \end{cases}$$

From the packet loss patterns, the probabilities of transitions were estimated using the following algorithms:

- **2-state Parameters Estimation:** The estimation of p_{12} and p_{21} are: $p_{12} = t_{c \to e}/n_1$

and $p_{21} = t_{e \to c} / n_0$, where $t_{c \to e}$ and $t_{e \to c}$ are the respective number of transitions from correct states to error states (i.e., $P_k = 0$ and $P_{k+1} = 1$) and from error states to correct states (i.e., $P_k = 1$ and $P_{k+1} = 0$), and n_0 and n_1 are the respective number of received and lost packets (i.e. the respective numbers of zeros and ones of P_k).

- **4-state Parameters Estimation:** In this case the values of the packet loss pattern P_k are divided into regions of two types: the first with lower packet loss (whose first and last values are zeros) and the second with higher packet loss (whose first and last values are ones) than certain threshold, e.g. 1%. Then, from the first region, p_{12} and p_{21} are estimated as explained in "2-state Parameters Estimation". Similarly, p_{43} and p_{34} are estimated from the second region. Finally, let the $t_{1st \to 2nd}$ be the number of transitions from the first region to the second; $t_{2nd \to 1st}$, the number of transitions from the second region to the first; n_{1st}, the number of received packets in the first region (zeros) and n_{2dn}, the number of lost packets in the second region (ones), then $p_{23} = t_{1st \to 2nd} / n_{1st}$ and $p_{32} = t_{2nd \to 1st} / n_{2nd}$.

From the packet loss patterns P_k (packet loss data traces) collected in the measurements, the respective gap and burst length distributions ($f_g(k)$ and $f_b(k)$) were obtained.

The probabilities of transitions were estimated from the sequence P_k. From this probabilities, the gap and burst length distributions of both 2-state and 4-state models, defined by Equations (6) and (7) for 2-state model and by Equations (17) and (18) for the 4-state model were obtained.

Figure 6 shows the empirical (measured) and theoretical distribution of burst and gap lengths of a representative packet loss data trace.

In Figure 6(a) it is shown that the burst length decays rapidly, e.g., to zero probability for burst of length lower than 5 packets. It is also observed that both two-state and four-state models can characterize this decay.

In Figure 6(b) can be seen that the gap length distribution decays slower than the burst length distribution. There exist gaps of tens and hundreds of packets with non-negligible probability and, in this case, the less flexible one-parameter formula of the two-state model cannot fit the measured distribution, in contrast with the four-state model, which fits it adequately.

Packet Loss Model Framework

In this work, it is used a description of VoIP packet loss based on microscopic and macroscopic packet loss behaviors (Raake, 2006).

In our studies, we analyzed packet loss patterns or packet loss data traces with different packet loss levels over particular periods or "time windows". Each "time window" can be represented by a microscopic packet loss period and all overall periods are represented by a macroscopic packet loss period. In order to simplify this packet loss description, the microscopic packet loss periods can be classified in two regions, one for lower and one for higher packet loss. So, the 2-state and 4-state Markov chains can be used for modeling the microscopic and macroscopic packet loss periods, respectively. Figure 7 shows some packet loss patterns extracted from VoIP test calls.

In Figure 7(a) we can see that packet loss is random, i.e., the packet loss pattern is represented by a microscopic packet loss period. On the other hand, in Figure 7(b) the packet loss is bursty, i.e., the packet loss pattern is represented by a concatenation of microscopic packet loss periods. In this figures, the microscopic packet loss periods with lower packet loss rate are de-

Figure 6. Empirical and theoretical distributions of: (a) burst length, and (b) gap length

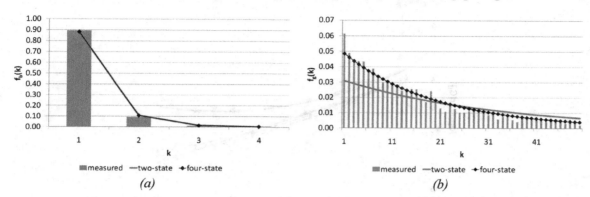

(a)   *(b)*

Figure 7. Packet loss patterns from VoIP test calls: (a) Random PLR, and (b) Bursty PLR

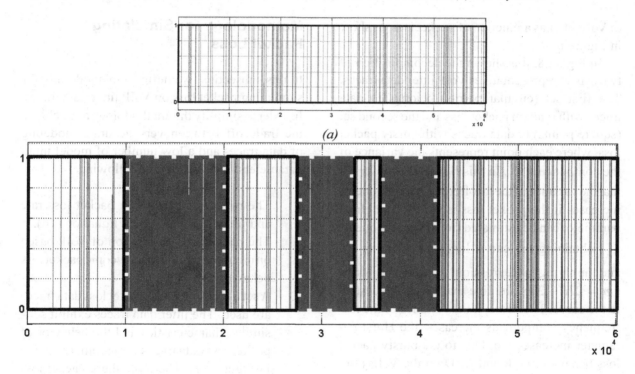

(a)

limited by the solid square, while the microscopic packet loss periods with higher packet loss rate are delimited by the dotted square.

Based on this packet loss behavior (random or bursty), we accomplished a detailed analysis of packet loss effects on the VoIP jitter. Furthermore, in this analysis we are motivated by two

factors arising from our own work: (a) the VoIP jitter can be modeled by self-similar processes with SRD or LRD, and (b) the VoIP jitter can be decomposed into a set of components C_i. Therefore, through a decomposition based on Haar wavelet it is observed the components behavior

Figure 8. Components behavior of jitter data traces as a function of packet loss

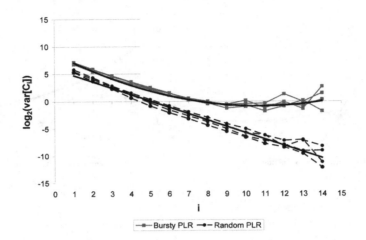

of VoIP jitter as a function of packet loss, as show in Figure 8.

In Figure 8, it is shown the decomposition of two sets of representatives VoIP jitter data traces. The first set (circular points) belongs to data traces with random packet loss and the second set (square points) to data traces with bursty packet loss, where each point represents the variance of the components C_i. In this figure, it is observed that the variance of the low frequency components increases if the packet loss is bursty. The Hurst parameter can be estimated from the components C_i, obtaining the curve $\log_2\left(Var\left[C_i\right]\right)$ vs. i and applying a regression to find the slope ($m = 2H - 2$)of the line that gives the best fit to the curve. Therefore, if the variance of the low frequency components increases, the Hurst parameter increases too. Due to the bursty packet loss behavior, we found LRD on the VoIP jitter data traces. So, by means of this decomposition it is shown a possible reason of the LRD presence in VoIP jitter.

Methodology for Simulating Packet Loss

In this subsection, we define a methodology for simulating packet loss on VoIP jitter data traces. In order to simplify this methodology and achieve the trade off between very accurate modeling of data traces and a low number of model input parameters, we consider the following:

1. The relationship between packet loss rate and jitter, summarized by Equation (20).
2. The packet loss description of VoIP based on microscopic and macroscopic packet loss behaviors.
3. A set of real jitter and packet loss data traces are used. The jitter data traces exhibit self-similar characteristics and the behavior of packet loss data traces is random, as shown in Figure 7(a). Therefore these packet loss patterns are represented for only one microscopic packet loss period with low level of *PLR*.
4. In order to incorporate *"n"* microscopic packet loss periods with high level of *PLR*, as it is shown in Figure 7(b), we generated packet loss patterns by means of the *4*-state Markov chain.

Table 2. Algorithm for simulating packet loss: (a) generating packet loss pattern, and (b) applying packet loss pattern

(a)	(b)

FOR $n = 1$ to $l - 1$
 	
 $P[n] = 0$ END FOR
 FOR $n = l$ to u
 IF (packet was lost)
 	
 $P[n] = 1$ ELSE
 	
 $P[n] = 0$ END IF
 END FOR
 FOR $n = u + 1$ to N
 	
 $P[n] = 0$ END FOR
	FOR $n = 2$ to N
	 IF ($P[n] = 1$)
	
	 $X[n] = X[n] + X[n-1]$ END IF
	 END FOR
	
	 $i = 1$ FOR $n = 2$ to N
	 IF ($P[n] \neq 1$) $\hat{X}[i] = X[n-1]$
	
	 $i = i + 1$ END IF
	 END FOR

5. In order to incorporate representative microscopic packet loss periods, the transition probabilities used in the *4*-state Markov chain, were estimated from real packet loss data traces as explained in "*4*-state **Parameters Estimation**".

Let $X = \left\{ X_t : t = 1,...,N \right\}$ be a VoIP jitter data trace with length N, self-similar (H parameter $0 < H_0 < 0.5$), and with a packet loss rate PLR_0.

The relationship between jitter and packet loss from (20) is used to apply "T" different packet loss patterns to X_t by means of the algorithm shown in Table 2.

By means of the above algorithm the new time series $\hat{X}^\tau$ are obtained, for $\tau = 0,1,2,...T-1$. For each $\hat{X}^\tau$ the PLR and H parameter were calculated, and the function $f\left(PLR_\tau, H_\tau \right)$ was generated.

Proposed Model

From our simulations, we found that the relationship between H parameter and the PLR can be modeled by a power-law function, characterized by three fitted parameters, as following:

$$H_M = \hat{H}_0 + \hat{a}\left(PLR \right)^{\hat{b}} \tag{29}$$

where H_M is the H parameter of the found model; $\hat{H}_0$, $\hat{a}$, and $\hat{b}$ are the fitted parameters; $\hat{H}_0$ is the H parameter when $PLR = 0$.

Simulation Results

In this section, simulation results are presented. The simulations are accomplished over VoIP jitter data traces corresponding to collected data sets.

Figure 9 illustrates the relationships between packet loss rate and Hurst parameter. This figure shows the empirical functions $f\left(PLR_\tau, H_\tau \right)$ that are obtained by simulations results and the function $f_{REAL}\left(PLR_\varepsilon, H_\varepsilon \right)$ that is generated by "E"

Figure 9. Relationship between packet loss rate and Hurst parameter: $f\left(PLR_\tau, H_\tau\right)$ *vs.* $f_{REAL}\left(PLR_\varepsilon, H_\varepsilon\right)$

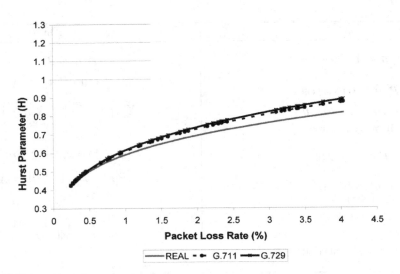

Table 3. Fitted parameters

$f\left(PLR_\tau, H_\tau\right)$	$\hat{H}_0$	$\hat{a}$	$\hat{b}$	MSE
G.711	0.0428	0.5659	0.2760	0.001474
G.729	0.0430	0.5716	0.2805	0.002305
$f_{REAL}\left(PLR_\varepsilon, H_\varepsilon\right)$	0.0429	0.5471	0.2475	

VoIP jitter data traces. The functions $f\left(PLR_\tau, H_\tau\right)$, result from applying "$T$" packet loss patterns to representative VoIP jitter data traces X_t; in these functions, each point represents the correspondence parameters PLR_τ and H_τ of a new time series $\hat{X}^\tau$. On the other hand, in the function $f_{REAL}\left(PLR_\varepsilon, H_\varepsilon\right)$, each point represents the correspondence parameters PLR_ε and H_ε of a jitter data trace X^ε, where $\varepsilon = 1, 2, ...E$, and "E" is the total number of collected jitter data traces.

The respective differences between the functions corresponding to simulation results $f\left(PLR_\tau, H_\tau\right)$ and the function $f_{REAL}\left(PLR_\varepsilon, H_\varepsilon\right)$, were quantified in terms of MSE.

Table 3 shows the fitted parameters and MSE between $f_{REAL}\left(PLR_\varepsilon, H_\varepsilon\right)$ and $f\left(PLR_\tau, H_\tau\right)$.

The results are summarized in Figure 9 and Table 3, and shows that a power-law model is suitable for describe the relationships between Hurst parameter and packet loss rate. As result of this analysis we conclude that the presented methodology for simulating packet loss, achieved the trade off between a very accurate modeling and a low number of model input parameters. Based on these results we proposed that the relationships found between PLR and H parameter can be good modeled by a power-law function with three fitted parameters ($\hat{H}_0$, $\hat{a}$, and $\hat{b}$).

FUTURE RESEARCH DIRECTIONS

In this section, we present the future research directions, summarized as following:

1.   The discovery of LRD (a kind of asymptotic fractal scaling) in VoIP jitter data traces can be followed by a further work detailing that investigates a possible multifractal behavior. The LD-diagram of a self-similar time series is a straight line. Then a linear regression can be applied in order to estimate the Hurst index or scaling parameter. On the other hand, when the LD-diagram of a self-similar time series cannot be modeled with a linear model, then the scaling behavior should be described with more than one scaling parameter (multifractal behavior) (Veitch et al, 1999).

2.   In the 4-state Markov model a "good" and "bad" state are distinguished and represent phases of lower and higher packet loss respectively. Both for the 'bad' and the 'good' state, an individual 2-state Markov model represents the dependency between consecutively lost or found packets. Therefore is necessary to find the accurate transitions probability between the two-state models, in order to incorporate representative microscopic periods. This transition probability can be found as follows: Since the most packet losses occur during temporal overload situations, we proposed incorporate the microscopic periods based on this behavior. The overload situations can be represented by means of a representative model of traffic volume. Therefore by the relationship between the traffic volume model and the overload situations we can define the transition probability between the two-state models. On the other hand, many researches have shown that the volume of IP traffic can be modeled by self-similar processes (Lelan

et al, 1994; Park & Willinger, 2000; Sheluhin et al, 2007).

3. N-packet FEC consists of that packet $n+1$ contains information about packet n, so that if packet n is lost, it can be approximately reconstructed from the associated information. Packet n cannot be reconstructed if there is no redundant information, i.e. when packet $n+1$ is also lost. The 1-packet FEC technique performance can be described as: it reduces the size of a burst of length k to $k-1$. The perceived *PLR* is proportional to the perceived average burst length, which in this case decreases by 1 (packet). With this correction scheme, the last N packets of a burst can be recovered and then, the perceived *PLR* of the end user is lower than the real *PLR* due to the network. Generally, the amount of redundancy is defined as a function of the *PLR*, e.g., it is not efficient to send redundant information if there are no missing packets. The FEC technique reduces the burstiness of packet loss, which affects the quality of a VoIP communication. The packet loss burstiness is considered by modeling network losses with finite-state Markov chains, which allow us to predict the perceived *PLR* when applying the N-packet FEC technique. Therefore, the characterization and modeling of packet loss can be used for the estimation the level of FEC redundancy (Estrada et al, 2009-2).

CONCLUSION

In this chapter, we have presented an introduction to the main concepts and mathematical background relating to *QoS* parameters and IP traffic nature.

Several parameters influencing voice quality on IP networks, particularly jitter and packet loss have an important impact. We analyzed the jitter and packet loss behavior of VoIP traffic by means of network performance measurements and simulations results, in order to provide a detailed characterization and accurate modeling of these *QoS* parameters.

As result of these analyses, we proposed that VoIP jitter can be properly modeled by means of self-similar processes with SRD or LRD. Through a decomposition based on Haar wavelet it is observed the components behavior of VoIP jitter as a function of packet loss and, by means of this decomposition it is shown a possible reason of the LRD presence in VoIP jitter.

On the other hand, the distributions of the number of consecutive received and lost packets, respectively named gap and burst, of a VoIP communication are modeled with discrete *2*-state and *4*-state Markov chains, respectively.

Furthermore, we used a description of VoIP packet loss based on microscopic and macroscopic packet loss behaviors, where these behaviors can be modeled by *2*-state and *4*-state Markov chains, respectively. Based on the above mentioned description, we have presented a methodology for simulating packet loss on self-similar VoIP jitter.

We proposed a new model that allows relating the *H* parameter with the *PLR* by means of a power-law function with three fitted parameters, summarized by Equation (29). Our results show that the presented methodology for simulating packet loss with various burstiness levels, achieved the trade off between a very accurate modeling and a low number of model input parameters ($P_{21}, P_{12}, P_{43}, P_{34}, P_{23}, P_{32}$). Simulation results show the effectiveness of our models in terms of *MSE*.

The proposed characterizations and models between main *QoS* parameters can be used by other researches as input to the design and evaluation of network, and implementation of *QoS* mechanisms on VoIP applications.

REFERENCES

Combs, G., et al. (2010). Wireshark: A network protocol analyzer. Retrieved from http:// www.wireshark.org/

Estrada, L., Torres, D., & Toral, H. (2009-1). *Variance error for finite-length self-similar time series*. Paper presented at the 7th International Conference on Computing, Communications and Control Technologies (CCCT) - In the Context of the 2nd International Multi-Conference on Engineering and Technological Innovation (IMETI), Orlando, Florida, USA. Estrada, L., Torres, D., & Toral, H. (2009-2). Description of a parameter-based optimization of the quality of service for VoIP communications. *WSEAS Transactions on Communications, 9*(8), 1042-1052.

ITU-T Recommendation G.114. (2003). *One-way transmission time*. Geneva, Switzerland: International Telecommunications Union.

ITU-T Recommendation G.1050. (2005). *Network model for evaluating multimedia transmission performance over Internet protocol*. Geneva, Switzerland: International Telecommunications Union.

ITU-T Recommendation H.323. (2007). *Packet-based multimedia communications systems*. Geneva, Switzerland: International Telecommunications Union.

Lee, H., & Lee, H. (2005). *A packet loss recovery scheme based on the gap statistics*. Paper presented at the International Conference on Information Networking (ICOIN), Jeju Island, Korea.

Leland, W. E., Taqqu, M. S., Willinger, W., & Wilson, D. V. (1994). On the self-similar nature of ethernet traffic (extended version). *IEEE/ACM Transactions on Networking, 2*(1), 1–15. doi:10.1109/90.282603

Leyva, L. (2004). Alliance FXO/FXS/E1 VoIP system. Retrieved from http:// www.cts-design.com

Park, K., & Willinger, W. (2000). *Self-similar network traffic and performance evaluation.* New York, NY: John Wiley & Sons, Inc. doi:10.1002/047120644X

Raake, A. (2006). Short- and long-term packet loss behavior: Towards speech quality prediction for arbitrary loss distributions. *IEEE Transactions on Audio, Speech, and Language Processing, 14*(6), 957–1968. doi:10.1109/TASL.2006.883231

Ramírez, J., & Torres, D. (2005). *A tool for analysis of Internet metrics.* Paper presented at the 2nd International Conference on Electrical and Electronics Engineering (ICEEE) and XI Conference on Electrical Engineering (CIE), Mexico, D.F.

Schulzrinne, H. (2003). *RTP: A transport protocol for real-time applications (RFC 3550).* Internet Engineering Task Force.

Sheluhin, O. I., Smolskiy, S. M., & Osin, A. V. (2007). *Self-similar processes in telecommunications.* Chichester, England: John Wiley & Sons Ltd.doi:10.1002/9780470062098

Sulkin, A. (2002). *PBX systems for IP telephony: Migrating enterprise communications.* New York, NY: McGraw-Hill Professional.

Toral, H., Torres, D., & Estrada, L. (2009). Simulation and modeling of packet loss on VoIP traffic: A power-law model. *WSEAS Transactions on Communications, 8*(10), 1053–1063.

Veitch, D., & Abry, P. (1999). A wavelet based joint estimator of the parameters of long-range dependence. *IEEE Transactions on Information Theory - Special issue on multiscale statistical signal analysis and its applications, 45*(3), 878-897.

Wickerhauser, M. V. (1994). *Adapted wavelet analysis from theory to software.* Natick, MA: IEEE Press.

Willamowius, J., et al. (2009). *OpenH323 gatekeeper: The GNU gatekeeper.* Retrieved from http:// www.gnugk.org/

Yajnik, M., Moon, S., Kursoe, J., & Towsley, D. (1999). *Measurement and modelling of the temporal dependence in packet loss.* Paper presented at the 18th International Conference on Computer Communications (IEEE INFOCOM), New York, NY.

ADDITIONAL READING

Chen, X., Wang, C., Xuan, D., Li, Z., Min, Y., & Zhao, W. (2003). Survey on QoS Management of VoIP. *Proceedings of the International Conference on Computer Networks and Mobile Computing.* (pp. 69-77). Washington, DC: IEEE Computer Society.

Gao, J., Cao, Y., Tung, W.-W., & Hu, J. (2007). *Multiscale Analysis of Complex Time Series: Integration of Chaos and Random Fractal Theory, and Beyond.* Hoboken, NJ: Wiley-Interscience.

ITU-T Recommendation G.711, (1993). Pulse Code Modulation (PCM) of Voice Frequencies. International Telecommunications Union, Geneva, Switzerland.

ITU-T Recommendation G.729, (2008). Coding of speech at 8 kbit/s using Conjugate-Structure Algebraic-Code-Excited Linear-Prediction (CS-ACELP). International Telecommunications Union, Geneva, Switzerland.

Postel, J. (1980). *UDP: User Datagram Protocol (RFC 768).* Internet Engineering Task Force.

Postel, J. (1981). *IP: Internet Protocol (RFC 791).* Internet Engineering Task Force.

Singh, R., & Ortega, A. (2002). *Modeling of Temporal Dependence in Packet Loss Using Universal Modeling Concepts.* Paper presented at the 12th Packet Video Workshop, Pittsburgh, PA.

Taqqu, M., & Teverovsky, V. (1998). *On estimating the intensity of long range dependence in finite and infinite variance time series. A Practical guide to heavy Tails* (pp. 177–217). Cambridge, MA: Birkhauser Boston Inc.

Toral, H., Torres, D., & Estrada, L. (2009). *Simulation and Modeling of Packet Loss on α-Stable VoIP Traffic*. Paper presented at the 9th International Conference on Multimedia, Internet & Video Technologies (WSEAS MIV), Budapest, Hungary.

Toral, H., Torres, D., Hernandez, C., & Estrada, L. (2008). *Self-Similarity, Packet Loss, Jitter, and Packet Size: Empirical Relationships for VoIP*. Paper presented at the 18th International Conference on Electronics, Communications, and Computers (IEEE CONIELECOM), Puebla, Mexico.

KEY TERMS AND DEFINITIONS

Hurst Parameter: This parameter expresses the speed of decay of the autocorrelation function of the self-similar time series.

Jitter: Jitter is the difference between two delay values. In this work, we called jitter to the difference between arrival times of successive voice packets that arrive on the receiver side.

Packet Loss Rate: The packet loss rate refers to packet loss probability and can be caused by a number of factors, for example, due to excessive network delay in case of network congestion.

Protocol: IP is a protocol of the Network Layer and has the task of delivering datagrams from the source host to the destination host solely based on their addresses.

Quality of Service: The quality of service is defined from two points of view: user and network. From the end user's perspective, the *QoS* is the collective effect of service performances, which determine the degree of satisfaction of a user of service. On the other hand, from the network's perspective, the term *QoS* refers to the network's capabilities to provide the *QoS* perceived by the end user.

Real-Time Transport Protocol: RTP is the protocol for transmitting delay-sensitive traffic across packet-based networks.

VoIP: Voice over Internet protocol is the real-time transmission of voice between two or more terminals, by using IP technologies over packet switched networks. A basic VoIP system consists of three parts, the sender, the IP networks and the receiver.

Chapter 2
End-to-End Dataflow Parallelism for Transfer Throughput Optimization

Esma Yildirim
Louisiana State University, USA

Tevfik Kosar
University at Buffalo (SUNY), USA

ABSTRACT

The emerging petascale increase in the data produced by large-scale scientific applications necessitates innovative solutions for efficient transfer of data through the advanced infrastructure provided by today's high-speed networks and complex computer-architectures (e.g. supercomputers, parallel storage systems). Although the current optical networking technology reached transport speeds of 100Gbps, the applications still suffer from the inadequate transport protocols and end-system bottlenecks such as processor speed, disk I/O speed and network interface card limits that cause underutilization of the existing network infrastructure and let the application achieve only a small portion of the theoretical performance. Fortunately, with the parallelism provided by usage of multiple CPUs/nodes and multiple disks present in today's systems, these bottlenecks could be eliminated. However it is necessary to understand the characteristics of the end-systems and the transport protocol used. In this book chapter, we analyze methodologies that will improve the data transfer speed of applications and provide maximal speeds that could be obtained from the available end-system resources and high-speed networks through usage of end-to-end dataflow parallelism.

DOI: 10.4018/978-1-61350-110-8.ch002

Copyright © 2012, IGI Global. Copying or distributing in print or electronic forms without written permission of IGI Global is prohibited.

INTRODUCTION

The data transfer throughput is a major factor that affects the performance of applications from many scientific areas (e.g. high-energy physics, bioinformatics, numerical relativity and computational fluid dynamics). The advancements in optical networking technology have gone beyond the achievable throughput values the applications get, however the same speed up is not seen in the application performance due to many reasons such as the protocol inadequacy, poorly tuned protocol parameters and underutilized capacity of the end-systems. The current protocols that are highly common (e.g. TCP) were originally not designed for high-bandwidth networks. Due to its additive increase multiplicative decrease policy, TCP takes a long time to fill the pipe of long-fat network pipes. Many protocols have been designed for high-bandwidth networks in the transport layer (Kola & Vernon, 2007; Jin et al, 2005; Floyd, 2003) to overcome this problem however they fail to replace TCP.

Other than transport layer protocols, some application-level solutions are proposed as well. Two of the very common methods are tuning buffer size and using parallel streams. While some buffer tuning methods need modification to the kernel (Cohen &Cohen, 2002; Semke, Madavi & Mathis, 1998; Torvalds et al, 2010; Weigle & Feng, 2001), the others are done at the application level (Jain, Prasad & Davrolis,2003; Prasad, Jain &Davrolis, 2004, Hasegawa et al 2001; Morajko, 2004). Although the buffer size parameter is properly tuned, it does not show a better performance than using parallel streams because parallel streams recover from packet loss quickly rather than a single stream with tuned buffer. They achieve high throughput by mimicking the behavior of individual streams and get an unfair share of the available bandwidth (Sivakumar, Bailey & Grossman, 2000; Lee et al, 2001; Balakrishman et al, 1998; Hacker, Noble & Atley, 2005; Eggert, Heideman & Touch, 2000; Karrer, Park &

Kim, 2006; Lu, Qiao & Dinda, 2005). However excessive usage of parallel streams reaches the network to a congestion point and it is hard to predict this point. The studies that try to find the optimal number of streams are so few and mostly based on approximate theoretical models (Hacker, Noble & Atley, 2002; Lu et al, 2005; Altman et al, 2006; Kola & Vernon, 2007}. They all have specific constraints and assumptions. Also the correctness of the proposed models is mostly proved with simulation results.

The foretold solutions to improve the throughput only remove the disadvantages of the protocols used. However, at some point the end-system resources become the source of bottleneck such as CPU, disk and NIC itself. Additional parallelism is needed through striping but the optimal level of striping is an open research area. The existing tools such as the GridFTP striped server (Allcock et al, 2005) and Dmover (Nathan et al, 2010) provide a means to utilize striping through multiple CPUs and nodes of an end-system architecture but they give the preference to the user to define the parallelism level. A dynamic and autonomic system that will decide this level depends on many factors.

In this book chapter we discuss many factors that affect the end-to-end application throughput such as the buffer size, parallel streams, CPU speed, disk speed and access methods in systems that use high-speed networks. The major purpose of this chapter is to provide insight to the characteristics of the end-systems that cause the bottleneck for throughput and to discuss future directions. We also present a method to optimize the parallel stream number and we have seen that this model gives very accurate results regardless of the type of the network.

BACKGROUND

TCP is the most widely used transport protocol but it may also be a major performance bottleneck in high-bandwidth networks because of its design goals. It is a transport layer protocol designed for optimizing the network bandwidth as well as providing fairness among the flows sharing the network. It has two phases that are named *slow start* and *congestion avoidance*. A congestion window is defined as the number of packets the sender is allowed to send. The higher the congestion window, the higher is the throughput. In the slow start phase the congestion window starts from 1 packet and is exponentially increased to utilize the throughput quickly until a packet loss event occurs. Then the congestion window is divided by half and starts to increase linearly. This is known as the additive increase - multiplicative decrease property (AIMD) (Tierney, 2005). When a timeout occurs the loop turns to the beginning congestion window size and enters the slow start phase again. This property of TCP ensures fairness, however it gives poor performance in terms of throughput. Therefore other methods are tried to compensate its poor performance such as using parallel streams and tuning buffer size.

Although the protocol used is a major factor in the transfer speed, with the development of current high-bandwidth networks, the bottlenecks over the end-systems have become the major factor that affects the upper limit to the data transfer speed. End-systems that invoke and receive data transfers may range from supercomputers to computational clusters or to hosts of varying capabilities (DOE, 2008). They have possible bottlenecks such as disk speed, disk schedulers, file systems, CPU load, MTU (Maximum Transmission Unit) and window size. However these bottlenecks could be overcome by proper tuning of the systems based on end system properties and architecture.

In a typical system that consists of end-systems and the network connecting them, the data transfer throughput depends on many factors. An example of such a system is given in Figure 1. The data transfer starts from the disk and reaches the memory, and then it is written to the network through the network interface card (NIC). The CPU, of course plays a major role in every part of those steps. In the figure, $Tnetwork$ presents the throughput of the network, $TSmem->network$ presents the memory-to-network throughput on the source, $TSdisk->mem$ presents the disk-to-memory throughput on the source; $TDnetwork->mem$ presents the network-to-memory throughput on the destination. Each step could cause the bottleneck that limits the transfer speed. In that case, the minimum of the optimized values will define the upper limit for maximal achievable throughput.

Network is the major source of bottleneck especially for low-bandwidth architectures. The systems connected with this kind of network, usually consist of single CPU/node, single disk access and NICs under or equal to 100Mbps. Figure 1 is an example of such architecture. The causes of the low throughput problem are many, could be directly or indirectly related to the network and could be listed as high latency, network traffic, underutilized transport protocol and untuned buffer size. While the first two problems are directly related to the network bottleneck, the latter two are related indirectly since these settings are done by the end-systems.

The end-systems that are connected with high-speed networks usually consist of parallel clusters, supercomputers or parallel storage systems. The first and foremost problem on those end-systems is again the protocol used. For example, TCP protocol is not designed for those types of networks and cannot utilize the most of it. Usage of parallel streams and buffer size could solve the problem in the application level. However usage of parallel streams or large buffer sizes places a burden on CPU as well as NIC. Luckily for parallel architectures multiple CPUs and NICs are available. In a typical distributed shared memory architecture, while the speed of the NIC on the head node is compatible to the speed of the network, the ones on the worker nodes may or may not. Considering that single disk access is available, the possible causes of bottleneck that may occur in such a system could be listed as CPU speed,

Figure 1. The end-to-end data transfer path

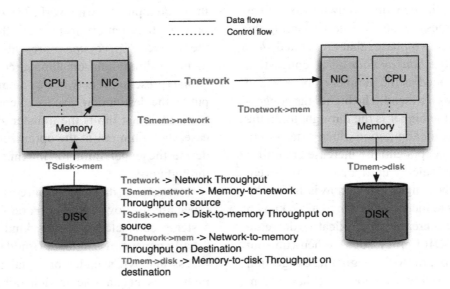

Tnetwork -> Network Throughput
TSmem->network -> Memory-to-network Throughput on source
TSdisk->mem -> Disk-to-memory Throughput on source
TDnetwork->mem -> Network-to-memory Throughput on Destination
TDmem->disk -> Memory-to-disk Throughput on destination

protocol settings and NICs that are not compatible to the speed of the network. The problems could be solved with CPU/node parallelism. Many parallel systems that are connected via high-speed networks have parallel storage systems. Disk access rate is a major source of bottleneck in single disk access systems. However in parallel storage systems, this bottleneck could be overcome by reading/writing data in stripes. While overcoming this bottleneck we could generate new bottlenecks since other parts of the system (e.g. CPU, NIC) may not keep up to it. In this case the possible causes of bottleneck could be listed as disk speed, CPU speed, protocol settings and NICs nodes.

In the literature there are only a handful examples that use CPU and Disk parallelism to eliminate the end-system bottleneck and there is no study that gives the optimal level of parallelism. However there are other methods that improve disk and CPU speed. Some of the optimizations to overcome the disk bottleneck are tuning I/O block size, tuning I/O scheduler and prefetching (Thomas, 2008). I/O block size defines the number of bytes read/written at a time from/to disk. I/O schedulers may perform different based on the load of the system and the characteristics of the transfers. While some schedulers work better than the others in busy machines, they can perform worse in idle machines. Also they differ in CPU usages as well. Prefetching can improve disk speed by reading ahead for large data sizes however it can increase access times for small data sizes. One of the techniques that are used to overcome the CPU bottleneck is interrupt coalescing. When there is a high interrupt rate usually on the head node of a supercomputer or cluster architecture only one interrupt is generated for multiple packets. Another technique is called IRQ bonding (Thomas, 2008) where specific interrupts are shared among the CPUs.

The GridFTP Striped Server (Allcock, 2005) provides an architecture, which supports striping and partial file transfer. According to this architecture data could be striped or interleaved across multiple servers as in a parallel file system or DPSS disk cache. Data sources and sinks may come in different forms such as clusters with local disks, clusters with parallel file systems, archival storage systems and geographically distributed data sources. One drawback of the architecture is

Figure 2. Effect of buffer size and parallel streams on average gridFTP throughput

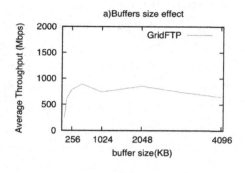
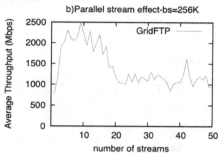

that the striping level is static. Once the server is configured only the striping level defined by the configuration is effective for all of the transfers. There is no option of dynamically selecting this number. Dmover (Simmel, 2008) is used to schedule bulk data transfers between GridFTP nodes. Dmover jobs contain the locations and paths of the files to be transferred. If a stripe count is specified, file transfers will occur in a striped mode. Both architectures provide tools to do parallelism and striping however do not provide the optimal level of parallelism. Dynamic decision of this number needs insight to many factors which in the following sections we analyze the effects of those factors in detail.

EFFECT OF BUFFER SIZE AND PARALLEL STREAMS ON THROUGHPUT

The buffer size is an important parameter that affects the transport layer protocol. It defines the number of packets that is on the fly before the sender waits an acknowledgement. The larger the buffer size is the higher is the throughput, however very large buffer sizes cause congestion that will increase the packet loss rate hence result in decrease in the throughput due to retransmissions. Buffer size is generally set to the *bandwidth-delay* product, which is the product of available band-

width and the round trip time. There are however variations about how the available bandwidth and round-trip time is measured. To better understand the effect of buffer size, we present the disk-to-disk GridFTP data transfers on two IBM cluster head nodes, which have 4Gbps NICs and 4-core processors in Figure 2. The average throughput starts to increase with small buffer sizes and it is at its peak value for 1M, but after that point it presents lower results. We can see that the buffer size is an important factor in throughput. However its performance is usually less than parallel streams due to the quick recovery of parallel streams from losses.

To understand the characteristics of throughput based on the buffer size and parallel streams parameters, we have conducted some experiments by ranging the buffer size between 64KB-4M and the parallel streams between 1- 50. The behavior of average throughput could be seen in Figure 3. The average throughput starts to increase as both parallel stream number and buffer size increase. It demonstrates higher values for high-buffer/low-stream number and low-buffer/high-stream number. The peak is reached with a stream number value between 5-10 and a buffer size value 256K-512K. After that point a sharp decrease is seen in throughput value and a large fluctuation for large buffer size and stream number values as well.

Figure 3. Buffer size vs parallel streams

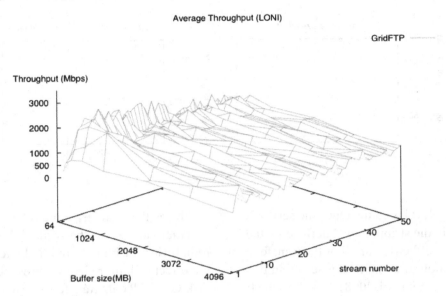

EFFECT OF PARALLEL STREAMS ON CPU UTILIZATION

Using parallel streams is a common method to remove the inadequacy of TCP protocol for long-fat networks. They provide multiple amounts of the throughput achievable by a single stream at the expense of losing fairness among other flows using the network. For uncongested networks this issue is not a problem which is often the case for high-speed networks because they usually have unused bandwidth due to improper use of end-systems. However using excessive number of parallel streams is also not a good way to utilize the resources. There are many reasons that prohibit the usage of excessive parallel streams. First reason is that, it could reach the network to a congestion point where packet loss rate increases and causes a drop-down in throughput. Another reason is that it could reach the end-system to its limits such as the CPU load and available NIC capacity.

In this section, we measure the effect of parallel streams on a multi-core node architecture in terms of CPU utilization by using GridFTP. Three different networks are used in the experiments conducted. The first network is a state-wide high-speed network of Louisiana which is called LONI (LONI, 2010). It has a 10Gbps backbone and connects 128 node Linux clusters with 4-8 core processors on each node. The latency of paths between clusters is short (e.g. up to 8msecs). The second network is the Teragrid (Teragrid, 2010) which is a nation-wide high-bandwidth network that has a 30 Gbps backbone. In the third setting, we use the inter-node connection to remove the effects of the network where the transfers are conducted between two I/O nodes of the same cluster.

In each case, we increase the number of parallel streams exponentially and measure the throughput as well as the CPU Utilization. Figure 4 presents the average memory-to-memory throughput of parallel streams. In general, the throughput increases as the stream number increases, after reaching its peak point, it either continues stable or starts to decrease either due to network or end-system bottlenecks. In each setting the nodes used have 10Gbps network interface henceforth we remove the possibility of NIC bottleneck.

To understand the source of the bottleneck, a second set of transfers is performed by adding

Figure 4. Effect of parallel streams on gridFTP throughput

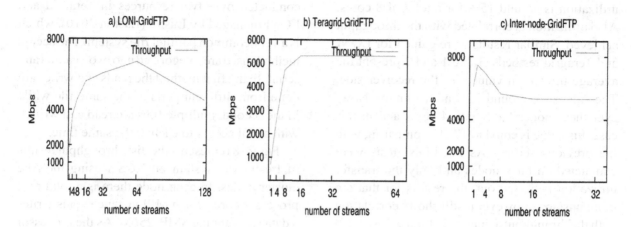

Figure 5. Effect of striping on gridFTP throughput

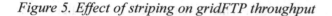

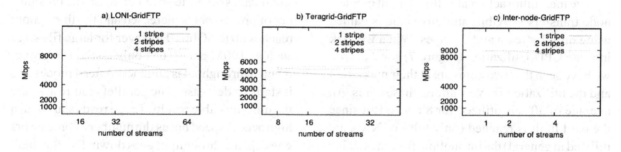

stripes and using multiple CPUs in addition to parallel streams. In each case, the parallel stream range that gives better throughput results is used. In Figure 5, there is a significant increase in throughput from single stripe to multiple stripes for LONI and Inter-node results. This indicates that CPU is a source of bottleneck and also excessive usage of stripes and parallel streams is the cause of drop-down in throughput. For Teragrid, since the results are so close to each other, it is difficult to say that multiple stripes will always give better results based on the network condition. The striping results are obtained only using a single node, yet it is sufficient to reach up to the network limit. We look into the CPU utilization results to find out why a single stripe is not sufficient.

In Figure 6, we present the CPU utilization of both sender and receiver side of Inter-node transfers. Two I/O nodes (Spider 21-22) of a cluster in LONI network are used. These nodes have 8 Intel processor cores. One important observation is that the utilization is higher in the receiver side (Spider22); hence it plays the ultimate role to set the achievable throughput limit. The sender (Spider22) starts with a 50% cpu utilization on single core and goes up to over 80% as the number of streams increases. The receiver utilization on the other hand is around 100% even for 1 stream and it pushes the limits of a single CPU as the stream number goes up. But it never uses more than two processors and a total of %140 percent CPU out of two cores. Furthermore the utilization of two cores is not even. Yet the throughput starts to decrease after 2 streams. In total, the receiver utilization is around 15% for a total of 8 cores. Also utilization is correlated with the throughput achieved. Similar results were gained for LONI and Teragrid testbeds. Table 1 and 2 present the average utilization values for the receiver side. The values are around 35% at maximum. However these nodes have only 4 cores and in this case this value is equal to 17.5% comparing with the previous setting. As the LONI tests were conducted on busy nodes and only the transfer utilization is parsed out, the results for that are more unstable, however it still shows correlation with the throughput achieved in Figure 5. We also have seen that only single core utilization was maxed out.

The maximum achievable throughput of internode transfers is 9Gbps and this value is gained using only 1 stream and 2 stripes. When we look into the CPU Utilization (Figure 7) for 2 stripes we have seen that two cores are at their maximum and the utilization is even among these cores. An average of 30% is utilized for 8 cores. But since the card limit is reached (only 90% of NICs are utilized in general) the throughput becomes stable around 9 Gbps. Comparing to the 7.5Gbps maximum throughput achieved with single stripe, using multiple CPUs is definitely an improvement.

EFFECT OF PARALLEL READ AND WRITE ON DISK THROUGHPUT

Disk is usually the slowest part of an end-system that is the general source of bottleneck in end-to-end data transfer. To provide faster data access speed multiple disks are stored and used in parallel and managed by parallel file systems. In this section, we analyze different access methods to data that is managed by parallel file systems by using MPI-IO (Gropp, Lusk & Thakur, 1999) and compare it to a local file system speed of a local hard drive of a node in Spider cluster. Parameters such as data size, stripe number and access method

affect the disk throughput. The experiments are conducted over two resources in Teragrid and LONI managed by Lustre (Lustre, 2010), which is a very common parallel file system. The access methods used are categorized into two: parallel and serial. In the first method the reads and writes are done from different parts of the same file while in the second, multiple files are read and written with serial access to each at the same time.

Figure 8 represents the disk throughput results of Lustre file system on NCSA using the Abe cluster nodes. In each node there is a total of 4 processor cores. Each MPI instance reads/writes a data size ranging 8MB-256M. As the processor number is increased, the total amount of data read or written is increased as well. For parallel write, small data size write speed increases as the number of processors is increased and the throughput reaches up to 6Gbps. However for large file sizes such as 100M and 256M only a slight improvement of throughput is obtained. After 4 processors it starts to decrease. The parallel read results are the most unstable results. Large reads start with a high access speed but as the number of processors goes up, the throughput goes down. But for small data sizes parallel reads make an improvement in terms of throughput going from 2Gbps to 4Gbps. The real benefit of the parallel file system is seen when we write to or read from different files at the same time. In Figure 8.c the throughput goes up to around 6Gbps even for large data sizes such as 100M and 256M. For small sizes it even reaches to 16Gbps. The serial read results do not depend on the data size and they provide similar throughput values and as the number of processors increases the read throughput continues to increase and reaches 60Gbps. Further increase in the parallelism level could increase this value more.

To define generic characteristics for the parallel access disk throughput we conducted the same experiments on a different cluster in LONI network. Figure 9 represents the MPI-IO results for Oliver cluster. Similar trends could be seen in the throughput curves except for the parallel read

Figure 6. Effect of parallel streams on CPU Utilization on inter-node gridFTP Throughput

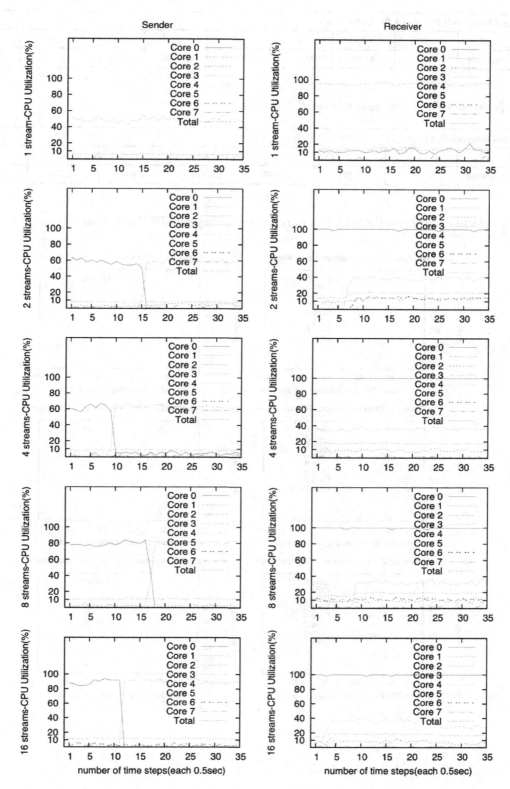

Table 1. LONI CPU Utilization vs Parallel Streams

Oliver-Poseidon(LONI) Receiver CPU Utilization								
Streams	1	2	4	8	16	32	64	128
Average Utilization	8,410	4,668	28,643	17,655	29,194	29,554	37,795	29,026

Table 2. Teragrid CPU Utilization vs Parallel Streams

Spider-Abe (Teragrid) Receiver CPU Utilization							
Streams	1	2	4	8	16	32	64
Average Utilization	2,140	7,781	13,897	25,178	32,692	34,774	32,841

Figure 7. Effect of stripes on CPU Utilization on inter-node gridFTP throughput

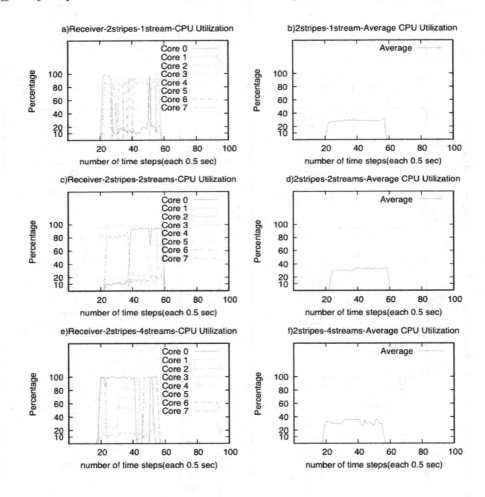

Figure 8. Abe cluster (NCSA) MPI-IO disk throughput

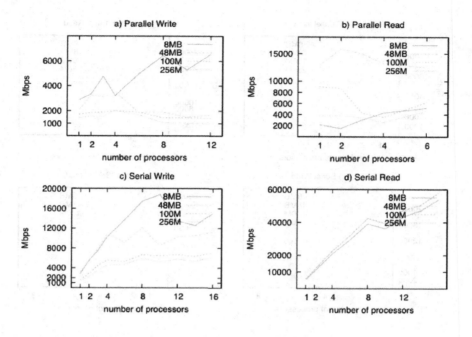

Figure 9. Oliver cluster (LONI) MPI-IO disk throughput

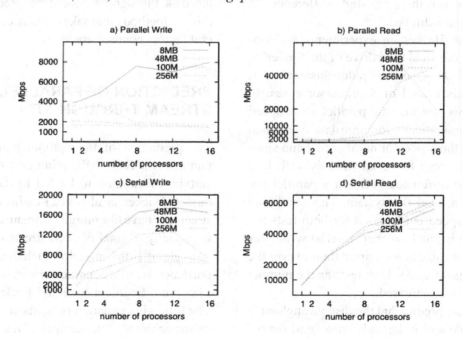

Figure 10. Spider21 (CCT/LSU) MPI-IO disk throughput

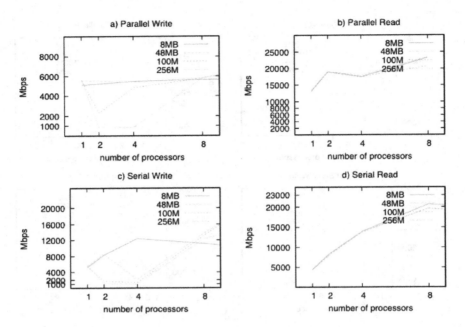

results. However, there are slight differences in the throughput achieved.

The local file system experiments are conducted over the local hard drive of the Spider21, which is an I/O node of the Spider cluster at CCT. The node has a total of 8 processor cores. In Figure 10, we see that the parallel write speed falls down dramatically for large data sizes when we increase the processor number to 2 and similar results are seen for serial write as well. This indicates the difference between a parallel file system and a local file system. The small data sizes write speed is increased for both tests but the increase is much steeper in serial write. For reads, the data size is not important however the read speed goes up for both tests as the number of processors is increased.

The results predict that the disk throughput is unpredictable and it depends on several factors such as the data size, the processor number, the disk deployment, the access method (serial/parallel), access type (read/write) and the file system. To model the end-to-end data transfer throughput,

the disk throughput should be predicted using mining methods that takes into account the several factors counted above.

PREDICTION OF PARALLEL STREAM THROUGHPUT

The prediction of the optimal parallel stream number is a very challenging task that requires certain information to be fed to the prediction model. Hacker et al (2002) claim that parallel streams behave like one giant stream that transfers in capacity of total of each streams' achievable throughput. In this model, the achievable throughput depends on three parameters: Round trip time, Maximum Segment Size and Packet Loss rate. The following equation presents an upper bound on the achievable throughput of n streams.

$$Th \leq n \frac{MSS}{RTT} \frac{c}{\sqrt{p}} \qquad (1)$$

RTT represents round trip time, *MSS* represents the maximum segment size, *p* represents the packet loss rate and *c* is a constant. However, this model only works for uncongested networks and assumes the packet loss rate is stable and same for each connection and does not increase as the number of streams increases. At the point the network gets congested, the packet loss rate starts to increase dramatically and the achievable throughput starts to decrease. The parameters become dependent on each other and Equation (1) turns into the following Equation:

$$Th_n \leq n \frac{MSS}{RTT_n} \frac{c}{\sqrt{p_n}} \tag{2}$$

Overall this model requires too much information that is also hard to gather and it does not give an answer to at what point the network will be congested.

Lu et al (2005) models the bandwidth of multiple streams as a partial second order equation and needs two different throughput measurements of different stream numbers to predict the others. The model tries to compute the relationship between *p*, *RTT*, and *n* by a partial second order equation. MSS and c are again considered as constants. We know that the packet loss rate increases exponentially when congestion occurs however the order of the exponent might not be known exactly but should be extracted dynamically. The relationship between the dynamic parameters of Equation (2) is presented in Equation (3):

$$p'_n = p_n \frac{RTT^2}{c^2 MSS^2} = a'n^{c'} + b' \tag{3}$$

When we insert p'_n in Equation (2) total throughput of *n* streams is represented as in Equation:

$$Th_n = \frac{n}{\sqrt{p'_n}} = \frac{n}{\sqrt{a'n^{c'} + b'}} \tag{4}$$

In this case, *c'* is the unknown order of the equation additional to *a'* and *b'*. To solve this equation, we need three measurements Th_{n1}, Th_{n2} and Th_{n3} on the throughput curve for stream values n_1, n_2 and n_3.

$$Th_{n_1} = \frac{n}{\sqrt{a'n_1^{c'} + b'}} \tag{5}$$

$$Th_{n_2} = \frac{n}{\sqrt{a'n_2^{c'} + b'}} \tag{6}$$

$$Th_{n_3} = \frac{n}{\sqrt{a'n_3^{c'} + b'}} \tag{7}$$

c' being to the power *n* makes the solving of the equation much harder. After several substitutions the following equations for *a'*, *b'* and *c'* are derived:

$$\frac{n_3^{c'} - n_1^{c'}}{n_2^{c'} - n_1^{c'}} = \frac{\dfrac{n_3^2}{Th_{n_3}^2} - \dfrac{n_1^2}{Th_{n_1}^2}}{\dfrac{n_2^2}{Th_{n_2}^2} - \dfrac{n_1^2}{Th_{n_1}^2}} \tag{8}$$

$$\tag{9}$$

$$a' = \frac{\dfrac{n_2^2}{Th_{n_2}^2} - \dfrac{n_1^2}{Th_{n_1}^2}}{n_2^{c'} - n_1^{c'}}$$

$$b' = \frac{n_1^2}{Th_{n_1}^2} - a'n_1^{c'} \tag{10}$$

The derivation of *a'* and *b'* depends on *c'*. To solve the first equation, we applied a mathematical root finding method called Newton's Iteration method. We revised the method to be suitable to our own problem:

$$c'_{x+1} = c'_x - \frac{f(c'_x)}{f'(c'_x)} \tag{11}$$

After x + 1 iterations we find a very close approximation to *c'*. Starting with a small number for c'_0 we continue to calculate through c'_{x+1}. The

Figure 11. Prediction of gridFTP Throughput by dynamic model equation order using Newton's Iteration

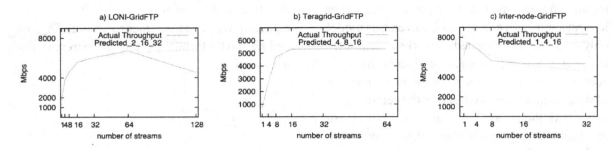

Figure 12. Prediction of gridFTP throughput in LAN, WAN, Internet2 ION

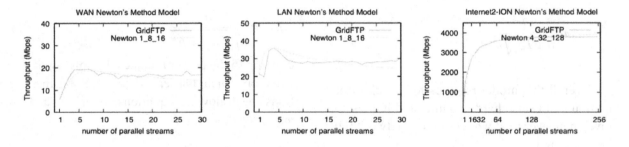

value of the most approximate c' depends on only f(c'), in this case the first equation above, and its derivative. After calculating a most approximate c' which is possible with only a few iterations, the value of a' and b' can easily be calculated.

In Figure 11, the application of the model on the memory-to-memory throughput curve of LONI, Teragrid and inter-node settings is presented. The actual throughput curve shows different characteristics for all of the settings. It always shows a logarithmic increase but after reaching its peak point it either goes stable or starts to fall down. However our model is able to predict the curve based on 3 different parallelism levels. The parallelism levels are chosen as powers of two which also helps using less number of data points. With the prediction model it is easy to find the optimal parallelism level by either taking the peak point of the curve or the point where the throughput increase falls below a certain threshold. A detailed analysis on the effect of selection of points is given in our previous paper (Yildirim, 2010).

To show the effectiveness of this model, we also present results regarding different types of networks other than high-speed networks presented in Figure 11. Those are regular wide-area Internet, local area network and a dedicated circuit-switched network Internet2-ION (Welshons, 2010) which has 10Gbps reservation capacity. The results are presented in Figure 12. The wide area experiments are done over a transoceanic link between LSU and University of Trento with a RTT of 150ms. The local area results belong to the two workstations in LSU while the Internet2 experiments are conducted between NCSA and CCT/LSU again however this time following a different path. Although the characteristics of the throughput curve differ, this model is able make a good prediction of throughput.

FUTURE RESEARCH DIRECTIONS

In this chapter, we have presented a mathematical model that can predict the optimal parallelism level, however it does not take into account other end-system specific bottlenecks such as the CPU, disk and NIC speeds. The need for a broader model that will take into account the architecture of the end-systems is emergent. There are software architectures, which provide the means that will make the application of such a model possible. However there is no existing study that will give optimal end-to-end parameter settings for maximal achievable throughput. The end-to-end data transfer throughput could be modeled as a specialized version of maximum flow problem. In a maximum flow problem the goal is to send as much flow as possible between two special nodes, without exceeding the capacity of any arc (Ahuja, Magnanti & Orlin, 1993). Considering the path of a data transfer is between two multi-node clusters, the disk and multi-core nodes of the clusters need to be modeled as nodes themselves with capacities. A model that will provide the optimal parallel stream number, optimal stripe number and the optimal node number by using minimum number of resources at their maximal capacities with minimum overhead will be a major development for areas such as scientific computing, grid computing and high-performance computing.

CONCLUSION

The inadequacy of the current transport protocols in utilization of the high-speed networks redirect the users to tune protocol parameters and use other means to improve the end-to-end data transfer throughput. The most important parameter that affects the throughput of TCP protocol is the buffer size. However it is outperformed by the more effective parallel streams that can recover from packet losses quickly. But as larger buffer sizes cause a decrease in throughput, using excessive parallel streams has also the same effect. Even using proper parallel stream numbers or buffer sizes may not let us fully utilize the available bandwidth of high-speed networks. The end-systems parameters

have a major role in this situation. We have seen in our experiments that parallel streams cannot fully utilize the multi-core CPUs in the current node architectures. In that case using multiple stripes can help even for memory-to-memory transfers. Even though the node CPU capacities are utilized through stripes, the NIC capacity could present a bottleneck. The disk is usually the slowest part of the system with large NIC capacities. However multiple stripes could also increase the disk read/write speed especially for parallel file systems. A model that will provide the optimal number of streams is presented in this chapter and it provides very accurate results for different types of networks. A broader model that will take into account the end-system bottlenecks and give the number of stripes per node and the number of node will provide a novel methodology for data transfer protocols and tools that aim utilization of high-speed networks which are increasing in capacity day by day.

REFERENCES

Ahuja, R. K., Magnanti, T. L., & Orlin, J. B. (1993). *Network flows*. Upper Saddle River, NJ: Prentice Hall.

Allcock, W., Bresnahan, J., Kettimuth, R., Link, M., Dumirescu, C., Raicu, I., & Foster, I. (2005). The Globus striped GridFTP framework and server. *Proceedings of the ACM/IEEE Conference on Supercomputing*, (p. 54).

Altman, E., Barman, D., Tuffin, B., & Vojnovic, M. (2006). Parallel TCP sockets: Simple model, throughput and validation. In *Proceedings of IEEE Conference on Computer Communications* (INFOCOM06), (pp. 1-12).

Balakrishman, H., Padmanabhan, V. N., Seshan, S., Katz, R. H., & Stemm, M. (1998). TCP behavior of a busy Internet server: Analysis and improvements. In *Proceedings of IEEE Conference on Computer Communications* (INFOCOM98), (pp. 252-262).

Cohen, A., & Cohen, R. (2002). A dynamic approach for effcient TCP buffer allocation. *IEEE Transactions on Computers, 51*(3), 303–312. doi:10.1109/12.990128

Eggert, L., Heideman, J., & Touch, J. (2000). Effects of ensemble TCP. *ACM Computer Communication Review, 30*(1), 15–29. doi:10.1145/505688.505691

Floyd, S. (2003). *RFC3649: Highspeed TCP for large congestion windows*. Retrieved July 31, 2010, from http:// www.ietf.org/ rfc/ rfc3649.txt

Gropp, W., Lusk, E., & Thakur, R. (1999). *Using MPI-2: Advanced features of the message-passing interface*. Cambridge, MA: The MIT Press.

Hacker, T. J., Noble, B. D., & Atley, B. D. (2002). The end-to-end performance effects of parallel TCP sockets on a lossy wide area network. In *Proceedings of IEEE International Symposium on Parallel and Distributed Processing* (IPDPS02), (pp. 434-443).

Hacker, T. J., Noble, B. D., & Atley, B. D. (2005). Adaptive data block scheduling for parallel streams. In *Proceedings of IEEE International Symposium on High Performance Distributed Computing* (HPDC05), (pp. 265-275).

Hasegawa, G., Terai, T., Okamoto, T., & Murata, M. (2001). *Scalable socket buffer tuning for high-performance Web servers*. In International Conference on Network Protocols (ICNP01), (p. 281).

Jain, M., Prasad, R. S., & Davrolis, C. (2003). *The TCP bandwidth-delay product revisited: Network buffering, cross traffic, and socket buffer auto-sizing*. *Technical report*. Georgia Institute of Technology.

Jin, C., Wei, D. X., Low, S. H., Buhrmaster, G., Bunn, J., & Choe, D. H. (2005). Fast TCP: from theory to experiments. *IEEE Network, 19*(1), 4–11. doi:10.1109/MNET.2005.1383434

Karrer, R. P., Park, J., & Kim, J. (2006). *Adaptive data block scheduling for parallel streams. Technical report*. Deutsche Telekom Laboratories.

Kelly, T. (2003). Scalable TCP: Improving performance in highspeed wide area networks. *Computer Communication Review, 32*(2), 83–91. doi:10.1145/956981.956989

Kola, G., & Vernon, M. K. (2007). Target bandwidth sharing using endhost measures. *Performance Evaluation, 64*(9-12), 948–964. doi:10.1016/j.peva.2007.07.001

Lee, J., Gunter, D., Tierney, B., Allcock, B., Bester, J., Bresnahan, J., & Tuecke, S. (2001). Applied techniques for high bandwidth data transfers across wide area networks. In *Proceedings International Conference on Computing in High Energy and Nuclear Physics* (CHEP01).

Lu, D., Qiao, Y., & Dinda, P. A. (2005). Characterizing and predicting TCP throughput on the wide area network. In *Proceedings of IEEE International Conference on Distributed Computing Systems* (ICDCS05), (pp 414-424).

Lu, D., Qiao, Y., Dinda, P. A., & Bustamante, F. E. (2005). Modeling and taming parallel TCP on the wide area network. In *Proceedings of IEEE International Symposium on Parallel and Distributed Processing* (IPDPS05), (p. 68b).

Morajko, A. (2004). *Dynamic tuning of parallel/ distributed applications*. Unpublished doctoral dissertation, Universitat Autonoma de Barcelona, Spain.

Prasad, R. S., Jain, M., & Davrolis, C. (2004). Socket buffer auto-sizing for high-performance data transfers. *Journal of Grid Computing, 1*(4), 361–376. doi:10.1023/B:GRID.0000037554.67413.52

Semke, J., Madhavi, J., & Mathis, M. (1998). Automatic TCP buffer tuning. *ACM SIG-COMM'98, 28*(4), 315-323.

Simmel, D., & Budden, R. (2008). *DMOVER: Scheduled data transfer for distributed computational workflows*. Paper presented at TeraGrid Conference, Las Vegas, NV.

Sivakumar, H., Bailey, S., & Grossman, R. L. (2000). Psockets: The case for application-level network striping for data intensive applications using high speed wide area networks. In *Proceedings IEEE Super Computing Conference* (SC00), (p. 63).

The LONI network. (2010). *Website*. Retrieved July 31, 2010, from http:// www.loni.org

The Lustre File System. (2010). *Lustre wiki*. Retrieved July 31, 2010, from http:// wiki.lustre.org

The Teragrid network. (2010). *Website*. Retrieved July 31, 2010, from http:// www.teragrid.org

Thomas, M. (2008). *Configuring servers for optimal I/O*. Talk given at Ultralight planets tutorial, Miami, FL.

Tierney, B. L. (2005). *TCP tuning techniques for high-speed wide-area networks*. Talk given at Networks for non-networkers 2 Workshop, Edinburgh, UK.

Torvalds, L., & the The Free Software Company. (2010). *The Linux kernel*. Retrieved July 31, 2010, from http:// www.kernel.org

US Department of Energy. (2008). *Advanced networking for distributed petascale science*. Technical report.

Welshons, K., Dorn, P., Hutanu, A., Holub, P., Vollbrecht, J, & Allen, G.(Design and implementation of a production dynamically configurable testbed. *Proceedings of TeraGrid2010*.

Yildirim, E., Yin, D., & Kosar, T. (in press). Prediction of optimal parallelism level in wide area data transfers. *IEEE Transactions on Parallel and Distributed Systems*.

ADDITIONAL READING

Altman, E., Barman, D., Tuffin, B., & Vojnovic, M. (2006). Parallel tcp sockets: Simple model, throughput and validation. In Proceedings of IEEE Conference on Computer Communications (INFOCOM06), pp. 1-12.

Hacker, T. J., Noble, B. D., & Atley, B. D. (2002). The end-to-end performance effects of parallel tcp sockets on a lossy wide area network. In Proceedings of IEEE International Symposium on Parallel and Distributed Processing (IPDPS02), pp. 434-443.

Lu, D., Qiao, Y., Dinda, P. A., & Bustamante, F. E. (2005). Modeling and taming parallel tcp on the wide area network. In Proceedings of IEEE International Symposium on Parallel and Distributed Processing (IPDPS05), pp. 68b.

Yildirim, E., Balman, M., & Kosar, T. (2008). Dynamically Tuning Level of Parallelism in Wide Area Data Transfers. Proceedings of International Workshop on Data-Aware Distributed Computing (DADC 2008)

Yildirim, E., Suslu, I. H., & Kosar, T. (2008). Which Network Measurement Tool is Right for You? A Multidimensional Comparison Study. Proceedings of IEEE/ACM Int. Conference on Grid Computing (Grid 2008)

Yildirim, E., Yin, D., & Kosar, T. (2009). Balancing TCP Buffer vs Parallel Streams in Application Level Throughput Optimization. Proceedings of International Workshop on Data-Aware Distributed Computing (DADC 2009.

Yin, D., Yildirim, E., & Kosar, T. (2009). A Data Throughput Prediction and Optimization Service for Widely Distributed Many-Task Computing. Proceedings of Many Task Computing in Grids and Supercomputers (MTAGS 2009)

Chapter 3
IPTV Challenges and Solutions in Metro Networks

Sajjad Zare
Sahand University of Technology, Iran

Akbar Ghaffarpour Rahbar
Sahand University of Technology, Iran

ABSTRACT

The Internet Protocol-based television (IPTV) uses digital TV technology and transmits TV and video contents over IP-based networks, where customers can have more choices in watching TV programs and interacting with it. In this chapter, different challenges and solutions proposed for IPTV are studied. We present an introduction to IPTV, its features, its applications, network factors for deploying IPTV, and an overview to IPTV networking infrastructure. Moreover, we study different factors in video coding that have an effect on optimizing the bandwidth and are robust against impairments. In addition, different challenges in IPTV over optical and wireless networks are reviewed. Besides, we study different solutions to improve VoD services. These methods use NVoD and TVoD to improve unicast services. We also study the methods that use features of networks and videos to improve multicasting services in IPTV. Finally, we discuss the methods to improve QoS in DSL and wireless networks.

INTRODUCTION

Digital Television is the most advanced version of Television technology improved in the last century. Digital TV provides customers more choices and interactivity. New technology called Internet Protocol-based Television (IPTV) uses

DOI: 10.4018/978-1-61350-110-8.ch003

digital TV technology and transmits it over IP based networks (Driscol, 2008), (Moawad, 2008). IPTV is a technique that transmits TV and video content over a network that uses the IP networking protocol. With increasing the number of users, performance becomes more important in order to provide interest in video content applications and relative services. The requirement for new video applications on traditional broadcast networks

Copyright © 2012, IGI Global. Copying or distributing in print or electronic forms without written permission of IGI Global is prohibited.

(cable, terrestrial transmitters, and satellite) opens a new perspective for the developed use of IP networks to satisfy the new service demands (Driscol, 2008).

Internet Protocol Television, IPTV, Telco TV, or broadband TV is delivering high quality broadcast television and/or on-demand video and audio content over a broadband network. On the other hand, IPTV is a mechanism applied to deliver old TV channels, movies, and video-on-demand contents over a private network. The official definition approved by the International Telecommunication Union focus group on IPTV (ITU-T FG IPTV) is as: "IPTV is defined as multimedia services such as television/video/audio/text/graphics /data delivered over IP based networks managed to provide the required level of quality of service and experience, security, interactivity and reliability" (Driscol, 2008, pp.2).

We shall study different challenges and solutions proposed for IPTV in this chapter. We first present a background on IPTV such as its features, its applications, network factors for deploying IPTV, and an overview to IPTV networking infrastructure. Then, we will discuss challenges of IPTV in different contexts, and state solutions for each challenge. We will also study the methods that use features of networks and videos to improve multicasting services in IPTV. We will discuss the methods proposed to improve QoS in DSL and wireless networks. Finally, we present future research directions and conclusion at the end of the chapter.

BACKGROUND

In this section, we provide definitions, discussions and networking infrastructures of the IPTV.

IPTV Features and Applications

In this subsection we shall discuss features and applications of IPTV. IPTV has a number of features as follows:

- Support for interactive TV: IPTV provides two-way communications facilities that allow service providers to deliver a complete sample of interactive TV applications. IPTV has some types of services such as live TV, high definition TV (HDTV), interactive games, and high speed Internet browsing.
- Time shifting: IPTV along with a digital video recorder is used for recording and storing IPTV content for later viewing.
- Personalization: IPTV supports two-way communications and permits end users to personalize their TV viewing habits by allowing them to decide what and when they want to watch a program.
- Low bandwidth requirements: Instead of delivering each channel to each end user, IPTV allows service providers to only transmit the channel that the end user has requested. This significant feature allows service providers to optimally use bandwidth of their networks.
- Accessible on multiple devices: Viewing of IPTV content is not limited to televisions. Consumers can use their PCs, mobile devices, and PDAs to access IPTV services (Driscol, 2008), (She et al., 2007), (Lambert et al., 2009), and (Ikeda, 2008).

The following list shows a number of IPTV applications, where each application needs different QoS requirements in order to be delivered in the best quality to end-users:

- Entertainment TV services (e.g., television channel and video-on-demand).
- Security (e.g., surveillance systems);
- Real-time communications (e.g., video telephony, teleconferencing);
- Interactive applications (e.g., interactive TV and gaming);
- Internet sharing and streaming (e.g., user-created video content and web-based

streaming to a desktop PC or mobile device);

- Corporate training and marketing videos (Driscol, 2008), (She et al., 2007), (Ikeda, 2008).
- Live video streaming (television channel) is one of the IPTV services.

Differences between IPTV and Internet TV

It is important to know the differences between IPTV and traditional watching of TV through Internet.

- Different Platforms: Internet TV uses the public Internet to deliver video contents to the end users, but IPTV uses secure dedicated private networks to deliver video content to customers. This private network is managed and operated by IPTV service providers. This is the main difference between ITV and IPTV that enables the IPTV service provider to apply its dedicated rules to the system.
- Geographical Reach: Networks are owned and controlled by service providers that cover a special geographical area. However, Internet has no geographical limitations and TV services can be accessed from any part of the world.
- Ownership of the Networking Infrastructure: When video is sent through Internet, some of the Internet protocols used to carry the video may get delayed or completely lost as video is transmitted through various networks. Therefore, the providers of video over the Internet cannot guarantee a TV viewing experience. However, IPTV is delivered over a networking infrastructure, which is typically owned by service providers. Owning the networking infrastructure allows telecom operators to engineer their systems to sup-

port the end-to-end delivery of high quality videos (Driscol, 2008).

Network Factors Associated with Deploying IPTV

The following is the list of factors that a network must support for IPTV services.

1. Network Dimensioning: IPTV distribution networks need high bandwidth capacity to support the transport of video contents. IPTV needs multiples of the bandwidth required to support voice over IP (VoIP) and Internet access services. The total bandwidth required to implement IPTV services depends on a couple of factors as (Driscol, 2008):
   - The number of IPTV multicast channels: It is noted that a single copy of each channel is sent from the IPTV data center to the distribution network. Once a channel is transmitted into the networking infrastructure, the multicast process handles the copying of channels and routing to individual IPTV subscribers. For example in a private network that implements IPTV, consider there are 10,000 subscribers of 100 standard definitions (SD) IP broadcast TV channels. If we assume that the provider uses H.264 to compress the channels, this generally needs a bandwidth requirement of at least 2 Mbps for each broadcasting channel. In this scenario where at least one subscriber is accessing each channel at a particular instance in time, the Next Generation Network (NGN) core distribution network will require 200 Mbps of bandwidth capacity (Driscol, 2008).
   - Inclusion of IP-VoD services: These types of services use unicast transmission techniques to provide com-

munications between the IPTV consumer devices and the on-demand video server. This type of service consumes a large amount of bandwidth and the network needs to synchronize this level of network traffic. Consider the same network of 10,000 end users and assume that 5% of the subscribers simultaneously use a VoD service. By assuming again that the H.264 compression standard is used, this translates to a peak usage on the network of 1 Gbps (10,000 × 5% × 2 Mbps) (Driscol, 2008).

2. IPTV Reliability: The IP networking infrastructure must be reliable at the event of device failure because in this case many services (multicast or unicast applications, VoIP and all services provided by this network) are interrupted. Redundant links should be used wherever possible (Driscol, 2008).

3. Fast Responsiveness: The network requires supporting minimum response times associated with channel zapping (refers to changing from one channel to another during TV viewing experience) (Driscol, 2008).

4. Predictable Performance: The video bit rate streams have variability nature due to different scenario complexities, which are delivered to an IPTV access device on a frame-by frame basis. Therefore, prediction of the exact requirements in video transmission is difficult, especially when the service is operating in real-time IPTV. Operators have to allocate appropriate network resources to overcome with variable bit rate streams (Driscol, 2008).

5. Levels of QoS: Since most IPTV services operate over a private IP broadband network, it is advisable to implement a QoS policy when delivering video contents to paying subscribers. A QoS system preserves a video signal and monitors the rate of impairments as it is transmitted over long distances. This

is to permit operators to provide services that require deterministic performance guarantees such as IP VoD and IP Multicast (Driscol, 2008).

Challenges for Delivering IPTV Streams

The use of delay-sensitive services such as interactive gaming, IPTV and Voice-over-IP (VOIP) continue to grow. The provision of QoS requirements in terms of loss, delay and jitter for these services are very difficult than for normal data (Jeong et al., 2008).

In addition to delay and jitter, IPTV streams are also sensitive to packet loss in such a way that a very little packet loss in an IPTV stream may cause a significant degradation in video quality (Asghar, Hood, & Faucheur, 2009). While digital video coding does not suffer from noise, typically found in analogue television systems, there are still two problems leading to packet loss: (1) access networks may suffer from packet loss due to the lack of bandwidth distributed among different services; and (2) packets may be lost in the core network due to congestion on certain network links (Lambert et al., 2009).

Overview of an IPTV Networking Infrastructure

Figure 1 shows a typical IPTV networking infrastructure with three main sections (Driscol, 2008):

*   IPTV data center (Headend): this center receives content from many sources such as content producers, local video, cable, terrestrial and satellite channels. The IPTV data center delivers the content through the distribution network to subscribers. This center must have a subscriber management system for accounting and profile purposes. The IPTV data center must provide security options as well.

Figure 1. IPTV networking infrastructure

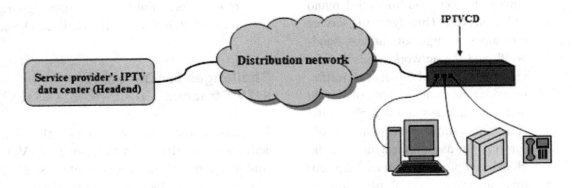

- Distribution network: this network obtains contents from IPTV data center and delivers them to subscribers. To deliver IPTV services, one-to-one connection is required. Because of large volume of video content in IPTV services, these types of networks must have high bandwidth. Since IPTV services are very sensitive to packet-loss, delay and jitter, these networks must ingratiate these factors as well.

- IPTVCD: IPTV Customer Device is an important component that allows a customer to use IPTV services. The IPTVCD is connected to the distribution network and receives contents and delivers them to customers. Since several services such as TV, telephone and Internet are presented in these networks, this device should be able to process, separate and send the relevant traffic of these services to associated devices. In addition, this device should receive requests from users and send them to the network.

IPTV Networking Infrastructure

IPTV network architecture consists of two sections: the last mile networks (i.e., access network) and centralized networks (i.e., core network). The last mile section can use a wide variety of networks, such as cable systems, copper telephone, wireless, and satellite networks to deliver advanced IPTV network services. The delivery of video over all these different types of networks has its own set of challenges (Driscol, 2008), (James, 2007).

IPTV Backbone Technologies

The backbone or core of an IPTV networking infrastructure is used to carry large bulk of video content at high speed rates between the IPTV data center and the last mile broadband distribution network. There are several different types of backbone transmission standards that has a number of specific features including data transfer speed and scalability. Three main backbone transmission technologies used in IPTV network infrastructures are ATM over SONET/SDH, IP over MPLS and metro Ethernet (Driscol, 2008). The core networks can connect IPTV data center to different types of access networks such as PON and WiMAX.

ATM Over SONET/SDH

Applications such as IPTV that need high bandwidth and low transmission delays can be supported by ATM. ATM will operate over different network media such as coaxial and twisted pair cables; however, it runs at its optimum speed over fiber cables. Here, ATM uses a physical layer called Synchronous Optical Network (SONET) to transport its cells over the backbone network, where SONET is a protocol that uses fiber media and provides high-speed transmission. The term Synchronous Digital Hierarchy (SDH) refers to the optical technology outside the United States. The SONET signal rate is measured by optical carrier (OC) standards (Driscol, 2008).

IP Over MPLS

Advanced Label Switch Routers (LSRs) is used to design an MPLS platform. These LSRs are responsible for establishing connection-oriented paths to specific destinations on the IPTV network. These virtual paths, called Label Switched Paths (LSPs), are configured with enough resources to ensure smooth transmission of IPTV traffic through an MPLS network. LSPs simplify and increase speed of routing of packets in the network because the packets are only controlled and inspected at the ingress nodes of the network. LSRs also identify network traffic types by adding an MPLS header onto the beginning of each IPTV packet. The header is added in the ingress LSR and removed by the egress LSR as it leaves the MPLS core network. MPLS routers use a number of local tables called Label Information Bases (LIBs) to determine details about the next hop along the route. In addition to testing the table, a new label is applied to the packet and forwarded to the appropriate router output port (Driscol, 2008).

Metro Ethernet

This core network uses connection orientated virtual circuits that allow IPTV service providers to guarantee the delivery of high quality video content within the core network. These dedicated links are called Ethernet Virtual Connections (EVCs) (Driscol, 2008). A metro Ethernet-based core network has some key technical features such as:

- It can resolve various requirements in the core networking technology such as resilience, high performance for delivering video content, and scalability (Driscol, 2008).
- Some of the modern Metro Ethernet networking components can operate at speeds up to 100 Gbps across long geographical distances. This feature enables providers to represent IPTV services at a desired platform (Driscol, 2008).
- The Metro Ethernet uses a complex recovery mechanism and therefore it is very good for IPTV services because video packets are very sensitive to packet loss (Driscol, 2008).

Last Mile Broadband Distribution Network Types

The network section located between the core network and the end-users' home needs enough bandwidth capacity to deliver video streams, on the other hand, providing this requirement is one of the primary challenges that IPTV service providers are experiencing (Driscol, 2008; She et al., 2007). There are mainly six different types of broadband access networks that can provide enough bandwidth for IPTV requirements (Driscol, 2008):

- With a network built with fiber
- With a DSL network
- With a wireless broadband connection
- With a cable TV network
- With a satellite-based network
- With Internet

IPTV over a Fiber Access Network

In this context, there are several network architectures based on the vicinity of fiber to end user's home (Driscol, 2008), (Kahabka, 2008):

- Fiber to the regional office (FTTRO)
- Fiber to the neighborhood (node) (FTTN)
- Fiber to the curb (FTTC)
- Fiber to the home (FTTH)
- Fiber to the apartment (FTTA)

These architectures typically use two different network technologies, PON and AON.

PON Networks

Passive Optical Network (PON) is a point-to-multipoint networking topology that can use light-waves of different colors to carry data across the network. This requires no electrical components between the IPTV data center and the destination point. A PON includes several components as Optical Line Termination (OLT) located at the IPTV data center and a number of Optical Network Terminals (ONTs) located at the end users side.

The OLT uses components such as fiber cable to connect one component to another and optical splitters to split an optical signal into multiple signals to deliver network traffic to the ONTs. The OLT manages the ONTs and responds to their requests. An ONT receives traffic in optical format, checks its address, converts the traffic into electrical signals, and sends the traffic toward different devices such as TV, PC and phones according to the type of traffic. PON can also support more wavelengths; therefore the capacity of this network can increase significantly (Driscol, 2008), (Kahabka, 2008), (Ikeda, 2008), (Zhang et al., 2009), (Nakanishi, Otaka, & Maeda, 2008).

AON Network

Active Optical Networks (AON) utilizes active elements (electrical components) such as Ethernet switches located between the IPTV data center and the endpoint of the fiber network. AON is a point to point optical network without splitter, where ONTs are directly connected to the Access Node (AN). Metro-Ethernet Switches, IP-Edge Rout-

ers, or Multi-Service Access Nodes (MSAN) with optical Ethernet interfaces are usually used for an AN unit (Kahabka, 2008). Bandwidth allocation in AON is better than PON and the increase of bandwidth in AON is simpler than PON. AON is more secure than PON since each ONT is directly connected to the AN and an ONT cannot receive the data belonging to other ONTs. Therefore, AON could be suitable for private network operators (Kahabka, 2008).

IPTV Over an ADSL Network

ADSL is a point-to-point connection network technology that uses exiting copper telephone lines to deliver high bandwidth services such as IPTV. It is named "asymmetric" because downstream bandwidth is more than the upstream bandwidth. This is due to the fact that transmission of data from the network to users is more than transmission of data by users to the network (Driscol, 2008). ADSL uses Frequency Division Multiplexing (FDM) to send and receive synchronous voice and data through a common link by means of dividing the range of frequency of telephone line into three sections:

- 0-4KHz for phone (because the range of frequency of human voice is usually between 3- 4KHz) and 4-25KHz is guarded band
- 25-200KHz is used for upstream traffic and 200-250KHz is also guarded band.
- 250KHz-1/1MHz is used for downstream traffic

There are several components that are used in an ADSL network (Driscol, 2008):

- An ADSL modem: located in the subscriber's home.
- A POTS splitter: The splitter divides the incoming signal into low and high frequen-

cies and sends it to a telephone and to the home network respectively.

- A DSLAM (Digital Subscriber Line Access Multiplexer): the DSLAM receives the subscriber's connections, aggregates them, and connects back to the central IPTV data center through a high speed fiber-based network backbone.

There are three main advantages for an ADSL network (Driscol, 2008):

- High speed compared with common modem
- Use of existing telephone line infrastructures
- Simultaneously using of network and phone

IPTV Over Wireless Networks

Video servers/encoders store audio/video (A/V) contents, encoded and compressed from live and pre-recorded programs. Video servers/encoders could be either centralized or distributed in core networks (Driscol, 2008), (She et al., 2007), (Hou et al., 2008). The A/V content from the source is formatted, compressed (mostly using MPEG-2 encoding and compression standard), and encapsulated as a service of Real time Transport Protocol (RTP). Currently, MPEG-4 standard with more performance is deployed and gradually used instead of MPEG-2 standard.

User datagram protocol (UDP) or transmission control protocol (TCP) is used to transport the payload and to turn it to the payload for internet protocol (IP) (Driscol, 2008), (She et al., 2007), (Hou et al., 2008). If metro Ethernet is used in the core network, the IP payload is encapsulated as Ethernet 802.3 and 10/100/1G Base-T traffic that travels through core networks. A WiMAX base station (BS) located at the edge of the core network receives 802.3 packets and the BS MAC de-capsulates Ethernet headers and encapsulates

the IP payload as 802.16 MAC PDUs and then into PHY PDUs (Retnasothie, Ozdemir, & Yucek, 2006), (Hou et al., 2008).

The 802.16 PHY prepares these PDUs for wireless links by performing FEC, symbol mapping and OFDM or other modulation schemes (Retnasothie, Ozdemir, & Yucek, 2006), (Hou et al., 2008).

IPTV Over Next Generation Cable TV Networks

With the advent of new services such as IPTV, cable TV operators have made large changes in their networks to support these services. Hybrid Fiber/ Coax (HFC) is a popular technology for cable TV networks to deliver video content to customers. In the HFC technology, the fiber-based section is as a backbone of the network to deliver huge amount of video streams to the coax-based section, where the coax-based section is an interface between the fiber-based section and customer's home (Driscol, 2008).

IPTV Over a Satellite-Based Network

Satellite networks can provide more bandwidth than terrestrial networks, appropriate for delivering triple-play services including digital video content, VOIP and high speed Internet access to customers. Many satellite network providers can deliver IP video contents using their networks to the cable and telecommunication head-ends and IPTV data centers.

The operations in a satellite network are as follows. The original content is received; aggregated and encoded with MPEG-2, MPEG-4 or Windows Media format; encrypted by satellite operator's video operations center; and then uploaded to the satellite. The content is relayed back down to the various video hubs that operate based on cable or telecommunication companies that have their own network infrastructure to deliver video content to customers (Driscol, 2008).

IPTV Over Internet

Video entertainment through Internet has grown up in recent years because of improved broadband speed, advances in compression technology, and great viewing choices. When watching a video in the Internet, the following operations are performed. At the streaming server, where the video is located, the video content is broken into IP packets, compressed and then transmitted across the Internet to the client PC. The PC has a suitable software that decompresses the video content an produces a live video for the client (Driscol, 2008). Table 1 compares different IPTV networking infrastructures with each other.

MAIN FOCUS OF THE CHAPTER

In this section we shall focus on challenges in IPTV under different contexts.

Video Coding

Since IPTV traffic is voluminous and sensitive to delay, jitter and packet-loss, it is necessary to use property of video streams to code a video in order to reduce the volume of the video and preserve its quality. In addition, due to voluminous data in IPTV, an A/V content should be compressed to match the capabilities of the channel and the decoding capabilities of the receiver. Audio and video are multiplexed into a single bitstream with a constant bit rate after being separately compressed (Appleby et al., 2006). On the other hand, since very little packet loss in an IPTV stream may cause a significant degradation in video quality, we study some methods to reduce this impairment.

The encoder usually operates in one of two modes: constant quality or constant bit rate. In the constant quality mode, the quality of frame sequences is kept the same by adjusting encoding parameters during the encoding process. A frame may contain different amount of information, for example, a frame related to news may have less information than a frame relevant to an action movie. As a result, some frames can be compressed much better than others. Therefore, the constant quality mode provides a vast variation in the number of bits required to represent each picture and a complex transmission management (Appleby et al., 2006). In the constant bit-rate mode, the encoder tries to stay close to the goal bit rate by manipulating the quality of frames, therefore this mode is a tradeoff between the quality and simplicity of transmission (Appleby et al., 2006). The constant bit rate mode generates variable quality that may be unacceptable. Therefore, the challenge is to manage the distribution of content that is very dynamic and its bit rate is highly variable.

Instead of both constant quality and constant bit-rate encoding, the bit rate can be adapted to network conditions (Appleby et al., 2006). The streaming server has a model of the client buffer so that the server can adapt the delivery rate due to the condition of the client buffers. In this method, the encoder codes each frame to a number of qualities. The encoder generates three types of frames: I-frame that has basic information, P and B frames that have partial information. The partial information is related to the detail of the scene that may not be even notable by human.

In adaptive bit-rate streaming, we cannot know which decoded frames can be used as references during encoding, and this is the main challenge for both video encoding and for the server. To solve this problem, switching from one quality stream to another should be limited to specific switching points. At these switching points, the relation of the video stream on the history of decoded pictures would be restricted. This restriction can be achieved by periodically encoding pictures as I-pictures (intra-pictures) (Appleby et al., 2006).

Assume that we have two different types of switching pictures such as Access Picture (AP) and Link Picture (LP). At each point where the switching pictures occurs, the server has the option to send either an AP switching picture and remain within the same stream, or send an LP switching picture and move to a higher or lower bandwidth according to the state of client buffer and network conditions that obtained by the server. Therefore if a client receives an AP switching picture, it assures that the server will stay in current stream. If the client receives an LP switching picture, it assures that the server will change its stream (Appleby et al., 2006).

In a broadcasting service in which the traffic of several programs is groomed into a single bitstream channel, a program can borrow bandwidth from another one. Each best-effort service receives a varying amount of the physically available bit rate; therefore if a streamed video traffic competes with other traffic for bandwidth, the available bit rate for any program stream will be unknown and time-dependent. Therefore, it is a good idea to add bandwidth assurance to the network infrastructure. This method has two disadvantages: (1) there may be a video sequence encoded at much higher quality than necessary; in this case the large amount of bandwidth is occupied spuriously; and (2) the reserved bandwidth may not be fully utilized because there may be an application that occupies less bandwidth than what is reserved for it. (Appleby et al., 2006).

Multicasting in IPTV

We study the property of networks and videos to support more IPTV multicast channels. Unlike traditional TV, in IPTV, an IPTV multicast channel is sent when at least one user requests it and for all users only one IPTV multicast channel is sent. For example, if 1000 users request the same TV channel, we do not send the requested TV channel in 1000 channels for each user separately. Instead, we send only one multicast channel for all of them. Since each user has different channel conditions due to channel fading in WiMAX, we use some methods in such a way that each user

receives video quality based on its capability (such as channel condition, type of device, …).

Unicasting in IPTV

VoD could be one of the main services that can be provided for IPTV. We study the methods that can optimize bandwidth usage and therefore can improve blocking probability and video quality. The VoD systems are divided into True-VoD (TVoD) and Near-VoD (NVoD). In TVoD, the video is transmitted by a unicast transmission. The main problem of TVoD system is its requirement for high bandwidth in order to transmit a requested video. To reduce high bandwidth requirement, some methods will be discussed. On the other hand, a video is transmitted by either a broadcast or a multicast transmission in NVoD (Lee et al., 2009).

Three main groups of NVoD are (1) batching: NVoD aggregates a group of requests that arrive close in time and serves all of them by one channel, (2) patching: where video requests are initially served by unicasting. When a request is synchronized to a multicast stream, the video request is joined to the multicast stream, and (3) broadcasting: where video is periodically broadcast into dedicated channels with a specified schedule (Lee et al., 2009).

QoS Improvements in IPTV

Congestion could be an important challenge in optical networks and DSL access links. Each packet loss that occurs in the congestion state produces visual artifacts in a video. On the other hand, in a wireless network, channel states are dependent on many conditions such as the distance between an SS and BS. Therefore, when sending a video on a wireless network such as IEEE 802.16, the mobile user may receive the video with an unstable quality that depends on its channel conditions.

Solutions and Recommendations

We shall discuss several solutions proposed for the challenges in each context in this section.

Video Coding

The first method that we study in this subsection is developed by Bell Technical lab (BT). This model is based on the human perception of the quality of video sequences. To optimize compression and as a result to optimize bandwidth, this model adjusts the encoder parameters based on the visual attention of human in such a way that parts of the scene that are more notable for human are encoded with more quality and more bandwidth are allocated for them. (Appleby et al., 2006).

As the second method, we study Scalable video coding (SVC) that has been the basic method since 20 years ago. In IPTV, video packet streams in IP-based networks are received by devices with different resolutions such as PC, SD, HD-ready and Full-HD TV. In addition, receivers in a wireless network have different channel conditions, and therefore, different capabilities to receive video packets. Consequently, scalability is needed (Wiegand, Noblet, & Rovati, 2009).

SVC codec encodes the video in different bit rates at different layers to match heterogeneous receivers based on three states: (1) Temporal scalability: in this state the encoder represents layers that are different in frame rate, (2) Spatial scalability: in this case the layers are different in frame size; and (3) Quality scalability: in this case the layers have the same frame rate and frame size but have different signal-to-noise ratio (SNR) (Wiegand, Noblet, & Rovati, 2009).

Another method uses the concept of scalable video coding to obtain a video with better quality. In this method, a frame is divided into two regions based on the motion activities with a threshold: the region with high motion activities (called region 1) form the base layer (encoded with better quality at higher frame rate), and the region with low motion (called region 2) form the enhancement layer. In each frame, only the blocks of the base layer are coded and the enhancement layer blocks are substituted with collocated blocks of the previous reference frame.

Note that SVC codec encodes a video with different bit rates at different layers, where each layer is called description. In the proposed Multiple Description (MD) coding, multiple independent descriptions based on quality-scalable video coding are produced for the blocks in the base layer. Then, multiple descriptions are transmitted over independent paths toward the destination. If all descriptions are transmitted without errors, then the receiver can produce a video with high quality. If one description is lost, the receiver can produce an acceptable video quality by another descriptions (Kim, 2006).

One can adjust a threshold in order to efficiently divide the regions. It is noted that the base layer is more important than the enhancement layer because the base layer has more information than the enhancement layer that belongs to low motion region. One can recover the enhancement layer by substituting of lost Macro Blocks (MB), i.e., a part of the frame, with rival MBs in other frames simplicity (Kim, 2006). Performance evaluation results show that the proposed MD coding can cope with packet losses because the reconstructed video quality can be maintained as long as both streams are not lost at the same time (Kim, 2006).

The fourth method to overcome packet loss and achieve better quality is to use the concept of SVC, in which when a packet loss occurs and a video is damaged, a new Network Adaption Layer (NAL) unit is inserted into the damaged video stream where the packet is lost. At the destination, the decoder uses different techniques such as Temporal Direct (TD), Frame Copy (FC), and Motion and residual Up-sampling (MRU) to recover the lost data (Lambert et al., 2009):

Temporal Direct (TD): In this method, motion vectors and reference indices are derived for

Figure 2. Motion vector inference using temporal direct (TD) mode

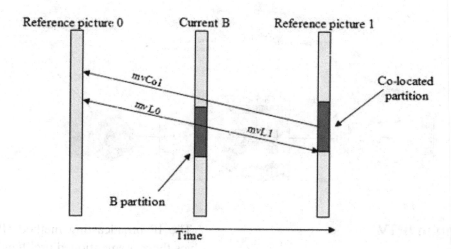

the lost macro-blocks using the TD macro-block mode (Lambert et al., 2009).

Figure 2 shows the temporal direct mode motion vector, when the current picture is temporally located between two reference pictures from the reference picture 0 (left hand) and 1 (right hand). We can conceal the current picture with two reference pictures by tracking objects in current picture within two reference pictures.

- **Frame copy:** A plain error concealment method in the case of a lost frame is achieved by repeating the last available frame. In other words, if the current frame is lost the previous received frame is repeated. This frame copy (FC) method can be achieved by copying the first frame in reference picture list 0. In this manner, the reference frame that is temporally closest to the lost frame is selected (Lambert et al., 2009).

- **Motion and residual up-sampling (MRU):** In this method, the motion and residual data of the reference layer are reused. The motion and residual data is up-sampled if necessary, and then the motion compensation step is executed at the enhancement layer (Lambert et al., 2009). Note that up-sampling is the process of increasing the sampling rate of a signal.

Note that one can use this method to cope with congestion by actively adapting video streams to avoid congestion. If congestion occurs, MRU replaces correct video packets with the new NAL units. This is because the congestion has occurred and we should drop packets. In this method, we replace them with NAL unit with fewer volume and recover them at the decoder to minimize the visual artifacts (Lambert et al., 2009). The advantage of this approach is that error concealment can be achieved using a decoder that has no support for error concealment. Moreover, the generation of these error concealing NAL units has a low complexity and can be executed in real time (Lambert et al., 2009).

The fourth method has a very high performance with low complexity. In addition, the visual result of the adjusted video bitstreams is equivalent with error concealment techniques that could be implemented in the decoder. In addition, no modifications are required at the decoder (Lambert et al., 2009). Video coding methods are compared in Table 2.

Figure 3. IP broadcasting system architecture

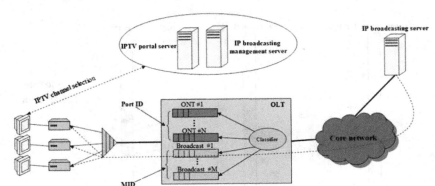

Multicasting in IPTV

Here, we shall discuss solutions proposed for multicasting of IPTV in PON and WiMAX network.

Multicasting of IPTV in PON networks

Two methods are discussed in this subsection for the support of multicasting IPTV traffic in PON. The first method, IP broadcasting, uses the nature of PON network to deliver multicast channels to IPTV terminals (Ikeda, 2008). This approach proposes an IP broadcasting system architecture which consists of a PON, IPTV terminals, and an IP broadcasting server. Note in a typical PON network, all ONTs share the bandwidth of the downstream link. When the OLT sends data to one of the ONTs, the data can be received by all ONTs. However, only the destination ONT receives the data based on the PON link ID. For example, the ID could be port ID in GPON or logical link ID (LLID) of GEPON (Ikeda, 2008). As a result, a packet of a multicast channel must be duplicated to all users of a multicast group in IPTV/PON. Repeating a video stream for each user of the multicast group, the bandwidth is wasted, and therefore, a large number of multicast channels cannot be supported (Ikeda, 2008).

The IP broadcasting method (Ikeda, 2008) solves the aforementioned problem by encapsulating the multicast packet into a broadcasting frame called Generic Encapsulation Method (GEM) frame with a multicast port ID. Therefore, by assigning a multicast port ID to all users of a multicast group, all of them can receive the multicast channel (Ikeda, 2008). Figure 3 illustrates the proposed IP broadcasting system architecture that consists of an IP broadcasting server, an IPTV network that contains core network, PON, and an IPTV terminal (Ikeda, 2008). The IPTV portal server provides the IPTV channel URL information to IPTV subscribers, which includes the IP broadcasting-type content, VOD-type content, and file download-type content (Ikeda, 2008).

An IP broadcasting management server manages the multicast addresses of IP broadcasting channels (Ikeda, 2008). When an IPTV terminal receives an IPTV channel URL from a remote TV controller or a keyboard, the terminal asks the IP broadcasting management server for the corresponding multicast address. After receiving the multicast address response, the IPTV terminal sends an IGMP join message to the ONT connected to the IPTV terminal as a channel request. When the ONT receives an IPTV channel selection request from the IPTV terminal, it will forward only the corresponding IP broadcasting channel to the IPTV terminal (Ikeda, 2008). Note that an

ONT may receive multiple IP broadcasting channels at the same time.

In a typical PON system, the IPTV channel selection time (the time between pressing a button in a remote controller and changing the channel) is specified by the transaction between an IPTV terminal and a multicast router that is already receiving multicast data. However in the proposed approach, the channel selection time is the transmission delay of a join message and the multicast data between an IPTV terminal and an ONT (Ikeda, 2008).

The second method, called Weighted Round Robin (WRR), tries to reduce the cost of the congestion in PON networks. Congestion is one of the main challenges in an optical network such as PON that results in packet loss, and packet loss leads to undesired visual effects in a video (Kwon et al., 2009). To achieve this goal, the WRR method gives special attention to reputable videos that have many advocates. The number of lost multicast packets is dependent on the number of receivers because if a multicast packet is lost, all the receivers of a multicast group cannot receive it. Therefore, in the WRR method, the multicast packets with more receivers are given larger weights and are preserved more than those with fewer receivers (Kwon et al., 2009). The WRR mechanism aggregates IPTV multicast flows into three classes with a classifier based on their weights to reduce the complexity of the OLT. A scheduler process these classes based on their weights (Kwon et al., 2009).

Multicasting of IPTV in WiMAX Networks

One of the main challenges of IPTV over WiMAX is that subscribers (SSs) experience different channel conditions due to channel fading and their distances to BS (Base Station) (She et al., 2007). This problem is due to the fact that SSs have different SNRs at the same time and support different modulation schemes. For example, if a

WiMAX network sends an IPTV channel with the 16QAM modulation to SSs, only those SSs with good channel conditions can support this modulation and can decode the received multicast signal. However, if a lower modulation scheme such as BPSK is used, SSs will force to encode videos in lower bit rates with lower quality. In this situation, those SSs with good channel conditions will only receive lower quality video, whereas they could receive higher quality video (She et al., 2007).

Superposition Coded Multicast (SCM) uses Scalable Video Coding (SVC) at the source and different modulations at the physical layer to solve this problem. For example, a 2-level SCM produces a base layer quality and an enhancement layer quality using SVC and then sends the base layer and the enhancement layer using BPSK and 16QAM modulations, respectively. Therefore, each SS can decode and obtain at least the base layer quality when it has the basic channel conditions. On the other hand, an SS with a good channel condition can decode both the base and enhancement layers and can obtain a better video quality (She et al., 2007).

One major limitation of the SCM is that an SS with a bad channel condition that partially receives higher quality layers is never able to use those data at the higher quality layer, and therefore, this data is useless (She et al., 2008). To overcome this problem, a new method has been presented in (She et al., 2008) that uses SVC at the source and Forward Error Correction (FEC) coding at the channel with different modulation schemes at the physical layer.

The new method encodes a Group of Frame (GoF) to different quality layers and the bitstream of each layer l is partitioned into source blocks of an equal length K_l symbols. Each segment of K_l symbols is then overspread into a series of N symbols using an FEC coding such as Reed-Solomon code. Each symbol is called a protected units (PU) and the size of each symbol is achieved by $m = \log_2^{(N+1)}$ where m is the size of the sym-

Figure 4. Generation of PUs of MDC packets based on modified Layered MDC with the decreasing ordering of K values from the lower layer to the higher one

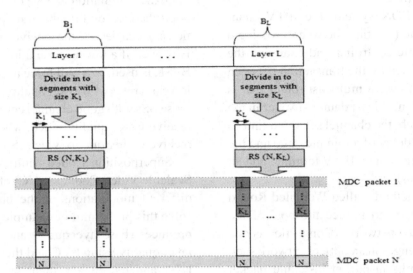

bol and N is number of all PUs (info + redundancy) (Jiang and Liu, 2009).

The value of K_l for partitioning layer l video bitstream is specified by a number of factors such as the importance of that layer for the final video reconstruction, the protection required by that layer in the transmission channel, and so on. At the last stage, PUs of each row in different quality layers are packetized in an MDC packet and PUs of different quality layers are modulated by different modulations. For example, the PUs of the base layer are transmitted with BPSK and PUs of higher layers are modulated with higher order modulation such as 16QAM. At the destination, an SS can recover a layer l if it receives equal or more than K_l partial MDC packets of that layer. A partial MDC packet of layer l is a section of the MDC packet that has PUs of that layer. Unlike the layered MDC, the new method allocates more protection overheads to a higher quality layer than to the lower one as showed in Figure 4. This is because of the integration of a modified layered MDC with superposition coding at the wireless channel (She et al., 2008).

To compare the IP broadcasting that uses Round Robin (RR) in its scheduling and the WRR, a PON network with a downstream bandwidth of 2.5 Gbps, an OLT with 32 ONTs, and 100 HTDV channels per ONT is taken into consideration, where the volume of each HDTV channel is 15Mbps. Average multicast packet loss percentage is 3.5% and 1.1% under IP broadcasting and WRR methods, respectively. Average queuing delay is 55μs, and 26μs under IP broadcasting and WRR methods, respectively. This shows the superiority of WRR over IP broadcasting.

To compare the methods discussed for WiMAX, a standard video sequence CARPHONE is encoded into bitstreams with two quality layers (i.e., $L = 2$) of 16 frames per GoF and the bit stream volume of layer 1 is B_1=1987712 and layer 2 is B_2 = 1278848. Then, the framework protects and multicasts the bitstreams with the design parameters N=255, K_1=233, and K_2=192. Channel fluctuations use Rayleigh fading from one WiMAX transmission frame after the other, while the channel state of a SS is unchanged during the period of a WiMAX transmission frame.

Figure 5. Broadcasting the video segments in the server, where s is the duration of a segment, t is the time that server starts broadcasting, and V is the duration of video

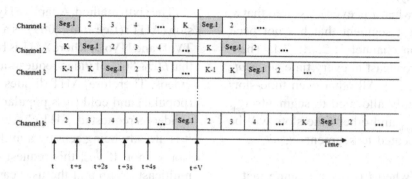

The other simulation parameters such as frame duration that is the time a WiMAX frame is sent is 2 ms, number of data subcarriers is 192, time slot duration that belong to a WiMAX network is 4 physical symbols, downlink and uplink subframe duration is 1 ms, FFT size is 256, OFDM symbol duration is 11.46 ns and average SNR (dB) of SS1 and SS2 is 10 and 28 respectively.

The peak SNR of received video in the legacy scheme is measured to be 9, whiles this term for SCM and modified layered MDC are 17 and 30, respectively. Therefore the modified layered MDC scheme achieves the best result and can provide better video quality for receivers.

Unicasting in IPTV

There are several methods to improve blocking probability and reduce bandwidth consumption. The first method, Staggered Broadcasting (SB) (Wong, 1988), is one of the simple methods in which a video is divided into k segments with duration s, where $s=V/k$ and V is the duration of the whole video. Then, each segment is broadcast on a separate channel. The bandwidth is divided into k equal channels and each channel broadcasts the video with the rate of consumption rate of video (r (bps)) repeatedly (see Figure 5).

In the SB method, when a client requests a video, it is randomly tuned to channel i. Assume that at this time channel i was recently broadcasting segment s_h. Then, the client computes the next channel that will start sending s_1 soon and switches to this channel. The client receives video from this channel and quits when the video is finished. The disadvantage of the SB method is its high service delay. If a client requests the video during broadcasting segment s_1, the client cannot receives the remainder of segment s_1 and must wait until the next broadca,…,) are broadcast on channel i (where $i>3$) consecutively.

T $m = \log_2^{(N+1)}$ he number of segments, n, must be $n=1+2^1+2^2+2^3+…+2^{k-1}=2^k-1$.

A client receives data from all k channels and stores them in a cache. The worst case of service delay in this method is $V/n=V/(2^k-1)$. Unlike SB and HB, this delay is exponentially reduced by increasing k.

The fourth method, Pagoda Broadcasting (PaB) (Paris, Carter, & Long, 1999), is similar to FB. The PaB allows more than one segment on each channel, however it is different from FB on transmission of segments on a channel. The PaB divides a video into n segments with equal size and bandwidth into k channels with equal rate. Each channel is logically divided into time-slots, each for duration of a segment. The time-slots are indexed as $slot_0$, $slot_1$, and so on. The broadcasting is performed as follows:

- Channel 1 broadcasts segment 1 (s_1) consecutively.
- Channel i (when i is even): assume that s_z is the earliest segment that has not been broadcast on channel 1, 2, ..., i-1. Then, it will be broadcast in every time slot $slot_{jz}$ (i.e., j=0, 1, ...). All other even time-slots will be equally allocated to segments s_{z+1}, s_{z+2}, ..., $s_{(3z/2)-1}$ and other time-slots will be equally allocated to segments s_{2z}, s_{2z+2}, ..., s_{3z-1}.
- Channel i (when i is odd): assume that s_z is the first segment that has been broadcast on channel i-1, and the earliest segment that has not yet been broadcast is $s_{3z/2}$. This segment is broadcast on channel i in every time-slot $slot_{j(3z/2)}$ $(j$=0,1,...). Each third slot is allocated to segments $s_{3z/2}$ to s_{2z-1}. The remainder slot is equally allocated to segments s_{3z} to s_{5z-1} in such a way that between each two consecutive pair of $s_{3z/2}$ slots there is exactly one instance of $2z$ segments.

For example, channel 2 will broadcast s_2, s_4, s_2, s_5, s_2, s_4, s_2, s_5, and so on. Channel 3 will broadcast s_3, s_6, s_8, s_3, s_7, s_9, s_3, s_6, s_8, s_3, s_7, s_9, s_3, etc.

In PaB, each client should be tuned to all channels in order to receive data from all of them, cache data and playback video when receives the first segment. In this method, the service delay decreases exponentially by increasing k.

The fifth method is Pyramid Broadcasting (PyB) (Viswanathan & Imielinski, 1995). Unlike the above methods, PyB divides a video into k segments with an increasing size. If the bandwidth allocated for each video is B, then this bandwidth is divided into k channels. Therefore, the broadcast rate is B/k on each channel. In PyB, channel 1 broadcasts s_1 consecutively, channel 2 broadcasts s_2 consecutively, and so on. A client can receive data from two channels at the same time. In general, the client downloads s_i from channel i and then plays it. The client should also tune to channel i+1 in order to download and store s_{i+1}

in its buffer. This method requires cache at the client side.

The sixth method, Adaptive Hybrid Transmission (AHT) (Lee et al.,2009), is a combination of TVoD and NVoD, where AHT is based on the fact that 60%-80% of video requests are for top 10-20 videos. Therefore, AHT divides videos into hot (popular) and cold (less popular) groups. When a video is requested, AHT checks to see whether it is already being sent by a multicast transmission or not. If yes, this request is joined to the multicast group and the user can download the requested video. Otherwise, if the video is highly requested, the video is chopped and allocated to multiple channels for multicasting purposes. If the requested video is not a highly requested video, it is transmitted by a unicast transmission. As shown in Table 3 the HB and PaB unicasting methods have low waiting time but require high bandwidth and storage at the client side. In the opposite side, the SB method has high waiting time but does not require bandwidth and storage at the client side. Assumptions for this simulation are as follows: VoD server bandwidth (number of channels) with unit r is 8 where r is the consumption rate of video, and the length of video is two hours.

QoS Improvements in IPTV

Here, some solutions shall be discussed in the context of congestion in optical networks and channel fading in wireless network.

Congestion Management Approaches

One solution to overcome congestion in DSL access links and minimize the cost of the congestion is to use different types of frames in a video stream. After video coding, there are three types of frames (Van et al., 2008):

- Intra-coded frame (*I*-frame) that is independent of any other frame.

Figure 6. A video sequence generated by a codec

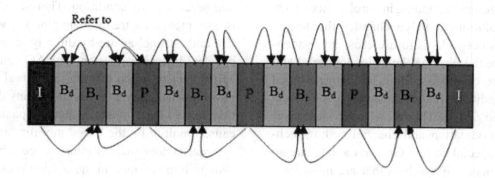

- Predictive-frame (*P*-frame) that is dependent on previous encoded I or P-frame.
- Bidirectional predictive frame (*B*-frame) that is dependent on two nearby frames.

It is noted that in the recent video codec, the *B*-frame is divided into two types of frames, B_r frame and B_d frame, where a B_r frame refers to its two neighbor B_d frames. In other words, a B_d frame depends on its neighbor frames. Therefore in all types of frames, a B_d frame does not refer to another frame. To encode an *I*-frame, we need more bits than *P* and *B*-frames since an *I*-frame needs more information than others. Therefore, an *I*-frame is the most important one followed by *P* and B_r and B_d frames, respectively (Van et al., 2008). This structure is shown in Figure 6.

In the intelligent packet drop method when congestion occurs, packets are eliminated based on their frame importance, i.e., this method eliminates the packets that have B_d-frame first followed by B_r-frame, and so on. If an *I*-frame is lost, a significant visual artifact is created in the received video. However, if a B_d-frame is lost, there is a partial visual artifact in the video. Therefore, the type of visual artifact is related to the types of lost frame. By the intelligent packet drop method, the number of significant visual artifacts can be reduced, but at the expense of increasing the number of partial visual artifacts. Note that recovering of a lost *I*-frame is impossible, where-

as partial visual artifacts can be repaired by effectively recovering lost B_d and B_r frames (Van et al., 2008).

The intelligent packet drop method also uses FEC and retransmission to protect important frames in error-prone physical layer. In the case of FEC, parity packets are added to a block of normal IPTV data packets. The proposed mechanism drops low priority packets during congestion (Van et al., 2008). Clearly, the packets that have been intelligently dropped because of congestion should not be retransmitted. This means that both the retransmission server and the retransmission client should be able to recognize the type of lost packets, i.e., which packets have been removed by the intelligent packet drop mechanism and which packets did not arrive at the receiver because of corruption. The solution is that the retransmission server serves a retransmission request only if the packet contains high priority information (Van et al., 2008).

CHANNEL FLUCTUATION MANAGEMENT APPROACHES

The following solution has been proposed for WLAN. However, we can use this solution to overcome channel fading in WMAN. For example, in the solution reviewed in subsection "Multicasting of IPTV in WiMAX Networks", SCM uses such idea to solve channel fading in wireless networks.

One solution to solve channel fluctuation in wireless networks is to use cross layer adaption, where the physical layer is monitored and the bit rate of video coding is changed based on the condition of the physical layer (Djama and Ahmed, 2007). The 802.11's physical layer prepares modulation and channel coding techniques. A special coding converts a data stream into a sequence of symbols that are modulated in amplitude, phase, or frequency of an analog signal. The complex modulations with high bit rates require a high Signal to Noise Ratio (SNR) to decode the symbols. Therefore, the complex modulations are more sensitive to noise than less complex modulations with low bit rates. Therefore, this method uses a complex modulation when the SS is close to the Access Point (AP), and a simple modulation when the SS is far from the AP (Djama and Ahmed, 2007).

To monitor physical layer and dynamically alter the bit rate of video coding, Rate Control Algorithm (RCA) (Djama and Ahmed, 2007) could be used. There are three types of RCAs: (1) Statistics-based RCA that maintains statistical information about the transmission condition; (2) SNR-based in which we should adapt rate with perceived SNR since SNR effect on the type of modulation scheme is directly related to the rate; (3) Hybrid RCA that is a combination of the two prior RCAs that takes their advantages and minimizes their disadvantages. The main disadvantage of the first two RCAs is that the rate changes continually due to the rapid change in channel conditions (Djama and Ahmed, 2007).

In the approach (Djama and Ahmed, 2007) proposed to overcome channel fluctuation, first, Adaption Gateway (AG) obtains information about user's terminal capabilities and user's profile. This information is used at the AG to generate the IPTV stream (trans-coding, trans-rating, etc.) based on the users requirements. Second, the AG continuously monitors the channel

condition experienced by a user and adapts bit rate based on this condition. Therefore, the AG is both media–aware by managing the video bit rate and channel-aware by directly accessing to physical layer information. The AG enables the adjustment of video bit-rate to the real channel bit-rate which may alter in reply to any degradation (e.g., signal strength quality, packet loss) caused mainly by the users' mobility and other external factors such as interference. The AG is usually implemented in the session/presentation layer (Djama and Ahmed, 2007).

FUTURE RESEARCH DIRECTIONS

We have studied many methods in this chapter, where each method can improve a feature of IPTV services. These methods reduce the impairments but cannot eliminate them at all. The following approaches could be research directions in future:

- Combination of the presented methods in this chapter to reduce or even eliminate the disadvantage and increase their advantages.
- Focusing on source coding to produce high video quality with low bulk based on the natures of a video. This is because by reducing volume of video traffic, the capacity of the network increases and the probability of congestion and BER reduces.
- Focusing on channel coding to reduce the effect of congestion and BER in optical networks and wireless networks, respectively. In this context, we should try to produce channel coding with high consistency so that if one section of traffic is lost due to congestion or BER, we can recover the lost section from received sections.
- Using characteristics of video to reduce the cost of congestion and BER. Since a video has different types of frames with different importances; we can eliminate the less im-

portant frames to preserve the video quality at the congestion state.

- Using cache server to reduce zapping time, retransmission of corrupted packets and adjusting its parameters (e.g., its location in the network) to reach the best performance results. In this context, we can place cache servers at different points in a network near to the users in order to reduce the zapping time and retransmission of the corrupted packet to preserve the video quality.
- Using header compression to reduce the header size. This can reduce BER and probability of congestion and can improve bandwidth usage. Note that IPTV packets are normally labeled with RTP/UDP/IP headers, resulting in a long header.

CONCLUSION

IPTV is a technique that transmits TV and video contents over a network that uses the IP networking protocol. IPTV network architecture consists of two a core backbone and an access network. The access network needs enough bandwidth capacity to deliver video streams. In this chapter, we have studied challenges in video coding, multicasting, unicasting and QOS and discussed different solutions for them.

The properties of video and networks have been studied that can improve the performance results in all solutions. For example, one solution in video coding section uses the degree of activities in video portions to code the video. In the muticasting section, the property of PON networks can be used, where each ONT receives traffic of other ONTs. In unicasting, this fact is employed that 60%-80% of video requests are for top 10-20 videos. Finally, we use this fact that a video stream contains different types of frames with different importances. Therefore, by eliminating unimportant frames, the video quality can be improved under congestion state.

REFERENCES

Appleby, S., Crabtree, B., Jeffery, R., Mulroy, P., & Nilsson, M. (2006). Video coding and delivery challenges for next generation IPTV. *BT Technology Journal*, *24*(2), 174–179. doi:10.1007/s10550-006-0056-3

Asghar, J., Hood, I., & Faucheur, F. L. (2009). Preserving video quality in IPTV networks. *IEEE Transactions on Broadcasting*, *55*(2), 386–395. doi:10.1109/TBC.2009.2019419

Djama, I., & Ahmed, T. (2007). A cross-layer interworking of DVB-T and WLAN for mobile IPTV service delivery. *IEEE Transactions on Broadcasting*, *53*(1), 382–390. doi:10.1109/TBC.2006.889111

Hou, F., Cai, L. X., She, J., Ho, P., Shen, X., & Zhang, J. (2008). A cooperative multicast scheduling scheme for multimedia service over IEEE 802.16 networks. *IEEE Transactions on Wireless Communications*, *8*(3), 1508–1519. doi:10.1109/TWC.2009.080417

Ikeda, H. (2008). Architecture and design of IP broadcasting system using passive optical network. *IEICE Transactions on Communications . E (Norwalk, Conn.)*, *91-B*(8), 2477–2484.

Jeong, H., Choi, J., Mo, J., & Kang, M. (2008). An adaptive loss-aware flow control scheme for delay-sensitive applications in OBS networks. *IEICE Transactions in Communications . E (Norwalk, Conn.)*, *91-B*(7), 2152–2159.

Jiang, G., & Liu, D. (in press). Analysis and implementation of FEC in 10G-EPON. *Higher Education Press and Springer.*

Juhn, L., & Tseng, L. (1997). Harmonic broadcasting for video-on-demand service. *IEEE Transactions on Broadcasting*, *43*(3), 268–271. doi:10.1109/11.632927

Juhn, L. S., & Tseng, L. M. (1998). Fast data broadcasting and receiving method for popular video service. *IEEE Transactions on Broadcasting, 44*(1), 100–105. doi:10.1109/11.713059

Kahabka, M. (2008). *AON vs. PON – A comparison of two optical access network technologies and the different impact on operations.* KEYMILE International GmbH, white paper.

Kim, J. (2006). Layered multiple description coding for robust video transmission over wireless ad-hoc networks. *Proceedings of World Academy of Science: Vol. 16. Engineering and Tech* (pp. 163–166). PWASET.

Kwon, Y. H., Choi, J. K., Choi, S. G., Um, T. W., & Jong, S. G. (2009). A weighted scheduling mechanism to reduce multicast packet loss in IPTV service over EPON. *ETRI Journal, 31*(4), 469–471. doi:10.4218/etrij.09.0209.0025

Lambert, P., Debevere, P., Cock, J. D., Macq, J. F., Degrande, N., Vleeschauwer, D.D., & Walle, R.V. (2009). Real-time error concealing bitstream adaptation methods for SVC in IPTV systems. *Springer Journal of Real-Time Image Processing*, 79-90.

Lee, J. M., Park, H., Choi, S. G., & Choi, J. K. (2009). Adaptive hybrid transmission mechanism for on-demand mobile IPTV over WiMAX. *IEEE Transactions on Broadcasting, 55*(2), 468–477. doi:10.1109/TBC.2009.2015605

Moawad, R. B. (2008, May). *IPTV over WiMAX: Overview on the video path from the server to the Wimax end-user.* Paper presented at the IEEE Lebanon Communications Workshop (LCW), Beirut.

Nakanishi, K., Otaka, A., & Maeda, Y. (2008). Standardization activities on broadband access systems. *IEICE Transactions on Communication. E (Norwalk, Conn.), 91-B*(8), 2454–2461.

O'Driscol, G. (2008). *Next generation IPTV services and technologies.* Hoboken, New Jersey: Wiley.

Paris, J. F., Carter, S. W., & Long, D. D. E. (1999, January). *A hybrid broadcasting protocol for video on demand.* Paper presented at ACM/SPIE Conference on Multimedia Computing and Networking, San Jose, CA.

Retnasothie, F. E., Ozdemir, M. K., & Yucek, T. (2006). *Wireless IPTV over WiMAX: Challenges and applications.* Paper presented at IEEE Wamicon (invited paper), Clearwater, FL.

She, J., Hou, F., Ho, P. H., & Xie, L. L. (2007). IPTV over WiMAX: Key success factors, challenges, and solutions. *IEEE Communications Magazine, 45*(8), 87–93. doi:10.1109/MCOM.2007.4290319

She, J., Yu, X., Hou, F., Ho, P. H., & Yang, E. H. (2008). A framework of cross-layer superposition coded multicast for robust IPTV services over WiMAX. *Proceedings IEEE Wireless Communications and Networking Conference,* (pp. 3139–44).

Van Caenegem, T. N. M., Struyve, K. O., Laevens, K., De Vleeschauwer, D., & Sharpe, R. (2008). Maintaining video quality and optimizing video delivery over the bandwidth constrained DSL last mile through intelligent packet drop. *Bell Labs Technical Journal, 13*(1), 53–68. doi:10.1002/bltj.20282

Viswanathan, S., & Imielinski, T. (1995). Pyramid broadcasting for video on demand service. In . *Proceedings of IEEE Multimedia Computing and Networking Conference, 2417,* 66–77.

Wiegand, T., Noblet, L., & Rovati, F. (2009). Scalable video coding for IPTV services. *IEEE Transactions on Broadcasting, 55*(2), 527–538. doi:10.1109/TBC.2009.2020954

Wong, J. W. (1998). Broadcast delivery. *Proceedings of the IEEE*, *76*(12), 1566–1577. doi:10.1109/5.16350

Zhang, C., Liu, D., Zhang, L., & Wu, G. (2009). *Controllable multicast for IPTV over EPON* (pp. 222–228). Higher Education Press and Springer.

ADDITIONAL READING

Arberg, P., Cagenius, T., Tidblad, O. V., Ullerstig, M., & Winterbottom, P. (2007). Network infrastructure for IPTV, Ericsson Review, No.3, 2007, from http:// www.ericsson.com/ ericsson/ corpinfo/ publications/ review/2007_03/ files/ 2_NetworkInfastructure.pdf.

Barbera, M., Gagliardi, G., & Romeo, S. (2005). The IPTV Challenge for Telco Operators, Accenture, 2005, from http:// www.iec.org/ newsletter/j an06_1/ analyst_1.pdf.

Cha, M., Choudhuryy, G., Yatesy, J., Shaikhy, A., & Moon, S. (2006). ” Case Study: Resilient Backbone Design for IPTV Services”, paper presented at the IPTV Workshop, International World Wide Web Conference, Edinburgh, Scotland, United Kingdom.

Chen, Y. F., Huang, Y., Jana, R., Jiang, H., Rabinovich, M., & Rahe, J. (2009). Towards capacity and profit optimization of video-on-demand services in a peer-assisted IPTV platform . *Springer, Multimedia Systems*, *15*, 19–32. doi:10.1007/ s00530-008-0127-z

Chien, W. D., Yeh, Y. S., & Wang, J. S. (2005). Practical channel transition for near-VOD services . *IEEE Transactions on Broadcasting*, *51*(3), 360–365. doi:10.1109/TBC.2005.852251

Chou, P. A., & Van der Schaar, M. (Eds.). (2007). “Multimedia over IP and Wireless Networks (Compression, Networking, and systems)” Elsevier, Academic press. Darwin, C. ” The Future of IPTV: Business and Technology Challenges “, Laurel Networks, white paper, from www. laurelnetworks.com.

Degrande, N., Vleeschauwer, D. D., & Laevens, K. (2008). Protecting IPTV Against Packet Loss: Techniques and Trade-Offs . *Bell Labs Technical Journal*, *13*(1), 35–52. doi:10.1002/bltj.20281

El-Sayed, M. L., Hu, Y., Kulkarni, S., & Wilson, N. (2006). Comparison of Transport Network Technologies for IPTV Distribution . *Bell Labs Technical Journal*, *11*(2), 215–240. doi:10.1002/ bltj.20171

Hermsmeyer, C., Valencia, E. H., Stoll, D., & Tamm, O. (2007). Ethernet Aggregation and Core Network Models for Efficient and Reliable IPTV Services . *Bell Labs Technical Journal*, *12*(1), 57–76. doi:10.1002/bltj.20217

Ho, K. M., Poon, W. F., & Lo, K. T. (2007). Performance study of largescale video streaming services in highly heterogeneous environment . *IEEE Transactions on Broadcasting*, *53*(4), 763–773. doi:10.1109/TBC.2007.908326

Hodis, F. (2008). IPTV Challenges and metrics. EXFO Corporate, Canada, white paper, 2008, from http:// documents.exfo.com/ appnotes/ anote174-ang.pdf.

House, B., Avenue, C., Laoghaire, D., & Dublin, C. Testing MPEG based IP video QoE/QoS. Shenick Network Systems, Ireland, white paper, from http:// www.shenick.com/pdfs/Testing_MPEG_IPTV_VOD_QOE.pdf.

Jain, R. (2005). I want my IPTV . *IEEE MultiMedia*, *12*(3), 95–96. doi:10.1109/MMUL.2005.47

Jennehag, U., Zhang, T., & Pettersson, S. (2007). Improving transmission efficiency in H.264 based IPTV systems . *IEEE Transactions on Broadcasting*, *53*(1), 69–77. doi:10.1109/TBC.2006.887167

Krogfoss, B., Sofman, L., & Agrawal, A. (2008). Caching Architectures and Optimization Strategies for IPTV Networks . *Bell Labs Technical Journal*, *13*(3), 13–28. doi:10.1002/bltj.20320

Lee, Y. C., Kim, J., Altunbasak, Y., & Mersereau, R. M. (2003). Layered coded vs. multiple description coded video over error-prone networks . *Elsevier, Signal Processing: Image Communication*, *18*, 337–356. doi:10.1016/S0923-5965(02)00138-8

Li, Z., & Herfet, T. (2009). MAC Layer Multicast Error Control for IPTV in Wireless LANs . *IEEE Transactions on Broadcasting*, *55*(2), 353–362. doi:10.1109/TBC.2009.2016502

Lian, S., & Liu, Z. (2008). Secure Media Content Distribution Based on the Improved Set-Top Box in IPTV . *IEEE Transactions on Consumer Electronics*, *54*(2), 560–566. doi:10.1109/TCE.2008.4560130

Lian, S., Sun, J., Liu, G., and Wang, Z. (2008). "Efficient video encryption scheme based on advanced video coding", Springer Science + Business Media, 38:75–89.

Luby, M. G., & Miller, J. W. "The Impact of Packet Loss on an IPTV Network", Digital Fountain., from http:// www.digitalfountain.com/ iptv.html.

Nagarajan, R., & Ooghe, S. (2008). Next-Generation Access Network Architectures for Video, Voice, Interactive Gaming, and Other Emerging Applications: Challenges and Directions . *Bell Labs Technical Journal*, *13*(1), 69–86. doi:10.1002/bltj.20283

Pompei, S., Rea, L., Matera, F., & Valenti, A. (2008). Experimental investigation on optical gigabit Ethernet network reliability for high-definition IPTV services . *Journal of Optical Networking*, *7*(5), 426–435. doi:10.1364/JON.7.000426

Siebert, P., Caenegem, T. N. M. V., & Wagner, M. (2009). Analysis and Improvements of Zapping Times in IPTV Systems . *IEEE Transactions on Broadcasting*, *55*(2), 407–418. doi:10.1109/TBC.2008.2012019

Tektronix (2007), A Guide to IPTV: The Technologies, the Challenges and How to Test IPTV, 2007 white paper, from www.tektronix.com/video_audio.

Uilecan, I. V., Zhou, C., & Atkin, G. E. (2007). *"Framework for Delivering IPTV Services over WiMAX Wireless Networks"*, *IEEE EIT 2007:vol* (pp. 470–475). Chicago: Illinois Institute of Technology.

Vleeschauwer, D. D., & Laevens, K. (2009). Performance of Caching Algorithms for IPTV On-Demand Services . *IEEE Transactions on Broadcasting*, *55*(2), 491–501. doi:10.1109/TBC.2009.2015983

Wiegand, T., Noblet, L., & Rovati, F. (2009). Scalable Video Coding for IPTV Services . *IEEE Transactions on Broadcasting*, *55*(2), 527–538. doi:10.1109/TBC.2009.2020954

Wu, M., Makharia, S., Liu, H., Li, D., & Mathur, S. (2009). "IPTV Multicast Over Wireless LAN Using Merged Hybrid ARQ With Staggered Adaptive FEC", I . *IEEE Transactions on Broadcasting*, *55*(2), 363–374. doi:10.1109/TBC.2009.2016500

Yiu, W. P. K., Jin, X., & Chan, S. H. G. (2007). "Challenges and Approaches in Large-Scale P2P Media Streaming", paper presented at the IEEE Computer Society, Hong Kong University of Science and Technology.

Zeng, Y., & Strauss, T. (2008). Enhanced Video Streaming Network with Hybrid P2P Technology . *Bell Labs Technical Journal, 13*(3), 45–58. doi:10.1002/bltj.20322

Zhu, Y., & Jue, J. P. (2009). Multi-Class Flow Aggregation for IPTV Content Delivery in IP Over Optical Core Networks . *Journal of Lightwave Technology, 27*(12), 1891–1903. doi:10.1109/JLT.2009.2022284

KEY TERMS AND DEFINITIONS

Channel Fading: Fading is deviation of the attenuation that a carrier-modulated telecommunication signal experiences over certain propagation media. The fading may vary with time, geographical position, distance from BS, weather condition, etc.

Congestion: Network congestion occurs when a link or node is carrying so much data so that its quality of service deteriorates. Typical effects include queuing delay, packet loss and the blocking of new connections

IPTV (Internet Protocol Television): IPTV can deliver high quality broadcast television and/ or on-demand video and audio content over a broadband network. On the other hand, IPTV is a mechanism applied to deliver old TV channels, movies, and video-on-demand contents over a private network.

PON (Passive Optical Network): PON is a point-to-multipoint metro optical network that has no active elements between the Optical Line Terminal (OLT) and the Optical Network Terminals (ONTs). All transmissions in a PON are between OLT and ONTs.

SVC (Scalable Video Coding): is a method that encodes a video in different bit rates at different layers to match heterogeneous receivers with different conditions based on three states temporal scalability, spatial scalability and quality scalability.

VoD (Video on Demand): IPTV supports two-way communications and permits end users to request their beloved video by allowing them to decide what and when they want to watch a video.

WiMAX: IEEE 802.16 working group has produced the Worldwide Interoperability for Microwave Access (WiMAX) that prepares a wireless solution in metropolitan area access networks. The WiMAX has a wide range coverage, high data rate, secured transmission and mobility supported at vehicular speeds.

Chapter 4
Utilization of Latency Measurements for Network–Based Applications

Mohammed Jubaer Arif
The University of Melbourne, Australia

ABSTRACT

Distributed computing, comprised of different components of an application located on different computers connected via network, has allowed value added services to provide enhanced user experience. Offering information based on geographic location of users of a distributed system is one of the newest and most notable advancements. Internet is the biggest distributed system present today, and finding the geographical location of the user on the Internet, commonly referred to as geolocation, is one of the challenging problems currently addressed by the research community. Of the two commonly used approaches, repository-based and measurement-based, this chapter primarily focuses on geolocating Internet hosts using the measurement-based approach. A measurement-based geolocation approach is based on the latency measurements between the distributed Internet nodes. Thus, this chapter conducts a systematic analysis of latency measurements between the Internet nodes. This chapter recognizes the importance of geolocation in distributed computing. As a result, it also presents a comparative study of existing repository-based and measurement-based geolocation approaches.

DOI: 10.4018/978-1-61350-110-8.ch004

Copyright © 2012, IGI Global. Copying or distributing in print or electronic forms without written permission of IGI Global is prohibited.

INTRODUCTION

The robust and scalable growth of the Internet has allowed different distributed services, such as email, electronic commerce and entertainment, to flourish rapidly. These applications often use latency measurements between Internet hosts in order to provide better services. Recently there have been many attempts to enhance these services in order to provide value added services to users. Providing services, using latency measurements between Internet hosts, based on users' physical location is one of the newest mechanisms. Identifying the physical location of the users on the Internet, commonly referred to as *geolocation*, is a non-trivial task. The Internet Protocol (IP) address, which is used to identify hosts on the Internet, does not have a direct association to the physical street address of the host. Moreover, the dynamic assignment of IP addresses complicates the matter as the same IP address can be found in different locations at different times.

Geolocation of Internet hosts enables a new wave of Internet applications which can be customized to serve users based on their physical location. Internet location information can be leveraged to improve user experience and determine business strategy. Some uses of such location-aware systems include load balancing and resource allocation between distributed Internet hosts, geographically targeted advertising on web sites, automatic selection of language to display web site content, web content delivery based on region, credit card fraud detection and providing emergency services for IP telephony. Whether the goal of an adopted geolocation technique is to show local advertisements on the web page or track Internet users in emergency situations, the accuracy of the localization system is vital. The accuracy requirements, however, vary from application to application.

In addition to being accurate, a geolocation technique is expected to be scalable, robust and efficient. The approaches of geolocating Internet hosts are broadly divided into two categories. The first, *repository-based* approach finds the location information based on a lookup. And the second, *Measurement-based* approach finds the location information based on the latency measurements from some fixed hosts to the targets. Repository-based approaches have an enormous overhead associated with creating and maintaining an up-to-date repository of location information of the ever growing lists of Internet hosts. On the other hand, measurement-based approaches produce fresh results based on latency measurements to targets from some fixed hosts. Though repository-based approaches may produce quite accurate results depending on the up-to-date and rich IP-to-location mapping dataset maintained, measurement-based approaches are more scalable, robust and efficient compared to repository-based approaches.

The goal of this chapter is to study measurement-based IP geolocation techniques that are applicable to the Internet. Therefore, initially it discusses about latency to distance relationship between Internet hosts. Then it discusses this relationship of the observed latency measurements between hosts with known locations, known as *landmark,* and the node to be geolocated, known as *target*, to constrain the possible location of the target. However, the task of finding an accurate model for latency to distance relationship between Internet hosts is not a trivial tasks mainly because of the variability in latency for a given distance. Thus, this necessitates capturing the variability in the proposed relationship, which should be taken into account in the geolocation algorithm.

MOTIVATION AND SCOPE

Latency refers to the delays of any kind incurred in processing and travelling of network data between Internet hosts. A low latency network is one that generally experiences small delays in time and a high latency network generally suffers

Figure 1. Repository-based geolocation approach

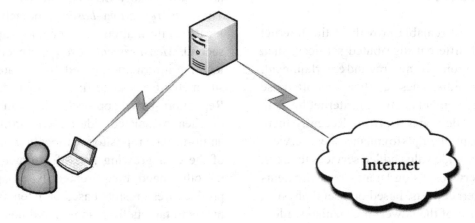

from long delays. Internet is the combination of all such small and long delay networks. Thus, utilization of latency for the benefits of distributed Internet technologies requires systematic analysis of latency measurements.

There are many usages of latency measurements for distributed Internet technologies. However, this chapter highlights the utilization of latency measurements in terms of host geolocation on the Internet. It identifies few key issues that make the study of Internet latency a challenging one. An important research problem that is addressed in this chapter is the analysis of a latency dataset that is collected from real Internet hosts. Such analysis helps to model the latency to distance relationship between Internet hosts.

CONTRIBUTION AND ORGANIZATION

The contribution of this chapter is threefold. First, it analyzes Internet latency measurements in order to better understand the Internet behavior. Second, it presents the existing geolocation approaches from the research domain. Finally, a comparative study is conducted between repository-based and measurement-based geolocation approaches

The reminder of the chapter is organized as follows: an overview of geolocation problem is presented in Section 4. Internet latency is analyzed in Section 5. Internet host geolocation approaches are detailed and compared in Section 6. Future research directions are discussed in Section 7. Finally the chapter is concluded in Section 8.

OVERVIEW OF GEOLOCATION PROBLEM

We start this section with an overview of a repository-based Internet host geolocation approach. Figure 1 shows a general diagram of a repository-based approach. As shown in the figure, in a repository-based approach a repository of IP-to-location is generated from the available sources on the Internet. When a user connects to the Internet, the IP address of the user's machine is forwarded to this IP-to-location repository for location information retrieval. Later, this location information is used by user's local or remote applications in order to provide location based services.

Figure 2 shows a general diagram of a measurement-based approach. As shown in the figure, in a measurement-based approach landmarks measure latencies to the target. Based on the observed latencies between landmarks and the

Figure 2. Measurement-based geolocation approach. In the left, landmarks measure latencies to the target; and in the right, landmarks constrain the target within approximated distances

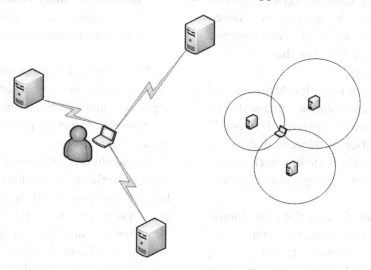

targets each landmark estimates a distance to the target from a predefined latency-distance relationship. Landmarks consider a circular region with the estimated distances and predict the target at a location where all the circular distances intersect. This single intersection point generation should be considered as the best case scenario as with highly variable Internet latency it is quite unexpected.

The latency between Internet hosts are generally measured using the Internet Control Message Protocol (ICMP) between the associated IP addresses of the hosts. Thus it is important to have a better understanding of both IP addresses and ICMP.

IP addresses are normally expressed as a dotted-decimal-number in order to make it easier for humans to remember. However Internet hosts transform these IP addresses to binary numbers to communicate. In IPV4 the four numbers in an IP address are called octets, because each of them has eight positions, i.e. 8 bits (in total 4 byte or 32 bits) when viewed in binary form, and such IP addresses take the form: 212.26.71.127. As Internet hosts, cell phones, and other consumer electronics expand their networking capability, the

smaller IPV4 address space is likely to run out. As a result the research community has come up with the notion of 16 byte (128 bits) long addresses known as IPV6. However, IPV6 is not widely used yet and at this stage it is not clear how IPV6 will behave with regard to Internet host geolocation. Thus this chapter focuses on geoloction in the IPV4 network.

One of the popular solutions to the scarcity problem of IPV4 is the deployment of a Network Address Translator (NAT) which associates a number of hosts to a single IP address. As a result, while assisting in the solution to the scarcity problem of IP addresses, NAT architectures complicate the problem of Internet host geolocation. Moreover, static and dynamic IP addressing makes the geolocation of Internet hosts challenging. Static addressing means each host is assigned a permanent IP address. On the other hand, in dynamic addressing the hosts use any available IP address within a range as defined by their Internet Service Provider (ISP).

ICMP is one of the core protocols of the TCP/IP protocol suite. It is widely used by hosts and routers to send notification of datagram problems back to the source. Tools such as ping use ICMP echo request packets to a destination IP address and wait for the ICMP echo response to reply to the source IP address. The time taken between the ICMP echo request and ICMP echo response is a measure of latency between the source and destination IP addresses.

This chapter attempts to geolocate hosts based on Internet latency measurements obtained from ICMP ping measurements between Internet IP addresses. We specifically address three open research challenges in relation to Internet host geolocation based on Internet latency measurements:

1. **Latency Model:** One of the most important points for a better measurement-based Internet host geolocation technique is to understand current Internet behavior through the analysis of latency between Internet hosts. An important research problem that we address in this chapter is the analysis of a latency dataset that we collected from real Internet hosts. Such analysis helps us model the latency to distance relationship between Internet hosts.

2. **Geolocation Accuracy:** A key factor related to Internet host geolocation is the accuracy of the approach which is measured in terms of *geolocation error*, the distance between actual and proposed location. In this chapter we discuss several algorithms for geolocation that produce different levels of accuracy. Our study suggests measurement-based approaches are capable of producing accurate results consistently than repository-based approaches.

3. **Scalability and Reliability:** Unpredictability of the Internet latency demands an Internet host geolocation technique to be scalable and reliable. The proposed geolocation approaches are expected to achieve the improved performance with acceptable measurement costs in order to scale on the Internet. At the same time the reliability of the proposed approaches depends on the

ability to produce consistent results. In this chapter we study both the issues in order to compare the accuracy of the existing geolocation approaches.

The relationship between these three challenges- latency model, geolocation accuracy and scalability and reliability- provide the focus for the research on Internet host geolocation in the IP network.

To conclude the section, Figure 3, presents an architectural diagram for locating targets with the help of distributed landmarks. These landmarks are physical servers of a distributed system and the target is a machine via which Internet users are connected to the Internet. The figure depicts a service where distributed servers of an organization geolocating a user in order to provide contents from the nearest server to the user. Each of the servers is consist of a geolocation engine along with other usual server components. This geolocation engine is a software component capable of measuring latency to target and use the measurement for locating the target. As the figure shows a client contacts any random server out of all the available servers in a request/response scenario and the geolocation engine of the contacted server initiate the geolocation. It notifies the other servers or landmarks while the client request is made and all the landmarks measures latency to the target or client from their respective geolocation engine. Finally, all these measurements are used to geolocate the client in the contacted server.

INTERNET LATENCY MEASUREMENTS

In this section we present our analysis of Internet latency.

The Internet consists of several Autonomous Systems (AS). An autonomous system is one network or sets of networks under the control of one or more network operators that help define the

Figure 3. Architectural diagram of geolocation in a distributed system

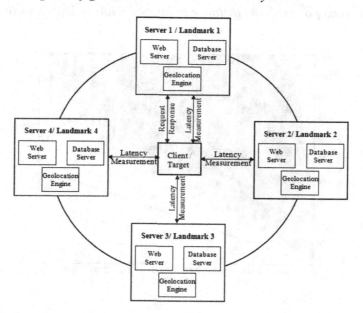

routing policy of the Internet. Routing between different AS is accomplished using the Border Gateway Protocol (BGP) -a protocol to share routing information. Different AS connect to each other either at public exchanges or at private peering points. The network path between two end-hosts typically traverses multiple AS. As a result, the characteristics of an end-to-end packet traversing path are very much dependent on the policies employed by all the AS between the source and the destination of the packets.

The Internet is the biggest network of all and is comprised of all different kinds of networks. Therefore, it is not expected that Internet latency will have a strict linear relationship with distances between hosts. Considering that Internet data packets in the majority of cases travel through optical fibers, the minimum latency between two nodes that are a distance d apart can be given by,

$$t_{min}(d) = d/c_{fiber} \quad eq..1$$

Here c_{fiber} is the maximum transmission speed of data through the fiber, which is approximately 2/3 the speed of light. As we show later, the latencies observed in real world Internet traffic are significantly higher than this lower bound due to factors such as routing policies between AS. Thus, the observed latencies are modeled as,

$$t(d) = t_{min}(d) + E(d) \quad eq. 2$$

where $t(d)$ is the observed latency for distance d and $E(d)$ is a noise term that accounts for network delays in the real measurement.

For our analysis of Internet latency we collected latency data over a period of month for our experiment from PlanetLab (PlanetLab), which is an experimental test-bed on the Internet for computer networking and distributed systems research. The latency data was generated via ICMP ping between our evenly distributed 50 landmarks in North America. Ping is a utility that sends a packet from a source to a destination and waits for a reply. The source host notes the local time on its clock as it transmits the packet in the network towards the destination. Each host that receives the packets checks the destination address to see if it matches their own address. If the destination address does not match the local host's address, the packet is forwarded to the network where the address resides. Once the destination host receives

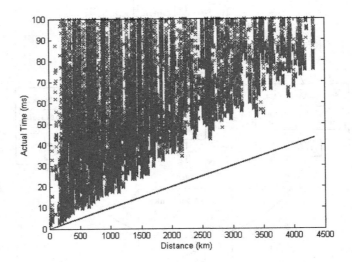

Figure 4. Distance-latency relationship between our landmarks generated with the traceroute tool. The straight line below the data points shows distance to latency relationship according to equation 1

the packets it sends a reply back to the source. The source again notes the time on the clock and notes the elapsed time as latency.

We also collected latency data between our landmarks using traceroute tool. Traceroute is a utility that traces a packet from source to destination, but additionally it will also show how many hops the packet requires to reach the destination and how long each hop takes. Traceroute works by sending packets with low time-to-live (TTL) fields. The TTL value specifies how many hops the packet is allowed before it is returned. When a packet cannot reach its destination because the TTL value is too low, the last host returns the packet and identifies itself. By sending a series of packets and incrementing the TTL value with each successive packet, traceroute finds out all the intermediary hosts and finally the destination. Like ping it also records the elapsed time from each hop and provides the latency information. We did not see any major differences in the measurements recorded by the ping and traceroute tools between end hosts.

The latency data between landmarks were collected over a period of one month, from September

23, 2008 to October 25, 2008. Over this period, we executed a script on each landmark, which generated ping commands originating from the particular landmark to every other landmark. At a given time, the originating landmark performed a three data packet ping to a selected destination landmark followed by a two-minute pause. Then the process continued with a new destination. After cycling through all destination landmarks the process was repeated. From the three observed ping times the minimum ping time was chosen as the measure of latency for modeling purposes.

The full dataset we gathered consists of approximately 150,000 latency-distance measurements. The number of measurements from each of our 50 landmarks was not equal due to certain ping commands not successfully completing from these PlanetLab nodes during the measurement collection period. The inter-landmark distance in the data covers the range 0.5km - 4331km.

In all the above mentioned latency datasets the Round-Trip Time (RTT)- the time required for a packet to travel from a specific source to a specific destination and back again- is used as the measure of latency. One could also use one-way

Figure 5. Distance to hop count relationship between our landmarks

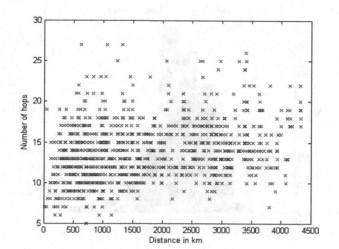

delay between source and destination as a measure of latency. However, measuring one-way delay between two hosts faces two major challenges. First, it requires access to both the end hosts for the measurements. Second, strict time synchronization between the two hosts is required. But measurement-based geolocation techniques focus on providing the location tracking service without having access to the client side. Thus, RTT is retained as a measure of latency throughout the chapter.

Analysis of Traceroute Dataset

In this subsection we analyze the dataset collected via the traceroute tool between landmarks.

First, we investigate the latency to distance relationship. Figure 4 shows the latency to distance relationship between our landmarks collected using the traceroute tool. It can be seen that there is a positive correlation between latency and distance. However, there is considerable variance in latency against a given distance.

We next examine the relationship between distance and hop count. Figure 5 shows distance to hop count relationship between our landmarks.

Figure 5 does not show a strong correlation between distance to hop count. A closer observation of the raw traceroute dataset reveals that the intermediate routers between a given pair of landmarks remain the same for the majority of the measurements.

Figure 6 shows the distribution of the hop count across all landmark pairs. Within our experimental region of North America all the nodes could reach each other with a minimum of five hops, maximum of 27 hops and an average of 14 hop counts.

Finally, from the traceroute dataset, we investigate how the hop count and latency are related. Figure 7 shows hop count and minimum latency between landmarks are weakly related. However, if the hop count is less than seven it tends to have lower latency. After the hop count exceeds seven, the latency measurements vary notably. This observation indicates that along with hop count, which always adds some additive delay at each hop to the final latency, other factors also influence latency. Various factors that could influence latency are discussed later.

The above observations endorse the use of latency measurements over hop count between

Figure 6. Hop count distribution of North America

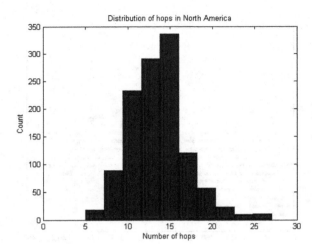

Figure 7. Hop count to latency relationship

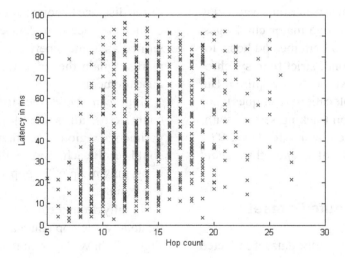

Internet hosts for geolocation approaches. This is because latency to distance demonstrates a positive correlation, whereas hop count to distance does not show any correlation. Thus, modeling latency data is likely to provide better distance constraint from the landmarks to the targets.

Analysis of Ping Dataset

In this section, we present the preliminary observations of the dataset collected using the ping tool in the real setting of PlanetLab (PlanetLab) and from the iPlane (iPlane) dataset, which is based on latency measurements between 68 landmarks spread around North America similar to our landmarks, using the ping tool. Figure 8 (a) shows a plot of the latency to distance (approximately 150,000 data points) gathered on the PlanetLab test-bed using 50 PlanetLab nodes in North America as landmarks. The solid line in Figure 8 (a) shows t_{min}(d) given by equation 1. Figure 9 (a) shows the histogram of observed distances for a given latency range (90.05ms-100.00ms) of the PlanetLab dataset. Similarly, Figure 8Figure 8: Distance-latency relationship *(a) between 50 PlanetLab landmarks (b) between 68 iPlane landmarks. The straight line below the data points shows the distance to latency relationship according to equation 1* (b) shows latency to distance data points between 68 iPlane landmarks collected at the same period of time as the PlanetLab dataset. iPlane landmarks are also distributed all across North America, similarly to PlanetLab landmarks. Figure 9 (b) shows the histogram of observed distances for a given latency range (99.40ms-103.89ms) in the iPlane dataset.

The following are five characteristics observed from these datasets (Figure 8 (a) and Figure 8(b)):

- The minimum latency observed is higher than the theoretical minimum given by equation 1.
- There is a positive correlation between latency and distance.
- A simple linear or non-linear relationship is not apparent in the dataset - the data is noisy as described by equation 2.
- Although an upper bound on distance for a given latency is apparent, a lower bound is not apparent. This is the case even for the data analyzed on a per landmark basis.
- For a given latency (or a latency range), some distances are more probable than other distances (Figure 8(a) and Figure 8 (b)).

The above observations are from one global distribution of latency measurements generated between all the landmarks from respective dataset.

Figure10 shows an example of the latency to distance relationship for a single landmark vn1. cs.wustl.edu at Washington University in St Louis. Similar observations to these in Figure 8 (a) of the combined distance-latency relationship are witnessed even for a per landmark basis distance-latency relationship.

Active and Passive Measurements

This section conducts further analysis on suitable types of latency measurements for network-based applications, such as, Internet host geolocation.

We discuss the suitability of active and passive measurement for measurement-based geolocation approaches. An active measurement refers to a real time latency measurement between Internet hosts that is gathered each time a geolocation action is to take place. On the other hand, a passive measurement refers to a prediction of latency between Internet hosts without initiating latency measurement between them. There are existing solutions available for Internet latency prediction (Dabek, 2004; Wong B. S., 2005; Madhyastha, 2006; Pietzuch, 2006; Francis, 2001). These solutions incur different levels of errors in their respective prediction mechanism. Therefore, a measurement-based geolocation approach is likely to consider an active measurement-based approach for geolocation in order to avoid any additional inaccuracies.

We further investigate the topic of active and passive measurements in terms of Triangle Inequality Violations (TIV) between respective PlanteLab and iPlane landmarks. TIV is the effect of packets between two nodes being routed on the longer or slower path between them when a shorter or faster path is available. As a result, presence of TIV may portray more significant latency inflation between a pair of nodes than expected. Therefore, prediction of latency between a landmark-target pair in comparison to another landmark-target pair may not be reliable in the presence of TIV.

Figure 8. Distance-latency relationship (a) between 50 PlanetLab landmarks (b) between 68 iPlane landmarks. The straight line below the data points shows the distance to latency relationship according to equation 1

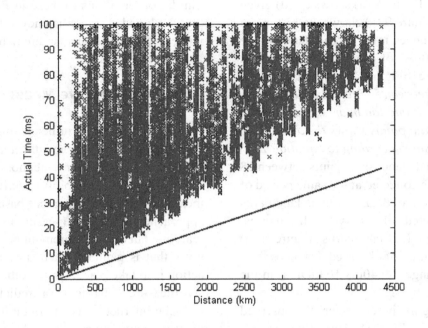

(a)

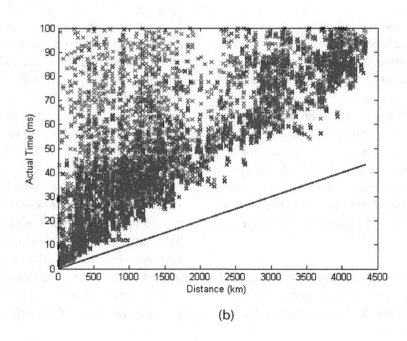

(b)

Figure 9. Histogram of distances (a) in the PlanetLab dataset for latency range 90.05-100.00 ms (b) in the iPlane dataset for latency range 99.40-103.89 ms

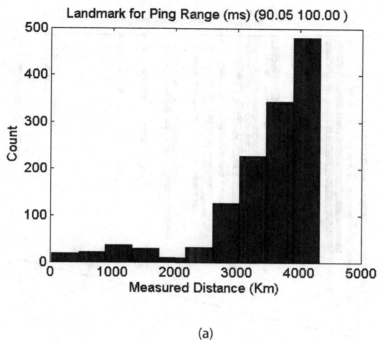

(a)

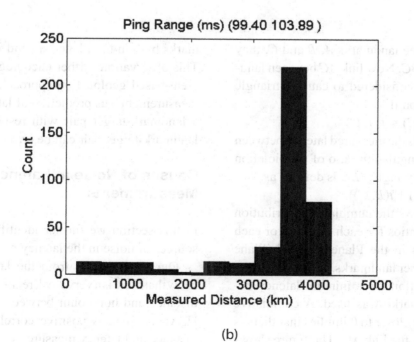

(b)

Figure 10. Distance-latency relationship for landmark vn1.cs.wustl.edu at Washington University in St Louis

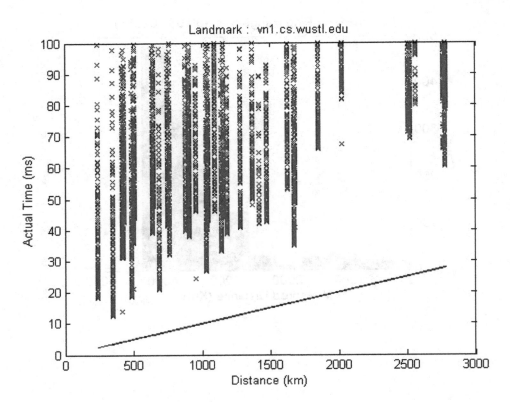

Given any three landmarks *A*, *B* and *C*, they form a triangle *ABC*. Now link *AC* between landmark *A* and *C* is considered to cause a triangle inequality violation if

$t(A, B) + t(B, C) < t(A, C)$

where t(X, Y) is the measured latency between X and Y. The triangulation ratio of the violation caused by *AC* in triangle *ABC* is defined as

$t(A, C)/(t(A, B) + t(B, C))$

Figure *11* shows the cumulative distribution of triangulation ratios for each link *AC* for each of the landmarks in the PlanetLab and iPlane dataset against other landmarks. In this triangulation ratio calculation the minimum latency between two landmarks was used. A cumulative distribution value closer to 0 implies that there is no TIV caused by the link AC. The figure shows there is significant TIV present amongst the land-

marks both in the PlanetLab and iPlane dataset. This observation further encourages a measurement-based geolocation approach to use active measurements, as prediction of latency between a landmark-target pair with respect to another landmark-target pair can be erroneous.

Causes of Noise in Latency Measurements

In this section we further identify the possible sources of noise in the latency measurements.

Our observations from the latency datasets show that there is a very weak relationship between distance and hop count between Internet hosts. However there is positive correlation between distance and latency measurements with considerable variance in latency for a given distance.

Figure 11. CDF of triangle inequality violations (TIV) between PlanetLab and iPlane landmarks

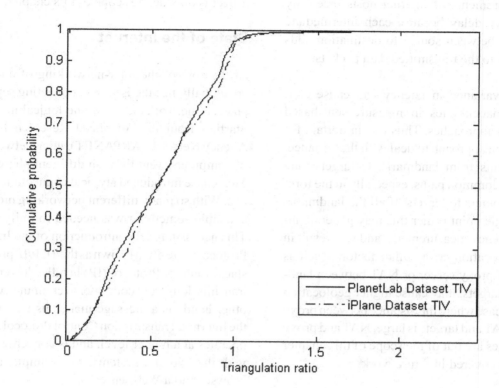

There are several factors that can contribute to the variance in Internet latency as observed in Figure 8 (a) and Figure 8 (b).

Heterogeneity is a key property that causes high variance in latency between Internet hosts. The heterogeneity ranges from the topology of the Internet to individual links that establish the connection between end hosts. The topology of the Internet is difficult to design because of its large size and it is constantly changing, resulting in changed routing policy. On the other hand, links on the Internet vary from a few hundred bytes modem links to significantly faster optical fiber links. As a result, the heterogeneity of the Internet is believed to cause higher variance in latency measurements.

Circuitous Routing is an integral part of Internet behavior. A data packet can take many routes between source to destination hosts based on the routing policy. The ever changing topology of the Internet adds more inflation to circuitous routing. Also, the Internet routes are asymmetric: i.e. the route from node A to B quite often differs from the route back from node B to A. As a result, one-way delay between Internet hosts could be preferable over RTT measurements. However, one-way delay confronts major hurdles as described earlier. Thus, it is believed, a circuitous route often causes higher variance in latency measurements.

Localized Delay is an important reason for higher variance in latency measurements. Localized delay may occur due to low-speed links and congestion in local nodes due to higher workload. It is to be noted that latency measurements of Internet hosts face only additive delay because each intermediate router between source to destination adds delays to the transmitted data packets.

Higher variance in latency can cause considerable inaccuracies in measurement-based geolocation approaches. Thus it is important for a geolocation approach to deal with the variance. Measurements from landmarks to targets may share some common paths, especially in the form of nearby routers to targets. If all the landmarks share a single point router this may generate inaccurate latency measurements and will result in higher geolocation error. Other factors, such as presence of proxy server or NAT between landmarks and targets, may cause higher geolocation error in the case where the distance between proxy server or NAT and targets is large. NAT and proxy related issues are out of the scope of this chapter and will be covered in future work.

INTERNET HOST GEOLOCATION

One interesting question in relation to all geolocation techniques is the ethical aspect of finding the physical location of users. In order to deal with this aspect the Internet Engineering Task Force (IETF) has a privacy working group called 'geopriv'. Geopriv continues to refine and analyze the authorization, integrity, and privacy requirements that must be met when representations of a location are created, stored and used. Geopriv details the privacy aspect in different Internet-drafts and/or Request For Comments (RFC). These documents emphasize protecting against unauthorized access to preserve the privacy of Internet users. Our observations and research suggest all the existing geolocaiton techniques proposed by the research community are aware of this ethical aspect. However, in this chapter we focus on the technical aspect of the geolocation

techniques and believe discussion of the ethical aspect is outside the scope of this chapter.

State of the Internet

At the core of the inter-networking of computers globally lies the issue of connecting separate physical networks to form one logical network. Starting from the Advanced Research Project Agency Network (ARPANET), inter-networking of computers went through different phases and each phase introduced atypical connection methods. With so many different networking methods available something was needed to unify them. This necessitated the introduction of the Internet Protocol Suite often known as the TCP/IP protocol stack. Internet Protocol (IP) handles lower-level transmissions from computer to computer. On the other hand, as a message makes its way across the Internet, Transmission Control Protocol (TCP) operates at a higher level, and is concerned only with the two end systems; for example, a Web browser and a Web server.

TCP/IP operates on the packet-switched network; in turn it embraces the best effort delivery service. In a best effort network all users obtain best effort service, meaning that they obtain unspecified variable bit rate and delivery time, depending on the current traffic load. When a message is sent from a source machine it starts traveling through intermediate routers. Each router on the path, based on their workload, available router interface and connectivity, forwards the message to the next router. The next routers can be in the straight line distance between the source and destination machine or they may be in a circuitous route. Finally, the message reaches the destination IP address via routers. It is also to be noted that routers exchange messages between them based on the IP address.

The best effort delivery service of IP is assisted by the higher layer protocol TCP in order to provide a guaranteed service. TCP ensures that all information transmitted from the source IP is received fully at the destination IP. However, TCP does not reserve any resources in advance and does not provide any guarantees regarding quality of service; for example, ensuring constant bit rate for applications such as Internet telephony. From this point of view, TCP can still be considered as a best effort service. On the other hand, the higher layer protocol User Datagram Protocol (UDP) is completely based on best effort delivery. UDP is very prominent for applications such as media streaming and online gaming where the extra connection messages and packet recovery features of TCP turn out to be a burden for the applications. Therefore latency measurements tools, such as ping and traceroute, preferably use UDP to take measurements between Internet hosts.

Notion of Geolocation on the Internet

As was discussed before, there is no one-to-one relationship between an IP and a physical address. Moreover, the dynamic assignment of IP addresses makes it even more difficult to track the location of an IP. There are several possible ways to determine the physical location of an IP address. From the context of the Internet, the simplest way might be to ask the user to provide the location information. However, such approaches are likely to be burdensome on the users and erroneous due to deliberate or accidental mistakes in the location information provided. Thus alternate approaches that evolve through technical solutions are required.

It is to be noted that Internet host localization is a more challenging task compared to the well-studied and related problems of wireless localization. This is primarily because the transmission characteristics in the Internet are more complex than those in the air. The most prominent wireless domain localization is the Global Positioning System (GPS). GPS, however, is ineffective indoors thus several research efforts were initiated for the indoor environment.

Different approaches to Internet host geolocation are detailed in the following sections.

Repository-Based Approaches

One of the intuitive approaches to host geolocation is comprehensive IP tabulation against physical locations, popularly known as the whois database, which can be used as a lookup table (Muir, 2006). However, because of the large number of available Internet hosts, such an approach is not likely to scale. Also, a lookup table is difficult to maintain and keep up-to-date, especially as it cannot take into consideration dynamic IP assignment. Other variants of comprehensive IP tabulation are whois lookup based on Autonomous Systems (AS) number (Gao, 2000; Muir, 2006), whois lookup by domain name (Muir, 2006) and voluntary DNS LOC records (Muir, 2006).

Three techniques for geolocation were proposed in IP2Geo (Padmanabhan, 2001): GeoTrack, GeoPing and GeoCluster. GeoTrack and GeoCluster are the two repository-based approaches in IP2Geo. GeoTrack uses traceroute information from a host to the target, which contains the list of routers encountered along the path. Using location hints from the DNS names of the routers along the path, the locations of the routers are determined. Of the routers whose locations are known, the closest one to the target is selected and its location is chosen as the target location. The accuracy of the technique depends on the distance from the target to the nearest router of known location.

GeoCluster is a database lookup technique that groups IP addresses to clusters based on geographical proximity. This information is combined with the user registration records from web-based services such as email services. This technique suffers from the general problems related to database lookup-based approaches, such as reliability, scalability and maintainability issues, and also unavailability of the user registration information for public access.

The recent data-mining based approach, Structon (Guo, 2009), is similar to GeoCluster except that it uses publicly available web pages instead of proprietary data sources in order to extract geolocation information. Structon uses a three-step approach. First, extracted geolocation information from web pages is associated with their IP addresses. Then this mapping information goes through multi-stage inference processes in order to improve the accuracy and coverage of its IP geolocation repository of different IP segments. Finally, those IP segments that are not covered in the first two steps are mapped with the location of the access router with the help of the traceroute tool. The accuracy of Structon implementation on the Internet depends heavily on the accuracy of extracted geographical mapping information. Moreover, with Structon, it is harder to get accuracy better than the granularity of city level.

Measurement-Based Approaches

GeoPing, the measurement-based approach of IP2Geo (Padmanabhan, 2001), works on the assumption that hosts that are geographically close have similar network delays with respect to other fixed hosts. By comparing the ping times to the target from a set of landmarks or probe machines with the ping times to a set of nodes at known locations, GeoPing estimates the target location to be the same as that of the node with a known location having the most similar ping values. Thus, the accuracy of GeoPing is limited by the distance to the nearest node with a known location.

Constraint-Based Geolocation (CBG) (Gueye, 2006) uses ping times from landmarks as a measure of delay. For each landmark a maximum distance bound for a given latency is derived using distance-to-ping relationships observed between landmarks. During geolocation the observed latencies from landmarks to the target are used to draw circles centered at each landmark based on the maximum distance bounds derived earlier. The target is assumed to reside in the convex region resulting from the intersection of circles, and the target location is estimated as the centroid of this convex region.

Similar to CBG, Topoloy-based Geolocation (TBG) (Basset, 2006) computes the possible location of the target as a convex region. In TBG the maximum distance bound is obtained based on the maximum transmission speed of packets in fibre, which gives a conservative estimate of the possible region. This region is further refined using inter-router latencies along the path between the target and the landmark, obtained from the traceroute command. The final target location is obtained through a global optimization that minimizes average position error for the target and the routers.

A relatively recent measurement-based technique for geolocation is Octant (Wong B. S., 2007). In contrast to other constraint based approaches that only limit the area where the target may be located, Octant also identifies areas where the target may not be located based on observed latencies (referred to as negative constraint). Octant expresses such information by considering two circles corresponding to the maximum and minimum distances from each landmark to the target which constrains the possible geographical area where the target may be located. Each landmark fits a convex hull to all of its delay-to-distance data points with other landmarks. Upper and lower facets of the convex hull correspond to the maximum and minimum distance bounds. Different weights are assigned to different geographical areas based on the number of intersections (higher weights assigned to larger numbers of intersections). The final estimated region is the union of all regions, where the weight exceeds a desired weight or the region size exceeds a selected threshold. A Monte-Carlo algorithm is applied to pick the best single point location from the final estimated regions. These estimated regions in Octant often end up being disconnected parts. Octant uses geographical and demographical constraints to improve the localization accuracy beyond its measurement-only solution.

The Statistical Geolocation of Internet Hosts (I.Youn, 2009) is a recent work in the domain of measurement-based Internet host geolocation that addresses the location tracking problem statistically. It consists of three steps. First, it generates an individual landmark profile with the latency measurements between each landmark to the other landmarks in the form of a scatterplot of latency-distance measurements. Second, using these profiles and in order to generate a latency-distance relationship, this approach approximates joint probability distributions of distance and latency using bivariate kernel density estimation. A Gaussian kernel is used for the estimation. Finally, it uses a force-directed algorithm to obtain the target location from the latency measurements between the landmarks and the target. In the iterative use of the force-directed algorithm, the resultant force moves the target location within the experimental region. This algorithm stops when the target position moves less than a prefixed threshold distance value and proposes the current position as the target location.

In this paper (Arif M. K., 2010), the applicability of Maximum Likelihood Estimation (MLE) technique is investigated for target geolocation on the Internet, based on a statistical model for Internet latency. The application of MLE for target geolocation was motivated by the probabilistic patterns observed in latencies between landmarks. From latency measurements gathered between landmarks over a period of time the conditional probability density function (PDF) was derived for latency given the distance travelled by packets. Using this PDF as the likelihood function this approach computed the MLE for a set of latency measurements from landmarks to the target to propose its most likely position.

Previous measurement-based geolocation techniques used the observed latencies from multiple landmarks to the target host to determine maximum bound or both the maximum and minimum bounds of the geographical region where the target host is located. Due to the large variance of Internet latency measurements, the region constrained based on such maximum-minimum bounds tends to be relatively large resulting in large estimation errors. GeoWeight (Arif M. K., 2010), which improves the geolocation accuracy by further limiting the possible target region by dividing the constrained region (between maximum and minimum distance) to sub-regions of different weights. The weight assigned to a sub-region indicates the probability of the target being in that sub-region; a higher weight indicating a more probable region. By considering latency measurements from multiple landmarks and computing the resultant weights of overlapping regions a better constrained target region can be obtained.

GeoWeight is the only approach among all the measurement-based approaches which incorporates all the five observations from section 5.2. Other approaches use only a different subset of these five observations.

Different Attributes of Comparison

In this section we compare the existing geolocation techniques in terms of different attributes. Accuracy indicates how accurate the technique is; Freshness describes how current the outcome is; Reliability illustrates the consistency in performance; Scalability analyzes the workload and possible point of failure of the approach; and Completeness discloses the certainty of the result. We believe these attributes are important for a geolocation approach for the following reasons:

- **Accuracy:** Producing an accurate target location can be considered as the most important attribute of a geolocation approach. An erroneous geolocation technique not only generates a wrong target location but also causes malfunctions in the applications using the inaccurate geolocation technique.
- **Freshness:** The outcome of a geolocation technique is only useful if the proposed location information represents the current

target location. Dynamic distribution of IP addresses requires constant updating or producing the results in real time. Out-of-date location information can cause critical problem for the applications using it.

- **Reliability:** A geolocation approach is expected to produce consistent results in spite of the possible anomalies present, either in the form of a falsified location record in repository-based approaches or higher latency variance in measurement-based approaches. Thus it is important to be able to track these inconsistencies in order to provide a reliable geolocation service.

- **Scalability:** An important metric for a geolocaiton approach is the amount of effort required to produce accurate location information. If the required effort is high this may outweigh the benefits of a geolocation service. Besides, a single point of failure can make a geolocation approach futile.

- **Completeness:** The capability for producing results is an important characteristic of a geolocation approach. Thus a geolocation approach can also be evaluated based on its certainty of producing results.

Two examples, IP-Whois from repository-based approach and OCTANT from measurement-based approach, are compared in terms of the attributes described earlier.

IP-Whois

- **Accuracy** Accuracy of a whois database largely depends not only on how exact the records are but also on how current the records are. Also, if the registered address represents a globally distributed organization or if an organization is given a large range of IP addresses, it affects the accuracy of whois services.

- **Freshness** Whois records need to be updated constantly otherwise the records become out of date. Unless a very recent time of update of the records is mentioned, it is likely that the whois service will produce outdated results.

- **Reliability** A whois record can be falsified intentionally or unintentionally. Constant update and verification of the records may help whois to produce reliable results.

- **Scalability** A considerable amount of effort is required for the automated and continuous update and verification of the whois record. Dynamic assignment of IP addresses makes it harder to maintain an up-to-date whois database. Unless a distributed replica of the same whois database is provided, IP whois is vulnerable to single point of failure.

- **Completeness** If the IP address is already recorded in the searched whois it can provide corresponding location information, otherwise it fails to provide any record.

OCTANT

- **Accuracy** Octant improves the geolocation accuracy over CBG by further constraining the possible target region. Within a possible target region Octant uses a Monte-Carlo algorithm to pick a single point that represents the most likely target location. Such exploration for a single point target location increases the geolocation accuracy for Octant.

- **Freshness** Octant requires measuring latency between landmarks periodically so that the maximum and minimum distance bounds given a latency measurement represent the current behaviour of landmarks in the present network condition.

- **Reliability** Being a measurement-based approach the performance of Octant is also susceptible to noisy Internet latency. Apart from this, the final regions for a possible target location generated by Octant end up

Table 1. Summary of the comparison of existing geolocation techniques with indicators high (H), medium (M) and low (L)

	Accuracy	Freshness	Reliability	Scalability	Completeness
Whois Look Up	M/L	M/L	M/L	L	L/M
DNS Look Up	M	H	M/L	L	L/M
GeoCluster	M	M	M	L	L
Structon	M	H	M	L	M
GeoPing	M	H	H	H	L
CBG	H/M	H	H	H	L
GeoBud	H	H	H	M	L
TBG	H	H	H	M	L
OCTANT	H	H	H	H	L
Statistical Geolocation	M	H	H	M	L
MLE	H	H	H	H	L
GeoWeight	H	H	H	H	L

being disconnected parts. This is due to Octant's simple model of possible target region generation from the maximum and minimum distance bounds.

- **Scalability** Octant requires maintaining up-to-date latency-distance relationship for individual landmarks. During geolocalization Octant uses the maximum and minimum distance bounds against a latency measurement from these latency-distance relationships and generates possible regions for the target. Octant is not susceptible to single point of failure as the landmarks in Octant are distributed and Octant can still produce result in case of few landmarks failure during geolocalization.
- **Completeness** Like other measurement-based approaches, Octant also assumes that the target will respond to an ICMP message.

Summary of Comparative Analysis

In this subsection we present a comparison between the existing geolocation approaches in Table 1 Summary of the Comparison of Existing

Geolocation Techniques with Indicators High (H), Medium (M) and Low (L). As shown in the table, H indicates high, M indicates medium and L indicates low. These three indicators for each technique are used in comparison to other existing geolocation techniques.

In summary, it is to be noted that the measurement-based approaches perform better in terms of accuracy and freshness. Measurement-based approaches are also comparatively reliable because repository-based approaches are susceptible to worn-out records. It is observed that the measurement-based approaches are more scalable as they require comparatively less effort and there is no single point of failure. Finally, certainty of the outcome of the measurement-based approaches can be low if the target is not responding to the latency measurements.

FUTURE RESEARCH DIRECTION

This chapter identified areas of distributed computing which can be benefited from the geolocation techniques. This chapter evaluated a large Internet latency data set and demonstrated the use of the latency for geolocating the Internet hosts in order to enhance user experiences of a distributed system. The core of the accuracy of a measurement-based geolocation approach is the ability to model a better latency-distance relationship given the higher variability of Internet latency against distance. In order to propose a more accurate latency model it is required to further investigate the impact of facts, such as, indirect routes and connectivity congestion between Internet hosts based on a much larger and a global scale latency data set. The outcome of such research is expected to produce quantification of richer connectivity between distributed Internet hosts, accurate prediction of latency between Internet hosts without extensive communications and a location aware web.

CONCLUSION

In this chapter we have analyzed Internet latency and discussed the usages of latency for measurement-based Internet host geolocation. We observed a positive latency to distance correlation between Internet hosts which is higher than the theoretical latency-distance relationship of optical fiber connectivity. A simple linear or non-linear relationship between latency and distance is harder to model with such noisy data. We further observed that an upper bound of distance for a given latency is more apparent than the lower bound of distance. Finally we witnessed, for a given latency, some distances are more probable than other distances.

Such thorough analysis of Internet latency is greatly helpful for the geolocation accuracy of measurement-based geolocation technique. It is observed that measurement-based approaches are capable of producing more accurate, reliable and scalable outcome. Available latency measurements during geolocation can also be used for other applications, such as, Voice over IP (VoIP) quality control. Therefore, it is believed the latency analysis presented in this chapter will not only

serve the geolocation technology but will also serve a wide variety of network-based applications.

REFERENCES

Arif, M. K. (2010). GeoWeight: Internet host geolocation based on a probability model for latency measurements. In *Proceedings of 33rd Australasian Computer Science Conference* (pp. 89-98). Brisbane, Australia: Australian Computer Society.

Arif, M. K. (2010). Internet host geolocation using maximum likelihood estimation technique. In *Proceedings of 24th IEEE Advanced Information Networking and Applications* (pp. 422-429). Perth, Australia: IEEE Computer Society.

Basset, E. J. (2006). Towards IP gelolocation using delay and topology measurements. In *Proceedings of 6th Internet Measurement Conference* (pp. 71-84). Rio de Janeiro, Brazil: Springer.

Dabek, F. C. (2004). Vivaldi: A decentralized network coordinate system. In *Proceedings of SIGCOMM Conference* (pp. 15-26). Portland, Oregon: ACM.

Francis, P. J. (2001). IDMaps: A global Internet host distance estimation service. *Journal of IEEE/ACM Transactions on Networking, 9*, 525-540. IEEE/ACM.

Gao, L. (2000). On inferring autonomous system relationships in the Internet. In *Proceedings of Global Telecommunications Conference (GLOBECOM)* (pp. 387-396). CA, USA: IEEE.

Gueye, B. Z. (2006). Constraint-based geolocation of Internet hosts. *Journal of IEEE/ACM Transactions-Networking, 14*, 1219-1232. IEEE/ACM.

Guo, C. L. (2009). Mining the Web and the Internet for accurate IP address geolocations. In *Proceedings of 28th IEEE INFOCOM Conference on Computer Communications* (pp. 2841-2845). Rio de Janeiro, Brazil: IEEE Communications Society. iPlane. (n.d.). *Recuperado el 2010, de iPlane: Latency measurements from University of Washington*. Retrieved from http:// www.mcs.anl.gov/ olson/ IPtoLL.html

Madhyastha, H. V. (2006). A structural approach to latency prediction. In *Proceedings of 6th ACM SIGCOMM Conference on Internet Measurement* (pp. 99-104). Rio de Janeiro, Brazil: ACM.

Muir, J. a. (2006). *Internet geolocation and evasion*. (Technical Report TR-06-05), School of Computer Science, Carleton University.

Padmanabhan, V. N. (2001). An investigation of geographic mapmapping techniques for Internet hosts. In *Proceedings of ACM SIGCOMM Computer Communication Review* (pp. 173-185). San Diego, CA: ACM.

Pietzuch, P. L. (2006). Network-aware overlays with network coordinates. In *Proceedings of 26th IEEE International Conference on Distributed Computing Systems Workshops (ICDCSW)* (pp. 12-12). Lisboa, Portugal: IEEE.

PlanetLab. (s.f.). *Website*. Retrieved from http:// www.planet-lab.org/

Wong, B. S. (2005). Meridian: A lightweight networkl service without virtual coordinates. In *Proceedings of ACM SIGCOMM* (pp. 85-96). Philadelphia, PA: ACM.

Wong, B. S. (2007). Octant: A comprehensive framework for the geolocalization of Internet hosts. In *Proceedings of 4th Symposium on Networked System Design and Implementation* (pp. 313-326). Cambridge, MA: USENIX.

Youn, I. (2009). Statistical geolocation of Internet hosts. In *Proceedings of 18th International Conference on Computer Communications and Networks* (pp. 1-6). CA, USA: IEEE.

KEY TERMS AND DEFINITIONS

Distributed System: It is a computer system where different components of an application are located on different computers and communicates between them via network.

Geolocation: Locating physical location of Internet hosts is referred to as Geolocation.

Internet Latency: Time taken for a data packet to travel between Internet hosts are known as Internet latency.

Internet Protocol (IP) Address: IP address is the logical address used to identify the Internet hosts.

Internet Technologies: Internet is the biggest distributed system and applications running on the Internet are known as Internet technologies.

Meaurement-Based Geolocation: Process to find the location information of the Internet hosts based on latency measurements.

Repository-Based Geolocation: Process to find the location information of the Internet hosts based on a database lookup.

Chapter 5
MINTCar:
A Tool Enabling Multiple Source Multiple Destination Network Tomography

Laurent Bobelin
CNRS, France

ABSTRACT

Discovering a network topology and inferring its performances for the client/server case is a well known field of study. However, client/server model is no longer accurate when dealing with Grids, as those platforms involve coordinated transfers from multiple sources to multiple destinations. In this chapter, we first review existing work, introduce a representation of the inferred knowledge from multiple sources and multiple destinations measurements that allows to obtain a well-posed problem, algorithms in order to reconstruct such a representation, a method to probe network, and give some experimental results.

INTRODUCTION

Nowadays institutional grid testbeds are composed of thousands of computing and data storage resources spread worldwide. Connectivity is ensured using either the Internet, or high bandwidth.delay networks such as GEANT (The GEANT website, retrieved 2010) in Europe, TeraGrid (The TeraGrid website, retrieved 2010) or Internet 2 (The Internet2 website, retrieved 2010) in US.

Data-intensive grid applications or even grid middleware itself usually deploy software and resources dedicated to bulk data transfer. For example, EGEE (The EGEE website, retrieved 2010) project uses a hierarchy of tiers. In such a hierarchy, each tier is a data storage center. Tier-0 is located close to the experiment place (for EGEE, at CERN, where data is produced). Tier-1 are national or institutional centers, tier-2 are located close to large computing centers, and tier-3 are located in labs. Tier-0 communicates to tier-1, tier-1s can communicate with every tier-1s and to a subset of tier-2s and tier-2s communicate to a subset of tier-2s and a subset of tier-3s. In such a case, the data transfer paradigm is no more a client/server one: each host is a source, a destination, or both, and each source communicates to a subset of destinations.

DOI: 10.4018/978-1-61350-110-8.ch005

Copyright © 2012, IGI Global. Copying or distributing in print or electronic forms without written permission of IGI Global is prohibited.

This overlay network is built on top of the real network. It implies that independent logical links can share some physical links. Therefore, it is mandatory to know capacity and topology of the underlying network in order to optimize communications between tiers. If not, some logically independent transfers may compete for the same physical network resource. Unfortunately, most of the time, physical topology is unknown. Moreover, existing monitoring tools like NWS (Wolski, Spring, & Hayes. 1999) or WREN (Lowekamp & al, 2003) only allow modeling basic interactions between transfers.

Internet topology discovery can be done using tools like traceroute (Jacobson, 1989) or traceroute-like measurements. The resulting topology is unlabeled. It is formed by matching IP address of network equipments belonging to the different observed paths. This method has drawbacks: multiple network router interfaces, as well as non-responding equipments, can lead to inaccurate results, and enforce to use dedicated techniques in order to bypass those problems and discover the topology, as in (Viger et al, 2008). Higher-level discovery can also be done using AS-level information provided by ISP using Looking Glass servers, as in (Subramanian et al, 2002). Anyhow those methods suffer the lack of relationships with performances of the links, as they only discover the physical links but not their capacities. In order to retrieve more relevant information, one can use techniques based on monitoring information of links load provided by routers in order to discover the topology to reconstruct the path of flows crossing the network (Zhang et al, 2003).

But all those methods use information that network administrators may not authorize access to. As a grid application runs on hosts owned by organizations applying different security policies, using such tools is most of the time unrealistic. Using application level measurements is then the most efficient way to discover the topology and infer network capacities. This is known in the literature as network tomography (Vardi, 1996).

NETWORK TOMOGRAPHY

Since the last decade, network tomography for the client/server case has been widely studied (see (Castro et al, 2004) for an overview). Resulting topology is a tree where each edge represents a set of physical objects. The root is the server, leaves are clients and inner nodes are disjunction points of paths between the server and its clients. Edges can sometimes be labeled with the capacity of routers and wires belonging to the sub-path represented by it. Packet train based techniques are used to infer disjunction point for a pair of path. Probing is done for each pair of paths. Reconstruction is done most of the time using statistical techniques to estimate likelihood. Roughly speaking, it consists to collapse 2 or more disjunction points into one when capacities of the sub-paths leading to those inferred points are similar. Unfortunately, this method relies on the assertion that the resulting topology is a tree. But a tree cannot characterize the network when multiple sources and multiple destinations are involved, as stated in (Bu, Duffield, & Lo Presti, 2002). New probing techniques, reconstruction algorithms and models must then be developed for this topology discovery and performances inference.

Network tomography is an inverse problem, as stated in (Vardi, 1996). Those problems consist in inferring the structure and characteristic of a system (i.e. the network) based only on its reaction to stimuli (i.e. end-to-end measurements). Canonical inverse problem solving consists in three steps:

- Find an accurate model for solutions, which may enable to pose the problem as a well-defined one (see (Hadamard, 1923) for a definition of it),

- Find a way to retrieve an initial set of observed data which enables reconstruction,
- Construct the solution using the data.

In order to have a well-defined problem, model must lead to a representation for a targeted network that exists and is unique. Then, if it exists a deterministic algorithm that can reconstruct a targeted network representation from end-to-end measurements, then the reconstructed solution is an exact representation of the targeted network (modulo the measurements errors bias, that can be considered as Hadamard' stability).

MINTCar (Metric Induced Network Topology - Construction, Analysis and Retrieval) is a tool that performs multiple sources multiple destinations network tomography. It is dedicated to the available bandwidth metric. It relies on a network model enabling to well-pose the problem, and implements algorithms and probing methods to perform the discovery and performance inference. The main goal of this book chapter is to give a general overview of the process leading to topology reconstruction.

RELATED WORK

This book chapter focuses mainly on topology discovery using only end-to-end measurements made actively for a given metric for the multiple source, multiple destination case, for the bandwidth metric. This section gives an overview of existing work dealing with network tomography. It is composed of three subsections, each of them covering one step of inverse problem solving.

Network Models

Network models used in network topology discovery can be separated in two different kinds: some are labeled and then depict the properties and behavior of the network, and some are unlabeled and depict network structure. In the later case,

even if some capacities in regard to a metric are known, it would not make sense, or it would be impossible, to label nodes or edges produced with values. Unlabeled and labeled topology discovery goals differ significantly. Labeled topology can be used by a distributed application in order to optimize its transfers. This also means that this discovery relies on a closed set of resources, which hosts the application processes. Unlabeled topology depicts the structure of the network and is more oriented toward analysis of the structure of the network.

Unlabeled Topology

Unlabeled topology can be separated in two kinds. The first kind is constructed by discovering the complete set of equipments and links deployed within the network. This IP-level topology discovery is most of the time designed for an open set of possibly non-cooperating hosts. The second one aims at discover the relationship between observed paths. This logical topology discovery then focuses on a closed set of cooperating host. This topology does not depict anymore the equipments belonging to the network, but a set of conjunction/disjunction points for paths.

Unlabeled IP-level topology discovery has been widely studied. As the resulting topology is similar to the real topology, it is sometimes named physical topology. As it relies on the idea of discovering the equipments and identifying them by their (IP) identity, there is not much work dealing with models, nor on accuracy of the reconstructed model (with some exception, as stated before). Readers interested in those methods can for example find further readings in the bibliography of (Latapy, Magnien, & Ouedraogo, 2008).

Some work can not fit into such a simple taxonomy. Authors of (Latapy, Magnien, & Ouedraogo, 2008) for example define an ego-centered topology view, based on the server view of the network. While focusing only on a single source/multiple destination case, they try to capture the dynamics of the routing and the topology of the network rather than a static description. Recently, works as (Hailiang et al, 2008) and (Ni et al, 2009) are using IP-level information to guide the metric induced topology inference. Authors of (Rabbat, Figueiredo, & Nowak, 2006) use identification of equipments along a route in order to reconstruct a whole topology. In their problem, while it is possible to know which equipments are belonging to a path, they are not able to identify the total order induced by the path they are considering. Their approach then relies on clustering techniques in order to identify the largest set of equipments shared by paths in order to infer sub-paths.

Unlabeled logical topology discovery has been also a subject of interest. The term logical topology has been formally defined by Bestavros in (Bestavros, Byers, & Harfoush, 2001) for the single source, single destination. They proved that it exists a unique representation of a given network as a logical topology that can be constructed by knowing the physical topology and the characteristics of a given platform.

Net Radar (Eriksson et al 2010) reconstructs an unlabeled topology using mainly RTT measurements correlations. While earlier versions of their reconstruction were only based on RTT measurements (Tsang et al, 2004), newer techniques are now based also on TTL and hop counts between hosts. Reconstructed topology is a tree, as RTT and TTL measurements are made from a single source. TTL gives an estimation of distance between hosts.

The ability to label or not the topology discovered is most of the time induced by the properties of the measured metric itself. (Bestavros, Byers, & Harfoush, 2001) first identifies the mandatory metric properties in order to reconstruct a labeled topology. Refinements of those mandatory properties, and identification of mandatory properties in order to aggregate trees produced by single source/multiple destination tomography from multiple sources have been done in the later (Bestavros,

Byers, & Harfoush, 2005). They have proved that for the multiple source multiple destination reconstruction using only single source multiple destination trees, strong assumptions have to be bone on both routing (symmetric routing for example) and on metrics (symmetric capacities for a link) used in order to properly reconstruct the whole topology from those data.

Labeled Topology

Little attention has been paid to correctly model interactions of paths as a labeled topology, as for client/server case, the produced topology is a tree. Paths outgoing from the same source forks just once, and so a disjunction point between paths can be identified by the capacity of the common sub-path two paths shares. These capacities can then be used in order to determine a partial order for the disjunction paths. This method leads to the construction of a tree, named Metric Induced Network Topology, or MINT (Bestavros, Byers, & Harfoush, 2001).

Authors of (Rabbat, Nowak, & Coates, 2004), have addressed the multiple source multiple destination case without considering the topology produced. They have focused on a way to discover a sub-path shared by paths: they have developed a method in order to detect if 4 paths going from a set of two sources to a set of two destinations share a common sub-path, or not. Then they aggregate sub-trees that share this topology. However this work lacks a valid network model: indeed, having a common sub-path is not a transitive property. This method does not hold for more than 2 trees representing sources/destination paths. Work based on network coding like (Duan, Cai, & Tian, 2009) relies on the cooperation of hosts inside the network, and suffer the same problem.

More flexible network models than a close-to-reality are appearing nowadays, for at least three reasons. First, it allows bypassing some tricky problems, such as reconstructing the total order induced by a path. It also allows, when chosen wisely, to deal with large scale topology discovery. Finally, it allows capturing more topology dynamics.

Authors of (Arifler, De Veciana, & Evans, 2007) deal with the tricky problem of common bottleneck discovery. With the help of passive measurements, they try to infer which groups of flows had correlated performances. It produces classes of flows that pass through the same bottleneck. The model used here is a grouping of paths into possibly overlapping classes.

Authors of (Eyraud-Dubois et al, 2007) are dealing with topology discovery, based on interactions between flows along paths. The model they use is a based on trees produced by a clustering of flows that interact, and then on cliques to produce a fully connected topology. The idea is to produce a network topology that will mimic the target network path relationships. The reconstructed topology is thus not really intended to reflect a topology close to the physical one.

Vivaldi (Dabek et al, 2004) is an example of network modeling in order to deal with large scale system. It consists in placing in a 3-dimensional space nodes according to the latency observed between them.

Probing Techniques

A rough taxonomy can be constructed based on the different existing techniques: it can be either active or passive, relying on network inner node cooperation or not, rely on direct probes made on the path considered or rely directly on equipments (router level) or upper level (AS level) information, it can be dedicated to one, two, or many path, sharing the same source/destination or not, it can give information about capacities of path for various metrics, and give different information about relationships between the considered paths.

MINTCar reconstruction mainly targets available bandwidth (as defined in (Jain, Dovrolis, 2004)) for which, in a different context, many

methods have been developed. As we are focusing on this metric, we give an overview of probing techniques developed around it, while focusing more on the information one need to reconstruct a topology based on available bandwidth: identifying bottlenecks by the set of paths sharing it rather than detecting it.

Detecting Bottlenecks

Many methods have been developed so far in order to detect shared bottlenecks for single source and multiple destinations. Probing can be either active (i.e. relying on active injection of packets through the network (Vardi, 1996), (Duffield et al, 2001), (Coates et al, 2002) or passive (inferring knowledge by the analysis of traffic traces (Padmanabhan, Qiu, 2002), (Arifler, De Veciana, & Evans, 2007), (Donnet, Friedman, & Crovella, 2005). Existing probes also target various metrics (mainly delay (Rabbat, Nowak, & Coates, 2004), but also bandwidth capacity (Dovrolis, Ramanathan, & Moore, 2001), (Dovrolis, Ramanathan, & Moore, 2004), available bandwidth (The UDPMon website, retrieved 2010) or RTT (Tsang et al, 2004). Finally probing can be dedicated to the identification of a bottleneck for a set of path sharing the same source or the same destination (Dovrolis, Ramanathan, & Moore, 2004), (The UDPMon website, retrieved 2010), (Tsang et al, 2004) (Padmanabhan, Qiu, 2002)(Vardi, 1996) (Duffield et al, 2001) (Coates et al, 2002) (Dovrolis, Ramanathan, & Moore, 2001)., or paths that does not share neither source nor destination (Rabbat, Nowak, & Coates, 2004) (Arifler, De Veciana, & Evans, 2007). Most methods produce good results in bottleneck discovery from one source to one or many destinations, with the limitation of bandwidth estimation given in (Jain, Dovrolis, 2004). However, it cannot scale to the case of estimating available bandwidth of a sub-path of paths coming from different sources to different destinations.

Identifying Bottlenecks

(Rubenstein, Kurose, & Towsley, 2002) introduced and studied the problem, by giving a method to estimate if flows were sharing the same bottleneck. The main idea was to determine if the packet arrival of the different flows were sharing the same distribution, using entropy-based estimators. If so, it means that the flows were crossing the same bottleneck link, and that this bottleneck is loaded at at least 80% of its capacity. This behavior has also been studied in (Dovrolis, Ramanathan, & Moore, 2004). Our probing technique shares Rubenstein's technique spirit. The main differences are the entropy-based estimator used, and the fact that MINTCar actively inject packets into the bottleneck link to reach the necessary load in order to identify it, while previous work detects only highly loaded bottlenecks.

(Rabbat, Nowak, & Coates, 2004) introduced what appears to be a close attempt to detect shared bottlenecks. 4 hosts, 2 sources a, b and 2 destinations x, y and the 4 paths between them $\left(p_{ax}, p_{bx}, p_{ay}, p_{by} \right)$ are considered. At a random time, each source sends packet to the first destination (x) then to the second one (y). The arrival order of each packet is observed at its arrival at the destination host. Then the arrival order is calculated for each injection by each destination: $a_x \leq 1$, 1 if the packet from source a has arrived before those of source b, -1 if not. The same holds for the calculation of α_y. Then the statistical arrival order $z = \left\{ a_x \neq a_y \right\}$ is calculated. As z equals to zero should happen only if the 4 paths share a common sub-path, this probe allows determining this property. The problem with such a measurement is that it is not related to any metric, but only gives a hint about topological property.

The second closest attempt has been done in (Harfoush, Bestavros, & Byers, 2009). The tool developed tries to evaluate the capacity of a well-known sub-path of a path. It is mandatory to know at least 3 paths outgoing from the same source: two paths containing the targeted sub-path, and one that separate from others just before the targeted sub-path begins. It means that this probing method is useful only when topology is already known. Moreover, it cannot handle paths with different sources.

Pathneck (Hu & al, 2004) is a tool that is able to evaluate available bandwidth for each link of a path. Together with IP identification of routers along the paths, it could be used to identify precisely bottleneck. However, it requires cooperation from inner nodes in the network, which is unrealistic on grid platform.

Reconstruction Algorithms

We consider existing algorithms from the view point of the accuracy. This accuracy can be influenced mainly by hypothesis and assumptions algorithm relies on, as well as the nature of the algorithm itself, or the probing technique used. Authors of (Eyraud-Dubois, Quinson, 2007) focused on accuracy and studied some algorithms using simulation. The approach guiding the following review here is different: while they try to compare results of experiments and real topology, we focus on accuracy of the reconstruction guaranteed by the model chosen. We also put an emphasis on the number of measurements needed to reconstruct a topology. Indeed, in network tomography computational steps are far less costly than probing the network and so classic complexity is not a real matter.

Single Source Multiple Destination

For client/server case, most of the tools actually use algorithms based on likelihood estimation (see (Castro et al, 2004) for an overview). Experiments shown good results in terms of accuracy for the single source/multiple destinations case. Those algorithms rely on a probing technique estimating the dependency of the capacities of a pair of path in order to infer the existence and capacity of a shared sub-path for a given metric. Reconstruction algorithms use this dependency and estimate the correlation of the performances of those shared sub-paths to eventually merge them. This correlation is done using a sensitivity parameter that fixes how similar should be performances in order to be considered as equal. This implies that the accuracy of reconstructed topologies is dependent from this parameter. If value of this parameter is too high, the produced topology will tend to have on single shared sub-path for all paths. If the value is too low, the topology produced will tend to be a binary tree. Likelihood estimation involves usually $o\left(n^2\right)$ probes where n is the number of destinations, as it needs to estimate the distance from the source to the disjunction point for each pair of paths.

Multiple Source Multiple Destination

Some algorithms rely on aggregation of single source/multiple destination trees. (Bestavros, Byers, & Harfoush, 2005) gives exact algorithms to produce a topology based on these points. However, the mandatory hypotheses are most of the time unrealistic (symmetric routing, metric symmetry). This work relies on tree matching without any other probing. The number of probes is then $o\left(mn^2\right)$ where m is the number of sources and n the number of destinations.

Authors of (Castro et al, 2004) algorithm uses a reliable estimator in order to aggregate trees; however, as stated before, the model of the reconstructed topology is valid only for two sources. The complexity is twofold: it requires $o\left(mn^2\right)$ to reconstruct all trees from the m sources to the n destination, plus an additive number of $o\left(m^2\right)$ measurements in order to estimate which part of the trees are sharing a sub-path.

(Arifler, De Veciana, & Evans, 2007) work is not intended to produce a representation of the topology, but classes of paths experiencing the same cross-traffic and bottlenecks. The notion of sensitivity as well as the fact that correlation is used can influence the classes produced. It does not require any probing, as it is based on passive measurements.

(Eyraud-Dubois et al, 2007) algorithm relies on producing a network that mimic the real network; from this point of view, their reconstruction allows to have an accurate topology. It requires a prohibitive $o\left(n^6\right)$ measurements in order to reconstruct the topology. Authors do not provide a realistic way to probe the network in order to retrieve the initial set of data on which the reconstruction is based.

Notation and Vocabulary

Hypothesis

Except when explicitly stated, we will assume that there is no cross traffic. Hereafter in this article, we will similarly assume that routing is consistent and stable. By the former, we suppose that routing function does not allow routing paths to join, fork, and join again. By the latter, we suppose that routing paths will not change during the whole probing process.

Network

We consider the network as an oriented graph $G = \left(V \cup S \cup R, E\right)$ where vertices V are network equipments (hops) such as routers, hub, etc., S the set of hosts which will behave like senders, R the set of hosts which will behave as receivers and E physical links between them ($E \subset V \cup S \times V \cup R$). We will note l_{ij} a directed edge from i to j. A host that is both a source and a destination will be considered as two different hosts, one source and one destination. Upon this graph, routing function defines a set of paths. If routing is consistent, there is a unique path between each source a and destination b. Indeed if two paths exist between a and b, that means that they have joined in a, then fork, and join again in b.

p_{ab} is the path from $a \in S$ to $b \in R$. This path is an ordered sequence $p_{ab} = \left\{ l_{ai}, l_{ij}, l_{jk}, ..., l_{qb} \right\}$ of directed edges $l_{ij} \in E$. We will use either link or edge in order to name such l_{ij}. Each directed edge of any path starts from the destination of the edge preceding it (if such an edge exists). A sub-path of p_{ab} is a sub-sequence of this sequence that satisfies the path definition between a source $a' \in S \cup V$ and a destination $b' \in V \cup R$. This sub-path is contained by p_{ab}.

The length of a path is the number of directed edges in the sequence. The set of all paths defined by the routing function between each source $s \in S$ and each destination $r \in R$ will be noted P_{e2e}. It is the set of end-to-end paths. We will call flow probes packets going through a path or sub-path.

A common sub-path to a set of paths P_s is a sub-path contained by each element of P_s. The common maximum sub-path of a set of paths P_s is the longest common sub-path of P_s. If consistency holds, the longest common maximum sub-path is unique for a given P_s. This sub-path will be noted $p_{maximum}^{P_s}$. We will say that paths contained in P_s admit a common maximum sub-path. The set of common maximum sub-path admitted by at least one subset of P will be noted Max^P.

Metric

A metric is a function whose initial domain is the set of flows and whose range is reals. As flows are defined over paths, the value obtained for a flow can label a path. We will note c_m^p the capacity of a path for the metric. For example, if the metric m is the delay, the capacity c_m^p of a path will be equal to the sum of the delay induced by each directed edge composing it.

Detectability

A capacity of a path p will be detectable if it exists a set of paths containing p such that probing over those paths can exhibit capacity of p. For example, if the metric is the throughput achievable by TCP flows on steady-state, then the capacity of a sub-path can be detected only if it is feasible to saturate this path. An undetectable capacity of a path can be for example a path inducing no delay for the delay metric, or a path with infinite capacity if the metric is the bandwidth.

Constant Metric

A metric will be constant with respect to measurement if the capacity c_m^p does not depend on the paths followed by probes that detect it. For example, if the metric is the delay induced by a path, the capacity of a sub-path common to a set of path will be the same for each of these paths. The ratio of achievable bandwidth between two co-occurring TCP flows on a same sub-path is a non-constant metric. Indeed, two TCP concurrent flows will share bandwidth according to their respective round trip time. Therefore, two pairs of TCP flows admitting the same common sub-path will not share the achievable bandwidth the same way, and will exhibit a different ratio.

Bounded Metric

A metric will be said to be bounded if the capacity of a (sub)path is determined by the lowest (or highest) capacity of all the links composing it. Most of bandwidth-based metric are bounded.

PROBLEM STATEMENT

Trees for the client/server case can be a misleading way of representing the network. Those trees fit on the real topology that can be retrieved by observing equipments deployed along path probed. Indeed disjunction points between paths are necessarily on one of those equipments.

However, reconstruction is done based on relationships between paths. Probing techniques in this case is a way estimate the dependency between performances of the two paths observed. Either they are independent, and so, there is no common sub-path to the two paths observed, or there is, and then one can infer from probing a value to label the common sub-path to those paths. Correlation is then used in order to reconstruct the whole tree. So, one can also see the reconstructed tree as preorder based on dependency between paths capacities outgoing from the same source, and not as a subgraph of IP topology. But disjunction does not make sense for the multiple source/ multiple destination case.

Reconstruction in this case should be based on another notion that can replace disjunction. An intuitive choice is the existence of sub-path, as in (Castro & al, 2004), in order to represent interactions between paths. If so, sub-paths set is the element set of the topology to produce. For disjunction points, preordering could be done easily by correlating the distance of disjunction points for pair of paths from the source. Another relation has to be chosen in order to preorder sub-paths. With sub-paths and with the consistency hypothesis, there is a unique possibly null common maximum sub-path for a given set of path.

Intersection of common maximum sub-paths for a set of sets of paths $\{P_1, ..., P_n\}$ is then the common maximum sub-path of the union set of the set of set, i.e. $P' = P_1 \cup ... \cup P_n$. So, inclusion is an interesting way to preorder sub-paths. This leads to the formal definition of the following model.

METRIC INDUCED NETWORK POSET

A Metric Induced Network Poset (MINP) is a poset $P^m = (X, \leq)$ formed from Max^P_{e2e}.

- X is defined by the relation $\forall i \in Max^P_{e2e}$, i detectable for the metric $m \Leftrightarrow i \in X$,
- $\leq$ is defined by the relation $\forall i, j \in X, i \subset j$ iff $j \leq y$
- Every element of $p \in X$ is labeled by its capacity c^p_m.

This model does not represent the real topology, but detectable common sub-paths and the set of longer (sub)paths in which they are included. It can be viewed as a topology of inclusion relationships of sub-path into end-to-end paths.

Model Properties

The model has interesting properties: in (Bobelin, Muntean, 2007) it is proved that it exists a unique representation for any target network, as well as proofs for the following properties. This representation can be reconstructed given all knowledge about network and routing deployed on it. This model also has three interesting properties in order to reconstruct this representation from end-to-end measurements:

Covering Rule

Given a set of paths P such that $\left(p_{max}^{P}\right| \neq 0$ no probe can exhibit two different p_{max}^{P}. This property trivially holds only if the metric is *constant* and paths are *stable*.

Grouping Rule for Bounded Metrics

Let two set of paths $P = P_{core} \cup \left\{p_a\right\} \cup P_{pivot}$, $P' = P_{core} \cup \left\{p_b\right\} \cup P_{pivot}$, $\left(P_{core}\right| \geq 0$. Suppose that each elements of P all share a common maximum sub-path, as well as elements of P' and P_{pivot}. If $\left\{p_a, p_b\right\} \cup P_{pivot}$ share a common maximum sub-path, then $P'' = P_{core} \cup \left\{p_a\right\} \cup \left\{p_b\right\} \cup P_{pivot}$ share a unique common maximum sub-path.

Moreover if the metric is bounded, then one can preorder the different common maximum sub-paths of each of those sets.

Sorting Rule for Bounded Metric

Given a bounded metric m and two sets of paths P and P', such that $\forall p \in P, \forall p' \in P', c_m^p < c_m^{p'}$ then no path of P' can share one of the common maximum detectable sub-path for all possible subsets of P.

This rule is intuitively simple: if a bottleneck has a lower capacity than the capacity of a path, then the path does not pass by this bottleneck.

PROBING TECHNIQUE

Algorithm described in section 6 uses a probing technique that establish if a detectable sub-path is shared by a set of paths, and, in case of multiple sub-paths, possible inclusion relationships between those sub-path. This section describes a probing technique dedicated to it.

Background

Most of detection and identification methods rely on packet dispersion. Suppose two packets are injected through a path p. Dispersion $\triangle_p^2$ is the time interval between reception of the last bit of the first packet and the first bit of the second packet. Dispersion is calculated for 2 or more packets. This dispersion, together with the variation of the injection rate is then used to calculate inner network properties, either capacity, one-way delay or available bandwidth.

Packets are most of the time injected back-to-back. Back-to-back means that the transmission of the last bit of a packet is followed immediately by the transmission of the first bit of the following packet. This type of injection are most of the time named packet pair for 2 packets, and packet train for more packets.

Let consider back-to-back packets. If there is no cross-traffic, the dispersion should only be due to the transmission time of the fist packet on the lower capacity link of the path. In this case, the dispersion $\triangle_p^2$ for the whole path p for 2 packets of size q can be expressed as follows:

$$\triangle_p^2 = \max_{i=0\ldots s} \tau_i = \frac{q}{\min_{i=0\ldots s} c_c^{l_i}}$$

Where τ_i is the transmission time at link i and $c_c^{l_i}$ is the capacity of the link. Cross-traffic influences dispersion. Let d_i^1 and d_i^2 be the delay induced by the queues of the hops along p, where d_i^1 is the waiting time in queue for m_1 at hop i and d_i^2 the waiting time in queue for m_2 after that m_1 has been transmitted. Dispersion δ_i^2 at hop i between two packets is then $\delta_i^2 = \tau_i^{m_1} + d_i^2$ if $\tau_i^{m_1} + d_i^1 \geq \delta_{i-1}^2$ or $\delta_{i-1}^2 + \left(d_i^2 - d_i^1\right)$ if not.

For the broader case of packet trains of size N going through path p of size s, the total dispersion

Figure 1. Cross-dependency of dispersion

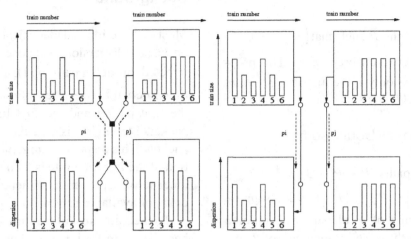

of the train is $\triangle_p^N = \Sigma_{k=1}^{N-1} \triangle_p^k$. If there is no cross-traffic, $\triangle_p^N$ depends only of the $\max_{i=0...s} \tau_i$. If there is, it depends on each δ_i^N for $i \in \left\{0...s\right\}$, which depends of the different d_i^k for $k \in \left\{0..N\right\}$.

This theoretical aspect has been extensively validated by both simulation and real life experiments in (Dovrolis, Ramanathan, & Moore, 2004) in an attempt to characterize relationships between capacity, available bandwidth, and packet trains dispersion. It is even used and validated in a way close to our in (Rubenstein, Kurose, & Towsley, 2002). Authors also showed that if the bottleneck link is heavily loaded (at least 80% of the capacity is used) $\triangle_p^N$ is no more reflecting the capacity of the link, but the distribution of cross-traffic.

OVERALL DESCRIPTION

MINTCar probing technique is based on this behaviour, as illustrated in figure 1. For each path considered, one has to estimate the available bandwidth. Then, one can inject at a random time within a period T a packet train whose size varies according to a certain function which has a distribution, different from the one assigned to

other paths. The packets trains coming from both sources must use almost all common bottleneck available bandwidth (it there is one) in order to make both dispersion dependent from each other. Two cases are depicted: on the left, we consider the case when paths p_i and p_j share a bottleneck link; on the right, there is no such link. Packet trains (numbered 1 to 6) are injected through the paths.

If there is a shared bottleneck common to the paths considered, then the different trains will sometimes collide, and as a result, distribution of values for $\triangle_{p_i}^N$ and $\triangle_{p_j}^M$ will be dependent. The similar reasoning holds for more than two paths.

Then, using accurate statistical estimator, it is possible to assess which arrival distributions depends of each other, and, by doing so, detect a shared bottleneck.

Determining Dependency

A way to determine dependency is to use information theory. Information theory and the related concepts of mutual information and independence are standard tools. In order to explain how to determine dependency as well as to enlight constraints induced by the use of negentropy on the practical probing process, we give here some classic definitions and relationships between concepts.

Negentropy and Induced Constraints on Random Variables

Dependency is the opposite of independence. Let y_1 and y_2 be two random variables whose values are reals. If an information about the value of one random variable does not give information about the value of the other, then the random variables y_1 and y_2 are said to be independent. Let $p_1(y_1)$ and $p_2(y_2)$ be the probability density function (pdf) of random variables y_1 and y_2 when y_1 and y_2 are considered alone (i.e. the marginal pdf of y_1 and y_2), and $p(y_{1,}y_2)$ be the joint probability density function of y_1 and y_2. If y_1 and y_2 are independent, then we following equation is true:

$$p(y_{1,}y_2) = p(y_1)p(y_2)$$

For an arbitrary number n of random variables, the independence condition can be extended as follows: the joint density of n random variables is the product of the n marginal densities of the variables.

In information theory, the entropy of a random variable can be interpreted as the degree of information that the observation of this random variable gives. The greater the entropy is, the greater the variable is random, unstructured. So, entropy can be viewed as the code length of this random variable. For a discrete random variable Y, entropy H can be defined as follow:

$$H(Y) = -\sum_i P(Y = a_i)\log(P(Y = a_i))$$

where a_i are the possible values of Y. If we extend this definition for a vector of random variables y for whose values are reals and whose density is $f(y)$, the differential entropy can be defined as follow:

$$H(y) = -\int f(y)\log(f(y))dy$$

This value tends to infinity when the variable can be considered as totally unstructured. In practice, in order to avoid such near-to-infinite values, one can use a slightly modified version of differential entropy called negentropy. The more the variable is random, the more negentropy will tend to zero. As a random variable whose distribution is gaussian is the "most random" of random variables, we use a gaussian random variable y_{gauss} to estimate negentropy $J(y)$:

$$J(y) = H(y_{gauss}) - H(y)$$

From a statistical point of view, negentropy is an optimal estimator for non-gaussianity. Using negentropy implies a constraint on random variable distribution, and so on packet dispersion-based measurements that must be achieved: their distribution must be non-gaussian. Moreover, negentropy is in practice difficult to calculate. So, methods to approximate negentropy are often used.

Authors of (Hyvärinen, Karhunen and Oja, 2001) suggest using an approximation based on the maximal entropy principle:

$$J(y) \approx \sum_{i=1}^{p} k_i \left[E\{G_i(y)\} - E\{G_i(\gamma)\} \right]^2$$

where k_i is a positive constant and γ a standard normal random variable. Random variable y must have a zero mean and a unit variance, and G_i must be non-quadratic functions. Constraints other random variables must be fulfilled by our probing process, and so use of the maximal entropy principle adds two other constraints on the practical probing process. Even if this approximation is rough, it remains always positive and equals zero if and only if y has a gaussian distribution.

For a quadratic G:

$$J(y) \propto \left[E\{G(y)\} - E\{G(\gamma)\} \right]^2$$

G function is often called contrast function. It allows enhancing the difference between "totally random" variables and others. Two functions are most of the time used. It is either:

$$G_1(u) = \frac{1}{a_1} \mathrm{logcosh}(a_1 u)$$

or

$$G_2(u) = -\exp\left(\frac{-u^2}{2} \right),$$

where $1 \le a_1 \le 2$ is a constant to set. The choice of either G_1 or G_2 depends most of the time of the random variable dynamics. Experiments we ran showed that in our case, the best contrast function is G_1 with $a_1 = 1$. Using this approximation, it is possible to estimate independence between many random variables by using its relationship to mutual information.

Mutual information I between m random variables $y_i \in y, i = 1 \ldots m$ can be defined by using differential entropy:

$$I(y_1, y_2, \ldots, y_m) = \sum_{i=1}^{m} H(y_i) - H(y)$$

Mutual information is a native measurement of dependency between random variables. It is always positive, and equals to zero if and only if the random variables considered are statistically independent. It can be interpreted by using the entropy interpretation as a code length.

$H(y_i)$ gives the code length of each y_i when they are coded separately, while $H(y)$ gives the code length when all the components are grouped within the same random vector, i.e. when all components y_i are coded within the same code. If all y_i are independent, they does not give any information on the others, so coding it separately will not let the code length grows.

An important property of mutual information is that, for an invertible linear transformation $y = Wx$:

$$I(y_1, y_2, \ldots, y_n) = \sum_i H(y_i) - H(x) - \log\left((\det W () \right.$$

If all y_i are decorrelated and normalized to unit variance, it means that $E\{yy^T\} = WE\{xx^T\}W^T = I$, so

$$\det I = 1 = \left(\det WE\{xx^T\}W^T \right) = (\det W)\left(\det E\{xx^T\} \right)(\det W^T)$$

so that means that $\det W$ must be a constant.

Moreover, if all y_i have a unit variance, entropy and negentropy differs only by their signs and a constant, so we have:

$$I(y_1, y_2, \ldots, y_n) = a - \sum_i J(y_i)$$

Where α is a constant not depending of W. This gives a relationship between negentropy and mutual information, that we can use to determine the mutual information degree shared by the results of our measurements.

Practical Dependency Determination and Random Variable Construction

Consider again example depicted in figure 1. In order to know if the mutual information grows if the paths share a common bottleneck, measurements are necessary: independent and simultaneous measurements. Independent measurements correspond to all random variables coded separately, and simultaneous measurements correspond to the case all variables are coded within the same code. To obtain those values, one can inject packet trains in all paths $p_i \in P$ considered sequentially: this will give values for random variables for each path. Each of those random variables will contain the $\triangle_{p_i}^{N_{p_i}}$ without any influence from other distribution. Let $y_{p_i}^{\{p_i\}}$ be the values obtained for a path p_i when packets are injected through this path only (i.e. the set of path containing p_i only).

Then, values when the different distributions possibly share information have to be obtained. To obtain it packet trains are injected through paths in P simultaneously. Let $y_{p_i}^{P}$ be the random variables obtained. Then it is possible to compute two mutual information values, one for simultaneous injection of packet train and one for independent injections. Let those values be

$$I_{ind}^{P} = I\left(y_{p_1}^{\{p_1\}}, y_{p_2}^{\{p_2\}}, \ldots, y_{p_n}^{\{p_n\}}\right) \quad \text{and}$$

$$I_{simult}^{P} = I\left(y_{p_1}^{P}, y_{p_2}^{P}, \ldots, y_{p_n}^{P}\right).$$ Comparing those values an information about independence of random variables contained, and so of independence of paths $p_i \in P$. Roughly speaking, if $I_{ind}^{P} < I_{simult}^{P}$, then it means that paths share a bottleneck.

Calculating Negentropy Approximation

The last step is to define how to make each random variable mean equals to zero, uncorrelate random variables and make them have a unit variance, in order to use negentropy approximation for mutual information approximation as defined earlier. The first step is usually named centering, and the two last steps are known as whitening. Centering consists simply in considering initial values minus their means. Whitening consists in a linear transformation of random variables vector x in order to obtain a new white vector $\tilde{x}$. White vector means a vector where each component is linearly uncorrelated with the others and has a unit variance. In other terms, the covariance matrix of $\tilde{x}$ must be equal to the identity matrix:

$$E\left\{\tilde{x}\tilde{x}^T\right\} = I$$

A method to obtain this is to do an eigendecomposition of the covariance matrix $E\left\{xx^T\right\} = BDB^T$, where B is the orthogonal matrix of eigenvectors of $E\left\{xx^T\right\}$ and D is the diagonal matrix of eigenvalues $D = \text{diag}\left(d_1, \ldots, d_n\right)$. $E\left\{xx^T\right\}$ can be estimated by using data samples $x(1), \ldots, x(T)$. White vector can now be expressed as:

$$\tilde{x} = BD^{-1/2}B^T x$$

Where the matrix $D^{-1/2}$ is easily calculated because $D^{-1/2} = \text{diag}\left(d_1^{-1/2}, \ldots, d_n^{-1/2}\right)$. It is easy to verify that using those transformations we now have $E\left\{\tilde{x}\tilde{x}^T\right\} = I$. Eigendecomposition implies that random variables must be linearly independent from each other. How to obtain values $\triangle_{p_i}^{N}$ in order to make the random variables is described in the next section.

Practical Probing

The overall process to determine if a set of path P share a bottleneck can be described as follow. First available bandwidth evaluation is determined for each path. This is necessary to determine the average packet train size for each path, as we must use almost all available bandwidth to have a dependency. This step is done by using a bulk data transfer-based technique implemented in a fork version of udpmon (the UDPMon website, retrieved 2010). Then, injection of packet train is done sequentially for each path, in order to determine the dispersion values for $y_{p_i}^{\{p_i\}}$ and determine I_{ind}^P .

Then, injection of packet train is done simultaneously for every subset of $P' \subseteq P$, in order to retrieve values for $y_{p_i}^{P'}$ and determine $I_{simult}^{P'}$ for each P'. Due to some properties of negentropy approximation and mutual information, those information are mandatory to determine if the whole set P share a bottleneck. Finally, mutual information values are calculated and dependency estimation is done. Packet train dispersion $\triangle_{p_i}^{N_{p_i}}$ when trains are injected non simultaneously on each path has to have a non-gaussian distribution, and each random variable should have linearly independent values, in order to measure the mutual information. The process for construction of such random variable is described hereafter.

Obtaining Non-Gaussian Distribution

In order to do so, injection of packet trains is repeated n times. Each time the number of packet in each train varies. For each path a different periodic function $s(i)$ is chosen. $s(i)$ which has a non-gaussian distribution. $s(i)$ will

at a step i give the length N of the packet train we have to inject (in packets), as depicted in figure 2.

Current version of our tool use one of sawtooth, sinusoid and square wave periodical functions. Those functions are sometimes used in order to show good results in using mutual information estimation from negentropy approximation, as their distributions are "really different".

Construction of random variables is done by measuring $\triangle_p^{s(i)}$, i.e. delay between the arrival of the first packet and the last packet of a train. If no cross-traffic occurs, by using varying size, we obtain at the destination values that reflect the size of the packet train. So, its distribution will be nearly the same as the distribution of the function we used. So, if there is no cross-traffic, we will obtain random variables for which the mutual information will be very small.

In practice, if there is cross-traffic, the distribution will be modified in an unknown way. If it is a "normal" cross-traffic, then the distribution could get closer to gaussian, but as we consider dispersion for a varying size of packet trains, it is really unlikely to happen. If the cross-traffic contains the cross-traffic produced by probing, i.e. packet trains with a well-chosen distribution for their sizes, and if the sum of this cross-traffic produced and the traffic we inject almost fully use the available bandwidth of the link, the distribution will contain information about this other distribution. Then both distributions will depend of each other.

Figure 2 depicts all parameters. All functions have the same set of parameters to set: packet size q, average size (in packets) N_m, period T, and amplitude A. We also need to determine average period of time between each packet train injection Γ. At each step i a delay lower than Γ before injection of the packet train is chosen randomly in order to avoid synchronization effects. Finally, to obtain random variables from the values ob-

Figure 2. Packet train injection

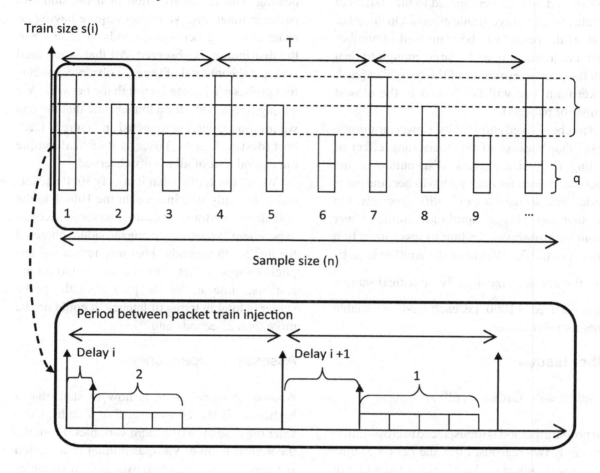

tained, we need also to choose a statistical sample size n.

The average period of time between each packet train injection (Γ) should be as short as possible, as it is a direct factor of the whole probe time, but it also should be able to allow to transmit large enough packet trains in order to measure their dispersion.

All other values are related with each other as:

$$N_m = \frac{c_{bw}^{l_i} * t_{train}^{N_m}}{q}$$

Where l_i is the bottleneck link and $t_{train}^{N_m}$ is the theoretic time of transmission of the whole packet train on the bottleneck link. $t_{train}^{N_m}$ Must be low, in order to perform as many as possible train injections in the shortest time possible, while having a sufficient number of large enough packets. In our tool, we arbitrarily choose to set $t_{train}^{N_m + \frac{A}{2}} = U_t = 2ms$, and calculate a trade-off between q and N_m from that. This value is sufficient to obtain enough packets to establish dependency for bottleneck having available bandwidth higher or equal to 10Mb/s. T is then chosen as $U_t * \left(P \right($ in order to avoid saturation.

T should be small compared to the statistical sample in order to avoid side effects. On the other hand, as the period can be expressed in number of packet trains, it must be large enough to deal with the coarse resolution of the burst size (each packet train size will be floored to the closest number of packets).

A has been fixed empirically. Lower amplitude means that because of the coarsening effect of sending fixed-size packets, distribution of the functions chosen for each path will become more similar, and so harder to identify precisely. On the other hand, bigger amplitude implies lower minimum size trains, leading to less interaction with cross-traffic. We chose the amplitude to be $\frac{1}{3}$ of the average size. Finally, statistical sample size *n* we used is 1000, i.e. each random variable contains 1000 values.

Other Issues

Dealing with Cross-Traffic

Our probing method is robust faced to cross-traffic for mainly two reasons. First, the period of time we choose to inject packets is at least an order of magnitude smaller than usually measured RTT on many paths. So, if flows are occurring simultaneously to our experiments, it distribution will not vary significantly within the time of injections.

The second reason is that modification of the distribution due to cross-traffic does not have a significant impact, as the pattern of injection does not have to be preserved at arrival. So, cross-traffic does not have a significant impact of our negentropy approximation estimation.

Dealing with Coarse Synchronization

Exact synchronization between hosts is a tricky problem. Synchronization in itself is tedious, and can lead to prohibitive initialization times. We chose to bypass this problem. As we are

dealing with the distribution of dispersion and periodic functions, we do not require having an exact matching between periods of time when the distribution is observed. All that is required is that at the interval of time we observe, concurrent probes are injected through the network. We simply inject flows for a longer time that the one we are observing, as depicted in figure3. Each host (dest A, B and C) uses as statistical sample the central part of all events observed.

We set our tool so that it injects 3000 packets trains, but only take in account the 1000th to the 2000th packets trains. It means that for a 6 seconds experiment, we are only using the values obtained for the 2-4 th seconds. That means that we implicitly suppose that even if a source has a long response time and/or the path from the probe starter is long in terms of latency, it could not be more than 2 seconds late.

Assessing Dependency

Another practical issue is how to state that a bottleneck is shared by a set *P* of *n* paths. Consider the case of two random variables. From the theoretical point of view, as mutual information is always increasing when two random variables are not independent, a sufficient condition could be $I_{simult}^{P} > I_{ind}^{P}$.

As negentropy approximation depends on random values from a gaussian random variable and as there is cross-traffic, there is a margin of error. So, it can happen that $I_{simult}^{P} > I_{ind}^{P}$ for values near zero.

Anyhow it is realistic to consider that above a certain threshold random variable exhibits shared information. So, conditions to establish if two random variables are dependent from each other are expressed by a threshold and the increase of mutual information:

Figure 3. Using only a subset of the total information obtained

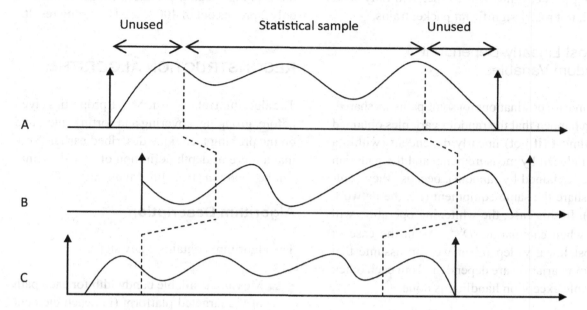

$$\frac{I^P_{simult}}{I^P_{ind}} > 1 + s_1 \text{ and } I^P_{simult} > s_2$$

where s_1 and s_2 are positive threshold to set by calibration. In order to retrieve relevant information for the algorithm given in section 6, we must establish a MINP for at least three paths.

First problem to address is to determine existence of a common bottleneck for all paths in the triplet. Suppose $P = \left\{p_a, p_b, p_c\right\}$. Consider for example the case of a bottleneck shared by two paths p_a and p_b that is not shared by p_c. If all paths in P share the same bottleneck, then I^P_{simult} will be higher than any values $I\left(y^P_{p_i}, y^P_{p_j}\right)$ where p_i, p_j so that $p_i \neq p_j$ and $p_i, p_j \in P$. So, for 3 paths, those have to be true, as well as:

$$\frac{I^P_{simult}}{max_{p_i, p_j \in P, p_i \neq p_j} I\left(y^P_{p_i}, y^P_{p_j}\right)} > s_3$$

Where s_3 is a threshold to set that must be greater than 1. This establishes if paths share bottleneck sub-path. In order to determine inclusion relation between sub-paths, one can do the following. For a triplet P of paths, we test if it has a bottleneck sub-path, and determine its capacity regarding to available bandwidth. We also do that for each subset of P. It allows us to determine relationships between bottlenecks for this triplet, because a bottleneck sub-path of lower capacity for a set of path P' than one of its superset P'' means that P' contains at least one more link than P'': the bottleneck link.

Unfairly Balanced Shared Bottlenecks

Some shared bottleneck can be shared by a set of paths P such that one path $p_i \in P$ has a large available bandwidth and other $p_j \in P\left\{p_i\right\}$ have a small one. In this case, distributions for paths in $P\left\{p_i\right\}$ will tend to be almost linearly dependent on the distribution of p_i, as p_i will inject important packet trains while other will only send small, not really significant packet trains.

Almost Linearly-Dependent Random Variables

If sources or destinations for some paths are shared, it can happen that the random variables obtained are almost (if not) linearly dependent (within a bias induced by measurements and the gaussian values obtained by random), because they actually share the same equipment (i.e. the network card). In this case, the whitening operation will fail, when calculating $D^{1/2}$. As in the case of almost linearly dependent we can assume that random variables are dependent from each other, a simple exception handling is done.

Experimental Results

We ran experiments without specific privileges, as any normal user. The figure 4 shows mutual information approximation values obtained by using negentropy approximation found for each of the 10 pairs of paths tested. Each experiment took 24 seconds of packet injection (6 seconds for the packet independent injection on each path, and 12 for the simultaneous injection), and computing time was negligible, for a total of 400 probes. The values obtained are ordered decreasingly.

Each curve represents the results obtained for one of the 10 pair of paths used. The two upper curves corresponds to a pair of path that shares the same source, and the other one the same destination. The two curves above the line correspond to pairs of paths sharing a common bottleneck, while having neither common destination nor sources. The 6 remaining curves represent pairs of paths of varying lengths but known to not share any bottleneck link in MAN. The threshold depicted by the line is the one used by our tool in order to determine dependency. As we can see,

the probing method produces robust results, as only 2 probes out of 400 leaded to wrong results.

RECONSTRUCTION ALGORITHM

The algorithm relies on the MINP properties given before, grouping, covering and sorting rules, and on the probing technique described earlier. Note that a more in-depth definition of this algorithm can be found in (Bobelin, Muntean, 2008).

Algorithm Description

The algorithm contains 2 key steps.

- Measure available bandwidth for each path of the targeted platform (i.e. each element of P_{e2e}). This allows ordering it by increasing available bandwidth.
- Iterates on the list of paths sorted by increasing capacity. Measure possible relationships with existing sub-paths that have already have been detected and that have a capacity similar to the path considered. If not, measure possible interactions with all paths.

Using the sorting rule for the bounded metric (as available bandwidth is bounded), sorting allows to constructs iteratively a MINP completely defined for the subset $P \subseteq P_{e2e}$, as there is no path of $P' = P_{e2e}P$ which will help to find an not detected shared sub-path of capacity lower than the path capacity. At each iteration step, relationship between already considered paths are established, and so the MINP currently reconstructed is then completely specified.

The second step of the above list consists in the following:

- If it exists an already detected sub-path that has a capacity similar to the current path

Figure 4. Mutual information approximation values for paths considered, ordered decreasingly

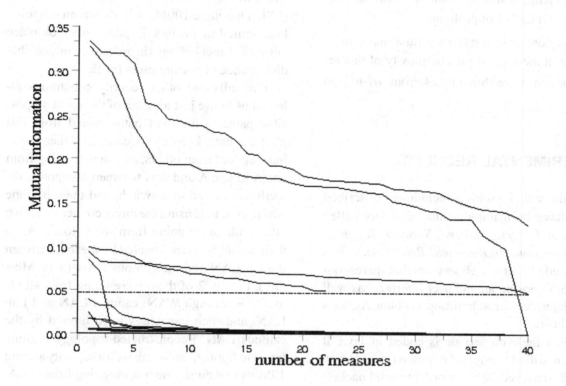

considered, then a probe is done, in order to check if the current path shares this sub-path with other paths. Probe should be done with each path sharing this sub-path. According to the grouping rule for the bounded metric, a probe should be done for each triplet of path. However, this can be shortened by choosing to execute probes only for a subset of the set of path sharing this sub-path. Fixing the number of maximum probe to test in order to consider all paths share the same sub-path allows having a constant number of measurements.

• If there is no sub-path detected with any of the already detected sub-paths, it means that either this path is independent from the already tested paths, or that it exists some sub-paths that have higher capacity that is

shared by some of the already tested path. Then an exhaustive probing is done with each path.

Performances

Complexity of this algorithm, in terms of computational steps, is polynomial, and is similar to the number of probes. Let n be the number of paths. Worst case occurs in the case when all paths are independent: each time a new path is considered, its relationships are probed with all already tested paths, leading to $\Sigma_{i=o}^{n} i$ tests, and so, $o\left(n^2\right)$ probes. However, this means that none of the paths considered are sharing any bottleneck, which is unlikely to happen. Best case occurs when all paths are sharing the same bottleneck: in this case, each time a new path is considered, it requires a constant number of probing with a fixed size subset of paths sharing this sub-path, thus leading to an $o(n)$ number of probing.

If we consider all paths within a platform of *m* hosts, it means that the complexity of this reconstruction algorithm ranges from $o(m^2)$ to $o(m^4)$.

EXPERIMENTAL RESULTS

Algorithms and probing techniques described above have been implemented in a tool called MINTCar (*Metric Induced Network Topology – Construction, Analysis and Retrieval*). It is a composed of a set of web services that are responsible for exposing an end user interface, as well as an interface for submitting probing requests to end hosts.

Whilst the web service is coded in Java, it calls a modified version of udpmon (the udpmon website, retrieved 2010) in order to send packets into the network. Probing scheduling as well as reconstruction is done by a reconstruction service.

We had deployed several sensors in different places in a campus (Luminy campus in Marseilles). The physical deployment and network underneath topology is illustrated in figure 5. Topology depicted here has been obtained by discussing with both campus administrators and local ones, and checked using traceroute. 6 computers were deployed (2 in each site we had access to). 2 sites (B and C on figure 5) were physically in a High Energy Physics lab (CPPM) but on different networks, site B on the lab LAN (limited to 100 bits/s), and site C on a network dedicated to EGEE experiments (with an outgoing link to Phocean WAN at 1Gb/s). There was a direct access between sites from B to C using a special gateway and then the lab's LAN. Due to security issues, the opposite way was going from

C to B passing through the WAN, then through the campus LAN, then the lab's LAN. Finally site A was located in a Computer Science school (ESIL) having a 100Mb/s LAN but an outgoing link limited to 10Mb/s. Experiments took place during summer holidays in order to avoid possible disturbance of normal users traffic.

Firewalls and other security constraints allowed us to use just a subset of the set of all possible paths. 6 different paths issued from this platform have been considered: 2 of them were independent from others, as one was going from site A to site A and was between computers directly connected to a switch, and the other one was from B to C using the direct connection. Two other paths were going from site C to site A, so their capacities were lowered by the link between the lab LAN and the campus LAN (a 10 Mb/s link). Finally 2 of them were going from site C to site B through WAN, campus LAN and Lab LAN, and their capacities were limited by the campus LAN. Reconstructed topology is illustrated in figure 6. Sub-path with a capacity around 10Mb/s was due to the link outgoing from site A, while the one with a capacity of almost 100 Mb/s was due to an inner campus LAN link.

ISSUES, CONTROVERSIES AND PROBLEMS

Key thing in our approach is the reconstruction of a unique and exact network representation. However, our tool can produce non-exact representation for mainly three reasons:

*   Error in probing the network. This can be either due to the method in itself, or because of changes in the network dynamics, either cross-traffic or routing changes. Cross-traffic is, by definition, something no one can have control on but should not affect our probing in itself. But it can imply an error in the initial available bandwidth

Figure 5. Experimental platform

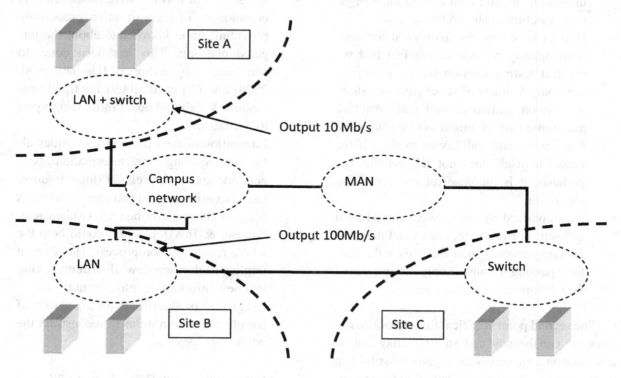

Figure 6. Reconstructed topology

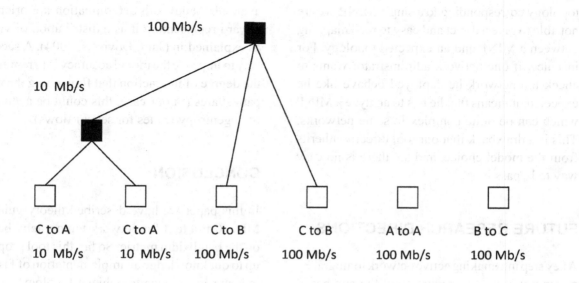

measurement, and then lead to false negative detection of shared bottleneck.

- Bias involved by the heuristical assumptions, mainly because of the fact that we are just testing relation with a new path with only a subset of set of path that share a common bottleneck sub path. Another assumption which might not be true is the consistence and stability of routing. If the model in itself does not rely on this hypothesis, it is the case for reconstruction algorithm.
- Bias involved by the network model used in itself. For example, our model does not capture sub-path such that this influences flow passing through it only if more than 1 flow is injected simultaneously.

The second point is critical for our tool nowadays, as consistency and stability may not be observed on large networks; anyhow this problem can be most of the time avoided using techniques such as the ones cited in the first point of our future research directions.

Another point is the abstract point of view that MINP gives on a network. As it exists many topology corresponding to a single MINP, we are not able to give a direct and easy to read mapping between a MINP and an expected topology. For instance, if one network administrator wants to check the network he deployed behave like he expected, it means that he has to analyze a MINP which can be quite complex in some networks. This is a drawback that our tool directly inherits from the model choice, and so, there is no easy way to bypass it.

FUTURE RESEARCH DIRECTIONS

A key step into making active network tomography a common use is the reduction of the number of measurements that one have to completely map the topology. 3 main axes exist:

- Integration of less intrusive measurements or guidance of reconstruction process by providing some knowledge about the targeted platform. This has been done, to some extent, by authors of (Hailiang et al, 2008) and (Ni et al, 2009) for traditional models. We should adapt those techniques to our model.
- Integration of new probing techniques allowing acquiring more information about network and paths relationships at once. Using existing proved and used techniques such as those described by (Rubenstein, Kurose, & Towsley, 2002) could help the whole reconstruction process. However, it implies to develop new algorithms taking that new information into account.
- Integration of algorithms for the choice of path to observe in order to reconstruct the whole topology.

A second interesting step is to focus more on the model ability to represent the real nature of the information obtained via measurements. Our current model considers that available bandwidth is not changing for a path. Nowadays work in available bandwidth determination are oriented toward representing it as a distribution of value as explained in (Jain, Dovrolis, 2004). A second way to improve the model accuracy is to represent the degree of interaction that flow going through path shares (in our case, this could be a storage of negentropy values for sets of flows).

CONCLUSION

In this paper we have described theory guiding MINTCar a tool for network tomography based on the bandwidth metric. So far, this tool propose up to our knowledge an implementation of fastest existing techniques to achieve topology reconstruction, and the only existing probing technique for multiple source multiple destination available bandwidth measurement.

Undergoing work has mainly three axes: enhancement of tool to support network monitoring, archiving and retrieving via a relational database, and implementation of fastest algorithm using multiple sources of information. The last point is a key for the success of network monitoring, as for now the tool cannot scale for large platform, due to prohibitive number of probes to realize. Using information such as traceroute-based information, it should be possible to reduce actual probing time drastically.

REFERENCES

Arifler, D., Veciana, G. d., & Evans, B. L. (2007). A factor analytic approach to inferring congestion sharing based on flow level measurements. *IEEE/ACM Transactions on Networking, 15*(1), 67–79. doi:10.1109/TNET.2006.890103

Bestavros, A., Byers, J., & Harfoush, K. (2001). *Inference and labeling of metric-induced network topologies.* (Technical Report BUCS-TR-2001-010), Boston University, Computer Science Department.

Bestavros, A., Byers, J., & Harfoush, K. (2005). Inference and labeling of metric-induced network topologies. *IEEE Transactions on Parallel and Distributed Systems, 16*(11), 1053–1065. doi:10.1109/TPDS.2005.138

Bobelin, L., & Muntean, T. (2007). *Metric induced network poset (MINP): A model of the network from an application point of view.* In First International Conference on Networks for Grid Applications (GridNets), MetroGrid Workshop, October 2007.

Bobelin, L., & Muntean, T. (2008). *Algorithms for network topology discovery using end-to-end measurements.* In International Symposium on Parallel and Distributed Computing, 47, (pp. 267–274).

Bu, T., Duffield, N., & Lo Presti, F. (2002). Network tomography on general topologies. *ACM SIGMETRICS*, 21-30.

Castro, R., Coates, M., Liang, G., Nowak, R., & Yu, B. (2004). Network tomography: Recent developments. *Statistical Science, 19*(3), 499–517. doi:10.1214/088342304000000422

Coates, M., Castro, R., Nowak, R., Gadhiok, M., King, R., & Tsang, Y. (2002). Maximum likelihood network topology identification from edge-based unicast measurements. *SIGMETRICS Performance Evaluation Review, 30*(1), 11–20. doi:10.1145/511399.511337

Dabek, F., Cox, R., Kaashoek, F., & Morris, R. (2004). Vivaldi: A decentralized network coordinate system. *Proceedings of the 2004 Conference on Applications, Technologies, Architectures, and Protocols for Computer Communications*, (pp. 15-26).

Donnet, B., Friedman, T., & Crovella, M. (2005). Improved algorithms for network topology discovery. In *Proceedings of PAM 2005*, (pp. 149-162).

Dovrolis, C., Ramanathan, P., & Moore, D. (2001). *What do packet dispersion techniques measure?* (pp. 905–914). In INFOCOM.

Dovrolis, C., Ramanathan, P., & Moore, D. (2004). Packet-dispersion techniques and a capacity-estimation methodology. *IEEE/ACM Transactions on Networking, 12*(6), 963–977. doi:10.1109/TNET.2004.838606

Duan, Q., Cai, W. D., & Tian, G. (2009). *Topology identification based on multiple source network tomography.* 2009 International Conference on Industrial and Information Systems, (pp. 125-128).

Duffield, N. G., Lo Presti, F., Paxson, V., & Towsley, D. F. (2001). *Inferring link loss using striped unicast probes* (pp. 915–923). In INFOCOM.

EGEE. (2010). *Website*. Retrieved from http://www.eu-egee.org/

Eriksson, B., Dasarathy, G., Barford, P., & Nowak, R. (2010). *Toward the practical use of network tomography for Internet topology discovery*. IEEE INFOCOM Conference 2010.

Eyraud-Dubois, L., Legrand, A., Quinson, M., & Vivien, F. (2007). *A first step towards automatically building network representations*. In 13th International European Conference on Parallel and Distributed Computing - Euro-Par 2007, (LNCS 4641, pp. 848–857).

Eyraud-Dubois, L., & Quinson, M. (2007). *Assessing the quality of automatically built network representations*. In Workshop on Programming Models for Grid Computing, CCGrid'07, Rio de Janeiro, 2007.

GEANT. (2010). *Website*. Retrieved from http://www.geant.net/

Hadamard, J. (1923). *Lectures on Cauchy's problem in linear partial differential equations*. Yale University Press.

Hailiang, L., Guangmin, H., Feng, Q., & Zhihao, Y. (2009). Network topology inference based on traceroute and tomography. *In Proceedings of WRI International Conference on Communications and Mobile Computing, volume 2*, (pp. 486–490).

Harfoush, K., Bestavros, A., & Byers, J. (2009). Measuring capacity bandwidth of targeted path segments. *IEEE/ACM Transactions on Networking, 17*(1), 80–92. doi:10.1109/TNET.2008.2008702

Hu, N., Li, L. E., Mao, Z. M., Steenkiste, P., & Wang, J. (2004). Locating Internet bottlenecks: Algorithms, measurements, and implications. In *SIGCOMM '04: Proceedings of the 2004 Conference on Applications, Technologies, Architectures, and Protocols for Computer Communications*, (pp. 41–54). New York, NY: ACM.

Hyvärinen, A., Karhunen, J., & Oja, E. (2001). *Independent component analysis*. John Wiley and Sons. doi:10.1002/0471221317

Internet2. (2010). *Website*. Retrieved from http://www.internet2.edu/

Jacobson, V. (1989). *Traceroute*. Retrieved from ftp://ftp.ee.lbl.gov/traceroute.tar.gz

Jain, M., & Dovrolis, C. (2004). Ten fallacies and pitfalls on end-to-end available bandwidth estimation. In *IMC '04: Proceedings of the 4th ACM SIGCOMM Conference on Internet Measurement*, (pp. 272–277). New York, NY: ACM.

Latapy, M., Magnien, C., & Ouédraogo, F. (2008). A radar for the Internet. *Proceedings of the 1st International Workshop on Analysis of Dynamic Networks* (ADN' 08), (pp. 901-908).

Lowekamp, B. B., Miller, N., Karrer, R., Gross, T., & Steenkiste, P. (2003). Design, implementation, and evaluation of the Remos network monitoring system. *Journal of Grid Computing, 1*(1), 75–93. doi:10.1023/A:1024039729687

Padmanabhan, V., & Qiu, L. (2002). *Network tomography using passive end-to-end measurements*. DIMACS Workshop on Internet and WWW Measurement, Mapping and Modeling, Piscataway, NJ, USA.

Rabbat, M., Figueiredo, M. A. T., & Nowak, R. D. (2008). Network inference from co-occurrences. *IEEE Transactions on Information Theory, 54*(9), 4053–4068. doi:10.1109/TIT.2008.926315

Rabbat, M., Nowak, R., & Coates, R. (2004). Multiple source, multiple destination network tomography. In *Proceedings of IEEE Infocom,* 2004.

Rubenstein, D., Kurose, J., & Towsley, D. (2002). Detecting shared congestion of flows via end-to-end measurement. *Journal IEEE/ACM Transactions in Networking, 10*(3), 381-395.

Subramanian, L., Agarwal, S., Rexford, J., & Katz, R. (2002). Characterizing the Internet hierarchy from multiple vantage points. In *Proceedings of IEE INFOCOM,* 2002.

Tatikonda, J. N. H. X. S., & Yang, Y. R. (2008). Network routing topology inference from end-to-end measurements. In Proceedings of The 27th Conference on Computer Communications. IEEE INFOCOM, (pp. 36–40).

TeraGrid. (2010). *Website.* Retrieved from http://www.teragrid.org/

Tsang, Y., Yildiz, M. C., Barford, P., & Nowak, R. D. (2004). *Network radar: Tomography from round trip time measurements.* In Internet Measurement Conference, (pp. 175–180).

Udpmon. (2010). *Website.* Retrieved from http://www.hep.man.ac.uk/ u/ rich/ net/

Vardi, Y. (1996). Network tomography: Estimating source-destination traffic intensities from link data. *Journal of the American Statistical Association, 91,* 365–377. doi:10.2307/2291416

Viger, F., Augustin, B., Cuvellier, X., Magnien, C., Latapy, M., Friedman, T., & Teixeira, R. (2008). Detection, understanding, and prevention of traceroute measurement artifacts. *Computer Networks: The International Journal of Computer and Telecommunications Networking, 52*(5), 998–1018.

Wolski, R., Spring, N. T., & Hayes, J. (1999). The network weather service: A distributed resource performance forecasting service for metacomputing. *Future Generation Computer Systems, 15*(5–6), 757–768. doi:10.1016/S0167-739X(99)00025-4

Zhang, Y., Roughan, M., Lund, C., & Donoho, D. (2003). An information-theoretic approach to traffic matrix estimation. Proceedings of the 2003 Conference on Applications, Technologies, Architectures, and Protocols for Computer Communications, (pp. 301–312).

KEY TERMS AND DEFINITIONS

Institutional Grid: Grid platform based on institution providing high performances resources such as clusters and storage facilities.

Inverse Problem: Problem consisting in inferring the structure and characteristic of a system based only on its reaction to stimuli.

Metric: A metric is a function whose initial domain is the set of flows and whose range is reals.

MINT: Metric Induced Network Topology. Topology discovered from the view point of one metric, that may not be an exact mapping of an IP topology.

Negentropy: Negative entropy, optimal estimator for non-gaussianity.

Network Tomography: Network properties or topology discovery using only end-to-end measurements.

Probe: Injection of flow into the network in order to estimates some properties of it.

Chapter 6
Service Provision Evolution in Self-Managed Future Internet Environments

Apostolos Kousaridas
University of Athens, Greece

Panagis Madgalinos
University of Athens, Greece

Nancy Alonistioti
University of Athens, Greece

ABSTRACT

Future Internet is based on the concepts of autonomicity and cognition, where each network element is able to monitor its surrounding environment, evaluate the situation, and decide the action that should be applied. In such context, the traditional service provisioning approaches necessitate a paradigm shift so as to incorporate the Cognitive Cycle. Towards this end, in this chapter, we introduce a Cognitive Service Provision framework suitable for Future Internet Networks. The proposed approach supports cognition by modeling a service as an aggregation of software components bundled together through a graph. Consequently, each service is composed by various components and is tailored to the operational context of the requestor. In order to prove the viability and applicability of the proposed approach we also introduce the enhancement of the IP Multimedia Subsystem through our Cognitive Service Provision framework. Finally, based on our work, we discuss future research directions and the link between service and network management.

FUTURE INTERNET NETWORKS

Future network systems design principles are based on high autonomy of network elements

in order to allow distributed management, fast decisions, and continuous local optimization. The Cognitive Cycle model, as it is depicted in Figure 1, is envisaged to be in the heart of Future Internet Elements and it leads to their autonomy (Kousaridas et al., 2010), (Ganek, 2003). A Future

DOI: 10.4018/978-1-61350-110-8.ch006

Copyright © 2012, IGI Global. Copying or distributing in print or electronic forms without written permission of IGI Global is prohibited.

Figure 1. Generic cognitive cycle model

Internet Element could be a network element (e.g., base station, mobile device), a network manager, or any software element that lies at the service layer.

The three distinct phases of the Generic Cognitive Cycle Model are the following:

- Monitoring process involves gathering of information about the environment and the internal state of a Future Internet Element. Moreover, the Monitoring process receives, internally or externally, feedback about the effectiveness of an execution that took place, after the last decision.

- Decision Making process includes the problem solving techniques for reconfiguration and adaptation, utilizing the developed knowledge model and situation awareness. The Decision Making supports the optimal configuration of each element, considering its hypostasis and the organization level that it belongs. Decision making mechanism identifies alternatives for

adaptation or optimization and chooses the best one, based on situation assessment, understanding of the surrounding context, and the preferences of the element. After decision making, the execution process undertakes to apply the decision that will change the behavior of the element.

- Execution process involves (self-) reconfiguration, software-component replacement or re-organization and optimization actions.

The scope of this book chapter is to discuss the challenges and describe the path for the evolution of the Future Internet services synthesis, delivery and adaptation, by exploiting the cognitive cycle paradigm. The cognitive cycle is placed at each network element that provides, consumes, or forwards one or more end-user services, and thus affects their performance and consequently users' experience. Even the software that undertakes to deliver (i.e. service provider) or consume (i.e.

user application) the respective end-user service (Service Layer) is designed following the cognitive cycle model and consequently interacts with the other cognitive cycles, thus affecting its behavior.

The continuous increase of the number of user equipments, in combination with the evolution of the traditional client/server model (Houssos, Gazis, & Alonistioti, 2003)0, for service provision towards more distributed application structures have paved the way for more advanced services. Especially, by taking into account that even simple users through their own devices (e.g., smart phones) can concurrently have the role of service consumer and service provider.

The rest of this chapter is organized as follows: In the following section the service management background is investigated, by presenting key research outcomes for service delivery, service publish and service discovery. Thereinafter, a platform independent and system agnostic framework for the evolution of the Future Internet service management is described, by adopting the cognitive cycle paradigm. In section 4, the baseline 3GPP IP multimedia sub-System (IMS) architecture is studied and its extensions in order to support the cognitive service provision framework are proposed. Finally, we conclude with future research directions and especially we discuss the cooperation between the service and network management, which is a major challenge that lies ahead.

SERVICE MANAGEMENT BACKGROUND

In the context of this section we will elaborate on the presentation of some key concepts of the service management area. We commence by providing a number of definitions which set the methodological and theoretical foundations of our work and proceed by identifying the state-of-the art paradigms of the area.

Our work is based on the assumption that a *Service* instantiates a specific functionality offered to a user by the execution of one or more applications ((Tselikas et al., 2003), (3GPP, 2006), (3GPP, 2009)). Therefore, we employ the notions of *Software Component* and *Application*. Specifically, a *Software Component (SW Component)* is a standalone software module that when combined appropriately with others form an *Application*. The latter comprises the software bundle that upon execution provides a *Service* to the users.

In order to capture and represent in a coherent manner the information related to a service we employ a number of profiles. Following a bottom-up approach we first define the *Software Component Profile (SW Component Profile)* which contains information regarding the requirements of a specific SW Component in terms of execution environment (both hardware and software platform) and collaboration with other SW Components. The latter identifies a specific part of the *Software Component Profile*, namely the *Binding Rules*. The *Application Profile* aggregates information deriving from various *SW Components Profiles* and provides information regarding the requirements posed for the successful provision of the identified *Application*. However the *Application Profile* contains additional, *Application* specific, information such as a provision/download URL. Finally, similarly to the *Application Profile*, a *Service Profile* comprises the aggregation of one or more *Application Profiles* as well as additional information related to charging and billing. A high level, UML based depiction, of this hierarchy is provided in Figure 2.

The fundamental entities that exist in every service provisioning framework are depicted in Figure 3. Initially, a *Service Provider*, which essentially comprises an actor, internal or external to the actual system, provides *Services* to terminals (end users) of one or more networks. The provision requires the initial registration of the service. The action of service registration essentially corresponds to the notion of *Service Publishing* which

Figure 2. High level depiction of the cognitive service provision framework concepts

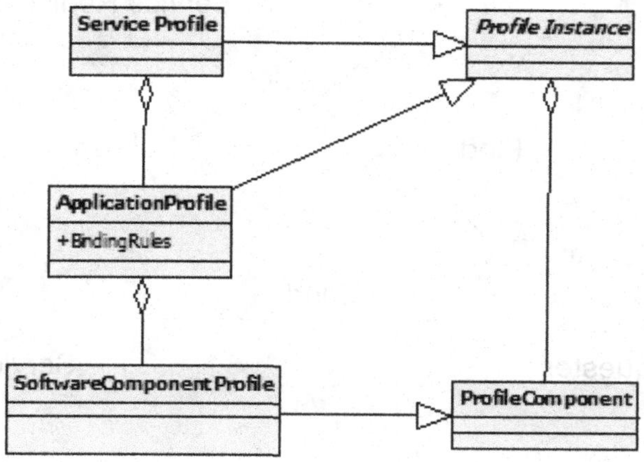

captures all functionality related to service registration and advertisement so a *Service* can become accessible and consumable by any *Service Requester*. The latter, discovers a *Service* by utilizing functionality identified by the concept of *Service Discovery*. Finally the service is delivered to the requestor through predefined protocols (*Service Delivery*) and can be adapted in order to match the requester's requirements (*Service Adaptation*). In the following paragraphs we attempt a short overview of the requirements posed by the *Service Publish, Service Discovery* and *Service Delivery* functionalities as well as state-of-the-art research in these areas, always from the perspective of a dynamically composed number of *Applications,* which upon deployment/composition provide a specific *Service* to a user.

Service Publish

The *Service Publish* aggregates all functionality related to the registration and possible advertisement of a service by a service provider. This module implements the following:

- *SW Component Profile* registration
- *SW Component* upload

- *SW Component Binding Rules* registration(Application Registration)
- *Application Binding Rules* registration(Service Registration)
- *Service Profile* registration

The most fundamental part of this procedure is the description of the procedure through which *SW Components* are bonded into *Applications* and *Applications* into *Services*. The implementation of this composition should provide two kinds of guarantee, namely, low computational cost and scalability. The former denotes the requirement for low delivery time with respect to the time required for the delivery of an off-the-shelf service, while the second the ability of a service to be composed of a large number of applications without imposing significant load compared to a lower cardinality composition approach.

Attempting to address these issues in the context of SELF-SERV (Benatallah et al., 2002), a declarative composition language has been defined. The idea is based on statecharts (Harel & Naamad, 1996) and supports the successful deployment of composite services (services composed of other services) as well as their concurrent or distributed execution. Each composite service is perceived

Figure 3. Traditional service provision approach

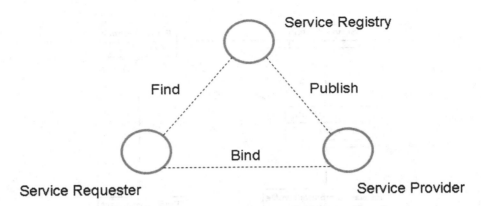

as a statechart, where states represent services and transition arrows between them simulate input and output. A more lightweight approach is outlined in (Lubell, 2001), where the use of RDF is considered for the description of networks of applications that involve discrete processes.

Service Discovery

The *Service Discovery* aggregates all functionality related to the discovery of a specific *Service* or a set of services by a registered client. The implementation of this action is directly influenced by the structure of the communication scheme. Therefore, two cases are distinguished, specifically centralized (traditional client-server communication) and ad hoc (peer to peer scheme).

There are several protocols and platforms which have been proposed and developed up-to-date with respect to the requirements posed by the discovery process. *Service Discovery* necessitates protocols which allow automatic detection of devices and services offered by these devices through communication networks. In addition, it dictates negotiation in terms of user preferences and terminal or network capabilities (e.g. profile Specification). Sun's JINI (Lubell, 2001), "Universal Description, Discovery and Integration" protocol (UDDI), IETF Service Location Protocols (SLP), UPnP, DNS-SD and Bluetooth's Service

Discovery Protocol (SDP) are some of the most important service discovery protocols that were designed for wired and wireless networks.

In the ad hoc case, the discovery phase becomes more elaborated, since virtually every peer of the network has to be queried. A straightforward approach would be the adaptation of well known content and query distribution techniques in peer to peer networks, such as those proposed in (Androutselis & Spinellis, 2004), (Zeinalipour-Yazti, Kalogeraki, & Gunopulos, 2004), or (Li & Wu, 2006). On the other hand a service discovery protocol specifically designed for mobile ad hoc networks such as GSD (Chacraborty et al., 2002), Konark (Helal et al., 2002) or HESED (Yang, Hassanein, & Mawji, 2006) could directly be adopted. However, the ad hoc network outlined previously is envisaged as being of low node cardinality with small lifetime.

Service Delivery

The *Service Delivery* aggregates all functionality related to the delivery of a specific service or a set of services to a registered client. The term delivery embraces all procedures involved from the selection of a service (right after the discovery phase) until its consumption by the client. The implementation of this action, as in the case of the *Service Discovery* is directly influenced by the structure of the communication scheme.

Web Services is one of the most important technologies, which incorporate the functions of the afore-discussed modules (Service publish, service discovery and service delivery). Web Services are a collection of protocols and standards used for exchanging data between applications or systems. Web services model uses Simple Object Access Protocol (SOAP), Web Services Definition Language (WSDL) and UDDI protocol, for service provision, service description and service discovery respectively. WSDL describes how to use the software service interfaces. A WSDL description is retrieved from the UDDI directory and the services are invoked over the World Wide Web using the SOAP, which is XML based, used for exchanging structured data and type information in a decentralized and distributed environment.

Web services allow programming language independence, and assure the desired platform interoperability and openness. Furthermore, the combination of semantic web and Web Services (OWL-S) provides greater automation for service provision, selection, invocation, composition and negotiation. The IP Multimedia Subsystem (IMS) is the service and session control platform, which allows the core network to be independent of a particular access technology (e.g. WLAN, UMTS), to support end-to-end QoS guaranteed connections, and to integrate mobility for all network applications.

COGNITIVE SERVICE PROVISION

In the context of this paragraph we will present in details the Cognitive Service Provision framework. As stated in the previous paragraph, the work is based on the following assumptions:

- An *Application* is considered as the composition of *Software Components*

- A *Service* is the user experience provided by the execution of one or more *Applications* or equally the functionality offered to the user by the execution.

Each service is modeled as a two level hierarchy graph (Figure 4). Each registered *Service Provider* enlists its *SW Components*, their binding-into-applications schemes as well as the applications' combination rules. In the upper layer the nodes represent the applications and links between them input and output information. The various paths defined between the Start and Finish nodes of the graph denote the various instantiations of this specific service. In the second layer, each application node is depicted as a graph, where this time nodes represent *SW Components*, links transfer of control from component to component and paths adapted versions of the same application.

The proposed hierarchical scheme for services' description gives us the capability to specify the architectural framework for Future Internet services provision in the context of a complex and distributed network environment, where the cognitive cycle paradigm is present. In the remaining of the paragraph we will provide a platform independent and system agnostic architecture (UML Modeling, Functional Blocks and Signaling) for the evolution of service delivery, discovery, adaptation and composition mechanism by capitalizing on the cognitive cycle model. The presentation follows a bottom-up approach; initially we present the fundamental operations outlined above and then we provide the holistic view of the framework and the employment of the cognitive cycle.

Service Publish

In the context of the CSP *Service Publish* operation each registered *Service Provider* enlists its *SW Components*, their binding-into-applications schemes as well as the applications' combination rules that will result in the provided services. Due

Figure 4. Service representation as a graph

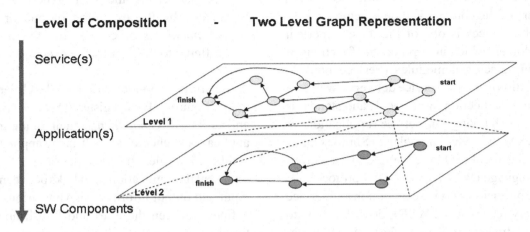

to the fact that our framework is targeting a large set of devices, ranging from personal computers to mobile phones, the representation should be lightweight and easily processed. Consequently the information is encoded with a set of adjacency matrixes. Figure 5 illustrates the registration of a service that is the result of the execution of an application made up of one component.

The *Stakeholder* logs into the systems and registers a new *SWComponent*. Essentially the registration triggers a series of events described by the action *modifyData*(). As soon as the operation is successfully concluded a reply is issued back at the stakeholder, who in turn starts inserting the binding-rules. The latter are dynamically placed in the graph and give the possibility to register a new *Service* through the *setServiceProfile*() action.

Rule-based approaches are combined in the process of service publishing. More specifically, the publishing system, based on the available binding information and the new service profile defines the service using only the available *SW Components* and *Applications* just like in (Basu, Wang, & Little, 2002). Moreover the arcs are populated with weights that are calculated using the quality criteria outlined in (Ponnekanti & Fox, 2002) together with policy rules defined by the

Service Provider. In addition the Web Ontology Language (OWL) which provides interoperability and inference features and in sequence the OWL Services (OWL-S (Yang, Hassanein, & Mawji, 2006)) ontologies is used to express detailed semantic information facilitating the subsequent service discovery mechanisms, by describing the meaning of the service through ontological annotation.

All the previous and forthcoming theoretical analysis is more effective by using a simple and efficient way of implementing the concepts of *SW Components*. It is obvious that the implementation of tens or hundreds of software modules is simply unaffordable and inapplicable in large scale communication environments. However, technologies such as AspectJ, JMangler and AspectS ((Zeng, 2003), (Kiczales et al., 2001), (Kniesel & Costanza, 2001)) allow the design of one simple component and its subsequent dynamic differentiation. In this way, one executable can represent a whole class of software modules.

The *Service Publishing* approach introduced by the proposed *Cognitive Service Provision Framework* is depicted in Figure 6. The heart of the system is the *ServicePublish* class, which implements the *ServicePublishInterface*. The latter is exploited by the Stakeholder in order to

Figure 5. Service publish module

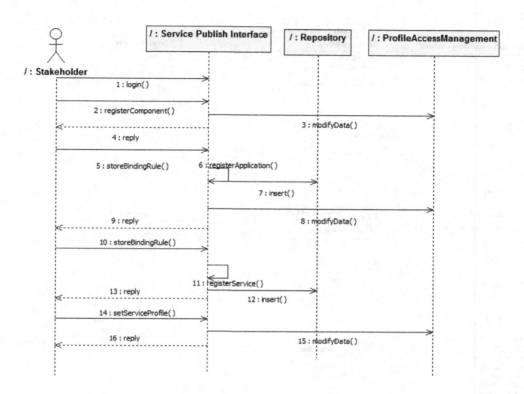

insert new services. The *Service* comprises the aggregation of the numerous *SWModules* and is described by a *ServiceProfile*.

Service Discovery

As explained in the previous section *Service Discovery* aggregates all functionality related to the discovery of a specific service or a set of services by a registered client and its implementation is influenced by the structure of the communication scheme; therefore, two cases are distinguished, centralized (traditional client server communication) and ad hoc (peer to peer scheme). The proposed protocol for the traditional client server model is presented in Figure 7. The ServiceDiscoveryModule of the client retrieves information from its local information base and requests a

service from the ServiceDiscoveryModule of the server. The latter, retrieves all available information and proceeds in a twofold filtering. At first, the rules are filtered and the available Applications are extracted. These Applications will serve as basis for the formulation of the final Service. Then, based on the issued request, a new filtering is applied which identifies the various Service compositions that can be offered to the requestor. The most important part of this procedure is the profile filtering. All nodes of the graph hierarchy outlined in the *Service Publish* are examined with respect to their hardware and software requirements. As a result, a set of nodes is removed together with their incoming and outgoing arcs. The aforementioned procedure is carried out from bottom to top. Specifically:

Figure 6. Service Publishing in the context of the proposed Cognitive Service Provision framework

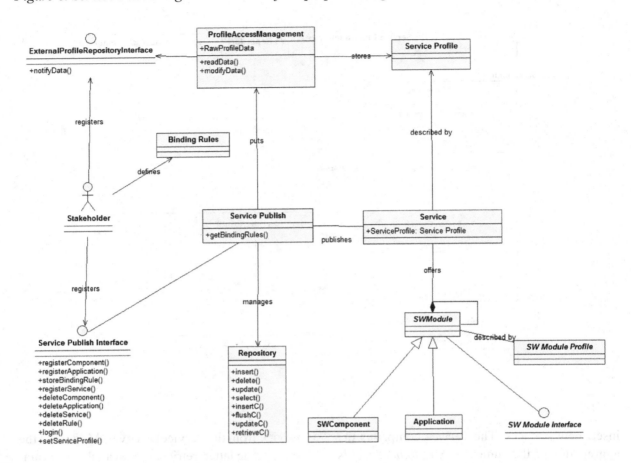

1. SW Component Level:
   ○ Each component is evaluated concerning its hardware and software requirements. All those that do not conform to the limitations posed by the execution system are removed.
   ○ The remaining components form the various application graphs.
2. Application Level:
   ○ Each application graph is examined for the existence of at least one path from start to finish. If no such path exists then the application is ignored.
3. Service Level:
   ○ The service graph is examined with the same procedure as above. If no

path exists from start to finish then the service cannot be provided, otherwise, all the existing paths depict various versions of the same service and are transmitted back to the querying node.

In the end, this procedure incorporates one more assessment step, namely the filtering of policy information. Therefore, services are defined in accordance with the rules provided by the current network operator, service provider and service consumer.

However, an ad hoc network outlined previously is envisaged as being of low node cardinality with small lifetime. Therefore, in the context of the

Figure 7. Service Discovery in a client-server query scheme

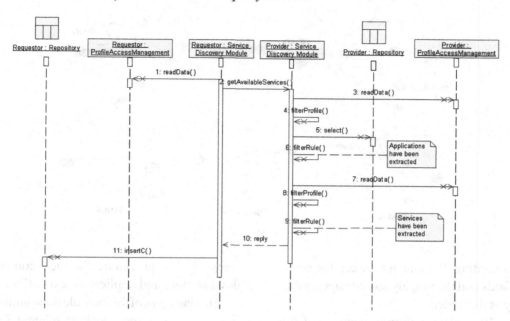

proposed *Cognitive Service Provision* framework, a simple store and forward technique together with caching is proposed.

Each peer upon necessitating a service initiates a query procedure in order to receive all services available in the vicinity. The query is forwarded by neighbor peers until it reaches a node that has already knowledge of available services. These services are stored in a cache memory repository. This event triggers a cache exchange between the querying device and the queried one, since the

Figure 8. An ad hoc network with new peers joining (red)

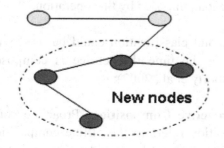

former could also be a service provider. A simple example is illustrated in Figure 8 and Figure 9. Initially two nodes are interconnected and form a small network which is expanded when four new devices (red circles) are connected to it. For simplicity reasons we assume than none of the new nodes can offer a service, therefore they have an empty service cache.

Thereinafter, one of the new peers requires a service. Since it cannot provide it to itself, initiates a query procedure. The query is forwarded by adjacent nodes until it reaches one with already populated cache. The generated reply is forwarded to all nodes of the query path until it reaches the source.

In order to ensure that a query is not endlessly forwarded in the network or get stuck in a loop, two simple techniques are used. Every query message has a predefined TTL, which is decreased by one every time it reaches a new node. Moreover, a query carries a specific identification number together with the MAC address of the initiating peer. These fields are stored in each peer's cache memory and checked whenever a message re-

Figure 9. Illustration of the query process

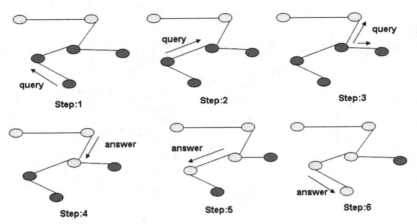

quires forwarding. If a match between the newly arrived fields and the already stored appears then the query is discarded.

Figure 10 depicts a simple example of this procedure. Profile filtering is carried out as in the client-server example presented previously, but this time, each peer decides locally based on its context information which services are supported for execution.

The *Service Discovery* approach introduced by the proposed *Cognitive Service Provision Framework* is depicted in Figure 11. The important functionality of the system is the *ServiceDiscovery*, which inherits and extends the *Decision-Making* class. The latter provides support for decision making actions which are required in the context of service discovery. Essentially, the *ServiceDiscovery* class retrieves information through the *Repository* and implements the actions of filtering as depicted in the *ServiceDiscovery-Interface*.

Service Delivery

Following the two envisaged cases of discovery, namely traditional client-server and ad-hoc/p2p schemes the *Service Delivery* is also studied in these contexts. In both cases three are the basic

steps of this procedure: service composition, downloading and application execution.

The basic part of this module is the implementation of the service composition scheme. Based on the analysis of the prior paragraphs, the following types of composition have been identified:

- **Server Side Composition:** The server takes charge of the binding procedure based on the available binding and context information. This approach is used when the terminal (user equipment) is not able to sustain the load imposed by this operation.
- **Client Side Composition:** The server forwards the binding rules and the components to the client machine. In this case, the client undertakes the binding procedure based on the forwarded binding information. This approach is followed when the terminal (user equipment) is able to sustain the load imposed by this operation.

A second classification could be used with respect to the time the service is composed (Chakraborty et al., 2002):

- **Proactive Composition:** Proactive composition refers to the offline composition of services on the provider side. This type

Figure 10. Service discovery process in an ad hoc network scheme

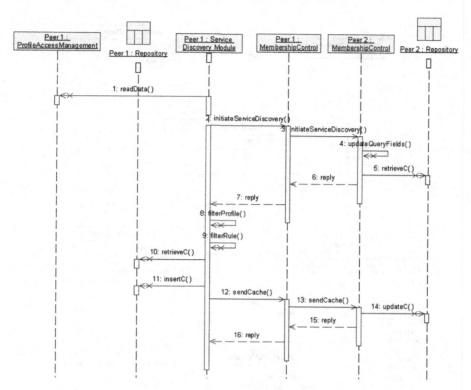

of composition is used when service composition is time consuming or the specific service is often requested.

- **Reactive Composition:** Reactive composition refers to the on-the-fly creation of a service upon request. It is employed in order to provide a personalized version of the service to the client.

The outlined classification schemes are not disjoint; on the contrary they can be combined as it is depicted in Table 1. The main difference between the service delivery process between an ad hoc network and a fixed topology lies in the fact that the proactiveness feature of a composition cannot be used as well as the delivery of an already composed set of applications. Consequently, peers on their own gather and combine the various *SW Components* into *Applications* and then into *Services*.

As far as execution is concerned, the following schemes are derived:

- **Centralized Execution:** All applications offering the requested service are executed locally.
- **Distributed Execution:** Applications offering the requested service are executed distributed and their results are aggregated in the client node. The idea is that the applications already exist somewhere and the client essentially instead of downloading them locally acts as the aggregator of the final output. It has to be stressed out however that the applicability of this execution scheme necessitates a set of robust machines, a stable network and synchronization according to the composition graph. Various implementation of this idea appear in (Chakraborty et al., 2002), (Chakrabory

Figure 11. Service Discovery in the context of the proposed Cognitive Service Provision framework

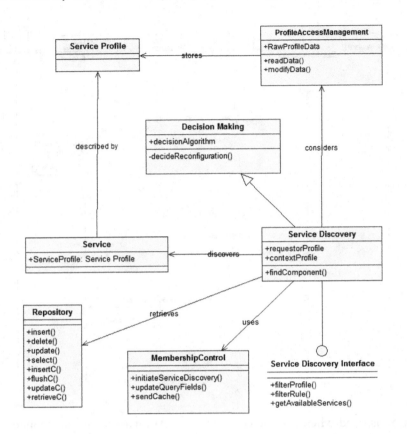

& Joshi, 2001), (Chakraborty, Yesha, & Joshi, 2004)

The client side, reactive composition and execution sequence chart is depicted in Figure 12, while Figure 13 provides an overview of our proposal. The main module in this case is the *SoftwareDownloadManager*, which undertakes all tasks related to the downloading of the software as well as the *BindingRules*. Additionally, the module is able to install and uninstall the software (i.e. delete an application) or in case of malfunctioning roll back to the previous stable situation or re-initialize the downloading session. The *ServiceDownloadManager* is triggered by the *ServiceDeliveryModule*.

Service Adaptation

Service Adaptation includes the procedures that upon their enforcement achieve to differentiate the result that a user experiences, through the

Table 1. Service composition schemes

	Proactive	Reactive
Server Side Composition	X	X
Client Side Composition	X	X

Figure 12. Service delivery (client side, reactive composition - central execution)

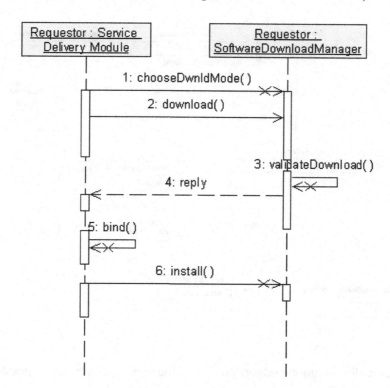

execution of one or more applications. The feature of adaptability is an important characteristic of pervasive services. An important phase of service adaptation procedure is the transition from the current state to the most suitable one of the entity being adapted, considering:

- The specified policies of the involved entities and the contextual environment
- Minimum effort from the provider and the client with the minimum consumption of resources.

The capability of *Services* to autonomously adapt to the context from which they are requested and in which they execute includes mechanisms, like:

- Dynamic adaptation of *Applications*

- Parameter level adaptation techniques
- Dynamic aggregation of components

It is straightforward therefore to consider that this differentiation can be triggered by various actions, such as:

- Change of the environment in which the *Application* is executed
- Change of the content consumed by the executed application
- Change of the *Applications* interactions that compose the *Service*
- Change of the *SW Components* that define one or more *Applications*

Two algorithms that can directly be applied to this problem are defined in (Yu & Lin, 2005) and (Yu and Kwei-Jay, 2005). Upon detecting a node

Figure 13. Service Delivery in the context of the proposed Cognitive Service Provision framework

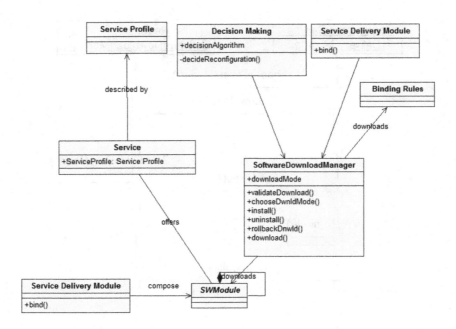

failure in the graph, the aforementioned algorithms backtrack to the closest node with outgoing arcs and try to find another path to the final destination. The general idea is largely based on the well known principal of optimality (Thomas et al., 2004) that is also used in the context of our work.

An example of this procedure is illustrated in Figure 14, Figure 15, and Figure 16. Upon delivery request, the paths on the applications and service graphs have been created and the service is being initialized. If we consider that one of the SW Components is not working properly and therefore the application in which it operates is also malfunctioning a remedy action should be triggered. The solution that will ensure service continuation lays in the selection of an alternate path either in the service graph or the in specific application graph where the malfunctioning component exists.

For example, the *Service Adaptation Module* may choose to completely ignore the problematic application and select another combination of applications for the service (alternate path in

the service composition graph), as it is depicted in Figure 15.

Alternatively, the adaptation may take place at level of the application graph. In this case the overlaying graph remains unaltered, and the malfunctioning application is adapted my changing the components combination sequence (alternate path in the application composition graph), as it is depicted in Figure 16.

One of the issues that has not been addressed by the aforementioned analysis is the decision process and specifically the reason for which a service version is selected from the set of available ones. In the discovery phase we can assume that the user chooses the service, while in the adaptation phase the device itself has to make the decision and select the new version.

A simple technique, which is employed in our framework, is to find the path with the highest node intersection comparing to the old one. High intersection provides smaller differentiation between the two versions of the service, namely the initial and the adapted one. The enhancement

Figure 14. Service Adaptation triggering - Component Failure (red signifies components/ applications in use)

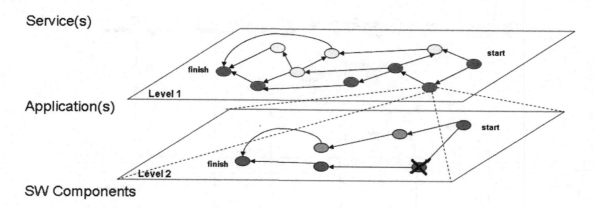

of weights in the graph will enable the use of path selection techniques such as Dijkstra's or Bellman's algorithms and consequently the definition of sophisticated service adaptation techniques.

Another issue that is discussed below is the location where the adaptation process takes place. It is straightforward to assume that the selection algorithm will be executed at the network node, where the required information is aggregated.

Consequently, in the ad hoc scenario, service adaptation takes place in the service consumer side, while in the client-server communication scheme it can take place either on the provider or on the consumer node. In both cases, if a SW Component is missing it can be downloaded from the possessing node. The flow charts of this procedure are depicted in Figure 17 and Figure 18. Figure 17 presents the messages that

Figure 15. Adaptation on the service composition layer (blue signifies adapted service)

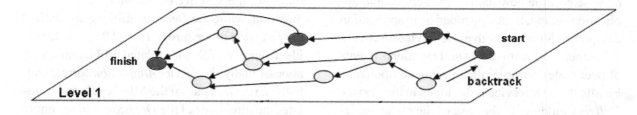

Figure 16. Adaptation on the application layer (green signifies adapted application - Level 1graph remains unaltered)

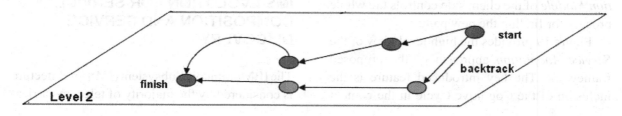

Figure 17. Service Adaptation in an ad hoc network scheme

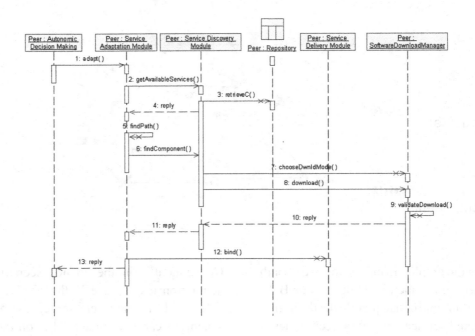

are exchanged in the case of an ad-hoc network. When a service adaptation action is triggered by the decision making module of a peer node the first step is to retrieve the list of the available services through the *Service Discovery* module. The *Service Adaptation* module of the initiating node selects the new path of the service and applications graph. If the download of an application component is necessary then the service discovery in cooperation with SoftwareDownload agents of peer nodes retrieves the missing components. Finally the new service is deployed in the *Service Delivery* module. In the case of the client-server scheme the steps are similar. The main difference is the process to retrieve the binding rules of the service and application layer graphs. The *Adaptation Module* of the client side controls the whole process for finding the new path.

Figure 19 provides the high level view of the *Service Adaptation* approach of the proposed framework. The key introduced feature is the inclusion of the Cognitive Cycle in the context of *Service Provision*. As the reader may notice, the Monitor-Decision Making-Execution approach is inherited by *Service Adaptation* and specialized for the case of *Service Provision*. The *Monitoring* process is implemented as *Service Monitor*, as specific entity which constantly monitors the validity of the binding of the application, while the *Decision Making* specializes the *Decision* procedure of the MDE cycle for the identification of *Service* related problematic situations. Finally, the *Service Adaptation* corresponds to the *Execution* part of the MDE cycle and translates the directives of the *Decision Making* entity to specific commands on the graph of the *SW Components*.

IMS EVOLUTION FOR SERVICE COMPOSITION AND SERVICE DISCOVERY

The IP Multimedia Subsystem (IMS) architecture is considered by the majority of telecom carriers

Figure 18. Service adaptation in a client server communication scheme (adaptation in client side)

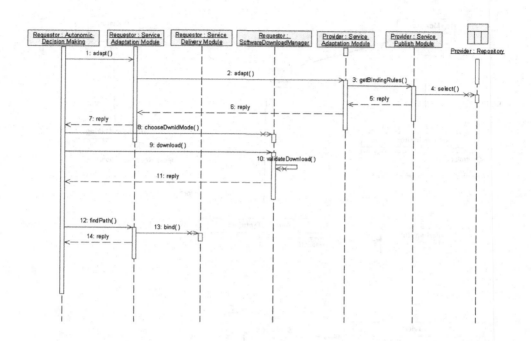

and service providers as the unifying technology, which brings wireless, wireline and Internet systems together into a seamless environment. IMS provides to the service providers the capability to integrate voice, video, data services as well as advanced services, and provide them on a single platform. Furthermore, IMS provides the opportunity for ubiquitous access for users regardless of service, terminal type or location as well as a uniform environment for billing. In this section the architectural and protocol aspects of the IMS architecture are described, while the evolution of the IMS infrastructure in order to incorporate the proposed hierarchical scheme for services' description and features of the cognitive service provision framework are presented.

IP Multimedia System

IP Multimedia System is an emerging technology, which main goal is to provide to the end user converged application services (data, speech) that

are based on the Internet Protocol (IP). IMS is an open and standardized architecture that attempts to integrate service provision by using features and advantages of both mobile communications and Internet world (Qadeer et al., 2009), (Loreto et al., 2010). The main protocols that constitute IMS are Session Initiation Protocol (SIP) (IETF RFC 3261), Session Description Protocol (SDP) (IETF RFC 4566), Diameter (IETF RFC 3588), and Real-time Transport Protocol (RTP) (IETF RFC 3550), while the main goals through IMS establishment are:

- to provide a common platform for the development, the provision, and the delivery of multimedia services,
- to offer fully integrated real and non-real time services,
- to facilitate the interaction between the user and the services that each user consumes,
- to assure the efficient classification of a group of user that are consuming the same

Figure 19. Service Adaptation in the context of the proposed Cognitive Service Provision framework

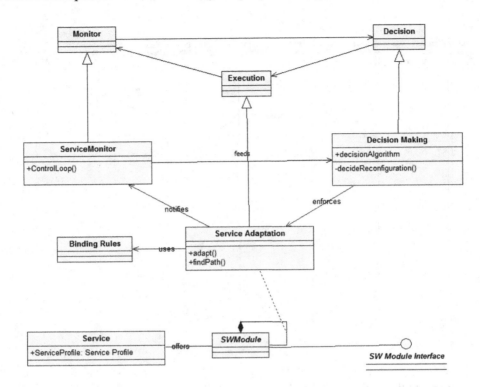

service, under one session or under multiple synchronized sessions.

As depicted on Figure 20, a high level IMS–enabled communications network architecture consists of four layers: a) the Application Layer, b) the core IMS Layer, c) the transport layer, and d) the network management layer. The transport layer includes all those wireless or wired access networks (e.g., LTE, Wifi, ADSL) that are available for the exchange of data packets (e.g., services) among the terminals of the end user and/or application servers. The Network Management (NM) layer comes into the scene in order to highlight the importance of the control of the NM system (NMS) on the transport layer and the necessity of collaboration between the NMS and the service management entities, as it is analysed in the following section. The main functional entities that constitute IMS are described as follows:

- The Home Subscriber Server (HSS) is the main data base of IMS. It is used to store and provide user profile information, security information as well as location information. It is also used for user authentication purposes as well as for services authorization support.
- The Proxy Call Session Control Functions (P-CSCF) server is the first contact interface for SIP messages from the IMS-enabled terminals to the rest IMS network. Terminal attaches to the P-CSCF prior to performing IMS registrations and initiating SIP sessions. P-CSCF operates as the local registrar and as the firewall for the infrastructure. P-CSCF undertakes a) to protect IMS by informing other IMS entities about user's identity, b) to act as the bridge between the visited networks and the home network of the end user, c) to provide

Figure 20. IP Multimedia Sub-System

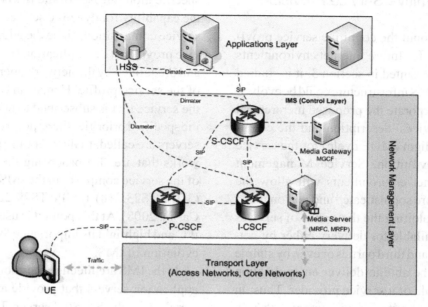

charging information in cooperation with the respective policy and charging control entities.

- The Interrogating CSCF (I-CSCF) server is at the edges of an administrative domain. Remote servers (i.e. remote P-CSCFs) discover I-CSCF through DNS calls and contact the latter in order to forward SIP messages to the respective domain. I-CSCF contacts HSS that is associated with in order to find the address of the S-CSCF, where it will select to forward the SIP messages and consequently serve the UE. Thus, S-CSCF could be used for load sharing purposes among multiple S-CSCF nodes.

- The Serving CSCF (S-CSCF) is the most important entity of the IMS infrastructure, where fundamental IMS functions are taking place and all SIP messages are passing through. S-CSCF is used as the local registar server for the users that have been served, and authorizes them by downloading (or updating) user's profile from the HSS. Furthermore, S-CSCF routes the SIP messages to the appropriate application server, by applying routing rules according to the service profile information and taking into account one or more initial Filter criteria (iFC). iFC are stored in the HSS, and provide information about the services that each user is subscribed to. More discussion about iFC is provided below.

- The media gateway and specifically the Media Gateway Controller Function (MGCF) is responsible to control a media gateway.

- The media server and specifically the Multimedia Resource Function Controller (MRFC) provides those functionalities for the adaptation and manipulation of services (e.g., transcoding).

The application Layer includes all application servers that provide an IMS service and interact with the S-CSCF server via SIP messages for control purposes. More information and details about the IMS building blocks and the specified interfaces are available in (3GPP TS23.228), (3GPP TS24.229), (3GPP TS23.218), (3GPP TS29.228).

IMS and Cognitive Service Provision

Taking into account the cognitive service provision framework for future Internet environments that has been presented in section 3, it is studied below how the IMS infrastructure could be evolved in order to incorporate the proposed hierarchical scheme for services' description and the cognitive cycle paradigm (MDE cycle) for the service management evolution. Service Management in future Internet environments will allow the provision of more sophisticated and personalized services, by exploiting the thousands of services that will be available for delivery either by network operators and third parties or even by simple users that will be able to deliver an application and have the role of a service provider. Thus, in a dynamic and ubiquitous environment with high user mobility, there is the need for the monitoring of the services ecosystem by incorporating also discovery mechanisms for service components (Figure 11). Based on the outputs of the service discovery phase, decision making and execution schemes for services composition are necessary for the realization of the hierarchical model as well as for more efficient reuse of distributed applications and services (Figure 19). Through services composition new sophisticated services will be developed by reusing and correlating existing service components/applications and thus avoiding the continuous specification of new services and the redundant development/delivery of the same application/service by multiple service provision points.

Specifically, the analysis hereinafter is focusing on the service discovery and service composition phase and how these two capabilities are affecting the structural features and the signalling of the IMS environment. Figure 21 illustrates the building blocks and interfaces that are introduced in the IMS architecture, following the design principles and the philosophy of IMS. The service discovery manager and service composer are incorporated in the IMS architecture as trusted SIP servers. The last specification releases of the IMS do not provide the capability for dynamic service discovery and service composition, since the address of the service providers (i.e. application servers) are static and predefined by the network operator in the iFC of the service profile. Hence, an end user knows the service that is subscribed to and according to the specified priorities the appropriate application servers are called. In the literature there are some works that are also proposing the incorporation of the service composer in the IMS infrastructure (3GPP TS23.218), (3GPP TS29.228), (Miguel & Carlin, 2008). At this point it is useful to describe iFC and highlight its importance for the proposed evolution of IMS.

In the IMS architecture the coordination of the application servers that provide a service is undertaken by the S-CSCF server. The latter coordinates the available application servers for the provision of a service based on the iFC information of the user profile. The service profile affects the routing of the SIP messages that are exchanged for the service provision. The profile of a service is always associated with a subscriber and includes one or more iFCs that have different priorities. iFC includes those information that will help the S-CSCF server to decide whether an application server should be invoked in order to deliver a service to the subscriber. The service profile is retrieved by the HSS server. The main entities of the iFC profile are depicted in Figure 22 (Poikselka & Mayer, 2009).

From the iFC structure it is obvious that composite services have not been taken into account. In the case that more than one application servers are involved the S-CSCF undertakes to forward the SIP message to the appropriate application server based on the "priority field" of the iFC. This mechanism allows only the sequential interaction between the application servers. Thus, a new functionality is necessary in the IMS architecture that will undertake to compose services (i.e. Service Composer) and will undertake the coordination of individual applications. Moreover,

Figure 21. Proposed scheme for the Dynamic Service Composition and Discovery in IMS

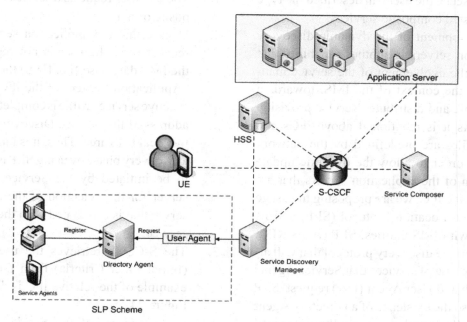

the update of the iFC structure is necessary in order to inform the S-CSCF, whether the requested service is a composite one or not. For that purpose, the parameter "Composite Service" could be introduced as a "Service Information" sub-field. This Boolean-type parameter (composite = 1, not-composite = 0) indicates whether the re-

quested service is a composite or not. In the case of a Composite Service the Service Composer undertakes to handle the request, according to the available services. The operator of the end user knows the initial constituent services of the requested composite service or alternatively in a

Figure 22. Initial Filter Criteria Information Model

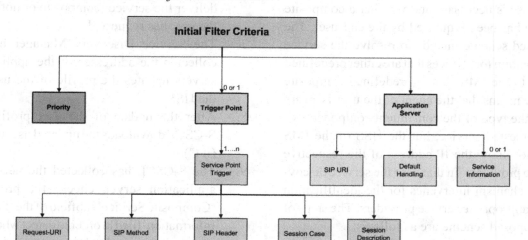

more future scene the user can described the type of the requested composite services.

The development of the dynamic discovery of application servers is another capability that will enable the evolvement of the service management, in the context of the IMS, towards a more dynamic and distributed service provision paradigm. As it is mentioned above iFCs and service profiles are predefined by the network operator. In order to allow the dynamic update or indication of the application servers that are described in the iFC, we are proposing the usage of the Service Location Protocol (SLP) and its integration with IMS entities. SLP (IETS RFC: 2608) is a service discovery protocol that will allow the searching of services that Service Agents (SA) publish and User Agent (UA) request. SLP considers also the existence of a Directory Agent (DA) that collects and stores locally discovered services and facilitates the UA discovery process by reducing searching time and signaling e.g., by sending unicast discovery messages instead of multicast packets. The application servers that are provided by after the SLP searching are recorded to the HSS data base in order to be available for other service provision requests.

The joint usage of the service discovery and service composition entities is described below and depicted in Figure 23, by using SIP messages. The IMS system checks whether a service discovery phase is necessary and whether a composite service has been requested by the end-user. The proposed scheme intends to resolve the service composition for services that are either predefined or not to the IMS. A non-predefined composite service means that the agent of the user is aware about the type of the constituent components of the requested service, but the HSS of the IMS does not know the IP address of the respective service providers. In that case the service discovery mechanism intervenes for the identification of the appropriate service providers. The steps of the proposed scheme are as follows:

1. The end user requests a service either composite or not.

2. In case that the application server that is requested by the user is not registered in the IMS data base (i.e. HSS) then the field "Application Server" of the iFC of the respective service profile is completed with the address of the Service Discovery server of the local IMS area. Thus, it is indicated that a discovery phase by using SLP is necessary to be initiated by the Service Discovery server for the detection of the application server that is associated with the requested service.

3. The S-CSCF retrieves the user's profile (Initial Filter Criteria) from the HSS. An example of the relative iFC is described in Figure 24.

4. If the address of the Service Discovery Manager has been indicated in the 'Server Name' field then C-SCSF calls the latter and indicates the type of the applications components that are required.

5. The Service Discovery Server sends a discovery request message to the User Agent in order to start searching for application servers.

6. The User Agent returns to the Service Discovery Manager the addresses of the application servers that have the ability to deliver the service (composite or not), that the user has requested.

7. The Service Discovery Manager having collected the addresses of the application servers updates the profile of the user on the HSS.

8. After the update of the user profile the S-CSCF downloads the updated user profile (iFC).

9. The S-CSCF has collected the necessary application server, checks the proposed 'Composite Service' subfield of the 'Service Information' filed in order to detect whether a composite service has been requested or not.

Figure 23. Signaling for the Discovery and composition of services

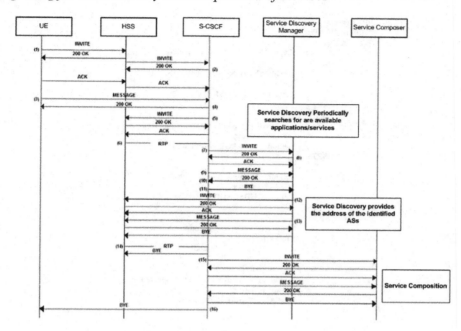

If 'Composite Service = 1' then the S-CSCF triggers the Service Composer entity, which undertakes to make the composition of the service and thereinafter S-CSCF contacts the services (application servers) that the user has requested.

The flexibility levels of the service management that could be introduced and efficiently implemented is a fundamental issue. The description of the services components that constitute a service, their priorities and in general the place for the publishing and description of a composite service (end user terminal or network operator side) are issues that affect the flexibility of the system and the changes that should take place to existing service provision platforms e.g., IMS.

CONCLUSION

From the above analysis it is obvious that new capabilities could be deployed for advanced ser-

vice provision. However the increased complexity for service management is one of the issues that should be addressed. For the fast evolution of the Future Internet services ecosystem it is necessary the specification of the interfaces among the various modules of the Cognitive Service Provision framework and mainly the provision of APIs and tools (e.g., Web 2.0 tools) that will allow the application developers to deploy fast and easy software components (*SW Components*) for both the service providers and the end users. Furthermore, there is the need of common information models for the uniform description of services and application as well as of a common representation scheme for the graph of services and the graph of software components.

The service management behavior is affected by the operation of the network management systems and vice versa. For that reason the federation and the cooperation of these two domains is a very important parameter and a challenge for future research. Before presenting how this link

Figure 24. iFC for service discovery activation

```
<InitialFilterCriteria>
    <Priority>0</Priority>
    <TriggerPoint>
        <ConditionTypeCNF>1</ConditionTypeCNF>
        <SPT>
            <ConditionNegated>0</ConditionNegated>
            <Group>0</Group>
            <Method>INVITE</Method>
        </SPT>
        <SPT>
            <ConditionNegated>0</ConditionNegated>
            <Group>0</Group>
            <Method>MESSAGE</Method>
        </SPT>
        <SPT>
            <ConditionNegated>0</ConditionNegated>
            <Group>0</Group>
            <Method>SUBSCRIBE</Method>
        </SPT>
        <SPT>
            <ConditionNegated>0</ConditionNegated>
            <Group>1</Group>
            <Method>INVITE</Method>
        </SPT>
        <SPT>
            <ConditionNegated>0</ConditionNegated>
            <Group>1</Group>
            <Method>MESSAGE</Method>
        </SPT>

        <SPT>
            <ConditionNegated>1</ConditionNegated>
            <Group>1</Group>
            <SIPHeader>
                <Header>From</Header>
                <Content>"joe"</Content>
            </SIPHeader>
        </SPT>
    </TriggerPoint>
    <ApplicationServer>
        <ServerName>sip:Discover_Manager@homedomain.com </ServerName>
    </ApplicationServer>
</InitialFilterCriteria>
```

could be used in practice it is useful to sketch out the future Internet network management systems.

The last decade there is a lot of literature and research work for the automation of network management by reducing the human intervention and handling complex situations. The self-management of Future Internet infrastructures necessitates the introduction of decision making techniques and the capitalization of the existing knowledge and policy frameworks, as it is depicted in Figure 25, where the cognitive cycle is also present for the automation of network management tasks. For efficient and scalable network management, where various stakeholders participate (network operators, service providers,

end users), a distributed approach is required. Dynamic network (re)-configuration, in many cases, is based on cooperative decision making of various Future Internet devices and distributed network management service components. Hints and requests/recommendations are exchanged among the layers, in order to indicate a new situation or an action for execution. The automated and dynamic incorporation of various layers/levels requirements (e.g., SLAs) into the management aspects, provides also novel features to network management capabilities. Moreover, the resolution of conflicting requests is an issue of situation awareness and elements' domain policy prioritisation.

Figure 25. Service and Network Management Cognitive Cycles interaction

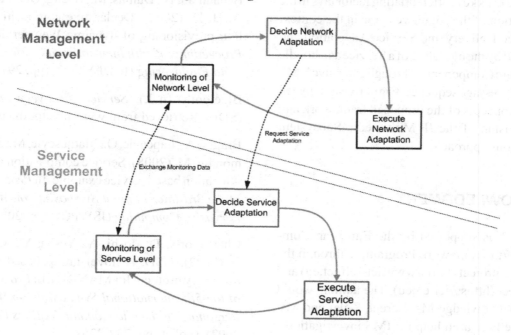

For the cooperation between the network and service management systems the following communication channels should be specified:

1. The first one is used for the exchange of monitoring data that is sensed locally either at the service or at network management level. The network management system could use service-level data as an input for the situation deduction and specifically for the identification of possible faults or optimization opportunities. Furthermore, service-level parameters could be used by the objective functions that the network management system should solve for the decision taking phase, according to the identified fault. On the other hand the service management level could exploit network-level monitoring data e.g., for the selection of the most efficient application server taking into account network conditions or for the building of the service path.

2. The second communication channel is used by the network management system in order to trigger service adaptations. Each network management system has a list of configuration actions that could be triggered as a remedy to a detected fault. Hence, service adaptation (e.g., service re-composition) is an additional configuration that could be triggered by the network management system.

Existing network management systems have limited capabilities for their cooperation with service management systems e.g., IMS. Hence, this could be considered as an important area for further research and specification.

In the context of this chapter we presented a novel approach for Service Provision which incorporates cognitive features and promotes itself as an ideal paradigm for the Future Internet era. Initially we discussed the challenges of the Future Internet Networks and then presented in details the proposed Cognitive Service Provision framework. Its key differentiating factor lays in the introduction of the cognitive cycle in the context of Service Delivery and Service Adaptation and supported by the modeling of a Service as a bundle of Software Components. Through extensive UML class and message sequence diagrams we analyzed the key concepts of the proposed framework and the extension of the IP Multimedia Subsystem through our approach.

ACKNOWLEDGMENT

This work is supported by the European Commission 7th Framework Programme through the Self-NET project (http://www.ict-selfnet.eu) and E3 project (https://ict-e3.eu). The authors would like to acknowledge Ms. Lorena Kolai and Ms. Penelope Loucareli help for IMS investigation.

REFERENCES

Androutselis, S., & Spinellis, D. (2004). A survey of peer-to-peer content distribution technologies. *ACM Computing Surveys, 36*(4), 335–371. doi:10.1145/1041680.1041681

Apostolos, K., Gérard, N., Julien, B., Vania, C., Vangelis, G., Tilemachos, R., & Nancy, A. (2010). An experimental path towards self-management for future Internet environments . In Tselentis, G., Galis, A., Gavras, A., & Krco, S. (Eds.), *Towards the future Internet - Emerging trends from European research* (pp. 95–104).

Basu, P., Wang, K., & Little, T. D. C. (2002). A novel approach for execution of distributed tasks on mobile ad hoc networks. In . *Proceedings of the IEEE Wireless Communications and Networking Conference, 2*, 579–585.

Benatallah, B., Dumas, M., Sheng, Q. Z., & Ngu, A. H. H. (2002). Declarative composition and P2P provisioning of dynamic Web services. In *Proceedings of 18th International Conference on Data Engineering* (ICDE) 2002, (pp. 297-308).

Bluetooth. (n.d.). *Service discovery protocol* (SDP). Retrieved from www.bluetooth.com

Brajdic, A., Lapcevic, O., Matijasevic, M., & Mosmondor, M. (2008). Service composition in IMS: A location based service example. In *Proceedings of the 3rd International Symposium on Wireless Pervasive Computing* (ISWPC), (pp. 208-212).

Chacraborty, D., Joshi, A., Yesha, Y., & Finin, T. (2002). GSD: A novel group based service discovery protocol for MANETS. In *Proceedings of the 5th International Symposium on Wireless Personal Multimedia Communications* (WPMC 2002). (vol. 1, pp. 232-236).

Chakraborty, D., Yesha, Y., & Joshi, A. (2004). A distributed service composition protocol for pervasive environments. In [WCNC]. *Proceedings of the IEEE Wireless Communications and Networking Conference, 4,* 2575–2580.

Chakrabory, D., & Joshi, A. (2001). *Dynamic service composition: State-of-the-art and research directions.* (Technical Report TR-CS-01-19), University of Maryland.

Cormen, T. H., Leirson, C. E., Rivest, R. L., & Stein, C. (2004). *Introduction to algorithms* (2nd ed.). MIT Press.

Dinsing, T., Eriksson, G., Fikouras, I., Gronowski, K., Levenshteyn, R., Pettersson, P., & Wiss, P. (2007). Service composition in IMS using Java EE SIP servlet containers. *Ericsson Review, 84*(3), 92–96.

DNS-SD. (2010). *Website.* Retrieved from http://www.dns-sd.org

Espinosa Carlin, J. M. (2008). Realizing service composition in the IP multimedia subsystem. In *Proceedings of the 1st. ITU-T Kaleidoscope Conference Innovations - Future Network and Services*. Geneva, Switzerland.

Ganek, A., & Corbi, T. (2003). The dawning of the autonomic computing era. *IBM Systems Journal, 42*(1), 5–18. doi:10.1147/sj.421.0005

3GPP. (2006). *TS 22.105: Services and service capabilities* (release 8).

3GPP. (2009). *TS 22.127: Service requirements for the open services access (OSA), stage 1* (release 7).

3GPP. (2010). TS29.228: IP multimedia (IM) subsystem Cx and Dx interfaces- Signaling flows and message contents.

3GPP. (2010). TS 23.218: IP multimedia (IM) session handling- IM call model, stage 2.

3GPP. (2010). *TS 23.228 v10.1.0: IP Multimedia Subsystem (IMS), stage 2*.

3GPP. (2010). TS 24.229: IP multimedia call control protocol based on session initiation protocol (SIP) and session description protocol (SDP), stage 3.

Harel, D., & Naamad, A. (1996). The STATE-MATE semantics of statecharts. *ACM Transactions on Software Engineering and Methodology, 5*(4), 54–64. doi:10.1145/235321.235322

Helal, A., Desai, N., Verma, V., & Lee, C. (2003). Konark: A service discovery and delivery protocol for ad-hoc networks. In *Proceedings of the IEEE Wireless Communication and Networking Conference* (WCNC 2003). (vol. 3. pp. 2107–2113).

Houssos, N., Gazis, V., & Alonistioti, A. (2004). Enabling delivery of mobile services over heterogeneous converged infrastructures. *Information Systems Frontiers, 6*(3), 189–204. doi:10.1023/B:ISFI.0000037875.51842.2b

IETF. (2010). Service location protocols (SLP). Retrieved from http://www.ietf.org/html.charters/OLD/ svrloc-charter.html

IETF RFC 3261. (2002). *SIP: Session initiation protocol*.

IETF RFC 3550. (2003). *RTP: A transport protocol for real-time applications*.

IETF RFC 3588. (2003). *Diameter base protocol*.

IETF RFC 4566. (2006). *SDP: Session description protocol*.

IETS RFC: 2608. (1999). *Service location protocol*.

Kiczales, G., Hilsdale, E., Hugunin, J., Kersten, M., Palm, J., & Griswold, W. G. (2001). An overview of AspectJ. In Proceedings of the 15th European Conference on Object-Oriented Programming, (pp. 327-355).

Kniesel, G., Costanza, P., & Austermann, M. (2001). JMangler-A framework for load time transformation of Java class files. In *Proceedings of the 1st IEEE International Workshop on Source Code Analysis and Manipulation Workshop*, (pp. 98–108).

Li, X., & Wu, J. (2006). Searching techniques in peer-to-peer networks. In Wu, J. (Ed.), *Handbook of theoretical and algorithmic aspects of ad hoc, sensor, and peer-to-peer networks* (pp. 613–642). Auerbach Publications.

Loreto, S., Mecklin, T., Opsenica, M., & Rissanen, H.-M. (2010). IMS service development API and testbed. *IEEE Communications Magazine, 48*(4), 26–32. doi:10.1109/MCOM.2010.5439073

Lubell, J. (2001). *Professional XML metadata*. Wrox Press.

OWL-S. (n.d.). *1.0 release*. Retrieved from http://www.daml.org/ services/ owl-s/ 1.0

Poikselka, M., & Mayer, G. (2009). *The IMS: IP multimedia concepts and services*, 3rd edition. ISBN: 978-0-470-72196-4

Ponnekanti, S. R., & Fox, A. (2002). *SWORD: A developer toolkit for Web service composition. Technical Report*. Stanford University.

Qadeer, M. A., Khan, A. H., Ansari, J. A., & Waheed, S. (2009). IMS network architecture. In *Proceedings of the International Conference on Future Computer and Communication* (ICFCC 2009). (pp. 329-333).

SOAP. (n.d.). *W3 specification*. Retrieved from http:// www.w3.org/ TR/ soap

Sun. (2010). *JINI*. Retrieved from http:// sun. com/ jini

Tselikas, N. D., Dellas, N. L., Koutsoloukas, E. A., Kapellaki, S. H., Prezerakos, G. N., & Venieris, I. S. (2007). Distributed service provision using open APIs-based middleware: OSA/Parlay vs. JAIN performance evaluation study. *Journal of Systems and Software*, *80*(5), 765–777. doi:10.1016/j. jss.2006.06.035

UDDI. (n.d.). *Universal description, discovery and integration protocol*. Retrieved from http:// www.uddi.org

UDDI specification. (2004). Retrieved from http:// www.oasis-open.org/ committees/uddi-pec/ doc/ spec/ v3/ uddi-v3.0.2-20041019.htm

UPnP. (n.d.). *Website*. Retrieved from http:// www.upnp.org

WSDL. (n.d.). *W3 specification*. Retrieved from http:// www.w3.org/ TR/ wsdl

Yang, Y., Hassanein, H., & Mawji, A. (2006). Efficient service discovery for wireless mobile ad hoc networks. In *Proceedings of the IEEE International Conference on Computer Systems and Applications*, (pp. 571–578).

Yu, T., & Lin, K.-J. (2005). Service selection algorithms for composing complex services with multiple QoS constraints. In *Proceedings of the 3rd International Conference on Service Oriented Computing* (ICSOC2005), (pp. 130-143).

Yu, T., & Lin, K.-J. (2005). *Adaptive algorithms for finding replacement services in autonomic distributed business processes* (pp. 427–434). Proceedings of Autonomous Decentralized Systems.

Zeinalipour-Yazti, D., Kalogeraki, V., & Gunopulos, D. (2004). Information retrieval techniques for peer-to-peer networks. *Computing in Science & Engineering*, *6*(4), 20–26. doi:10.1109/ MCSE.2004.12

Zeng, L., Benatallah, B., Dumas, M., Kalagnanam, J., & Sheng, Q. Z. (2003). Quality driven Web services composition. In Proceedings of the 12th International Conference on World Wide Web, (pp. 411–421).

Section 2
Wireless Sensor Networks and Applications

Chapter 7
Evaluating the Performance of the IEEE 802.15.4 Standard in Supporting Time–Critical Wireless Sensor Networks

Carlos Lino
Universidad Politécnica de Valencia, Spain

Carlos T. Calafate
Universidad Politécnica de Valencia, Spain

Pietro Manzoni
Universidad Politécnica de Valencia, Spain

Juan-Carlos Cano
Universidad Politécnica de Valencia, Spain

Arnoldo Díaz
Instituto Tecnológico de Mexicali, México

ABSTRACT

The performance of wireless sensor networks (WSNs) at monitoring time-critical events is an important research topic, mainly due to the need to ensure that the actions to be taken upon these events are timely. To determine the effectiveness of the IEEE 802.15.4 standard at monitoring time-critical events in WSNs, we introduce a routing scheme based on drain announcements that seeks minimum routing overhead. We carried out a novel performance evaluation of the IEEE 802.15.4 technology under different conditions, to determine whether or not near-real-time event monitoring is feasible. By analyzing different simulation metrics such as packet loss rate, average end-to-end delay, and routing overhead, we determine the degree of effectiveness of the IEEE 802.15.4 standard at supporting time-critical tasks in multi-hop WSNs, evidencing its limitations upon the size and the amount of traffic flowing through the network.

DOI: 10.4018/978-1-61350-110-8.ch007

Copyright © 2012, IGI Global. Copying or distributing in print or electronic forms without written permission of IGI Global is prohibited.

INTRODUCTION

The IEEE 802.15.4 standard (IEEE 802 part 15.4, 2006) has gained great popularity in recent years in applications characterized by low-rate data transfers and strict power consumption requirements.

The ZigBee specification (ZigBee Alliance, 2008) builds upon the IEEE 802.15.4 standard, to provide the appropriate support for building monitoring applications in wireless sensor networks. In particular, it makes use of the physical (PHY) and medium access control (MAC) layers defined by the IEEE 802.15.4 standard, and defines the upper levels of the protocol stack - network and above - that the 802.15.4 standard does not cover, thus offering seamless communication with sensors, actuators and other small devices for measuring and controlling tasks that do not require high bandwidth, but require low power consumption and latency.

The MAC layer plays an important role in determining the efficiency of the bandwidth sharing in wireless channels and the energy cost of the communication (Gutiérrez, Callaway & Barrett, 2003). The IEEE 802.15.4 is a standard that defines the level of physical and medium access control for wireless personal area networks with low data rate transmissions (LR-WPAN). The 802.15.4 standard is intended for applications that require secure communication with low data transmission rate, while maximizing the battery lifetime. The current version was adopted in 2006.

Among the potential applications of the IEEE 802.15.4 technology we have time-critical event monitoring, in which the delivery time of recorded information is of utmost importance (e.g. fire, gas escape, and intruder detection). The main requirement imposed on WSNs when supporting time-critical event monitoring is that data must travel throughout the network within a short-time interval. Therefore, the worst-case delay becomes a critical issue, and it is determined by the environment and the configuration of the

WSN in terms of network topology, number of nodes, and node density.

WSNs supporting time-critical event monitoring applications are characterized by stricter requirements compared to other applications. In the former, the sensor nodes must react immediately upon the detection of an event, sending the sensed data to the drain in the shortest possible time. Notice that the relevance of the data is directly related to the response time of the WSNs (e.g., when tracking an intruder). Thus, for an effective support of time-critical event monitoring, the time needed to transfer the data packets from the sensor nodes to the drain is of utmost importance. Since end-to-end delay depends on factors such as a) the technology used, b) the routing protocol, c) the mean and worst-case number of hops, and d) the load over the network; the combined effect of these factors must be analyzed to determine the viability of a solution at supporting different critical-event monitoring applications.

In this chapter, we provide a detailed performance analysis of the IEEE 802.15.4 standard when supporting time-critical applications over wireless sensor networks.

BACKGROUND ON PERFORMANCE OF WSN APPLICATIONS

In the literature, we can find a lot of work that addresses the behaviour and performance of WSN applications. Nevertheless, only a few researchers have addressed the evaluation of the performance of IEEE 802.15.4 standard in supporting time-critical event monitoring. Zheng and Lee (Zheng & Lee, 2006) conducted a study to obtain the performance of various features, such as beacon and non-beacon modes, network autoconfiguration, tree formation and association, coordinator relocation, and orphans nodes for WSNs based on the IEEE 802.15.4 standard. They had previously described some application scenarios to show the potential of 802.15.4, including an overview of the standard and focusing on its feasibility and functionality in supporting ubiquitous networking (Zheng & Lee, 2004).

Chehri *et al.* (Chehri, Fortier & Tardif, 2007) introduced an architecture for surveillance and monitoring of mine safety. However, instead of specifying the wireless network topology used, they merely assessed the feasibility of using low-power WSN technology.

Concerning real-time WSNs, Chen *et al.* (Chen *et al.*, 2006), for the tracking of multiple targets using multi-sensor fusion, proposed an algorithm that converts the binary detection into fine positioning reports using spatial correlation. The algorithm is applied to the real-time tracking of an unknown number of people moving through an outdoor field, monitored by a WSN. They also analyzed the 802.15.4 standard, both analytically and in a simulation environment, to determine to what degree the standard satisfies the specific requirements in real-time industrial automation.

Lu *et al.* (Lu et al., 2003) described and evaluated an architecture for real-time communication in large-scale wireless sensor networks, for monitoring and control purposes. On the other hand, He *et al.* (He et al., 2005) introduced the VigilNet architecture, a large-scale sensor network system which tracks, detects and classifies targets in a timely and energy-efficient manner. VigilNet is applicable in military operations, where events of interest occur at a relatively low rate and the duration of significant events is very short.

DESCRIPTION OF IEEE 802.15.4

The IEEE 802.15.4 (IEEE 802 part 15.4, 2006) is a standard that defines the physical and medium access control, for wireless personal area networks with low rates of data transmission (LR-WPAN) layers. The 802.15.4 standard is intended for applications that require secure communication with low data transmission rate while maximizing the battery lifetime. The Zigbee specification (ZigBee Alliance, 2008) builds upon the 802.15.4 standard to provide a complete solution for building wireless sensor networks. In particular, it defines the upper levels of the protocol stack -network and application- that the 802.15.4 standard does not cover.

The IEEE 802.15.4 standard defines the physical layer specifications (PHY) and media access control (MAC) support for devices that consume minimal power and typically operate within a personal operating space (POS) of 10 m. Wireless links under the 802.15.4 standard can operate in three different license-free frequency bands, known as scientific, medical, and industrial (ISM) bands. The maximum data rates supported are 250 kbps in the 2.4 GHz band, 40 kbps in the 915 MHz band, and 20 kbps in the 868 MHz band. A total of 27 channels are allowed in the 802.15.4, including 16 channels in the 2.4 GHz band, 10 channels in the 915 band and one channel in the 868 MHz band.

TYPES OF DEVICES

The IEEE 802.15.4 standard is designed to work with two device types: Reduced Function Devices (RFDs) and Full Function Devices (FFDs). The FFDs have the ability to communicate with any device in the network within its communication range, whereas the RFDs are only able to communicate directly with FFDs. Each network consists of multiple FFDs and RFDs, with one of the FFDs designated as the coordinator of the Personal Area Network (PAN). The FFDs can operate in three different ways: device, coordinator, and PAN coordinator. The RFDs can operate only as a device.

The FFD devices can be used in any topology, and are capable of coordinating the network and communicating with other devices. Since the RFDs cannot become network coordinators, they can only communicate with a coordinator of the network and thus a star topology is created. A device in an802.15.4 network can use either a 64

Figure 1. Networks topologies supported in ZigBee

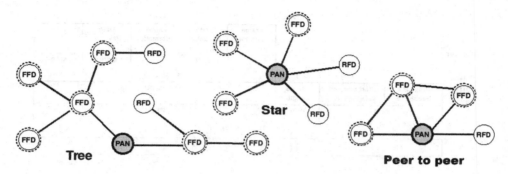

bit address or a 16 bit short address, which is assigned during the association process. Notice that, even when relying on short addresses, an 802.15.4 network has a capacity for 65,535 devices (2^{16}-1).

NETWORK TOPOLOGIES

ZigBee support three different network topologies: star, peer-to-peer, and tree. Figure 1 illustrates these three topologies.

In the star topology, the communication is established between the node devices and the coordinator of the PAN. The PAN coordinator can be connected to a main power supply, while the node devices are usually battery powered. Applications that can benefit from this topology include home automation, computer peripherals, toys and games. When a FFD is activated for the first time, it can establish its own network and become the PAN coordinator. In the peer-to-peer topology there is also a PAN coordinator. Unlike the star topology, any device can communicate with any other device that is within its range, and the network can be self-organized. Among the applications that can make use of this topology are: industrial control and monitoring, wireless sensor networks, and monitoring of inventories. It also allows multiple hops to route messages from any device to any another device within the network, thereby providing reliability in multihop routing. The tree topology is a special case of

peer-to-peer network in which most of the devices are FFDs, and where a RFD device can connect to a network tree as a leaf node at the end of the branch. The FFD can act as a coordinator, providing synchronization to other devices and coordinators. However, only one of the coordinators can become the PAN coordinator.

STRUCTURE OF DATA FRAMES

The 802.15.4 standard defines four types of frames, including: a) the beacon frame used by the coordinator, b) the data frame used for all data transfers, c) the receipt acknowledgment frame used to confirm successful frame reception, and d) the controlled MAC frame used to handle all peer-to-peer transfers.

The ZigBee protocol supports beacon and non-beacon enabled modes. However, the beacon frame adds a new level of functionality to the network. The communication from a coordinator and a node is indirect. The coordinator stores the messages and announces pending messages in the beacon frame. The nodes are most of the time in sleep state, and periodically wake up to check if they have pending messages from the coordinator, waiting for the beacon frame. If not, they go back to sleep state, with a consequent saving of energy. The beacon frames are important in the mesh and cluster tree networks, to keep all nodes synchronized without requiring that the nodes

Figure 2. Data frame of IEEE 802.15.4

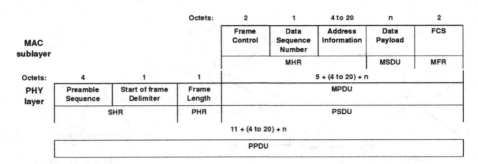

consume too much battery power, listening for long periods of time.

At the physical layer, the basic transmission frame is called PPDU (Phy Protocol Data Unit). The PPDU format begins with a synchronization header (SHR, Synchronization HeadeR), followed by a physical layer header to indicate the length of the package (PHR, Phy HeaR), and then the physical layer service data unit (PSDU, PHY Service Data Unit).

The acknowledgment frame provides the active information exchange between the receiver and the sender, to verify that the packet was received without errors. This short package uses the *quiet time*, specified by the standard, to send a short packet immediately after data packet transmission.

The MAC command frame is a mechanism for remote control or to configure the devices. Allows a centralized network manager to configure devices individually, no matter how large the network is.

Figure 2 shows the format of an 802.15.4 data frame. A MAC frame, also known as a MAC Protocol Data Unit (MPDU), consists of a MAC header (MHR), the MAC data service unit (MSDU) and the MAC footer (MFR).

The first field in the header is the frame control field, and indicates the MAC frame type that is being transmitted. In general, we could say that it characterizes the contents of the data frame. Since a data frame may contain variable information about the source and the destination, the address field size can vary between 4 and 20 bytes.

The payload field is also of variable length, and the maximum value of the MAC data payload field is equal to (127 bytes) - (25 bytes) = 102 bytes. The MPDU is then passed to the PHY as the PHY data frame payload, i.e., PSDU. The PSDU is prefixed with a synchronization header (SHR) and a PHY header (PHR), that together with PSDU conform the PHY data packet, i.e., PPDU (IEEE 802, Part 15.4, 2006).

DRAIN ANNOUNCEMENT BASED ROUTING SCHEME FOR WSNS

A protocol for wireless sensor networks should enable auto-configuration, allowing that its operation does not require personal attention. Unlike mobile ad hoc networks, sensor networks do not have large mobility requirements. It also differs from other wireless networks, such as WLAN, which were designed to have a greater transmission range and, therefore, require a constant power source. The design criteria of a routing protocol for sensor networks depends directly on the implementation and on its performance, which could be measured through metrics such as latency, data loss and routing load.

In this section, we briefly describe some of the best-known routing protocols for ad hoc networks. Moreover, we show different drain announcement based routing schemes (DABRs), and introduce the new proposed routing scheme.

DIFFERENCES BETWEEN THE DRAIN ANNOUNCEMENT BASED ROUTING SCHEMES AND SOME EXISTING ROUTING PROTOCOLS

Routing protocols are classified according to the way they establish routes to the target node. They can be classified into three categories: proactive, reactive and hybrid protocols. In the case of proactive protocols, all routes are calculated before they are needed. In the case of reactive protocols, the routes are discovered and established as requested, i.e., the protocol finds a route to reach a target node, when a node needs to send it some information. Finally, hybrid protocols combine the advantages of proactive and of reactive routing, initially establishing some routes proactively and discovering reactive routes when new nodes are activated. According to the classification of the protocols, the routing schemes based on the drain announcement are categorized as a proactive protocol, since the path to the target node is built before is needed. For this reason, in this section we review only the most important proactive protocols proposed in the literature, in order to specify the differences with respect to the routing scheme we propose. These protocols are the DSDV (Destination Sequence Distance Vector) (Perkins & Bhagwat, 1994), the WRP (Wireless Routing Protocol) (Murthy & Garcia-Luna-Aceves, 1996), and the OLSR (Optimized Link-State Routing Algorithm) (Jacquet et al., 2001).

In the DSDV protocol, neighbor nodes periodically exchange their full routing tables to estimate the distance to the other nodes that are not neighbors. The amendments made to the DSDV protocol solve the routing loop problem by introducing sequence numbers for determining new routes. Although DSDV only provides a route for each destination, it always chooses the shortest path based on the number of hops to the destination. The DSDV protocol uses two types of update messages: a larger (full-dump) message and a small (incremental) message. Full-dump messages carry all the available routing information, whereas incremental update messages carry only the routing information changed since the last full dump.

The WRP protocol differs from DSDV in that it uses a set of tables whose main objective is to keep more accurate routing information. Each node is responsible for maintaining four tables: distance table (DT), routing table (RT), link cost table (LCT), and a message retransmission list (MRL). The MRL table is used to manage the delivery of routing update packets. Each table entry contains the sequence number that identifies the route update packet, a retransmission counter, an array of agreement with one entry per neighbor, and a list of units sent in the update packet. The table also stores which units should be retransmitted, and which neighbors are yet to acknowledge an update message. The nodes are reported including changes to the routes through the update packets. These packets are sent between neighbors and contain the elements to update the routes. The nodes send these packets when they process the update packets received from other neighbors, or when they detect a change in the link to a neighbor. If a node is not sending messages, it must periodically broadcast a HELLO package. When a node receives a HELLO message from a new node, the node will be added to the routing table and a copy of its routing table will be sent to the new node.

The OLSR protocol was designed with the aim of reducing the size of control messages and to minimize the overhead of the flooding of control traffic. Using HELLO messages, nodes find their one and two hop neighbors through their responses. The sender node can then select its multipoint relays (MPR), which are one hop away nodes that offer the best route to the two hop nodes. Each node has an MPR selector set, which describes the nodes that have selected it as an MPR node. This protocol uses topology control (TC) messages along with MPR forwarding to disseminate neighbor information throughout the

Table 1. Comparative of the routing schemes

Protocol	Properties					
	Each node maintains a routing table	Each node maintains an entry in routing table	Upgrade routes	Identification of the next hop to destination	Stored the number of hops to target	Broadcast to update routes
DSDV	Yes	No	By the algorithm	Yes	Yes	**By nodes**
WRP	4 tables are used	In the 4 tables	Very often using HELLO messages	Yes	Yes	**No, messages to neighbors**
OLSR	Yes	No	With HELLO messages and TC messages	Yes	Is calculated	**No, messages to neighbors**
DABR	No	Yes	Defined at the beginning	Yes	Yes	**Drain**

network. Also, the OLSR uses host and network association (HNA) messages to disseminate network route advertisements in a similar way the TC messages advertise host routes.

Table 1 shows a comparison of the routing protocols discussed in this section, where we include our proposed routing scheme.

Overview of the Drain Announcement Based Routing Scheme

The drain announcement based routing (DABR) intends to reduce the route discovery overhead incurred by the sensor nodes that require sending the sensed information to its destination. The proposed algorithm also reduces the end-to-end delay by minimizing the routing traffic in the communication channels.

To explain the DABR scheme, we should first mention that our target WSN environment is based on a multi-hop, single-drain scheme, where sensor nodes are distributed with a density that is close to the transmission range inherent to the IEEE 802.15.4 technology (10 meters). In the case of the drain node, this may be a fixed or mobile node with the ability to communicate and receive information sent from the different sensor nodes. The deployment of sensor nodes in these applications can be either random or manual, being that

the relative location of sensor nodes is closely related to the performance of the routing protocol.

Below are the major steps taken by the proposed drain announcement based routing scheme:

1. The drain node is announced via broadcast messages with sequential sequence numbers.
2. Drain neighbor nodes (nodes within the transmission range of the drain) receive the drain announcement.
3. Neighbor nodes store the path towards the source node (drain), and they rebroadcast the message to all their neighbor nodes.
4. If a node receives a message containing a route towards the drain more than once, it gives preference to routes that contain the least number of hops towards the drain node and, afterward, it gives preference to the highest sequence numbers.
5. Each entry in the routing table is associated with a lifetime timer, during which the route will remain valid.
6. The routes are refreshed through periodic drain announcements that are propagated to all nodes.
7. The path information is maintained in the routing table of each node until the link with the neighbor nodes is lost or until the timeout is triggered.

Figure 3. Propagation of broadcast sent by the drain

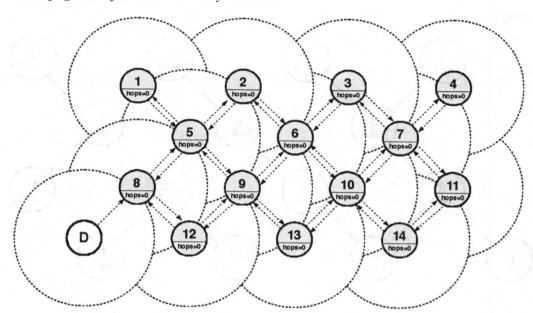

In Fig. 3 we can observe how the drain node (*D*) initiates the process by sending a broadcast message, which is only received by the node that is within its transmission range (node *8*). Node 8 will store the route to the drain and will forward it using a broadcast message to its neighbor nodes (nodes *5* and *12*), which will repeat the same procedure.

Fig. 4 shows the routes and the number of hops required for each node to reach the drain. For instance, node *8*, which received the first broadcast, is one hop away from the drain, whereas nodes *5* and *12* require two hops to reach the drain.

The proposed path discovery algorithm adopted by the drain announcement based routing scheme for WSNs, is shown below. The input parameters of the algorithm are: the drain node identifier (*Sink_ID*), the interval to send broadcast messages and to refresh the route in all sensor nodes (*interval*), and the stop time (*stop_time*), which represents how long the simulation will run (assuming that the algorithm is used to perform a simulation). Within the main body of algorithm,

we can observe a loop where function *DrainNotify* is invoked, Through the use of this function, nodes can discover the routes to the drain node using broadcast communication, as explained previously. The loop finishes when the execution time is equal to the input parameter *stop_time*. We also show the body of the *DrainNotify* function. It can be observed that the drain node will broadcast messages to all sensor nodes. When these packets are received by all nodes, they will be able to determine the path toward the drain node.

```
Input: Sink_ID, interval, stop_time
Variables: packet, time, broadcast_id
BEGIN
    time = 0
    broadcast_id = 0
    REPEAT
        DrainNotify(Node_sink)
        time += interval
    UNTIL (time < stop_time)
END
```

Figure 4. Number of hops to reach the drain, as recorded by the nodes, after the drain broadcasted the first message

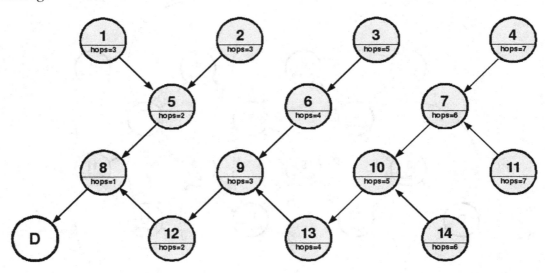

```
FUNCTION DrainNotify(Node_source)
    VAR broadcast_id, request, rtable,
packet
    packet.Node_source = Sink_ID
    packet.Node_dst = broadcast_addr
    packet.msg_type = DRAIN_ANNOUNCEMENT
    packet.msg_seqnum = broadcast_id++
    packet.hop_count = 0
    broadcast(packet)
END DrainNotify
```

When relying on the aforementioned routing mechanism to create and maintain routes, any sensor node willing to send or forward a report packet to the drain operates by using standard procedures: it consults its routing table to see if there is a valid path towards the drain, and then sends the information using that route. In case that no route is available, all traffic is discarded until a route is restored. Notice that when doing critical-event monitoring tasks, near-real-time feedback from the network is expected, and buffering data for long periods of time becomes meaningless.

The implementation of the DABR protocol in the ns-2 simulator is focused on scenarios where the drain and sensor nodes are fixed, distributed in a grid within a physical space. Depending on the configuration of the event to simulate, the routing protocol sends a broadcast to discover routes immediately after the sensor nodes are associated with the drain node, and maintaining those paths during the whole simulation time in those cases where it is unlikely that the sensor nodes are disabled or lose the route; otherwise, periodic announcements are generated by the drain node to maintain the routes updated.

SIMULATION RESULTS

To evaluate the performance of the IEEE 802.15.4 standard in supporting the time-critical WSNs, we used the ns-2 network simulator (The Network Simulator – ns-2, 2008). The methodology followed for conducting the tests was the following: we implemented and validated our routing protocol for WSNs (described before) using the ns-2 network simulator. In each scenario, there is a single drain node which is randomly positioned and which assumes the role of PAN. The transmission range used for all nodes was the maximum allowed by the 802.15.4 standard,

Table 2. Simulation parameters for set of experiments #1

Number of nodes	200
PHY/MAC	IEEE 802.15.4/2.4 GHz band
Traffic type	CBR
Simulation time	600 seconds
Simulation area	140x140 meters
Sensor topology	Grid
Routing protocol	Drain announcement based routing scheme for WSNs
Transmission range	10 meters
Packet size	50 bytes
Number of traffic sources	20
Traffic load	0.33, 1, 2, 10, 20 and 66.66 pkt/s

i.e., 10 meters, and the radio propagation model is two-ray ground. Other parameters related to the scenario setting are shown in Table 1 and Table 2, each one reflecting a set of experiments. Our simulation experiments were based on a series of repetitions, changing parameters on each experiment, in order to achieve a holistic performance assessment of IEEE 802.15.4 standard.

Next, we describe the main configuration differences between the two sets of the experiments carried out. In the first set of experiments, we generated a scenario with 200 nodes in a grid, where the number of sensors generating traffic was 20, which were randomly selected. The number of packets generated per second used was: 0.33, 1, 2, 10, 20 and 66.66 packets per second. In the second set of experiments, we analyzed the scalability of the network by using 40, 80, 120, 160, 200 and 400 sensor nodes, maintaining the number of source nodes fixed at 20, with a data rate of a packet every 0.33 seconds.

For each experiment we obtained three different metrics: the packet loss rate, the average end-to-end delay, and the routing overhead.

Concerning to the *packet loss rate*, it indicates the percentage of data packets transmitted that are

not received successfully. This metric is obtained according to the following equation:

$$Loss(\%)= (Number\_of\_data\_packets\_lost/ Number\_of\_data\_packets\_sent)*100$$

Concerning to the second metric, *average end-to-end delay*, it allows us to know the time it takes for a message to travel from the originating sensor to the drain node, and it is obtained using the following equation (Marandin, 2009):

$$Avg\_delay=\Sigma_i(Reception\_time_i-Transmission\_time_i)/Total\_number\_of\_data\_packets\_received$$

Finally, the third metric, *normalized routing load (NRL)*, is defined as the ratio between the number of routing packets transmitted and the number of data packets received, and it is obtained using the equation shown next:

$$NRL=Number\_of\_control\_packets\_sent/ Number\_of\_data\_packets\_sent$$

EVALUATING THE IMPACT OF NETWORK TRAFFIC

In this first set of experiments, we analyzed the behavior of the WSN when increasing the amount of traffic injected per source. The parameters used in these simulation experiments can be observed in Table 2. We used a fixed number of traffic sources and increased the packet injection rate on a per-source basis.

Figure 5(a) shows the performance achieved with the drain announcement based routing protocol. With respect to the percentage of data loss, it increases quite sharply for low load values, reaching about 32% loss when injecting 1 packet per second per source, for a total load of merely 8 Kbit/s (notice that the maximum data rate for IEEE 802.15.4 is of 250 Kbit/s when operating in the 2.4 GHz band). When traffic increases to values

Figure 5. Packet loss ratio (a) and average end-to-end delay (b) when varying load

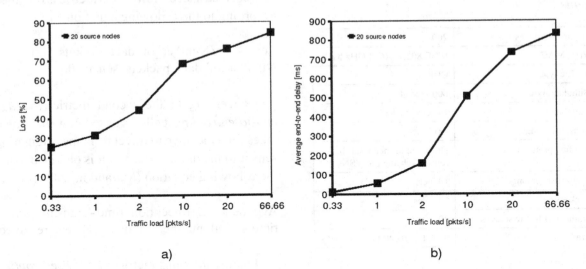

a)   b)

Figure 6. Number of routing/injected packets (a) and normalized routing load (b) when varying the packet injection rate on a per-source basis

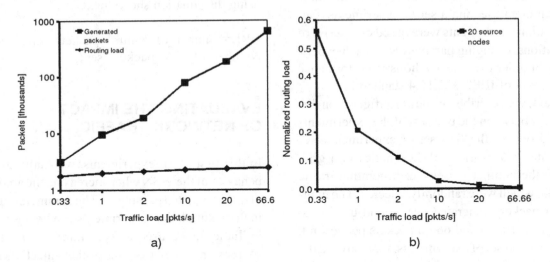

a)   b)

greater than 10 packets per second, the percent of loss increases drastically, reaching almost at 90% of packet loss when the traffic load is of 66.66 packets per second.

Figure 5(b) shows the obtained results for the average end-to-end delay when varying the load. We can see that the average delay keeps a direct relationship with the load, being that delay values

become prohibitive for near-real-time responsiveness (<500 ms) when sources were injecting 10 pkt/s each.

Concerning routing overhead, Figure 6 (a) shows the routing load for increasing traffic load. We find that the routing load increases slightly with traffic due to occasional malfunctioning related to congestion.

Table 3. Simulation parameters for set of experiments #2

Number of nodes	40, 80, 120, 160, 200 and 400
PHY/MAC	IEEE 802.15.4/2.4 GHz band
Traffic type	CBR
Simulation time	600 seconds
Simulation area	63x63, 91x91, 112x112, 133x133, 140x140 and 200x200 meters
Sensor topology	Grid
Routing protocol	Drain announcement based routing scheme for WSNs
Transmission range	10 meters
Packet size	50 bytes
Number of traffic sources	20
Traffic load	0.33 pkt/s

Figure 6(b) shows the normalized routing load for the range of packets transmitted (0.33, 1, 2, 10, 20 and 66.66 packets/second). We can observe that, as the traffic load increases, the routing overhead remains mostly the same. This leads to a steep decay in the normalized routing overhead of our proposal.

Scalability of our Approach

In this second set of experiments, we analyzed the scalability of the WSN when varying the total area of the simulation, while maintaining the sensor density fixed. Thus, when the area was increased, we proportionally increased the number of sensors to maintain the sensor density at 10000 sensors per square kilometer.

The simulation parameters for this set of experiments are shown in Table 3. Compared to the previous experiments, the total load is now fixed since we do not vary the number of sources nor the load injected per source.

Figure 7(a) shows the packet loss ratio for the different scenarios analyzed. We can appreciate losses increasing from 6.5% to 13.7% for the set of scenarios simulated. Notice that the percentage of data loss increases almost linearly with the scenario size/number of nodes, being the loss rate itself considered moderate, although not prohibitive for our target application.

Concerning the end-to-end delay metric, the results obtained are shown in Figure 7(b). The average delay increases from 46 milliseconds (40 nodes) up to 319 milliseconds (400 nodes). At his point, it is worth mentioning that the average end-to-end delay depends significantly on the position of the source nodes with respect to the drain node. Anyway, under no circumstances did it surpass the 500 ms, a threshold value below which we believe near-real-time monitoring can be achieved adequately.

Figure 8(a) shows the routing load when increasing the number of nodes/scenario size. Notice that, despite the number of generated data packets remains approximately the same for all tests, the routing load increases proportionally to the number of nodes, as expected. In particular, as depicted by the normalized routing load chart in Figure 8(b), its growth approaches the threshold of one, beyond which there will be more routing packets than data packets in the network, which can be problematic since channel resources are scarce.

Figure 7. Packet loss ratio (a) and average end-to-end delay (b) when varying the number of nodes per scenario

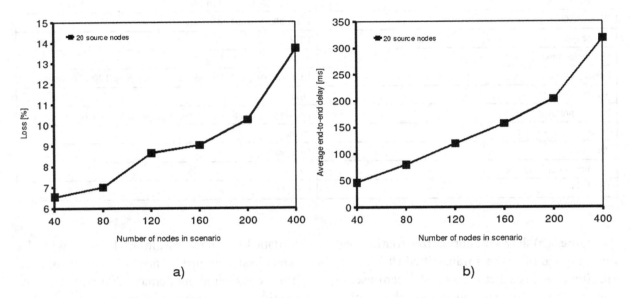

a)

b)

Figure 8. Number of routing/injected packets (a) and normalized routing load (b) when varying the number of nodes per scenario

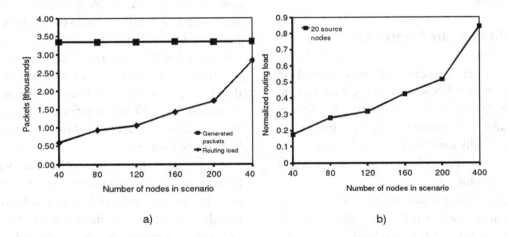

a)

b)

FUTURE RESEARCH DIRECTIONS

Many of the available research works focus on specific protocol layers, missing a more global overview. Thus, we believe that having an application-layer perspective of performance is of utmost importance. For this reason, developing

tools to generate events which can be used as input to simulators, and then developing tools to obtain application-layer results based on simulation data is necessary to develop high-quality research in this field prior to actual deployment.

With respect to generating time-critical events, such tools should integrate representative classes of time-critical events in WSNs, including intruder tracking and gas/fire propagation monitoring. Intruder-based events could be supported by offering several mobility patterns and options. In the case of gas/fire propagation events, both indoor and outdoor scenarios could be considered.

Another interesting issue about routing protocols is the consideration of drain node mobility. Most of the current protocols assume that the sensor nodes and sink are stationary (Akkaya & Younis, 2003). However, there might be situations, such as battle environments, where the drain needs to be mobile. In such cases, an appropriate routing protocol is needed to update the routes to the drain node. The development of a new routing protocol must be able to handle the overhead of routing due to the mobility of the drain, thus providing a minimum delivery time of packets.

CONCLUSION

In this chapter, we make a performance analysis of the IEEE 802.15.4 standard to assess its effectiveness at supporting time-critical event monitoring applications. To achieve this goal, we developed a routing protocol based on drain announcements that reduces the amount routing traffic on the network to a minimum. Our main purpose was to reduce interference of control traffic upon data traffic as much as possible.

In general, our simulation measurements showed that, despite the performance results in terms of loss rate, end-to-end delay and routing overhead were not overly satisfactory, the performance of the IEEE 802.15.4 standard was adequate to achieve reliable support for time-critical event monitoring.

In order to have a comprehensive overview on the performance of the IEEE 802.15.4 standard in supporting time-critical wireless sensor networks, we defined three sets of tests where the purpose was to assess: (i) the saturation threshold when varying the number of sensors generating traffic,

(ii) the saturation threshold when varying the load injected per node, and (iii) the scalability limits when increasing the size and the number of sensors in the network.

The results from the first set of tests show that with only seven active sensors injecting a minimal load, the loss rate was already above 20%, although delay values remained below 500 ms even with 40 sources of traffic. Concerning the second set of tests, we find that loss and delay are extremely sensitive to the load injected per node, increasing drastically even for very low load values. Delay values experienced similar growth, and the increase in terms of control traffic evidenced that the network suffers from some stability limitations. Finally, the third set of tests showed that all load, delay and routing overhead increased almost linearly with the number of nodes that comprised the WSN, although the range of values for delay and loss were not prohibitive for our target application.

Overall we found that the IEEE 802.15.4 is a technology that imposes strong limitations in terms of the amount of traffic that can be supported in a WSN environment. Thus, we consider that it can be used to support time-critical event monitoring applications as long as two basic conditions are met: (i) the WSN is not simultaneously being used to perform other measurements such as temperature, humidity, etc., or these can be disabled during the monitoring process; (ii) when the monitoring process is active, the number of nodes simultaneously active and their updating frequency should be very low to reduce the total load in the WSN to a minimum.

REFERENCES

Akkaya, K., & Younis, M. (2003). *A survey on protocols for wireless sensor networks. Ad Hoc networks*. Elsevier.

Chehri, A., Fortier, P., & Tardif, P. M. (2006). *Security monitoring using wireless sensor networks.* Annual Conference on Communication Networks and Services Research.

Chen, P., Oh, S., Manzo, M., Sinopoli, B., Sharp, C., & Whitehouse, K. Sastry, S. (2006). *Instrumenting wireless sensor networks for real-time surveillance.* International Conference on Robotics and Automation, ICRA 2006.

Gutiérrez, J. A., Callaway-Jr, E. H., & Barrett-Jr, R. L. (2003). *Low-rate wireless personal area networks. Enabling wireless sensors with IEEE 802.15.4. Standards Information Network.* IEEE Press.

He, T., Vicaire, P., Yan, T., Luo, L., Gu, L., Zhou, G., ... Abdelzaher, T. (2005). *Achieving real-time target tracking using wireless sensor networks.*

IEEE 802, Part 15.4. (2006). *Wireless medium access control (MAC) and physical layer specifications for low-rate wireless personal area networks* (WPANs). IEEE Computer Society.

Jacquet, P., Mühlethaler, P., Clausen, T., Laouiti, A., Qayyum, A., & Viennot, L. (2001). Optimized link state routing protocol for ad hoc networks. *Proceedings IEEE International Multi Topic Conference: Technology for the 21st Century.*

Lu, C., Blum, B. M., Abdelzaher, T. F., Stankovic, J. A., & He, T. (2003). *Rap: A real-time communication architecture for large-scale wireless sensor networks.* Real-Time and Embedded Technology and Applications Symposium.

Marandin, D. (2009). *Simulation of IEEE 802.15.4/ ZigBee with network simulator 2* (NS-2). Retrieved October 2009 from http://www.ifn.et.tu-dresden. de/~marandin/ZigBee/ZigBeeSimulation.html

Murthy, S., & Garcia-Luna-Aceves, J. J. (1996). An efficient routing protocol for wireless networks. *Mobile Networks and Applications,* 1.

Perkins, C., & Bhagwat, P. (1994). *Highly dynamic destination-sequenced distance-vector routing (DSDV) for mobile computers.* SIGCOMM Conference on Communications Architectures, Protocols and Applications, vol 24.

The Network Simulator. (2008). *NS-2.* Retrieved January 2010 from http://www.isi.edu/nsnam/ns/

Zheng, J., & Lee, M. J. (2004). Will IEEE 802.15.4 make ubiquitous networking a reality? A discussion on a potential low power, low bit rate standard. *IEEE Communications Magazine,* 42.

Zheng, J., & Lee, M. J. (2006). *A comprehensive performance study of IEEE 802.15.4 sensor network operations. IEEE Press.* Wiley Interscience.

ZigBee Alliance. (2008). *Network specification.* Retrieved January 2010 from http://www.zigbee.org/ZigBeeSpecificationDownloadRequest/ tabid/311/Default.aspx

ADDITIONAL READING

Abdalhaq, B. (2004). A methodology to enhance the prediction of forest fire propagation. PhD thesis, Universitat Autònoma de Barcelona, España.

Ad, M., Royer, E. M., Perkins, C. E., & Das, S. R. (1999). Ad hoc on-demand distance vector (aodv) routing.

Akyildiz, I. F., Su, W., Sankarasubramaniam, Y., & Cayirci, E. (2002). A survey on sensor networks. *Communications Magazine, IEEE, 40*(8), 102–114. doi:10.1109/MCOM.2002.1024422

Alazzawi, L. & Elkateeb, A. (2008). Performance evaluation of the wsn routing protocols scalability. J. Comp. Sys., Netw., and Comm., 2008:1–9.

Alexandridis, A., Vakalis, D., Siettos, C. I., & Bafas, G. V. (2008). *A cellular automata model for forest fire spread prediction: The case of the wildfire that swept through spetses island in 1990.* Elsevier. Applied Mathematics and Computation.

Baronti, P., Pillai, P., Chook, V., Chessa, S., Gotta, A., & Hu, Y. (2007). Wireless sensor networks: A survey on the state of the art and the 802.15.4 and zigbee standards. *Computer Communications*, *30*(7), 1655–1695. doi:10.1016/j.comcom.2006.12.020

Cam, T., Boleng, J., & Davies, V. (2002). A survey of mobility models for ad hoc network research.

Dousse, O., Tavoularis, C., & Thiran, P. (2006). Delay of intrusion detection in wireless sensor networks. In MobiHoc '06: Proceedings of the 7th ACM international symposium on Mobile ad hoc networking and computing, pages 155–165, New York, NY, USA. ACM.

He, T., Krishnamurthy, S., Stankovic, J. A., Abdelzaher, T., Luo, L., Stoleru, R., et al. (2004). Energy-efficient surveillance system using wireless sensor networks. In MobiSys '04: Proceedings of the 2nd international conference on Mobile systems, applications, and services, pages 270–283, New York, NY, USA. ACM.

He, T., Vicaire, P., Yan, T., Luo, L., Gu, L., Zhou, G., et al. (2006). Achieving real-time target tracking using wireless sensor networks. In 12th IEEE Real-Time and Embedded Technology and Applications Symposium (RTAS'06), pages 37–48. IEEE.

Himoto, K., & Tanaka, T. (2008). Development and validation of a physics-based urban fire spread model. Elsevier. Fire safety journal.

José. García, A. B., Corredor, I., López, L., Hernández, V., & da Silva, A. (2008). Guaranteeing QoS in Wireless Sensor Networks, chapter 9. Taylor & Francis Inc.

Lee, J. S. (2006). Performance evaluation of ieee 802.15.4 for low-rate wireless personal area networks. Consumer Electronics. *IEEE Transactions on, 52*(3), 742–749.

Li, D., Wong, K. D., Hu, Y. H., & Sayeed, A. M. (2002). Detection, classification, and tracking of targets. *IEEE Signal Processing Magazine, 19*(2), 17–29. doi:10.1109/79.985674

Lu, C., Blum, B. M., Abdelzaher, T. F., Stankovic, J. A., & He, T. (2002). Rap: A real-time communication architecture for large-scale wireless sensor networks. Real-Time and Embedded Technology and Applications Symposium, IEEE, 0:55–66.

Miyashita, M. (2004). A line in the sand: a wireless sensor network for target detection, classification, and tracking. *Computer Networks, 46*(5), 605–634. doi:10.1016/j.comnet.2004.06.007

Perkins, C. E., Royer, E. M., Das, S. R., & Marina, M. K. (2002). Performance comparison of two on-demand routing protocols for ad hoc networks. *Personal Communications, IEEE, 8*(1), 16–28. doi:10.1109/98.904895

Rehm, R. G. (2008). The effects of winds from burning structures on ground-fire propagation at the wildland-urban interface. 12:477–496.

Ruiz, L. B., & Siqueira, I. G. Leonardo, Wong, H. C., Marcos, J., & Loureiro, A. A. F. (2004). Fault management in event-driven wireless sensor networks. In MSWiM '04: Proceedings of the 7th ACM international symposium on Modeling, analysis and simulation of wireless and mobile systems, pages 149–156, New York, NY, USA. ACM.

Sankarasubramaniam, Y., Akan, O. B., & Akyildiz, I. F. (2003). Esrt: event-to-sink reliable transport in wireless sensor networks. In MobiHoc '03: Proceedings of the 4th ACM international symposium on Mobile ad hoc networking & computing, pages 177–188, New York, NY, USA. ACM.

Shah, S., Khandre, A., Shirole, M., & Bhole, G. (2008). Performance evaluation of ad hoc routing protocols using ns2 simulation. Society, I. E. E. E. C. (2006). Part 15.4: Wireless Medium Access Control (MAC) and Physical Layer (PHY) Specifications for Low-Rate Wirelees Personal Area Networks (WPANs). IEEE Computer Society, ieee std 802.15.4 2006 edition.

Stam, J. and Fiume, E. (1995). Depicting fire and other gaseous phenomena using diffusion process. ACM 701-4/95/008:7.

Sullivan, A. L. (2007). A review of wildland fire spread modelling, 1990-present 2: Empirical and quasi-empirical models.

Wang, X., Lizier, J., Obst, O., Prokopenko, M., & Wang, P. (2008). Spatiotemporal anomaly detection in gas monitoring sensor networks. In Verdone, R . In Networks, W. S. (Ed.), *Lecture Notes in Computer Science* (*Vol. 4913*, pp. 90–105). Berlin, Heidelberg: Springer Berlin Heidelberg.

Yu, L., Wang, N., & Meng, X. (2005). Real-time forest fire detection with wireless sensor networks. In Proceedings. 2005 International Conference on Wireless Communications, Networking and Mobile Computing, 2005., volume 2, pages 1214–1217. IEEE.

Chapter 8
Data Gathering with Multi–Attribute Fusion in Wireless Sensor Networks

Kai Lin
Dalian University of Technology, China

Lei Wang
Dalian University of Technology, China

Lei Shu
Osaka University, Japan

Al-Sakib Khan Pathan
International Islamic University, Malaysia

ABSTRACT

This chapter addresses the problem of data gathering with multi-attribute fusion over a bandwidth and energy constrained wireless sensor network (WSN). As there are strong correlations between data gathered from sensor nodes in close physical proximity, effective in-network fusion schemes involve minimizing such redundancy and hence reducing the load in wireless sensor networks. Considering a complicated environment, each sensor node must be equipped with more than one type of sensor module to monitor multi-targets; hence, the complexity for the fusion process is increased due to the existence of various physical attributes. In this chapter, by investigating the process and performance of multi-attribute fusion in data gathering of WSNs, we design a self-adaptive threshold to balance the different change rates of each attributive data. Furthermore, we present a method to measure the energy-conservation efficiency of multi-attribute fusion. Then, a novel energy equilibrium routing method is proposed to balance and save energy in WSNs, which is named multi-attribute fusion tree (MAFT). The establishment of MAFT is determined by the remaining energy of sensor nodes and the energy-conservation efficiency of data fusion. Finally, the energy saving performance of the scheme is demonstrated through comprehensive simulations. The chapter concludes by identifying some open research issues on this topic.

DOI: 10.4018/978-1-61350-110-8.ch008

Copyright © 2012, IGI Global. Copying or distributing in print or electronic forms without written permission of IGI Global is prohibited.

INTRODUCTION

With the advancements in distributed computing and Internet technologies, networks such as wireless sensor networks (WSNs) are increasingly finding their usage in various distribute computing applications. In the dual role of wireless communication technology and chip fabrication technology, WSNs appeared for different types of tasks (Vuran, Akan, & Akyildiz, 2004), (Bettstetter & Hartmann, 2005). This kind of network can interact with the physical environment and with data processing and wireless communication ability; the sensor nodes in the network can accomplish complex monitoring tasks. The sensor nodes are not traditional simple perception device and transforming the physical signal to digital signal, but a physical unit integrated with perception module, data processing module and wireless communication module. These nodes are expected to be inexpensive and can be deployed in a large number in harsh environments, which implies that the sensors are typically operating unattended without any human intervention for most of the network's lifetime. Each sensor node has its control area to monitor the surrounding environment by perception equipment, optical equipment, chemical analysis equipment, and electromagnetic equipment. Certainly, some special functions can be achieved by setting some functional equipment. WSN has become an important technology with scientific research and practical value in the application of military scouting, industrial production monitoring, city management, ecological monitoring, forest fire monitoring, medical care, disaster rescue, terrorism presentation, and dangerous area domination (Baunach, Kolla, & Mühlberger, 2007).

Figure 1 shows the connecting architecture of Internet and WSNs. It is said that Internet changes the communication method among people while WSNs connect the logical and physical worlds together. By the combination of Internet and WSN,

WSNs change the interaction between people and nature. People can appreciate the world directly from the combination of these two networks and extend the current function of network and further explore the world.

After the network is deployed, the sensor nodes monitor and collect various environmental data by distributed computing (Sahoo, Hsieh, & Sheu, 2007), (Shon et al., 2009). The sensory data are transmitted to the sink node by multi-hop method. It can be seen that the sensor node has the double functions of terminal and routing for collecting and processing data. Currently, some crucial technologies in WSNs are poorly developed while the great challenge is the limitation of energy supply, computing capacity, and network communication bandwidth. Therefore, one of the essential research problems is how to effectively utilize limited resources to achieve high performance in data gathering.

Considering the high deployment density of sensor nodes, content redundancy of transmitted sensory data can occur during data gathering process. If all of the redundant packets are transmitted, the energy and bandwidth will be heavily wasted. For the sake of improving the resource utilization, data fusion is employed in WSNs (Ruth et al., 2006), (Li & Mohapatra, 2007), (Pantazis et al., 2008), which brings some benefits: Firstly, the data fusion can save energy consumption. As the monitoring area is overlapped, data fusion process can delete abundant data and save overall transmission energy. Secondly, more accurate data can be obtained. Considering the cost, the accuracy of one sensor node is not high. The correctness cannot be guaranteed only by gathering data from several sensor nodes, some data have to be acquired by monitoring multiple sensor nodes deployed on the same target area. Thirdly, the data fusion is beneficial for improving data gathering efficiency. The reduction of data transmission can enhance the wireless channel efficiency by decreasing the transmission congestion, conflict,

Figure 1. Connecting architecture of Internet and WSNs

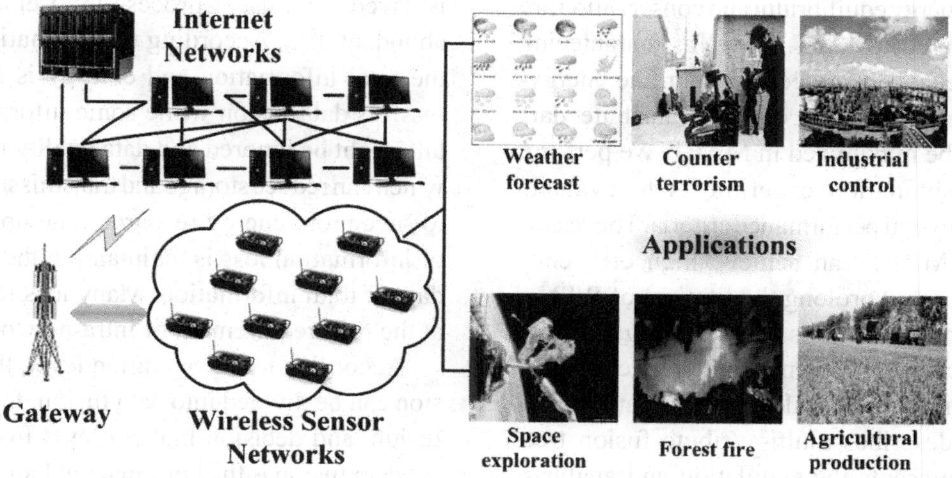

and time delay. Data fusion can combine with many network protocols. For example, the collected data can be filtered step by step. In the network layer, many routing protocols combine the data fusion mechanism to reduce the data transmission. For these reasons, data fusion has become an indispensable technology for WSNs.

With the development of WSN, data fusion is starting to be used in combination with other technologies, such as fusion-driven routing. In WSNs, routing is not only responsible for data gathering, but also providing the foundation of data fusion, time synchronization, and target location (Wang, Yu, & Shang, 2005). The performance criterion of a fusion-driven routing method is whether it can remove the unnecessary links and utilize the energy efficiently. To avoid energy holes caused by excessive energy consumption of partial sensor nodes, the establishment of routing method should guarantee both energy equilibrium and maximum reduction in energy consumption and prolong the lifetime of the whole network. Additionally, as the sensor node is equipped with multi-type sensors, if the network adopt heterogeneous node, then the difference of gathered data has higher requirement for data fusion. Even if the homogeneous data

are adopted, the new problem will also be caused due to the different types of data. In this case, the importance of our research is to find out how to fuse data under homogeneous networks, which is a major work published in (Lin et al., 2010).

In this chapter, the current related schemes are summarized and compared. Then, we discuss the data fusion process in both homogeneous and heterogeneous WSNs, and analyze the negative effect of a multi-attribute change rate difference on the fusion process. Based on the analysis, we propose a self-adapting threshold to solve this problem. This method can balance different change rates of each attributive data. Furthermore, we analyze the energy-conservation efficiency of multi-attribute fusion in data gathering. For multi-attribute fusion, the correlations of packets required for fusion is much lower than those of single-attribute fusion. In this case, the computing cost for the complicated fusion process cannot be simply neglected. We consider both the effect of multi-attributes and the cost of data fusion in our research. Then, we present a method to measure the energy-conservation efficiency of multi-attribute fusion. In combination with multi-attribute fusion and routing, we propose a new energy equilibrium routing scheme, viz., multi-attribute fusion routing (MAFT). Energy equilibrium and conservation are both considered in MAFT. As well as guaranteeing some degree of energy equilibrium, the energy-conservation efficiency of multi-attribute data fusion can be maximized in MAFT. We perform extensive simulation experiments to evaluate MAFT by several performance criteria. The results show that MAFT can achieve high efficiency performance and prolong the lifetime of WSNs.

The remainder of this chapter is organized as follows. Section 2 presents some related works. Section 3 introduces multi-attribute data fusion. Section 4 describes multi-attribute fusion tree. Section 5 presents the simulation and analysis. We summarize our work and conclude the chapter in Section 7 after mentioning the future research directions in Section 6.

BACKGROUND

Our work is closely related to the data fusion mechanism, energy efficient routing, and energy balancing design in WSN. We will give a brief review of the works in these three aspects.

The Related Work in Data Fusion in WSN

In WSNs, the purpose of data fusion is saving energy consumption and prolonging the network lifetime. By eliminating abundant data in the network and forming much efficient data after fusion, the network flux and energy consumption can be reduced. The data fusion can be classified from different viewpoints. There are three types of typical data from; (1) information content, (2) the relationship between data fusion, and (3) application data semantic meaning.

According to the information content before and after fusion process, the data fusion can be divided into lossless fusion and loss fusion. In lossless fusion, all the detailed data information is saved. The usual process is to eliminate the abundant data. According to information theory, the total information and entropy is limited by lossless data fusion while some information detail might be ignored and data quality is reduced, which can reduce storage and transmission amount to save more energy resource. The upper bound of information loss is maintaining the necessary data of total information. Many loss fusions aim at the data requirement of intra-network.

According to the operation level, the data fusion can be divided into data fusion, feature level fusion, and decision-making level fusion. Here, the data fusion is the bottom level facing direct to data. In the target identification application, it is also called pixel-level fusion. The operation target includes pixel data classification, combination, and reduction of the abundant data. The feature-level fusion abstracts some data characterization and decision-making level fusion can complete the judgment and classification. By some simple logical operation, the final decision can be obtained. As the calculating power and energy are limited for sensor node, there is less decision-making level fusion process in the current applications of WSNs.

According to the semantic of data, the data fusion can be divided into application of dependent fusion and independent fusion. The dependent fusion should understand the semantic of data from the application layer and obtain the maximum compression. However, this may result in a large information loss. Additionally, the semantic problem of multi-layer causes more difficulty to protocol stack. For the independent fusion, the understanding of the data semantic of application layer is not necessary since it can fuse the data from data link layer directly. This technology realizes the data fusion as an independent level and simple relationships between different layers. As the data fusion is preceded by the data from different layers, these methods will not loss any information. However, the data fusion efficiency is lower than that of the dependent fusion.

Krishnamachari et al. investigated the impact of data aggregation on various networking metrics by surveying the existing data aggregation protocols in WSNs (Krishnamachari, 2002). Intanagonwiwat et al. proposed a novel approach that adjusts aggregation points in order to increase the amount of path sharing and reduced energy consumption (Intanagonwiwat et al., 2002). The results suggested that greedy aggregation could achieve up to 45% energy savings over opportunistic aggregation in high-density networks, without adversely impacting latency or robustness. Pattem et al. proposed several data aggregation techniques to study the performance of various data aggregation schemes across the range of spatial correlations (Pattem, Krishnamachari, & Govindan, 2004). The analysis and simulations revealed that the characteristics of optimal routing with compression did depend on the level of correlation. Specially, there existed a practical static clustering scheme which could provide near-optimal performance for a wide range of spatial correlations. Yu et al. employed the data aggregation tree to extract the packet flow (Yu, Krishnamachari, & Prasanna, 2004). Goel et al. proposed a hierarchical matching algorithm, which resulted in an aggregation tree with simultaneous logarithmic approximation for all concave aggregation functions (Goel & Estrin, 2003). In this model, each node can theoretically obtain the joint entropy of its sub-tree to achieve the maximal aggregation ratio. Anandkumar et al. (2009) presented a novel formulation for optimal sensor selection and in-network fusion for distributed inference known as the prize-collecting data fusion (PCDF) in terms of the optimal trade-off between the costs of aggregating the selected set of sensor measurements and the resulting inference performance at the fusion center (Xing et al., 2009). PCDF is then analyzed under a correlation model specified by a Markov random field (MRF) with a given dependency graph. For a special class of

dependency graphs, a constrained version of PCDF reduces to the prize-collecting Steiner tree on an augmented graph. In this case, an approximation algorithm is given with an approximation ratio that depends only on the number of profitable cliques in the dependency graph.

The Related Work in Routing in WSN

To improve the routing efficiency, it is important to eliminate unnecessary wireless communication link and generate a routing method with highly efficient data transmission. Perrig et al. presented SPINS as the first adaptive data centered routine protocol (Perrig et al., 2002). Before this protocol transmits the real data, the sensor nodes announce the metadata with the describing information for collective use. Unless there are some relevant requirements, it would transmit the data in purpose. SPINS could solve the inner-burst, overlap, and resource exhaustion in extensive calculation to obtain good energy efficiency. The topological change is local, and it is only necessary for the sensor node to get information about the neighboring sensor nodes. Intanagonwiwat et al. presented the directed diffusion arithmetic which is a kind of data diffusion in data naming with a group of properties of the sensor node for naming its generated data (Intanagonwiwat, Govindan, & Estrin, 2000). The terminal sensor nodes send out the inquiring operation in property combination, such as object name, interval time, duration time, position range and so on. The inquiring message would be diffused by announcement, and each sensor node could cache the message and aggregate the data by the arithmetic of generating the minimum tree. At last, the inquiring message would explore the whole network, suit the original data, and receive the data chosen by the named variable gradients in a higher frequency routine. Directed diffusion need not complete the topology by the adoption of feedback strategy, so it is a kind of highly energy efficient protocol. Lindsey et al. presented a scheme called PEGASIS (Power-Efficient Gathering in Sensor Information Systems) that each node could receive information from its neighbors and send to its neighbors (Lindsey, Raghavendra, & Sivalingam, 2002). The data gathered by nodes in each round have to be collected and transmitted to the base station by only one designated node in order to reduce energy consumption and to extend the lifetime of the WSN. PEGASIS considers energy delay as an optimization metric per round of data gathering in WSNs. Yao et al. studied a system named COUGAR for detecting and apperceiving the data inquiring capability (Yao & Gehrke, 2002). They presented a kind of mistaken allowance and extensible arithmetic of calculating the aggregating function, explored the ideology to express the sensor networks as database, and discussed how to apply the distributed inquire treatment technique in apperceiving data inquiring process. Madden SR et al. investigated the data inquiring technique in WSNs, presented a dynamic adjusting sequence inquiry processing and multi-inquiry in managing the sensor networks, realized the aggregating function in sensor networks by applying the database, brought forward a method to run the function in low energy, distributed wireless sensor networks environment and developed an apperceiving database system named TinyDB (Madden et al., 2002), (Madden et al., 2005). Govindan et al. worked over the calculating method of aggregating function in WSNs, advanced an energy saving arithmetic named tree configuration and verified the great influence of wireless communication arithmetic to the calculated performance by experiment (Govindan et al., 2002). Cristescu et al. proved that the minimum-energy data gathering problem is NP-complete by applying the reduction set-cover problem, and claimed that the optimal result is an approximation based on a combination between the SPT (shortest path tree) and TSP (traveling salesman path) (Cristescu, Beferull-Lozano, & Vetterli, 2004). Luo, Liu, & Das (2006) proposed

a routing algorithm called minimum fusion Steiner tree (MFST) for data gathering with aggregation in wireless sensor networks. MFST not only optimizes data transmission cost but also incorporates the cost for data fusion, which was significant for emerging sensor networks with the vectorial data and security requirements. They further found that fusion costs were comparable to those of communications for certain applications (Luo et al., 2006). Motivated by the limitations of MFST, they designed a novel routing algorithm, called adaptive fusion Steiner tree (AFST) for energy efficient data gathering in sensor networks.

The Related Work in Energy Balancing in WSN

Most sensor nodes are unable to communicate with the sink node directly because of their limited communication capacity. As a result of this limitation, multi-hop routing has become the basic method for data gathering in WSNs. In this way, intermediate nodes deplete their energy faster when they take more tasks, such as relaying the received data or completing the fusion process to curtail the network load. Therefore, the occurred energy hole prevents remote data from being sent further to the sink node. The avoidance of the energy hole in WSNs has attracted a lot of attention and some valuable results have been reported in recent years. Powell, Leone, and Rolim (2007) proposed a centralized algorithm to compute the optimal parameters for WSNs and proved that these parameters maximize the network lifetime. Olariu and Stojmenovic (2006) investigated theoretical aspects of the uneven energy depletion phenomenon in sink-based wireless sensor networks. Wu et al. explored the theoretical aspects of the non-uniform node distribution strategy that addresses the energy hole problem in WSNs. They proposed a distributed shortest path routing algorithm tailored for the proposed non-uniform node distribution strategy (Wu &

Chen, 2008). Zhang and Shen (2009) formulate the energy consumption balancing problem as an optimal transmitting data distribution problem by combining the ideas of corona-based network division and mixed-routing strategy together with data aggregation.

MULTI-ATTRIBUTE DATA FUSION IN WSN

In this section, we will describe the multi-attribute data fusion in WSN in detail. First, the system models are described. Then, the fusion process is discussed and a self-adaptive threshold is designed to balance the different change rates of each attributive data. Finally, the energy-conservation efficiency of multi-attribute data fusion is discussed.

System Models

Network Model

We assume that all the nodes are uniformly distributed in a circular area of radius. Only one sink node is located at the center of the area. All the nodes have the same initial energy budget. In data gathering, the maximum communication distance is also the same for all nodes. Each node has a unique ID number and knowledge of its geographical location. Without loss of generality, we make the following assumptions in this paper:

- All the sensor nodes and the sink node remain stationary after deployment.
- Except for the sink node, all the sensor nodes are isomorphic with the same initial energy, computation capacity and data fusion capacity. The sink node has no limitations of energy and computation capacity.

- Based on the distance to the receiver, the sensor nodes can adjust the transmission power to save energy consumption.
- When the sensor nodes have no tasks, they can switch to the sleeping state to save energy consumption.

Fusion Model

Similar to (Luo, Liu, & Das, 2006), (Luo et al., 2006), a data fusion model is employed in our research, where the sensor nodes are required to send their data constantly. In this model, if a node v needs to receive the data sent from node u,, which is marked as $w(u)$.. The total data amount after fusion process at node v is expressed as:

$$w(v) = \max(\tilde{w}(v), w(u)) + \min(\tilde{w}(v), w(u))(1 - \rho) \quad (1)$$

Where $\tilde{w}(v)$ represents the data amount generated by node v. ρ represents the data correlation between node u and v,, which is affected by data attribute.

Energy Model

We assume that all the nodes have the same initial energy E_0,, while only the sink node is without energy limitation. Similar to (Heinzelman, Chandrakasan, & Balakrishnan, 2002), the energy consumption of transmitting one bit data over distance d is $e_t(d) = \varepsilon_{elec} + \varepsilon_{amp} \cdot d^k$, where ε_{elec} and $\left(ID_u, ID_v\right)$ are the energy spent by transmitter electronics and transmitting amplifier, respectively. k ($k \geq 2$) is the propagation loss exponent. Consequently, the energy dissipation in receiving one bit data is $e_r = \varepsilon_{elec}$.. Data fusion process can introduce the extra energy consumption, which is represented by e_f.. Specially, the fusion cost

Figure 2. Data fusion in homogeneous network

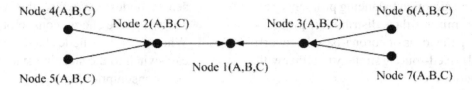

Figure 3. Data fusion in heterogeneous network

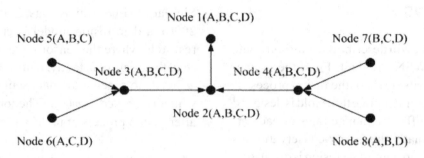

will be increased with the using of encryption and other security mechanisms.

Data Fusion in Homogeneous and Heterogeneous WSNs

According to the configuration of sensor nodes, wireless sensor network can be divided into two types: homogeneous and heterogeneous WSNs. For the former, all the sensor nodes are exactly the same. For the latter, there are more or less individual differences among nodes. In our research work, the heterogeneous WSNs is composed of nodes equipped with different sensors. In the following, we will take an example to explain the fusion process in homogeneous and heterogeneous WSN.

In homogeneous WSN, the attributes, length, and structure of packets generated by each sensor node are exactly the same. As shown in Figure 2, each node generates three kinds of attributive data, represented by type A, type B, and type C. In such a case, the part with same attribute in packets

can be fused according to the requirement set by users in data gathering.

In heterogeneous WSNs, the attributes of the packets generated by different nodes are not the same, which increases the difficulty of the fusion process. As shown in Figure 3, there are four kinds of sensors in the network, which can separately generate four kinds of attributive data represented by types A, B, C, and D. Each node is equipped with three kinds of sensors. Figure 3 shows the data gathering and fusion process for nodes 5, 6, 7 and 8. The attributive data in packets generated by them are types A, B, and C; types A, C, and D; types B, C, and D; and types A, B, and D. For easy illustration, the packets generated by nodes 1, 2, 3 and 4 are not shown in this figure. Although the data attributes of these nodes are not identical, there is still some redundancy if some of the same attributes exist. For example, node 3 can fuse the components of type A and C which coexist in packets generated by node 5 and 6. This shows that data fusion can still be used to

Figure 4. Packet structure of PHY layer

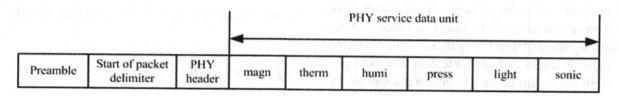

reduce redundancy in a heterogeneous WSN if the same attributes exist in different packets.

Self-Adaptive Threshold

Under a complex environment, it is necessary for WSNs to monitor multi-targets. To achieve this purpose, each sensor node needs to be equipped with more than one kind of sensor, such as magnetometer sensor, thermal sensor, humidity sensor, pressure sensor, light sensor, sonic sensor, etc. These sensors can monitor the environment separately or cooperatively. As a result, the generated packets contain multi-attribute data. The packet structure of the physical layer is shown in Figure 4. When the data attributes in one packet are different, some of them could have a high ratio of changes while others might remain stable. When these packets are extracted or synthesized, the different change rates of the attributes makes the fusion process more complicated. Additionally, although data fusion can reduce redundant data and hence curtail network load, the energy consumption of the fusion process needs to be considered.

The most usual and basic method used in data fusion is to set a threshold. In this way, the sensor node can make a judgment to determine whether to transmit the packets. If the difference between the last transmitted packet and the current prepared packet is less than the threshold, then the current packet will not be transmitted. Hence, the unnecessary data transmission is avoided.

As mentioned above, the sensor node often needs to be equipped with more than one kind

of sensor, which can gather different monitoring data. Compared with separate transmission of each attributive data, the transmission of multi-attribute data packed in one packet can reduce the network flow. If all attributive data in packets still adopts the same threshold, the data with a low change rate will also be transmitted along with the packet when the threshold is low and this will waste the network energy and bandwidth. If the threshold is high, the packets will be transmitted at a low frequency and this might result in the loss of valuable data. To solve this problem, we design a self-adaptive threshold to balance the change rate of different attributive data.

We use T_1 and T_2 represent the upper and lower limits of self-adaptive threshold, which can be set according to the real application. In data gathering, the self-adaptive threshold of i attributive data, denoted by T_i, is calculated as:

$$T_i = T_1 + (1 - I_i) \times \frac{\sum M_i(T_2 - T_1)}{M} \quad (2)$$

Where, M is the total transmission number of the packets, M_i represents number of packets transmitted only caused by the i attributive data. I_i represents the importance of the i attributive data, which can be set according to the real application in the range of 0 to 1. $\sum M_i / M$ reflects the change rate of attributive i data. To calculate T_i, the sensor nodes need to cache each packet for a certain period. Obviously, the attributive data with higher change rate will obtain a higher threshold, which leads to a stronger restrict. In this way, the passive transmission of insensitive data can be reduced. It should be noted that the arrangement of threshold value must be restricted to avoid the loss of available data. For example, if all the transmission of packets are caused by only one kind of attributive data, then $M = \sum M_i$. Here, the threshold of this attributive data is calculated by equation (3):

$$T_i = T_1 + (1 - I_i)(T_2 - T_1) = (1 - I_i)T_2 + I_iT_1 \tag{3}$$

It can be seen from equation (3) that if T_2 is set too high, some available data might be lost. On the contrary, if T_2 is set too low, the efficiency of the threshold to balance different attributive data will be reduced.

Energy-Conservation Efficiency of Multi-Attribute Data Fusion

In WSN, the main task of data fusion is to reduce the unnecessary data transmission for the sake of reducing energy consumption. The energy-conservation efficiency of data fusion is mainly dependent on the correlation among different data. Here, the correlation coefficient is denoted by ρ. For example, in the case of fusing two packets, the length of the generated packet after fusion will be decreased with increasing the correlation of data in the two packets.

Additionally, it is also affected by energy consumption of fusion process. Specially, data fusion cannot save the energy of network anymore when the energy consumption reaches a certain degree. In the following section, we will analyze the energy-conservation efficiency of data fusion.

To measure the energy-conservation efficiency of data fusion, both the cost of transmission and fusion are considered, denoted by $T(e_k)$ and

$F(e_k)$, respectively. $T(e_k)$ is the energy consumption of transmission on edge e_k and can be calculated as:

$$T(e_k) = G(e_k) \cdot t(e_k) \tag{4}$$

Where $G(e_k)$ represents the total data amount of transmission, and $t(e_k)$ represents the energy consumption of transmitting one bit data. The value of $t(e_k)$ is given by the model in section 3.3.

$F(e_k)$ represents the energy consumption of fusion process and is given by:

$$F(e_k) = H(e_k) \cdot f(e_k) \tag{5}$$

Where $H(e_k)$ represents the total data amount of data fusion, and $f(e_k)$ represents the energy consumption of fusing one bit data. The value of $f(e_k)$ is affected by the chosen fusion algorithm.

Without the loss of generality, we make the following hypothesis: When sensor node u transmits packet to node v, the node v is responsible for fusing the data of itself and received data. $D(u)$ and $D(v)$ represents data amount of node u and v before fusion, respectively. $\hat{D}(v)$ represents the generated data amount after fusion. If node u and v generate one same attributive data and the correlation of node u and v is ρ_{uv}, we have:

$$\hat{D}(v) = \max(D(u), D(v)) + \min(D(u), D(v)) \cdot (1 - \rho_{uv}) \tag{6}$$

In our research work, for any $e_k \in E$, $t(e_k) = t(e)$ and $f(e_k) = f(e)$. The packet of node u sent to v includes m kinds of attributive data, so $D(u)$ can be written as:

Box 1.

$$E_2(v) = \left[\sum_{i=1}^{m} D(u_i) + \sum_{j=1}^{n} D(v_j)\right] \cdot f(e) + \left[\sum_{i=1}^{m} D(u_i) + \sum_{j=1}^{n} D(v_j) - \sum_{i=j} \min\left[D(u_i), D(v_j)\right] \cdot \rho_{uv} \cdot g_i\right] \cdot t(e)$$

$$= \left[\sum_{i=1}^{m} D(u_i) + \sum_{j=1}^{n} D(v_j)\right] \cdot \left[t(e) + f(e)\right] - \sum_{i=j} \min\left[D(u_i), D(v_j)\right] \cdot \rho_{uv} \cdot g_i \cdot t(e) \qquad (12)$$

$$D(u) = \sum_{i=1}^{m} D(u_i) \qquad (7)$$

The data generated by node v includes n kinds of attributive data, so $D(v)$ can be written as:

$$D(v) = \sum_{j=1}^{n} D(v_j) \qquad (8)$$

According to whether node v proceeds data fusion or not, there are two cases. One is node v does not fuse data but transmits the packets received and those that are generated by itself directly, thus the total data amount transmitted by node v marked as $D'(v)$ can be written as:

$$D'(v) = D(u) + D(v) = \sum_{i=1}^{m} D(u_i) + \sum_{j=1}^{n} D(v_j) \qquad (9)$$

At this time, the energy consumption of node v marked as $E_1(v)$, is expressed in equation (10):

$$E_1(v) = D'(v) \cdot t(e) = \left(\sum_{i=1}^{m} D(u_i) + \sum_{j=1}^{n} D(v_j)\right) \cdot t(e) \qquad (10)$$

On the contrary, if node v fuses the received and local packets. According to the data fusion model in section 3.2, the total data amount after fusion is expressed in equation (11):

$$\hat{D}(v) = \sum_{i=1}^{m} D(u_i) + \sum_{j=1}^{n} D(v_j) - \sum_{i=j} \min\left[D(u_i), D(v_j)\right] \cdot \rho_{uv} \cdot g_i \qquad (11)$$

Where, g_i represents the effect of data attribute on correlation. Obviously, $\hat{D}(v)$ decreases with increasing ρ_{uv}, which causes the reduction of energy consumption for the transmission of node v. At this time, the total energy consumption of sensor node v is written as: (see Box 1).

It can be deduced that the energy-conservation efficiency of multi-attribute fusion at node v is:

$$U(v) = E_1(v) - E_2(v)$$

$$= \sum_{i=j} \min\left[D(u_i), D(v_j)\right] \cdot \rho_{uv} \cdot g_i \cdot t(e) - \left(\sum_{i=1}^{m} D(u_i) + \sum_{j=1}^{n} D(v_j)\right) \cdot f(e) \qquad (13)$$

Above all, the energy-conservation efficiency of data fusion is determined by both the correlation among nodes and the energy consumption of fusion process. If the energy consumption of fusion is too high or the correlation among nodes is too low, the data fusion may not save energy for WSNs. The energy-conservation efficiency of data fusion can be used to optimize the establishment of routing and determine how to proceed the data fusion.

It should be noticed that what we measure is the energy consumption between two nodes which can communicate directly. In fact, the unavoidable packet collision and loss exist, which can cause data retransmission that can increase energy consumption. In our research work, the quality of communication is less considered so we ignore the effects of packet collision and packet loss. Actually, this kind of influence can be quantified by increasing $t(e)$. Additionally, the cost of computing energy-conservation efficiency is also ignored, since this cost is much lower compared to complicated fusion process and will not influence the overall performance of WSN.

MULTI-ATTRIBUTE FUSION TREE

In this section, we propose an energy equilibrium routing method for WSN, which is named multi-attribute fusion tree (MAFT). The establishment of MAFT is determined by the remaining energy of sensor nodes and the energy-conservation efficiency of data fusion. The purpose of our design is to balance and save energy in WSNs.

Problem Statement and Design Purpose

For ease of exposition, we define the following two terms:

Definition 1. Energy equilibrium means that nodes in the network use up their energy simultaneously.
Definition 2. Change rate of data means the change speed of data content per unit time.

Now we begin to formulate the problem. For a given data-gathering sensor network, including the source nodes set S and sink node, each source node needs to send its data to sink node. Due to the limitation of communication ability of sensor nodes, the farthest source nodes from the sink node need m hops to send the data to sink node. The sensor node set S_l represents the nodes with

l hops, where $\sum_{l=(1,2,\cdots,m)} S_l = S$ and S_0 is the sink node. Each source node belonging to S_l needs to select one forwarding node from S_{l-1} in the range of its communication area. Our objective is to design a routing protocol that can balance and minimize the energy consumption when delivering data from all source nodes in S to the sink node. This problem can be formulated as follows:

$$\begin{cases} \min \sum_{u \in S_l} \sum_{v \in S_{l-1}} e_{uv} \cdot x_{uv}, \quad l = \left(1,2,3,\ldots,m\right) \\ s.t. \quad for\ \forall u \in S_l, \ \sum_{v \in F_u} x_{uv} = 1 \\ \quad E_v \geq E_k, \ u,k \in F_u \end{cases}$$

$$(14)$$

Where x_{uv} represents whether the connection is existed between node u and v. When node v is the forwarding node of node u, then $x_{uv} = 1$, otherwise, $x_{uv} = 0$. e_{uv} represents the energy consumption on the edge from node u to v, consisting of three parts: node u transmitting data, node v receiving and fusing data. It can be denoted as:

$$e_{uv} = D(u) \cdot t(e) + D(u) \cdot r(e) + [D(u) + D(v)] \cdot f(e)$$

E_v represents the energy level of node v. For $\forall u \in S_l$, $F_u \in S_{l-1}$ represents the backup nodes set for forwarding nodes, which can directly communicate with node u as shown in the shadow of Figure 5.

In equation (14), the first constraint specifies that the source node u in S_l has only one forwarding node. The second constraint is to guarantee forwarding nodes are the nodes with the highest energy level among the backup nodes.

The above optimization problem is not easily to be solved because of the conflicts between energy equilibrium and energy conservation. Although

Figure 5. Backup nodes set for the forwarding nodes

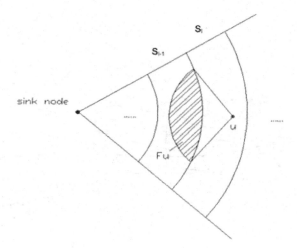

some of the nodes can guarantee the lowest energy consumption of network, the remaining energy of these nodes may be low and result in their quick death. For avoiding the energy hole, we will give priority to the object of energy equilibrium. It will be described in detail in the following section.

Multi-Attribute Fusion Tree Design

Multi-Attribute Fusion Tree

In wireless sensor network, the routing is responsible for gathering the information from the sensor nodes to the sink node. Each sensor node can play double function role like relay and terminal in traditional network. Since both the energy supply and computing ability are limited, the main target for routing research is focusing on how to establish a highly efficient routing protocol to maximize the network lifetime. Additionally, the establishment of routing should have the characteristic of low complexity and serviceability.

For these reasons, we establish a multi-attribute fusion tree (MAFT). The network is divided into N coronas, denoted by $C_1, C_2, C_3, \cdots, C_N$ as shown in Figure 6. For the sake of guaranteeing not to lose the packets, the width of coronas should

be less than the maximum communication range of nodes. In data gathering, nodes belonging to a corona $\{C_{i-1} | i \neq R\}$ will forward packets generated by both themselves and nodes from corona $\{C_j | (i+1) \leq j \leq R\}$. Each sensor node in corona C_i ($2 \leq i \leq N$) can find its forwarding node from the corona C_{i-1} while the nodes in corona C_1 can communicate with the sink node directly. Each forwarding node needs to cache the received packets for a certain period. This routing can be constructed only with local information by distributed process. The location of each node is not necessary in this process. Additionally, MAFT can support both the active and passive data gathering. In active data gathering, each sensor node transmits the packets by the pre-install rules. Different with active data gathering, each sensor node in passive data gathering will not transmit the packets until it receives an inquire message.

Problem Optimization

If the energy equilibrium is not considered in equation (1), it means the second constraint is ignored. The optimization object is simple to save the energy of network in maximum. According to

Figure 6. Division of sensor nodes hops in network

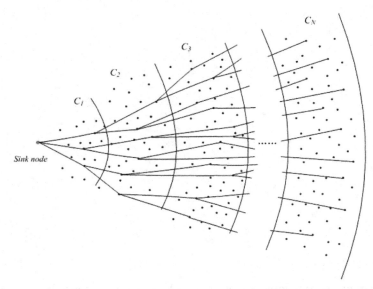

the simplified optimization object, the remaining energy of the selected forwarding node maybe low, and they have to undertake more tasks. Although the total energy consumption of the whole network is lowest at a particular time, the partial nodes using up energy early will speed up the death of network. So, it must first consider the energy equilibrium.

However, the absolute energy equilibrium cannot be realized in real application. We adopt a simple method to ensure the energy equilibrium with a certain degree, which is to select those nodes with higher remaining energy as forwarding nodes to undertake more tasks. As described in the second constraint of equation (1), when the forwarding node of node u is to be selected, the nodes with higher remaining energy in F_u are first selected, denoted as F_u', here $F_u' \in F_u$. Then, the nodes in F_u' which can meet the needs of optimization are selected as forwarding nodes. The detailed selection process is described in section 4.2(C). Now, equation (14) is simplified as follows:

$$\begin{cases} \min \sum\limits_{u \in S_l} \sum\limits_{v \in F_u'} e_{uv} \cdot x_{uv}, & l = (1,2,3,\cdots m) \\ \quad s.t \ \ for \ \forall u \in S_l, \quad \sum\limits_{v \in F_u'} x_{uv} = 1 \end{cases}$$

$$(15)$$

Theorem 1: The bigger $U(v)$ is, the little $\sum\limits_{u \in S_l} \sum\limits_{v \in F_u'} e_{uv} \cdot x_{uv}$ is.

Proof: $\sum\limits_{u \in S_l} \sum\limits_{v \in F_u'} e_{uv} \cdot x_{uv}$ represents the total energy consumption of sending the data generated by all sensor nodes to sink node. If there is no fusion process, the total energy consumption will be the highest. If ignoring the energy consumption of sink node, the energy consumption for sending the data generated by $\forall u \in S_l$ to sink node can be calculated as:

$$e_u = l \cdot D(u) \cdot t(e) + (l-1) \cdot D(u) \cdot r(e) \qquad (16)$$

$$\sum_{u\in S_i}\sum_{v\in F_u} e_{uv}\cdot x_{uv} = \sum_{u\in S_i} e_u = \sum_{u\in S_i}[l\cdot D(u)\cdot t(e)+(l-1)\cdot D(u)\cdot r(e)]$$

(17)

Obviously, the bigger $U(v)$ is, the little $\hat{D}(v)$ is, and then the little $\sum_{u\in S_i}\sum_{v\in F_u} e_{uv}\cdot x_{uv}$ is.

Theorem 1 is proven.

Selection of Next-hop Forwarding Node

As illustrated above, it is suggested that the selected forwarding nodes from the backup nodes with higher remaining energy ought to maximize energy-conservation efficiency, since each sensor node might have more than one backup node to be chosen as forwarding node. Assume that there are H backup nodes for node u, denoted by $\{v_1, v_2, v_3, \ldots v_H\}$. Now, the most important thing is to select the proper forwarding node from them. As described in section 4.2(B), both remaining energy and energy-conservation efficiency are considered during the selection. We define energy-conservation efficiency of multi-attribute fusion as and it can be calculated by each sensor node using equation (13). If we only consider it, the backup node with the highest $U(v_j)$ will be chosen. For example, if one forwarding node represented by v_r is selected, it should meet the following equation (18):

$$U(v_r)\geq U(v_j) \qquad v_r\in H \qquad (18)$$

However, it will break the energy equilibrium in WSNs. For the sensor nodes in WSNs are usually stable, the data correlation of nodes are also fixed so that the $U(v_j)$ of each backup node seldom changes. It means v_j will be chosen as the forwarding node repeatedly, which increases its energy consumption and accelerates its death. To avoid the energy hole appeared in WSN, the remaining energy of node must be considered in priority.

As the remaining energy of nodes decreases continuously, the information can not be exchanged frequently. We divide the initial energy E_0 into grades to measure the remaining energy of nodes. Using energy grade, the sensor node needs to inform its neighbor nodes when its energy grade decreases, which means each node only needs to update its information of energy grade for no more than $G-1$ times. Obviously, this method can significantly reduce the energy consumption of communication.

When all backup nodes are determined, it first compares the energy grade of backup node, and then selects the node with highest energy grade. If there are more than one backup node with highest energy grade, the further selection is based on the $U(v_j)$. If there are still nodes existed with the highest $U(v_j)$ during the further selection, then a random node among them will be selected.

Establishment of MAFT

The establishment of MAFT is started from the sink node with broadcasting an advertisement (ADV) message. The nodes receiving this message belong to the corona C_1. Then, the nodes in corona C_1 broadcast their ADV including the information of their ID, serial number of coronas, and the current energy grade. The nodes who receive the message from corona C_1 belong to corona C_2. The process is continued until the whole network is divided into N concentric coronas. In broadcasting transmission, the nodes in corona C_i are unavoidable to receive the ADV messages from the nodes in the same or the outer corona C_{i+1}. To avoid duplicate recording, the sensor nodes need to compare their serial

Figure 7. Illustration of MAFT

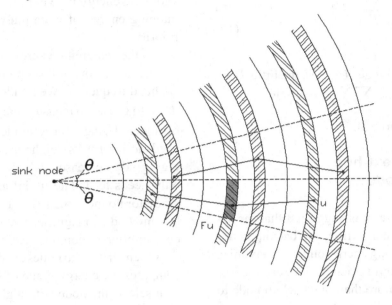

number of corona with those in ADV, and abandon the ADV from corona C_i and C_{i+1}.

For further balancing the energy, we divide each corona into many sub-zones as Figure 7. The data is transmitted between the corresponding sub-zones in two neighbor coronas. For example, the backup nodes set F_u for node u are all the nodes in pink area.

Generally, the sensor nodes will receive more than one ADV message sent from the inner corona. These nodes will become the backup nodes for forwarding nodes. The selection process of the forwarding nodes starts from the nodes in corona C_N to sink node. The selection results should be informed to the chosen nodes.

Figure 8 shows the selection process of forwarding nodes. $N_f(u)$ represents the forwarding node of node u. $M(v)$ represents the ADV message of node v, including $\left(ID_v, S_v, G(v)\right)$.

In WSNs, the energy consumption is impossible to be absolutely in equilibrium. Therefore, the routing needs to be reconstructed after a certain period. The period depends on many factors;

such as the application environment, the initial energy level of sensor nodes, and so on.

SIMULATION AND NUMERICAL RESULTS

In this section, we evaluate the energy saving performance of the proposed MAFT. Our simulation experiments are organized as follows: Firstly, we describe the experimental environment. Secondly, we demonstrate the energy saving performance of the proposed scheme in the energy consumption and number of live nodes of network; Thirdly, we investigate the performance of the design based on the different parameters of d_c and d_s.

Experimental Environment

In this section, we evaluate the performance of the MAFT via simulation experiments under NS2. We assume that 300 sensor nodes are uniformly deployed into a circular area with diameter of

Figure 8. Selection process of forwarding nodes

```
1: Initialize i=0

2: for ∀u∈S do

3:     if M(v)=TRUE, Sᵤ=Sᵥ+1 then

4:         Fᵤ←v

5:         for all v∈Fᵤ do

6:             if G(v)>G(z), ∀z∈Fᵤ then

7:                 i++

8:                 mark vᵢ= v
```

Table 1. Parameters in simulation

Parameters	Value
Initial energy	2J
Communication bandwidth	1Mbps
Delay time	25μs
Energy consumption/circuit	50nJ/bit
Energy consumption of amplifier	d <87m, 10 pJ/bit·m² d ≥87m, 0.0013 pJ/bit·m⁴
d_c	20m
d_s	25m
Energy consumption of data fusion	20nJ/bit

200m. All the sensor nodes are the information source and can be the forwarding nodes. The original packet is 500 bytes generated by each sensor node. Each packet consists of three kinds of attributive data. The basic parameters used in the simulations are shown in Table 1.

Experimental Result and Analysis

We employ d_s and d to represent the maximum correlation distance between nodes and the space distance between two sensor nodes, respectively.

If $d \geq d_s$, the correlation coefficient between nodes is 0, otherwise, it is given by $\rho = \left(1 - d / d_s\right) \times f \times g_i$. In our experiments, g_i of three given data attributes in packets is corresponding to $g_i = 0.6, 0.8, 1.0 (i = 1, 2, 3)$. f represents the effect of fusion algorithm on data correlation, which is set as 1 in the whole simulation. We compared the MAFT with MTE-F, where MTE-F adds the data fusion process based on MTE (Minimum Transmitted Energy). The main idea of MTE is that all nodes send packets using

Figure 9. Energy consumption of network

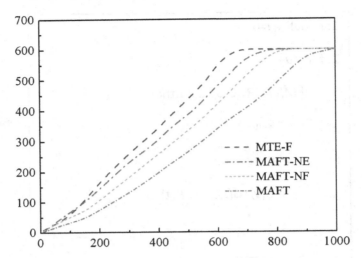

the minimum power, that is to say, send packets to their nearest neighbor nodes. For further analysis, we also add MAFT-NE and MAFT-NF for comparison. Compared with MAFT, the main difference is that the remaining energy is not considered in MAFT-NE while the energy-conservation efficiency of data fusion is not considered in MAFT-NF.

Figure 9 shows the total energy consumption under different protocols. It can be seen that the total energy consumption in MAFT is the lowest at the same time with the consideration of both energy-conservation efficiency of data fusion and remaining energy. MAFT-NF shows more total energy consumption than MAFT, which does not consider energy-conservation efficiency of data fusion. Compared to MAFT and MAFT-NF, MAFT-NE shows much more total energy consumption without considering the remaining energy. MTE-F shows the most total energy consumption among the four protocols.

Figure 10 shows the number of alive nodes with different protocols. In MAFT, the dead time of the first node and the last node are both later than the others. MAFT-NF is sensitive to the energy change of network. Hence, it shows better

performance than MAFT-NE. MTE-F still shows the worst performance.

Figure 11 reflects the effect of d_c on the lifetime of network with different protocols, where d_s is fixed at 25m. It can be seen that the lifetime of MAFT is always the longest at the same d_c and the peak appears when d_c is 20m. When d_c is less than 20m, the number of routing hops between sensor nodes and sink node increases with decreasing d_c. When d_c is over 20m and less than 25m, the correlation coefficient ρ decreases with increasing d_c. When d_c reaches 25m, the correlation coefficients ρ of MAFT, MAFT-NE, and MAFT-NF arrive to zero. As MAFT-NE only considers the fusion efficiency, the lifetime of MAFT-NE drops at the fastest pace. Since the data packages are transmitted to their neighbor nodes in MTE-F, the real communication distance is not determined by d_c. The fusion process is still available on MTE-F which results in a slow drop of lifetime. It can be seen that the lifetime of MTE-F is above than that of MAFT-NE when d_c is higher than 40m.

Figure 12 reflects the effect of d_s on the lifetime of network with different protocols, where

Figure 10. Number of alive nodes

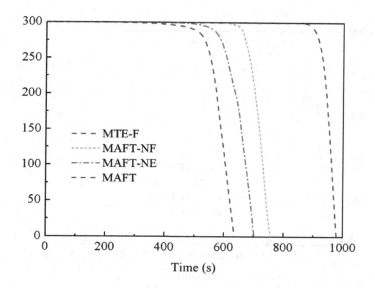

Figure 11. Effect of d_c on the lifetime of network

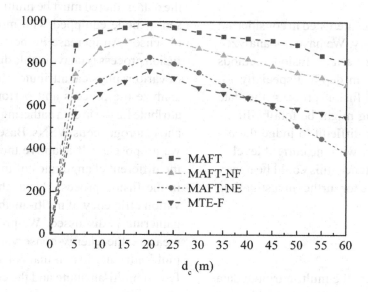

d_c is fixed at 20m. When d_s is less than 20m, the energy consumption will not benefit from data fusion in data gathering since ρ is 0 now. However, MAFT and MAFT-NF still exhibit longer lifetime than the other two protocols. MTE-F shows better performance than MAFT-NE, this is because of the higher sensitivity of MAFT-NE to the effect of d_s on correlation coefficient than MTE-F. On the contrary, when d_s is higher than 20m, ρ decreases with increasing d_s. At this time, MAFT still exhibits the best performance.

Figure 12. Effect of d_c on the lifetime of network

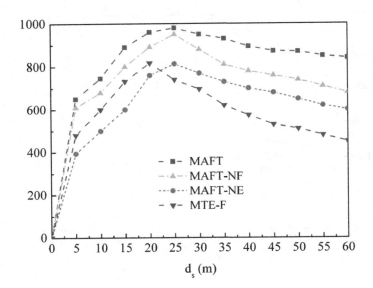

FUTURE RESEARCH DIRECTIONS

As a future work, we are interested in considering the data fusion efficiency. We have not analyzed the interaction among various fusion methods on relation coefficient in depth. Especially for decision-making level fusion process, the data types before processing might be totally different. In fact, it is really difficult to judge the accurate fusion efficiency with the current level of knowledge we have. Hence, this could be a very attractive research issue for further investigation.

CONCLUSION

In this chapter, we study the multi-attribute data fusion in WSN. As there are strong correlations between data gathered from sensor nodes in close physical proximity, the effective in-network fusion schemes involve minimizing such redundancy and hence reducing the load in wireless sensor networks. Therefore, the routing method should support data fusion for fusion-driven routing. Here, data are fused along the routing path toward the sink node. Under a complicated environment, the data gathered must be multi-attribute for each sensor node equipped with more than one kind of sensor. An increase in the complexity for the fusion process is unavoidable due to the existence of various physical attributes. In this chapter, we analyze the process and performance of multi-attribute fusion in data gathering for homogeneous and heterogeneous WSNs. Based on the analysis, we propose a self-adaptive threshold to balance the different change rates of multi-attribute data in the fusion process. Next, the energy-conservation efficiency of multi-attribute fusion in data gathering is discussed. We present a method to measure the energy-conservation efficiency of multi-attribute fusion that considers both the effect of multi-attribute and the cost of data fusion. Then we propose an energy equilibrium routing method, viz., multi-attribute fusion tree (MAFT). In MAFT, both energy equilibrium and conservation are considered. Finally, we perform extensive simulation experiments to evaluate MAFT by several performance criteria. The results show that MAFT can save energy and prolong the network lifetime.

REFERENCES

Anandkumar, A., Meng, W., Lang, T., & Swami, A. (2009). Prize-collecting data fusion for cost-performance tradeoff in distributed inference. In *Proceedings of IEEE INFOCOM* (pp. 2150-2158). Rio de Janeiro, Brazil.

Baunach, M., Kolla, R., & Mühlberger, C. (2007). *Beyond theory: Development of a real world localization application as low power WSN.* In 32nd IEEE conference on local computer networks (pp. 872-884), Dublin, Ireland.

Bettstetter, C., & Hartmann, C. (2005). Connectivity of wireless multihop networks in a shadow fading environment. *Wireless Networks, 11*(5), 571–579. doi:10.1007/s11276-005-3513-x

Cristescu, R., Beferull-Lozano, B., & Vetterli, M. (2004). On network correlated data gathering. [Hong Kong, China.]. *Proceedings - IEEE INFOCOM, 4,* 2571–2582.

Goel, A., & Estrin, D. (2003). Simultaneous optimization for concave costs: Single sink aggregation or single source buy-at-bulk. In *Proceedings of ACM-SIAM Symposium on Discrete Algorithms* (pp. 499-505). Baltimore, MD.

Govindan, R., Hellerstein, J. M., Wei, H., Madden, S., Franklin, M., & Shenker, S. (2002). *The sensor network as a database.* (Technical Report 02-771), Computer Science Department, University of Southern California, USA.

Heinzelman, W. B., Chandrakasan, A. P., & Balakrishnan, H. (2002). An application-specific protocol architecture for wireless microsensor networks. *IEEE Transactions on Wireless Communications,* 660–670. doi:10.1109/TWC.2002.804190

Intanagonwiwat, C., Estrin, D., Govindan, R., & Heidemann, J. (2002). *Impact of network density on data aggregation in wireless sensor networks.* In 22nd International Conference on Distributed Systems (pp. 457-458), Vienna, Austria.

Intanagonwiwat, C., Govindan, R., & Estrin, D. (2000). Directed diffusion: A scalable and robust communication paradigm for sensor networks. In *Proceedings of the 6th Annual International Conference on Mobile Computing and Networking* (pp. 56-67). Boston, MA: ACM.

Krishnamachari, B. (2002). The impact of data aggregation in wireless sensor networks. In *Proceedings of International Workshop on Distributed Event-Based Systems* (pp. 575-578).

Li, J., & Mohapatra, P. (2007). Analytical modeling and mitigation techniques for the energy hole problem in sensor networks. *Pervasive and Mobile Computing, 3,* 233–254. doi:10.1016/j.pmcj.2006.11.001

Lin, K., Wang, L., Li, K., & Shu, L. (2010). Multi-attribute data fusion for energy equilibrium routing in wireless sensor networks. *KSII Transactions on Internet and Information Systems, 4*(1), 5–24. doi:10.3837/tiis.2010.01.001

Lindsey, S., Raghavendra, C., & Sivalingam, K. (2002). Data gathering algorithms in sensor networks using energy metrics. *IEEE Transactions on Parallel and Distributed Systems, 13*(9), 924–935. doi:10.1109/TPDS.2002.1036066

Luo, H., Liu, Y., & Das, S. K. (2006). Routing correlated data with fusion cost in wireless sensor networks. *IEEE Transactions on Mobile Computing, 5*(11), 1620–1632. doi:10.1109/TMC.2006.171

Luo, H., Luo, J., Liu, Y., & Das, S. K. (2006). Adaptive data fusion for energy efficient routing in wireless sensor networks. *IEEE Transactions on Computers, 55*(10), 1286–1299. doi:10.1109/TC.2006.157

Madden, S., Franklin, M. J., Hellerstein, J. M., & Hong, W. (2005). TinyDB: An acquisitional query processing system for sensor networks. [TODS]. *ACM Transactions on Database Systems, 30*(1), 122–173. doi:10.1145/1061318.1061322

Madden, S., Szewczyk, R., Franklin, M. J., & Culler, D. (2002). Supporting aggregate queries over ad-hoc wireless sensor networks. In *Proceedings of the Fourth IEEE Workshop on Mobile Computing Systems and Applications* (pp. 49-58). Callicoon, NY: IEEE Computer Society.

Olariu, S., & Stojmenovic, I. (2006). Design guidelines for maximizing lifetime and avoiding energy holes in sensor networks with uniform distribution and uniform reporting. In *Proceedings of IEEE Conference on Computer Communications (INFOCOM'06)* (pp. 1-12). Barcelona, Catalunya, Spain.

Pantazis, N. A., Vergados, D. D., Miridakis, N. I., & Vergados, D. J. (2008). *Power control schemes in wireless sensor networks for homecare e-health applications*. In 1st International Conference on Pervasive Technologies Related to Assistive Environments (pp. 1100-1107) Athens, Greece.

Pattem, S., Krishnamachari, B., & Govindan, R. (2004). *The impact of spatial correlation on routing with compression in wireless sensor networks*. In Third International Symposium on Information Processing in Sensor Networks (pp. 28-35). Berkeley, CA: ACM.

Perrig, A., Szewczyk, R., Wen, V., Culler, D., & Tygar, D. (2002). SPINS: Security protocols for sensor networks. *Wireless Networks Journal (WINE)*, 521-534.

Powell, O., Leone, P., & Rolim, J. (2007). Energy optimal data propagation in wireless sensor networks. *Journal of Parallel and Distributed Computing, 67*, 302–317. doi:10.1016/j.jpdc.2006.10.007

Ruth, A. P., Jason, M., Abu, B., Ashok, K., & Magdy, B. (2006). *Multisensor data fusion schemes for wireless sensor networks*. In CAMPS 2006-International Workshop on Computer Architecture for Machine Perception and Sensing (pp.136-141). Montreal, Canada: IEEE Computer Society.

Sahoo, P. K., Hsieh, K., & Sheu, J. (2007). *Boundary node selection and target detection in wireless sensor network*. In IFIP International Conference on Wireless and Optical Communications Networks (WOCN '07), (pp. 1-5). IEEE Computer Society, Singapore.

Shon, T., Koo, B., Choi, H., & Park, Y. (2009). *Security architecture for IEEE 802.15.4-based wireless sensor network*. In 4th International Symposium on Wireless Pervasive Computing (ISWPC'09), (pp. 1-5), Melbourne, VIC, Australia.

Vuran, M. C., Akan, O. B., & Akyildiz, I. F. (2004). Spatio-temporal correlation: Theory and applications for wireless sensor networks. *Computer Networks, 45*(3), 245–259. doi:10.1016/j.comnet.2004.03.007

Wang, J., Yu, H., & Shang, Z. (2005). Research on reliable link layer communication in wireless sensor networks. In *Proceedings of the 2005 International Conference on Communications, Circuits and Systems* (pp. 417-421), Hong Kong, China.

Wu, X., & Chen, G. (2008). Avoiding energy holes in wireless sensor networks with non-uniform node distribution. *IEEE Transactions on Parallel and Distributed Systems, 19*(5), 710–720. doi:10.1109/TPDS.2007.70770

Xing, G., Tan, R., Liu, B., Wang, J., Jia, X., & Yi, C. (2009). *Data fusion improves the coverage of wireless sensor networks*. In International Conference on Mobile Computing and Networking (pp. 157-168), Beijing, China.

Yao, Y., & Gehrke, J. (2002). The cougar approach to in-network query processing in sensor networks. *SIGMOD Record, 31*(3), 9–18. doi:10.1145/601858.601861

Yu, Y., Krishnamachari, B., & Prasanna, V. K. (2004). *Energy-latency tradeoffs for data gathering in wireless sensor networks*. In IEEE INFOCOM 2004 - Conference on Computer Communications - Twenty-Third Annual Joint Conference of the IEEE Computer and Communications Societies (pp. 244-255). Hong Kong, China.

Zhang, H., & Shen, H. (2009). Balancing energy consumption to maximize network lifetime in data-gathering sensor networks. *IEEE Transactions on Parallel and Distributed Systems, 20*(10), 1526–1539. doi:10.1109/TPDS.2008.252

KEY TERMS AND DEFINITIONS

Data Change Rate: Change rate of data means the change speed of data content per unit time.

Energy Equilibrium: Energy equilibrium means that nodes in the network use up their energy simultaneously.

Chapter 9
Security Issues on Outlier Detection and Countermeasure for Distributed Hierarchical Wireless Sensor Networks

Yiying Zhang
Shenyang Institute of Engineering, China

Lin He
Korea University, South Korea

Lei Shu
Osaka University, Japan

Takahiro Hara
Osaka University, Japan

Shojiro Nishio
Osaka University, Japan

ABSTRACT

Outliers in wireless sensor networks (WSNs) are sensor nodes that launch attacks by abnormal behaviors and fake message dissemination. However, existing cryptographic techniques have difficulty in detecting these outliers, which makes outlier recognition a critical and challenging issue for reliable and secure data dissemination when outliers exist in WSNs. This chapter is concerned about detection and elimination problems of outlier. To efficiently identify and isolate outliers, we present a novel "Outlier Detection and Countermeasure Scheme" (ODCS), which consists of three mechanisms: (1) An abnormal event observation mechanism (AEOM) for network surveillance; (2) An exceptional message supervision mechanism (EMSM) for distinguishing fake messages by exploiting spatiotemporal correlation and consistency; (3) An abnormal frequency supervision mechanism (AFSM) for the evaluation of node behavior. The chapter also provides a heuristic methodology which does not need the knowledge of normal or malicious sensors in advance. This property makes the ODCS not only to distinguish and deal with various

DOI: 10.4018/978-1-61350-110-8.ch009

Copyright © 2012, IGI Global. Copying or distributing in print or electronic forms without written permission of IGI Global is prohibited.

dynamic attacks automatically without advance learning but also reduces the requirement of capability for constrained nodes. In our solution, the communication is limited to a local range, such as one-hop or a cluster, which can reduce the communication frequency and circumscribe the session range further. Moreover, the chapter also provides countermeasures for different types of attacks, such as the rerouting scheme and the rekey security scheme, which can separate outliers from normal sensors and enhance the robustness of network, even when some nodes are compromised by adversary. Simulation results indicate that our approach can effectively detect and defend the outlier attack.

INTRODUCTION

Wireless sensor networks (WSNs) can effectively employ different applications by collecting sensory information in unattended and often adversarial environments such as enemy detection in battle fields, or fire monitoring in urban areas (Aggarwal, 2001). Therefore, the security provision of confidentiality and authentication is a critical requirement for many wireless sensor network applications. However, sensor nodes are highly constrained in transmission power, on-board energy, processing capacity and storage, which requires careful resource management. Due to these limited resources and operation in hostile environments, WSNs are subjected to numerous threats and are vulnerable to attacks from inside, e.g., outliers (Akyildiz et al., 2002), (Sheng et al., 2007), (Liu, Cheng, & Chen, 2007), (Zhang et al., 2010), or from outside, e.g., eavesdropping (Bandyopadhyay & Coyle, 2003).

In this chapter, we focus on the outliers. The outliers are severely destructive to the function of WSNs. Since the outliers usually occupy the same network source as normal nodes, they can easily manufacture the fake messages or tamper with the real messages to impact the performance of network. However, the traditional techniques, such as cryptographic encryption, authentication etc., cannot detect and eliminate all attacks.

Although most of previous security works focus on outside attacks and try to establish a credible relationship among sensor nodes in WSN based on the traditional cryptography (Akyildiz et al., 2002), (Bandyopadhyay & Coyle, 2003), (Bellare, Canetti, & Krawczyk, 1996), (Branch et al., 2006), (Breunig et al., 2000), (Chan, Perrig, & Song, 2003), (Chang & Kuo, 2006), (Chen et al., 2002), (David et al., 2004), (Deng, Han, & Mishra, 2005), which cannot support sufficient protection from all attacks, especially outliers from outlier. Thus, it becomes very urgent and challenging to design an outlier detection scheme. In this chapter, we present a novel outlier detection scheme as well as a series of countermeasures.

PROBLEM STATEMENT

Outliers (also called Inside attacker) in WSNs are some sensor nodes controlled by adversary, they do not perform tasks as normal nodes but exhibit different types of abnormal behaviors, e.g., dropping received messages from their neighbors, forwarding messages to enemy, broadcasting redundant messages, and disseminating fake messages (Akyildiz et al., 2002), (Liu, Cheng, & Chen, 2007). The outlier has the same network resource as a normal sensor node, but its behaviors are different. Typically, outliers are compromised and remote-controlled by adversary. Outliers also attack WSNs by tampering with messages transferred in WSNs or generating bogus messages and forwarding them to critical nodes (e.g., aggregation nodes or sink node), which typically reduces network performance in terms of reliability and security because of the following consequences (Bandyopadhyay & Coyle, 2003):

1. Wasting network bandwidth;
2. Increasing energy consumption;
3. Interfusing illegal messages into sensory data streaming;
4. Causing communication obstruction or dynamic holes.

However, although the outliers seriously threat the network, they are difficult to be detected by traditional cryptographic techniques for the attacks come from network inside (Ash & Moses, 2005). Outliers usually could obtain all or part of the security materials, such as keys, which makes it easy for the outlier to tamper with, inject or eavesdrop messages in network. Thus, it is critical to establish an efficient secure and reliable scheme to detect and prevent outliers. The conventional methods such as encryption, authentication, etc. have the ability to protect the correctness and integrity in WSN. However, they cannot withstand outliers' attacks.

Outliers usually attack the network via two ways:

1. Disseminating fake messages in the network
2. Tampering with transmission of the network

To address this challenging issue, we propose a novel Outlier Detection and Countermeasure Scheme (ODCS) to detect and handle outliers in a hierarchical WSN (e.g., a clustered WSN (Banerjea, 1996)). Moreover, due to high density in the network topology, sensor observations are highly correlated in the space domain. The nature of the physical phenomenon constitutes the temporal correlation between each consecutive observation of a sensor node. These spatiotemporal correlations along with the collaborative nature of the WSN bring significant potential advantages for the development of efficient communication protocols well-suited for the WSN paradigm. Therefore, we adopt the hierarchic network. Compared with previous works (Akyildiz et al., 2002), (Liu, Cheng,, & Chen, 2007), (Bandyopadhyay and Coyle, 2003),

(Bellare, Canetti, & Krawczyk, 1996), (Branch et al., 2006), (Breunig et al., 2000), (Chan, Perrig, & Song, 2003), (Chang & Kuo, 2006), (Chen et al., 2002), (David et al., 2004), (Deng, Han, & Mishra, 2005) for outlier detection in WSNs, ODCS has the following scientific research contributions:

- Firstly, we utilize the spatiotemporal correlation in neighborhood activities as well as the statistical similarity, which provides a heuristic methodology and does not need the knowledge about normal or malicious sensors in advance. This property makes ODCS not only to distinguish and deal with various dynamic attacks automatically without advance learning, but also to reduce the requirement of capability for constrained nodes.
- ODCS can reduce energy consumption and improve reliability by: 1) the communication is limited in a local range, e.g., 1-hop neighbor-communication; 2) cluster head can authenticate and manage member nodes based on the cluster-architecture, which not only reduces communication frequency but also circumscribes the session range further.
- ODCS can not only handle exceptional messages but also abnormal behaviors.
- ODCS provides a rerouting scheme and a rekey security scheme respectively for different types of attacks, which can separate outliers from normal sensors and enhance the robustness of network, even when some nodes are compromised by adversary.

RELATED WORKS

Outlier detection usually is a research issue in data management (Chen et al., 2002), (Du, Wang, & Ning, 2005), (Eschenauer & Gligor, 2002), (Ferreira et al., 2005), (Handy, Haase, & Timmermann, 2002), (Hawkins, 1980), (Hill, Minsker,

& Amir, 2007). Hawkins (1980) defines outlier as an observation that deviates a lot from other observations, and can be generated from a different mechanism. Most of previous works focus on the following four aspects (Ash & Moses, 2005): 1) detection of exceptional message, 2) detection of abnormal behavior in routing, 3) detection of intrusion in wireless networks, and 4) detection of both exceptional message and abnormal behavior.

Detection of Exceptional Message

Detection of exceptional message focus on the messages that are remarkably different from other messages transferred in WSN. Once the adversaries deploy the outliers in network successfully, they can control them to tamper with the messages and disseminate these fake messages in network.

Akyildiz et al. (2002) develop a solution that: 1) allows flexibility in a heuristic to detect outliers; 2) works in-network with communication load the proportional outcome; 3) is robust with respect to data and network change. The solution adopts a technique based on distance similarity to identify global outliers in sensor networks. This technique attempts to reduce the communication overhead by a set of representative data exchanges among neighboring nodes. Each node uses distance similarity to locally identify outliers and then broadcasts the outliers to neighboring nodes for identification. The neighboring nodes repeat the procedure until all sensor nodes in the network eventually agree on the global outliers. This technique can be flexible in respect to multiple existing distance-based outlier detection techniques. However, the technique does not adopt any network structure so that every node uses broadcast to communicate with other nodes in the network, which will cause too much communication overhead. Consequently, it does not scale well to the large-scale networks. Also, it does not work well for the fine-granularity event with limited samples as well as considers without the region correlation of data.

Hu, Perrig, and Johnson (2003) propose a distance-based technique to identify n global outliers in continuous query processing applications of sensor networks. This technique reduces communication overhead as it adopts the structure of aggregation tree and prevents broadcasting of each node in the network. Each node in the tree transmits some useful data to its parent after collecting all the data sent from its children. The sink then roughly figures out top n global outliers and floods these outliers to all the nodes in the network for verification. If any node disagrees on the global results, it will send extra data to the sink again for outlier detection. This procedure is repeated until all the nodes in the network agree on the global results calculated by the sink. This technique considers only one-dimensional data and the aggregation tree used may not be stable due to the dynamic changes of network topology.

Bellare, Canetti, and Krawczyk, (1996) identifie faulty sensor(s) using the aggregation tree including the maximum (max) and minimum (min) values of the sensed attribute and their locations. Therefore, if any sensor reports a data value outside the [min, max] range, it can be identified as a faulty sensor. Breunig et al. (2000) compute a running average and compare it with a threshold, which can be adjusted by a false alarm rate. However, on one hand, Bellare's and Breunig's schemes have not ability to distinguish exceptional values which are different from other nodes in the same place and same time. On the other hand, Banerjeea's and Li's schemes only focus on the deviation of data but ignore the quantity of messages, even there may be exceptional quantity messages whose values are in the certain range. Our solution improves the immunity of network from abnormal behaviors, and can protect the network not only from the devastation of data but also the wrong behavior of nodes.

Detection of Abnormal Behavior

Detection of abnormal behavior aims to identify the attacks, e.g., spoofing, sinkhole or DoS attack. With these types of attacks, outliers attack network by abnormal output, such as large message sending. Some related works (Chan, Perrig, & Song, 2003), (Ishida, Kakuda, & Kikuno, 1992) have been conducted for WSNs.

Chan, Perrig, and Song (2003) propose an in-network outlier cleaning approach that is accomplished during multi-hop data forwarding process and uses neighboring relation. This approach guarantees that outliers can be either corrected or removed from further transmission. In this paper, there are two in-network outlier cleaning techniques for data collection applications of sensor networks. One technique uses wavelet analysis specifically for outliers such as noises or occasionally appeared errors. The other technique uses dynamic time warping distance-based similarity comparison specifically for outliers that are erroneous and last for a certain time period. In this technique, each node transforms raw data into the wavelet time-frequency domain and identifies the high-frequency data measurements as outliers and corrects them using proper wavelet coefficients. The long segmental outliers can be detected and removed by comparing the similarity of two sensing series of the neighboring nodes within 2 forwarding hops. The proposed techniques take advantage of spatiotemporal correlations of sensor data for identifying outliers. A drawback of this technique, however, is its dependency of a suitable pre-defined threshold that is not obvious to define.

Ishida, Kakuda, and Kikuno (1992) present two techniques based on Dynamic naive Bayesian Networks (DBNs) to identity local outliers in environmental sensor data streams. The naive Bayesian classification technique is utilized to detect outliers' misbehavers in WSNs and also uses the spatiotemporal correlations, which are very important for detecting outliers with high accuracy. This technique uses DBNs to fast track changes in dynamic network topology of sensor networks. One technique assumes that there is only a measured state variable existing in the multivariate data and the current state can be determined only depending on its historical state. This technique identifies outliers by computing the posterior probability of the most recent data values in a sliding window. The data measurements that fall outside the expected value interval are considered as outliers. The other technique uses a more complex DBN including two measured state variables for outlier detection. This technique makes it possible to operate on several data streams at once.

Detection of Intrusion in Wireless Networks

Detection of intrusion in wireless networks is studied in (David et al., 2004), (Deng, Han, & Mishra, 2005). David's work (2004) is the first work on intrusion detection in wireless ad hoc networks. A new architecture is investigated for collaborative statistical anomaly detection, which provides protection from attacks. In Deng's (2005) approach, an intrusion alarm is raised when the number of failures exceeds a predefined threshold. In this work, multiple rules are defined, and a decision is made based on a simple summation of the rule application results. Various solutions that deploy machine learning techniques appeared recently. These solutions support the idea that machine learning techniques offer higher level of flexibility and adaptability. However, these techniques consume significant resources. Moreover, the feature sets they deploy mostly include those features whose values are known to change under the influence of an attacker, or are known to be weak spots. This is their major deficiency, as relying on these features only the known attacks or their variations can be detected. Comparing with previous works in this section, our countermeasures can defend various attacks much better, and require no prior knowledge on normal/malicious sensor activities.

Detection of Both Exceptional Message and Abnormal Behavior

Generally, outlier attacks the networks by multiple attributes simultaneously, i.e. by both exceptional message and abnormal behavior, such as disseminating large numbers of fake messages. Liu, Cheng, and Chen (2007) proposed an Insider Attacker Detection Scheme in WSNs (IADS) which can detect the outlier in both sides.

IADS assumes each sensor can listen on the channel for activities of direct neighbors intermittently. Based on spatial correlation, i.e., sensors should behave similarly in the close proximity, IADS divides the process of detection into four phases: 1) information collection phase. In this phase, each sensor monitors its every direct neighbor's networking behaviors and models these behaviors in a q-component attribute vector. 2) false information filtering phase. A sensor is no reliable, if its trust value is lower than minimum value. 3) outlier detection. According to the value of vector, sensor calculates the distance with its each neighbor by Mahalanobis distance. 4) Majority vote. Each nodes will announce all identified outliers to its neighbors (maybe larger than 2-hop). According to these advertisements, sensor can calculate a proportion which indicates how many sensors consider a sensor *is* an outlier. The majority vote combines decisions to report the result to the base station.

However, due to the limited-resource of WSN, IADS is still not suitable for WSN for some weaknesses. Firstly, the establishment of attribute vectors needs globe or large-range information and much communication, which is difficult or impractical for most of applications in WSN. In our solution, we adopt the hierarchical network model which localizes the communication and just needs a small sample space according to the spatiotemporal correlation. Secondly, to authenticate the outlier, IADS introduces too many sensors to communicate with each other, which consumes high energy and high communications. In our solution, we detect outliers in cluster head and authenticate them by one-hop neighbors with few communications. Finally, IADS only considers the spatial correlations but ignore the temporal correlation, which reduces the accuracy of detection, especially when new event happens. In our solution, we employ the spatiotemporal correlation which can distinguish the event or the attacker early.

In short, most existing related works are for ad hoc network and just focus on incomplete protection, which makes it insufficient for defending various attacks from outlier. Therefore, our solution provides a more consummate scheme, which can detect and defend attacks from outliers in these three aspects.

System Model

Network Model

We consider a WSN consisting of a base station and large numbers of sensor nodes. The considered WSN can be represented as a graph G (V, E), where $V = \{v_i | v_j, ..., v_{|V|}\}$ is a finite set of sensor nodes (vertexes) and $E = \{e_i | e_j, ..., e_{|E|}\}$ is a finite set of links (edges), $E \subset V \times V$. Here, vertex v_i denotes a sensor node; and suppose that an edge e_{ij} indicates a communication link between the two given sensors v_i and v_j, where $e_{ij} \in E$.

> **Definition 1** *Direct Neighbor Node*: given $\forall v_i, v_j \in V$ (i≠j), if $\exists e_{ij} \in E$, v_j is called as v_i's direct neighbor node (1-hop-node). Let $N(v_i)$ represents the set of all v_i's direct neighbor nodes.

Moreover, the hierarchical architectures have high performance (Bandyopadhyay, 2003) as follows: 1) Extension of the network lifetime; 2) Reduced energy consumption by each network sensor node; 3) Reduced quantity of messages transferred in network by data aggregation. Thus, we choose a hierarchical architecture as the network model. In our network, we propose that the all sensor nodes can self-organize into clusters which are charged by a cluster head (also call as *CH*).

The Hierarchical Architecture

Let C_i and CH_i represent a cluster and a cluster head, respectively. Thus, $V = \bigcup_{i=1}^{n} C_i$, and $C_i \cap C_j$ = ø. Each sensor node x has a unique id ID_x and can send/receive messages to/from $N(ID_x)$. All nodes in a cluster are reachable by the cluster head through either direct communication or multi-hop relaying, which only uses short distance radio for transmission (Akyildiz et al., 2002). However, for the energy efficiency, the normal nodes have been forbidden to communicate with the base station directly. The cluster head collects and aggregates the data from its member nodes, and forwards them to the base station.

Considering the energy efficiency and security of WSN, the cluster head election algorithm is adapted as equation (1) (Main & Savitch, 1997), (Malan, Welsh, & Smith, 2004), (Medhi, 2002). In the initial phase, a node itself decides whether it can become a candidate CH according to the energy level and a random algorithm. A node with more energy has a high probability to be elected as a CH. To become a CH, it needs another parameter generated by each node randomly, and the number should be between 0 and 1.

$$T(n) = \begin{cases} \frac{p}{1-p[r \mod (1/p)]}[\eta+(i\times p)(1-\eta)], & \forall n \in \text{“} \\ 0, & otherwise \end{cases} \quad (1)$$

Where $T(n)$ is probability function of electing itself as *CH*; p is the percentage of *CH*s; r denotes the current round number; η represents the remaining energy level percentage; i is the sum of rounds that a node is idle, and it is reset to 0 when it is

elected as *CH*. Γ is the set of nodes that have not been *CH*s in the $1/p$ rounds recently.

THE SECURITY FOUNDATION

Due to the open communication and harsh environment of WSN, the network is subjected to numerous threats and vulnerable to attacks. It is very important to establish a secure communication infrastructure. A typical scheme is the random key predistribution, in which each node is preloaded with an initial key as the seed for key management (Medhi, 2002), (Perrig et al., 2002), (Rafaeli & Hutchison, 2003), (Zhu, Setia, & Jajodia, 2006). Moreover, a sensor node deployed in a security critical environment must be manufactured to prevent possible break-in attacks at least for a short time interval when captured by an adversary; otherwise, the adversary could easily compromise all the sensor nodes and then threaten the network.

To provide the security, networks typically are based on cryptographic operations that involve keys. In the chapter, a key system is presented, which supports not only confidentiality but also authentication for the messages exchanged by nodes in the WSN. Since the network is established based on hierarchical architecture, single key system is not appropriate for all the secure communication. In our solution, we support five types of keys for each sensor nodes to protect each phase: an initial key, a master key, a pair-wise key, a cluster key and a network key.

- *The initial key.* Every sensor node will be assigned an initial key generated by the base station in the initial phase of deployment. The initial key provides the primal and basal security environment for network. Using the initial key as the seed key, each node can generate a master key by a one-way hash function. Afterwards, the initial key will be erased to ensure that the

Table 1. The different keys in our solution

Key	Function	Range
Initial key	As a seed to generate the master key, it will be erased after being used.	Overall network
Master key	Generated by initial key, it is the seed for the pairwise key.	A sensor node
Pairwise key	The key shared between two neighbor nodes provides a secure communication link for pair nodes.	Between pair nodes
Cluster key	The key shared between the cluster head and member nodes provides a secure communication link between cluster and its member.	Inside of a cluster
Network key	The key shared between the cluster heads and the base station protects the communication between them.	Between the cluster head and the base station

adversaries have no the ability to deduce other keys by the initial key. The initial key is a temporary key and will be released later.

- *The master key*. Each sensor node can generate a master key using by the initial key. The master key is a unique key for each node. The node will establish the secure relationship with its immediate neighbor nodes (one-hop nodes) based on the master key.
- *The pairwise key*. Each sensor node will establish a secure link with its immediate neighbor nodes. The pairwise key is shared with pair neighbor nodes and encrypt/decrypt the messages exchanged between them. Since the master key is unique, the pairwise key is various, which makes it very difficult to obtain the entire pairwise key for adversaries.
- *The cluster key*. A cluster key is a key shared by sensor nodes in the same cluster. Different from pairwise key, the cluster key is generated by cluster head and its member nodes. Since the cluster key has higher affection in the network, it will be rekeyed when the cluster head detected outlier.
- *The network key*. A network key is for the security of communication between the cluster head and the base station. After the formation of cluster, cluster head aggregates the data from other member nodes

and forward them to the base station. During the process, cluster head encrypts/decrypts the messages by the network key with the base station.

In the summary, the key system includes the considered five types of keys. In our key system, we protect each phase in communication. However, the key operations mostly happen locally, and both the cluster key and pairwise key are based on the master key (generated by initial key), which makes the system efficient.

Establishing the Pair-Wise Key

The security foundation is that each sensor node x can establish pair-wise keys with $N(ID_x)$, which is also used as the security foundation for research work in (Krontiris et al., 2008), (Laneman & Wornell, 2003), (Larsen & Marx, 2000), (Medhi, 2002), (Perrig et al., 2002), (Rafaeli & Hutchison, 2003). We assume there exists a lower bound on the time interval T_{min} that is necessary for an adversary to compromise a sensor node, and the time interval T_{est} for a newly deployed sensor node to discover its immediate neighbors is smaller than T_{min} ($T_{min} > T_{est}$), especially in the initial phase of deployment (Perrig et al., 2002).

Definition 2 *One-Way Cryptographic Hash Function $f_K(x)$:* $f_K(x)$ is a one-way cryptographic hash function which utilizes node

x's identification ID_x and previous key K as parameters to generate a new key via a deterministic procedure, which can take an arbitrary block of data and returns a fixed-size bit string.

The base station generates an initial key K_I and loads each node with this key in time interval T_{est}. When sensor nodes are deployed in WSN, each node u can use K_I and hash function f to generate its master key $K_u = fK_I (ID_u)$. Once having gotten master key, nodes will erase K_I. Note that the processing will be finished in T_{est}, the adversaries have no ability to eavesdrop the network and get K_I. After the time interval T_{est}, although adversary could compromise a node, it just obtains the materials of key of the compromised node but not K_I and information of other nodes.

Definition 3 MAC(key, msg): is a cryptographic message authentication code (*MAC*) of message *msg* using a symmetric key *key*. A MAC algorithm accepts a secret key and an arbitrary-length message as input to be authenticated, and outputs a *MAC*.

Afterwards, node u broadcasts an advertisement message $(ID_u, Nonce_u)$ containing a nonce $Nonce_u$, and waits for v $(v \in N(_u))$ to respond with ID_v. Once a neighbor node v accepts the advertisement message, it will respond node u with $\{ID_v, MAV(K_v, ID_v \mid Nonce_u)\}_{K_I}$ encrypted by K_I as follows.

$$u \rightarrow N(u) : \{ID_u, Noncue_u\}_{K_I}$$

$$v : K_{vu} = f_{K_u}\{ID_v\}$$

$$v \rightarrow u : \{MAC(K_{vu}, ID_v)\}_{K_u}$$

At the same time, v can also generate the master key $K_v = fK_I (ID_v)$. Node u computes its pairwise key, K_{uv} as $K_{uv} = fK_v (ID_u)$, with v; also to the neighbor node v, K_{vu} as $K_{vu} = fK_u (ID_v)$. Thus, each node can use its neighbor nodes' IDs and pairwise key to decrypt the encrypted message by its neighbors, which means that every node can be authenticated by its immediate nodes.

Establishing the Cluster Key

The cluster key establishes a secure link between member nodes and the cluster head. Similar to pair-wise keys, the cluster key is generated based on the master key and pairwise key.

After the forming of clusters, each cluster head CH_i sends an advertisement message *adv* attaching its initial master key K_{CH}^0 to all cluster member nodes. Once the member sensor node u ($u \in C_i$, $u \neq CH_i$) accepts *adv* and obtains K_{CH}^0, it generates an initial cluster key K_{CH}^u as $K_{CH}^u = f_{K_u}(ID_{CH})$ and send it as a reply message encrypted by K_{CH}^0 back to CH_i. Then the cluster head can decrypt them. The security foundation provides an initial secure environment for network and will be utilized by other mechanisms.

$$CH_i \rightarrow * : \{ID_{CH}, K_{CH}^0\}_{K_I} \qquad 1.$$

$$u : K_{CH}^u = f_{K_u}(ID_{CH}) \qquad 2.$$

$$u \rightarrow CH_i : \{ID_u, K_{CH}^u\}_{K_{CH}^0} \qquad 3.$$

After these steps, each sensor node u has established a pairwise key with each its neighbors and also obtained the cluster key from the cluster head. Furthermore, each of them erases the initial key K_I, which makes the adversaries have no the ability to obtain the master key.

Establishing the Network Key

The network key provides the secure transmission between the cluster head and the base station. In the hierarchical WSN, the cluster head obtains very significant information as the collector. Therefore, it is very necessary to ensure the security for reporting of the cluster head.

Generally, once a node is elected as the cluster head, it sends an application message encrypted by K_I to base station to register its ID as a cluster head. Afterwards, the base station generates a new key and sends it to the cluster head as the cluster key. The detailed processing in the base station is beyond the scope of this work.

Problem Formulation

Outlier detection is a long studied problem in data analysis. Although there are several papers give the definitions of outlier (Bay & Schwabacher, 2003), (Branch et al., 2006), (Hawkins, 1980), most of them suppose the WSN as a large dataset and just focus on the aspect of data deviation as well as ignore the behaviors of sensor node. Since the data usually has the characteristic of localization, it cannot be fully representative of the entire information without any sensor nodes' information, e.g. position. In this section, the definitions are given from wireless sensor network aspect on both the data deviation and behavior difference.

Suppose there are m clusters, $C_1, C_2, ..., C_m$ in a WSN. Given $\forall v_j \in C_i$ ($1 \leq j \leq |C_i|$), let d_j represent the message from v_j; and f_j represents the sending messages frequency of v_j. Here now formally defines the outlier problem addressed in this chapter. As mentioned earlier, an outlier represents a node whose observation is behaviorally distant from the rest of nodes on either content of messages or number of messages in WSN. The two types of definitions of outliers are as follows.

F Attacker

Definition 4 $F(t)$ attacker (also called F attacker): Given the frequency list is $f_1, f_2, ..., f_n$ ($n > 0$). Let $\overline{f} = \frac{1}{n} \sum_{i=1}^{n} f_i$, and $\overline{F}(f) = |f - \overline{f}|$. A node is called an $F(t)$ outlier, that is, F outlier, if $\overline{F}(f) > t$, where t is a threshold which defines the deviation toleration of frequency.

The definition of $F(t)$ indicates the deviation of frequency sent messages. Although the choice of the disclosure frequency does not affect the security of the system, it is an important performance factor, especially in disclosure of sensor node behavior.

G Attacker

Definition 5 $G(d, th)$ attacker (also call G attacker): Given the sorted data list $d_1, d_2, ..., d_k, ...$. We have $|d_1 - d| \leq |d_2 - d| \leq ... \leq |d_k - d| \leq ...$. Let $G^k(d) = |d_k - d|$ represent the distance between data d and its k-th nearest neighbor $(K\text{-}NN)(d_k)$. A node is called an $G(d, th)$ outlier, if $G^k(d) > th$. Where th is a threshold which represents the deviation between two messages.

The definition of $G(d, th)$ describes the deviation of content sent messages based on the k-th nearest neighbor (K-NN) (Ramaswamy, Rastogi, & Shim, 2000). Considering the situation that outlier can attack the network by tampering with messages or disseminating fake messages, it is very necessary to support the detection mechanism for $G(d, th)$ outlier. Furthermore, the WSNs usually encounter the spatiotemporal correlation (Vuran, Akan, & Akyildiz, 2004), which makes the identification process locally.

In defiance of the cryptological protection, outliers launch attack via tampering with packets or sending abnormal quantity of packets, which disseminates untruthful messages or causes abnormal traffics.

In addition, due to the resource-constrained sensors and the loose infrastructure of network, detection of outlier is not trivial. Our solution employs a hierarchical architecture which can efficiently collect and analyze messages into cluster heads for the wireless sensor network. Based on this architecture and the detection approach, we propose corresponding algorithms for detection of outliers with parameters *t* and *th* for Definitions 4 and 5, respectively. Considering the variety of applications in wireless sensor network, we adopt a heuristic method to generate these parameters.

Attacks Model

Outliers can attack WSNs in various ways, we survey some attacks under outliers for WSNs. In the descriptions below, note the difference between attacks that try to manipulate user data directly and attacks that try to affect the underlying transmission topology.

Provocateur Attack

In Provocateur attack, a provocateur is a sensor node compromised by adversary and hide in the network as a spy. Different from the passive attack of eavesdropping, provocateur takes the initiative to spread fake messages in the network or eavesdrop aggregated data to the adversary. The outlier usually launches provocateur attack by tampering with or generating fake messages or eavesdrop messages.

Sink-Hole Attack

Sink-Hole attacks are based on the idea that the nodes controlled by adversary attract surrounding nodes with unfaithful routing information, and then alters the data passing through it. In a Sinkhole attack, an outlier tries to draw all or as much as possible traffic from a particular area, by making itself look attractive to the surrounding nodes with respect to the routing metric. Sinkhole attacks typically work by making a compromised node look especially attractive to surrounding nodes with respect to the routing algorithm. For instance, an adversary could spoof or replay an advertisement for an extremely high quality route to a base station.

Hello Flood Attack

In *hello flood* attack, nodes broadcast *hello* messages to inform one-hop neighbors of their presence, which makes that an adversary can lunch a *hello flood* and disseminate them from an outlier. These replayed *hello* packets reach nodes that the originating node cannot communicate with directly. Any node that uses the originating node as the next hop in a route but that is not within that node's radio range would not be able to reliably forward traffic.

DoS Attack

Denial of service attack (DoS) in WSNs is a critical security issue. In this chapter, we focus on defending against such as path-based DoS attack. With this type of attack, outliers overwhelm sensor nodes with either replayed packets or injected spurious packets and attempt to disrupt, subvert, or destroy a network, which makes WSN be affected on both the functionality and the overall performance, and a large amount of energy will be consumed.

Selective Forwarding Attack

WSNs are usually multi-hop networks and assume that the participating nodes could forward the messages faithfully. Outliers, however, can refuse to route certain messages and drop them. An outlier interested in suppressing or modifying packets originating from a select few nodes

Figure 1. The framework of ODCS

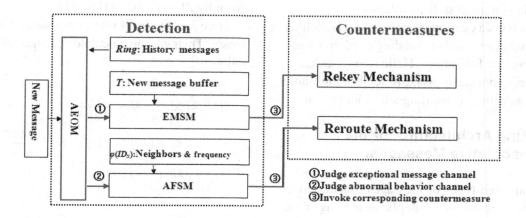

can reliably forward the remaining traffic and limit suspicion of her wrongdoing. If they drop all the packets through them, then it is called as Black Hole Attack (Karlof & Wagner, 2003). If they selectively forward the packets, it is called selective forwarding. Selective forwarding attacks are typically most effective when the outlier is explicitly included on the path of a data flow. An outlier launching a selective forwarding attack will likely follow the path of least resistance and attempt to include itself on the actual path of the data flow.

DETECTION MECHANISMS IN ODCS

In this section, we will introduce the strategy to detect outlier and provide the corresponding countermeasures in next chapter. According to the problem formulation, there are two types of attackers: *G* attacker and *F* attacker. We then propose a scheme for outlier detection. Based on different behaviors of attackers, the detection mechanism can invoke different identification algorithm to verify the doubted nodes.

The proposed Outlier Detection and Countermeasure Scheme (ODCS) consists of four mechanisms: 1) Abnormal Event Observation Mechanism (AEOM); 2) Exceptional Message

Supervision Mechanism (EMSM); 3) Abnormal Frequency Supervision Mechanism (AFSM); and 4) countermeasures which will be introduce in detail next chapter.

The several mechanisms can work cooperatively as follows. When a new message arrives at the cluster head, the AEOM will authenticate it. Afterward, the AEOM uses a trigger-mechanism which can discover abnormal events and trigger relevant mechanisms. Once the AEOM detected abnormal event, it will trigger EMSM or AFSM. The EMSM and the AFSM are responding for abnormal behavior and exceptional message respectively. Once the EMSM and the AFSM confirmed the event, the countermeasure mechanism supports some efficient solutions. In Figure1, M, T and $\varphi(ID_x)$ are some assistant data sources and described later.

Abnormal Event Observation Mechanism (AEOM)

For perceiving the abnormal events (Wang, Xu, & Liu, 1999), (Wu et al., 2007), (Xu, Heidemann, & Estrin, 2001), (Yang et al., 2008), (Zhang & Chen, 2006) and invoking corresponding mechanisms, we design the AEOM that is sensitive to abnormal events. In WSN, outlier controlled by adversary typically acts different with normal nodes in abnormal style as follows.

An adversary can attack network by launching abnormal event, such as sending excessive messages to cause DoS attack, Hello flood attack, etc, or dropping normal message to achieve Sink-hole attack, selective forwarding attack and so on.

The Ring Architecture for the Representative Messages.

There are two types of messages transferred in network in freshness: the duplicate messages; the fresh messages. The duplicate messages mean that the messages are usually sent and authenticated. It is only necessary to judge whether forward them according to the frequency. Thus, it is very important to collect and cluster the representative messages.

Considering the limited storage of sensor, a storage architecture, a ring named M is designed to store the latest history messages as the data frame of reference (Zhang et al., 2008). Here history messages indicate those representative and recent accepted messages by cluster head.

Suppose M store records circularly. In M, the fresh messages will be arranged in the ring orderly, which will flush old messages when it has been filled. Let $M = \{m_i \mid m_1, m_2, ..., m_{|M|}\}$, which is a dynamic set exchangeable. Here m_i, a tuple with the format as <*msg, freq, tstamp*>, is the property of message type. And *msg* denotes the content of the representative message, for example, if there are 5 types of messages, M would store 5 representative messages ($M = \{m_1, m_2, ..., m_5\}$); and *freq* indicates the frequency of m_i ($1 \leq i \leq |M|$), which indicates that how many this type of messages it has been sent; and *tstamp* is the timestamp of the nearest sent message.

Moreover, according to queuing theory in M/M/1 queuing system, in cluster head, the random arrival pattern of message from inside cluster is in line with Poisson distribution, and the probability of an arrival in a time interval of length $h > 0$ is given by Zhao (2003, p311-331).

Here λ is the birth rate of messages for each sensor. Then we can calculate L, length of M, as follow:

$$e^{-\lambda h}(\lambda h) = \lambda h(1 - \lambda h + \frac{(\lambda h)^2}{2!} - ...)$$
$$= \lambda h - (\lambda h)^2 + ... + (-1)^{n+1}\frac{(\lambda h)^n}{(n-1)!} + ...$$
$$= \lambda h + o(h)$$

$$(2)$$

$$L = \frac{T}{e^{-\lambda h}(\lambda h)} = Te^{\lambda h}(\lambda h) \qquad (3)$$

Here T is the service time of cluster head. Normally, the service time is the capability that cluster head can deal with all messages in M. However, in initial phase, we can set the default value of M as half of the number of nodes within the cluster (Zhao, 2005). According to equation (2) and (3), we can decide the length of M.

With the constant arrival of messages, the items in M will be updated when the message arrives. During the collecting process, messages can be clustered into at most L types, that is, the comparison for distinguishing new message scan the ring at most L times too. In next applications, M as the objective dataset can support the simplicity and efficiency of outlier detection.

Outlier Detection for G Attacker

In the hierarchical WSN, the cluster head has the relationship as tree structure with its members. Thus, the cluster head is responsible for collecting information from member nodes. According to the spatiotemporal correlation in WSN, single node in a cluster has lower chance to catch an event independently. Based on the above fact and according to the definition 5, the message from the inside cluster will be authenticated in the cluster head. This subsection just focuses on the deviation of content.

When a new message m_{new} coming from the cluster member arrives at cluster head, it can be authenticated by similarity function with M. According to Definition 5 and (Zhao & Karypis, 2005), (Zhen, Yuan, & Myong-Soon, 2006), we have a set as follows:

$$G(m_{new}) = \{G^i(m_{new}) \mid G^1(m_{new}), G^2(m_{new}),...,G^{|M|}(m_{new})\}$$
$$= \{|\, m_i - m_{new} \,|\, ||\, m_1 - m_{new} \,|, |\, m_2 - m_{new} \,|,...,|\, m_{|M|} - m_{new} \,|\}$$

(4)

In equation (4), $G^i(m_{new})$ denotes the divergence between the new message and normal messages. According to equation (4), this distance measurement is appropriate in cases where messages are defined as "different", if they are different from others on contents. Suppose we have a certain threshold th. Given $\forall\, i,\ (1 \leq i \leq |M|),\ m_{new}$ should be an exceptional message: a fake or new message, if $G^i(m_{new}) > th$.

Outlier Detection for F Attacker

Outliers can attack the network in variety ways. Besides attack in content, outliers can also attack the network by misbehaviors, e.g., Outliers can launch attack with abnormal transmission frequency, e.g. too high or too low. This attack is mainly manifested in the exceptional frequency of sent message, or incorrect targets (receivers).

To detect the exceptional behavior from outlier, we can adopt k-means algorithm (Jun, Jeong, & Kuo, 2005) according to definition 4. Firstly, in Euclidean space, the mean of transmission in a cluster can be computed by equation (5) as follows:

$$t = \frac{1}{|M|} \sum_{m_i \in M} m_i.freq$$

(5)

Here t denotes the mean of history message frequency. Given a cluster C_k, a sensor node $v_i \in C_k$,

the *threshold*, the differentia between a node message and the cluster mean (centroid) in frequency, can be computed by equation (6) as follows:

$$diff(C_k, t) = \sqrt{\sum_{i=1}^{|C_k|} (w_{v_i} - t)^2}$$

(6)

Here w_{v_i} denotes the frequency of one type of message from node ID_i. In other words, it indicates how many messages that node v_i has sent and different from *freq* which denotes the frequency of one type of message for a cluster. If $diff(C_k, t)$ is greater than the threshold value, it means that the node has sent too many or too few messages and is considered as an Outlier candidate. Cluster head then invokes AFSM mechanism to identify it further.

Exceptional Message Supervision Mechanism (EMSM)

Having detected the exceptional messages, the AEOM invokes the EMSM to further identify whether the messages are fake. The EMSM mechanism is responsible for distinguishing false or fake messages to identify outliers.

Analysis of G Attacker

Based on the facts that nodes in WSNs are often in spatiotemporal correlation (Jun, Jeong, & Kuo, 2005), EMSM can utilize the characteristic to classify messages and distinguish suspicious messages. The identification of new message has hysteresis, that is, we have no ability to identify a new type of message until we can collect sufficient evidence from the subsequence new messages. Identifying a new type of message should meet the following conditions:

1. the new message should have similar messages;

2. the similar messages should be from different senders in the same cluster;

3. the new subsequence messages have a short interval with that new message, for example a period;

The first condition requires that the new message is not independent. In accordance with the facts, it is low probability that only single node in the cluster detects the event for the high-density deployment of sensor nodes; and the single node is unauthentic in WSN. According to the description above, the second condition ensures that the event has localization. That is, the sensor nodes which have neighboring relationship have the high possibility to monitor the same event. Also, the third condition shows that the detection has synchronization. The algorithm of EMSM meets all the above requirements.

Identify G Attacker

Due to the constrained storage in WSN, a temporal *Buffer* named S is designed for accumulating several subsequent messages as the frame of reference. Let $S = \{(s_i, w_i) \mid (s_1, w_1), (s_2, w_2), ..., (s_{|T|}, w_{|S|})\}$. Here, s_i indicates a fresh message; w_i is the frequency of s_i. According to the cosine similarity, we can compute the similarity between m_{new} and s_i, and then identify the m_{new}'s attribute by using equation (6). Since the S is temporal, it requires that all identification should be end in a period and the space will be released.

According to definition 5, the idea of k-NN is extremely simple and yet quite effective in many applications, e.g., text classification. We can choose different suitable methods for different applications. The key component of a k-NN algorithm is the distance/similarity function, which is chosen based on applications and the nature of the data. For relational data, the Euclidean distance is commonly used. For text documents, cosine similarity is a popular choice.

Given a similarity function $\gamma()$ which indicates the distance between two messages ; and the $\Gamma()$ presents the minimum of the distance between m_{new} and the sequent message set S as equation (7).

$$\Gamma(m_{new}, S) = \min\{\gamma(m_{new}, s_i) = \mid m_{new} - s_i \mid \mid s_i \in S\}$$

$$(7)$$

If $\Gamma() \leq threshold$, there should be one $s_i \in S$ which similar to m_{new}. If the similar messages also come from different nodes, m_{new} will be considered as a new type message and added to M; otherwise, it will be considered as a fake message. And the node will be marked as an Outlier. At the same time, cluster head will inform its members and base station (BS).

Abnormal Frequency Supervision Mechanism (AFSM)

Having detected the abnormal frequency of a node, the AEOM invokes the AFSM to further identify whether the node is an F attacker. The AFSM mechanism is responsible for distinguishing weather a node is an F attacker by employing a one-hop authentication mechanism.

Analysis of F Attacker

According to discussion, the Outliers often behave abnormally. Most of the behaviors are as follows:

1. Tampering with messages from other members;

2. Dropping the messages which need to be forwarded to cluster head or other members, such as sink-hole attack and Selective Forwarding attack;

3. Broadcasting redundant messages to waste energy and cause communication traffics, e.g., DoS attack;

4. Eavesdropping messages and leaking them to adversary. AFSM focuses on detecting these types of attacks.

Subsequently, for authenticating an outlier candidate, we propose a 1-hop neighbor authentication mechanism. According to Definition 1, each node ID_x which keeps its $N(ID_x)$ can get w_{ID_i} that indicates the frequency of node $ID_j \in N(ID_x)$ and store them in a queue. Let $\varphi(ID_x) = \{(ID_j, w_{ID_j}) | (ID_1, w_{ID_1}), (ID_2, w_{ID_2}), \ldots, (ID_m, w_{ID_m})\}$, here φ denotes a queue of the outlier candidate ID_x's neighbor nodes; m is the amount of ID_x's neighbor nodes.

In statistics, a standard score indicates how many standard deviations an observation is above or below the mean. It is a dimensionless quantity derived by subtracting the population mean from an individual raw score and then dividing the difference by the population standard deviation. This conversion process is called standardizing or normalizing; however, "normalizing" can refer to many types of ratios; see normalization (statistics) for more. The standard deviation is the unit of measurement of the z-score (Liu, 2001).

Identify F Attacker

According to *z*-score theory, the z-score method transforms an attribute value based on the mean and the standard deviation of the attribute. That is, the z-score of the value indicates how far and in which direction the value deviates from the mean value of the attribute, expressed in units of the standard deviation of the attribute. Therefore, we can provide correct judgment based on the z-score method in equations (8), (9) and (10) as follows:

$$\mu_{ID_x} = \frac{1}{m} \sum_{j=1}^{m} w_{ID_j}, \qquad (8)$$

$$\sigma_{ID_x} = \sqrt{\frac{1}{m-1} \sum_{j=1}^{m} (w_{ID_j} - \mu_{ID_x})^2} \qquad (9)$$

$$\overline{\varphi_{ID_x}} = \left| \frac{w_{ID_x} - \mu_{ID_x}}{\sigma_{ID_x}} \right|, \qquad (10)$$

Where μ_{ID_x} and σ_{ID_x} denote the mean and standard deviation of the neighbors of ID_x respectively; and the $\overline{\varphi_{ID_x}}$ represents the distance between the outlier and the population mean of $\varphi(ID_x)$ of the standard deviation. If $\varphi(ID_x)$ is negative when the $\overline{\varphi_{ID_x}}$ is below the mean, the node will be reported to cluster head as a real outlier. Otherwise, the neighbors suggest cluster head to cancel the identification of outlier candidate.

Furthermore, if w_{ID_i} is high enough for collection, which means the cluster head has gotten sufficient messages and then informs its members to pause or delay transmission. In this situation, if the member nodes still transfer messages out of controlling, it should be considered as an outlier.

COUNTERMEASURES IN ODCS

Since the outliers are not detectable and many of them attack network without decryption of messages (Liu, Cheng. & Chen, 2007), it is insufficient to defend against the outlier only by cryptography-based techniques. We can do nothing to rescue the outliers (compromised nodes), then we should provide a good scheme to reduce the impact of the outliers on the network as much as possible. Once a normal node has been compromised as an outlier, we assume the adversary also obtains all materials of outlier including keys. In this section, we will present the cooperating algorithms to filer the outlier. According to different attacks, the cluster head can invoke different corresponding mechanism and defend against the attacks.

A Common Filter Function Based on ID-identification

Once having identified the outlier out, the cluster head would broadcast $ID_{attacker}$ (the ID of attacker) to other the cluster members. The alarm announcement should be not known by outlier. However, due to the open communication, it is very difficult to avoid the outlier, when the alarm happens.

In the chapter, we design a new function $\Psi()$ which supports a filter approach to filter the outlier as well as deliver the notice message to normal nodes. The function is as follow.

$$\Psi(ID_x) = \prod_{i=1}^{m}(ID_x - ID_i), \qquad (11)$$

When the cluster head broadcasts the control message, each node is designed to utilize function (11) to decide acceptance or not after receiving the control message. $ID_{attacker}$ cannot recover the new key because $\Psi(ID_{outlier}) = 0$, and it has no the ability to decrypt the control messages. The function should be not very complex, because each node just collects and computes the nodes' ID in the same cluster. Each sensor node in WSN has an ID list which stores all IDs in the same list and their statuses, such as is it an outlier, has it been a cluster head and so on. When a node has been announced as an outlier, each sensor node will mark it as an outlier.

Defend Against the Message Dissemination Attack from G Attacker

Typically, G attacker attacks the network by disseminating the exceptional messages, such as the tampered messages, the fake messages.

Firstly, identified by above approaches and authenticated by cluster head ID_i, the outlier $ID_{attacker}$ will be announced in the cluster. Then the normal node u will decrypt the messages to obtain the outlier's ID $ID_{attacker}$, and evade the messages from $ID_{attacker}$. Suppose CH, u, o indicate the cluster head, normal member node and outlier respectively, the process is as follow.

$$CH \rightarrow * : MAC(K_{CH}^*, ID_{attacker})$$

u: $\Psi(ID_{attacker}) \neq 0$, *update the ID list and mark attacker; afterwards, u rejects those messages from o*;

o: $\Psi(ID_{attacker}) = 0$, *do nothing*.

Furthermore, G attacker can also attack the network by tampering with the messages transferred in network, which means the attacker has obtained the security things, such as key, and can decrypt the messages. Thus, it is necessary to rekey, which will be described in next section in detail.

Defend Against the Provocateur Attack from G Attacker

The provocateur attack aims to eavesdrop the messages to the adversaries, which will disclose the information if they also obtain the relative keys. To defend against the provocateur attack, we present a rekey mechanism that can support dynamic key to protect the network and filter the attackers (Zhang, 2008). Once the cluster head detects an attacker, it will inform the overall member nodes to rekey. Then the new generated cluster key replaces the obsolete one. In our solution, the rekey mechanism provides a continuous protection which makes the network has the ability of resilience to outlier.

The Situations for Rekeying

In the chapter, we adopt the rekey approach with the trigger-mode. According to the different situation, the generation of communication keys is the responsibility of the communication parties (i.e., the cluster head, the base station). In all cases, the key generating part must be trusted by all key-receiving nodes.

The cluster head invokes rekey mechanism under two situations:

1.   When the cluster head detects the outlier;
2.   When the cluster head sent a certain quantity of encrypted messages.

The Rekey in the Cluster Head

During the operation of WSN, if a node is identified as a G attacker, the security materials will be obtained by adversaries. Then the cluster head informs the overall cluster member nodes to rekey. And the new generated cluster key replaces the obsolete cluster key. Thus, although the outlier node has disclosed keys, the network is still safe. In addition, the rekey happens within a cluster but not the whole network, which achieves the energy conservation.

Considering the common key K_I has been released in the initial phase, the cluster head will generate new common key in the cluster for rekeying. The process of rekeying in the cluster head is as follow.

Based on the jth master key of cluster head K_{CH}^j (the initial master key is K_{CH}^0), we generate a new nonce $Nonce_{CH}^{j+1}$ for the new master key K_{CH}^{j+1} asequation (12).

$$K_{CH}^{j+1} = f_{K_{CH}^j}(ID_{CH} \mid Nonce_{CH}^{j+1}) \qquad (12)$$

Once the $(j+1)^{th}$ key K_{CH}^{j+1} is generated, the cluster head will distribute the key as well as disclose the outlier. The process is shown as follow:

$$CH \rightarrow * : ID_{attacker}, \{ID_{CH}, K_{CH}^{j+1}\}_{K_{CH}^j} \qquad 1.$$

$$u : \psi(ID_{attacker}) = \begin{cases} true, do \ nothing \\ flase, decrypt \ new \ cluster \ key \ K_{CH}^{j+1} \end{cases} \qquad 2.$$

$$u : K_{CH}^{u^{j+1}} = f_{K_{CH}^{j+1}}(ID_{CH}) \qquad 3.$$

$$u \rightarrow CH : \{ID_u, K_{CH}^{u^{j+1}}\}_{K_{CH}^{j+1}} \qquad 4.$$

As the process shows, for rekeying normal nodes as well as filtering outlier, the cluster head CH sends a control message to inform its member u to rekey. The control message contains the ID of outlier. The sensor nodes in the cluster can avoid the outlier using by function Ψ (). Thus the network becomes secure by eliminating the outliers and retains the normal nodes.

In addition, the rekey locally happens within a cluster, which improves the energy efficiency.

The Rekey in the Base Station

According to (Zhu, Setia, and Jajodia)'s work (2006), when the cluster head sent a certain quantity of encrypted messages (more than $2^{2k/3}$, k is the length of key), the key will be no longer safe. Because the adversaries maybe also poach the same number of messages, they have the ability to decrypt the message and obtain the node keys. The whole network tends to compromise. Therefore, when the quantity of messages sent by the cluster head is close to $2^{2k/3}$, such as $2^{2k/3}$ -1, the cluster head must rekey in time. And then every cluster head perform rekey and update the schedule in the meantime.

The network key between base station and cluster head will be changed according to the quantity of messages from the cluster head, where the interval between n_i and n_{i+1} is one threshold. Considering that different cluster head sends reports to base station in different time with different frequency, we just rekey for the cluster head which sent sufficient messages but not all cluster heads.

Figure 2. To defend against the Sinkhole attack

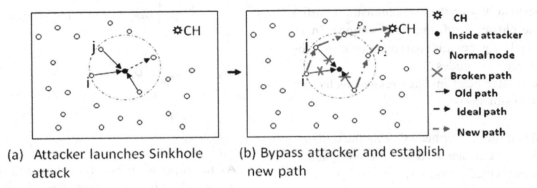

(a) Attacker launches Sinkhole attack   (b) Bypass attacker and establish new path

Different from the cluster head, base station should have special algorithm for the new key generation (however, we will ignore the algorithm for that the chapter only focuses on the outliers without authenticating by external authentication center such as the base station.), because the base station usually is thought as the credible part.

Defend Against the Deviant Frequency Attack from F Attacker

Since the *F* attacker typically lunches the deviant frequency attack, such as DoS attack and Sink-hole attack, which attacks the network by abnormal sending. An outlier can inject bogus broadcast packets to force sensor nodes to perform expensive verifications or messages forwarding, thus exhausting their limited battery power. To inhibit the behavior of the outlier, we will adopt the principle of avoidance.

The Implement of Avoidance for F Attacker

To defend against the DoS attack and the sinkhole attack, the nodes in the set of $\varphi(ID_{attacker})$ would exchange the old route information for establishing the new path. Either the DoS attack or the Sinkhole attack attempts to change the number of messages in the network to influence the net-

work's security. We design a reroute approach to prevent the attack.

In Figure 2, the attacker will attract normal nodes as a fake aggregator and drop the messages from them.

Let ID_i, $ID_j \in \varphi(ID_{attacker})$, they and $N(ID_i)$, $N(ID_j)$ know the outlier $ID_{attacker}$. There were two ideal paths originally:

P_1: $ID_i \rightarrow ID_{attacker} \rightarrow \ldots \rightarrow CH$
P_2: $ID_j \rightarrow \ldots \rightarrow CH$

As shown in Figure 2, to prevent from attacker, ID_i in P_1 will rejoin new path P_2 as $ID_i \rightarrow ID_j \rightarrow \ldots \rightarrow CH$.

The Reroute Approach for Implement

Considering the relationships among neighbors and cluster members are typically hierarchical, we choose breadth-first traversal (*BFT*) algorithm to establish new route. Since the communication in wireless sensor network has broadcasting characteristic and the cluster has very limited member nodes, *BFT* is very easily to be deployed.

Firstly, node ID_i checks its neighbor list $N(ID_i)$ to find the suitable next hop node, such as the nearest node by distance. Then, it sends a reroute message to the candidate next-hop node which will reply the message with the path information (e.g., the strong path of the node). ID_i decides whether it is a suitable node as the next-hop node according to the information of the node, such as

Table 2. Pseudo-code for finding next-hop node

Algorithm pseudo-code for finding next-hop node
1: INPUT $N(ID_i)$
2: NextNode = ø
3: Dist = ∞ // Initialize with a big value
4: **for** j = 1 **to** $\mid N(ID_i)\mid$ {
5: **if** ($ID_j \neq ID_{attacker}$) {
6: if ($ID_j = ID_{CH}$) {
7: Found the path;
8: **return** ID_{CH}; //found the path and end the process
9: }
10: **if** Dist>distance(ID_i, ID_j) {//distance of two nodes
11: Dist=distance(ID_i, ID_j)
12: NextNode = ID_j
13: }
14: }
15: }
16: **return** NextNode

the reputation or the signal strength. We repeat this process until establish a new route to cluster head. The algorithm for finding next-hop node is shown in Table 2.

According to the return information, the sender node establishes a secure route to the cluster head. The route steers clear of the outlier, which defends against the message lost or the traffic jam from attacks.

SECURITY ANALYSIS AND SIMULATION

In this section, we analyze the security and performance of our mechanisms in ODCS. Comparing with previous works, we focus on the outlier detection, and present corresponding countermeasures to defend against the exceptional message attack and abnormal behavior attack. Thus, we discuss the security of the network under attack by outlier and protection under the key system. Therefore, we analyze the performance of the countermeasures compared with the related works.

Security Analysis

Firstly, we establish a secure environment by a random key pre-distribution, which makes sensor nodes secure the link among immediate neighbors as well as supports the friendly relations among them in initial phase. In the initial phase, every node establishes and shares pair-wise keys with its direct neighbors. The pair-wise keys are used for securing communications that require privacy or source authentication. For example, a node can use its pair-wise key to secure the transmission of its sensor readings to an aggregation node. Note that the use of pair-wise keys precludes passive participation.

Furthermore, considering the integrity of security, the ODCS also supports the cluster key and the network keys which protect the communication between normal nodes and cluster head as well as the communication between the cluster head and the base station. Under the protection of these three types of keys, the network provides the tolerance on security, that is, even some nodes compromised as the outliers by adversary, other areas in network are also safe. Moreover, we also support the rekey mechanism for different outliers, which can generate new key for cluster nodes or the cluster head.

Table 3. Analysis on immunity

Attacks Types	LEACH	IADS	ODCS
Selective-Forwarding	×	×	√
Sink-Hole attack	×	√	√
Sybil attack	×	√	√
Worm-Hole	×	√	√
HELLO Flood	√	√	√
Provocateur attack	×	×	√

Secondly, in ODCS, EMSM uses similarity approach and spatiotemporal correlation to prevent against the tampered messages or fake messages dissemination from malicious nodes. Based on the *K-NN* distance and a similarity formula, EMSM can detect the outlier out by the distinguished bogus messages efficiently. By adjusting the threshold value, EMSM can distinguish the messages in different granularities. Moreover, different from most of previous works, our solution considers not only the deviation in data but also the localization of data. In WSN, the data usually has no independence, that is, most of data is relative, especially in geographical correlation. Since the data from single node are not credible, comparing with the history messages and current messages respectively, EMSM can identify those new messages from exceptional message sent from outliers. The EMSM effectively defends against tampering with message attack.

Finally, AFSM focuses on detecting the abnormal frequency of node. Besides the exceptional message attack, the outlier also can lunch the attack by misbehavior. Essentially, the abnormal behaviors often cause the traffic unconventionality in WSN by dropping or bursting messages or forwarding messages to discrediting targets. Computing the deviant frequency out, AFSM can locate the outlier and invoke the rekey mechanism. For rekeying the cluster, AFSM sends the control messages with filter function that can bypass the indicated sensors. AFSM can defend against the Hello flood attack, the sinkhole attack and

provocateur attack, etc. Table 3 compares the performances of LEACH, IADS and ODCS in immunity.

Simulation

We evaluate the performance of supervision mechanisms. According to the requirements of LEACH, we designed a sensor network simulation incorporating with a hierarchical sensor network as the foundational environment by using C++ and MATLAB. We take a temperature monitoring system as the simulation objective.

The Simulation Environment

In our simulation, we establish a 100m * 100m sensor network, 100 nodes are set to detect the temperature in the region from 8:00 AM to 4:00 PM. Detailed parameters of the simulations are same as in. We assume that the outliers are distributed uniformly in the network. The outliers' misbehaviors are mainly expressed by tampering with messages.

The Implement of Simulation

Firstly, we establish and observe the attack models: 1) the mixed data model, the outliers can attack network with mixed data (higher or lower than normal value); 2) the high-data model, the outliers attack the network with fake messages which are higher than normal value. Since the low-data

Figure 3. The mixed-data model

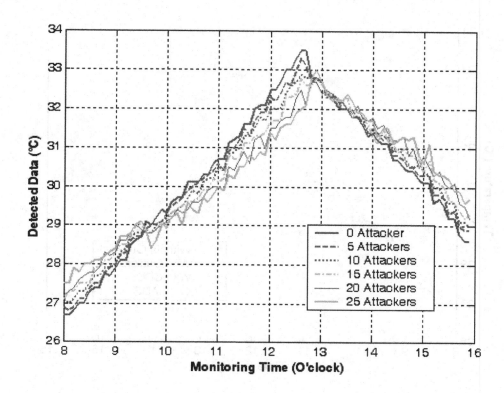

model is similar to the high-data model, we only discuss the two models. We assume that outliers are very intelligent that they can send bogus messages mixed with normal messages.

Figure3 shows a mixed-data model where outliers send about 80% fake messages. With the increase of the amount of the outlier, the data-lines deviate from normal curve increasingly. If outliers exceed 15%, the deviation is almost 0.5°C, which indicates the outliers seriously impact the results.

Furthermore, we employ and evaluate both ODCS and LADS on the mixed data attack model. Figure4 shows the results of ODCS vs IADS in different degree attacks, e.g. with 10 outliers and 25 outliers, respectively. Although the two mechanisms have similar functions, the results however show ODCS has higher performance. In Figure4, there are 10 outliers in the network. Both ODCS and IADS all can effec-

tively detect and avoid the outliers. And the ODCS curve is closer to the normal curve than IADS curve, which indicates ODCS has higher precision than IADS.

Figure5 shows our approach can efficiently detect the outliers. When the outliers are below 30% in network, the amount of detection outlier is almost 95% by ODCS as well as 90% by IDAS. Typically, ODCS limits the communication range in one-hop local, but ODAS generally employs multi-hop (e.g., two-hop) sensors, which sometimes entangles more different events simultaneously and makes error judgment.

In the Figure5, the error detection of ODCS is about 5%. And for the error rate, there are two main reasons: firstly, the nodes have fault or are interfered by outside interference, and the detection will be affected. In this situation, some sensors will emit interfered messages, which causes

Figure 4. ODCS vs IADS (with 10 outliers)

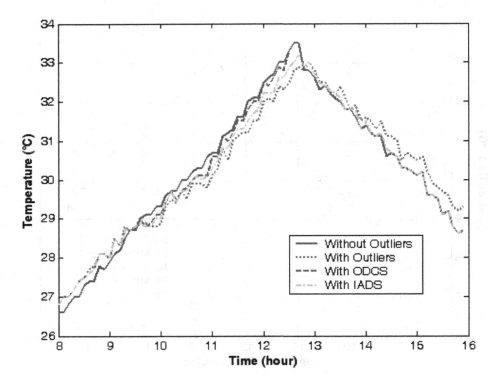

easily error judgment, sometimes even the amount of detection is more than the amount of actual outlier; secondly, if there are more than two outliers in a cluster and send the fake messages at the same time, the supervision work becomes more difficult. In that situation, the spatiotemporal correlation cannot work well, especially when the outliers send similar messages. However, if the outliers are not neighbors or send different messages, we can distinguish them well by using the supervision mechanism.

Furthermore, IADS and ODCS adopt different network models which lead the different performances, such as in communication and energy consumption. In IADS, they adopt the neighbor nodes authentication mechanism; meanwhile, our solution, ODCS collects and aggregates the information in cluster head, which reduce the communication among nodes.

As shown in Figure 6, for detecting and identifying outliers, IADS should exchange the many attribute vectors to obtain the properties of network behaviors, which consumes more energy in the initial phase than ODCS. At the same time, ODCS just forms clusters and elects the cluster head. In communication, IADS sends about two times packets than ODCS does.

Furthermore, with the operations of detection, once IADS detected outlier, the nodes exchange the attribute information to distinguish the attacker and then there are more nodes (usually more than two-hop neighbor nodes) to vote whether the candidate attacker is real or not; meanwhile, ODCS just identifies the candidate attacker in cluster head with the history information and the subsequent information according to spatiotemporal correlation. As the simulation results in Figure 6, with increase of outlier, IADS

Figure 5. The results of detection

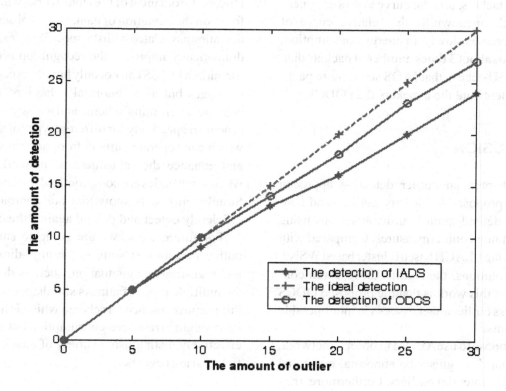

Figure 6. The number packets and energy consumption for detecting attacker with different number of attackers

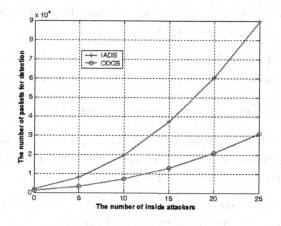 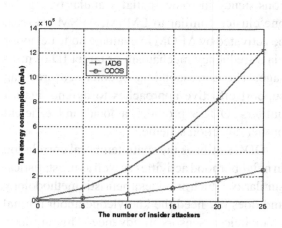

needs to exchange more and more packets to identify attackers, and the curve grows exponential growth; meanwhile, the relative curve of ODCS increases slowly. In energy consumption, IADS sends about 3 times number of packets than ODCS. It is because that IADS sends more packets to authenticate the attackers than ODCS.

CONCLUSION

In this chapter, an outlier detection approach ODCS is proposed to identify outliers and consequently defend against outlier attacks by using corresponding countermeasures. Compared with other existing LEACH based (cluster based WSNs) security solutions, the significant research contribution of this work is that the proposed ODCS can address outlier attack issues via interoperable mechanisms.

We propose to use AEOM to observe network. AEOM can distinguish the abnormal event and identify the potential outliers. Furthermore, triggered by AEOM, EMSM can distinguish the exceptional message by using distance measurement based on spatiotemporal correlation and consistency in some spatial granularity, e.g., in one cluster. Similar to EMSM, AFSM also can be activated by AEOM to evaluate node behavior via a frequency mechanism or target ID of message. The corresponding countermeasures can support effective approaches to defend against outliers. ODCS provides a local and efficient outlier detection scheme.

ODCS utilizes the spatiotemporal correlation in neighborhood activities as well as the statistical similarity, which provides a heuristic methodology and does not need the knowledge about normal or malicious sensors in advance. This property makes ODCS not only distinguish and deal with various dynamic attacks automatically without advance learning, but also reduce the requirement of capability for constrained nodes. In ODCS, we can reduce energy consumption and improve reliability for the localization communication. Different from most of previous works which just focus on the deviation of data, ODCS observe the deviation associated with the specific nodes, which dramatically improves the recognition accuracy for outlier. ODCS can not only handle exceptional messages but also abnormal behaviors. ODCS provides a rerouting scheme and a rekey security scheme respectively for different types of attacks, which can separate outliers from normal sensors and enhance the robustness of network, even when some nodes are compromised by adversary. Simulation results show that our approach can efficiently detect and defend against the outlier.

For future work, we are going to study the outlier detection scheme in the high-dimension and high-frequency situation, such as detecting the multiple types of attacks simultaneously. For this purpose, we need a scheme which is not only lightweight in resource-consumption but also can effectively distinguish a variety of attack modes from various events.

REFERENCES

Aggarwal, C. C., & Yu, P. S. (2001). *Outlier detection for high dimensional data.* In SIGMOD '01, New York, NY, USA.

Akyildiz, I. F., Su, W. L., Sankarasubramaniam, Y., & Cayirci, E. (2002). A survey on sensor networks. *IEEE Communications Magazine, 40*(8), 102–114. doi:10.1109/MCOM.2002.1024422

Ash, J. N., & Moses, R. L. (2005). *Outlier compensation in sensor network self-localization via the EM algorithm.* In ICASSP.

Bandyopadhyay, S., & Coyle, E. J. (2003, April). *Energy efficient hierarchical clustering algorithm for wireless sensor networks.* Paper presented at Proceeding of IEEE INFOCOM'03, San Francisco, USA.

Banerjea, A. (1996). A taxonomy of dispersity routing schemes for fault tolerant real-time channels. *Proceedings of ECMAST, 26*, 129–148.

Banerjeea, T., Xiea, B., & Agrawal, D. P. (2008). Fault tolerant multiple event detection in a wireless sensor network. *Journal of Parallel and Distributed Computing, 68*(9), 1222–1234. doi:10.1016/j.jpdc.2008.04.009

Bay, S. D., & Schwabacher, M. (2003). *Mining distance-based outliers in near linear time with randomization and a simple pruning rule.* Paper presented in KDD '03, New York, NY, USA.

Bellare, M., Canetti, R., & Krawczyk, H. (1996). *Keying hash functions for message authentication. Paper presented in Advances in Cryptology Crypto '96, Lecture Notes in Computer Science.* Springer-Verlag.

Branch, J. W., Szymanski, B. K., Giannella, C., Wolff, R., & Kargupta, H. (2006, July). *In-network outlier detection in wireless sensor networks.* Paper presented at IEEE ICDCS'06, Lisboa, Portugal.

Breunig, M. M., Kriegel, H.-P., Ng, R. T., & Sander, J. (2000). *LOF: Identifying density-based local outliers.* Paper presented in SIGMOD '00, New York, NY, USA.

Chan, H., Perrig, A., & Song, D. (2003, May). *Random key predistribution schemes for sensor networks.* Paper presented in IEEE Symp. Security and Privacy, Berkeley, CA, USA.

Chang, R. S., & Kuo, C. J. (2006). An energy-efficient routing mechanism for wireless sensor networks. *Advanced Information Networking and Applications (AINA'06) IEEE, 2,* 18-20.

Chen, B., Jamieson, K., Balakrishnan, H., & Morris, R. (2002). Span: An energy-efficient coordination algorithm for topology maintenance in ad hoc wireless networks. *ACM Wireless Networks Journal, 8*(5).

David, M., Tax, J., Robert, D., & Ridder, D. D. (2004). *Classification, parameter estimation and state estimation: An engineering approach using MATLAB.* John Wiley and Sons.

Deng, J., Han, R., & Mishra, S. (2005). *Intrusion-tolerant routing for wireless sensor networks.* Elsevier Journal on Computer Communications.

Du, W., Wang, R., & Ning, P. (2005, May). *An efficient scheme for authenticating public keys in sensor networks.* Paper presented in 6th ACM Int'l. Symp. Mobile Ad Hoc Networking and Computing (MobiHoc'05), Urbana-Champaign, IL.

Eschenauer, L., & Gligor, V. (2002, November). *A key management scheme for distributed sensor networks.* Paper presented at 9th ACM Conf. Computer and Communications Security (CCS'02), Washington.

Ferreira, A. C., Vilac, M. A., Oliveira, L. B., Habib, E., Wong, H. C., & Loureiro, A. A. F. (2005, April). *On the security of cluster based communication protocols for wireless sensor networks.* Paper presented in 4th IEEE International Conference on Networking (ICN'05), Reunion Island.

Handy, M. J., Haase, M., & Timmermann, D. (2002). *Low energy adaptive clustering hierarchy with deterministic cluster-head selection.* Paper presented in the 4th IEEE Conf. on Mobile and Wireless Communications Networks. Stockholm: IEEE Communications Society.

Hawkins, D. M. (1980). *Identification of outliers.* Chapman and Hall.

Hill, D. J., Minsker, B. S., & Amir, E. (2007). *Real-time Bayesian anomaly detection for environmental sensor data.* Paper presented in the 32nd Congress of the International Association of Hydraulic Engineering and Research.

Hu, Y., Perrig, A., & Johnson, D. B. (2003, March). *Packet leashes: A defense against wormhole attacks in wireless networks.* Paper presented at 22nd Annual Joint Conf. IEEE Computer and Communications Societies (INFOCOM'03), San Francisco, CA.

Ishida, K., Kakuda, Y., & Kikuno, T. (1992, November). *A routing protocol for finding two node-disjoint paths in computer networks.* Paper presented in Internation Conference on Network Protocols

Jun, M. C., Jeong, H., & Kuo, C. J. (2005). *Distributed spatiotemporal outlier detection in sensor networks.* In SPIE.

Karlof, C., & Wagner, D. (2003, May). *Secure routing in wireless sensor networks: Attacks and countermeasures.* Paper presented in First IEEE International Workshop on Sensor Network Protocols and Applications (SNPA 03).

Krontiris, I., Dimitriou, T., Giannetsos, T., & Mpasoukos, M. (2008). Intrusion detection of sinkhole attacks in wireless sensor networks. ALGOSENSORS 2007. *LNCS, 4837,* 150–161.

Laneman, J. N., & Wornell, G. W. (2003). Distributed space-time-coded protocols for exploiting cooperative diversity in wireless networks. *IEEE Transactions on Information Theory, 49,* 2415–2525. doi:10.1109/TIT.2003.817829

Larsen, R. J., & Marx, M. L. (2000). *An introduction to mathematical statistics and its applications* (3rd ed.).

Liu, F., Cheng, X. Z., & Chen, D. C. (2007, May). *Insider attacker detection in wireless sensor networks.* Paper presented in INFOCOM 2007, 26th IEEE International Conference on Computer Communications, (pp. 1937-1945). Anchorage, Alaska, USA.

Liu, M. J. (2001). *Studies on knowledge discovery methods.* Unpublished Ph.D. Dissertation, Nankai University, Tianjin.

Main, M., & Savitch, W. (1997). *Data structures and other objects using C.* Addison-Wesley.

Malan, D. J., Welsh, M., & Smith, M. D. (2004, October). *A public-key infrastructure for key distribution in TinyOS based on elliptic curve cryptography.* Paper presented in Proc. 1st IEEE Int'l. Conf. Sensor and Ad Hoc Commun. and Networks (SECON'04), Santa Clara, CA.

Medhi, J. (2002). A single server Poisson input queue with a second optional channel. *Queueing Systems, 42*(3), 239–242. doi:10.1023/A:1020519830116

Perrig, A., Szewczyk, R., Wen, V., Culler, D., & Tygar, J. D. (2002). SPINS: Security protocols for sensor networks. *Wireless Networks Journal, 8*(5), 521–534. doi:10.1023/A:1016598314198

Rafaeli, S., & Hutchison, D. (2003). A survey of key management for secure group communication. *ACM Computing Surveys, 35*(3), 309–329. doi:10.1145/937503.937506

Ramaswamy, S., Rastogi, R., & Shim, K. (2000). *Efficient algorithms for mining outliers from large data sets.* Paper presented in SIGMOD '00, New York, NY, USA.

Sheng, B., Li, Q., Mao, W. Z., & Jin, W. (2007). *Outlier detection in sensor networks.* International Symposium on Mobile Ad Hoc Networking & Computing, Montreal, Quebec, Canada, (pp. 219-228).

Vuran, M. C., Akan, O. B., & Akyildiz, I. F. (2004). Spatiotemporal correlation: Theory and applications for wireless sensor networks. *Computer Networks Journal, 45*(3), 245–259. doi:10.1016/j.comnet.2004.03.007

Wang, K., Xu, C., & Liu, B. (1999). *Clustering transactions using large items*. Paper presented in the Eighth Intl. Conf. on information and Knowledge Management (CIKM'99).

Wu, W. L., Cheng, X. Z., Ding, M., Xing, K., Liu, F., & Deng, P. (2007). Localized outlying and boundary data detection in sensor networks. *IEEE Transactions on Knowledge and Data Engineering, 19*(8), 1145–1157. doi:10.1109/TKDE.2007.1067

Xu, Y., Heidemann, J., & Estrin, D. (2001). *Geography-informed energy conservation for ad hoc routing*. Paper presented in the Seventh Annual ACM/IEEE International Conference on Mobile Computing and Networking.

Yang, W. C., Zhang, Y. Y., Kim, K. B., Kim, D. S., Cui, M. Y., Xue, M., & Park, M. S. (2008). *VSCF: A vote-based secure cluster formation scheme*. Paper presented at IEEE International Conference on Networking, Sensing and Control (ICNSC 2008), Sanya.

Zhang, Y., & Chen, L. (2006, September). *In-network outlier ceaning for data collection in sensor networks*. Paper presented in 1st International VLDB Workshop on Clean Databases (CleanDB'06), Seoul, Korea.

Zhang, Y. Y., Park, M. S., Chao, H. C., Chen, M., Shu, L., & Park, C. H. (2010). *Outlier detection and countermeasure for hierarchical wireless sensor networks*. IET Information Security (SI), 2010.

Zhang, Y. Y., Yang, W. C., Kim, K. B., Cui, M. Y., & Park, M. S. (2008). *A rekey-boosted security protocol in hierarchical wireless sensor network*. Paper presented at 2008 International Conference on Multimedia and Ubiquitous Engineering (MUE), Busan, Korea.

Zhang, Y. Y., Yang, W. C., Kim, K. B., & Park, M. S. (2008). *Outlier detection in hierarchical wireless sensor network*. Paper presented at 2008 3rd International Conference on Innovative Computing Information and Control, Dalian, China

Zhao, Y., & Karypis, G. (2003). Empirical and theoretical comparisons of selected criterion functions for document clustering. *Machine Learning, 55*, 311–331. doi:10.1023/B:MACH.0000027785.44527.d6

Zhao, Y., & Karypis, G. (2005). Hierarchical clustering algorithms for document datasets. *Data Mining and Knowledge Discovery, 10*(2), 141–168. doi:10.1007/s10618-005-0361-3

Zhen, F., Yuan, P., & Myong-Soon. (2006, June). *Efficient clustering of data gathering in wireless sensor networks*. Paper presented in the 8th International Conference on Electronics, Information, and Communication (ICEIC), Ulaanbaatar, Mongolia.

Zhu, S., Setia, S., & Jajodia, S. (2006). LEAP+: Efficient security mechanisms for large-scale distributed sensor networks. *ACM Transactions on Sensor Networks, 2*(4), 500–528. doi:10.1145/1218556.1218559

KEY TERMS AND DEFINITIONS

F **Attacker:** The node sends messages with abnormal frequency.

G **Attacker:** The node sends abnormal messages.

Hierarchical Wireless Sensor Network (HWSN): In hierarchical wireless sensor network, the sensors can self-organize clusters. In the cluster, there is a node named cluster head which collects and aggregates the data from its member nodes, and forward them to the base station.

Key Management:To provide the security: wireless sensor networks typically are based on cryptographic operations that involve keys.

MAC: Message authentication code (*MAC*).

Outliers: Also call Inside attacker, in wireless sensor networks are some sensor nodes controlled by adversary, they do not perform tasks as normal nodes but exhibit different types of abnormal behaviors, e.g., dropping received messages from their neighbors, forwarding messages to enemy, broadcasting redundant messages, and disseminating fake messages.

Chapter 10
Computationally Efficient Cooperative Public Key Authentication Protocols in Ubiquitous Sensor Network

Abedelaziz Mohaisen
University of Minnesota Twin Cities, USA

Tamer AbuHmed
Inha University, South Korea

DaeHun Nyang
Inha University, South Korea

ABSTRACT

The use of public key algorithms to sensor networks brings all merits of these algorithms to such networks: nodes do not need to encounter each other in advance in order to be able to communicate securely. However, this will not be possible unless "good" key management primitives that guarantee the functionality of these algorithms in the wireless sensor networks are provided. Among these primitives is public key authentication: before sensor nodes can use public keys of other nodes in the network to encrypt traffic to them, they need to make sure that the key provided for a particular node is authentic. In the near past, several researchers have addressed the problem and proposed solutions for it as well. In this chapter we review these solutions. We further discuss a new scheme which uses collaboration among sensor nodes for public key authentication. Unlike the existing solutions for public key authentication in sensor network, which demand a fixed, yet high amount of resources, the discussed work is dynamic; it meets a desirable security requirement at a given overhead constraints that need to be provided. It is scalable where the accuracy of the authentication and level of security are merely dependent upon the desirable level of resource consumption that the network operator wants to put into the authentication operation.

DOI: 10.4018/978-1-61350-110-8.ch010

Copyright © 2012, IGI Global. Copying or distributing in print or electronic forms without written permission of IGI Global is prohibited.

INTRODUCTION

Public key cryptographic algorithms have been discarded from consideration as a solution for securing wireless sensor network (WSN) due to their long execution time (Chan et al., 2003). On the other hand, symmetric key algorithms have been intensively studied in the context of securing WSN due to their computational feasibility on the typical sensor nodes (Chan et al., 2003, Du et al., 2003, Eschenauer & Gligor, 2002, Liu & Ning, 2003, Perrig et al., 2002). However, recent results of operating public key algorithms on typical sensor nodes have shown a relevant and satisfactory efficiency. For example, Gura et al. in (Gura et al., 2004, Wander et al., 2005) introduced efficient implementation and measurements that show practicality of elliptic curve cryptography (Koblitz et al., 2000) and RSA (Rivest et al., 1983) signatures' verification; by showing that the ECC signature verification consumes 1.62 seconds on the 8-bit ATMega128 processor, which is the de facto standard processing unit in many commercialized sensor platforms (Crossbow Tech. Inc, BTnode Project). In addition, Watro et al. developed a limited public key architecture (called TinyPK) and provided an evaluation of practicality by measuring resources required per sensor to perform typical public key operations (i.e., signing, encrypting and decrypting) per sensor node in (Watro et al., 2004). The efficiency of key distribution in TinyOS based on ECC (Koblitz et al., 2000) is studied and measured on typical sensor nodes as shown by Malan et al. (Malan et al., 2004). All of these measurements, and recent studied, advocated the applicability of public key cryptography in the context of sensor network, and refuted the argument on the inefficiency of such algorithms for securing wireless sensor networks.

Indeed, public key algorithms have many advantages over the symmetric key algorithms, especially when deployed for WSNs. For example, while the resiliency to nodes compromise and connectivity of the sensor network security overlay are two critical issues in the latter type of algorithms, they are not a concern at all when using public key cryptography. This is, the compromise of a single node would reveal information related to that compromised node (its private key) and the ability of a node to encrypt a message to another node is subject to the knowledge of other nodes public key, making every node able to encrypt messages to arbitrary nodes in the sensor network without pre-existing knowledge of the destination. However, to make use of such algorithms, public key authentication is required. Worse, conventional public key authentication algorithms are inefficient for WSNs, for that WSNs are resources-constrained and such algorithms require more resources than that can be afforded by such networks.

Public key algorithms operate in a way that does not require a node to know other node's private key in order to encrypt a message intended for that node. However, before encrypting a message for the designated node, say Bob, the node wishing to encrypt the message, say Alice, needs to know Bob's public key in advance in order to be able to encrypt that message to him. Because of that, public key authentication is required to makes sure that Alice is encrypting for Bob using Bob's authentic public key. In the traditional networks, the public key authentication is performed using public key infrastructure and digital certificates, which are used for distributing public keys signed by the private of a centralized authority, acting as a trusted third party. Furthermore, when a node, Alice, wants to check the authenticity of the public key, she simply verifies the signature on the public key of Bob against the public key of the trusted authority, and thus realizes the authenticity of public keys. However, due to the special nature of the WSNs including, including the fact that the existence of such centralized authority in fully decentralized WSN is almost impossible, such solution is insufficient for these networks (Mohaisen et al., 2007). The naive solution to the problem is to store public keys of every other sensor node in each node in the network in a pre-deployment phase thus requiring each node fetch the authentic key of the node at the running time. However, such solution would require large amount of memory, which is not available to sensor nodes. Replacing keys by their hash values would reduce the memory requirements of such solution greatly, but not to the degree that such solution would be possible for sensor networks, for the same limited memory requirements reason. Obviously, storing the keys or their hashed values require a high magnitude of memory which is impractical for the case of WSN. Accordingly, any solution to the problem should consider greatly reducing the memory requirements from those posed by the previously mentioned solutions.

To this end, this chapter considers the problem of public key authentication in context of WSNs. We first review related work in the literature introducing solutions for the problem, and discuss the extent to which these works succeed in the solving the problem. We then discuss another solution for the problem that aims to further meet the special nature of the WSN, which is basically the limited amount of resources available for each sensor node. The solution in introduced in the form of protocols that use a distributed and cooperative voting mechanism to perform authentication. Also, our contribution relies in that we do not use any heavy cryptographic operations to authenticate a key where each sensor node stores only a limited number of hashed keys for a set of different nodes' keys. We introduce additional scenarios related to public key authentication in WSN and show in details the efficiency of presented protocols.

The rest of the chapter is organized as follows: section 2 introduces the related work. Section 3 introduces the initial protocol for public key authentication in WSN. To overcome the problem of tossing, section 4 introduces two undeviating protocols. In section 5, we discuss some extensions

for our protocol such like multi-hop authentication, security level determination and dynamic resistance, and power awareness through MAC-based implementation. The evaluation of our protocols' accuracy, analysis and applications are in section 6 and section 7 respectively. Finally, concluding remarks are drawn in section 8.

RELATED WORKS

There has been several works in the literature on the problem of public key authentication in the context of sensor networks. The problem was first addressed by Benenson (Benenson 2005) where the author investigated how to apply public key authentication in WSN for authenticating node queries. The solution introduced is based on Elliptic Curve Cryptography (ECC) and it used the Public Key Infrastructure (PKI) approach to issue a certificate for every user of the sensor networks through a certification authority (CA). The CA has its own private/public key pair and each node is preloaded with a certificate of its public key along with the public key of the CA. Thus, when a sensor node contacts other node, it sends a certificate of its public key which is signed by the CA private key. Hence, the recipient sensor node verifies the received certificate with the CA public key. As previously mentioned, the shortcoming of this solution is mainly in the fact that authentication assumes a trusted third party in the WSN, which is hard to consider in many realistic scenarios. Furthermore, such approach incurs high communication and computation overhead to each sensor node, since the certificate should be transmitted and verified by sensor nodes.

Public key authentication solution which could be appropriate for sensor networks has been firstly studied in by Du et al. in (Du et al., 2005). In Du et al.'s scheme, Merkle hash tree is used for authenticating the public keys of the entire network. The Merkle hash tree (Merkle, 1980) is a binary tree of n leaves that represent the different nodes' hashed keys. Each internal parent node, until the root, stores a hashed value of its corresponding children data blocks. In (Du et al., 2005), each node stores a set of $\log_2(n)+1$ hashed values (which are selected from the corresponding leaf to the root of the tree according to the details in (Merkle, 1980)). Once Bob's key authentication is required by Alice, Alice receives Bob's hashed values and his public key. Locally, Alice performs several hashing computations on the received values and compares the resulting root with preloaded root that she owns. Depending on whether the calculated final hashed value (that corresponds to the root in the tree) is equal to the stored root at Alice's side or not, Alice determines whether to admit Bob's key or not. For the communication versus memory tradeoff and optimization, Du et al. also utilized the deployment knowledge for splitting Merkle tree into several sub-trees which is referred as the Merkle forest. In the Merkle forest, each split of the tree reduces the used memory by one key. Du et al's work greatly reduces the required memory (over the naive schemes) but results in an additional computation overhead at the side of each node equivalent to $\log_2(n)+1$ hashing computations. In addition, the above solution is not scalable: to construct the original Merkle hash tree, the whole leaves nodes need to be fixed in advance which prohibit additional nodes from joining or leaving the network at the run time, a feature that is essential in WSNs' dynamics.

Ren et al. (Ren et al., 2007) introduced Bloom Filter-based Authentication Scheme (BAS) scheme. In BAS, the trusted authority generates the public keys for all network nodes, and then uses Bloom filter to map and compress public keys into a specific size vector less than the total size of WSN public keys. Bloom filter is a space-efficient randomized data structure for representing a set in order to support membership queries (Mitzenmacher, 2002). As the vector of bloom filter is uploaded to each sensor node, the sensor is capable of authenticating the public keys of other nodes by querying its bloom filter. BAS scheme has a false positive problem inherited from Bloom filter structure, where the public key could be authenticated though it is not a valid public key. Also, when public keys are revoked, the trusted party needs to send the updated bloom filter for all sensor nodes in order to prevent the authentication of revoked public keys. This obviously incurs communication overhead as frequent as the revocation happens in WSN. Ren et al. (Ren et al., 2007) extend BAS scheme and also introduced a robust broadcast authentication scheme called Hybrid Authentication Scheme (HAS) which is based on Bloom filter and Merkle hash tree in order to increase network users compared to the case of BAS scheme. However, since the Merkle hash tree requires fixed number of users to be predetermined before the WSN deployment, it is not scalable and a new user can only be added after revoking an old user. Worse, the whole design assumes the existence of a trusted third party in the WSN to run the protocol.

Recently, Wang et al. (Wang et al., 2009) introduced another approach for public key distribution which is used for broadcast authentication in WSN. Wang et al.'s basic scheme assumed that each node will hold N short-term public keys that are encrypted by N different symmetric keys. The symmetric keys are generated from hash chains, where $\text{key}_i = H(\text{key}_{i+1})$. When the time reaches t_i, the key P_i becomes alive, so that the base station needs to disclose the encryption key key_i to sensor nodes. By doing so, each sensor node at time t_i will broadcast massages signed by P_i and concatenated to the encryption of the P_i. As the symmetric key is generated by hash chain, each node can simply verify it using a preloaded $\text{key}_0 = H(\text{key}_1)$ in order to decrypt and obtain P_i. To this end, sensors use the hash chain to authenticate the symmetric key, and then use this symmetric key to decrypt the encrypted public key P_i of each sensor that is already stored in its memory. Since the basic scheme needs sensors to have enough memory to carry all public keys, Wang et al. proposed A Progressive Public Key Distribution Scheme (PPKD). In PPKD, some public keys have to be distributed by the base station after the deployment. Using the hash chain approach used in the basic scheme, the base station broadcast P_i's hash before its lifetime t_i, along with a signature produced using P_{i-1}'s private key. Sensors can authenticate the hash using P_{i-1}, and later authenticate P_i using the hash. This approach has a problem in a lossy communication environment; where sensors fail to receive one public key. In such case, such sensors are unable to authenticate any future public key. Furthermore, while not explicitly assumed, the role played by the base station is equivalent to that played by other trusted parties in other systems, which limit the usability of the design in many real world contexts.

Assumptions and Notation

Through this chapter, we assume a wireless sensor network with the following properties:

1. Hundreds of sensor nodes are deployed within the same radio range or within the same functional cluster; an example of this deployment is in (Bapat et al., 2005). The network size depends on the MAC layer but not on the physical layer, which rationalizes this assumption (Karl & Willig, 2005).
2. The different nodes in the network, or at least the group of nodes which participate in a given authentication operation, can overhear every traffic between any pair of nodes for a given time slot. This assumption is valid in many low duty cycle MAC protocols; such like S-MAC (Ye et al., 2004), and T-MAC (Van Dam & Langendoen, 2003). Practically, this overhearing is necessary to make the

nodes decide whether to relay a frame or not when it is not for them. As well, it differs in the WSN from the corresponding in the ad hoc network due to the low duty cycle (Van Dam & Langendoen, 2003, Ye et al., 2004). Thus, we assume that the scheduled nodes to be awake are enough to assist in performing the authentication operation for a specific key.

3. The public key of an arbitrary node is deliverable from any node to other nodes while attackers reside in the same geographical area or within the same radio coverage range. Also, interception and modification of frames, including authentication frames, are possible during one-hop transmission only if attackers know who is about to send traffic and not possible otherwise (Schaller et al., 2007).
4. The attackers have the ability to inject forged frames during the authentication operation which might affect the decision of authentication if the number of successfully injected forged frames is greater than a threshold value.
5. The chances for performing a Sybil attack (Zhang et al., 2005) on this particular protocol, in which an attacker can send several messages from the same device using different addresses (i.e., attacker with several identities and using single physical entity), is negligible because the authentication should be performed within t period that consider the transmission delay and the sum of processing delays for the specified frames from the concerned authentication group's nodes.

Through the rest of the chapter, the following notation in Table 1 is used. Other notation is defined at the time it is used, as well.

Table 1. Notations

Notation	Description
n	network size in node
m	number of attacker's injected frames
k	ideal # of frames to carry out the authentication
$\hat{k}$	# of authentication frames including redundancy
σ	deviation of the size of the authentication group
ε	practical deviation due to σ $(\varepsilon = \lceil \sigma \rceil)$
p_s	authentication success probability
p_f	authentication failure probability
$e_{p\|\sigma}$	error in p_a or p_f due to the deviation σ
s_i, s_j	two sensor nodes (the communicating parties)
P_i	public key of node s_i
K_i	hash value of P_i which is equal to hash($ID_i \mid P_i$)
AREF	Authentication REsponse Frame
ARF	Authentication Request Frame.

AUTHENTICATION PROTOCOL

The protocols that we study in this chapter mainly utilize the overhearing in the wireless environment. In brief, these protocol work as follows: for a sensor node with desirable information to be authenticated (e.g. public key information in this case, and other information in other applications), the information to be authenticated is preloaded in a set of nodes and recalled when authentication is needed to perform a majority voting in a distributed manner and judge the authenticity of the received information. In more details, our protocols consist of two phases: the initialization phase in which the information to be authenticated is preloaded in some sensor nodes, and the online authentication phase in which the authentication is performed. In the following, we review the details of both phases.

Initialization Phase

In the initialization phase, Trusted Authority (TA) randomly selects $\hat{k}$ number of nodes and installs the public key information of a node i (K_i) to the $\hat{k}$ nodes; where $\hat{k} = H(ID_i \mid P_i)$ and H is a one way hash function. The offline initialization phase is as follows:

1. For each node $s_i \in \{s_1, \ldots, s_n\}$, trusted party computes $K_i \leftarrow H(P_i \parallel ID_i)$. Then it loads P_i and $K_i \leftarrow H(P_i \parallel ID_i)$ into s_i.

2. The trusted party selects a subset $G_i \subset \{s_1, \ldots, s_n\}$ of $\hat{k}$ nodes, and loads each node $s_j \in G_i$ with the public information $K_i \leftarrow H(P_i \parallel ID_i)$ of node s_i.

An algorithmic description of the offline initialization phase is shown in Algorithm 1. Notice

Algorithm 1. An algorithmic description of the offline initialization phase

---

Algorithm 1: PrimInit phase

Input : **nodes of the network** $\{s_1, \dots, s_n\}$ with their identifiers

$\{ID_1, \dots, ID_n\}$ and corresponding public keys $\{P_1, \dots, P_n\}, \hat{k}$

Output: Public key of each node is loaded into sets of nodes of size $\hat{k}$.

for each $s_i \in \{s_1, \dots, s_n\}$ *do*

compute $K_i \leftarrow H(P_i \| ID_i)$;

select set $G_i \subset \{s_1, \dots, s_n\}$ (size of G_i is $\hat{k}$);

for each $s_j \in G_i$ *do*

Load $K_i \leftarrow H(P_i \| ID_i)$;

---

that the TA's role is limited to the initialization phase and does not take part in the real authentication protocol.

Online Authentication Protocol

The procedure of this protocol is shown in Algorithm 2. The procedure is explained in the following. First, s_j sends ARF requesting P_i of s_i which implicitly indicates the need for authenticating K_i. Node s_i and all nodes in the group G_i reply to s_j's ARF with AREF messages by sending K_i that they store. Node s_i differs in that it sends P_i also with its AREF reply message. Node s_j receives replies from the different nodes until the end of the time window t. After that, node s_j proceeds to the voting by checking if the numbers of received AREF messages are higher than a threshold or not (considering σ as will be shown later). If the number is higher, s_j performs a majority voting to admit K_i if the number of received K_i copies from the nodes in G_i that are equal to the copy received from s_i is greater than $k/2$. If this fails, the authentication process is performed again. Otherwise, each node in G_i performs the authentication independently and determine to keep K_i or not according to a coin tossing. Figure 1 shows the ARF-AREF general

interaction. Note that, if we consider p as the probability of head, then $p = k/n$, where k herein is the number of nodes that will keep K_i on average.

Hurdle of Deviation

The coin tossing that determines whether a node will keep or remove its own copy of K_i follows a binomial distribution with a variance σ^2. Based on σ, the future authentication operations for the same K_i will be affected. For any binomial distribution with a probability p, the variance is $\sigma^2 = np(1-p)$. By setting $p = k/n$ we find that $\sigma = [k(1 - k/n)]^{0.5}$. Note that, this value would have an impact on the accuracy p_s and p_f. Also, the deviation σ greatly depends on k even for the different n. To solve this problem, we discuss two undeviating protocols.

UNDEVIATING AUTHENTICATION PROTOCOLS

To overcome aforementioned deviation, we modify the protocol so that we do not need a coin tossing in its operation. This modification relies on predefining the set of nodes which will reply in the next authentication for the same key. The

Figure 1. Single-hop and Multi-hop models of cooperative public key authentication protocols (a) Single-hop model. Incoming arrows to s_j represent replies from the overhearing nodes in group G including some from potential attackers. (b) Multi-hop model. The authentication within the same coverage area is performed using the single hop model and nodes that belong to the intersection of two areas act as intermediate authenticators.

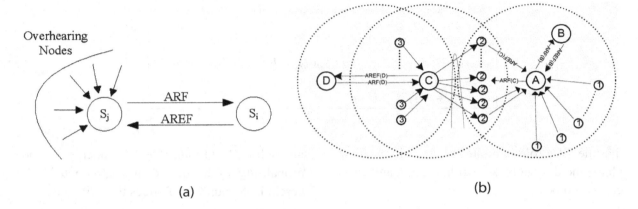

(a) (b)

offline phase is different from the former protocol but the same for each of the modified protocols as shown in Algorithm 3. In this initialization phase, the hashed key K_i is loaded into the memory of c different groups of nodes each of size $\hat{k}$. The following two subsections include the online part for two discussed protocols considering the initialization in Algorithm 3 as a first step, which is a slight modification of the previous offline phase.

C-rounds Authentication Protocol

The first protocol's operation life is limited to c rounds where c is a number that determines the overhead required for the protocol deployment. An algorithmic description of this protocol is in Algorithm 4. Firstly, the concerned node (say s_j) sends AREF with the current authentication round, r, which is initiated to 1. Each node in G_r replies with an AREF message that contains K_i while s_i replies with K_i and P_i as well. The same majority voting is performed on the received responses with the time t as explained earlier in

Algorithm 4. If the authentication fails, the nodes of the current round in G_r delete the stored K_i, r is increased by one, and a new request with a new r is performed again. At the same time, each node performs the same authentication and determines whether to keep K_i or not without interacting with the concerned nodes s_i and s_j. In this protocol, no tossing is required to determine whether to keep K_i or not since the group of the assisting nodes is predefined and the authentication is held in the same way in all of these nodes determining certainly whether to keep K_i or not. Upon the failure of the protocol due to that more than $k/2$ attacker's authentication frames are injected, the request is reset and the frames in the current group are deleted.

Long Living Authentication Protocol

The long living protocol is similar to the protocol in Algorithm 4, however it differs in that no deletion is performed after finishing the authentication process. When K_i authentication is required by node s_j, node s_j firstly sends a request as $\langle r, req \rangle$

Algorithm 2. An algorithmic description of the Online Authentication Protocol

---

Algorithm 2: PrimOnline phase.

Input: G group of nodes of size $\hat{k}$, $\hat{k}$ as desirable number of sensor nodes
Output: Information K_i installed into a given group M of nodes.

s_j : Broadcast $\langle \text{ARF} \rangle$;

s_i : reply to s_j with K_i and P_i;

Each node in G_i replies to s_j with K_i;

s_j : **set** $init\_time \leftarrow s_j.current\_time$;

s_j : **set** $b\_index \leftarrow 1$;

while $init\_time + t \neq s_j.current\_time$ *do*

s_j .buffer[b_index] $\leftarrow$ received $< K_i >$;

set $b\_index \leftarrow b\_index + 1$;

If $| s_j.\text{sizeof}(\text{buffer}) - k | \leq \varepsilon$ *then*

If count (recFrom (G_r)=RecFrom (s_i)) $> k/2$ *then*

accept K_i, break
else
reject K_i

Each node in G_r : delete K_i;
else

s_j : perform the above procedure again

for each node $s_x \in G$ *do*
perform the voting on overheard frames (line 4 to 19) ;
perform coin tossing and get the result
If result= head *then*
keep K_i;
else
delete K_i;

---

where r is a *random integer* such that $0 < r \leq c$. Upon the authentication success, the information K_i is kept in each node G_r. If the authentication fails, the information is kept in the current group and another r is randomly picked from the same interval to select another group to assist in the authentication. The limit of this modification is that the attacker can monitor the communication traffic between the nodes and get some inference on the groups' assignment with some certainty so he can inject fake authentication frames without delay. However, the protocol's advantage is obvious in guaranteeing authentication of K_i for longer time.

EXTENSIONS

In this section, we introduce further extensions to our protocols. First, we discuss a multi-hop authentication protocol. Then, to provide dynamic security levels according to attack possibilities, we introduce a dynamic authenticating group size assignment. Finally, we discuss implementation issues of the protocol including integrating it into the MAC layer for power awareness and power saving.

Algorithm 3. An algorithmic description of the offline initialization phase in the undeviating authentication Protocols

---

Algorithm 3 UDInit phase

Input: Network nodes $\{s_1, \ldots, s_n\}$ ans their identifiers $\{ID_1, \ldots, ID_n\}$, set of public keys of associated with nodes and identifiers as $\{K_1, \ldots, K_n\}$, $\hat{k}$, counter r

Output: Public key information P_i is installed into the groups $\{G_1, \ldots, G_c\}$ where each G of size $\hat{k}$. Each group is distinguished by the counter value r.

for each $s_i \in \{s_1, \ldots, s_n\}$ *do*

compute $P_i \leftarrow H(K_i \| ID_i)$;

select $G_1, \ldots, G_c : G_i \subset \{s_1, \ldots, s_n\}$, size of G_i is $\hat{k}$;

set $r \leftarrow 1$;

for each $G_x \in \{G_1, \ldots, G_c\}$ *do*

pair $\langle r, P_i \rangle$;

for each $s_j \in G_x$ *do*

load $\langle r, P_i \rangle$;

set $r \leftarrow r + 1$;

Multi-Hop Authentication Protocol

All the previously introduced protocols perform well for single hop authentication but have limits when nodes are deployed in a wide geographical area with different coverage zones (see Figure 1) requiring a multi-hop operation. To do so, a slight modification is introduced at the expense of some additional overhead. The nodes within the same coverage area such as A and B (in Figure 3) can perform the single hop authentication via the assisting groups within the same coverage zone (i.e., numbered by "1"). For nodes A and C, an arbitrary node in C's coverage which is authenticated to A (one of those numbered as "2") can perform the authentication and transfer such authentication to A updating the authenticity of C. The same operation is performed for three and more hops authentication (e.g., A and D). Note that the intermediate authenticators in an intersecting coverage area needs to be trusted (or at least previously authenticated) in order to avoid malicious node's authentication.

Proactive Protocol: Dynamic Group Size

Our protocols' security depends on $\hat{k}$ and k which are determined in advance and might be inferred by an attacker. An attacker who knows these parameter in advance, especially for the c-rounds protocol, can perform an exhaustive flooding which will not only result in authentication failure but also introduce a vulnerability in the form of DoS attack (Wood & Stankovic, 2002). To overcome this problem, we set $\hat{k}$ to a larger value than the value required for the normal authentication. Initially, a fraction of $\hat{k}$ is used to participate in the authentication. Once a possibility of attack is measured (e.g., derived from DoS detection scheme running along with the authentication protocols), all of the nodes in the network are

Algorithm 4. An algorithmic description of the c-rounds authentication Protocol

Input: Initialization in algorithm 3, G_r, k, ε, t, and $\hat{k}$

Output: A key Information K_i is authentication and authentication counter r is updated for next authentication.

s_j : set $r \leftarrow 1$;

s_j : Broadcast $\langle r, \text{ARF} \rangle$;

s_i : reply to s_j with K_i and P_i;

Each node G_r : reply to s_j with $< r, P_i >$;

s_j : set init_time $\leftarrow s_j$.*current_time*;

s_j : set $b\_index \leftarrow 1$;

While init_time $+ t \neq s_j$.*current_time do*

s_j . buffer[b_index] $\leftarrow$ received $< r, P_i >$;

set $b\_index \leftarrow b\_index + 1$

If $| s_j.sizeof(buffer) - k | \leq \varepsilon$ *then*

If count(recFrom(G_r)=recFrom(s_i)) $> k/2$ then

accept K_i, Break;

else

reject K_i ;

$\{s_1, \ldots, s_{\hat{k}}\} \in G_r$: delete K_i ;

Else s_j : $r \leftarrow r + 1$

s_j : Broadcast $\langle r, \text{ARF} \rangle$

s_j : perform the above procedure

Each $s_i \in G_r$: simultaneously receives the authentication frames within t and performs voting (lines 11 to 22).

Figure 3. The authentication success, p_s, for different $\hat{k}$ values and $k = 20$

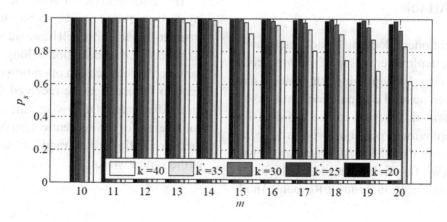

Figure 2. MAC frame modifications for power awareness and flooding attack resistance in our proposed protocol

AER	AC	Data	Source MAC	Destination MAC
00	0	Data (routing, localization, raw sensed data, etc)		
01	1	Unavailable		
10	1	160 bit hash value		Public key
11	1	160 bit hash value		unavailable

AC   : authentication code. | Unavailable: does not exist in the used frame.
AER : authenticating request / response. | Public key: 160 or 1024 bit public key.

Table 2. Flags and their indication

AER	AC	frame Identification
00	0	data frame
01	1	request frame
10	1	response frame from the concerned node
11	1	response frame from the assisting group

notified and $\hat{k}$ is set to a larger value than the initial one. By dynamically setting $\hat{k}$ to larger and smaller values, we can balance the security/ communication requirement. The additional overhead for this scenario is in the memory requirement for storing larger $\hat{k}$ number of K_i while the maximum communication is bounded by the largest fraction size of assisting nodes.

Power Awareness and Flooding Attack

The aforementioned flooding attack motivates an interesting deployment issue of our protocols for energy saving. By deploying our protocols in the MAC layer, several computations and unsolicited authentication frames can be avoided. To make this deployment possible, we introduce a slight modification on the MAC frame as shown in Figure 2. Two flag fields are added which are the ARR (Authentication Request/Response) and

AC (Authentication Frame) with their meanings shown in Table 2. Based on AC values, the frames in the network are classified into authentication and normal data frames. Based on ARR, the frames are classified into authentication request (ARF) and authentication response (AREF) frames from the concerned node (which will include the copy of the public key information itself) and authentication response from the set of the assisting authentication nodes.

By performing the different checks at the MAC layer, the required energy for passing unsolicited frame to upper layers will be avoided. In addition, if the received information belongs to an already canceled authentication operation due to authentication failure then the received frames are directly discarded. Otherwise, this information is considered for the authentication operation. Further verification will be required on this extension in the future works.

ANALYSIS AND EVALUATION

Analysis

Recall $n, \hat{k}, k, p_s, p_f, \sigma$ and m defined above and define a and b as the number of real authentication frames and attacker's authentication frames respectively. Also assume that the probability of attackers' frames delivery and the real assisting group is equally likely. The probability for any combination of a and b in k given m and $\hat{k}$ is defined as (where $a + b = k$) the combination of a out of k and the combination of b out of m by the combination of the sum of a and b ou of the sum of $\hat{k}$ and m

$$p = \frac{\binom{\hat{k}}{a}\binom{m}{b}}{\binom{\hat{k} + m}{a + b}} = \tag{1}$$

The probability of authentication success, p_s, is equal to the probability that a is greater than or equal to $k/2$ which can be defined as:

$$p_s = p(a \geq k/2) = \sum_{i=0}^{k/2} p(a = \frac{k}{2} + i) = \sum_{i=0}^{k/2} \frac{\binom{\hat{k}}{k/2+i}\binom{m}{k/2-i}}{\binom{\hat{k}+m}{k}} \tag{2}$$

However, since the summation applies only for the numerators for the components inside of it, we can simply and further define the model for $\hat{k} \geq k$ and $m \geq k/2$. When $m \leq k/2$, $p_s = 1$, to get:

$$p_s = \left\{ \binom{\hat{k}+m}{k}^{-1} \right. \tag{3}$$

For simplicity, in the following analysis, we consider that $m > k/2$ unless otherwise is mentioned. We can similarly show that the authentication failure probability, p_f, is $p_f = 1 - p_s$

$$p_f = 1 - p(a \geq k/2) = p(a < k/2)$$

$$= \sum_{i=1}^{k/2} p(a = k/2 - i) = \sum_{i=1}^{k/2} \left(\frac{\binom{\hat{k}}{k/2-i}\binom{m}{k/2+i}}{\binom{\hat{k}+m}{k}} \right) \tag{4}$$

However, according to the deviation introduced earlier due to the coin tossing, p_f and p_s may differ slightly. By plugging the deviation values in the model above in Eq (1), we get

$$p_{(\sigma)} = \frac{\binom{\hat{k}+|\sigma|}{a}\binom{m}{a}}{\binom{\hat{k}+m+|\sigma|}{a+b}} \tag{5}$$

Accordingly, the results in (2) and (4) can be written with regard to $|\sigma|$ as:

$$p_s' = \sum_{i=0}^{k/2} p_{(\sigma)}(a = k/2 + i) = \sum_{i=0}^{k/2} \frac{\binom{\hat{k}+|\sigma|}{k/2+i}\binom{m}{k-i}}{\binom{\hat{k}+m+|\sigma|}{k}}, \tag{6}$$

$$p_f' = \sum_{i=1}^{k/2} p_{(\sigma)}(b = \frac{k}{2} + i) = \sum_{i=1}^{k/2} \frac{\binom{\hat{k}+|\sigma|}{k/2-i}\binom{m}{k+i}}{\binom{\hat{k}+m+|\sigma|}{k}} \tag{7}$$

Now, we define the error in authentication probability (with respect to p_s) as

$$e_{p_s|\sigma} = |p_s' - p_s| \tag{8}$$

Note that the error in authentication failure due to σ $e_{p_f|\sigma} =| p_f' - p_f |$ is equal to $e_{p_s|\sigma}$ since:

$$e_{p_s|\sigma} =| p_s' - p_s |=| 1 - p_f' - (1 - p_f) |$$
$$=| p_f' - p_f |= e_{p_f|\sigma} \tag{9}$$

Demonstration and Simulations

To evaluate the performance of our protocols, we performed an intensive simulation aiming to demonstrate the resistance of our protocols against the flooding attacking within the time constraints. To evaluate the authentication success probability, we perform the authentication process repeatedly for 100 times with the specified parameters. For each round, the authentication success is counted as `1' and the failure is counted as zero where the overall authentication probability is expressed as the averaged successes to whole number of trials (that is, the summation of `1's divided by a 100). Figure 3 shows the theoretically derived authentication success probability p_s for different authenticating group size and varying attackers packets. Note that, as long as the number of the attackers' packets are less than the group size, a satisfactory p_s is obtained (i.e., $p_s > 0.6$)

To study the impact of the deviation σ in the aforementioned theoretical model, we simulate the case of two protocols with the different initialization and obtain the impact of σ as the difference between two authentication success probabilities driven as above (shown in Figure 4). Such probability is tightly close to the theoretically driven formula above (shown in Figure 4). As the authenticating group size grows, σ grow as well (shown in Figure 4).

Overhead Evaluation

We evaluate the protocols in terms of communication, computation, and memory overhead.

- **Memory:** the memory is required for storing the public key of a given node in a set of k different sensor nodes. Considering the early notation of the network size, the required memory per one authentication $M = 160 \times k$ bit. For c-rounds protocol, the required memory is $M = 160 \times k \times c$ bit.
- **Computation:** the computation in terms of processing time is required for one hash calculation and k-160- bit hash values comparisons to check their equality. Such comparisons are performed using a simple exclusive or operation ($\oplus$) for the received hashes and compare the result with zero. Such processing requires $(20Ck)/(f)$ 8-bits exclusive or operations, where C is a constant determined by the 8-bit words comparison efficiency on the concerned processor, the 20 represents the hash value in 8-bit words (=160/8), f is the frequency of the sensor node in Hertz and k is the aforementioned authentication parameter.
- **Communication:** for the early defined k and the typical length of hash function's output $|K_i|$, the required communication overhead is $|K_i| \times k + 1024$ bit for both the single hop authentication at averag

A brief listing of all of our proposed protocol overhead evaluation is as follows

- **Memory.** For the three proposed authentication protocols, each node requires $160\,\hat{k}$ bit, $160c\,\hat{k}$ bit, and $160(\hat{k}+c)$ bit in the primary, c-round, and multi-hop protocols, respectively, where $c = (h-1)k_0$. Also, the long living protocol requires $160c\,\hat{k}$ bit to run authentication process as in c-round protocol case.
- **Communication:** the communication required to authenticate node in all single

Figure 4. Impact of deviation on authentication success probability (a) The authentication success, p_s with and without σ for $n = 1000$, $\hat{k} = k = 20$ and varying m (b) The error of authentication due to σ when $n = 1000$ for $k = 10, 20$ (c) Simulation versus theoretical error estimation

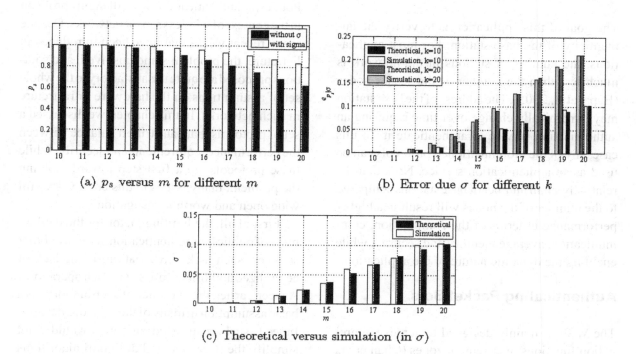

(a) p_s versus m for different m

(b) Error due σ for different k

(c) Theoretical versus simulation (in σ)

hop protocols is $160 \hat{k}$ bit. However, the communication required in case of multi hop protocol is $160(\hat{k} + c)$ bit.

To give insights on the impact of our scheme compared to the state-of-art related work in lietrature by Du et al. in terms of computation and communication overhead, we evaluated our primary protocol, RSA, ECC, and Du et al.'s, which resulted in the following:

- **Computation**: following the computation model mentioned before, our primary protocol requires $2 \times 10^{-2} k + 7.2$ (ms). However, we found that RSA, ECC, and Du et al protocols require 430 (ms), 1620 (ms), and $7.2k + c$ (ms), respectively.
- **Communication**: the required communication overhead of our primary protocol

is $160 \hat{k} + |K_i|$ bit; the RSA, ECC, and Du et al protocols require 1024, 320, and 160 $\hat{k} + |K_i|$ bit, respectively.

Given the computation and communication evaluations of the related schemes mentioned above, we estimated numerical comparison between our scheme and Du et al in terms of the communication and computation for the following parameters: $n = 1000$; $k = \log_2 1000 = 10$. Both of our scheme and Du et al. scheme require 2624 bit communication overhead in the case of using RSA encryption and 1760 bit in the case of ECC encryption. However, Du et al. scheme needs 72 (ms) in both RSA and ECC encryption setting which is much more than our scheme computation overhead. Our scheme computation overhead is 8.155 (ms) in case of RSA setting and 7.518 (ms) in the case of ECC setting.

ADDITIONAL APPLICATIONS

Authenticating the Base Station

The goal of this application is to verify the authenticity of the base station. For most applications, the number of stations in the network is much less than the number of the sensor nodes (Bapat et al.,2005). The address of the base station may dynamically change over time requiring an authentication service to authenticate it. In this case, any of the aforementioned protocols can be used as an authentication service. Note that the relatively small number of base stations compared to the number of the nodes will result in a higher performance in terms of the computation, communication, average memory and security, while enabling the dynamic nature of the application.

Authenticating Packet Sets

The WSN is mainly designed to achieve aggregation functions over remote zones (Chan et al., 2007). In this model, we let the base station send context command packets that require the node to perform a specific sensing job based on the category of the command itself (Ahn and Kim, 2006). In such cases, the space of those commands is a limited set and can be considered as a categorical command set. As of the early application, benefiting from the relatively smaller number of command categories over the number of the nodes in the network, any of the early introduced algorithms can be used to verify the authenticity of any command by requesting its authentication via pre-defined set of nodes that save the command in their memory.

DIRECTIONS FOR FURTHER RESEARCH

Public key authentication is a challenging problem in the context of wireless sensor networks. Despite many recent works that have been introduced in lietrature, the problem stand unsolved, and solutions proposed are quite unsatisfactory to the whole set of assumptions on the hardware infrastrcture in such networks. In this chapter, we discussed a set of protocols that can strike a balance between the performance requirements and security. While these protocols are a first step towards solving the problem, many issues in this context are still wide open and worth investigation.

First of all, the limiting factor for the deployment of public key authentication, as well as other services, such as key revocation, is the lack of centralized authorities to assist in such operations. As seen earlier, the existence of such authority is a basic assumption in many of the previous designs. Indeed, such centralized authority would a lot simplify the operation and design of algorithms that are hard to conceive without of them. It worth further investigation to look for the potential of these solutions in real-world sensor network settings. Potentially, such sensor networks could be in an industrial, less hostile settings.

Second, we anticipate public key algorithms by themselves are not going to be used for encryptyion and decryption of the whole traffic between sensor nodes, but are meant to simplify the problem of symmetric key distribution among sensor nodes, which are then used for encrypting the traffic between sensor nodes. Accordingly, this calls for the design of architectures that consider "authenticated key distribution" as a solution for the problem in hand. Such primtives, if found, would solve both problems of authentication and distribution at the same time.

Third, and sepcific to the design of the protocols discussed in this paper, we find that design that tries to weigh the collaboration between sensor nodes to provide security primitives would enable several security threats, such as the Sybil attack and some types of the Sybil attack. While these problems by themselves are issues of concern in the general context of secure distributed systems, it is worthwhile ot investigate the extent to which these can be problematic with the discussed designs.

Fourth, our understanding of the solution to the problem of public key authentication is in a lot of cases limited to the known type of public key cryptographic algorithms (such as RSA, ECC, among others). It is worth mentioning, however, that there has been a lot of progress on the development of public key algorithms, and primitives, specific to resources limited devices. Such works are based on new and old assumptions are more fit to the sensor network settings. Examples of such work can be found in (Camenisch et al., 2006)

Specific to hardening attacks on the discussed protocols in this chapter, we mention a few directions. First, light-weight puzzles (Schaller et al., 2007) can be used to harden the overhearing of the public key information by attackers and reduce their chances for injecting fake authentication frames. Second, it will be interesting to have concrete formulation for the energy saving due to deploying our protocols in the MAC layer. Third, radio coverage issues in relation with multi-hop authentication protocol and proactive group size are interesting to discover.

CONCLUSION

Since the Public key cryptography is now computationally feasible to sensor networks, public key authentication is a very important issue for security in sensor networks. In this chapter, we have discussed the problem of applying efficient public key authentication in WSN. Also, we introduced a novel family of authentication protocols for public key authentication with farther applications in wireless sensor network. Even of the initial deviation based on the nature of the protocol, detailed analysis has shown its practicality for properly selected protocol parameters. We extended our protocol to multi-hop authentication fashion and studied the authentication accuracy in both cases.

REFERENCES

Ahn, S., & Kim, D. (2006). Proactive context-aware sensor networks. In *Proceeding of EWSN* (pp. 38-53).

Bapat, S., Kulathumani, V., & Arora, A. (2005). Analyzing the yield of exscal, a large-scale wireless sensor network experiment. In *Proceeding of ICNP* (pp. 53-62).

BTnode Project. (2010). *Eth Zurich*. Retrieved from www.btnode.ethz.ch/

Camenisch, J., Hohenberger, S., Kohlweiss, M., Lysyanskaya, A., & Meyerovich, M. (2006). *How to win the clonewars: Efficient periodic n-times anonymous authentication*. ACM Conference on Computer and Communications Security 2006 (pp. 201-210).

Chan, H., Perrig, A., Przydatek, B., & Song, D. X. (2007). SIA: Secure information aggregation in sensor networks. *Journal of Computer Security*, *15*(1), 69–102.

Chan, H., Perrig, A., & Song, D. X. (2003). Random key predistribution schemes for sensor networks. In *Proceeding of IEEE Symposium on Security and Privacy* (pp. 197-213).

Crossbow Tech. Inc. (n.d.). *Website*. Retrieved from http://www.xbow.com/

Du, W., Deng, J., Han, Y. S., Varshney, P. K., Katz, J., & Khalili, A. (2003). A pairwise key predistribution scheme for wireless sensor networks. *ACM Transactions on Information and System Security Journal, 8*(2), 228–258. doi:10.1145/1065545.1065548

Du, W., Wang, R., & Ning, P. (2005). An efficient scheme for authenticating public keys in sensor networks. In *Proceedings of MobiHoc* (pp. 58-67).

Eschenauer, L., & Gligor, V. D. (2002). A key-management scheme for distributed sensor networks. *In Proceeding of ACM CCS* (pp. 41-47).

Gura, N., Patel, A., Wander, A., Eberle, H., & Shantz, S. C. (2004). Comparing elliptic curve cryptography and RSA on 8-bit CPUs. In *Proceeding of CHES* (pp. 119-132).

Karl, H., & Willig, A. (2005). *Protocols and architectures for wireless sensor networks*. John Wiley & Sons Ltd. ISBN-13 988-0-470-09510-2

Koblitz, N., Menezes, A., & Vanstone, S. A. (2000). The state of elliptic curve cryptography. *Journal of Designs . Codes and Cryptography, 19*(2/3), 173–193. doi:10.1023/A:1008354106356

Liu, D., & Ning, P. (2003). Establishing pairwise keys in distributed sensor networks. In *Proceedings of ACM CCS* (pp. 52-61).

Malan, D. J., Welsh, M., & Smith, M. D. (2004). A public-key infrastructure for key distribution in tinyos based on elliptic curve cryptography. *In Proceedings of First IEEE Int. Conf. on Sensor and Ad Hoc Comm. and Networks* (pp. 71-80).

Merkle, R. C. (1980). Protocols for public key cryptosystems. In *Proceedings of IEEE Symposium on Security and Privacy* (pp. 122-134).

Mitzenmacher, M. (2002). Compressed Bloom filters. *IEEE/ACM Transactions on Networking, 10*(5), 613–620. doi:10.1109/TNET.2002.803864

Mohaisen, A., Nyang, D., Maeng, Y., & Lee, K. (2007). Structures for communication-efficient public key revocation in ubiquitous sensor network. In *Proceedings of the International Conference on Mobile Ad-hoc and Sensor Networks* (pp. 822-833).

Perrig, A., Szewczyk, R., Tygar, J. D., Wen, V., & Culler, D. E. (2002). Spins: Security protocols for sensor networks. *Wireless Network Journal, 8*(5), 521–534. doi:10.1023/A:1016598314198

Ren, K., Lou, W., & Zhang, Y. (2007). Multi-user broadcast authentication in wireless sensor networks. In *Proceedings of SECON* (pp. 223-232)

Rivest, R. L., Shamir, A., & Adleman, L. M. (1983). A method for obtaining digital signatures and public-key crypto-systems. *Communications of the ACM Magazine, 26*(1), 96–99. doi:10.1145/357980.358017

Schaller, P., Capkun, S., & Basin, D. A. (2007). Bap: Broadcast authentication using cryptographic puzzles. In *Proceedings of ACNS,* (pp. 401-419).

Van Dam, T., & Langendoen, K. (2003). An adaptive energy-efficient mac protocol for wireless sensor networks. In *Proceedings of SenSys* (pp. 171-180).

Wander, A., Gura, N., Eberle, H., Gupta, V., & Shantz, S. C. (2005). Energy analysis of public-key cryptography for wireless sensor networks. In *Proceedings of PerCom* (pp. 324-328).

Wang, R., Du, W., Liu, X., & Ning, P. (2009). ShortPK: A short-term public key scheme for broadcast authentication in sensor networks. *ACM Transactions on Sensor Networks, 6*(1), 1–29. doi:10.1145/1653760.1653769

Watro, R. J., Kong, D., Fen Cuti, S., Gardiner, C., Lynn, C., & Kruus, P. (2004). Tinypk: Securing sensor networks with public key technology. In *Proceedings of SASN* (pp. 59-64).

Wood, A. D., & Stankovic, J. A. (2002). Denial of service in sensor networks. *IEEE Computer Magazine*, *35*(10), 54–62.

Ye, W., Heidemann, J. S., & Estrin, D. (2004). Medium access control with coordinated adaptive sleeping for wireless sensor networks. *IEEE/ACM Transactions on Networking*, *12*(3), 493–506. doi:10.1109/TNET.2004.828953

Zhang, Q., Wang, P., Reeves, D. S., & Ning, P. (2005). Defending against sybil attacks in sensor networks. In *Proceedings of ICDCS Workshops* (pp. 185-191).

Chapter 11
RNST:
Precise Localization Based on Trilateration for Indoor Sensor Networks

Guangjie Han
Hohai University, China

Wen Shen
Hohai University, China

Chuan Zhu
Hohai University, China

Lei Shu
Osaka University, Japan

Joel Rodrigues
University of Beira Interior, Portugal

ABSTRACT

The key problem of location service in indoor sensor networks is to quickly and precisely acquire the position information of mobile nodes. Due to resource limitation of the sensor nodes, some of the traditional positioning algorithms, such as Two-Phase Positioning (TPP) algorithm, are too complicated to be implemented and they can not provide the real-time localization of the mobile node. We analyze the localization error, which is produced when one tries to estimate the mobile node using trilateration method in the localization process. We draw the conclusion that the localization error is the least when three reference nodes form an equilateral triangle. Therefore, we improve the TPP algorithm and propose Reference Node Selection algorithm based on Trilateration (RNST), which can provide real-time localization service for the mobile nodes. Our proposed algorithm is verified by the simulation experiment. Based on the analysis of the acquired data and comparison with that of the TPP algorithm, we conclude that our algorithm can meet real-time localization requirement of the mobile nodes in an indoor environment, and make the localization error less than that of the traditional algorithm; therefore our proposed algorithm can effectively solve the real-time localization problem of the mobile nodes in indoor sensor networks.

DOI: 10.4018/978-1-61350-110-8.ch011

Copyright © 2012, IGI Global. Copying or distributing in print or electronic forms without written permission of IGI Global is prohibited.

INTRODUCTION

Wireless Sensor Networks (WSNs) have been attracting increasing research interest given the recent advances in miniaturization, low-cost and low-power design. WSNs hold the promise of many new applications in the area of monitoring and control. Spatial localization (determining physical location) of a sensor node is an example of critical service for context-aware applications in WSNs. Examples include target tracking, intrusion detection, wildlife habitat monitoring, climate control, and disaster management (Fengyuan Ren, Haining Huang & Chuang Lin, 2003). Most of the applications are related to the positions of sensor nodes: sensing data without the position information of the sensor nodes are not useful, thus self-localization is the basic application in a WSN (Fubao Wang, Long Shi & Fengyuan Ren, 2005). Sensor nodes often need to determine their further actions based on their physical locations. To precisely obtain the position information of a mobile node is the key of the location service, therefore how to efficiently and precisely acquire the mobile nodes' position information, and being able to provide the location service to the user, is one of the important problems in WSNs.

In an indoor environment, one of the major challenges for researchers is to localize the sensor nodes with relatively high localization precision. For military radio networks, knowing the precise location of each person with a radio can be critical. In offices and in warehouses, object localization and tracking applications are possible with large-scale ad-hoc networks of wireless tags. Existing geo-location systems such as GPS do not always meet the operational (e.g. power), environmental (e.g. indoors) or cost constraints in indoor sensor networks. It is also impractical to configure the position information for every node in an indoor environment. Therefore, reference nodes with their positions are vital aspects of nearly every localization system; the mobile nodes get their own positions based on the position information

of reference nodes using localization techniques, including RSSI, AoA, ToA/TDoA, etc. In the past few years, a number of positioning algorithms have been proposed to reduce the localization error of the mobile nodes. Many researches dealt with the node localization issues without taking into account the freference node" parameter, however reference node placement also strongly affects the quality of spatial localization (N. Bulusu, et al., 2001; N. Bulusu, et al., 2003).

In this chapter, we analyze the localization error, which is produced when one tries to estimate the mobile node using trilateration method in the localization process. We draw the conclusion that the localization error is the least when three reference nodes form an equilateral triangle. Our analysis provides theoretical foundation for purposefully selecting the suitable reference nodes to reduce the localization error in indoor sensor networks. We improve the TPP algorithm and propose a novel RNST positioning algorithm, which can satisfy the real-time localization requirement of the mobile nodes. We also implement our proposed RNST algorithm using the network simulator OPNET and actual Zigbee sensor platform, and make a comparison with the TPP algorithm. The experimental results show that our algorithm can effectively meet real-time localization requirement of the mobile nodes with limited resources. Moreover our algorithm can also guarantee the minimum localization error within a short time period and effectively meet the localization precision requirement of the mobile nodes. Compared to the existing approaches, RNST algorithm is able to quickly estimate the position of the mobile node based on the received packets. To the best of our knowledge, this is the first comprehensive work on reference node selection algorithm based on trilateration.

This chapter is organized as follows. In Section 2, we list the related work in more details. In Section 3, we present the theoretical background of our proposed RNST algorithm. We present our RNST algorithm and analyze the reasons of the localization error in Section 4. The simulation results and performance analysis are shown in Section 5. Finally, in Section 6 we summarize our results and predict future work.

RELATED WORK

Since many applications need to know where objects or persons are and various location services need to be provided, the localization problem has received considerable attention in the past. Many localization approaches have been proposed specifically for sensor networks, which are generally classified into two phases (Fubao Wang, Long Shi & Fengyuan Ren, 2005). The first phase mainly focuses on localization schemes tightly-coupled to infrastructure frameworks, such as RADAR, Active Bat, Active Badge, Smart Rooms, etc. The second phase mainly focuses on localization schemes loosely-coupled to infrastructure-less frameworks, including Cricket (Priyantha NB, Chakraborty A & Balakrishnan H, 2000), Self-Positioning Algorithm (SPA) (Capkun S, Hamdi M & Hubaux J-P, 2002), Convex Position Estimation (CPE) (Doherty L, 2000), Ad hoc Positioning System (APS) (Koen Langendoen & Niels Reijers, 2003), Cooperative ranging (Beutel J, 1999) and TPP (Savarese C, Rabay J & Langendoen K, 2002) algorithm, Ad-hoc localization system (Savvides A, Han C-C & Srivastava MB, 2001) and N-hop Multilateration Primitive (NMP) (Avvides A, Park H & Srivastava MB, 2002), Generic Localized Algorithms (GLA) (Meguerdichian S, Slijepcevic S, Karayan V & Potkonjak M, 2001), MDS-MAP(Shang Y, Ruml W, Zhang Y & Fromherz MPJ, 2003), etc. Recently researchers have focused on iterative precision algorithm, such as Cooperative ranging, TPP algorithm and N-hop multilateration primitive. The position information of the unknown node is initially estimated using the traditional algorithms, and is improved by iterative computation in the next phase. However, in order to get high localization precision, the tra-

ditional algorithms require too much processing power and energy. It is impractical to implement them in mobile nodes with limited resources, and these algorithms can not meet the real-time localization requirement of a mobile node. The above-mentioned localization schemes do not consider the effect of geometrical relationship among reference nodes (except (N.Bulusu, et al., 2001; N.Bulusu, et al., 2003) and (Y.Zou & K.Charkrabarty, 2003; TheinLai Wong, et al., 2004; Jennifer Yick, et al., 2004; V.Isler, 2006)), which, however, strongly affects the quality of localization.

In (Priyantha NB, et al., 2000), the researchers only give some guiding instructions of reference node placement in Cricket indoor localization schemes. In (N.Bulusu, et al., 2001), the researchers analyze three adaptive reference node placement algorithms (Random, Max and Square-grid) using a mobile human or robot agent for localization based on RF-proximity, and they also evaluate different placement algorithm against both coverage and localization issue. In (N.Bulusu, et al., 2003), the researchers propose HEAP (an incremental reference placement algorithm) for low density regimes and STROBE (an adaptive density algorithm) for high density regimes. The localization precision can be improved by moving the nodes or adding some new nodes by a mobile human or robot agent based on the simulation results. The researchers in (Y.Zou & K.Charkrabarty, 2003; TheinLai Wong, et al., 2004; Jennifer Yick, et al., 2004) propose some spherical localization schemes to achieve the tracking task by adding or moving nodes by outside forces (manpower or robot). It is impractical or infeasible to precisely locate by adding or moving reference nodes in an indoor environment. There are also some limitations to be used in real applications. Volkan (V.Isler, 2006) proposes an approximation algorithm for placement and distributed deployment of sensor camera teams, which form right-angled triangle based on triangulation to track the mobile nodes. However, the algorithm needs heavy computa-

Table 1 Summary of the related work

Localization algorithms	Placement of Anchor node	Localization Error	Localization time	Energy Consumption	Localization Algorithm
F.Wang, et al.,	Random	Biggest	Longest	Average	RADAR
Capkun S, et al.,	Random	Bigger	Longest	Much	SPA
Avvides A et al.,	Random	Bigger	Longer	Much	NMP
L.Koen, et al.,	Random	Bigger	Longer	Much	APS
Doherty L	Random	Average	Longer	Much	CPE
Meguerdichian S, et al.,	Random	Average	Longest	Much	GLA
Shang Y, et al.,	Random	Average	Longer	Much	MDS-MAP
Savarese C, et al.,	Random	Less	Longest	Much	TPP
P.NB, et al.,	Corner	Bigger	Average	Average	Cricket
N.Bulusu, et al.,	Square-grid	Bigger	Longer	Average	Random, Max and Square-grid
N.Bulusu, et al.,	Mobile robot	Bigger	Longer	Average	HEAP,STROBE
Y.Zou, et al.,	Mobile robot	Average	Longer	Average	Spherical localization
V.Isler	Right-angled triangle	Average	Average	Average	Right-angled triangle

tions and communications, so it hardly satisfies real-time localization requirement of the mobile nodes. The idea of equilateral triangulation, based only on intuition though, was briefly mentioned (D.Niculescu & B.Nath, 2003) in designing Ad Hoc Positioning Systems Using AoA. The summary of the related work is listed in Table 1.

THEORETICAL BACKGROUND

Consider three distinct reference nodes $p_i = (x_i, y_i), i = 1, 2, 3$ in $\mathbb{R}^2$. We want to calculate the coordinate (x_0, y_0) of an unknown node p according to r_i (the distances between p_i and p). We have the following system of equations based on trilateration location method.

$$\begin{cases} (x_0 - x_1)^2 + (y_0 - y_1)^2 = r_1^2 \\ (x_0 - x_2)^2 + (y_0 - y_2)^2 = r_2^2 \\ (x_0 - x_3)^2 + (y_0 - y_3)^2 = r_3^2 \end{cases} \tag{1}$$

Solving system (1), we derive the position of unknown node p.

$$\begin{cases} x_0 = \dfrac{1}{\Delta}(2T_1(y_1 - y_3) - 2T_2(y_1 - y_2)) \\ y_0 = \dfrac{1}{\Delta}(2T_2(x_1 - x_2) - 2T_1(x_1 - x_3)) \end{cases} \tag{2}$$

where

$$\Delta = 4((x_1 - x_2)(y_1 - y_3) - (x_1 - x_3)(y_1 - y_2)),$$

$$T_1 = r_2^2 - r_1^2 - x_2^2 + x_1^2 - y_2^2 + y_1^2 \text{ and}$$

$$T_2 = r_3^2 - r_1^2 - x_3^2 + x_1^2 - y_3^2 + y_1^2.$$

If the Δ is equal to 0, three reference nodes are on a straight line and the unknown node can not be determined. The above analysis indicates that an unknown point p can be determined by three reference nodes p_1, p_2 and p_3 if these three nodes are not on a straight line.

Theorem 1

$\Delta = 0$ if and only if p_1, p_2 and p_3 are on a straight line.

Proof

We first prove the sufficiency part. Suppose p_i's are on a straight line. There are two cases for this assumption. For the first case, the three points are on the same line $x = a$. In this case, one checks Box 1.

For the second case, the three points are on the same line $y = kx + b$. It follows that

$$\frac{y_1 - y_2}{x_1 - x_2} = \frac{y_1 - y_3}{x_1 - x_3} = k$$

So in this case (see Box 2). This proves the sufficiency part.

We then prove the necessity part. Suppose that

$$\Delta = 4\big((x_1 - x_2)(y_1 - y_3) - (x_1 - x_3)(y_1 - y_2)\big) = 0$$

If $x_1 = x_2$, then necessarily $y_1 \neq y_2$, otherwise $p_1 = p_2$, contradicting the fact that the three reference points are all distinct. It follows that $x_1 = x_3$. So we conclude p_1, p_2 and p_3 are on the same line $x = a$, where $x_1 = x_2 = x_3 = a$.

Similar if $x_1 = x_3$, one can also derive that $x_1 = x_2$, so again the three points are on a straight line. In the following we assume that $x_1 \neq x_2$ and $x_1 \neq x_3$. We can rewrite $\Delta = 0$ as

$$\frac{y_1 - y_2}{x_1 - x_2} = \frac{y_1 - y_3}{x_1 - x_3}$$

In this case one can check that the three points p_i's are on the straight line

$$y = kx + b$$

where $k = \dfrac{y_1 - y_2}{x_1 - x_2}$ and $b = \dfrac{y_1 x_2 - y_2 x_1}{x_2 - x_1}$

Remark 1

The above analysis indicates that an unknown point p can be determined by three reference points p_i's if these three points are not on a straight line. In real application, we can place the reference point to form a sharp triangle to make sure Δ to be relatively large.

In real applications, we can place the reference nodes to form a sharp triangle to make sure Δ to be relatively large. Moreover nodes p_1, p_2 and p_3 should not be too close to each other, otherwise Δ will become too small for estimating the un-

Box 1.

$$\Delta = 4\big((x_1 - x_2)(y_1 - y_2) - (x_1 - x_3)(y_1 - y_2)\big) = 4\big((a - a)(y_1 - y_3) - (a - a)(y_1 - y_2)\big) = 0$$

Box 2.

$$\Delta = 4\big((x_1 - x_2)(y_1 - y_3) - (x_1 - x_3)(y_1 - y_2)\big) = 4\big(k(x_1 - x_2)(x_1 - x_3) - k(x_1 - x_3)(x_1 - x_2)\big) = 0$$

known node. Intuitively this is easily understandable: three nodes will act like just one node if they are too close to each other, so they will not effectively determine the position of an unknown node. Previously we assume that the measurement of the distance is absolutely precise, however inevitably the measurement error will exist.

As explained above, any three reference nodes can give us an estimation of (x_0, y_0). Solving Equation (1) associated with all the possible three reference nodes, we obtain the estimated coordinates of $(x_0, y_0) : (x_0^{(1)}, y_0^{(1)}), \cdots\cdots, (x_0^{(n)}, y_0^{(n)})$. Then $\bar{x}, \bar{y}$, defined as $\bar{x} = \dfrac{1}{n} \sum_{i=1}^{n} x_0^{(i)}$, $\bar{y} = \dfrac{1}{n} \sum_{i=1}^{n} y_0^{(i)}$, is the collective average of these n estimations. During this process, the *localization error* is defined to be $\Delta r = \sqrt{\Delta x^2 + \Delta y^2}$, where $\Delta x = |x_0 - \bar{x}|$, $\Delta y = |y_0 - \bar{y}|$.

As shown in Figure 1, if there exists the localization error, three circles can form a small region, the size of the small region can be regarded as the size of the localization error (Guangjie Han, 2004). Thus, if we can reduce the size of the small region, then we can also decrease the size of the localization error. Under the above-mentioned assumption, Eq.1 will not give the precise computation for the unknown node. In fact as we shall analyze in the sequel, the exact solution for the unknown node will be located in a neighborhood of the node given by Eq.1. In the following we assume that the error will range between $(-\varepsilon, \varepsilon)$.

Another very interesting interpretation of Δ is that it is twice the area of the triangle $p_1 p_2 p_3$, which will be denoted by $area(p_1 p_2 p_3)$ in the sequel.

Theorem 2

$$| \Delta | = 2 area(p_1 p_2 p_3)$$

Figure 1. Region of localization error

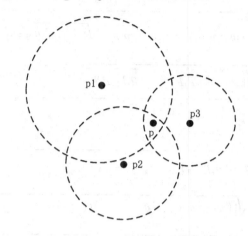

Proof

Note that

$$| \Delta | = 2 area(p_1 p_2 p_3) = | \overrightarrow{p_1 p_2} || \overrightarrow{p_1 p_3} | \sin \theta$$

where $\theta = \angle(\overrightarrow{p_1 p_2}, \overrightarrow{p_1 p_3})$, Simple calculations will show (see Box 3), where $(\cdot)$ denote the dot product of two vectors. Notice that

$$| \overrightarrow{p_1 p_2} |^2 = (x_1 - x_2)^2 + (y_1 - y_2)^2 ,$$

$$| \overrightarrow{p_1 p_3} |^2 = (x_1 - x_3)^2 + (y_1 - y_3)^2 ,$$

$$(\overrightarrow{p_1 p_2} \cdot \overrightarrow{p_1 p_3})^2 = ((x_1 - x_2)(x_1 - x_3) + (y_1 - y_2)(y_1 - y_3))^2$$

the calculation can go on as follows in Box 4. This establishes the claim in the theorem.

Previously we assume that the measurement of the distances are absolutely accurate, however inevitably the measurement error will exist. In the following we assume that the error will range between $-\varepsilon$ and ε. In other words, when the distance between two points are measured to be r, the true value could be any real number between $r - \varepsilon$ and $r + \varepsilon$.

Box 3.

$$2area(p_1p_2p_3) = |\overrightarrow{p_1p_2}||\overrightarrow{p_1p_3}|\sqrt{1-\cos^2\theta} = \sqrt{|\overrightarrow{p_1p_2}|^2|\overrightarrow{p_1p_3}|^2 - |\overrightarrow{p_1p_2}|^2|\overrightarrow{p_1p_3}|^2\cos^2\theta}$$

$$= \sqrt{|\overrightarrow{p_1p_2}|^2|\overrightarrow{p_1p_3}|^2 - (\overrightarrow{p_1p_2}\cdot\overrightarrow{p_1p_3})^2}$$

Box 4.

$$2area(p_1p_2p_3)$$

$$= \sqrt{((x_1-x_2)^2+(y_1-y_2)^2)((x_1-x_3)^2+(y_1-y_3)^2) - ((x_1-x_2)(x_1-x_3)+(y_1-y_2)(y_1-y_3))^2}$$

$$= \sqrt{(x_1-x_2)(y_1-y_3)-(x_1-x_3)(y_1-y_2))^2} = |\Delta|$$

Under the above assumption, Formula 1 will not give the exact estimation for the unknown point. In fact as we shall analyze in the sequel, the exact solution for the unknown point will be located in a neighborhood of the point give by Formula 1.

Now for $i = 1, 2, 3$ we define (see Box 5).

Note that when $\varepsilon_i = 0$, $\cap_i C_{p_i}$ will consist of one point, which corresponds to the point given by Eq.1. However if these is measurement error, namely when $\varepsilon_i > 0$, $\cap_i C_{p_i}$ will be a region with positive area. We denote the circle $\{(x,y) \mid (x-x_0)^2 + (y-y_0)^2 = \varepsilon^2\}$ by S_p. Let l_{p,p_i} be the straight line passing through both p and p_i, then l_{p,p_i} shall intersect with S_p at two points $q_{i,1}$ and $q_{i,2}$. For $j = 1, 2$, we denote the line passing through $q_{i,j}$ and tangent to S_p by

$\bar{l}_{q_{i,j}}$. Then the region $\bar{C}_{p_i}$ shall be the region in between the two lines $\bar{l}_{q_{i,1}}$ and $\bar{l}_{q_{i,2}}$, as shown in Figure 2.

When the measurement error ε is relatively small, at certain neighborhood of p, C_{p_i} can be linearized and approximated by $\bar{C}_{p_i}$ and $area(C_{p_i})$ can be approximated by $area(\bar{C}_{p_i})$. Certainly an optimal configuration of the three reference nodes will minimize $C = \cap_i area(C_{p_i})$ (approximately $\bar{C} = \cap_i area(\bar{C}_{p_i})$ when ε is small). We shall prove that when the reference nodes are placed in a symmetrical way, the optimal configuration can be achieved.

Box 5.

$$C_{p_i} = \{(x,y) \in \mathbb{R}^2 \mid (x-x_i)^2 + (y-y_i)^2 \le (r_i+\varepsilon_i)^2, (x-x_i)^2 + (y-y_i)^2 \ge (r_i-\varepsilon_i)^2\} \tag{3}$$

Figure 2. Analysis of localization error

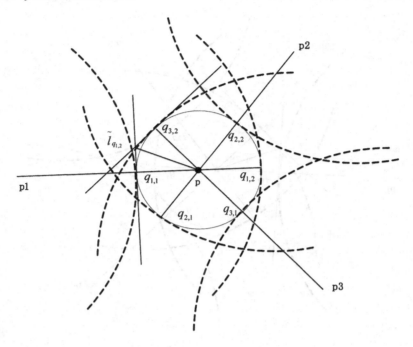

Definition 1

A subset $S \subset \mathbb{R}^n$ is called a convex set if for any two points $p \in S$ and $q \in S$, and for any real number t with $0 \le t \le 1, tp + (1-t)q \in S$.

Consider a convex set S and a continuous function f defined on S, the convex function has obvious geometrical significance, which is illustrated in Figure 3.

In Figure3, we can see that, when $f(x)$ represents a convex function, the circular arc between a two random points $(x_1, f(x_1))$ and $(x_2, f(x_2))$ must be under their chord.

Definition 2

f is called a convex function if for any two points $p \in S$ and $q \in S$, and for any real number t with $0 \le t \le 1$,

$$f(tp + (1-t)q) \le tf(p) + (1-t)f(q)$$

f is said to be strictly convex if

$$f(tp + (1-t)q) < tf(p) + (1-t)f(q).$$

Lemma 1

For a smooth function f defined on a convex set $S \subset \mathbb{R}^n$, f is convex if and only if $f''(x) \ge 0$ for any x in S and f is strictly convex if and only if $f''(x) \ge 0$ for any x in S.

Lemma 2

For a convex function f defined on S, and for m points $p_1, p_2, ..., p_m$,

$$f(\frac{1}{m}(p_1 + p_2 + \cdots p_m)) \le \frac{1}{m}(f(p_1) + f(p_2) + \cdots + f(p_m))$$

If f is a strictly convex function, the equality holds if and only if $p_1 = p_2 = ... = p_m$.

Figure 3. Representation of convex function

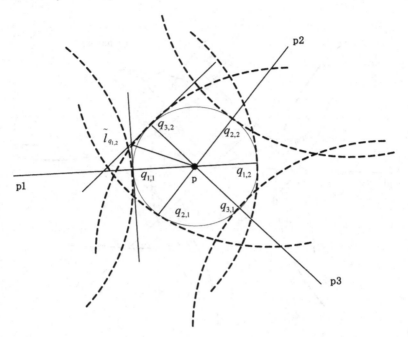

Let $\alpha_{i,j}$ be the angle between $\overrightarrow{pp_i}$ and $\overrightarrow{pp_j}$ in Figure 2. Then we have

Theorem 3

$area(\tilde{C}_{p_i})$ reaches its minimum when $\alpha_{1,2} = \alpha_{2,3} = \alpha_{3,1} = \pi / 3$. In other words, symmetrical reference nodes (in the sense of the angle direction) form an optimal configuration.

Proof

Simple computations will lead to

$$area(\tilde{C}) = 2\varepsilon^2(\tan \frac{\alpha_{1,2}}{2} + \tan \frac{\alpha_{2,3}}{2} + \tan \frac{\alpha_{3,1}}{2}).$$

Note that

$$\alpha_{1,2} + \alpha_{2,3} + \alpha_{3,1} = \pi.$$

Since $(\tan x)'' = 2 \tan x(1 + \tan x) \geq 0$ when $0 \leq x \leq \pi / 2$. We derive Box 6. The equality holds when

$$\alpha_{1,2} = \alpha_{2,3} = \alpha_{3,1} = \pi / 3. \qquad \square$$

Box 6.

$$area(\tilde{C}) = 6\varepsilon^2 \frac{1}{3}(\tan \frac{\alpha_{1,2}}{2} + \tan \frac{\alpha_{2,3}}{2} + \tan \frac{\alpha_{3,1}}{2}) \geq 6\varepsilon^2 \tan \frac{\alpha_{1,2} + \alpha_{2,3} + \alpha_{3,1}}{6} = 6\varepsilon^2 \tan \frac{\pi}{6}$$

Figure 4. Topology copy of reference point coordinate

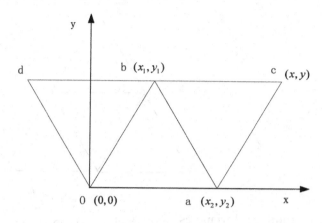

Remark 2

The above analysis indicates that an unknown point p can be determined by three reference points p_i's if these three points are not on a straight line. In real application, we can place the reference point to form a sharp triangle to make sure Δ to be relatively large. Moreover p_1, p_2 and p_3 should not be too close to each other, otherwise Δ will become too small for estimating the unknown point. Intuitively this is easily understandable, since too close three points feel like almost just one point, which will not be able to determine an unknown point. In other words, the optimal configuration is reached when the reference nodes are placed symmetrically.

Theorem 4

In an indoor environment, when the distance between the reference point and the unknown point is beyond the transmission range, additional reference points are required to add near our unknown point. So that, there would form a new equilateral triangle. The locations of the added reference points could be calculated through the original reference node.

Proof

In order to simplify the question, the reference points are put as Figure4 shown. As we can see, the locations of the three vertexes in the equilateral triangle Δabo are known, while the location of point c and d are unknown. So the locations of the circle, point a and point b are $(0,0)$, $(x_2,0)$ and $(\frac{x_2}{2},y_1)$ respectively. According to the relative location of the equilateral triangle, we can get the location of c is $(\frac{3}{2}x_2,y_1)$ and the location of d is $(-\frac{x_2}{2},y_1)$.

Then, when deploying the reference points, once knowing a equilateral triangle's location, we can locate the rest points. These points are located precisely. Then we can locate other points through repeating this process. Theoretically, every equilateral triangle can get its location. However, the indoor environment is a confined space. Therefore, we can deploy the reference points intentionally.

Theorem 5

When an equilateral triangle is used to location unknown point, we can get a minimum location

Figure 5. Expansion of reference node

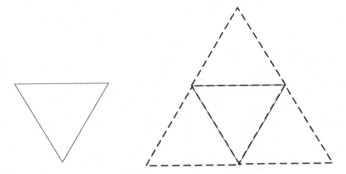

error. While the number of equilateral triangles which participate locating the unknown point is rising, the location error decreases. That means the location error converges.

Proof

When $n = 1$, according to Theorem 1, one equilateral triangle will get a minimum location error. We can use an area C_{p1} to express the possible area of the unknown node; When $n = 2$, we add one more area C_{p2} on the base of the original C_{p1}. For each equilateral triangle, the location error is independent. C_{p2} also represent the possible area of the unknown node. Therefore, if we add one additional equilateral triangle in locating, the possible area of the unknown node would be $\bigcap_{i=1}^{2} C_{pi} = C_{p1} \cap C_{p2}$, that means the possible area of location error is a set that shared by the two given sets. So we have $\bigcap_{i=1}^{2} C_{pi} \subseteq C_{p1}$ or $\bigcap_{i=1}^{2} C_{pi} \subseteq C_{p2}$. Assuming that the location error of the second equilateral triangle $C_{p1} \subseteq C_{p2}$, then $\bigcap_{i=1}^{2} C_{pi} \subseteq C_{p1}$. In that case, the location with two equilateral triangles will get a lower error than the location with only one. When $n > 2$, the location error is the union of sets formed by n equilateral triangles, where

$$\bigcap_{i=1}^{n} C_{pi} = C_{p1} \cap C_{p2} \cap \cdots \cap C_{pi} \cap \cdots \cap C_{pn};$$

therefore the location error of the unknown node is

$$\bigcap_{i=1}^{n} C_{pi} \leq \min\{C_{p1}, C_{p2}, \cdots, C_{pi}, \cdots, C_{pn}\};$$

from which we can see that as the number of equilateral triangles increase, the location error falls to get a more accurate location.

So, we can conclude that the location error decreases when using multi equilateral triangles to locate unknown node. The location error is convergent.

In order to get more precise position information of the mobile nodes in indoor sensor networks, we can place three reference nodes, which form an equilateral triangle. If the coverage area of the sensor network is too large, we also need to place new reference node in adjacent position of the original equilateral triangle to extend the coverage area of the reference nodes, as shown in Figure 5.

As shown in Figure 5, we place a new reference node based on the original equilateral triangle, which form a new equilateral triangle. Based on the geometrical relationship of equilateral triangle, the position information of the new node can be calculated. Since the cost of reference node is expensive, so we should place the reasonable number of reference nodes to decrease the localization error of the unknown node.

Figure 6. Placement of reference node

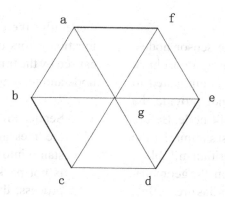

Table 2. TPP algorithm

Step 1	A mobile node broadcasts a location message to its neighboring reference nodes, and then the reference nodes return a confirmed location message containing $\{ID, T_{send}, (a,b)\}$, where ID denotes the ID of reference node, T_{send} denotes the sending time by reference node, and (a,b) denotes the coordinate of reference node.
Step 2	The mobile node receives many location messages of reference nodes, and then it calculates the distances between the mobile node and every reference node.
Step 3	As for each three reference nodes, the mobile node judge if the three reference nodes are on a straight line.
Step 4	Compute the estimated locations of the mobile node using any three reference nodes that are not a straight line.
Step 5	Finally, the mobile node calculates the average location value.

Certainly we want to use as few reference nodes as possible and decrease the localization error to the greatest extent.

In Figure 6, we place 7 reference nodes, which consist of 8 equilateral triangles, including 6 small equilateral triangles, they are

$$\triangle abg, \triangle cbg, \triangle cgd, \triangle dge, \triangle gef, \triangle afg$$

and two big equilateral triangles, they are $\triangle ace, \triangle bfd$. Thus, we can place 8 equilateral triangles using 7 reference nodes. In our scheme, we can fully use the fact that the equilateral triangle is the best location strategy to reduce the localization error of the mobile nodes during the localization process.

Table 3. RNST algorithm

Step 1	A mobile node broadcasts a location message to its neighboring reference nodes, then the reference nodes return a confirmed location message containing $\{ID, T_{send}, (a,b)\}$, where ID denotes the ID of reference node, T_{send} denotes the sending time by reference node, and (a,b) denotes the coordinate of reference node.
Step 2	The mobile node calculates the distances between each pair of nodes and judge if any of the three reference nodes can form "almost" equilateral triangle.
Step 3	Compute the estimated locations of the mobile node using each of the possible equilateral triangles.
Step 4	Finally, the mobile node calculates the average location value.

RNST Algorithm and Localization Error Analysis

Due to resource limitation of the sensor nodes, some of the traditional positioning algorithms, such as TPP algorithm, are too complicated to be implemented and they can not provide the real-time localization of the mobile node. Before introducing our algorithm, we first summarize the procedure of traditional TPP algorithm in Table 2.

As analyzed in previous section, the geometrical relationship of reference nodes has great effect on the localization error of unknown node; however, TPP algorithm does not consider this factor. In this section, we improve the TPP algorithm, and propose RNST positioning algorithm which can provide real-time localization service. In our algorithm, we position the reference nodes to form an equilateral triangle in an indoor environment to minimize the localization error and improve the real-time localization performance. During our localization process, a mobile node can purposefully select suitable reference nodes to estimate its position; the procedure of our proposed algorithm is listed in Table 3.

Remark 3

In real applications, we can not place the reference node in the strictly style of equilateral triangle. There exists some minor error with the theoretical value of the reference node. In Table 3, "almost" equilateral triangle means for other scenarios, it may vary depending on the nature of the application.

In real applications, the localization error always exists, no matter what location scheme or advanced location technique we use. In (Guangjie Han, 2004), the author mentions the reasons of the localization error based on multilateration, which mainly consist of time measurement error and the error caused by geometrical relationship of reference nodes. As we mentioned before, we mainly analyze the latter in this paper.

Time Measurement Error

Generally, there are several impact factors in location errors using mobile equipments which caused by the transmission between the reference node and the unknown node.

- Sender Processing Delay: On transmitting the message, the node inserts the time-stamp into the message. Since the message is not packed yet, we need some relative process, the time of pack message by the sender is denoted as $Time_{SPD}$;
- Sender Delay: If the processor is busy when the data packet is packed and ready to send, the packet will store in a buffer, wait to be transmitted. We denote $Time_{SD}$ as the time of storing data packets in the buffer;
- Sending Time: There is a fixed length message as well as data speed when transmitting a message. This delay could be calculated as $Time_{ST}$;
- Propagation Time: The transmission time between the transmission node and the receiving node, represents as $Time_{PT}$;
- Receiver Processing Time: On receiving the message, the receiving node need some time to process relative operation. The time delay is denote as $Time_{RPT}$.

So that the total transmission delay between the transmission node and the receiving node is

$$Time_{total} = Time_{SPD} + Time_{SD} + Time_{ST} + Time_{PT} + Time_{RPT}$$

$Time_{ST}$ can be calculated through the total number of bytes which were sent from the sender. While $Time_{SPD}$, $Time_{RPT}$ and $Time_{SD}$ are not stationary. Transmission delay is a major delay among these uncertain delays. Besides, there would be also information loss during the transmission. If the sender re-transmits the message, there would be a greater increasing of the round-trip time of the location error.

The location error mentioned above is caused by the time measurement in location process, which can be improved by communication protocol and time synchronization between different nodes. Meanwhile, time synchronization will continue to adjust the different time resolution, which requires time synchronization irregularly. We can use synchronization to decrease the location error caused by the time measurement.

In a WSN Environment, there is time inconsistency between the reference node and the unknown node after a period of time. The location error caused by this time inconsistency could be limited time synchronization between nodes. Therefore, we need time synchronization between the reference node and the unknown node to ensure their consistency. Time synchronization plays an important role in estimate the distance between different nodes. The process of time synchronization is as follows, firstly the reference node broadcast the synchronization information through the broadcast packets. All the other node detect the time delays and set their own time as sum of the time stamp in the broadcast packet and the time delay to each node. In that case, we can keep time synchronization between the receiving nodes and the transmission node.

Generally, the time measurement error caused by time delay can be improved by communication protocol between nodes.

- $Time_{SPD}$ and $Time_{SD}$ will get time stamp when the transmission channel is idle. In that case we can decrease these two delay $Time_{SPD} = 0$ and $Time_{SD} = 0$:
- $Time_{PT}$ The synchronization is transmitted by wireless electric wave in the indoor location process. The transmission speed is 300m/μs. We assume that the distance between nodes in indoor environment is limited, so we can safely ignore the transmission time, $Time_{PT}=0$:

- $Time_{ST}$ could be divided into two parts, the first part is the transmission of synchronic signals, the second part is the transmission of synchronic message. Since each message contains a fixed length as well as data speed, the delay $Time_{ST}$ can be calculated:
- $Time_{RPT}$ can measure delay through the time stamp of the local receiver. If the receiving node records a time stamp when the time synchronization information arrives and records another one when adjusting the time of the receiving node. The delay here is the deviations of the two time stamps.

As $Time_{SPD} = 0$, $Time_{SD} = 0$ and $Time_{PT} = 0$, the signal transmission error between nodes is $Time_{total} = Time_{ST} + Time_{RPT}$. In that case, the transmission protocol between nodes could efficiently decrease the signal transmission error.

As shown in Figure 7, the transmitting node and the receiving node synchronic at the signal initial stage. The transmitting node insert its own time stamp $Time_{sender}$ into the message, then the receiving node records its local time stamp $Time_{rts1}$ on receiving the synchronic signal from the transmitter. It records another time stamp $Time_{rts2}$ after receiving the information. Therefore, we can get $Time_{ST}$ and $Time_{RPT}$.

The time of receiving is

$$Time_{receive} = Time_{sender} + Time_{ST} + (Time_{rts2} - Time_{rts1})$$

where $Time_{rts2}$ and $Time_{rts1}$ are the time stamps recorded by the receiving node.

For each $Time_{ST}$, if we could aware the number of message transmitted meanwhile the signal speed is fixed, the time of receiving can also be expressed as $NUM_{packet} \times Time_{signal}$, where NUM_{packet} represents the number of messages, $Time_{signal}$ represents the time of sending single message. Then

Figure 7. Propagation error between synchronization signals of two nodes

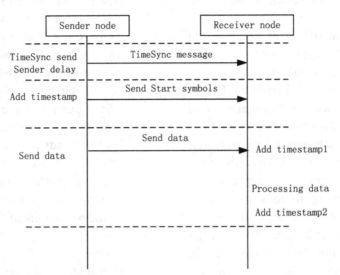

$$Time_{receive} = Time_{sender} + NUM_{packet} \times Time_{signal} + (Time_{rts2} - Time_{rts1})$$

The receiving node continues to adjust its own clock in the synchronic process in order to achieve the time synchronization between nodes. In that case, the transmission time between nodes would be more precise on condition that the nodes are time synchronization. At the same time, we can avoid the location error of the unknown node caused by the time difference between nodes.

Geometrical Error

As mentioned above, in the process of locating unknown node, the location error minimizes when the three reference node form an equilateral triangle. If the shape of the triangle formed by the reference nodes is random, we need to discuss the difference between the error area caused by random reference nodes and error caused by the best reference nodes. A quantitative analysis is shown to analyze how to minimize the location error by consciously deploying the reference nodes.

Lemma 6.

$$\int_0^{\frac{\pi}{2}} \ln(\sin x)dx = \int_0^{\frac{\pi}{2}} \ln(\cos x)dx = -\frac{\pi \ln 2}{2}$$

Proof

Consider the following variable change

$$x = \frac{\pi}{2} - t$$

Apply the variable change, we obtain

$$\int_0^{\frac{\pi}{2}} \ln(\sin x)dx = -\int_{\frac{\pi}{2}}^0 \ln(\cos t)dt = \int_0^{\frac{\pi}{2}} \ln(\cos x)dx,$$

Which establish the identity

$$\int_0^{\frac{\pi}{2}} \ln(\sin x)dx = \int_0^{\frac{\pi}{2}} \ln(\cos x)dx.$$

Since

$$\sin x = 2 \sin \frac{x}{2} \cos \frac{x}{2},$$

We have Box 7. Now we apply the change of variable

$$x = 2t$$

to the second term in the above equality, we obtain

$$\int_0^{\frac{\pi}{2}} \ln \sin \frac{x}{2} dx = 2 \int_0^{\frac{\pi}{4}} \ln \sin t\, dt = 2 \int_0^{\frac{\pi}{4}} \ln \sin x\, dx. \tag{5}$$

Then we apply the change of variable

$$x = \pi - 2t$$

to the second term in the above equality, we obtain

$$\int_0^{\frac{\pi}{2}} \ln \cos \frac{x}{2} dx = -2 \int_0^{\frac{\pi}{2}} \ln \sin t\, dt = 2 \int_{\frac{\pi}{4}}^{\frac{\pi}{2}} \ln \sin x\, dx. \tag{6}$$

Combining Equation 4, 5, 6, we have,

In other words, we obtain the claim in the lemma

$$\int_0^{\frac{\pi}{2}} \ln(\sin x)\, dx = -\frac{\pi \ln 2}{2}$$

An interesting problem is how much the equilateral triangle placement of the reference nodes can improve the precision than the random placement or Square-grid placement of the reference nodes. In the following, we show that the localization precision can be remarkably improved if the best placement is employed.

As shown above, the error region size $\tilde{C}$ is equal to

$$area(\tilde{C}) = 2\varepsilon^2 (\tan \frac{\alpha_{1,2}}{2} + \tan \frac{\alpha_{2,3}}{2} + \tan \frac{\alpha_{3,1}}{2}) \tag{7}$$

The minimum area $area(\tilde{C}) = 2\sqrt{3}\varepsilon^2$ can be attained when $\alpha_{1,2} = \alpha_{2,3} = \alpha_{3,1} = \pi/3$. We now calculate the $E(area(\tilde{C}))$ (the expectation of $area(\tilde{C})$) when the reference nodes are randomly selected, using the fact that $\alpha_{1,2} + \alpha_{2,3} + \alpha_{3,1} = \pi$.

Now,

$$E(area(\tilde{C})) = 2\varepsilon^2 E(\tan \frac{\vec{x}}{2} + \tan \frac{\vec{y}}{2} + \cot(\frac{\vec{x}}{2} + \frac{\vec{y}}{2}))$$

where $(\vec{x}, \vec{y})$ is a random vector with uniform distribution on the following region:

$$D = \{(x,y) \mid x \geq 0, y \geq 0, x + y \leq \pi\}.$$

Therefore, the probability density function of $(\vec{x}, \vec{y})$ is $p(\vec{x}, \vec{y}) = 2/\pi^2$. Then (see Box 8).

Box 7.

$$\int_0^{\frac{\pi}{2}} \ln(\sin x)dx = \int_0^{\frac{\pi}{2}} \ln\left(2\sin \frac{x}{2} \cos \frac{x}{2}\right)dx = \int_0^{\frac{\pi}{2}} \ln 2 dx + \int_0^{\frac{\pi}{2}} \ln\left(\sin \frac{x}{2}\right)dx + \int_0^{\frac{\pi}{2}} \ln \cos \frac{x}{2} dx. \tag{4}$$

Applying necessary change of variables, we calculate the error region size

$$E(area(\tilde{C})) = (\frac{24}{\pi} \ln 2)\varepsilon^2 .$$

Thus, the equilateral placement of the reference nodes can greatly improve the estimation than randomly placement of the reference nodes by

$$\beta = \left\{(\frac{24}{\pi} \ln 2)\varepsilon^2 - 2\sqrt{3}\varepsilon^2\right\} / (\frac{24}{\pi} \ln 2)\varepsilon^2 = 34.9\%$$

As for the Square-grid placement, if we choose three reference nodes, then we have

$$area(\tilde{C}) = 2\varepsilon^2(\tan\frac{45}{2} + \tan\frac{45}{2} + \tan\frac{90}{2}) = 3.657\varepsilon^2$$

Therefore, the estimation is improved by 5.3%. Based on the above analysis, the localization error of our proposed scheme is the least when the equilateral triangle placement is employed. The unknown node can purposefully select the suitable reference nodes to reduce the localization error during the localization process in WSNs.

PERFORMANCE ANALYSIS AND COMPARISON

We have implemented our proposed RNST algorithm and TPP algorithm both in the network Simulator OPNET version 10 and on the Zigbee sensor platform, respectively.

Design of Experiments

To testify our proposed RNST algorithm, we design the experiment consisting of several phases. First, we test the real-time localization using the Zigbee sensor platform. The goal of this test is used to prove if our RNST algorithm can effectively meet the real-time localization requirement of the mobile nodes with limited resources in an indoor environment. Second, we track a mobile node using our proposed RNST algorithm and the TPP algorithm in a room. Finally, we compare and analyze the data obtained from our experiments.

In our experiments, 21 reference nodes are uniformly distributed based on equilateral triangle in a region of $21m \times 15m$, the distance between adjacent nodes is $4.6m$ and 1 mobile node is also randomly located in the same area, as shown in Figure 8. Generally, the reference nodes of the traditional algorithm are placed according to square-grid or random placement, however in order to compare the performance of our algorithm with that of the traditional algorithm, the same simulation environment is adopted in our experiments.

Localization Error Analysis

In the traditional positioning algorithms, such as TPP algorithm, an unknown node first randomly selects several reference nodes to compute its initial position, then iteratively improves the localization precision using the position information of more reference nodes. In our test, we run the simulation 100 times and averaged data over these 100 runs. In the following, we compare the localization error of the unknown node with

Box 8.

$$E(area(\tilde{C})) = \frac{4\varepsilon^2}{\pi^2} \iint_D \tan\frac{x}{2} + \tan\frac{y}{2} + \cot(\frac{x}{2} + \frac{y}{2})dxdy = \frac{4\varepsilon^2}{\pi^2}(-2\int_0^\pi \ln\cos\frac{x}{2}dx - 4\int_0^\pi \ln\sin\frac{x}{2}dx)$$

Figure 8. Simulation environment

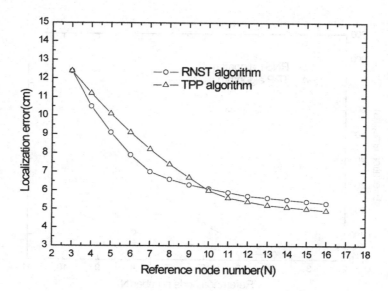

Figure 9. Comparison of localization error

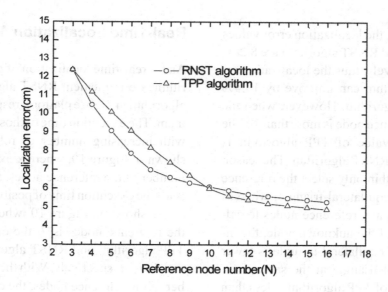

increasing the number of the reference nodes using RNST algorithm and TPP algorithm, respectively, as shown in Figure 9, where x-axis represents the number of the reference nodes, and y-axis represents the localization error of the mobile node.

As shown in Figure 9, with increasing number of the reference nodes, the localization error value of the unknown node decreases drastically in the beginning, however the curve becomes almost flat afterwards. When the number of the

Figure 10. Comparison of location time

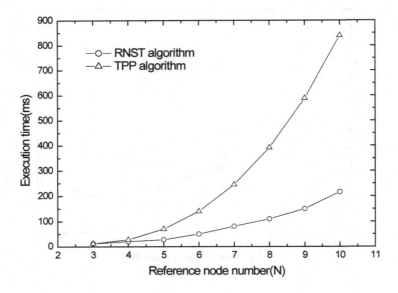

reference nodes is 7, the localization error values of TPP algorithm and RNST algorithm are 8.2*cm* and 7.1*cm,* respectively, thus the localization error of RNST algorithm can improve by 13.4% than that of TPP algorithm. However, when the number of the reference node is more than 10, the localization error value of TPP algorithm is smaller than that of RNST algorithm. The reason is that RNST algorithm only select the reference nodes which form equilateral triangle, whereas TPP algorithm uses any reference nodes to calculate the position of the unknown node, the increasing number of equilateral triangle is fewer than non-equilateral triangle at the same time, thus the error value of TPP algorithm is less than that of RNST algorithm when the number of the nodes involved in the position estimation of the unknown node gets more than certain threshold. Apparently compared to TPP algorithm, our proposed RNST algorithm can greatly decrease the localization error in a shorter period of time.

Real-Time Localization Analysis

As for real-time localization of positioning algorithm, we implement RNST algorithm and TPP algorithm in Zigbee platform respectively and test them. The execution time of those two algorithms with increasing number of reference nodes is shown in Figure 10, where x-axis represents the number of the reference nodes, and y-axis represents the execution time of positioning algorithm.

As shown in Figure 10, when the number of the reference nodes is 7, the execution time of TPP algorithm and RNST algorithm are 245*ms* and 75*ms*, respectively. With the increasing number of the reference nodes, the execution time of TPP algorithm is exponentially increasing, whereas the execution time of RNST algorithm is only slowly increasing. On the other hand, in order to get precise position information, TPP algorithm needs heavy computation and communication. TPP algorithm needs to consume much more energy than RNST algorithm. At the same time, the computational complexity of TPP algorithm is much bigger than the one of RNST algorithm with the increasing number of the reference nodes. Thus, our proposed RNST algorithm can efficiently meet the real-time localization requirement of the mobile node in an indoor environment.

It is important to guarantee smaller localization error and meet the real-time localization requirement of the mobile node at the same time during the localization process. The balance point of two effect factors is that the number of reference node is 7 based on the analysis of experimental data, as shown in Figure 8.

When the mobile node covers 7 reference nodes (polygon $bcefhi$ in Figure 11), the transmission radius of the mobile node is equal to l, here l is the length of the side of equilateral triangle. When the mobile node covers 6 reference nodes (equilateral triangle $\triangle ach$), the transmission radius of the mobile node is equal to $2\sqrt{3}l / 3$; when the mobile node covers less than 5 reference nodes, the transmission radius of the mobile node is less than l, so the minimum transmission radius of the reference node is equal to $2\sqrt{3}l / 3$. We can also calculate that the maximum transmission radius of the reference node is equal to

$3\sqrt{3}l / 4$, thus the transmission range of the reference node is $2\sqrt{3}l / 3 \leq R_{scope} \leq 3\sqrt{3}l / 4$, where R_{scope} denotes the transmission range of the reference node. Therefore, in the real application of an indoor environment, we can adjust the coverage area of the mobile node is not more than 7 reference nodes and also guarantee the localization error of the mobile node is the least and meet the high real-time localization requirement of the mobile node.

The total location time of a mobile node T_{all} can be represented using

$$T_{all} = T_{execution} + T_{delay} + T_{propagation}$$

where $T_{execution}$ denotes the execution time of the positioning algorithm, T_{delay} denotes the delay time of signal transmission, $T_{propagation}$ denotes the time difference of transmission between the reference node and the mobile node. Typically, the walking speed of an adult is 0.7m/s in an indoor environment. The side length of equilateral triangle is 4.6m in the simulation environment, then the optimal transmission range of the mobile node

Figure 11. Transmission scope of reference point signal

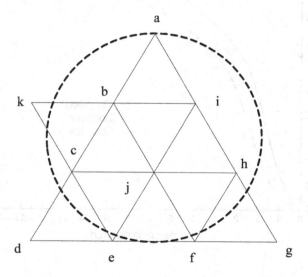

is $2\sqrt{3}l / 3 \leq R_{scope} \leq 3\sqrt{3}l / 4$, so we can calculate that the time range of signal transmission is $11.9ms \leq T_{propagation} \leq 17.1ms$. When the number of reference node chosen by the mobile node is 7, the execution time of our proposed algorithm $T_{execution}$ is $75ms$; however the execution time of the TPP algorithm is $245ms$ in the same condition and can not guarantee the real-time localization. If our algorithm can meet the real-time localization of the mobile node and the effective positioning time T_{all} is less than $100ms$, thus the range of signal transmission delay is $7.9ms \leq T_{delay} \leq 13.1ms$, which shows that our algorithm can effectively guarantee the real-time localization.

In the analysis above, we only consider the execution time of our proposed algorithm. In the real application, we also need to consider some other factors, such as the time difference of signal transmission. When the number of reference node chosen by the mobile node is 7, the update rate of positioning algorithm is about 9~10 times/second, thus our proposed algorithm can effectively meet the positioning requirement for an indoor environment.

Positioning Algorithm Evaluation

We place the reference nodes according to Figure 8 and simulate RNST algorithm under the following three different conditions: (1) No interference signal, only location signal; (2) Location signal and little noise signal; (3) Location signal, little noise signal and interference signal. We randomly choose 200 nodes to run simulation 500 times and average data over these 100 runs. In order to evaluate the algorithm performance, we compare the estimated values obtained from our simulation experiment with the actual values, the localization error distribution condition of RNST algorithm as shown in Figure 12, where x-axis represents the localization error value, and y-axis represents the percentage of reading with error less than x-axis.

Figure 12. Localization precision of RNST algorithm

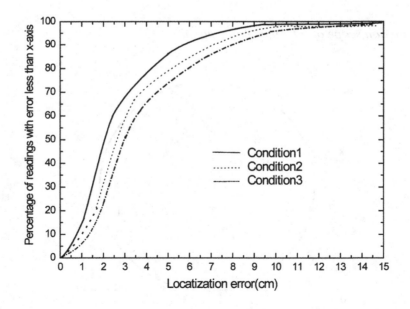

As shown in Figure 12, the localization error of RNST algorithm is less than 7.1cm in the 95% confidence level, which is high localization precision, and the localization precision of RNST algorithm in different condition is shown in Table 4.

As shown in Table 4, the localization error of RNST algorithm reaches 7.1cm in the 95% confidence level of condition one. The bigger interference is, the small localization error is. The simulation results are better suitable for the real conditions of an indoor environment. We also simulate to track the path of the mobile node in a room. The mobile node is tracked in the environment of Figure 8 using RNST algorithm and TPP algorithm respectively, the tracking path comparison of both algorithms is shown in Figure

13, where x-axis represents the length of the room, and y-axis represents the width of the room.

As shown in Figure 13, based on the estimated and actual tracking path, the path of our proposed RNST algorithm is a little closer to the actual tracking path than that of TPP algorithm. However, when the mobile node is located in the border of the room, since only a few reference nodes are involved in the computation of the position of the mobile node, thus the localization error of the mobile mode is bigger. The comparison of the mobile node's RMSE is shown in Figure 14, where x-axis represents the number of the test point, and y-axis represents the value of RMSE. Based on the comparison of RMSE changing trend, we draw the conclusion that it also coincides with in Figure 13.

Table 4. Performance of RNST algorithm

Test condition	Readings return (%)	95% confidence level (cm)
1	93	7.1
2	75	8.2
3	62	10.6

Figure 13. Comparison of mobile node tracking path

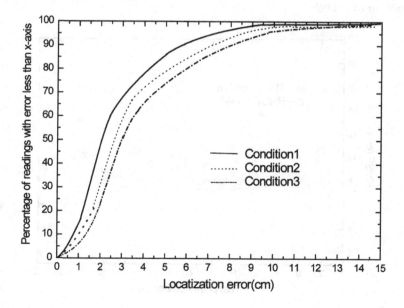

As expected from above-mentioned analysis, we conclude that RNST algorithm can meet the real-time localization requirement of the mobile node with limited resources in an indoor environment, and make the localization error of RNST algorithm less than that of the traditional TPP algorithms.

FUTURE RESEARCH DIRECTIONS

In recent years, the localization problem of WSNs has raised many innovative solutions and ideas. However, the research in the field is still in a start-up phase. The chapter raises interesting questions for future research directions: we plan to extend our RNST algorithm to outdoor environment. We also plan to conduct further research on the deployment problem of the reference nodes based on other positioning techniques. We also combine the advantages of RNST and TPP algorithm to enhance the localization error in the next research phase. We believe that in addition to the existing research subjects of the localization algorithms, the possible hot research is listed as follows: (1) Evaluation the performance model of localization algorithms,

and improve the reference node selection and filtering mechanisms to reduce the positioning time of the unknown nodes. (2) Deploy the randomly nodes on the surface of the actual land-based, research the positioning performance of actual land. (3) Research a novel localization algorithm which suitable to the resource-constrained sensor nodes, and reduce the localization error which caused by random distribution of the nodes. (4) Research a self-adjustment localization algorithm in the mobile network environment, simulation the localization algorithm performance in the low mobility of the sensor node. (5) Research the optimal path planning which the mobile anchor node can traverse the entire network. (6) Research the security localization of the WSNs, and so on.

CONCLUSION

In this chapter, we analyze the localization error of a mobile node and draw the conclusion that the localization error is the least when three reference nodes form an equilateral triangle. The equilateral triangle placement of the reference nodes can greatly improve the position estimation than the

Figure 14. Comparison of RMSE

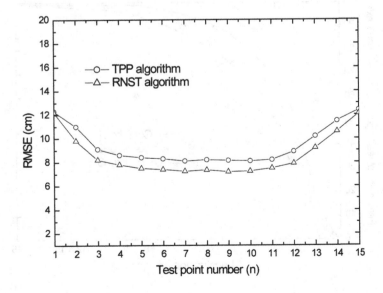

random placement or the Square-grid placement of the reference nodes. We improve the TPP algorithm and propose a novel RNST algorithm for the mobile node in indoor sensor networks. The simulation results show that our proposed RNST algorithm can greatly improve the localization precision of the mobile node, meanwhile satisfying the time constraints and guaranteeing the minimum localization error in a short period.

REFERENCES

Avvides, A., Park, H., & Srivastava, M. B. (2002). The bits and flops of the N-hop multilateration primitive for node localization problems. *In: Proc. of the 1st ACM Int'l Workshop on Wireless Sensor Networks and Applications*, (pp. 112-121). Atlanta, GA: ACM Press.

Beutel, J. (1999). *Geolocation in a Pico radio environment*. Berkeley, CA: UC Berkeley.

Bulusu, N., Heidemann, J., & Estrin, D. (2001, April). Adaptive beacon placement. In *Proc. of the 21st International Conference on Distributed Computing Systems (ICDCS-21)*, Phoenix, Arizona, USA, (pp. 489–498).

Bulusu, N., Heidemann, J., Estrin, D., & Tran, T. (2003). Self-configuring localization systems: Design and experimental evaluation. *ACM Transactions on Embedded Computing Systems (TECS). Special Issue on Networked Embedded Systems*, *3*(2), 24–60.

Capkun, S., Hamdi, M., & Hubaux, J. P. (2002). GPS-free positioning in mobile ad-hoc networks. *Cluster Computing*, *5*(2), 157–167. doi:10.1023/A:1013933626682

Clouqueur, T., Phipatanasuphorn, V., Ramanathan, P., & Saluja, K. K. (2002, September). Sensor deployment strategy for target detection. In *Proc. of the First ACM International Workshop on Wireless Sensor Networks and Applications*, (pp. 42-48).

Doherty, L. (2000). *Algorithms for position and data recovery in wireless sensor networks*. Berkeley, CA: University of California Press.

Han, G. (2004). *Research on reference point selection of locating service in ubiquitous computing*. Shenyang: Northeastern University.

Isler, V. (2006). Placement and distributed deployment of sensor teams for triangulation based localization. In *Proc. of IEEE International Conference on Robotics and Automation*, (pp. 3095–3100).

Langendoen, K., & Reijers, N. (2003). Distributed localization in wireless sensor networks: A quantitative comparison. *Journal of Computer Networks*, *43*, 499–518. doi:10.1016/S1389-1286(03)00356-6

Meguerdichian, S., Slijepcevic, S., Karayan, V., & Potkonjak, M. (2001). Localized algorithms in wireless ad-hoc networks: Location discovery and sensor exposure. In *Proc. of the 2nd ACM Int'l Symp. On Mobile Ad Hoc Networking & Computing*, (pp. 106-116). Long Beach, CA: ACM Press.

Niculescu, D., & Nath, B. (2003, March). Ad hoc positioning system (APS) using AOA. In *Proc. of IEEE International Conference on Computer Communication (INFOCOM)*, (pp. 1734-1743).

Priyantha, N. B., Chakraborty, A., & Balakrishnan, H. (2000). The Cricket location-support system. In *Proc. of the 6th Annual Int'l Conf. on Mobile Computing and Networking*, (pp. 32-43). Boston, MA: ACM Press.

Ren, F., Huang, H., & Lin, C. (2003). Wireless sensor networks. *China Journal of Software*, *14*(7), 1282–1291.

Savarese, C., Rabay, J., & Langendoen, K. (2002). Robust positioning algorithms for distributed ad-hoc wireless sensor networks. In C. S. Ellis (Ed.), *Proc. of the General Track of the Annual Conference on USENIX*, (pp. 317-327). Monterey, CA: USENIX Press.

Savvides, A., Han, C.-C., & Srivastava, M. B. (2001). Dynamic fine-grained localization in ad-hoc networks of sensors. In: *Proceedings of the 7th Annual on Mobile Computing and Networking*, (pp. 166-179). ACM Press.

Shang, Y., Ruml, W., Zhang, Y., & Fromherz, M. P. J. (2003). Localization from mere connectivity. In *Proc. of the 4th ACM Int'l Symp. On Mobile Ad Hoc Networking & Computing*, (pp. 201-212). Annapolis, MD: ACM Press.

Wang, F., Shi, L., & Ren, F. (2005). Self-localization systems and algorithms for wireless sensor networks. *China Journal of Software*, *16*(5), 857–868. doi:10.1360/jos160857

Wong, T.-L., Tsuchiya, T., & Kikuno, T. (2004, March). A self-organizing technique for sensor placement in wireless micro-sensor networks. In *Proc. of the 18th International Conference on Advanced Information Networking and Application (AINA'04)*, Fukuoka, Japan, vol.1, (pp. 78-83).

Yick, J., Bharathidasan, A., Pasternack, G., Mukherjee, B., & Ghosal, D. (2004). Optimizing placement of beacons and data loggers in a sensor network – A case study. In *Proceedings of the IEEE Wireless Communication and Networking Conference (WCNC)*, (pp. 2486-2491).

Zou, Y., & Charkrabarty, K. (2003). Sensor deployment and target localization based on virtual forces. In *Proc. of the IEEE Infocom Conference*, (pp. 1293-1303).

ADDITIONAL READING

Alan Mainwaring, J. Polluters & R Szewczyk. (2002). Wireless Networks for Habitat Monitoring, In: *Proc. of the 1st ACM Intermionasl Workshop on Wireless Sensor Networks and Applications*, 88-97.

Baggio, A., & Langendoen, K. (2008). Monte Carlo Localization for Mobile Wireless Sensor Networks. *Ad Hoc Networks*, ▪▪▪, 718–733. doi:10.1016/j.adhoc.2007.06.004

ChaiHo Ou & KuoFeng Ssu. (2008). Sensor Position Determination with Flying Anchors in Three-Dimensional Wireless Sensor Networks. *IEEE Transactions on Mobile Computing*, ▪▪▪, 2008.

Chen, H. (2008, October). A Novel Centroid Localization Algorithm for Three-Dimensional Wireless Sensor Networks. *In: Proc. of International Conference IEEE WiCOM '08*, 1-4.

Chen, W., Li, W., & Heng, S. (2006). Weighted Centroid Localization Algorithm Based on RSSI for Wireless Sensor Networks. *Journal of Wu Han University of Technology*, *30*(2), 265–268.

Dai, G., Zhao, C., & Qiu, Y. (2008). A Localization Scheme Based on Sphere for Wireless Sensor Network in 3D. *Acta Electronics Sinica*, *36*(7), 1297–1303.

Dan, W. (2006). *Localization of Wireless Sensor Network*, Southwest Jiaotong University, Master Thesis.

de Oliveira, H. A. B. F., Nakamura, E. F., & Loureiro, A. A. F. (2005, October). Directed Position Estimation: A Recursive Localization Approach for Wireless Sensor Networks, *In: Proc. of the 14th International Conference on Communications and Networks*, 557-562.

Girod, L., Bychovskiy, V., Elson, J., & Estrin, D. (2002). Locating Tiny Sensors in Time and Space: A Case Study, *In: Wemer B, ed. Proc. of the 2002 IEEE Int'l Conf. on Computer Design: VLSI in Computers and Processors*. Freiburg: IEEE Computer Society, 214-219.

Girod, L., & Estrin, D. (2001). Robust Range Estimation using Acoustic and Multimodal Sensing, *In: Proc. of the IEEE/RSJ Int'l Conf. on Intelligent Robots and Systems (IROS 01)*. Maui: IEEE Robotics and Automation Society, 3, 1312-1320.

Han, G. (2009). *Deokjai Choi & Tam Van Nguyen* (pp. 1017–1027). Reference Node Selection Algorithm and Localization Error Analysis for Indoor Sensor Networks, Wireless Communications and Mobile Computing.

Hao, Yu. (2006). *Target Localization and Track Based on the Energy Source*, Master's Thesis, Fudan University.

Harter, A., Hopper, A., Steggles, P., & Ward, P. (1999). The Anatomy of a Context-aware Application, *In: Proc. Of the 5th Annual ACM/IEEE Int'l Conf. on Mobile Computing and Networking*, Seattle: ACM Press, 59-68.

He, T. Chengdu Huang & Blum B M. (2003). Range Free Localization Schemes for Large Scale Sensor Networks, *In: Proc. of the International Conference on MobiCom*. San Diego: ACM Press, 81-95.

He, T., Huang, C. D., & Blum, B. M. (2003, September). Range-Free Localization Schemes in Large Scale Sensor Networks, *In: Proc. of the 9th Annual International Conference on Mobile Computing and Networking (MobiCom2003)*, 81-95.

Hu, Z., Gu, D., & Song, Z. (2008, July). Localization in Wireless Sensor Networks Using a Mobile Anchor Node, *In: Proc. of the 2008 IEEE/ASME International Conference on Advanced Intelligent Mechatronics*, 602-607.

Koutsonilas, D., Das, S. M., & Charlie, H. U. Y. (2007). Path Planning of Mobile Landmarks for Localization in Wireless Sensor Networks. *Computer Communications, 30*(13), 577–2592.

Kuang XingHong, Shao HuiHe & Feng Rui. (2008). A New Distributed Localization Scheme for Wireless Sensor Networks. *Acta Electronics Sinica, 34*(2), 344–348.

Lai, X., Wang, J., & Zeng, G. (2008). Distributed Positioning Algorithm Based on Centroid of Three-dimension Graph for Wireless Sensor Networks. *Chinese Journal of System Simulation Technology, 20*(15), 35–42.

Lazos, L., & Poovendran, R. (2006). HiRLoc: High-Resolution Robust Localization for Wireless Sensor Networks. *IEEE Journal on Selected Areas in Communications, 24*(2), 233–246. doi:10.1109/JSAC.2005.861381

Li, C. (2006). *Wireless Sensor Network Self-Positioning Technology*, Southwest Jiao Tong University, Master Thesis. Fubao Wang, Long Shi & Fengyuan Ren, Self-localization Systems and Algorithms for Wireless Sensor Networks, *Journal of Software, 16*(5), 858-859.

Li, H., Bu, Y., & Han, X. (2009). Path Planning for Mobile Anchor Node in Localization for Wireless Sensor Networks. *Journal of Computer Research and Development, 46*(1), 129–136.

Li, J., Wang, K., & Li, L. (2009). Weighted Centroid Localization Algorithm Based on Intersection of Anchor Circle for Wireless Sensor Network. *Journal of Jilin University Engineering and Technology Edition, 39*(6), 1235–1241.

Li, X., Xu, Y., & Ren, F. (2007). *Wireless Sensor Network Technology*. Beijing Institute of Technology Press.

Li, Zhaobin, & Wei, Zhanzhen & FengLin Xu. (2009). Enhanced Centroid Localization Algorithm and Performance Analysis of Wireless Sensor Networks. *Sensors and Actuators, 22*(4), 563–566.

Lin, J., Liu, H., & Li, G. (2009). Study for Improved DV-Hop Localization Algorithm in WSN. *Application Research of Computers, 26*(4), 512–516.

Lingxuan Hu & Evans D. (2004). *Localization for Mobile Sensor Networks Mobile*. USA: Computing and Networking.

Liu, K., Wang, S., & Zhang, F. (2005, September). Efficient Localized Localization Algorithm for Wireless Sensor Networks. *In: Proc. of the 5th International Conference on Computer and Information Technology*, 21-23.

Liu, M., Wang, T., & Zhou, Z. (2009). Self-localization Algorithm for Sensor Networks of Sparse Anchors. *Computer Engineering, 35*(22), 119–121.

Tiantian Liu, Hongda Chen & Guo Li. (2009). Biomimetic Robot Fish Self-positioning Based on Angle and Acceleration Sensor Technology. *Robot Technology and Application*, 435-440.

Liu, Y. (2006). *Distributed Mobile Localization Algorithms of WSN*, Master's thesis, Hunan Technology University.

Lu ke, Zhang jun & Wang gang. (2007). Localization for Mobile Node Based on Sequential Monte Carlo. *Journal of Beijing University of Aeronautilcs and Astronautics, 33*(8), 886-889.

Luo, R. C. Ogst Chen & Pan S H. (2005). Mobile User Localization in Wireless Network Using Grey Prediction Method. *In: Proc. the 32nd Annual Conference of IEEE Industrial Electronics Society (IECON 2005)*, Raleigh, USA:IEEE Press, 2680-2685.

Lv, L., Cao, Y., Gao, X., & Luo, H. (2006). Three Dimensional Localization Schemes Based on Sphere Intersections in Wireless Sensor Network. *Beijing Posts and Telecommunications University, 29*, 48–51.

Neuwinger, B., Witkowski, U., & Ruckert, U. (2009). Ad-Hoc Communication and Localization System for Mobile Robots, *FIRA. LNCS, 5744*, 220–229.

Ogawa, T., Yoshino, S., Shimizu, M., & Suda, H. A New Indoor Location Detection Method Adopting Learning Algorithms, *In: Proc. of the First IEEE International Conference on Pervasive Computing and Communications*, Texas,USA:IEEE Press, 525-530.

Qin, W., Feng, Y., & Zhang, X.-T. (2009). Localization Algorithm for Wireless Sensor Network Based on Characteristics of Energy Attenuation. *Journal of Chinese Computer Systems, 30*(6), 342–347.

Qiu, Y., Zhao, C., & Dai, G. (2008). Wireless Sensor Network Node Position Technology. *Chinese Journal of Computer Science, 35*(5), 672–676.

Rui, L. (2008). *Underwater GPS Location Technology*, Xi'an Electronic Science and Technology University, Master's Thesis.

Rui Huang & Zaruha Gergety V. (2007). Static Path Planning for Mobile Beacons to Localize Sensor Networks, *In: Proc. of IEEE PerCom*, Piscataway, 323-330.

ShiJian Li, CongFu Xu & Yang Yang. (2008, February). Getting Mobile Beacon Path for Sensor Localization. *Journal of Software, 19*(2), 455–467.

Jian Shu, Linlan Liu & Yubin Chen. (2009). A Novel Three-dimensional Localization Algorithm in Wireless Sensor Networks, *Wireless Communications and Mobile Computing*, 24-29.

Sun, L., Li, J., & Yu, C. (2005). *Wireless Sensor Network*. Beijing: Tsinghua University Press.

Sun, P., Zhao, H., & Han, G. (2007). Chaos Triangle Compliant Localization Reference Node Selection Algorithm. *Journal of Computer Research and Development, 44*(12), 1987–1995. doi:10.1360/crad20071201

Uchiyama, A. (2007). Ad-hoc Localization in Urban District. In *Proc. of IEEE INFOCOM, 2306-2310*. Sae Fuji & Kumiko Maeda.

Wang, G., Tian, W., & Jia, W. (2007). Location Update Based on Local Routing Protocol for Wireless Sensor Networks. *Chinese Journal of High-tech Communications, 17*(6), 563–568.

Wang, J., Huang, L., & Xu, H. (2008). A Novel Range Free Localization Scheme Based on Voonoi Diagrams in Wireless Sensor Networks. *Journal of Computer Research and Development, 45*(1), 119–125.

Wang, S., Hu, F., & Qu, X. (2007). *Wireless Sensor Networks Theory and Applications.* Beijing University of Aeronautics and Astronautics Press.

Wang, Y., Huang, L., & Xiao, M. (2009). Localization Algorithm for Wireless Sensor Network Based on RSSI-verify. *Journal of Chinese Computer Systems, 30*(1), 456–462.

Yu, G., Yu, F., & Feng, L. (2008). A Three Dimensional Localization Algorithm Using a Mobile Anchor Node under Wireless Channel, Neural Networks, *In: Proc. of the International Joint Conference on Neural Networks,* 477-483.

Yu, H., Chen, X., & Fan, J. (2007). Gauss-Newton Method Based on Energy Target Localization. *Computer Engineering and Applications, 43*(27), 124–126.

Zhang, L. Q., Zhou, X. B., & Cheng, Q. (2006). Landscape-3D: A Robust Localization Scheme for Sensor Networks over Complex 3D Terrains, *In: Proc. of the 31st IEEE Conference Local Computer Networks (LCN),* IEEE Computer Society Press, Tampa, FL, 239-246.

Zhao, H., Feng, Y., Luo, J., & Yang, K. (2007). Mobile Node Localization Algorithm of Wireless Sensor Network. *Hunan Science and Technology University, 34*(8), 74–77.

Zheng, Shijue, & Kai, Li & ZhenHua Zheng. (2008). Three Dimensional Localization Algorithm Based on Nectar Source Localization Model in Wireless Sensor Network. *Application Research of Computers, 25*(8), 114–118.

Zhongxiang, M., & Baoye, S. (2009). HWC Localization Algorithm of Wireless Sensor Network. *Computer Engineering, 35*(7), 104–109.

KEY TERMS AND DEFINITIONS

Indoor Sensor Networks: A sensor network consists of multiple detection stations called sensor nodes, each of which is small, lightweight and portable in an indoor environment. A sensor network is a group of specialized devices with a communications infrastructure intended to monitor and record conditions at diverse locations.

Localization: A technique for determining the location of a node in Sensor Networks

Localization Error: The distance difference between real position and estimated position is produced when a node tries to estimate another node in the localization process.

Mobile Node: A mobile node is any mobile device that can be used to make a remote or portable connection to other nodes. The location of this kind of node may frequently be changed, although a mobile node can also be a router in Sensor Networks.

Reference Node: A reference node with a GPS model can provide its location information to other unknown node during the localization process.

RNST Algorithm: Reference Node Selection algorithm based on Trilateration (RNST), which can provide real-time localization service for the mobile nodes in an indoor environment. RNST estimates the mobile node using trilateration method in the localization process.

TPP Algorithm: The location information of the unknown node is initially estimated using the traditional algorithms, and is improved by iterative computation in the next phase.

Chapter 12
A WSN–Based Building Management Framework to Support Energy–Saving Applications in Buildings

Antonio Guerrieri
University of Calabria, Italy

Giancarlo Fortino
University of Calabria, Italy

Antonio Ruzzelli
University College Dublin, Ireland

Gregory O'Hare
University College Dublin, Ireland

ABSTRACT

Using wireless sensor networks (WSNs) for auditing and managing the energy consumption in a building is an emerging research area that includes a number of novel applications such as activity pattern recognition, adaptive load shifting, and building energy profiling in domestic and industrial settings. This chapter defines the specific requirements for applications of energy management in the building context and proposes a novel framework for building management (BMF) to support heterogeneous platforms. To allow flexible node activity grouping, BMF defines roles and operations derived from the mathematical set theory, while it optimizes transmissions through a mechanism of adaptive packet size. BMF has been implemented and tested in TinyOS. Results show an increase in reliability with respect to existing transmission schemes that can be traded off to reduce energy consumption.

DOI: 10.4018/978-1-61350-110-8.ch012

Copyright © 2012, IGI Global. Copying or distributing in print or electronic forms without written permission of IGI Global is prohibited.

INTRODUCTION

The worldwide call for energy reduction, demonstrated by various international policies, is accelerating the introduction of energy saving techniques. It is recognized that buildings consumption accounts for more than 40% of worldwide energy use and has faster grown rate than transportation and industry energy consumption. Reducing energy consumption of buildings requires generating energy awareness among residents and controlling devices within the building. Strong evidences suggest that occupants can actively adapt their behaviour to energy saving with suitable feedback, support, and incentives, reducing significantly and cost-effectively energy use without impacting adversely their comfort (Stern, 1999).

To achieve this goal, the use of wireless sensor networks to audit buildings and control equipment represents a viable and more flexible solution to traditional building monitoring and actuating systems (BMAS), which require retrofitting the whole building and therefore are difficult to implement in existing structures. In contrast, solutions based on WSN (Akyildiz et al., 2002; Akyildiz & Vuran, 2010) for monitoring buildings and controlling equipment, such as electrical devices, heating, ventilation and cooling (HVAC), can be installed in existing structures with minimal effort. This should enable monitoring of space usage and energy (electricity, gas, water) while facilitating the design of techniques for intelligent device actuation. In order to achieve this, WSN-based building auditing necessitates devising a dedicated management framework for (1) the management of a range of cooperating networked entities, (2) the profiling of the energy spent and (3) the development of applications for controlling the energy consumption in buildings.

This paper proposes a Building Management Framework (BMF), which is a domain-specific framework for energy saving techniques in buildings. The contribution of the framework is twofold:

from one side the BMF assists the application developer with an extensible Application Programming Interface (API) to allow profiling the energy of the building and subsequently control the existing HVAC and electrical equipment. From the other side, the BMF is a network practitioner in the sense that facilitates the deployment of heterogeneous nodes, management and maintenance of the network operation. This is achieved by providing a set of embedded functionalities and a corresponding middleware at the base station (BS) side. Moreover, we demonstrate some advantages resulting from a reduction of the bytes sent over the air, during configuration phase achieved through an optimization of the configuration packets. BMF is currently implemented in TinyOS (Levis, 2006) and supports the interoperation of TelosB (Polastre, Szewczyk, & Culler, 2005), Tyndall (Barton et al., 2006), Epic (Jiang et al., 2009), and KMote (Madabhushi, 2007) platforms with heterogeneous sensing capabilities.

The chapter is organized as follows: we first introduce the main requirements for a building energy auditing system for office buildings highlighting the unsuitability of some existing frameworks when used in the context of building monitoring. Then we introduce BMF and describe its main components and processing levels. Following, the chapter provides some initial performance analysis before some future works and the conclusions.

BUILDING MANAGEMENT: REQUIREMENTS AND OBJECTIVES

Many new structures incorporate energy management systems such as intelligent lighting, HVAC control systems that allow profiling the energy spent in the building. However, a much larger portion of existing buildings do not have any energy monitoring retrofitted. WSNs represent an appropriate solution to allow energy monitoring in such buildings. For example this would allow quantifying and understanding how the energy is spent throughout the building to better direct investment for energy-efficient solutions. The first step in order to reduce the energy consumption in a building is to measure how and where the energy is spent. As each building is unique, we need to define how data gathering on energy consumption can be obtained. This should clearly reflect how energy is spent in relation to how an infrastructure is being used:

- **Electricity**: Monitoring electricity consumption is achieved through electrical socket sensors such as ACme (Jiang et al., 2009), Tyndall (Barton et al., 2006) or Episensor (Episensor, 2009), which can be provided with a 1-phase or 3-phase current transformer (CT) clamp for the electricity monitoring of the whole building or a portion of it. Moreover, such platforms can be provided with an actuation layer to activate/deactivate electrical equipment remotely.
- **Lighting**: Light sensing is a common capability provided by WSN platforms. For an accurate monitoring of light utilization the wireless sensors should be placed: (1) in the proximity of luminaries to identify artificial lighting activity, (2) nearby windows to identify natural lighting, (3) on working desk to monitor the luminosity perception of occupants during their work activity. Considering that the ideal luminosity condition in an office should be from 500 to 1000 Lux, sensing desk luminosity allows estimating whether a certain light should be on or off.
- **HVAC**: Temperature sensors placed on the input and output pipes of the heater can provide accurate measurements of each heater activity. Moreover, ambient temperature sensors are distributed in several parts of the structure to monitor the ambient temperature of the working environment. Finally, vibration sensors on top of air conditioning systems are also used to monitor the activity of HVAC.
- **Occupants**: Wireless sensor network producers such as Tyndall and Episensor, provide reed switch for detecting the opening and closing of doors and windows. In addition, passive infrared (PIR) module can be used to sense people presence in certain parts of the building. Moreover, camera sensors, such as cyclop camera mounted on TelosB (Erickson et al., 2009) can even be used to sense the number of people in a room.

For example Figure 1 shows the principal monitoring activity that can be achieved through sensor networks to allow deriving comprehensive energy utilization in an office space. The reported set of nodes (ACme, Tyndall, Episensor, TelosB) can cover a wide range of energy monitoring applications.

RELATED WORK

In this section several works related to Building Management end Energy Management in buildings will be overviewed and compared.

In iSense (Padmanabh et al., 2009) authors developed a system to monitor and schedule conference room management. There are two aspects of the legacy conference room management solution. Firstly, the conference rooms are not utilized properly. Secondly the electricity is consumed even when it is not required. Doing some experiments they found that the current utilization of the conference room is close to 67%. This is because in case of cancellation of the meeting, the same is not updated in the calendar system. People also don't update the calendar if the meeting is over before the schedule time. The wireless sensor network based system which they have developed can sense the various ambience parameters in each conference room and transmit

Figure 1. Example of energy monitoring in an office space

the same to an application server to detect physically whether meeting is going on or not. It also sends alert to switch off the light and the heating/cooling system. So they get two advantages. There will be more meeting hours effectively which increases the utilization of conference room. However main aspect is that they reduced the electricity consumption. What iSense presents is an application that is completely achievable using the BMF with a difference in the flexibility that the BMF gives allowing to reconfigure at runtime the nodes in the conference rooms since every room needs different configurations to make the system working properly.

In LightWise (Delaney et al., 2009) a WSN aims to evaluate lighting control systems in existing office buildings. Office occupancy detection, ambient light and the state of lighting system are identified in order to understand the waste of energy of the lighting system. In this case waste of energy is intended as the energy used to power on the luminaires if the ambient light from the windows was enough or if the office is unoccupied. In LightWise all nodes were programmed to periodically send every few seconds the data of ambient lighting, luminaire state and presence detection. Indeed, the application required only a subset of those parameters by each node. With no BMF in place the developer was incapable to address the nodes according to their functions and request parameters at runtime. Only stopping the application and reprogramming the nodes accordingly could in fact, achieve this. This resulted in long development period and a large amount of useless data transmitted and extra energy spent. In general, the heterogeneous type of nodes needed to monitor a building requires dedicated development and management tool to facilitate the deployment and re-configuration of nodes at runtime. BMF addresses this issue via organizing nodes in groups, which share logical properties such as location, sensing devices and reporting targets. With BMF the developer could declare three groups for ambient light nodes, state of light detection nodes, occupancy detection nodes. The group can then be associated to their location, e.g. a room or an open space office. This allows configuring each group to send only the data needed or average against the other nodes sharing the same functionality or being dynamically reconfigured at any time. In general, using BMF, developers can achieve a significant reduction of transmitted bytes and an increase of packet reliability.

Similar grouping provided by BMF was proposed in Abstract Region (AR) (Welsh & Mainland, 2004), which defines "Neighbourhood relationship" between nodes in the network. A major difference is that AR targets data sharing among a neighbourhood while managing a sensor network in a building requires grouping nodes that may be located in areas far apart from each others. Furthermore, the frequent downstream communication (from BS to nodes), which is common for BMAS due to device actuation and control makes AR unsuitable for BMAS. A framework for BMAS requires flexible node addressing in several part of the building that goes beyond neighbourhood data sharing. The downstream communication is key as devices may be activated/deactivated dynamically. Therefore addressing nodes by dynamic groups is crucial to reduce the network load and improve the efficiency in BMAS.

An interesting approach to general purpose query processing is proposed by TinyDB (Madden et al., 2005). However TinyDB shows major issues in dynamic group management and it is developed specifically for Mica platform. TinyDB provides a simple, SQL-like interface to specify the data to extract from the network, along with additional parameters, like the rate at which data should be refreshed. Given a query specifying data interests, TinyDB collects that data from motes in the environment and routes it out to a PC. TinyDB uses long configuration packets, because the nodes receive every time the whole queries. Vice versa, BMF supports optimized length configuration packets to query the nodes and is designed to be platform independent and already supports many TinyOS platforms and sensors. Platform independence is a further important aspect in building monitoring, mainly due to the multitude standard communication protocol used for building monitoring, such as WirelessHART, Modbus and KNX, which requires seamless plug-in interoperability between platform and sensor vendors. These motivates the

design of a domain-specific building management framework, namely BMF, which will be discussed in details in the next sections.

In the Table 1 a comparison among TinyDB, AR and BMF is shown. In particular, while TinyDB is defined like a query processor for Sensor Networks, AR is a Programming Framework and BMF is an Application Framework. Both TinyDB and BMF are self-contained: they don't need the programming of embedded code for the sensor nodes whereas in AR the programmer has to write code to be deployed on the nodes using a particular language. Since every application is deployed every time in AR, it doesn't support request mechanism and it doesn't provide a user interface to remotely configure network parameters. Vice versa, both TinyDB and BMF allow sending requests to the nodes through a Java API. However, they provide two dissimilar request mechanisms: TinyDB supports SQL-like queries while the BMF uses a particular type of Request 4-Tuple, as detailed in this paper. This allows in-network processing and is based on multi-hop protocols for data dissemination and collection.

Another important distinction is that BMF fully supports the dynamic group management, which allows to dynamically address physical and logical groups, whereas TinyDB can merely set some parameters like one Group at deploying time, while AR can only manage a node neighbourhood defined on the basis of radio hops and distance.

BUILDING MANAGEMENT FRAMEWORK

Building Management Framework (BMF) is a domain-specific framework for flexible distributed sensing and actuation in buildings. BMF addresses specific building requirements that are not addressed in general-purpose frameworks for WSNs. In particular, the main features of BMF are:

Table 1. Comparison among TinyDB, Abstract Regions and BMF

	TinyDB	Abstract Regions	BMF
Description	Query Processor for Sensor Networks	Programming Framework	Application Framework
Requires the user to write embedded C code for sensors	NO	YES, simplified.	NO
Request mechanism	SQL-like queries	NO	Request 4-Tuple
User Interface	Java API	NO	Java API
In-network processing algorithms	In-network processing optimized to merge data from different nodes when possible	Services for in-network processing	In-network processing only on node
Multi Hop Communication	YES, done in TinyDB	YES	YES, using Collection and Dissemination TinyOS protocols
Supported Platforms	Mica motes with TinyOS 1.1	Mica motes	TelosB, Tyndall25, Epic motes with TinyOS 2.1
Managing by dynamic groups (smart address)	NO (if a group is known a priori, it can be set at deploying time)	NO. Groups are defined like Regions of nodes in a Neighbourhood (radio hops and distance)	YES
Network Synchronization	YES, to allow the nodes to wake up all together	NO	NO

- *An ad-hoc communication protocol based on variable length packets*, which allows saving bandwidth and reducing communication latency;
- *Run-time node reconfiguration*, which enables to switch over different applications at run-time through transmission of configuration packets;
- *Flexible group organization*, which supports setting and change of group affiliations for the nodes at run-time;
- *Adaptive node addressing*, which aims to optimize the downstream communication so allowing to send packets to a node, a group or a set of groups;
- *Dynamic device actuation*, which allows activating or modifying the state of actuators, plugged into the nodes, through over-the-air messages;
- *In-node store and pre-elaboration of sensed data*, which enables nodes to transmit data features, instead of raw data, to the BS so saving bandwidth and allowing

many nodes to share the same radio channel (Gravina et al., 2008);
- *Heterogeneous sensor platform support*, which allows compilation and deployment of BMF on different platforms transparently.

The BMF has been tested on several platforms including TelosB, Tyndall25, Epic, and KMote. The following subsections presents organization and programming of the building sensor network and then delves into the software architecture of BMF.

Sensor Network Organization and Programming

The BMF dynamically organizes the nodes of the building sensor network in groups. A group is defined as a not-empty collection of nodes:

$$G_i = \{node_1^i, node_2^i, ..., node_n^i\} \neq \varnothing. \qquad (1)$$

In particular, a group formalizes either logical or physical properties of nodes. Examples of properties are: location (e.g. dining room), monitoring activity (e.g. heater monitoring), the presence of a specific sensing device onboard (e.g. passive infrared detector). Indeed, a node can belong to more than one group. Every node knows its group membership through the reception of configuration packets sent by the BS. A group membership can therefore be dynamically changed at any moment.

Operating on groups yields high flexibility when addressing nodes, while a dynamic node addressing scheme allows sending packets to a specific node or a group. Clearly, transmitting to several nodes simultaneously saves bandwidth. Node addressing is formalized with the following regular expression:

$$N \mid ([NOT] \ G \ [TSO \ [NOT] \ G]*). \qquad (2)$$

Where N is an element of the set of the nodes in the building sensor network, G is an element from the set of the groups, TSO is a theory set operator (e.g. union, intersection, difference) and NOT is the negation. BMF relies on the Dissemination protocol (Levis et al., 2004) for downstream communication. Through this, nodes can receive packets sent from the BS and, by simply analyzing the packet destination field representing target nodes or groups, the node decides if the packet is to be handled (the node belongs to the destination field) or discarded (the node does not belong to the destination field).

The upstream communication relies on the Collection Tree Protocol (Levis et al., 2004) that allows delivering packets sent from nodes to the BS, which is set as root of the tree.

Figure 2 shows an example of an office space in which nodes are deployed highlighting models of grouping and relations that is possible to realize in BMF. In particular, the Group "Lamps" includes sensors placed close to lamps to monitor lamps activity. The "Occupancy" Group includes all the nodes that have an infrared sensor detecting movements in a room. The "Open Space" Group is composed of all the nodes in the Open Space room. Once the groups are defined, nodes can be manipulated through set theory operations. In the figure are shown examples of union and intersections: the intersection between the Groups "Open Space" and "Lamps" addresses all the lamps which are placed in the Open Space; the intersection between "Open Space" and "Occupancy" is for all the nodes which have an infrared sensor and are placed in the Open Space; the last example points to both nodes close to the lamps and nodes with an infrared sensor that are in the Open Space.

Sensing and actuation activity of the building sensor network can be programmed through queries (also called requests) sent from the BS to the nodes. A request R is formalized as the following quadruple:

$$R = \ < OBJECT, \ ACTION, \ RATE, \ LIFETIME >, \qquad (3)$$

Where OBJECT is a specific sensor or actuator belonging to a node, ACTION is the action to be executed on OBJECT, RATE is the frequency action execution, LIFETIME is the duration of the reiterated actions. In particular: (i) if OBJECT is a sensor, ACTION can be a request for either raw sensed data or threshold notification (e.g. if the sensed data overtakes a given threshold, a notification is sent); (ii) if the OBJECT is an actuator, ACTION represents the actuation of a specific parameter of the actuator (e.g. in case of a led, ACTION can activate the led toggling).

Instances of requests derived relative to Figure 2 for the "Lamps Group" is as follows:

$$R_1 = \ < LIGHT, \ AVARAGE \ ON \ SENSED \ DATA, \ 1 \ MIN, \ 1 \ DAY >. \qquad (4)$$

This requests to all the nodes near the lamps to transmit every minute the average value read by the light sensor in a whole day. The request (4)

Figure 2. Example of grouping and relations in BMF

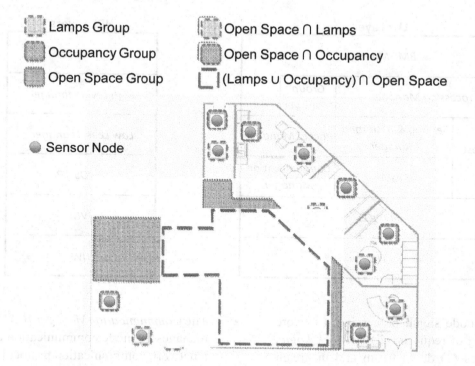

can be used to understand when a lamp is on or off. An alternative method is to use the threshold mechanism in BMF which results in reducing the number of packets sent from the nodes to the BS:

$$R_2 = <\text{LIGHT, TRANSITION THRESHOLD}\ (x)\ \text{ON SENSED DATA, 1 MIN, 1 DAY}>. \quad (5)$$

In (5) the nodes nearby the lamps are requested to check every minute for one day if the reading from the light sensor has exceeded the threshold x. This ACTION may be used to reduce the number of packets sent over the network.

Software Architecture

BMF is basically organized into two levels of processing logics: Low-Level Processing (LLP) and High-Level Processing (HLP). While the LLP resides on the sensor nodes, HLP resides at the

BS side, which is usually a laptop, workstation or PDA.

The implementation of BMF has been carried out on TinyOS (Levis, 2006) through the nesC language (Gay et al., 2003) due to their availability for many sensor platforms and flexibility to meet specific application needs. The BS side of the framework is implemented in Java. LLP and HLP are described in the following subsections. Figure 3 shows a layered view of the LLP and HPL logics which highlights the main components of the BMF that will be detailed in the following subsections.

Low-Level Processing (LLP)

LLP is the node-level part of BMF and is implemented in TinyOS 2.1. LLP (see Figure 4) supports two types of logics: (i) *Node Logic*, which provides (1) acquisition of data from sensors, (2) execution of actions on actuators plugged into

Figure 3. Layered view of the BMF

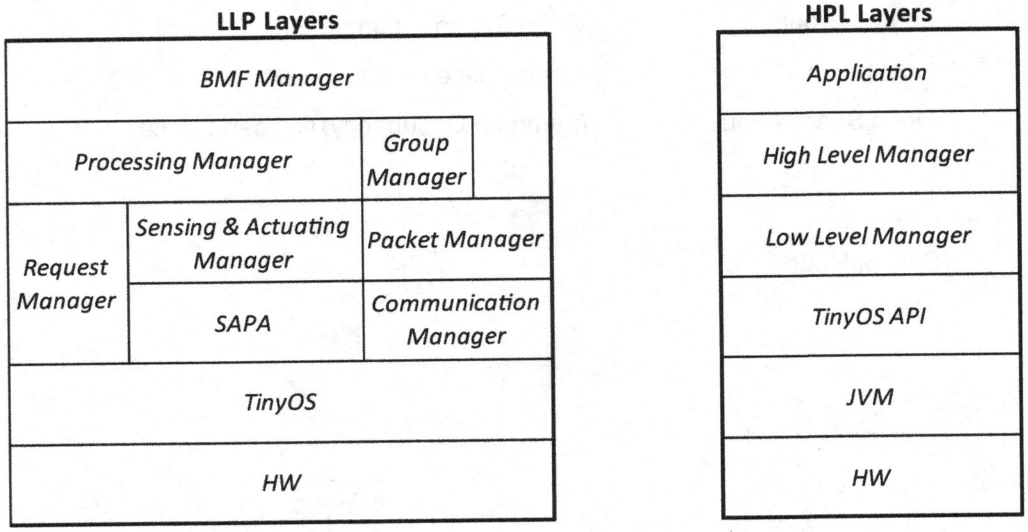

LLP Layers

BMF Manager		
Processing Manager		Group Manager
Request Manager	Sensing & Actuating Manager	Packet Manager
	SAPA	Communication Manager
TinyOS		
HW		

HPL Layers

Application
High Level Manager
Low Level Manager
TinyOS API
JVM
HW

nodes, (3) in-node signal processing; (4) store and scheduling of requests; (ii) *Network Logic*, which provides (1) downstream and upstream routing, (2) packet parsing, (3) construction and transmission; (4) dynamic node addressing; (5) group management.

The modular structure of LLP allows separation of concerns for all the key functions so that, in case of changes to a single component, this can be replaced with no modifications to other components. The structure consists of the following main modules:

- The *PacketManager (PaM)*, which handles packets of the application level protocol of BMF. It parses received packets (sent by the BS) and builds packets to be transmitted (to the BS);
- The *GroupManager (GM)*, which manages the group membership of a node. A node can belong to several groups at the same time and its membership can be dynamically updated on the basis of packets sent by the BS;

- The *CommunicationManager (CM)*, which manages the node communication through a network communication protocol.
- The *BMFManager (BMFM)*, which is the central component of the framework. BMFM receives events every time a packet arrives from the network and every time some data to be sent is ready. In the first case, it interprets the packet by means of PaM and dispatches the packet to the handling component; in the latter case, it builds the packet through PaM and dispatches it to CM to send it to the BS;
- The *RequestManager (RM)*, which stores the BS requests and schedules them according to execution rate and lifetime;
- The *Sensing&ActuatingManager (SAM)*, which is a dispatcher that forwards sensor reading and actuation requests to the right sensor/actuator driver. To allow extensibility, sensors and actuators communicate with a generic platform version of the drivers.
- The *Sensor, Actuator & Platform Abstraction (SAPA)*, which is a layer that allows addressing different types of sen-

Figure 4. LLP component diagram

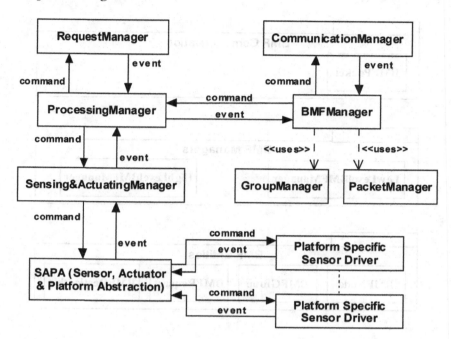

sors/actuators in a platform independent way. SAPA guarantees interoperability between TinyOS-based platforms and sensing/actuation devices by creating a common API used to abstract from different low-level hardware sensor and actuator drivers. By using SAPA to address a sensor, SAM only needs to request for a generic sensor, which is automatically linked to the platform specific one at compilation time.

- The *ProcessingManager (PM)*, which manages all the requests for sensing and/or actuation coming from the network or from internal components. In particular, PM handles an internal queue of one-shot requests. In accordance with the request type, PM (i) interacts with RM to schedule the periodical request; (ii) interacts with SAM to read a sensor or actuate a command; (iii) computes some functions on the acquired data; (iv) checks sampled values to set a timer. Furthermore, an event

allows PM to forward data destined to the BS via the BMFM.

Note that only RM, SAPA and CM are based on TinyOS components while SAM, PaM, PM, GM and BMFM are built on top of the other components. This allows higher and lower layers to be independent of the TinyOS components and therefore can be easily ported to non-TinyOS platforms.

High-Level Processing (HPL)

The High-Level Processing (HLP) logic of BMF is implemented at the base station side and consists of a Java API which allows configuring group memberships and issuing requests to the nodes and waiting for data/info packets from the building sensor network. The API is organized according to three main packages shown in Figure 5 and explained below.

The *BMF Entities* package contains the classes formalizing the concepts of node, group,

Figure 5. HLP package diagram

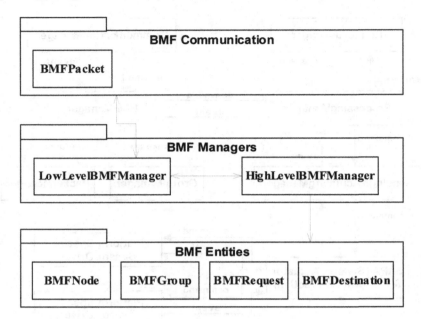

request and destination. In particular, the *BMF-Node* class contains information about the nodes in the network; the *BMFGroup* class stores the nodes belonging to groups; the *BMFRequest* class formalizes the quadruple in Eq.(3). Each BMFRequest object has a destination field representing the destination of a request.

The *BMF Communication* package allows sending and receiving packets (*BMFPacket*) to/from the building sensor network according to the application-level Building Management Framework Communication Protocol (BMFCP). BMFCP therefore supports the communication between HLP and LLP to configure and monitor the building sensor network in an effective manner. In particular, the BMFRequests to be sent to the building sensor network are codified as BMFPackets. The BMFPackets can be formed, depending on the specific request or the specific data from the nodes, by different fields having a different amount of bytes. The BMFCP is developed to send over-the-air variable length packets containing only the meaningful bits of the significant fields. Thus, the BMFCP optimizes

transmissions saving battery on the single nodes and network bandwidth so allowing more nodes to share the same radio channel.

The *BMF Manager* package provides classes that facilitate the construction of BMF-based applications. In particular, an application can be built atop either a *LowLevelBMFManager* or a *HighLevelBMFManager*. In the former, packets to be sent can be managed in a special-purpose way. In the latter, applications transparently reuse the default LowLevelBMFManager and rely on the HighLevelBMFManager, which provides a few methods to configure and monitor the building sensor networks.

PERFORMANCE EVALUATION

In order to show energy-efficiency and reliability of BMF, the performance evaluation is achieved by comparing the ad-hoc communication scheme of BMF (hereafter referred as Variable Length – VL scheme) with the conventional TinyOS communication, which is based on fixed-length

Figure 6. Nodes disposition in the Clarity Lab

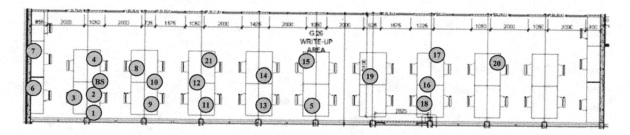

packets (hereafter referred as Fixed Length – FL scheme). This is achieved by measuring packet loss and energy in transmission for several experiments in a building sensor network formed of 22 TelosB nodes. Figure 6 shows the placement of nodes for the experiment. The experiments were executed in the Clarity-Centre Lab at University College Dublin. In order to experiment a real multi-hop network, nodes were deployed in the main open space office of about 30m in length and about 6.5m in width. In the figure, nodes are tagged with their ID or with "BS" for the Base Station. To note that the laboratory includes several research groups and testing were done in the presence of other sensor networks operating on different radio channels with respect to the one of the experiment.

Sensor node activity has been set-up as follows: (i) packets are sent from each node at a mean rate of 1 per second; (ii) the radio duty-cycle is set to less than 1% to guarantee network longevity of several months; (iii) for the FL scheme packets are all 20 bytes long whereas for the VL scheme, packets are between 12 and 20 bytes.

In Figure 7a the packet loss per node computed for the VL and FL schemes is reported. Note that the VL mechanism mitigates significantly packet loss caused by the low duty-cycle. This allows an average increase of 10% in transmission reliability with respect to the FL without affecting the energy consumption (see below). An important result is that, by leveraging on the VL mechanism, the framework can achieve lower duty-cycle therefore

saving energy against classic FL transmissions. In Figure 7b the average transmission energy per second per each node is shown. This evaluation is carried out by using an Energy component (Ruzzelli et al., 2009) able to calculate, by monitoring the right pins of the microcontroller, how long the radio is sending and listening to the radio channel. As can be noted, average energy consumption is basically invariant with respect to the VL and FL schemes apart from cases (see node 19) in which nodes are heavily used as routers.

Moreover, to evaluate the energy expenditure of the system, we monitored the battery levels of the sensor nodes of the system under two specific operating modes: (1) light, temperature and humidity are acquired every second and sent to the BS after acquisition; (2) light and temperature are acquired every second, aggregated through the average feature, and transmitted to the BS every minute. Thus, while in the first operating mode raw data acquired from all sensors included in the sensor nodes are sent, in the second operating mode only two sensors are selected and data coming from sensors are aggregated before their transmission to the BS. In both the operating modes, the monitored voltage is sent every minute and the duty cycle of the radio of the sensor nodes is set to 0.5%. Tests were carried out by using TelosB sensor nodes with 2 Ni-MH batteries of 1.2V and 2500mAh each and for a period of 12 hours for each test.

The obtained results are reported in Figure 8. In particular, as can be noted better performances

Figure 7. (a) Packet loss evaluation; (b) energy evaluation

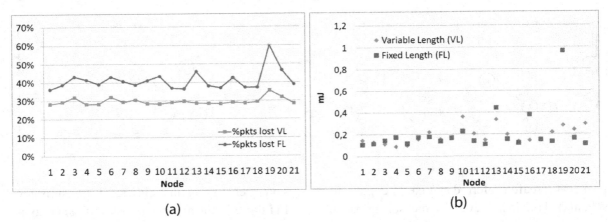

(a)   (b)

Figure 8. Comparison of the mean battery voltage by using the BMF and sending raw data

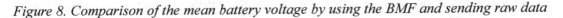

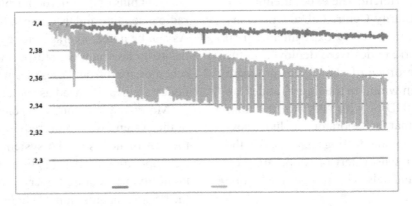

are obtained by using BMF. It is worth noting that the trend of the mean voltage in the first operating mode (raw data) is highly irregular due to the frequent raw data transmission that can affect the acquisition of the voltage value; in fact, such phenomenon is very limitedly appreciated in case of the second operating mode as data transmission to the BS is less frequent.

Finally, considering the battery voltage trends on a 12 hours monitoring period and a linear battery consumption until the voltage value of 2.1V (which is the minimum operating voltage for cc2420 radio) a mean battery duration can be computed for the two described cases: (1) less than 100 hours; (2) around 400 hours.

FUTURE WORKS

Our vision is that future buildings will be monitored and automated through WSNs managed by flexible and efficient frameworks like the BMF. This vision is supported by experimental results we are obtaining by exploiting BMF for building monitoring.

The following future works can be envisaged:

- *Software enhancement of the BS*. The BS side of the BMF can be re-designed following the OSGi paradigm in order to provide more modularity than the actual API and support enhanced services for configuration and data post-elaboration.

- *Multi-Base Station networks.* The BMF is not suitable for big buildings, where WSN can be composed by many nodes and packets can be sent to a base station from nodes many hops far away, so creating a network overloading with the loss of too many packets and with very high battery consumption to route/replicate packets in the network. In this case, a Multi-Base Station system can significantly reduce the energy spent in the network extending (consequently) its life. The BSs in the system have to cooperate to monitor the whole building.

- *Use of energy harvesting and self powered nodes.* Even if the BMF is optimized to make the life of the batteries in the nodes of a network very long, sometimes it is very difficult to change batteries, especially if nodes are in places difficult to reach. This is the reason because the BMF will support nodes capable to harvest energy by themselves, like was done in (Gupta et al., 2010), and nodes integrated in powered objects like lamps or appliances to form smart objects.

- *Network security.* Security of data is very important for privacy reasons. The BMF will use stable and well tested security algorithms by using the AES (Advanced Encryption Standard) 128 algorithm included in the cc2420 radio chip and integrating the ZigBee stack in the future release.

- *Energy saving applications.* The development of advanced energy recommendation systems atop BMF to give feedback to users about energy consumption.

CONCLUSION

This paper has presented the Building Management Framework (BMF), a flexible framework for the support of Building Management and Actuation Systems based upon WSNs. BMF is motivated by the specific characteristics of applications for intelligent buildings, which require a fully versatile framework for addressing, reprogramming and supporting platforms and application plug-in at runtime. BMF supports heterogeneous platforms, flexible node activity grouping, dynamic setting of roles and operations with ability to optimize transmissions through adaptive packet sizing. In contrast to generic management framework for sensor networks, BMF is a domain-specific framework tailored for sensor network applications in buildings. This is achieved through an embedded set of modules implemented in TinyOS and a flexible Java API to interface with the network and collect data. The paper detailed an initial performance evaluation of BMF that demonstrated reliability and energy improvement against the TinyOS dissemination routing mechanism. The paper highlighted how the framework can be effectively used in the context of modeling energy in an office space scenario.

REFERENCES

Akyildiz, I. F., Su, W., Sankarasubramaniam, Y., & Cayirci, E. (2002). Wireless sensor networks: A survey. *Computer Networks: The International Journal of Computer and Telecommunications Networking, 38*(4), 393–422.

Akyildiz, I. F., & Vuran, M. C. (2010). *Wireless sensor networks*. John Wiley & Sons, Inc.

Barton, J., Hynes, G., O'Flynn, B., Aherne, K., Normana, A., & Morrissey, A. (2006). 25mm sensor–actuator layer: A miniature, highly adaptable interface layer. *Journal: Sensors and Actuators A, 132*, 362–369. doi:10.1016/j.sna.2006.04.004

Delaney, D., O'Hare, G., & Ruzzelli, A. G. (2009). Evaluation of energy-efficiency in lighting systems using sensor networks. In *the Proceeding of 1st ACM Workshop On Embedded Sensing Systems For Energy-Efficiency In Buildings (BuildSys 2009)*, Berkeley, CA, USA.

Episensor. (2009). *Website*. Retrieved from http://www.episensor.com

Erickson, V. L., Lin, Y., Kamthe, A., Brahme, R., Surana, A., & Cerpa, A. E. … Narayanan, S. (2009). Energy efficient building environment control strategies using real-time occupancy measurements. In *the Proceeding of 1st ACM Workshop On Embedded Sensing Systems For Energy-Efficiency In Buildings (BuildSys 2009)*, Berkeley, CA, USA.

Gay, D., Levis, P., von Behren, R., Welsh, M., Brewer, E., & Culler, D. (2003). The nesC language: A holistic approach to networked embedded systems. In *the Proceeding of the ACM SIGPLAN conference on Programming language design and implementation (PLDI'03)*, San Diego, California, USA.

Gravina, R., Guerrieri, A., Fortino, F., Bellifemine, F., Giannantonio, R., & Sgroi, M. (2008). Development of body sensor network applications using SPINE. In *Proceeding of the 2008 IEEE International Conference on Systems, Man, and Cybernetics (SMC 2008)*, Singapore.

Gupta, V., Kandhalu, A., & Rajkumar, R. (2010). Energy harvesting from electromagnetic energy radiating from AC power lines. In *Proceeding of the 6th ACM Workshop on Hot Topics in Embedded Networked Sensors (HotEMNETS 2010)*, Killarney, Ireland.

Jiang, X., Dawson-Haggerty, S., Dutta, P., & Culler, D. (2009). Design and implementation of a high-fidelity AC metering network. In *Proceeding of the 8th ACM/IEEE International Conference on Information Processing in Sensor Networks (IPSN09) Track on Sensor Platforms, Tools, and Design Methods (SPOTS 09)*, San Francisco, CA, USA.

Levis, P. (2006). *TinyOS programming*. Retrieved from http:// csl.stanford.edu/ ~pal/ pubs/ tinyos-programming.pdf

Levis, P., Patel, N., Culler, D., & Shenker, S. (2004). Trickle: A self-regulating algorithm for code maintenance and propagation in wireless sensor networks. In *the Proceeding of the First USENIX/ACM Symposium on Networked Systems Design and Implementation (NSDI '04)*, San Francisco, CA, USA.

Madabhushi, N. (2007). *KMote - Design and implementation of a low cost, low power hardware platform for wireless sensor networks*. Retrieved from http:// www.cse.iitk.ac.in/ ~moona/ students/ Y5111028.pdf

Madden, S. R., Franklin, M. J., Hellerstein, J. M., & Hong, W. (2005). TinyDB: An acquisitional query processing system for sensor networks. *ACM Transactions on Database Systems*, *30*(1), 122–173. doi:10.1145/1061318.1061322

Padmanabh, K., Mallikarjuna, A., Vanteddu, R., Siva, S. S., Kumar, K. A., & Chevuru, S. … Paul, S. (2009). iSense: A wireless sensor networks based conference room management system. In *the Proceeding of 1st ACM Workshop On Embedded Sensing Systems For Energy-Efficiency In Buildings (BuildSys 2009)*, Berkeley, CA, USA.

Polastre, J., Szewczyk, R., & Culler, D. (2005). Telos: Enabling ultra-low power wireless research. In *the Proceeding of the 4th International Symposium on Information processing in sensor networks*, Los Angeles, CA, USA.

Ruzzelli, A. G., Dragone, M., Jurdak, R., Muldoon, C., Barbirato, A., & O'Hare, G. M. P. (2009). In *Proceeding of European Workshop on Sensor Networks (EWSN)*, Cork, Ireland.

Stern, P. C. (1999). Information, incentives and pro-environmental consumer behavior. *Journal of Consumer Policy*, *22*, 461–478. doi:10.1023/A:1006211709570

Welsh, M., & Mainland, G. (2004). Programming sensor networks using abstract regions. In *the Proceeding of the 1st USENIX/ACM Symposium on Networked Systems Design and Implementation (NSDI'04)*, San Francisco, CA, USA.

KEY TERMS AND DEFINITIONS

Building Energy Management: Management of the energy of a building with the aim to optimize the energy expenditure.

Building Management Framework: A framework allowing to manage a Wireless Building Sensor Network which provides specific functions and facilities to monitor and/or controlling sensors and actuators.

Data Dissemination/Collection Protocols: Network protocols used in many types of network to disseminate/collect data. Usually the dissemination starts from a Base Station and reachs any node in the network through multi-hop paths. On the contrary, the collection drives data from nodes to a Base Station.

Group-based Request: A request addressed to a specific group which includes nodes with the same logical or physical scope.

In-Node Signal Processing: Data processing executed on a node in a Wireless Sensor Network to (pre)elaborate data acquired from sensors.

Wireless Building Sensor Networks: Wireless Sensor Networks optimized for building monitoring and maintenance. In particular, these networks are specialized for the monitoring and controlling of specific parameters for buildings.

Wireless Sensor Networks: Wireless Sensor Networks are groups of specialized transducers with a wireless radio intended to monitor and record conditions at diverse locations. A Wireless Sensor Network consists of multiple detection stations called sensor nodes, each of which is small, lightweight and portable.

Section 3
Next Generation Distributed Systems

Chapter 13
Publish/Subscribe Techniques For P2P Networks

Cuong Pham
University of Massachusetts, USA

Duc A. Tran
University of Massachusetts, USA

ABSTRACT

P2P is a popular networking paradigm in today's Internet. As such, many research and development efforts are geared toward services that can be useful to the users of P2P networks. An important class of such services is that based on the publish/subscribe paradigm to allow the nodes of a network to publish data and subscribe data interests efficiently. This chapter is focused on the techniques that enable these services in P2P networks.

INTRODUCTION

A publish/subscribe networking system is one in which the nodes can serve the role of a publisher or a subscriber to publish data or subscribe for data of interest, respectively. The publish/subscribe model differs from other request/response models in that a query of the former model is submitted and stored in advance, for which the result may not yet exist but the query subscriber expects to be notified if and when the result later becomes available. The publish/subscribe model is thus suit-

able for search applications where queries await future information, as opposed to the traditional applications where the information to be searched must pre-exist.

Enabling publish/subscribe services in peer-to-peer (P2P) networks is a topic that has received a lot of attention in recent years. As P2P can be adopted for distributed networking as an effective way to share resources, minimize server costs, and promote boundary-crossing collaborations, a publish/subscribe functionality should be useful to these networks. For example, a monitoring operator in a P2P-based geographical observation network (Teranishi et al., 2008) will be able to

DOI: 10.4018/978-1-61350-110-8.ch013

Copyright © 2012, IGI Global. Copying or distributing in print or electronic forms without written permission of IGI Global is prohibited.

subscribe a query to receive alerts of fire occurrences so that necessary rescue efforts can be dispatched quickly; or, in a P2P-based scientific information sharing network (Shalaby & Zinky, 2007), a subscriber will be notified when new scientific information is published.

Usually, a publisher node does not know who is interested in its data, and, vice versa, a subscriber node does not know where in the network its data of interest is available. Thus, a challenging problem is to design mechanisms for the subscribers and publishers to find each other quickly and efficiently. A simple way is to broadcast each query to all the nodes in the network or to employ a centralized index of all the queries subscribed and information published. This mechanism is neither efficient nor scalable if applied to a large-scale network.

Consequently, a variety of distributed publish/subscribe mechanisms have been proposed. They follow two main approaches: gossip-based and structure-based. The first approach is designed for any unstructured networks, in which the subscriber nodes and publisher nodes find each other via exchanges of information using the existing peer links, typically based on some form of randomization. The other approach organizes the nodes into some overlay structure and develops publish/subscribe methods on top of it. Examples of such an overlay are those based on Distributed Hash Tables (e.g., CAN (Ratnasamy et al., 2001), Chord (Stoica et al., 2001). The gossip-based approach's advantage is its applicability to any unstructured network, while the structure-based approach is favored for better efficiency.

This chapter provides a survey on the publish/subscribe techniques for P2P networks. First, we will provide some necessary preliminaries. We then discuss several representative techniques in each of the following categories: structure-based, gossip-based, and a hybrid of these two. We conclude the chapter with some remarks.

PRELIMINARIES

Peer-to-Peer Networks

A P2P network is a decentralized network of equivalent-role nodes. A node can serve in either a "server" role or a "client" role, or both, depending on circumstances. Unlike traditional client/server networks, P2P networks have no limit for growth and no single point of failure. The capability to share resources and the freedom to join and leave the network at any time are among the properties that make P2P networks very popular on the Internet today.

There are two main types of P2P networks: structured and unstructured. In unstructured P2P networks, e.g., [Gnutella] and [Freenet], the links between nodes are formed in an ad hoc manner without any predefined structure. Unstructured P2P networks are easy to maintain under network dynamics. They are fully decentralized with a high degree of fairness. However, they are not efficient in search operations. Search in a unstructured network usually requires broadcasting of the query, thus incurring a high communication cost.

Structured P2P networks are designed for better search operations. In such a network, the nodes are arranged in an overlay structure which provides efficient routing and lookup mechanisms. Distributed Hash Tables (DHT) is the most popular structure for structured P2P networks (e.g., CAN (Ratnasamy et al., 2001), Chord (Stoica et al., 2001), Pastry (Rowstron & Druschel, 2001), and Tapestry (Zhao et al., 2004). As CAN is used later in this chapter, let us describe briefly how it works. In CAN (abbr. of "Content Addressable Networks"), the network is viewed virtually as a multi-dimensional geometric space, called the CAN space, in which each node is assigned a location. The CAN space is partitioned into rectangular zones and the node location assignments are determined such that there is only one node in each zone. An overlay neighbor link is created between two nodes if their zones are adjacent.

Figure 1. CAN: (left) indexing & retrieval; (right) construction & routing

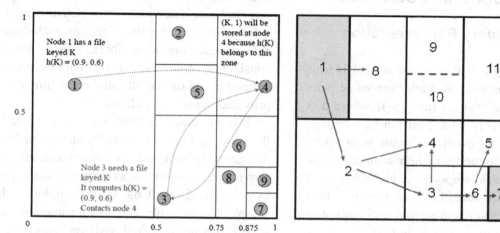

The control overhead for each node is therefore small because a node only needs to keep track of its neighbors and the number of these neighbors is at most twice the CAN space dimensionality which is a constant.

Data storage and retrieval in CAN work as follows. Each data object is hashed into a location in the CAN space and its index is stored at the node whose zone contains this hash location. When a query for an object is initiated, the hash location of the object is computed and the query is sent to the node owning this location and thus can find the object there. Routing to a location in the CAN space is based on geometry-based greedy routing via the overlay neighbor links: in each forwarding step, the message is always forwarded to a neighbor node that is closer to the destination node, geometrically. The distance between two nodes, which defines "close-ness", is computed using their corresponding CAN locations.

Figure 1(left) provides an illustration of indexing and retrieval in a two-dimensional CAN network. Here, the CAN space is a square [0, 1] x [0, 1]. Each node (1→9) owns a zone, which is a rectangle. Node 1 has a file associated with key K. The pointer (K, 1) (meaning that node 1 has a file with key K) is stored in the node whose zone contains h(K) - the hashing location of K, which

is node 4. Once a node 3 request a file with key K, it needs to route the query to location h(K) and thus will reach node 4, where every file with key K will be found. Routing from node 3 to node 4 is by relaying via neighbor nodes, greedily getting as close geometrically to the destination as possible.

Figure 1(right) illustrates the construction and routing procedures of CAN. Suppose that node 10 want to join the CAN network. This node chooses a random location, which, we suppose, currently resides in the zone of node 9. Node 10 then contacts node 9 and asks for a share of the latter' zone. Node 9 halves its zone into two smaller zones, retaining one and giving the other to node 10. Routing in CAN is even simpler. Suppose that node 1 is looking for some data, whose hashing location is in the zone of 7. Node 1 chooses among its neighbors the one node that is geometrically closest to 7 to forward the message; in this case, node 2. Node 2 then repeats the same procedure. Eventually, the routing path from node 1 to node 7 is 1→2→3→6→7.

The advantage of structured P2P networks is their scalability and lookup efficiency. However, they incur the cost of constructing and maintaining the overlay structure, most of which are due to node departures, arrivals, or failures.

PUBLISH/SUBSCRIBE SERVICES

Event and Query Representation

An event in a publish/subscribe system is usually specified as a set of d attribute-value pairs $\{(attr_1, v_1), (attr_2, v_2), ..., (attr_d, v_d)\}$ where d is the number of attributes, $\{attr_1, attr_2, ..., attr_d\}$, associated with the event. For example, consider a P2P network to monitor fire in a large region. Each peer records temperature, humidity, wind speed, and air pressure in its area over time, thus d is four – representing these four data attributes: $attr_1$ = 'temperature', $attr_2$ = 'humidity', $attr_3$ = 'wind speed', and $attr_4$ = 'air pressure'. In generic expression, the constraints in a query can be specified in a predicate of disjunctive normal form – a disjunction of one or more condition clauses, each clause being a conjunction of elementary predicates. Each elementary predicate, denoted by $(attr_i ? p_i)$, is a condition on some attribute $attr_i$ with '?' being the filtering operator. As used in the literature of publish/subscribe techniques, a filtering operator can be a comparison operator (one of $\{=, <, >\}$) or a string operator such as "prefix of", "suffix of", and "substring of" if the attribute is of string type. Thus, to be notified of all locations with temperature above 100°F, humidity below 20%, and wind speed above 50 mph, no mater what air pressure, the query can be expressed as ('temperature' > 100) AND ('humidity' < 20) AND ('wind speed' > 50). An event x satisfies a query q, denoted by $x \in q$, if and only if x satisfies all the elementary predicates specified in at least one condition clause of q.

The publish/subscribe scheme above allows a flexible way to specify a query as a disjunction of any number of conjunctive clauses and the filtering operator '?' can be any of the aforementioned, including the string operators. However, for simplicity of implementation, most schemes assume that a query is a single conjunctive clause of elementary predicates that can only use the comparison operators $\{=, <, >\}$. This form of query can thereffore be called the rectangular form because if an event is modeled as a point in a d-dimensional coordinate system, each dimension representing an attribute, a query can be considered a d-dimensional box with the vertices defined based on the attribute constraint values provided in the query clause.

It is sometimes a tedious process to specify the lower and upper bounds for all the attributes of a query. In such cases, it is more convenient to provide an event sample as the query and request to be notified of all the events similar to this sample. For example, consider a camera remote surveillance network deployed over many airports to detect criminal suspects. If a particular suspect is searched for, his or her picture is submitted as a subscription to the network in hopes of finding the locations where similar images are captured. A query of this kind can be represented by a sphere, in which the sample is the center of the sphere and similarity is constrained by the sphere's radius. This query is said to have the spherical form.

Subject-Based vs. Content-Based

There are two main types of publish/subscribe designs: subject-based or content-based. In the subject-based design, events are categorized into a small number of known subjects. There must be an event attribute called 'subject', or something alike, that represents the type of the event and a query must include a predicate ('subject' = s) to search only events belonging to some known subject s. The occurrence of any event of subject s will trigger a notification to the query subscriber. The subscription and notification protocols are mainly driven by subject match rather than actual-content match.

The content-based design offers a finer filtering inside the network and a richer way to express queries. A subscriber wants to receive only the events that match its query content, not all the events that belong to a certain subject (which could result in too many events). For example, many Bostonians are only interested in the Celtics and do not want to be bothered by any event published regarding the Lakers. A query with subject "NBA" would result in receiving all US professional basketball events including those about the Celtics and the Lakers. A content-based query is therefore more desirable. A node upon receipt of a query or event message needs to extract the content and makes a forwarding decision based on this content. We can think of the subject-based model as a special case of the content-based model and because of this simplification a subject-based system is less challenging to design than a content-based system is.

STRUCTURE-BASED PUBLISH/ SUBSCRIBE TECHNIQUES

A popular approach among structure-based publish/subscribe techniques is to employ a Distributed Hash Table (DHT) to build an overlay structure on top of the P2P network. This overlay provides efficient methods to route queries and events to their corresponding nodes that are determined based on the hashing function. The goal is that the node storing a subscription and that receiving a satisfactory event are either identical or within a proximity of each other. Scribe (Castro et al., 2002) uses Pastry (Rowstron & Druschel, 2001) to map a subscription to a node based on topic hashing, thus those subscriptions and data objects with the same topic are mapped to the same node. Instead of Pastry, the CAN (Ratnasamy et al., 2001) and Chord (Stoica et al., 2001) DHT structures are employed in (Gupta et al., 2004) and (Terpstra et al., 2003), respectively. A technique that can be used atop any such DHT structure was proposed in (Aekaterinidis & Triantafillou, 2005). Non-DHT techniques also exist, such as Sub-2-Sub (Voulgaris et al., 2006) and R-tree-based (Bianchi et al., 2007).

To illustrate the structure-based approach, we discuss how publish/subscribe services can be deployed in a P2P network structured using the CAN overlay (Ratnasamy et al., 2001) discussed earlier in this chapter. Although CAN is an efficient overlay for traditional retrieval in P2P networks, deploying a publish/subscribe service on top of CAN is not as straightforward. From the database perspective, because we typically model a data object as a point and a query as a range of points, we need to address the range indexing problem in publish/subscribe systems. From the networking perspective, due to its range, a subscription query may be replicated at multiple nodes to wait for notification of all possible matching data objects. Hence, the number of subscriptions stored in the network can be large, resulting in not only high communication cost to replicate the subscriptions, but also high storage cost for each node and long time to match an object against a subscription query. We need to minimize unnecessary replications, yet at the same time store the queries in the network intelligently so that data notification remains efficient.

Because of the low dimensionality of the CAN space, another challenge to a CAN-based publish/ subscribe system is due to the mismatch between the CAN dimension and the data dimension. Data can, and usually, be of high dimension, such as in applications searching documents, multimedia, and sensor data, which normally are associated with many attributes. It is difficult to hash similar high-dimension data objects into zones in a low-dimension space which are close to each other, making the search for a continuous range of data highly inefficient.

Meghdoot (Gupta et al., 2004) is a CAN-based publish/subscribe technique that works for multi-dimensional data space. In Meghdoot, each subscription query in d dimensions is mapped a point in 2d dimensions and the P2P network is virtualized in a CAN space of 2d dimensions. In the case that d is large, the CAN dimension is large, making CAN very inefficient. In addition, Meghdoot does not allow publish/subscribe applications with different data dimensions to run on the same CAN network.

Next, we describe a technique (Tran & Nguyen, 2008) using Random Projection (RP) to map queries and events to appropriate rendezvous nodes in the network. This technique can deploy a publish/subscribe application of any data dimensionality on any existing CAN network.

RP Based Publish/Subscribe

Suppose that the data (event) space D is d-dimensional, and CAN space is k-dimensional. The idea of RP is to project a d-dimensional data object in the original data space onto the CAN space to get a new data object in k dimensions such that the distance between two data objects after the projection remains within a small constant factor of the original distance.

Let $\{u_1,...,u_k\}$ be k random vectors, each being a d-dimensional orthonormal vector. Consider a subscription query Q = (s,r), which is a sphere centered at point $s \in D$ with radius r, asking for all events that are within a distance r from the sample event s. Projecting this sphere on the k random vectors, we obtain a k-dimensional hyper-rectangle $u(Q) = u_1(s, r) \times u_2(s, r) \times ... \times u_k(s, r)$, where each edge $u_i(s, r)$ is the interval $[<s, u_i> - r, <s, u_i> + r]$ (here, $<.,.>$ denotes the inner product of two vectors). The center of this rectangle is the point $center_u(Q) = (<s, u_1>, <s, u_2>, ..., <s, u_k>)$.

A strategy for query subscription is to store the query q in the nodes V_i whose CAN-zone, denoted by $zone(V_i)$, intersects Q's CAN-projection (i.e., $zone(V_i) \cap u(Q) \neq \varnothing$). This strategy can be implemented as follows:

1. Use CAN routing to send Q to the node V_Q such that $zone(V_Q)$ contains $center_u(Q)$.
2. Each node V that receives Q forwards this query to each neighbor node V' such that $zone(V') \cap u(Q) \neq \varnothing$; node V' follows the same procedure as V does.

When an event x becomes available, using CAN routing, we advertise x to the node V_x such that $zone(V_x)$ contains the point $u(x) = (<x, u_1>, <x, u_2>, ..., <x, u_k>)$. It is obvious that if x satisfies a query Q, then $u(x)$ must be a point inside rectangle $u(Q)$. Consequently, $zone(V_x)$ must intersect $u(Q)$ and the query Q must have been stored at node V_x. Thus, given an event x and subscription query Q, that match each other, they are guaranteed to always find each other at some rendezvous node.

The above strategy allows for quick and cost-effective event notification because each event is advertised to only one node. However, there might incur a large amount of subscription replicas in the network. Since subscription queries are likely to overlap, we should take advantage of this property to minimize their replication in the network. Observe that if query Q' covers query Q, it must be true that $u(Q')$ covers $u(Q)$. Therefore, if a new query Q is covered by an existing query Q', the nodes that the new query is mapped to must have already stored the existing query. Because those events that satisfy Q' will be returned to notify Q' anyway, which can be filtered to match Q, there is no need to replicate query Q further. Based on this observation, a more efficient strategy is proposed in (Tran & Nguyen, 2008), which differs from the aforementioned strategy in that a query Q is not replicated at a node if this node has stored an existing query Q' such that $u(Q')$ contains $u(Q)$. The query subscription for a query Q works in detail as follows:

1. Use CAN routing to send Q to the node V_Q such that $zone(V_Q)$ contains $center_u(Q)$.
2. If there does not exist a query Q' currently stored at node V_Q such that $u(Q')$ covers $u(Q)$:
   - Node V_Q will store Q and is called the *home node* of Q, denoted by *home(Q)*.
   - Forward Q to adjacent nodes whose zone intersects Q. Such a node V' performs the following steps:
     - Store Q at V'

Figure 2. Query subscription and event notification

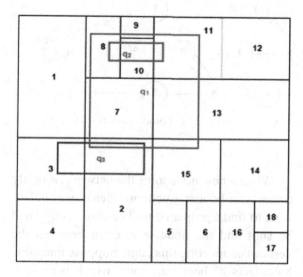

- For each existing query Q' stored at V' such that $u(Q)$ covers $u(Q')$, remove query Q' from node V'
- Forward Q to adjacent nodes whose zone intersects Q as in step b)

3. If node V_Q stores a query Q' satisfying the condition of 2), query Q will be routed to and stored at node *home(Q')*.

To illustrate this revised strategy, we consider the following scenario. In Figure 2, queries q_1, q_2, q_3 are submitted into the network at times in that order. Query q_1 is submitted first, which intersects the zones of nodes 7, 13, 11, 9, 10, 8, and 2. Therefore, q_1 is stored at these nodes and the home node of q1 is node 7 (because the projection center $center_u(q_1)$ lies in the zone of node 7). When q_2 is submitted, it is sent to node 10 whose zone contains the projection center of q_2. Because node 10 already stores query q_1 and $u(q_1)$ covers $u(q_2)$, query q_2 will be stored at the home node of query q_1, i.e., node 7 only; hence, a significant reduction in subscription load. When

query q_3 is submitted, because its projection is not covered by any other's, it is stored at nodes 2 and 3 because their zones intersect $u(q_3)$, node 2 serving as the home node of query q_3.

When an event x becomes available, the notification procedure works as follows:

1. Use CAN routing to advertise x to the node V_x such as $u(x) \in zone(V_x)$
2. For each query Q stored at node V_x such that $u(x) \in u(Q)$, forward x to node *home(Q)* – the home node of Q. At each home node V that receives x, search for and notify all the queries that match x and that call V home.

For example, continuing the previous illustration with Figure 2, suppose that an event x satisfying query q_2 is available such that $u(x)$ lies in the zone of node 11. An advertisement will be sent to node 11, where it is found that $u(x) \in u(q_1)$. Consequently, the advertisement of x is routed to the home node 7 of query q_1, where we will find query q_2.

GOSSIP-BASED PUBLISH/SUBSCRIBE TECHNIQUES

Structure-based techniques are capable to grow the network and adaptable to network dynamics, but they incur an additional cost to maintain the overlay. In addition, some of these techniques require different overlays for different publish/subscribe applications. The gossip-based approach (Terpstra et al., 2007), (Wong & Guha, 2008), (Gkantsidis et al., 2006) can work with any unstructured networks and thus does not have these limitations.

The word "gossip" gives the intuition of its use in publish/subscribe techniques: subscriber nodes and publisher nodes find each other by gossiping with their respective neighbors. An example is to use random walks. A query follows a random walk in the network and is replicated at each node

Figure 3. Random multi-graph example

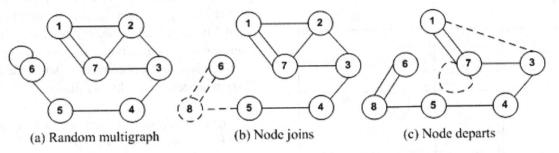

(a) Random multigraph   (b) Node joins   (c) Node departs

visited. Another random walk is used to publish an event. If these two random walks are long enough, they have a good chance to intersect. As such, there is a high probability that an event will reach every query and thus find all the matching queries. The tradeoff, however, is due to the high cost (communication, storage) to disseminate each query or event. The main question, therefore, is how to design a gossiping mechanism that offers the best balance between efficiency and effectiveness. BubbleStorm (Terpstra et al., 2007) is a recent technique aimed to address this challenge.

BubbleStorm

BubbleStorm replicates each query in a given number of nodes within a number of hops from the source. This set of nodes called a query bubble. Similarly, an event is also replicated in an event bubble. These bubbles need to be large enough to share at least a rendezvous node where the query and event can find each other.

To reach a given bubble size, nodes chosen to disseminate a query (or event) should be independent and the bubbles should be formed without cycles. For this purpose, a random multi-graph is proposed, in which self-loops and double-edges are allowed and a node's degree is proportional to its bandwidth. Figure 3(a) illustrates a random multi-graph of 7 nodes. The degree of node 1 is 3, of node 7 is 4, etc.

When a new node joins the network, it firstly contacts the bootstrap node and then uses a random walk to find a proper edge. The chosen edge will be split and the node is inserted between the vertices connecting this edge. Suppose that node 8 contacts its bootstrap node, which is node 3, and eventually found an edge between node 5 and 6. The creation of new links is illustrated in Figure 3(b). If a node leaves, its neighbors need to adjust their connections to maintain degrees. For example, in Figure 3(c), node 2 departs from the network and as a result new links (2-3, 7-7) are created to maintain the degrees of nodes 2, 3, and 7.

The communication primitive used by BubbleStorm to replicate queries and events in the bubbles is called BubbleCast. BubbleCast defines a split factor f which controls how many neighbor nodes should receive a forwarded query or event. Suppose that a query, starting at a node V needs to be replicated at n_q nodes. Node V will store a replica of the query and forwards the query to f neighbor nodes, chosen randomly. Each such a neighbor node is responsible for $(n_q - 1)/f$ remaining replicas of the query; the same replication procedure as at node V is applied. The dissemination of an event is similar.

Figure 4 provides an example of how BubbleCast works. In this example, suppose the number of replicas for a query is 17, and the split factor is 2. Each time, the number of replicas is reduced by 1 and then divided by split factor 2. From the initial

Figure 4. How BubbleCast works

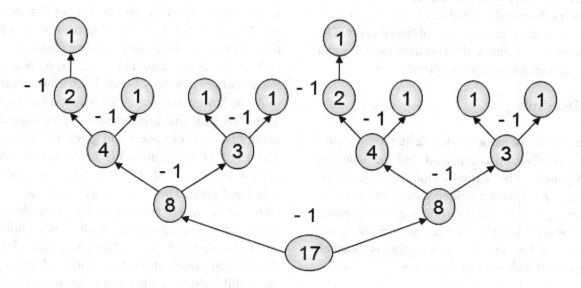

subscriber, the number of remaining replicas is 17-1 = 16, divided by split factor of 2. Each new forwarder will continue with 8 as the number of replicas, including itself. The process continues until the number of replicas becomes 1. So the procedure will end up with totally 17 replicas as the desired size of the bubble. This process is the hybrid of random walks and flooding.

Choosing a desirable bubble size is a key factor of BubbleStorm. It is proposed that if a query is replicated at $n_q = O(sqrt(n))$ nodes and an event is disseminated to $c^2 n/n_q$ nodes, the probability that the query and the event can find each other at an intersection of their bubbles is $1-exp(c^2)$, where c is the certainty factor (e.g., c = 3 → probability = 99.99%).

HYBRID PUBLISH/ SUBSCRIBE TECHNIQUES

The gossip-based approach offers more flexibility than the structure-based approach because the former requires no overlay structure in advance and allows queries and events to be expressed

in any format. On the other hand, as queries and events are spread randomly in the network, there is no guarantee that they will meet each other. To make any gossip-based system effective, we need to publicize the queries and events widely in the network, leading to the trade-off between efficiency and effectiveness. In addition to that, the guarantee that every query meets every event is unnecessarily strong. Indeed, we only need to guarantee that ever query meets every *matching* event.

In this section, we introduce Pub-2-Sub (Tran & Pham, 2010), a technique combining the strengths of both structure-based and gossip-based approaches. Pub-2-Sub can be considered a hybrid approach that can work in any unstructured P2P network, yet having the efficiency of structure-based techniques. It allows any number of independent publish/subscribe applications to run simultaneously on the same underlying P2P network. Because Pub-2-Sub is based on directed routing, it has the potential to be more efficient than the gossip-based approach. Pub-2-Sub results in lower storage and communication costs in comparison to BubbleStorm. In terms of computation cost, Pub-2-Sub requires only a node in the network that needs to evaluate its local queries to find those matching a given published event. The technique also incurs small notification delay and is robust under network failures.

Pub-2-Sub

Pub-2-Sub is based on two key design components: the virtualization component and the indexing component. The virtualization component assigns to each node a unique virtual address. The indexing component determines the corresponding subscription and notification paths for given queries and events, in which routing is based on the virtual addresses of the nodes.

Virtualization

A virtualization procedure can be initiated by any node to result in a "virtual address instance" (VA-instance), where each node is assigned a virtual address (VA) being a binary string chosen from $\{0, 1\}^*$. Suppose that the initiating node is S^*. In the corresponding VA-instance, denoted by $INSTANCE(S^*)$, we denote the VA of each node S_i by $VA(S_i: S^*)$. To start the virtualization, node S^* assigns itself $VA(S^*: S^*) = \varnothing$ and sends a message inviting its neighbor nodes to join $INSTANCE(S^*)$. A neighbor S_i ignores this invitation if already part of the instance. Otherwise, by joining, S_i is called a "child" of S^* and receives from S^* a VA that is the shortest string of the form $VA(S^*: S^*) + '0*1'$ unused by any other child node of S^*. Once assigned a VA, node S_i forwards the invitation to its neighbor nodes and the same VA assignment procedure continues repeatedly. In general, the rule to compute the VA for a node S_j that accepts an invitation from a node S_i is that $VA(S_j: S^*)$ is always the shortest string of the form $VA(S_i: S^*) + '0*1'$ unused by any other child node currently of S_i.

Eventually, every node is assigned a VA and the VAs altogether form a prefix-tree rooted at node S^*. We call this tree a VA-tree and denote it by $TREE(S^*)$. For example, Figure 5 shows the VA-tree with VAs assigned to the nodes as a result of the virtualization procedure initiated by node 1. The nodes' labels (1, 2, ..., 24) represent the order they join the VA-tree. Each time a node joins, its VA is assigned by its parent according to the VA assignment rule above. Thus, node 2 is the first child of node 1 and given $VA(2: 1) = VA(1: 1) + '1' = '1'$, node 3 is the next child and given $VA(3: 1) = VA(1: 1) + '01' = '01'$, and node 4 last and given $VA(4: 1) = VA(1: 1) + '001' = '001'$. Other nodes are assigned VAs similarly. For example, consider node 18 which is the third child of node 8 (VA '011'). The VA of node 18 is the shortest binary string that is unused by any other child node of node 8 and of the form $VA(8: 1) + '0*1'$. The other children 16 and 17 already occupy '0111' and '01101', therefore the VA of node 18 will be '011001'.

In $INSTANCE(S^*)$, each node S_i is associated with a "zone", denoted by $ZONE(S_i: S^*)$, consisting of all the binary strings str such that: (i) $VA(S_i: S^*)$ is a prefix of str, and (ii) no child of S_i has VA a prefix of str. In other words, among all the nodes in the network, node S_i is the one whose VA is the maximal prefix of str. We call S_i the "designated node" of str and use $NODE(str: S^*)$ to denote this node. For example, using the virtual instance $TREE(1)$ in Figure 7, the zone of node 11 (VA '00101') is the set of binary strings '00101', '001010', and all the strings of the form '0010100...', for which node 11 is the designated node.

Indexing

Pub-2-Sub supports publish/subscribe applications that can have any data dimensionality and allows any number of them to run on the network simultaneously, whose dimension can be different from one another. For ease of presentation, we assume for now that events are one-dimensional.

Figure 5. Pub-2-Sub: virtualization & indexing

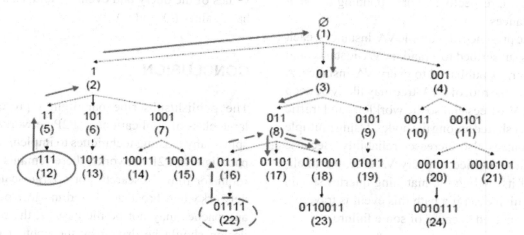

In Pub-2-Sub, an event x is expressed as a k-bit binary string (the parameter *k* should be chosen to be larger than the longest VA length in the network). A query Q is represented as an interval $Q = [q_l, q_h]$, where $q_l, q_h \in \{0, 1\}^k$, subscribing to all events x belonging to this interval (events are "ordered" lexicographically). As an example, if k = 3, the events matching a query *['001', '101']* are *{'001', '010', '011', '100', '101', 111'}*. Supposing that every node has been assigned a VA as a result of a virtualization procedure initiated by a node S^*, we propose that (i) each query Q is stored at every node S_i such that $ZONE(S_i: S^*) \cap Q \neq \emptyset$; and (ii) each event x is sent to *NODE(x: S*)* – the designated node of string x. It is guaranteed that if x satisfies Q then Q can always be found at node *NODE(x: S*)* (because this node's zone must intersect Q). The routing of queries and events to their destination nodes is facilitated by the VA structure based on the matching between the node VAs and query/event content.

Figure 5 shows an example with k = 7. Suppose that node 12 wants to subscribe a query Q = *['0110001', '0110101']*, thus looking to be notified upon any of the following events *{'0110001', '0110010', '0110011', '0110100', '0110101'}*. Therefore, this query will be stored at nodes *{8, 17, 18}*, whose zone intersects with Q. For example, node 8's zone intersects Q because they both contain '0110001'. The path to disseminate this query is $12 \rightarrow 5 \rightarrow 2 \rightarrow 1 \rightarrow 3 \rightarrow 8 \rightarrow \{17, 18\}$ (represented by the solid arrow lines in Figure 11). Now, suppose that node 22 wants to publish an event x = < *'0110010'*>. Firstly, this event will be routed upstream to node 8 – the first node that is a prefix with *'0110010'* (path $22 \rightarrow 16 \rightarrow 8$). Afterwards, it is routed downstream to the designated node *NODE('0110010': 1)*, which is node 18 (path $8 \rightarrow 18$). Node 18 searches its local queries to find the matching queries. Because query Q = *['0110001', '0110101']* is stored at node 18, this query will also be found. The storage and communication costs for a query's subscription depend on its range; the wider the range, the larger costs.

Multiple VA Instances

Because query subscription and event notification procedures are based on the VA-tree, the root node and those nearby become potential hotspots. To alleviate this bottleneck problem, a solution is to build, not one, but multiple VA instances. We can build *m* VA-instances initiated by dedicated nodes randomly placed in the network $\{S_1^*, S_2^*, ..., S_m^*\}$. After *m* virtualization procedures, each node S_i will have *m* VAs, *VA (S_i: S_1^*), VA(S_i: S_2^*), ..., and*

$VA(S_i: S_m*)$, respectively corresponding to the m VA-instances.

In the presence of multiple VA-instances, each query is subscribed to a random VA-instance and each event is published to every VA-instance. A node near the root of a VA-tree may likely be deep in other VA-trees and so the workload and traffic are better shared among the nodes. Using multiple VA-instances also increases reliability. Because an event is notified to every VA-tree, the likelihood of its finding the matching queries should remain high even if a path this event is traveling is disconnected because of some failure.

Multi-Dimensionality

In the description of Pub-2-Sub we have expressed an event as an one-dimensional k-bit binary string and a query as an one-dimensional interval. In practice, however, an event can have multiple attributes and as such it is usually represented as a numeric value in d dimensions where d is the number of attributes. To specify a subscription, a query is often specified as a d-dimensional rectangular range of values. Pub-2-Sub can work with events and queries of this general form.

First, we need a hash mechanism f that hashes a d-dimensional value x to an one-dimensional k-bit binary string $x^f = f(x)$ and a d-dimensional range Q to an one-dimensional interval $Q^f = f(Q)$ of k-bit strings such that if $x \in Q$ then $x^f \in Q^f$. For this purpose, we propose to use a (k/2)-order Hilbert Curve mapping (Lawder & King, 2000). This mapping preserves not only the containment relationship but also the locality property. Thus, small Q in the original space is mapped to small Q^f in the one-dimensional space with a high probability.

Then, to subscribe a query Q we use the hash interval Q^f. Similarly, to publish an event x we route it to the designated node of x^f. When the event x reaches this node, locally stored queries are evaluated to find those matching x; the query evaluation with the event is based on the original values of the query and event (Q and x), not the hash values (Q^f and x^f).

CONCLUSION

The publish/subscribe paradigm represents a large class of applications in P2P networks. Despite many existing techniques to implement this paradigm in P2P networks, there remains much room for future research. For a large-scale P2P network where broadcast-based and gossip-based approaches may not be the best fit, the routing design should be driven by the content of the message being routed so as to limit the scope of propagation. On the other hand, content-based routing if enabled by a structured overlay might incur considerable costs to maintain the structure. Since P2P networks may be of different types (small vs. large, unstructured vs. structured, static vs. dynamic) and the application to deploy may also have its own characteristic (low vs. high query rate, low vs. high event rate, subject-based vs. content-based, etc.), it is difficult to choose a publish/subscribe design that works well in every practical case. Thus, rather than trying to find a "perfect" design universally, it would be better to categorize the networks and applications into similarity-based groups and design the "best" technique for each group. For example, for P2P-based cooperative networks in which the nodes are supposed to be functional most of the time and failures should not happen too often, a technique like Pub-2-Sub presented in this chapter is a good design candidate. Data grid networks and institutional collaborative networks can take full advantage of this technique.

It is also important to develop a publish/subscribe middleware package that provides a set of common services to most publish/subscribe network/applications no matter their categories, and another set of services each customized toward a specific category. This middleware should provide convenient tools for the middleware designer to add new service components to the existing architecture, such as a new language for query and event description and a new implementation for routing, data aggregation, or an event matching algorithm. It should also give the application developer freedom and a convenient API to choose the publish/subscribe service configuration that is best for the context of the deployment. Middleware development for publish/subscribe applications in P2P networks remains ad hoc and isolated. It should be given high priority in the future research towards publish/subscribe services in P2P networks.

REFERENCES

Aekaterinidis, I., & Triantafillou, P. (2005). Internet scale string attribute publish/subscribe data networks. In CIKM '05: Proceedings of the 14th ACM *International Conference* on Information and *Knowledge Management*, (pp. 44–51). ACM Press.

Bianchi, S., Felber, P., & Gradinariu, M. (2007). *Content-based publish/subscribe using distributed r-trees* (pp. 537–548). In Euro-Par.

Castro, M., Druschel, P., Kermarrec, A., & Rowstron, A. (2002). SCRIBE: A large-scale and decentralized application-level multicast infrastructure. *IEEE Journal on Selected Areas in Communications, 20*(8), 1489–1499. doi:10.1109/JSAC.2002.803069

Gkantsidis, C., Mihail, M., & Saberi, A. (2006). Random walks in peer-to-peer networks: Algorithms and evaluation. *Performance Evaluation, 63*(3), 241–263. doi:10.1016/j.peva.2005.01.002

Gnutella. (n.d.). *Home page*. Retrieved from http://gnutella.wego.com

Gupta, A., Sahin, O. D., Agrawal, D., & Abbadi, A. E. (2004). Meghdoot: Content-based publish/subscribe over p2p networks. In Middleware '04: Proceedings of the 5th ACM/IFIP/USENIX *International Conference* on Middleware, (pp. 254–273). New York, NY: Springer-Verlag New York, Inc.

Lawder, J. K., & King, P. J. H. (2000). Using space-filling curves for multidimensional indexing. In BNCOD 17: Proceedings of the 17th British National Conference on Databases, (pp. 20–35). London, UK: Springer-Verlag.

Ratnasamy, S., Francis, P., Handley, M., Karp, R., & Shenker, S. (2001). A scalable content addressable network. In ACM SIGCOMM, San Diego, CA, August 2001, (pp. 161–172).

Rowstron, A., & Druschel, P. (2001). *Pastry: Scalable, distributed object location and routing for large-scale peer-to-peer systems*. In IFIP/ACM International Conference on Distributed Systems Platforms (Middleware), Heidelberg, Germany, November 2001, (pp. 329–350).

Shalaby, N., & Zinky, J. (2007). *Towards an architecture for extreme p2p applications*. In Parallel and Distributed Computing and Systems Conference (PDCS), Cambridge, MA, November 2007.

Stoica, I., Morris, R., Karger, D., Kaashock, M., & Balakrishman, H. (2001). *Chord: A scalable peer-to-peer lookup protocol for Internet applications*. In ACM SIGCOMM, San Diego, CA, August 2001, (pp. 149–160).

Teranishi, Y., Tanaka, H., Ishi, Y., & Yoshida, M. (2008). A geographical observation system based on p2p agents. In PERCOM '08: Proceedings of the 2008 Sixth Annual IEEE International Conference on Pervasive Computing and Communications, (pp. 615–620). Washington, DC: IEEE Computer Society.

Terpstra, W. W., Behnel, S., Fiege, L., Zeidler, A., & Buchmann, A. P. (2003). A peer-to-peer approach to content-based publish/subscribe. In DEBS '03: Proceedings of the 2nd international workshop on Distributed eventbased systems, (pp. 1–8). New York, NY: ACM Press.

Terpstra, W. W., Kangasharju, J., Leng, C., & Buchmann, A. P. (2007). Bubblestorm: Resilient, probabilistic, and exhaustive peer-to-peer search. In *SIGCOMM '07: Proceedings of the 2007 Conference on Applications, Technologies, Architectures, and Protocols for Computer Communications*, (pp. 49–60). New York, NY: ACM.

Tran, D. A., & Nguyen, T. (2008). *Publish/subscribe service in can-based p2p networks: Dimension mismatch and the random projection approach*. In IEEE Conference on Computer Communications and Networks (ICCCN'08). Virgin Island, USA: IEEE Press.

Tran, D. A., & Pham, C. (2010). Enabling content-based publish/subscribe services in cooperative P2P networks. *Journal of Computer Networks*, *54*(11). doi:10.1016/j.comnet.2010.02.003

Voulgaris, S., Rivire, E., Kermarrec, A.-M., & van Steen, M. (2006). *Sub-2-sub: Self-organizing content-based publish subscribe for dynamic large scale collaborative networks*. In 5th Int'l Workshop on Peer-to-Peer Systems (IPTPS 2006), 2006.

Wikipedia. (n.d.). *Freenet*. Retrieved from http://en.wikipedia.org/ wiki/ Freenet

Wong, B., & Guha, S. (2008). Quasar: A probabilistic publish-subscribe system for social networks. In Proceedings of The 7th International Workshop on Peer-to-Peer Systems (IPTPS '08), Tampa Bay, FL, February 2008.

Zhao, B. Y., Huang, L., Stribling, J., Rhea, S. C., Joseph, A. D., & Kubiatowicz, J. (2004). Tapestry: A resilient global-scale overlay for service deployment. *IEEE Journal on Selected Areas in Communications*, *22*(1), 41–53. doi:10.1109/JSAC.2003.818784

Chapter 14
A P2P–Based Strongly Distributed Network Polling Solution

Cristina Melchiors
Federal University of Rio Grande do Sul, Brazil

Dionatan Teixeira Mattjie
Federal University of Rio Grande do Sul, Brazil

Carlos Raniery Paula dos Santos
Federal University of Rio Grande do Sul, Brazil

André Panisson
Federal University of Rio Grande do Sul, Brazil

Lisandro Zambenedetti Granville
Federal University of Rio Grande do Sul, Brazil

Liane Margarida Rockenbach Tarouco
Federal University of Rio Grande do Sul, Brazil

ABSTRACT

Several activities are employed in network management to ensure correct network operation, including administration, monitoring, and provisioning of network devices. Among them, one of the most CPU- and bandwidth-intensive tasks is network polling. Although this task has to be performed in several real network management situations, it presents serious scalability and fault tolerance drawbacks if executed using traditional management architectures such as centralized or weakly distributed ones. It demonstrates the importance of investigating alternative architectures. This chapter presents a strongly distributed architecture for network polling. This architecture follows a P2P-based distributed management model, looking at P2P as an infrastructure that can be used to provide support for management operations to be accomplished in a highly distributed way. The chapter presents the polling architecture design, discusses the implemented prototype and the performance evaluation carried out to validate the approach, and provides a comparative analysis of the architecture with two other distributed polling approaches.

DOI: 10.4018/978-1-61350-110-8.ch014

Copyright © 2012, IGI Global. Copying or distributing in print or electronic forms without written permission of IGI Global is prohibited.

INTRODUCTION

Several activities are employed in network management to ensure correct network operation, including activities for administration, maintenance, and provisioning of network devices (Commer, 2006; Clemm, 2007). Among these activities, one of the most CPU- and bandwidth-intensive tasks is network polling, used for network monitoring. This activity is performed by a network manager entity, which periodically requests status and performance information from a typically large set of network agent entities. The collected information enables, for example, the detection of critical conditions that require some reaction from the management system in order to lead the managed infrastructure back to a stable, safe state. It also can be used to collect periodic performance data for statistical and trending analyses.

When carried out using traditional management models, based on centralized and weakly distributed management paradigms (Martin-Flatin, Znaty & Hubaux, 1999; Martin-Flatin, 2003; Schönwälder, Quittek & Kappler, 2000), the employment of polling to monitor modern, high speed networks becomes a critical issue because the volume of generated traffic and the processing power required to deal with this management information is prohibitive. Given that, polling tends to be avoided as much as possible, or even replaced by other methods, such as instrumenting managed devices to automatically send a notification when anomalous situations are internally detected.

However, avoiding polling activity is not possible in many situations. It occurs, for example, when a management application must monitor the status of a device variable that does not generate events. It also happens when the notification itself is sent via an unreliable transport mechanism such as the User Datagram Protocol (UDP) as used by the Trap messages in the Simple Network Management Protocol (SNMP) (Harrington, Presuhn & Wijnen, 2002). In fact, it occurs frequently, as can be observed in recent investigations (Schönwälder, Pras, Harvan, Schippers & van de Meent, 2007) on the actual use of SNMP, in which SNMPv2 confirmed notifications (Inform messages) (Harrington, Presuhn & Wijnen, 2002) were rarely found in SNMP usage in actual production networks. In addition, such research work (Schönwälder, Pras, Harvan, Schippers & van de Meent, 2007) has confirmed that traditional, polling-based network monitoring responds for most of the SNMP traffic generated. This means that although alternatives for polling do exist, traditional polling is still extensively employed.

Nevertheless, polling architectures of traditional management models are not feasible to be used in modern networks. In such traditional architectures, the polling of all devices is executed by a single or few management stations. This causes serious scalability problems because there is a large overload of management traffic in the management stations as well as in the links close to them. Moreover, such architectures have fault tolerance problems because, if the communication between the managed device and the management stations is lost, the monitoring of all devices managed by this station is interrupted. This way, alternative approaches have to be investigated to execute polling-based network monitoring in current days.

A promising alternative for distributed management systems is peer-to-peer (P2P) technology (Lua, Crowcroft, Pias, Sharma & Lim, 2005; Androutsellis-Theotokis & Spinellis, 2004). P2P systems are largely used today in distributed systems, in a large range of application fields, including file sharing, communication, collaboration, distributed computing and distributed storage. Such systems operate based on virtual networks (called P2P overlay networks) composed of heterogeneous nodes (peers) and virtual links between such nodes. Because of its features, it can be analyzed as a technology that provides support for the distribution of network management operations to a large number of peers, bringing benefits such as scalability, fault tolerance, flexibility and collaboration among human administrators in a co-operative management overlay (Granville, Rosa, Panisson, Melchiors, Almeida & Tarouco, 2005).

This chapter covers the use of a P2P-based strongly distributed management architecture for network polling. Such an architecture follows a P2P-based distributed management model, looking at P2P as an infrastructure that can be used to provide support for management operations to be accomplished in a highly distributed approach. The architecture distributes the periodic polling management actions across the entire network in a scalable way, and provides a more fault tolerant service.

The architecture has also been conceived to support the polling of network devices in a very flexible way, as required by real current networks. It is able to manage not only modern and flexible devices, but also devices that offer only rigid and limited native management functions, and so do not have support to be instrumentalized to run additional software that contains new overlay or polling functions. Nowadays, this situation occurs in a large number of networks, due to the large device heterogeneity and the elevated presence of devices that only support traditional management protocols. An example is the monitoring of devices that just support SNMP-based management and so, cannot be modified to run new functions that will include them directly in an overlay network. As this limitation is not detailed in some approaches conceived for distributed device monitoring, it represents an important flexible feature of the architecture presented. Besides, the architecture supports the polling configuration of different sets of management information from each managed device, with different polling parameters (*e.g.*, monitoring frequency, event generation, threshold alarm value, information storage). This ability and related flexibility are important for the management of current, real networks, since those networks offer a large number of network services

and, this way, require the acquisition of different information for the management of each one.

The remaining of this chapter is organized in four main sections. The *Background* section provides definitions and discussions about P2P technology, network management and research works that employed P2P technology for network management. The *P2P-Based Distributed Network Polling Approach* section presents the use of the P2P-based strongly distributed management architecture for network polling activity. Its first subsection discusses the limitations of network polling in current days, followed by the subsections that present the P2P-based distributed management model and the management environment. The remaining subsections present the strongly distributed network polling architecture itself, discussing its structure, the implementation and evaluation developed to validate the architecture, and the comparative analysis of the architecture and two other approaches. The *Future Research Directions* section discusses emerging network management trends and needs. Finally, the *Conclusion* section presents the concluding remarks.

BACKGROUND

This section provides definitions and discussions to improve the understanding of this chapter. The first section presents network management concepts and introduces distributed network management systems. The second section presents P2P technology, discussing its definitions and system groups. Finally, the third section discusses the use of P2P technology for network management.

Network Management

Network management (Clemm, 2007; Commer, 2006; Hegering, Abeck & Neumair, 1999; Udupa, 1996) involves several activities performed to improve the operation, administration, and maintenance of network devices. Such activities can be organized in five functional areas, according to the most established functional reference model (FCAPS): fault management, configuration management, accounting management, performance management and security management.

Fault management activities include network status monitoring and reacting with the appropriate action when a fault is detected. Configuration management activities involve the actions performed to set up managed devices. Accounting management activities are used to get network resource utilization information, keep this information registered, control user quotes, and bill users. Performance management activities involve monitoring and optimizing network performance. Finally, security management activities are performed to ensure access to management information and managed resources according to the appropriate security levels, checking the network to detect intrusion attempts and keeping a register of security information.

The status and performance monitoring activities are part of fault and performance functional areas. These activities aim to get network information in order to check if the network is operating properly. The information is obtained from the network through two ways: periodically polling the network to collect device information, and receiving event notifications sent from managed devices. Both functionalities can be employed to manage the network. However, in some situations, event notification reception can not be performed or is not enough. It happens, for instance, when the information that the system wants to obtain is not reported by the device through a notification event. It also occurs when the notification is very relevant to the management system but it is sent using an unreliable transport mechanism such as the User Datagram Protocol (UDP). In these situations, the network monitoring has to be carried out periodically by polling the network to collect the required information.

Network management is performed through network management systems. The first tradi-tional network management systems were based on an entity with a manager role and a set of entities with an agent role, following the typical manager-agent management model and the centralized management paradigm. Some years later, with the increasing complexity of network management requirements, this model has been extended to more sophisticated architectures, introducing entities that follow manager and agent roles simultaneously, originating the distributed management paradigms (Martin-Flatin, Znaty & Hubaux, 1999; Martin-Flatin, 2003; Schönwälder, Quittek & Kappler, 2000).

Distributed management paradigms can be grouped in weakly and strongly distributed paradigms (Martin-Flatin, 2003). In weakly distributed paradigms, the network management processing is distributed to a small group of nodes in the network. In strongly distributed paradigms, the management operations are also decentralized to the agents in the system, involving a large number of entities.

P2P Technology

Peer-to-peer (P2P) systems (Androutsellis-Theotokis & Spinellis, 2004; Lua, Crowcroft, Pias, Sharma & Lim, 2005; Milojicic, Kalogeraki, Lukose, Nagaraja, Pruyne, Richard, Rollins & Xu, 2003) operate using a virtual network created over a physical computer network. Such an overlay network (P2P network) is composed of software nodes called peers, which can act as resource consumers (clients) and resource providers (servers) simultaneously. P2P systems are characterized by the sharing of computational resources (such as content, storage, CPU cycles, etc) without requiring the intermediation of a centralized server. Figure 1 presents a schema of a P2P network executing over a physical network infrastructure.

Several definitions have been presented for P2P systems in the literature, and there is no consensus on the exact definition to be used. Some

Figure 1. P2P network

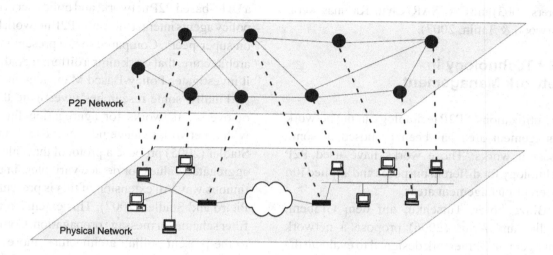

definitions (Androutsellis-Theotokis & Spinellis, 2004) consider the architecture and the characteristics of the system and exclude those systems that depend on one or more globally centralized servers for their basic operation (such as Napster, which uses a global search index). Other definitions (Milojicic, Kalogeraki, Lukose, Nagaraja, Pruyne, Richard, Rollins & Xu, 2003) are less restrictive about the architectures followed by the systems, focusing on the characteristics and functionalities provided by the technology. The explanation of P2P technology discussing the sharing of decentralized resources located in several network nodes is also employed by other authors (Gong, 2001; Chan, Karunasekera, Harwood & Tanin, 2007), while others (Arnedo-Moreno & Herrera-Joancomarti, 2009) emphasize the collaboration of P2P network nodes to provide basic network services such as content sharing, storage or CPU processing.

This chapter follows those definitions that emphasize the characteristics and functionalities provided by P2P technology. Accordingly, P2P technology involves resource sharing across several network nodes, in a way that peers offer their resources to the network and receive other resources. Those resources include content,

CPU processing, storage, connectivity, the ability to interact with some other kind of network resource, etc. This way, P2P technology can be used as support for network node collaboration, in order to provide important network services such as network resource indexing and searching, data sharing, and communication functionalities for applications. It can also be used to provide support for more complex services and functionalities, such as P2P-based distributed storage services with sophisticated techniques and data redundancy (Williams, Huibonhoa, Holliday, Hospodor & Schwarz, 2007; Hasan, Anwar, Yurcik, Brumbaugh & Campbell, 2005), and P2P-based publish-subscribe notification services (Courtenage & Williams, 2006; Gupta, Sahin, Agrawal & Abbadi, 2004; Chirita, Idreos, Koubarakis & Nejdl, 2004), among others.

P2P systems can be classified into two main groups: P2P applications and P2P infrastructures. P2P applications are closed P2P systems not intended to be easily extendable and targeted to a specific purpose, such as file sharing, distributed computing, collaboration or communication. P2P infrastructures are general purpose systems aimed at providing basic P2P services that enable the execution of developed applications over the P2P network, such as JXTA (Gong, 2001; Halepovic & Deters, 2003) and CAESAR (Chan, Karunasekera, Harwood & Tanin, 2007).

P2P Technology in Network Management

The utilization of P2P technology in the network management area has been proposed in some research works. Those works have used P2P technology for different purposes and applied it to different management areas.

Binzenhöfer, Tutschku, auf dem Grabem, Fiedler and Arlos (2006) propose a network management framework designed to evaluate the Quality of Service (QoS) and general network information using tests. The framework aims to offer information to a central network monitoring system, complementing it. P2P technology is used in such a framework to provide logical connectivity among framework agents and to enable a framework agent to find another one in reasonable time. Compared to the polling architecture presented in this chapter, that framework has a different purpose, since it is not conceived to provide periodic polling; instead, it obtains network information enabling local tests in framework agents and distributed network tests with other framework agents.

State and Festor (2003) propose a network management framework that uses JXTA (Gong, 2001; Halepovic and Deters, 2003) P2P infrastructure services such as search, announcement and communication channels. Such a framework uses Java Management Extensions (JMX) technology (Sun Microsystems, 2002) to structure devices and service agents. Compared to the present polling architecture, that work focuses on different topics, not exploring periodic polling monitoring functionality.

Kamiensky, Sadok, Fidalgo, Lima and Ohlman (2006) propose a framework for Policy-Based Management (Strassner, 2004) that employs a network of policy servers and policy agents.

Policy servers interact in the framework through a DHT-based P2P network; and policy servers and policy agents interact through a P2P network based on super-peers. Compared to the present polling architecture, that work aims a different goal, since it investigates Policy-Based Management.

Finally, some researches investigate the use of overlay networks for aggregation functions with a network management purpose. Dam and Stadler (2005) propose a protocol that calculates aggregated values for device variables, in a continuous way. An extension of this is presented by Pietro and Stadler (2007). This extension uses a filter schema for message propagation. Compared to the present polling architecture, those works are similar in the sense that the three focus on obtaining network managed information. However, those works proposed in the literature have different purposes and aim to obtain information for a different use, since they explore computing aggregated values of the information (such as a global sum, minimum or average). In contrast, the present polling architecture aims to collect a variable set of management information from several devices, obtaining results like the ones accomplished with traditional commercial management platforms, but following a more fault tolerant, scalable and flexible approach than the one followed by traditional platforms, as will be further discussed. Additionally, the present work focuses and discusses explicitly how to obtain information from devices that can not be instrumentalized to run additional functions and specifically consider such a requirement in the polling architecture.

P2P-BASED NETWORK POLLING APPROACH

This section presents P2P-based network polling approach. The first section discusses issues and problems for performing network polling activity in current networks. The next two sections introduce the P2P-based distributed network management model followed by the polling architecture and the management environment that materializes this model and which is used by the polling architecture. The remaining sections introduce and discuss the strongly distributed network polling architecture itself. Initially, it presents the polling architecture, including its structure and services. Next, it discusses the prototype developed and the evaluation performed to verify the feasibility of the architecture. Finally, it presents a comparative analysis of the polling architecture and two other approaches that can be employed for polling.

Network Polling Issues and Problems

Network monitoring through periodic polling is one of the most essential functionalities of network management. As previously discussed, this activity is part of fault and performance management areas, being a fundamental function to detect faults and performance problems in networks.

In the initial management systems, based on the centralized network management paradigm, the polling functionality was performed by a single management station. This station was responsible for periodically collecting information from all the managed resources of the network. This approach has as benefit its simplicity. However, with the increase of the network size, such an approach presented serious scalability problems because the management station concentrates all the management processing. Moreover, the network links close to the station become overloaded, as the management traffic becomes concentrated on this node. In addition to scalability issues, the approach also presents severe fault tolerance drawbacks, as the management station represents a single point of failure.

In order to reduce such limitations, the management was decentralized to a small number of nodes, originating weakly distributed management systems. These systems are characterized by a small number of nodes that perform the management activities. Typical examples of such systems are the traditional commercial network management platforms, which follow the weakly distributed hierarchical management paradigm (Martin-Flatin, 2003). In these platforms, there is a main management station and a small group of secondary management stations that perform some activities, including the polling of network devices.

However, weakly distributed management systems also present limitations with the increase of the network size. Management processing is still concentrated on few nodes, generating scalability drawbacks. Additionally, in case of failure in communication between a management station and some part of the network, the monitoring of all those devices is interrupted. These drawbacks demonstrate the need of employing a strongly distributed architecture for network polling in modern networks.

Some strongly distributed approaches have been proposed for network management (Martin-Flatin, 2003; Schönwälder, Quittek & Kappler, 2000; Melchiors, 2010), including the one based on Script MIB (Schönwälder, Quittek & Kappler, 2000; Levi & Schönwälder, 2001), one of the technologies applied to strongly distributed management more researched in the area. However, although such strongly distributed approaches have been proposed since several years ago, few examples of their concrete utilization in production networks are found today. These issues demonstrate the need to investigate an alternative strongly distributed approach to network polling.

As previously discussed, the strongly distributed polling architecture presented in this chapter is based on P2P technology. This technology has been largely used in real, production networks today, being applied to several application areas such as file sharing, collaboration, distributed computing, distributed storage, etc. This way, P2P seems to be a promising technology to be investigated as support for a strongly distributed polling architecture.

P2P-Based Distributed Network Management Model

The strongly distributed polling architecture presented in this chapter follows the P2P-based distributed management model (Granville, Rosa, Panisson, Melchiors, Almeida & Tarouco, 2005; Melchiors, Granville & Tarouco, 2009). This model looks at P2P as an infrastructure that can be used to offer support for management operations to be accomplished in a highly distributed way. In this perspective, services introduced by P2P networks provide innovative features that can be used to improve the way to perform management operations.

The model is composed of entities responsible for management operations and communication. Each entity represents a peer in the P2P overlay network, and the set of all peers of the overlay forms the management system. The peers in the management overlay can play different roles, representing a different type of management entity.

The model is composed of four types of entities:

- **Network administrator interface (NAI) entity**, which provides applications to human network administrators;
- **Management services (MS) entity**, which provides generic management services to other peers;
- **Managed resources control (MRC) entity**, responsible for the communication with the managed resources agents, executing management activities on such resources;
- **P2P network connectivity (PNC) entity**, which represents generic peers that compose the P2P network and do not provide management functionalities. Such peers improve P2P network connectivity and services, adding further peers to the P2P

network in addition to peers with management functionalities.

The management activities can be performed in the model by a single peer or by a group of peers, according to the *P2P group concept*. A group, in this context, represents a virtual entity formed by a dynamic set of peers that shares a common set of policies and interests. This way, a group can be seen as a single entity to the rest of the P2P overlay network. This unified vision allows additional functionalities to be provided by the groups, such as the load distribution and fault tolerance mechanisms supported by the management environment architecture described later.

Management Environment

The polling architecture is designed over a management environment that materializes the P2P-based distributed management model discussed in the previous section. This management environment is based on the environment initially proposed in (Melchiors, Granville & Tarouco, 2009) with improvements over that one.

The management environment contains services and applications that provide functionalities which enable the effective management of the network, including: (*i*) network management services and applications, which contain, for instance, the polling services presented in this document; (*ii*) maintenance services and applications, which provide maintenance facilities to the distributed environment, such as deployment and updating component services; and (*iii*) P2P-based structural services, which provide P2P-based special and sophisticated services to the distributed environment, such as *P2P-based distributed storage* and *P2P-based publish-subscribe notification* services. The *P2P-based structural services* are used by all the services and applications of the management environment. As will be discussed later, two *P2P-based structural services* are required from the management environment by the polling architecture: the notification service and the storage service.

Those elements are developed in the management environment over a *P2P infrastructure layer*. This layer executes P2P organization and communication primitives (including overlay maintenance, auto-organization and communication mechanisms) and provides P2P services. The layer should be implemented using some previously developed P2P infrastructure, such as JXTA (Gong, 2001; Halepovic & Deters, 2003). The P2P infrastructure selected for the management environment should offer the basic services of a traditional P2P substratum, such as peer and resource indexing and searching. Moreover, this infrastructure should offer general purpose functionalities that enable the development of complex applications over the infrastructure (Paller & Kokkinen, 2008; Chan, Karunasekera, Harwood & Tanin, 2007), including the support for file sharing and storage, and the support for service invocation, as provided by several P2P infrastructures and middlewares (Chan, Karunasekera, Harwood & Tanin, 2007; Paller & Kokkinen, 2008; Brogi, Popescu, Gutiérrez, López & Pimentel, 2008; Gong, 2001). Service invocations can be seen, in this context, as a mechanism to enable the sharing of the logical and the computational resources among P2P network nodes. The infrastructure should also support the concept of *peer groups* or be extended to support such a feature in a way that a service can be offered by both a *peer group* or by a *single peer*, enabling, respectively, the support for **peer group services** and **peer services** in the architecture.

Additionally, the P2P infrastructure for *peer groups* is extended in the management environment to provide fault tolerance (Granville, Rosa, Panisson, Melchiors, Almeida & Tarouco, 2005) and load balancing (Panisson, Rosa, Melchiors, Granville, Almeida & Tarouco, 2006) support. The fault tolerance support provides features carried out by groups in order to improve service availability. This is achieved by implementing a mechanism that guarantees even when peers join and leave dynamically, the group always has at least one member. The load balancing support enables the distribution of management activities among all the peers of a group in a transparent way. The distribution can consider several factors, including peer load, peer memory consumption, peer reliability, link traffic load and number of hops between the peer and the managed resource, etc.

P2P-Based Strongly Distributed Network Polling Architecture

The strongly distributed architecture for network polling follows the previous P2P-based distributed management model. The architecture distributes the polling actions across several *network administrator interface* (NAI), *management service* (MS) and *managed resources control* (MRC) entities, providing improved scalability, fault tolerance, and flexibility. This section presents the strongly distributed polling architecture, discussing the polling activities, their structures and the services involved.

Polling Activities

The polling architecture divides the polling actions into two main activities: polling configuration and periodic polling execution. It is divided into two activities in order to separately and specifically manage each one of the stages involved in polling. The polling configuration activity represents the task that configures the polling in the entities that will periodically collect the information. This activity is executed one time for each set of devices being monitored in the environment, and can be executed again later to change the monitoring configuration parameters or to include new devices to be managed. The periodic polling execution activity represents the task that is executed regularly by the entities responsible for collecting the management information.

The polling configuration activity is started by a *NAI entity*, in which the network administrator, using some application, configures the parameters of the polling operation, such as devices and information to be monitored, polling frequency, alarm notification (enabled or not), threshold value to generate alarm notifications (if enabled), information storage (enabled or not), etc. This entity interacts with a *MS entity group* and informs the polling parameters defined by the network administrator. The *MS entity group* identifies which *MRC entity groups* are responsible for the control of each device configured in the polling and interacts with these groups indicating the polling configuration parameters that they should execute. Each one of the *MRC entity groups* executes configuration activities on its own. The configuration activity is executed in order that all *MRC entity groups* responsible for a resource informed in polling are configured. Each *MRC entity group*, then, will execute the polling of the resources that it is responsible for. The periodic polling execution can be started immediately after configuration or after some time period defined in the configuration parameters. Additionally, if the *NAI entity* wants to receive event notifications related to that polling, it subscribes itself as a subscriber of these events in the *P2P-based publish-subscribe notification* service of the management environment. If other entities also want to receive such events, they can also subscribe themselves.

The periodic polling execution activity involves, in each polling cycle, two steps: to periodically request the information from the managed devices according to configured intervals; and to compare the values received with pre-defined thresholds, generating actions when these thresholds are crossed (if configured), as well as storing these values (if configured).

Polling Services and Compositions

The polling architecture structures the two main polling activities as a set of *peer group services*, and service compositions of such services. The polling *peer group services* are designed using the *peer group service* support made available by the management environment. Each *peer group service* in the architecture is responsible for performing some specific action. A *peer group service* can accomplish its function without calling another service, or can depend on other additional services in order to fulfill its actions, defining service compositions.

Two kinds of dependencies between services are defined in the architecture presented: *local dependency* and *general dependency*. *Local dependency* represents a constraint so that the called service must be executed in the same peer that the service invoking it. This constraint is necessary in some contexts because of special performance or implementation requirements. *General dependency* represents the invocation of a service without constraints. Local dependency is related to the consumer service: a service can be invoked with local dependency by a consumer service, and be invoked remotely by another consumer service.

The service composition for each main activity involved in polling (polling configuration and periodic polling execution) is shown in figure 2. The notation used in the figure is derived from the one proposed in (OMG, 2008): the collaboration diagram (ellipses) represents the service composition and each service is represented by its interface (rectangles). Some services involved in these compositions are specific to polling. Other services execute general functions and can also be used by other management activities.

Each polling service is designed in the management environment through a specific software component, which is supported by all *peer group* members in the case of *peer group services*. Considering *peer group services* that offer specific polling functions, the *peer group* typically involves a small or medium set of peers of the P2P network, according to the service characteristics. Otherwise, *P2P-based structural services* are designed as P2P-based environment services,

Figure 2. Polling service compositions

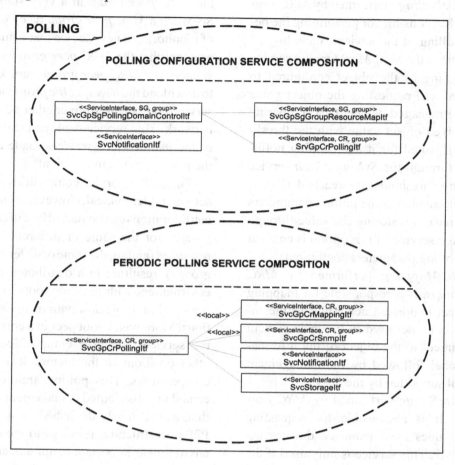

in a similar way as regular P2P network services. This way, these services typically involve all P2P network peers of the management environment.

The services involved in polling compositions are:

- **SvGpMsPollingDomainControl**: performed by *MS peer groups*. This service is responsible for (*i*) interacting with the *SvGpMsGroupResourceMap* service in order to obtain the *MRC peer groups* in charge of the devices to be polled; (*ii*) interacting with the services of these *peer groups* to inform the polling parameters.
- **SvGpMsGroupResourceMap**: performed by *MS peer groups*. Responsible for iden-

tifying the *MRC peer group* in charge of controlling each specific managed device. According to the P2P infrastructure used, this service can be designed to obtain this information by different ways, taking benefits of the P2P-based environment: it can use the P2P infrastructure resource location service to request groups in charge of each device; it can get this information from the P2P infrastructure storage service; it can get this information using manually configured mapping data. With the service independence provided by the environment, the design used in it does not affect the other polling services.

- *SvGpMrcPolling*: performed by *MRC peer groups*. Responsible for performing the periodic polling of the devices, including (*i*) getting from the *SvGpMrcMapping* service the mapping of the object configured to be polled; (*ii*) requesting the object value from the managed device; (*iii*) comparing the received object value with the thresholds established for it and sending notifications through the *SvNotification* service when the thresholds are reached (if this option is enabled in the polling parameters configured); (*iv*) storing the value through *SvStorage* service (if this option is enabled in the polling parameters configured).

- *SvGpMrcMapping*: performed by *MRC peer groups*. It is responsible for mapping the object expressed according to the information model used in the management environment to the object of the information model followed by the management protocol supported by the device.

- *SvGpMrcSnmp*: performed by *MRC peer groups*. It is responsible for requesting object values from managed devices using SNMP. This service is only used if the managed device uses this management protocol.

- *SvNotification*: represents the *P2P-based publish-subscribe notification* service, provided as a P2P-based structural service of the management environment. It is responsible for sending event notifications.

- *SvStorage*: represents the *P2P-based storage* service, provided as a P2P-based structural service of the management environment. It is responsible for the distributed storage of the information of the management environment.

Use of the *SvGpMrcMapping* service and the *specific protocol interaction* service (*e.g.*, *SvGpMrcSnmp* for SNMP-based devices) enables the extension of the management capabilities of the *MRC peer group* in a very simplified way. So, when a *MRC peer group* receives the charge of monitoring a new device that is managed by a protocol that the *MRC peer group* still does not support, the *MRC peer group* members just need to download the new *specific protocol interaction* service component from another peer in the P2P network. This service deployment can make use of the *maintenance services* made available by the management environment.

The polling service composition of each main activity is hierarchical. However, multiple polling configurations can be started by different *MS peer groups*, for the same or different management resources (and so, the same or different *MRC peer groups*), resulting in a distributed management environment with multiple roots to hierarchical trees and multiple destinations to event notifications. Moreover, a root peer in a composition can run services for other compositions, assuming other positions in the hierarchical tree of such compositions. This polling architecture is executed in a distributed management environment that, as previously described, is supported by a P2P infrastructure. It brings to the management environment important communication and collaboration facilities which provide support for these distribution characteristics of the polling architecture.

Example of Network with Polling Services

Figure 3 presents an example of a network with polling services. In the network, the polling configuration is requested by peer *NAI001* and peer *NAI002*. The *SvGpMsPollingDomainControl* and *SvGpMsGroupResourceMap peer group* services are served by some peers represented at the right of the figure. The network devices are managed by two *MRC peer groups*: *MRCG001* and *MRCG002*. In the figure, for example, the *MRCG001 group* manages switch SA, switch SB, router RA and the devices connected to them, while the *MRCG002*

Figure 3. Example of network and its polling services

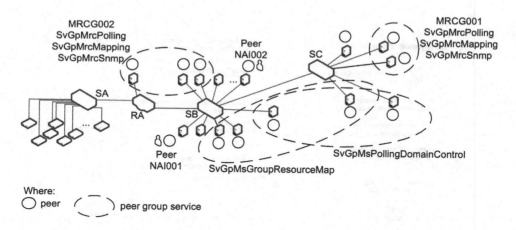

group manages switch SC and the devices connected to it. The *SvStorage* and *SvNotification* services are not represented in the figure: they are served by all network peers. Additionally, in order to not overload the figure, the peer connections of the P2P network were not represented.

Architecture Implementation and Evaluation

The network management environment and its polling architecture were implemented using the ManP2P framework (Panisson, Rosa, Melchiors, Granville, Almeida & Tarouco, 2006), a network management framework that follows an initial P2P-based distributed management model (Granville, Rosa, Panisson, Melchiors, Almeida & Tarouco, 2005). This framework uses the Java language and a JXTA P2P general purpose infrastructure (GONG, 2001; Halepovic & Deters, 2003) and follows a component-based architecture. It provides software components called *Management Components*, controlled by a *Container*, for applications to implement management functionalities in the peers.

The polling services that form the present polling activities have been implemented through a set of *Management Components*. The components implemented and their interactions are described

in Figure 4. This figure also follows a notation derived from (OMG, 2008).

In this document, the focus is on the polling architecture and polling services. The notification service has been implemented through a basic publish/subscribe mechanism in which one service is initiated for each *MRC group*, served by a single peer. The storage service has been implemented through the file storage system in the peer itself, and also one service is initiated to serve each *MRC peer group*. The *SvGpMsGroupResourceMap* has been designed using a local manually configured mapping file. The management environment service architecture makes it possible for each service to be improved in an independent and transparent way, since the service interface be respected. Each service was implemented with a single peer in the group. The SNMP model was used as information model for environment managed objects. This model can be replaced with the adaptation of *SvGpMrcMapping*.

Evaluation

In order to evaluate the feasibility of the polling architecture, some experiments were performed using the prototype developed. These experiments analyzed some performance parameters in each polling activity that is part of polling architecture.

Figure 4. Polling service components

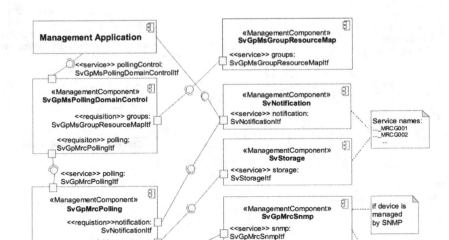

The first experiment presents performance measures for the polling configuration activity. The evaluation was performed using 11 virtual machines (VM), with 128Mb of RAM each, running on a Core2 2,4 GHz computer. Each VM hosted one peer: 1 peer with an authentication service, 1 peer with the *SvGpMsPollingDomainControl* service, 1 peer with the *SvGpMsGroupResource-Map* service, and 1 up to 8 peers in the remaining VMs running the *SvGpMrcPolling* and the other MRC services, besides the *SvNotification* and *SvStorage* services. As previously mentioned, MRC services are served by a group of peers, but in this evaluation, it has been assigned only one peer representing each group. The polling configurations were invoked by an application running on a Pentium IV/ Windows XP computer.

We begin testing the scalability of a polling configuration varying the number of *MRC peer/ groups* being configured (1, 2, 4 and 8). Each *MRC group* was configured to poll a set of 64 SNMP agents, resulting in up to 512 pollings configured when using 8 groups. Two performance parameters

were measured: response time to configure the full set of SNMP agents in all *MRC peers* (measured by the application that invoked the polling configuration) and the sum of all network traffic generated during configuration by all peers involved (measured through tcpdump (TCPDUMP, 2010) processes). The response time represents an important evaluation parameter in polling configuration activity experiments because it should be verified if the response time to configure polling as a strongly distributed activity is feasible for it to be used in management operations, as discussed later. Moreover, the network traffic parameter represents an important measure because, if a high traffic volume is generated to configure the activity, it can cause network problems.

Figure 5 presents the mean response time and mean network traffic resulting from 30 samples executed for each number of *MRC peer/groups*. As can be seen in the figure, both results are linear functions of the number of groups being configured. The configuration is done a few times in a regular polling management task, sometimes

Figure 5. *Mean response time (a) and mean network traffic (b) in polling configuration*

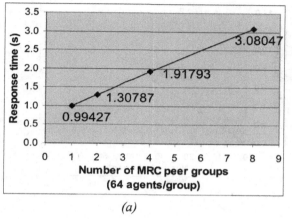

(a)

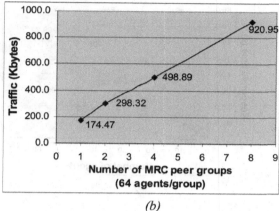

(b)

only once for each polling set. However, a quick polling configuration of new devices is important for the management administrators to be capable of analyzing some new network information in special situations, and it could become a drawback for a strongly distributed polling architecture when compared to centralized or weakly distributed architectures. The experiment results show that the present architecture supports such quick configuration (3.08s for configuring the monitoring of 512 devices), as required. Moreover, the *MRC groups* are configured sequentially by the algorithm at *SvGpMsPollingDomainControl*: this way, in situations in which a quicker configuration is demanded, this algorithm can be improved by parallelizing the interactions with *MRC groups*. So, for instance, with the parallelization of four *MRC groups* being configured by turn, it could result in a response time for configuring the monitoring of 512 devices at around 1.3s. Concerning network traffic, its values are related to the use of JXTA infrastructure, which uses text-encoded messages and contains JXTA (Halepovic & Deters, 2003) traffic control messages overhead. Although a high value was found for a single *MRC group* (64 agents), the network traffic presents a smaller increase with the inclusion of more MRC groups.

As previously discussed, the configuration activity is done only a few times in the polling task, and, so, its traffic causes a time-limited impact on network links. If demanded, improvements of such values can be evaluated by compressing XML JXTA messages or using other P2P infrastructures besides JXTA, in order to investigate lower bandwidth consumer P2P infrastructures.

The second experiment presents the performance evaluation of the periodic polling activity carried out by a *MRC peer group*. The evaluation was made using 4 VMs, with 128 Mb memory, installed on a Core2 2,33 GHz computer. Each VM hosted one peer: 1 peer with an authentication service, 1 peer with each MS service, and 1 peer, responsible for the periodic polling itself, with the *SvGpMrcPolling* service (that directly invokes *SvGpMrcMapping* and *SvGpMrcSnmp*), besides the *SvNotification* and *SvStorage* services, initiated for this group.

Now, we tested the scalability of the periodic polling activity as a function of the number of devices polled by one *MRC group*. Two performance parameters were measured. First one, the response time to perform the polling of the full set of agents, using only one Java thread (all device requests being done sequentially). Second,

Figure 6. Mean response time (a) and mean network traffic (b) in periodic polling

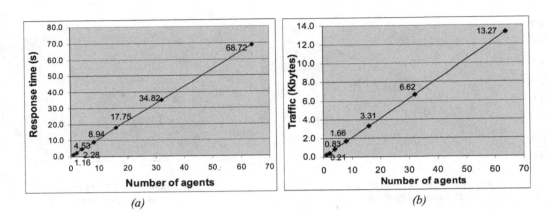

(a)   *(b)*

the network traffic generated in network links to retrieve device information using SNMP. The storage service traffic was not considered, since this implementation focuses on polling services and the storage service is able to be invoked directly, as it is in the peer itself. Notifications were not generated and their traffic was not included.

Figure 6 presents the results of this experiment, requesting the SNMP objects ifInOctets and ifOutOctets of one interface of each agent. As a single *MRC peer/group* is used in the experiment, the response time and network traffic are linear functions of the number of agents monitored. The increase of managed SNMP agents (managed devices) through the use of the additional *MRC groups* will result in the parallelization of the response time, since each *MRC group* will perform the polling of only those devices that it is responsible for. This way, with a large number of *MRC groups* being used, as supported and expected in the proposed architecture, the response time to manage a large number of managed devices will not be increased, since the polling of such groups will be executed in parallel. Concerning network traffic caused by additional *MRC peer groups* included, the *MRC peer groups* placement definition and the mapping of managed resource-*MRC group* according the network topology enable that network traffic generated by the periodic polling

of each *MRC group* to be restricted to the links close to the managed resources.

Besides such measure tests, an additional evaluation was performed in order to identify bottlenecks in response time of periodic polling activity. It showed that the socket closing operation took a mean time of 1,002 milliseconds versus a total mean time of 1,074 milliseconds to handle all the polling processing of each agent. In order to improve this time, a deeper analysis of this topic can be done in future work. Besides, the response time can be reduced by increasing the Java threads s pool at the *SvGpMrcPolling* service. Initial experiments executed for polling 64 agents with 5 Java threads resulted in a mean response time of 14,594 milliseconds (30 samples), versus 68,720 milliseconds for just one thread. The number of pool threads can be adjusted in an independent way in each peer, according to the resources available.

The present polling architecture enables a strong distribution of *MRC peer groups* responsible for periodic polling. This way, distributing the *MRC peer groups* and defining agent-to-group mappings according to the network topology can result in agents being periodically monitored by entities much closer than in previous centralized or weakly distributed approaches. As a consequence, it reduces the CPU processing and network traffic in connectivity devices and network links.

Polling Architecture Comparative Analysis

In order to analyze additional aspects of the present polling architecture, we compared it with other distributed management approaches that could be used for network polling. We have opted to perform a qualitative comparison among the approaches. A qualitative evaluation based on characteristics and functionalities has been chosen instead of a quantitative evaluation because: it is able to discuss more aspects; and the scalability and other performance parameters issues are highly related to the distribution paradigm used. So, a quantitative comparison of the strongly distributed polling architecture presented here with the traditional polling architectures would not provide the best information to fully evaluate the present approach since it would compare different distribution paradigms, which have different scalability results, and better scalability results for strongly distributed approaches. Moreover, that comparison would not take into account other important non-quantitative, functional aspects that should be evaluated, such as the control level required from other entities, entity communication support, fault tolerance, flexibility, ease of design and implementation, etc. Regarding a quantitative comparison with a strongly distributed management approach, as these approaches have rarely been used in real, production networks management, a quantitative comparison would not be effective. Moreover, this comparison would also not take into account the other aspects that should be compared.

Therefore, a qualitative evaluation was chosen, comparing the present polling architecture with two other distributed management approaches that could be used for network polling: the model followed by widely used traditional commercial network management platforms, and the Script MIB (Schönwälder, Quittek and Kappler, 2000; Levi & Schönwälder, 2001). These approaches were selected because they represent different and representative distributed management models.

The model followed by commercial network management platforms is composed of a main management station and some few collecting management stations which retrieve management information from the network devices. This model has been widely used in network management and is one of the most traditional network management models. The Script MIB defines a SNMP MIB designed to delegate management functions to distributed managers. It has been defined by the IETF Distributed Management (disman) Working Group (IETF, 2010). This approach represents one of the more researched and discussed strongly distributed management approaches in the literature.

In the comparison, the management entity that typically asks for polling will be referred to as *top-level manager* (TLM). The other management entities that execute functions to configure polling will be referred as *mid-level managers* (MLM). Within these, the entities that specifically perform the periodic polling requests will be called *collector mid-level managers* (CMLM).

The goal of the methodology followed by the analysis was to compare important and representative functional characteristics of distributed management approaches in order to distinguish their structure, operation, requirements, benefits and limitations. In order to do so, an examination of distributed management approaches was performed and eight characteristics were selected for analysis. Each management approach was then analyzed according to these characteristics.

The results are summarized in Table 1 and discussed in the following of this section.

1. **Monitoring**. In the traditional platform model, the monitoring of network managed devices is performed by the main station (TLM) and collecting stations (CMLM). In the Script MIB architecture, delegated scripts can implement polling functions. Finally, in the P2P-based architecture, *group services* in peer entities implement polling functions,

Table 1. Analysis summary

Characteristic	Management Approaches		
	Traditional Platforms Model	**Script MIB**	**P2P-based Polling Architecture**
1) Monitoring	Performed by main station (TLM) and collecting stations (CMLMs).	Delegated scripts can implement polling functions.	Services implement polling functions, including a periodic polling control service executed by *MRC entities* (CMLMs).
2) Distribution level	Weakly distributed	Strongly distributed	Strongly distributed
3) Functions provided for TLM to control CMLM. CMLM control level required from TLM	Typically, functions for CMLM control are not provided to main station (TLM). Collecting management stations (i.e., CMLM) are configured directly by user, not by TLM.	Functions for CMLM control are provided by Script MIB objects. TLM typically has to execute control functions over script execution at CMLMs, such as transfer or request script installation, inform parameters, start it, get results, etc.	Functions for CMLM control are implemented through service operations provided by the requested service interface. TLM sends information through service operation parameters. Each service performs its operation and calls other services if required to perform its functions.
4) Communication between management entities involved in polling	Through SNMP messages (such as SNMPv2 Inform) and platform specific messages.	Through Script MIB objects	Through service operations
5) Placement of CMLMs	Medium distance from managed devices.	Can be placed closely to the managed devices.	Can be placed closely to the managed devices.
6) Scalability	Medium	Higher	Higher
7) Fault tolerance	Medium	Medium	Higher
8) Ease of implementation	According to the platform API.	Medium	High because of the management environment structure.

including a periodic polling control service.

2. **Distribution level.** The traditional platform model is suited for weakly distributed polling architectures; Script MIB is well suited for weakly and strongly distributed polling architectures (Schönwälder, Quittek and Kappler, 2000). The P2P-based architecture is designed for strongly distributed polling architectures, but is also well suited for weakly distributed, if desired.

3. **Functions provided for TLM controlling CMLM.** CMLM control level required from TLM. In traditional platforms, the collecting stations typically have to be configured directly. With Script MIB, a lot of functions to manage the script execution are offered to TLM. On the other hand, the TLM needs to perform high control over the script execution at CMLM: typically, it will have to

verify if the CMLM already has the script module that performs the polling, and it will transfer or request such transfer in contrary; it will inform script execution parameters; it will control the script execution; it will get script execution results, etc. In the P2P-based architecture, the functions for controlling the service execution are provided through service operations defined in service interfaces. There are no restrictions about these operations, so, if required, service operations that provide specific control functions can be implemented. Usually, the architecture requires very low control from TLM because the CMLMs and other MLMs are designed to have improved independence and have themselves control over how to perform their own functions. The TLM (or MLM when there is a service calling another one) only has to inform the function parameters:

the service operation is all controlled by the service itself. So, the Script MIB requires the TLM to perform a lot more control over the MLMs: the P2P-based architecture provides more independence and autonomy to MLMs.

4. **Communication between management entities involved in polling.** In traditional platforms, communication is typically provided through specific platform messages. SNMPv2 Inform messages are also used to report events from collecting stations to the main station. In the Script MIB, the communication between the TLM and MLMs is done through the SNMP protocol and Script MIB objects. The results of polling functions are also collected through Script MIB objects. On the other hand, in the P2P-based architecture the communication between these entities is done through management environment messages and service operations. The results of management functions can also be collected through service operations.

5. **Placement of CMLMs.** In the traditional platforms model, the collecting stations are placed at a medium distance from the managed devices, because a small number of stations are used. With a different approach, both in the Script MIB and P2P-based architectures, the CMLMs can be placed closer to the managed devices. It is required only that the MLMs be equipped with an SNMP agent with Script MIB support or equipped with a MRC peer, respectively.

6. **Scalability.** The scalability in both the Script MIB and P2P-based architectures is improved by the placement of CMLMs closer to the managed devices. Moreover, when compared to centralized and weakly distributed approaches (including the traditional platform model), both Script MIB and P2P-based architectures enable the utilization of a large number of CMLMs, distributing the management traffic and processing. Compared to the Script MIB, the P2P-based

architecture scalability is enhanced because the TLM does not have to perform control operations over the MLMs, reducing the processing and traffic on this manager even more. Furthermore, the support for *peer group services* provided by the management environment improves scalability because load distribution methods can be used among the members of the group.

7. **Fault tolerance.** The fault tolerance issues need to be evaluated considering the different fault situations, including situations when a TLM goes down, when a CMLM goes down, and when faults occur in the communication channels. When a TLM goes down, in traditional platforms model, the polling operation is typically continued in the other stations (CMLMs). However, if some devices are monitored by the TLM itself, the monitoring of these devices is interrupted. In the Script MIB, according to the script implementation, the CMLMs can have some functions interrupted, since a lot of control is required from TLM for the CMLMs to operate. In the P2P-based architecture, a fault in TLM does not affect the *periodic polling* operation at all, as it is executed only by collector entities (*MRC groups*) and such entities are autonomous and do not demand any control from TLM. Additionally, even for the *polling configuration* activity, the architecture is fully independent of a specific TLM entity: the architecture is conceived considering that any TLM peer can request a polling configuration. This way, even the polling configuration can be changed during a TLM fault. Considering now a scenario in which a TLM is operating correctly and one CMLM goes down, the polling operation is continued in the other collector entities in all three approaches. In those situations, traditional platforms typically provide ways for the main station to start the polling of some information of the

usually large number of devices that were managed by the fault collecting station. However, such polling supports only some basic information, limiting their management. On the other hand, in the P2P-based architecture, through the strong distribution provided and large number of collector entities (*MRC groups*) used, the fault tolerance is improved since only a small number of devices are affected by a fault in one collector entity, reducing its damages. Furthermore, in this architecture, the support provided by the use of *peer group services* brings fault tolerance improvement because if one of the peers of the *group service* goes down, other peers of the group can assume the complete polling functions of the fault peer, continuing all the collector entity operations. Finally, considering the situations in which faults occur in the network communications channels causing communication interruption, the strongly distributed approaches (Script MIB and P2P-based architectures) have improved fault tolerance since the strong distribution enables collector entities to be placed closer to managed devices, reducing the situations in which the communication is interrupted in the links between the CMLM entity and each device that it is in charge of. In addition, in the P2P-based architecture, the support provided by the use of *peer group services* improves fault tolerance since the network communication interruption often does not affect all the *MRC peer group* members, and so, another peer can assume the functions of the peer that no longer has communication to the devices managed.

8. **Ease of design and implementation of polling functions.** In the traditional platforms model, it depends of the platform structure and API. This way, it is not clearly comparable with the other two approaches. In the Script MIB, there is no restriction about what program language to choose, but it is

limited to script functions. In the P2P-based architecture, the focus on the service based model and service composition makes the design and implementation of new services much easier than in other approaches, since all the management environment services can be reused though service composition. Moreover, any information model can be chosen, which improves its flexibility.

This way, the P2P-based distributed architecture shares the advantages resulting from the distribution already present in other strongly distributed architectures, with additional improvements in several features. Furthermore, the P2P-based architecture advantages include its higher flexibility, simplified service deployment, improved fault tolerance, improved load balancing through the use of *group services*, easy design and implementation of new management services with the use of a management structure with granular services that can be reused by others, etc.

FUTURE RESEARCH DIRECTIONS

As previously discussed, the monitoring of today's networks present critical scalability and fault tolerance issues if it is based on centralized or weakly distributed hierarchical models. It requires the use of strongly distributed polling architectures as the one presented in this document.

Besides such limitations, an additional problem emerges nowadays: the increasing need to manage services across several administrative domains. This occurs, for instance, when it is necessary to manage Quality of Service (QoS) requirements in a network path that crosses through several administrative domains. This can be demanded by services that perform the transmission of large amounts of data with QoS requirements. An example is a videoconference transmission that is transmitted to different destinations. Another example occurs in grid computing systems

(Kovalenko & Koryagin, 2009; Krauter, Buyya & Maheswaran, 2002), which aggregates resources from several administrative domains. Network infrastructure status and performance information are important for grid systems tasks such as job scheduling, monitoring and migration (Caminero, Rana, Caminero & Carrión, 2007), since that information enables network conditions to be considered when evaluating the performance of applications running in the grid system.

The emerging need to manage devices across several administrative domains originates a specific requirement for network management systems: the utilization of management models that do not employ authority and subordination relations for the interactions between management entities (Melchiors, 2010). This requirement occurs because each administrative domain is responsible for the management of its own network. So, it is not acceptable that a domain to order a management action for another domain: each domain must have the autonomy to decide if it will or will not execute a management action requested by another domain, demanding management system entity interactions that do not involve authority and subordination relations.

This requirement is supported by the present polling architecture. The *polling architecture* is flat about control aspects. Some activities are executed following a structure, as in the polling configuration activity, in which one service requests services of other entities. However, this structure is employed only to define the sequence of actions involved in the activity: it does not imply the authority of the entity requesting the action over the other entity, since the entity that receives the request is an autonomous entity and the polling architecture does not define an obligation of the entity in attending to the request.

In order to provide mechanisms to support the choice of the entity to attend (or not) to the requests received, mechanisms based on Policy-Based Management (PBM) (Strassner, 2004) can be employed through the development of additional polling services. In this approach, each *MRC entity group* that receives a polling configuration request (through *SvGpMrcPolling* service) can make use of PBM to evaluate whether it chooses to service the request or not. The use of this control in the present polling architecture has as benefit its simplification since the control can be restricted to the polling configuration activity only, being performed by each *MRC entity group* that receives a service request. The *MRC entity group* then evaluates whether it will or will not execute the action required and, if it chooses to do so, it configures its internal mechanisms to include the polling of the devices informed in the polling configuration request. If, however, the *MRC entity group* chooses not to execute the action requested, its services are not configured for polling those devices and the periodic polling activity is not affected.

This way, the present polling architecture can be employed to monitor the network information of multiple, independent administrative domains, such as, for instance, the monitoring of QoS requirements of the network infrastructure used by grid computing systems. The architecture provides a cooperative approach in which entities of one administrative domain can request services for entities of other domains respecting the emerging requirement of supporting the network administrative domain's autonomy.

CONCLUSION

In network computer monitoring, the periodic polling of managed devices is essential in several situations. Nevertheless, the traditional polling architectures, based on centralized and weakly distributed paradigms, are not viable to be kept in modern network management, since they present serious scalability and fault tolerance drawbacks.

This chapter presented a P2P-based strongly distributed polling architecture. The discussed architecture supports polling network devices in a very flexible way, as required by real current Internet networks, including support to collect different management variables from each management device and the ability to get management variables from devices that contain rigid and limited management functions.

The experiments performed demonstrated the appropriate response time and network traffic for both *polling configuration* and *periodic polling* activities of the present architecture, illustrating its feasibility for this network management functionality. Moreover, the approaches comparison demonstrated the benefits of using the present approach for network polling. This way, through the strong distribution of management entities and the device to *MRC entity group* mapping provided, the present architecture can be used to reduce network traffic and improve scalability in the polling network management operation. Moreover, the architecture discussed increases fault tolerance for the polling operation, as discussed in the comparison analysis. In addition, other benefits are provided by the present polling architecture, such as the very low level of control required by *MRC entities*, the easy design and implementation of new management services, the improved flexibility and the simplified service deployment, among others.

REFERENCES

Androutsellis-Theotokis, S., & Spinellis, D. (2004). A survey of peer-to-peer content distribution technologies. *ACM Computing Surveys*, *36*(4), 335–371. doi:10.1145/1041680.1041681

Arnedo-Moreno, J., & Herrera-Joancomarti, J. (2009). A survey on security in JXTA applications. *Journal of Systems and Software*, *82*, 1513–1525. doi:10.1016/j.jss.2009.04.037

Binzenhöfer, A., Tutschku, K., auf dem Graben, B., Fiedler, M., & Arlos, P. (2006). A P2P-based framework for distributed network management. In M. Cesana & I. Fratta (Eds.), *Wireless systems and network architectures, LNCS 3883* (pp. 198-210). Heildelberg, Germany: Springer.

Brogi, A., Popescu, R., Gutiérrez, F., López, P., & Pimentel, E. (2008). A service-oriented model for embedded peer-to-peer systems. *Electronic Notes in Theoretical Computer Science*, *194*(4), 5–22. doi:10.1016/j.entcs.2008.03.096

Caminero, A., Rana, O., Caminero, B., & Carrión, l. (2007). An autonomic network-aware scheduling architecture for Grid computing. In B. Schulze, O. Rana, J. Myers, W. Cirne (Eds.), *Proceedings of the 5th International Workshop on Middleware For Grid Computing* (pp. 1-6). New York, NY: ACM.

Chan, L., Karunasekera, S., Harwood, A., & Tanin, E. (2007). CAESAR: Middleware for complex service-oriented peer-to-peer applications. In K. Goschka, S. Dustdar, F. Leymann, & V. Tosic (Eds.), *Proceedings of the Workshop on Middleware for Service Oriented Computing* (pp. 12-17). New York, NY: ACM.

Chirita, P. Idreos, S., Koubarakis, M., & Nejdl, W. (2004). Publish/subscribe for RDF-based P2P networks. In C. Bussler, J. Davies, D. Fensel, & R. Studer (Eds.), *The Semantic Web: Research and applications, First European Semantic Web Symposium, LNCS 3053* (pp. 182-197). New York, NY: Springer.

Clemm, A. (2007). *Network management fundamentals*. Indianapolis, IN: Cisco Press.

Commer, D. E. (2006). *Automated network management systems: Current and future capabilities*. Upper Saddle River, NJ: Pearson Prentice Hall.

Courtenage, S., & Williams, S. (2006). *The design and implementation of a P2P-based composite event notification system.* In 20th International Conference on Advanced Information Networking and Applications - Volume 1, AINA'06 (pp. 701-706). Washington, DC: IEEE Computer Society.

Dam, M., & Stadler, R. (2005). *A generic protocol for network state aggregation. Radiovetenskap och Kommunikation.* Linköping.

Gong, L. (2001). JXTA: A network programming environment. *IEEE Internet Computing, 5*(3), 88–95. doi:10.1109/4236.935182

Granville, L. Z., Rosa, D. M., Panisson, A., Melchiors, C., Almeida, M., & Tarouco, L. M. R. (2005). Managing computer networks using peer-to-peer technologies. *IEEE Communications Magazine, 43*(10), 62–68. doi:10.1109/MCOM.2005.1522126

Gupta, A., Sahin, O. D., Agrawal, D., & Abbadi, A. E. (2004). Meghdoot: Content-based publish/subscribe over P2P networks. In H. A. Jacobsen (Ed.), *Middleware 2004, Proceedings of the International Middleware Conference* (pp. 254-273). New York, NY: Springer.

Halepovic, E., & Deters, R. (2003). The costs of using JXTA. In N. Shahmehri, R. L. Graham, & G. Carroni (Eds.), *Proceedings of the 3rd International Conference on P2P Computing* (pp. 160-167). Los Alamitos, CA: IEEE Computer Society.

Harrington, D., Presuhn, R., & Wijnen, B. (2002). *An architecture for describing simple network management protocol (SNMP) management frameworks. (RFC 3411, STD 62). Internet Engineering Task Force.* IETF.

Hasan, R., Anwar, Z., Yurcik, W., Brumbaugh, L., & Campbell, R. (2005). A survey of peer-to-peer storage techniques for distributed file systems. In H. Selvaraj (Ed.), *Proceedings of the International Conference on Information Technology ITCC 2005, volume II* (pp. 1-9). Los Alamitos, CA: IEEE Computer Society.

Hegering, H. G., Abeck, S., & Neumair, B. (1999). *Integrated management of networked systems: Concepts, architectures, and their operational application.* San Francisco, CA: Morgan Kaufmann.

IETF. (2010). *Distributed management (disman).* Retrieved October 1, 2010, from http://datatracker.ietf.org/wg/disman/charter

Kamienski, C., Sadok, D., Fidalgo, J. F., Lima, J., & Ohlman, B. (2006). On the use of peer-to-peer architectures for the management of highly dynamic environments. In *Proceedings of the Fourth IEEE International Conference on Pervasive Computing and Communications Workshops* (p. 135-140). Los Alamitos, CA: IEEE Computer Society.

Kovalenko, V. N., & Koryagin, D. A. (2009). The Grid: Analysis of basic principles and ways of application. *Programming and Computer Software, 35*(1), 18–34. doi:10.1134/S0361768809010046

Krauter, K., Buyya, R., & Maheswaran, M. (2002). A taxonomy and survey of grid resource management systems for distributed computing. *Software, Practice & Experience, 32*, 135–164. doi:10.1002/spe.432

Levi, D., & Schönwälder, J. (2001). *Definitions of managed objects for delegation of management scripts. (RFC 3165). Internet Engineering Task Force.* IETF.

Lua, K., Crowcroft, J., Pias, M., Sharma, R., & Lim, S. (2005). A survey and comparison of peer-to-peer overlay network schemes. *Communications Surveys & Tutorials, 7*(2), 72–93. doi:10.1109/COMST.2005.1610546

Martin-Flatin, J. P. (2003). *Web-based management of IP networks and systems.* Chichester, UK: John Willey & Sons.

Martin-Flatin, J. P., Znaty, S., & Hubaux, J. P. (1999). A survey of distributed enterprise network and systems management paradigms. *Journal of Network and Systems Management, 7*(1), 9–26. doi:10.1023/A:1018761615354

Melchiors, C. (2010). *Gerenciamento de Redes Fortemente Distribuído Utilizando a Tecnologia P2P*. Unpublished doctoral dissertation, Federal University of Rio Grande do Sul, Porto Alegre, Brazil.

Melchiors, C., Granville, L. Z., & Tarouco, L. M. R. (2009). P2P-based management of collaboration communication infrastructures. In S. Niiranen, J. Yli-Hietanen & A. Lugmayr (Eds.), *Open information management: Applications of interconnectivity and collaboration* (pp. 343-373). Hershey, PA: Information Science Publishing.

Milojicic, D. S., Kalogeraki, V., Lukose, R., Nagaraja, K., Pruyne, J., & Richard, B. … Xu, Z. (2003). *Peer-to-peer computing*. (Tech. Report HPL-2002-57). Palo Alto, CA: HP Laboratories Palo Alto.

OMG. (2008). *UML profile and metamodel for services (SOA-Pro), revised submission. (*OMG Document ad/2008-05-03). Needham.

Paller, G., & Kokkinen, H. (2008). Modular, service-oriented API for peer-to-peer middleware. In *Proceedings of the International Conference on Mobile Wireless Middleware, Operating systems, and Applications* (pp. 1-6). Brussels, Belgium: ICST.

Panisson, A., Rosa, D., Melchiors, C., Granville, L. Z., Almeida, M., & Tarouco, L. M. R. (2006). Designing the architecture of P2P-based network management systems. In P. Bellavista, & C. Chen (Eds.), *Proceedings of the 11th IEEE Symposium Computers and Communications* (pp. 69-75). Los Alamitos, CA: IEEE Computer Society.

Pietro, A., & Stadler, R. (2007). A-GAP: An adaptive protocol for continuous network monitoring with accuracy objectives. *IEEE Transactions Network Services Management, 4*(1), 2–12. doi:10.1109/TNSM.2007.030101

Schönwälder, J., Pras, A., Harvan, M., Schippers, J., & van de Meent, R. (2007). SNMP traffic analysis: Approaches, tools, and first results. In *Proceedings of the 10th IFIP/IEEE International Symposium Integrated Network Management* (pp. 323-332). IEEE Press.

Schönwälder, J., Quittek, J., & Kappler, C. (2000). Building distributed management applications with the IETF script MIB. *IEEE Journal on Selected Areas in Communications, 18*(5), 702–714. doi:10.1109/49.842986

State, R., & Festor, O. (2003). A management platform over a peer to peer service infrastructure. In *Proceedings of the 10th International Conference on Telecommunications* (pp. 124-131). Piscataway, NJ: IEEE Press.

Strassner, J. C. (2004). *Policy-based network management*. San Francisco, CA: Morgan Kaufmann.

Sun Microsystems. (2002). *Java management extensions (JMX) instrumentation and agent specifications*. Palo Alto, CA: Sun Microsystems.

TCPDUMP. (2010). *TCPDUMP/LIBCAP public repository*. Retrieved October 15, 2010, from http:// www.tcpdump.org

Udupa, D. K. (1996). *Network management systems essentials*. New York, NY: McGraw Hill.

Williams, C., Huibonhoa, P., Holliday, J., Hospodor, A., & Schwarz, T. (2007). Redundancy management for P2P storage. In B. Schultze, R. Buyya, P. Navaux, W. Cirne, & V. Rebello (Eds.), *Proceedings of the Seventh IEEE International Symposium on Cluster Computing and the Grid* (pp. 1-8). IEEE Computer Society.

KEY TERMS AND DEFINITIONS

Centralized Network Management Paradigm: Network management paradigm that centralizes all the management processing in a single management entity.

Distributed Network Management Paradigms: Network management paradigms that distribute management processing to some or several network nodes.

JXTA: General-purpose, open-source P2P infrastructure based on Java, largely used in P2P systems developing.

Network Periodic Polling: Network management activity that involves periodically collecting management information from managed devices.

Peer-to-Peer (P2P) System: System that operates based on virtual network nodes and by virtual links among nodes, forming P2P overlay networks.

Peer-to-Peer (P2P) Infrastructure: P2P approaches developed to provide basic P2P services and applications that enable the development and execution of other applications over the P2P network.

Script MIB: Distributed approach that defines a SNMP MIB designed to delegate management functions to distributed managers.

Chapter 15
Service–Oriented Networking for the Next Generation Distributed Computing

Qiang Duan
Pennsylvania State University, U.S.A.

ABSTRACT

With the rapid development of various emerging technologies, such as Web services, Grid computing, and cloud computing, computer networks have become the integrant of the next generation distributed computing systems. Networking systems have a significant impact on distributed application performance; therefore, they must be integrated with other computational resources in distributed computing systems to support the requirements of high-performance distributed applications. This chapter presents a new Service-Oriented Networking (SON) paradigm that enables the integration of networking and distributed computing systems. The SON applies the Service-Oriented Architecture (SOA) principle and employs network virtualization for abstracting networking resources in the form of network services, which can be described, discovered, and composed in distributed computing environments. This chapter particularly discusses network service description and discovery as key technologies for realizing the SON, and describes a network service broker system for discovering the network services that meet the performance requirements of distributed applications. A general modeling approach to describing network service capabilities and an information updating mechanism are also presented in this chapter, which can improve the performance of the network service broker system in heterogeneous and dynamic networking environments.

DOI: 10.4018/978-1-61350-110-8.ch015

Copyright © 2012, IGI Global. Copying or distributing in print or electronic forms without written permission of IGI Global is prohibited.

INTRODUCTION

The past decade has witnessed many exciting developments in the area of distributed computing. Some of the most significant progresses in this field include Web services, Grid computing, and Cloud computing, which have enabled the utilization of a wide variety of distributed computational resources as a unified resource. These emerging distributed computing technologies, with the rapid development of new networking technologies, are changing the entire computing paradigm toward a new generation of distributed computing.

The notion of Web services evolved from the concept of software-as-a-service, which first appeared as the application service provider model. Web services extend the software-as-a-service concept to include the delivery of complex business processes and transactions as services. When comparing Web services to Web-based applications we may distinguish the following key differences: Web services act as resources to other applications that can request and initiate those Web services with or without human intervention; Web services are modular, self-aware, and self-describing applications; Web services are more flexible and manageable than Web-based applications; and Web services may be brokered or auctioned (Papazoglou, 2008).

Grid computing started off in the mid-90s to address large-scale computing problems using a network of resource-sharing commodity machines that deliver the computation power affordable only by supercomputers and large dedicated clusters at that time. The idea is to federate the heterogeneous computational resources across geographically distributed institutions and make them to be utilized as a unified resource by various applications. Grid computing was initially developed by the high-performance computing community with its own standard specifications. Then Web services have been gradually adopted into the key technologies and standards for Grid computing.

Cloud computing is a relatively recent term that can be defined as a large scale distributed computing paradigm that is driven by economics of scale, in which a pool of abstracted, virtualized, dynamically-scalable computing functions and services are delivered on demand to external customers over the Internet (Foster et al., 2008). A Cloud is massively scalable and can be encapsulated as an abstract entity that delivers different levels of services to customers outside the Cloud. Cloud services can be dynamically configured and delivered on demand.

Cloud computing is closed related to Grid computing. Though having different technical details, they share essentially the same vision – to reduce the cost of computing, increase reliability, and enhance flexibility of managing computing infrastructures. Both Cloud computing and Grid computing need to manage large scale facilities, to enable customers to discover, request, and use computing resources provided by central facilities, and to implement highly parallel computations on those resources. Cloud computing can be viewed as the next evolution step after Grid computing in the field of distributed computing.

Data communications play a crucial role in all the aforementioned emerging distributed computing systems. Federation and coordination of geographically distributed computational resources to deliver better-than-best-effort services is a key feature of both Web services and Grid computing. Cloud services are typically accessed through communication channels provided by computer networks. Networking performance has a significant impact on the end-to-end service quality experienced by the applications and customers supported by these distributed computing systems. Therefore, communication networks with Quality of Service (QoS) provisioning capabilities become an indispensable ingredient of the next generation high-performance distributed computing systems.

However there exists a gap between the demands of the emerging distributed computing for data communications and the services that can be offered by traditional networking systems. The expectations of high-performance distributed computing include predictability in networking performance, coordination of both computing and networking resources, and application-driven control, management, and configuration of networking systems to match end-to-end distributed computing requirements. However, traditional networks were designed specifically to support a narrow range of precisely defined communication services. These services were implemented on fairly rigid infrastructures, with minimal capabilities for ad hoc reconfiguration. Supporting functions, like operations, managements, and security, in traditional networks were also specifically designed and customized to facilitate a particular type of service. Therefore, the provisioning of networking services and management of underlying network systems are tightly coupled, and limited by evolution of the underlying network platform. Reengineering networking systems to provide new services for supporting emerging distributed systems and various new applications is slow and static. Also networking resources are managed separately from the management of computing resources; thus lacking an optimization of resource utilization.

Therefore the next generation distributed computing requires integration between distributed computing systems and networking systems, which allows computer networks to be involved in distributed computing environments as "full participants" just like other computing resources such as CPU capacity and memory/disk space. A key feature for such integration lies in flexible and effective interaction between distributed computing systems and networking systems. Such interaction enables networking resources to be exposed to distributed applications as commodity service components and to be composed with computing resources into composite distributed services that meet the application requirements.

The Service-Oriented Architecture (SOA) and network virtualization, which will be discussed in more details in the next two sections, are two significant recent progresses in the fields of distributed computing and networking respectively. The SOA serves as a key architectural principle for the emerging distributed computing systems and network virtualization is expected to play a crucial role in the next generation networks. Though initially developed in two relatively independent fields, the SOA and network virtualization together provide a promising approach to integrating networking and distributed computing systems; thus may significantly contribute the next generation distributed computing.

This chapter presents a new Service-Oriented Networking (SON) paradigm that applies the SOA with network virtualization for integrating communication networks into distributed computing environments. This chapter will first give an overview of the SOA and a briefly introduction to the notion of network virtualization. Then the chapter will describe the service-oriented networking paradigm and discuss how application of the SOA principle with network virtualization facilitates the integration of networking and distributed computing systems. This chapter will also investigate key technologies for realizing the SON and particularly describe a network service broker system for network service description and discovery, which are two key elements for implementing in SON. A general model for describing network service capabilities and a scalable mechanism for updating service descriptions are also discussed in this chapter for improving the performance of the network service broker in SON.

THE SERVICE-ORIENED ARCHITECTURE

The SOA is described in (Channabasavaiah, Holley & Tuggle, 2003) as "an architecture within which all functions are defined as independent services with standard interfaces that can be called in defined sequences to form business processes."

The SOA can be considered as a philosophy or paradigm to organize and utilize services and capabilities that may be under the control of different ownership domains. A *service* in the SOA is a computing module that is self-contained (i.e., the service maintains its own states) and platform-independent (i.e., the interface to the service is independent with its implementation platform). Services can be described, published, located, orchestrated, and programmed through standard interfaces and messaging protocols. The technologies providing the desired functionality of a service are hidden behind the service interface. This guarantees that external components neither know nor care how services perform their functions.

The common principles that are mostly related to service-orientation include service reusability, service contract, service abstraction, service composability, service autonomy, and service discoverability. Since the service functionality is accessed through standard interface and internal implementations are transparent to users, a service can be reused as a building block for constructing various systems. Services share a formal contract that describes each service and defines the terms of information exchange for service interaction. Services adhere to a communication agreement collectively defined by one or more service description documents. Services represent an abstraction of the underlying logic, which hides the internal implementations and expose its functionality via the service contract. Services are composable and a collection of services could be orchestrated and composed into a single new service. Services are also autonomous modules that have a high level control over its underlying runtime environment. Services can be discovered by service users (including other services) through some sort of standard mechanism for publishing and searching service descriptions.

The key elements of SOA and their interactions are shown in Figure 1. A service provider publishes a machine-readable document called *service description* at a service registry. The service description gives descriptive information about the functions provided by the service and the interfaces for utilizing such functions. When a service customer, either an application or another service, needs to utilize computing resources to perform a certain function, it starts a service discovery process to locate an available service that meets its requirement. Typically a service broker handles service discovery for service customers by searching the service descriptions published at the registry and selecting a service that matches the criteria specified by the customer. The broker may select and consolidate multiple singles service into a composite service to meet the customer's requirements. After discovering a service, the service customer contacts the service provider and invokes the service by following the interface defined in the service description.

A key feature of SOA is the *loose-coupling* interactions among heterogeneous systems in the architecture. The term "coupling" indicates the degree of dependency any two systems have on each other. In loosely coupled interactions, systems need not know how their partner systems behave or are implemented, which allows systems to connect and interact with each other more freely. Therefore, loose coupling of heterogeneous systems provides a high level of flexibility and interoperability for building integrated, cross-platform, inter-domain computing environments. It is this feature that makes the SOA very effective for integrating various heterogeneous computing systems.

The keys to realizing SOA include service description, service publication, service discovery, service composition, and message delivery. Although SOA could be implemented in different ways, currently the Web services technologies and standards are widely adopted as the major implementation environment for the SOA. The standard for Web service description is Web Service Description Language (WSDL) (Chinnici et al., 2007), which defines the XML grammar

Figure 1. Key elements of the SOA and their interactions

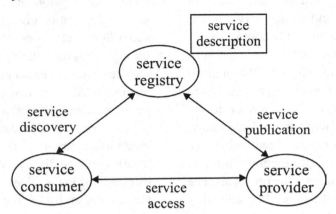

for describing services as a collection of communicating endpoints capable of exchanging messages. Web service publication is achieved by Universal Description Discovery and Integration (UDDI) (Clement et al., 2004), which is a public directory with standard interfaces for publishing and searching service descriptions. Web service composition describes the execution logic of service-based functions by defining their control flows. The Business Process Execution Language (BPEL) (Barreto et al., 2007) is a standard for Web service composition. Simple Object Access Protocol (SOAP) (Gudgin et al., 2007) is a standard transport protocol for exchanging messages among Web services. All the above Web service technologies and standards are based on Extensible Markup Language (XML), which is a general-purpose markup language that facilitates data sharing across different systems and applications.

NETWORK VIRTUALIZATION

Network virtualization is one of the most significant recent developments in the networking area. Recently numerous network-based computing applications have been developed and deployed on top of the Internet, and these applications have a wide spectrum of networking requirements.

The highly diverse network application requirements have motivated research on various new networking technologies and even alternative architecture for the next generation Internet. The idea of virtualization was first proposed to be applied in networking area as an approach to developing virtual testbeds for the evaluation of new networking technologies (Anderson et al., 2005). For example in PlanetLab (Bavier et al., 2004) and GENI (GENI Planning Group, 2006) projects, network virtualization was employed to build open experimental facilities for researchers to create customized virtual networks for evaluating new network technologies and architecture. Then the network research community realized that fundamental changes must be made in the Internet architecture to allow heterogeneous networking systems to coexist on top of a shared infrastructure platform. Toward that objective, the role of virtualization in the Internet has been shifted from an evaluation tool to a fundamental diversifying attribute of the inter-networking paradigm (Turner & Taylor, 2005).

Essentially network virtualization follows a well-tested principle – separation of policy from mechanism – in the inter-networking environment. In this case, network service provisioning is separated from data transportation mechanisms; thus dividing the traditional roles of Internet

Service Providers into two entities: infrastructure providers who manage the physical network infrastructures, and service providers who create virtual networks for offering end-to-end services by aggregating networking resources from multiple network infrastructures (Chowdhury & Boutabak, 2009).

Infrastructure providers (InPs) are in charge of operations and maintenance of physical network infrastructures and offer their resources through programmable interfaces to different service providers instead of providing direct services to end users. Service providers (SPs) lease networking resources from multiple InPs to create virtual networks and deploy customized protocols in the virtual networks by programming the resources in multiple infrastructures. A virtual network is a collection of virtual nodes connected together by a set of virtual links to form a virtual topology, which is essentially a subset of the underlying physical topology. Each virtual node could be hosted on a particular physical node or could be a logical abstraction of a networking system. A virtual link spans over a path in the physical network and includes a portion of the networking resources along the path. Figure 2 illustrates a network virtualization environment, in which the service providers SP1 and SP2 construct two virtual networks by using resources from the infrastructure providers InP1 and InP2.

Network virtualization will bring a significant impact on all stakeholders in the networking areas. The best-effort Internet today is basically a commodity service that gives network service providers limited opportunities to distinguish themselves from competitors. Network virtualization offers a rich environment for innovations. This can stimulate the development of a wide range of new Internet services and will also drive investment in the core network infrastructure components needed to deliver new services. In a network virtualization environment, SPs are released from the requirement of purchasing, deploying, and maintaining physical network equipments, which

significantly lower the barrier to entry of the Internet service market. Network virtualization also enables a single SP obtain control over the entire end-to-end service delivery path across network infrastructures that belong to different domains, which will greatly facilitate the end-to-end QoS provisioning.

Recently network virtualization has attracted extensive interest from both academia and industry. New network architecture was proposed in (Turner & Taylor, 2005) for diversifying the Internet, which enables various meta-networks built on top of a physical substrate. The CABO Internet architecture proposed in (Feamster, Gao, & Rexford, 2007) decouples network service providers and infrastructure providers to support multiple network architectures over shared infrastructures. The EU FP7 4WARD project has also adopted network virtualization as a key technology to allow the future Internet run virtual networks in parallel (Niebert et al., 2008). Some standard organizations are also embracing the notion of network virtualization into their standard specifications. For example the Next Generation Network (NGN) architecture defined by ITU-T follows a key principle of separating service-related functions from underlying transport-related technologies (Song et al., 2007). The Open Mobile Alliance (OMA) recently developed an Open Service Environment (OSE) that delivers network services by composing standard service enablers, which are virtualization components of networking resources (OMA, 2009). An overview of more research efforts and progresses in the area of network virtualization can be found from the survey given in (Chowdhury & Boutabak, 2009).

SERVICE-ORIENTED NETWORKING

This section presents a new service-oriented networking paradigm that applies the SOA principle and employs network virtualization to enable integration of networking and distributed computing

Figure 2. Illustration of a network virtualization environment

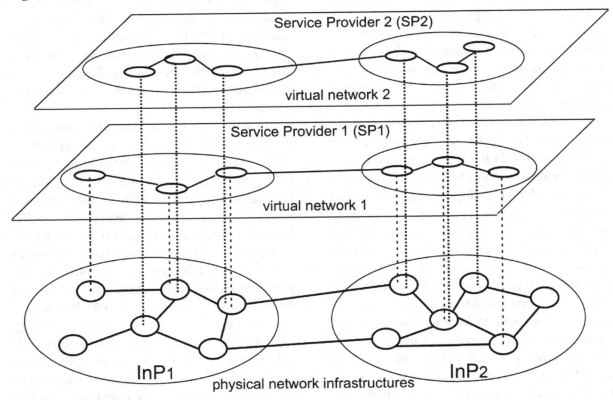

systems. Through such integration, networking resources and other types of computational resources merge seamlessly into a network-based distributed computing platform for meeting the requirements of various distributed applications.

In general key functions of a distributed computing system include data processing, data storage, and data communications among the processing and storage components distributed across the system. Currently SOA-based distributed computing systems mainly focus on virtualizing and encapsulating the resources and capacities of data processing and storage functions into services. Data communication functions are provided by the underlying networking systems, which are typically managed independently with the distributed system. Networking systems are becoming the integrant of the next generation distributed computing systems. Therefore encapsulating networking resources also in form of services by following the same SOA principle will enable distributed systems to view and manage all functional components, including data processing, storage, and communications, through a uniform mechanism. In this way, the conventional SOA-based distributed systems will be extended to a composite distributed service provisioning platform in which services can be abstract modules of both computing and networking resources. This new networking paradigm that encapsulates networking resources into network services by following the SOA principle is referred to as *Service-Oriented Networking* (SON) in this chapter.

Network virtualization embraces the SON paradigm and plays a significantly role in realizing the SON for networking and computing integration. Network virtualization de-couples data transportation functions provided by network infrastructures from network service provisioning functions that utilized by distributed systems. Such de-coupling allows networking resources to be accessed through standard and programmable interfaces, and enables networking resources to be virtualized and encapsulated into network services offered by network infrastructures. Though developed independently with the SOA and distributed computing, principles and practices of network virtualization can be brought into SOA-based distributed computing systems in the SON paradigm. Network virtualization provides a means to present abstracted networking capabilities to upper-layer software, including distributed computing systems and applications. This allows for the use of networking capabilities without having to address the specific dependencies of certain types of low-level network protocols and hardware. Because of the heterogeneity of network protocols, equipments, and technologies, exposing networking capabilities to upper layer distributed systems without virtualization would lead to unmanageable complexity. The abstraction of networking resources through the virtualization-based SON paradigm can address the diversity and significantly reduce complexity of the integration of networking and distributed computing.

A layered architecture of the SON for networking and distributed computing integration is shown in Figure 3. At the bottom of this architecture is the resource layer, which consists of physical infrastructures that provide both networking resources and computational resources. Above the resource layer is the virtualization layer. At this layer network virtualization enables the resources in network infrastructures to be encapsulated into networking services, just as the abstraction of computational resources into computing services, both by following the SOA principle. The service provisioning layer is above the virtualization layer and below the application layer. This layer discovers and selects both networking services

and computing services, and synthesizes them into composite distributed services that match the requirements of various distributed applications. This figure shows that in SON networking resources are virtualized, accessed, and managed through a unified mechanism as computational resources like CPU capacity and memory/disk space. Therefore networking services are integrated with computing services into a composite distributed service provisioning platform for supporting the requirements of various applications.

The network virtualization-based SON paradigm provides multiple benefits to the next generation distributed computing. SON supports a wider range of data communication services with more attributes than the services that can be offered by traditional networking technologies. In SON, networking resources, virtualized and encapsulated in SOA-compliant services, may be combined in almost limitless ways with other service components that abstract both computational and networking resources; thus greatly expanding the services that can be offered by the composite distributed computing platform to various applications. SON offers the ability to match application requirements to communication services through discovering and selecting the appropriate networking services, and composing them with computing services. SON de-couples underlying network infrastructures from upper-layer service provisioning; thus allowing new distributed applications to be developed and deployed without being limited by the evolution of underlying networking technologies.

The SON paradigm may also lead to a new model for Internet service and distributed computing service delivery. Figure 3 shows that in SON the provisioning of networking services and computing services, which used to be offered separately by the traditional networking and distributed computing systems, merge into one provisioning layer for composite distributed services. This convergence of service provisioning in SON enables a new service delivery model

Figure 3. Layered architecture of SON for networking and distributed computing integration

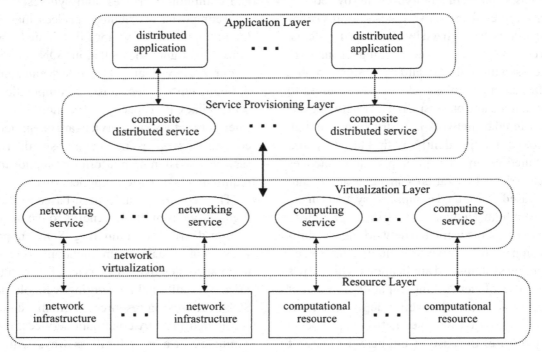

in which the roles of traditional network service providers (for example AT&T and Verizon) and distributed computing service providers (for example Google and Amazon) merge together into one role of generic service provisioning. The new service delivery model may stimulate innovations in service development and create new business opportunities in the market of Internet-based distributed computing services and applications.

As service description and discovery being key technologies for realizing the SOA, description and discovery of network services are keys to implementing the SON paradigm. A distinguishing feature of network services is their capabilities of guaranteeing a certain level of networking QoS. Therefore a network service description should provide sufficient information about the networking capability that can be offered by the service. In addition, network service discovery and composition must select and synthesize the appropriate network services for meeting the end-to-end networking performance required

by distributed applications. The SON, as a new technology for integrating computer networks and distributed computing systems, involves inter-discipline research collaboration across the two communities of distributed computing and networking.

The currently available technologies for Web service description and discovery must to be enhanced to meet the special requirements of SON. The WSDL specification focuses on providing functional information about services and UDDI standard lacks an effective mechanism to publish and search service features such as service provisioning capabilities. Recently World Wide Web Consortium (W3C) developed WS-Policy (Vedamuthu et al., 2007) and WS-PolicyAttachment (Bajaj et al., 2007) specifications for describing non-functional characteristics of Web services. WS-Policy aims to provide a general-purpose framework and model for expressing service characteristics such as requirements, preference, and capabilities as policies. WS-PolicyAttachment defines a mechanism to associate the policy expressions with the existing WSDL standard. The WS-Agreement specification (Andrieux, 2007) developed by the Open Grid Forum (OGF) defines a protocol between service providers and service users for establishing and managing service level agreements. Although significant progresses toward QoS-enable Web/Grid service description and discovery have been made in the aforementioned developments, description of network service capabilities and discovery of network services for meeting performance requirements are left open as domain-specific fields in those specifications.

The networking research community has also started exploring application of the service-orientation concept to enhance network service provisioning. The authors of (Baroncelli & et al., 2005; Martini & et al., 2005) introduced a service plane to enhance utilization of automatically switched transport networks. In (Verdi & et al., 2006) a service layer employing Web services technology was adopted in a service-oriented management scheme to enhance network management. The authors of (Mambretti & et al., 2006) proposed a virtualization service layer to enable dynamic light path service provisioning in an intelligent optical network. A User Controlled Light Path (UCLP) system developed in (Grasa & et al., 2008) provides a Web services-based network virtualization framework to enable users to build their own applications without dealing with the complexity of the underlying technologies. An application-driven network control mechanism was developed and evaluated in (Martini & et al., 2009), which applies the SOA principle in the resource management of GMPLS-controlled optical networks to enable QoS control on a per-application basis.

Though some interesting research results have been obtained in this interdisciplinary area, network service capability description, performance-based network service discovery and composition, and network service information publication and updating are still important opening issues that need extensive investigation. The rest of this chapter presents a network service broker system as a key component in the SON for network service discovery, and also discusses technologies for describing and updating information about network service capabilities in large scale dynamic networking environments.

NETWORK SERVICE BROKER SYSTEM

Discovering the appropriate network services that meet distributed application requirements plays a crucial role in SON. Through SOA-based network virtualization in SON, upper-layer distributed applications can utilize the data communication capacities provided by underlying network infrastructures as network services. A network service broker, acting as a mediator between network infrastructures and distributed applications, simplifies the process of matching application requirements to available networking capabilities by aggregating offers from multiple network infrastructures.

The structure of a network service broker system for SON is shown in Figure 4. The system consists of a Network Service Broker (NSB), a Network Service Registry (NSR), Network Service Providers (NSPs), and Network Service Consumers (NSCs). The network service providers here could be the SPs in network virtualization who provide end-to-end network services, or network infrastructure providers that offer infrastructure services. A network service consumer could be a distributed computing application or another service that needs to access networking resources. Each network service provider compiles a service description and publishes the description at the network service registry. Whenever a distributed application needs to utilize the underlying networking resources for data communications, the application becomes a service consumer and submits a network service request to the service

Figure 4. Structure of a network service broker system for service-oriented networking

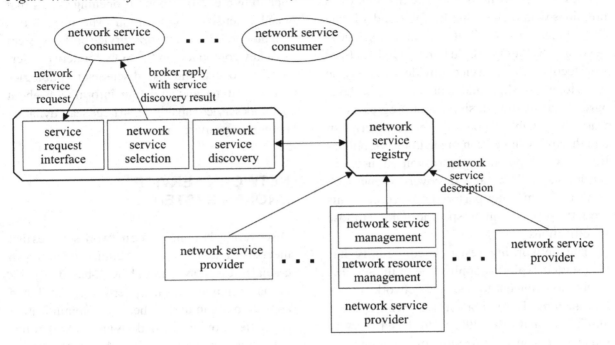

broker. The broker searches the network service descriptions published at the service registry and discovers the appropriate network service that meets the networking requirements for the application. After receiving the service discovery result from the broker, the application will be able to access the discovered network service through the interface described in the service description.

Each network service provider is required to implement two functional modules for supporting SON: a Network Service Management (NSM) module and a Network Resource Management (NRM) module. The NSM module serves as the interface between the internal implementation of the network service and its surrounding environment. The main functions of NSM include registering the network service to the service registry, collecting network state information from the NRM module to compile a network service description, and publishing the service description at the service registry. The network states collected by the NSM module include the currently available networking resources and capacities in

the network infrastructure, which will be embedded in the network service description published at the service registry. The NSM module is also responsible for updating the network service description at the service registry when the network state information (such as the available networking capacity) changes. The NRM module manages the networking resources that belong to the service provider in order to guarantee the networking QoS required by each consumer of this service.

The network service broker comprises three modules: Service Request Interface (SRI), Network Service Discovery (NSD), and Network Service Selection (NSS). When a service consumer needs to discover a network service, the consumer submits a network service request to the service broker through the SRI interface. In order for the service broker to conduct performance-based network service discovery and selection, the service request submitted to the broker should specify the following three aspects of demand information: a) the source and destination addresses for the data communication; b) the networking performance required by the service consumer, such as the minimum bandwidth and maximum delay for data transportation; c) the characteristics of the traffic load for the network service. The traffic load characteristics are needed by the service broker to estimate the achievable networking performance of the discovered network services under the traffic load.

On receiving the network service request, the service discovery module (NSD) of the network service broker accesses the service registry to find all available network services that support data communication from the source to the destination specified in the service request. These network services are selected as candidate services. For each candidate service, the service selection module (NSS) uses the networking capacity information published in its service description and the traffic load characteristics specified in the service request to evaluate the achievable networking performance that the service can offer to the consumer. Then the NSS module compares the predicted performance with the requirements given in the service request and selects the service that meets all performance requirements given by the consumer. If multiple candidate network services meet the requirements, selection among them is based on other criteria such as service cost or load balance. After selecting a network service, the network service broker will send a reply message through the SRI interface to notify the service consumer the result of network service selection. Then the consumer may contact the selected network service provider to negotiate a Service Level Agreement (SLA). The NRM module in the selected network service may need to allocate a certain amount of networking resources for QoS provisioning in order to guarantee the SLA. After resource allocation, the NSM module in the same network service will accordingly update the network capability states and republish an updated service description at the service registry to reflect the latest networking capability offered by the service provider. Other functions of the service broker system, including publishing network service descriptions, maintaining service descriptions at the registry, searching the registry for candidate network services, and negotiating and establishing a SLA, can be implemented based on the current SOA standards and technologies. The interaction procedure for network service description and discovery is shown in Figure 5.

NETWORK SERVICE DESCRIPTION AND INFORMATION UPDATING

A key extension to the currently available service description specifications to support network service des in SON is to include descriptive information about data transport capabilities offered by network infrastructures. Such descriptive information also forms the basis of performance-based network service discovery, selection, and composition. A main challenge to describing network service capabilities comes from the heterogeneity of the networking systems that will be utilized by the next generation distributed computing. Emerging distributed applications could be built on top of various networking systems including both fixed and mobile networks, both wired and wireless networks, both IP-based packet switching networks and alternative connection-oriented networks. Furthermore, data communications for a distributed application could traverse across multiple networks with different implementations. Therefore, network service description requires a general approach that is agnostic to specific networking technologies and architecture. Another challenge lies in the scale and complexity of the underlying networking systems for the next generation distributed computing, which may span across different network domains with a multilevel hierarchical structure. This requires high level aggregation and abstraction of networking resources in network service description.

This section presents a general model for describing service capabilities of various network

Figure 5. The interaction procedure for network service description, discovery, and selection

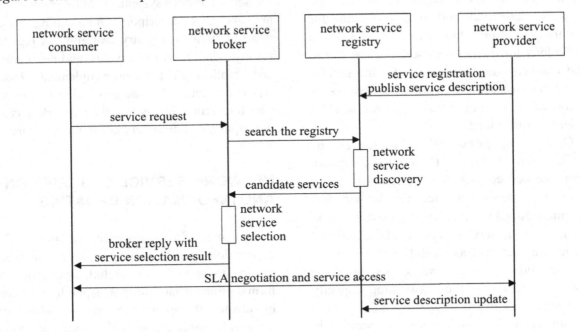

infrastructures. The core functions offered by a network service can be categorized into two aspects: the connectivity supported by the service and the data transportation capacity for each connection provided by the service. Connectivity can be described by enumerating all the pairs of source and destination between which the network infrastructure can transport data. Transport capacity of the connection from a source to a destination needs to be described by a set of parameters. The service capability of a networking system with m ingresses and n egresses can be modeled by an $m \times n$ matrix $\mathbf{C}$. The element $\mathbf{c}[i, j]$ of this matrix gives a descriptor for the data transportation capacity offered by the networking system from the ingress i to the egress j. In general the element $\mathbf{c}[i, j]$ is a vector that consists of multiple parameters that describe data transport attributes, for example the available bandwidth and the transmission delay on the network route from the ingress i to the egress j. A possible descriptor that can be used as the element $\mathbf{c}[i, j]$ in the matrix $\mathbf{C}$ is the service curve guaranteed by the networking system

for data transportation from the ingress i to the egress j (Duan & Lu, 2009). A service curve, as defined in network calculus (Boudec & Thiran, 2001), gives a lower bound of the amount of data transportation that a network service offers from an ingress to an egress during an arbitrary time interval. A service curve guaranteed by a network route is independent with the implementation technologies of the route; thus can be used as a general descriptor for networking capabilities of various network services.

Currently there are mechanisms available for measuring and managing network state information, for example the technologies reported in (Kind & et al., 2008) and (Prasad & et al., 2003). Various approaches are also available to aggregate low-level network states into a high-level abstraction (Uludag & et al., 2007). The methods of collecting and aggregating network state information are implementation dependent and may vary in different network infrastructures, but the matrix $\mathbf{C}$ with a capability descriptor as each element provides all network service providers with a general approach to describing their networking capabilities in service descriptions.

In a large scale dynamic networking environment such as the Internet, the states and capacity information of various networking systems change frequently. Therefore keeping the latest network service descriptions at the service registry is significant for discovering and selecting the appropriate network services. However, republishing the entire service description whenever a network state change occurs may cause a large amount of communication and management overhead between service providers and the service registry. This makes the service registry a performance bottleneck in the network service broker system. In order to solve this problem, an event-driven subscription-notification mechanism can be applied to reduce the overhead caused by frequent service description update; thus improving the overall performance of the network service broker system.

Event-driven processing introduces a subscription-notification pattern for SOA implementations. In this pattern an information producer sends one-way notification messages to one or more interested receivers. A notification message typically carries information about an event that has occurred. The message receivers must register to the producer before receiving notifications. The OASIS Web Service Notification (Graham, Hull, & Murray, 2006) is a family of related specifications that define a standard approach to notification using a topic-based subscription-publication mechanism. This mechanism can be employed in the network service broker system for improving the performance of service description updating. The network service registry can subscribe to a network service provider and specify a set of network states as subscription topics. Then, the service registry will receive a notification message from the service provider whenever a change occurs to a network state that is subscribed as a topic. A threshold can also be set to each subscription topic so that an update notification is triggered only when the amount of change in that topic is greater than the threshold. In this way, the network service registry can obtain the latest network state and capability information for network discovery and selection without being overloaded by frequent service description update. Since the notification message contains only the changed states instead of the entire service description and an update only happens when a network state changes more than a pre-specified threshold, this updating mechanism can greatly reduce communication and management overhead.

The interaction procedure for network service description and discovery with event-driven information update is shown in Figure 6. When a network service provider publishes its network service description for the first time at the service registry, the service registry subscribes to the service provider for receiving notifications of network state changes. The service registry can specify a set of network states as subscription topics. After this registration-subscription procedure completes, the network service registry will be notified whenever a specified subscription topic is changed in the network service. Then the description for this network service will be updated accordingly at the service registry.

The performance of the network service broker system could be further improved by reducing the information updating overhead through a technology for partial service description publication. This technology allows network service providers to publish only a part of their service descriptions at the service registry. This part of description could include information such as the network types, network service operators, and also connectivity information such as a list of source-destination pairs between which a network service offers data transportation. The published part of description is relatively stable for typical networks and does not need frequent update. If a network service is selected as a candidate service, then the NSS module in the service broker will contact the NSM module in the service provider

Figure 6. The interaction procedure for network service description, discovery, and selection with event-driven information update

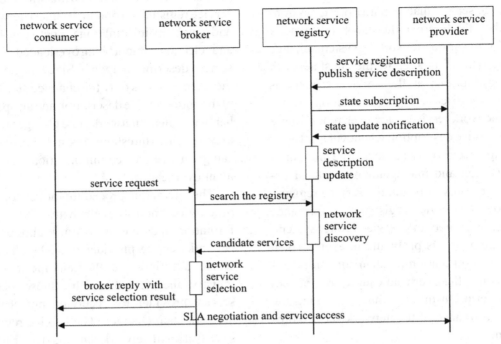

Figure 7. The interaction procedure for network service description, discovery, and selection with partial publication of network service description

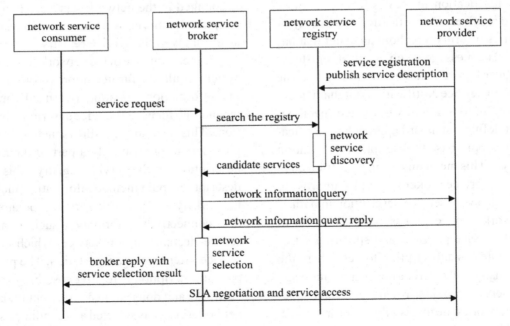

to retrieve additional information needed for service selection, for example retrieving information about the available bandwidth and transmission delay on a network route for performance evaluation. In this way dynamic state information of each network service is maintained within the service provider instead of at the service registry; thus can be updated in real time without generating communication overhead between the service provider and the service registry. The partial publication technology can be used together with the event-driven update mechanism. Update on the published part of description can be implemented by the notifications from the network service provider. Since only the relatively static part of description is published at the registry, the update frequency and the messaging load will be further reduced. Figure 7 shows the interaction procedure for network service description, discovery, and selection with partial service description publication.

CONCLUSION

With the rapid development of various emerging distributed computing technologies such as Web services, Grid computing, and Cloud computing, computer networks become the integrant of the next generation distributed computing systems. Therefore, integration of networking and distributed computing systems becomes an important research problem for building the next-generation high-performance distributed information infrastructure. The SOA will serve as a architectural principle for the next generation distributed computing and network virtualization is expected to play a crucial role in the future Internet. The SOA together with network virtualization offer a promising approach to integrating networking resources into distributed computing systems.

This chapter presents a new SON paradigm that applies the SOA principle and employs network virtualization to enable the integration between computer networks and distributed computing systems. The SON virtualizes networking resources offered by various network infrastructures and encapsulates them in the form of services by following the SOA principle. Network services can be discovered and selected by distributed computing systems, and can also be composed and orchestrated with other computational resources into composite distributed services to support various distributed applications. Network virtualization plays a significant role in SON by decoupling network service provisioning from specific data transportation technologies and allowing network infrastructures to be accessed as services. This chapter particularly discusses network service description and discovery as key technologies of SON and describes a network service broker system as a key component for implementing network service description and discovery. A general approach to describing network service capabilities and an information updating mechanism are also discussed in this chapter for improving performance of the service broker system in heterogeneous and dynamic networking environments

REFERENCES

Anderson, T., Peterson, L., Shenker, S., & Turner, J. (2005). Overcoming the Internet impasse through virtualization. *IEEE Computer*, *38*(4), 34–41.

Andrieux, A., Czajkowski, K., Dan, A., Keahey, K., Ludwig, H., Nakata, T., ... Xu, M. (2007). *Web services agreement (WS-agreement) specification*. Open Grid Forum (OGF) Recommendation.

Bajaj, S., Curbera, F., Hondo, M., Kaler C., Maruyama, H., Nadalin, A,. ... Shewchuk, J. (2006). *Web services policy attachment* (WS-policy attachment). World Wide Web Consortium (W3C) Recommendation.

Baroncelli, F., Martini, B., Valcarenghi, L., & Castoldi, P. (2005). A service oriented network architecture suitable for global Grid computing. *Proceedings of IEEE Conference on Optical Network Design and Modeling*, (pp. 283-293).

Barreto, C., Bullard, V., Erl, T., Evdemon, J., Jordan, D., & Kand, K. (2007). *Web services business process execution language (WS-BPEL) v 2.0. Organization for the Advancement of Structured Information Standards (OASIS)*. Specification.

Bavier, A., Bowman, M., Chun, B., Culler, D., Karlin, S., & Muir, S. … Wawrzoniak, M. (2004). Operating system support for planetary-scale network services. *Proceedings of the 1st Symposium on Network System Design and Implementation*, (pp. 253-266).

Boudec, J. L., & Thiran, P. (2001). *Network calculus: A theory of deterministic queuing systems for the Internet*. Springer Verlag.

Channabasavaiah, K., Holley, K., & Tuggle, E. (2003). *Migrating to a service-oriented architecture*. IMB DeveloperWorks.

Chinnici, R., Moreau, J., Ryman, A., & Weerawarana, S. (2007). *Web services description language (WSDL) v 2.0*. World Wide Web Consortium (W3C) Recommendation.

Chowdhury, N., & Boutabak, R. (2009). Network virtualization: State of the art and research challenges. *IEEE Communications*, *47*(7), 20–26. doi:10.1109/MCOM.2009.5183468

Clement, L., Hately, A., Riegen, C., & Rogers, T. (2004). *Universal description, discovery and integration (UDDI) v 3.0. Organization for the Advancement of Structured Information Standards (OASIS)*. Specification.

Duan, Q., & Lu, E. (2009). Network service description and discovery for the next generation Internet. *International Journal of Computer Networks*, *1*(1), 46–65.

Feamster, N., Gao, L., & Rexford, J. (2007). How to lease the Internet in your spare time. *ACM SIGCOMM Computer Communications Review*, *37*(1), 61–64. doi:10.1145/1198255.1198265

Foster, I., Zhao, Y., Raicu, I., & Lu, S. (2008). Cloud computing and Grid computing 360-degree compared. *Proc. of the 2008 Grid Computing Environment Workshop*.

GENI Planning Group. (2006). GENI design principles. *IEEE Computer*, *39*(9), 102–105.

Graham, S., Hull, D., & Murray, B. (2006). *Web services base notification (WS-BaseNotification) v 1.3*. Organization for the Advancement of Structured Information Standards (OASIS) specification.

Grasa, E., Junyent, G., Figuerola, S., Lopez, A., & Savoie, M. (2008). UCLPv2: A network virtualization framework built on Web services. *IEEE Communications*, *46*(3), 126–134. doi:10.1109/MCOM.2008.4463783

Gudgin, M., Hadely, M., Mendelsohn, N., Moreau, J.-J., Nielsen, H. F., Karmarkar, A., & Lafon, Y. (2007). *Simple object access protocol (SOAP) v 1.2. World Wide Web Consortium (W3C)*. Specification.

Kind, A., Dimitropoulos, X., Denazis, S., & Claise, B. (2008). Advanced network monitoring brings life to the awareness plane. *IEEE Communications*, *46*(10), 140–146. doi:10.1109/MCOM.2008.4644132

Mambretti, J., Lillethun, D., Lange, J., & Weinberger, L. (2006). Optical dynamic intelligent network services (ODIN): An experimental control-plane architecture for high-performance distributed environments based on dynamic lightpath provisioning. *IEEE Communications*, *44*(3), 92–99. doi:10.1109/MCOM.2006.1607871

Martini, B., Baroncelli, F., & Castoldi, P. (2005). A novel service-oriented framework for automatic switched transport networks. *Proc. of IFIP/IEEE Symposium on Integrated Network Management*, (pp. 295-308).

Niebert, N., Baucke, S., Khayat, I., Johnson, M., & Ohlman, B. (2008). The way 4WARD to creation of a future Internet. *Proc. of the IEEE 19th International Symposium on Personal, Indoor and Mobile Radio Communications*.

Papazoglou, M. P. (2008). *Web services: Principles and technology*. Pearson Prentice Hall.

Prasad, R., Murray, M., Dovrolis, C., & Claffy, K. (2003). Bandwidth estimation: Metrics, measurement techniques, and tools. *IEEE Network, 17*(6), 27–35. doi:10.1109/MNET.2003.1248658

Song, J., Chang, M. Y., Lee, S. S., & Joung, J. (2007). Overview of ITU-T NGN QoS control. *IEEE Communications, 45*(9), 116–123. doi:10.1109/MCOM.2007.4342866

The Open Mobile Alliance (OMA). (2009). *OMA service environment*, version 1.0.5.

Turner, J., & Taylor, D. E. (2005). Diversifying the Internet. *Proc. of the IEEE 2005 Global Communication Conference*.

Uludag, S., Lui, K.-S., Nahrstedt, K., & Brewster, G. (2007). Analysis of topology aggregation techniques for QoS routing. *ACM Computing Surveys, 39*(3), paper 7.

Vedamuthu, A., Orchard, D., Hirsch, F., Hondo, M., Yendluri, P., Boubez, T., & Yalçinalp, Ü. (2007). *Web services policy (WS-policy) framework v 1.5*. World Wide Web Consortium (W3C) Recommendation.

Verdi, F. L., Duarte, R., Lacerda, F. C., Medeira, E., Cardozo, E., & Magalhaes, M. (2006). Provisioning and management of inter-domain connections in optical networks: A service-oriented architecture-based approach. *Proc. of IEEE Conference of Network Operations and Management*.

Chapter 16
Long–Term Evolution (LTE):
Broadband–Enabled Next Generation of Wireless Mobile Cellular Network

Bing He
Aviat Networks Inc., USA

Bin Xie
InfoBeyond Technology LLC, USA

Sanjuli Agrawal
InfoBeyond Technology LLC, USA

David Zhao
CERDEC, USA

Ranga Reddy
CERDEC, USA

ABSTRACT

With the ever growing demand on high throughput for mobile users, 3G cellular networks are limited in their network capacity for offering high data services to a large number of users. Consequently, many Internet services such as on-demand video and mobile TV are hard to be satisfactorily supported by the current 3G cellular networks. 3GPP Long Term Evolution (LTE) is a recently proposed 4G standard, representing a significant advance of 3G cellular technology. Attractively, LTE would offer an uplink data speed up to 50 Mbps and a downlink speed up to 100 Mbps for various services such as traditional voice, high-speed data, multimedia unicast, and multimedia broadcasting. In such a short time, it has been broadly accepted by major wireless vendors such as Verizon-Vodafone, AT&T, NTT-Docomo, KDDI, T-Mobile, and China Mobile. In order for high data link speed, LTE adapts new technologies that are new to 3G network such as Orthogonal Frequency Division Multiplexing (OFDM) and Multiple-Input Multiple-Output (MIMO). MIMO allows the use of more than one antenna at the transmitter and receiver

DOI: 10.4018/978-1-61350-110-8.ch016

Copyright © 2012, IGI Global. Copying or distributing in print or electronic forms without written permission of IGI Global is prohibited.

for higher data transmission. The LTE bandwidth can be scalable from 1.25 to 20 MHz, satisfying the need of different network operators that may have different bandwidth allocations for services, based on its managed spectrum. In this chapter, we discuss the major advance of the LTE and its recent research efforts in improving its performance. Our illustration of LTE is comprehensive, spanning from the LTE physical layer to link layer. In addition, the LTE security is also discussed.

INTRODUCTION

Long-Term Evolution (LTE)(3GPP TS 36.300) is a cellular network technology for mobile phone systems, which has a history of almost thirty years. The cellular network capacity can be defined as the average throughput (or data bit rate) per user which is the key issue in providing high quality services for users. It is well known that cellular network suffers from the limited network capacity, especially with the increase in the number of users in the network. This drives the cellular networks towards Broadband Wireless Access (BWA) such as LTE for providing high-speed wireless access over a wide area while satisfying the Quality of Service (QoS) requirement for a variety of services.

Figure 1 illustrates the milestones of cellular technologies from the second generation (2G) to the fourth generation (4G) and shows the increase of the network capacity. Before 2G, the first generation (1G) of cellular network is analog FDMA system, developed in the early of 1980. The use of digital modulation such as TDMA (Time Division Multiple Access) is the significant progress of the 2 generation (2G), as compared to 1G. GSM (Global System for Mobile Communications) is the most popular 2G system, representing the huge success of 2G. Most GSM networks (in Europe) operate in the 900 MHz or 1800 MHz bands. However, the 850 MHz and 1900 MHz bands were used in Canada and the United States. In the 2G mobile system, roaming and security are enhanced with the support of user handoff from a base station (BS) to a neighboring BS.

The 2G cellular system with the addition of General Packet Radio Service (GPRS) and En-

hanced Data Rates for GSM Evolution (EDGE) is mostly referred as the 2.5G. The original GSM is limited by its network capacity and the per user data rate is scaled by several kbits/s. Upon the original GSM system, the packet data capability is added for packet-oriented mobile data service by means of GPRS in 1997. GPRS provides data rates of 56 kbit/s or more. In 1999, EDGE further improved the speed data transmission. EDGE is also known as Enhanced GPRS (EGPRS) and is first deployed on the GSM system in 2003. The Evolved EDGE typically offers bit-rates of 400kbit/s.

UMTS is one of the third generation (3G) of mobile communication and is the first version is release in 1999 (release99 (R99)). Most of the UMTS systems use Wideband Code Division Multiple Access (WCDMA), which achieves a higher speed and supports more users compared to TDMA. It supports the maximum theoretical data rate of 21 Mbit/s and the user can expect a rate up to 384 kbit/s for R99 handsets and 7.2 Mbit/s for HSDPA handsets in the downlink connection. CDMA2000 EV DO is another 3G technology that is operated on the IP-based backbone. Its downlink achieves up to 2.4 Mbit/s with Rev. 0 and up to 3.1 Mbit/s with Rev. A. The uplink rate for Rev. 0 can operate up to 153 kbit/s while Rev. A can operate at up to 1.8 Mbit/s. The CDMA2000 EV-DO Rev. A and EV-DO Rev. B are considered as the 3.5G technology, offering high data rates for users. High-Speed Downlink Packet Access (HSDPA) is alternative 3.5G network developed based on the UMTS for higher data transfer speeds and capacity. The HSDPA downlink speeds achieve 1.8, 3.6, 7.2 and 14.0 Mbit/s and HSPA+ achieves higher data rate with speeds of up to 42

Figure 1. LTE evolution path

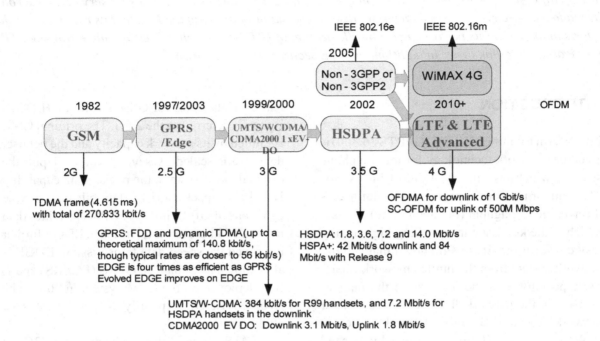

Mbit/s downlink and 84 Mbit/s with Release 9 of the 3GPP standards.

All of the above 2G, 2.5G, 3G, 3.5G, and LTE technologies are standardized by 3GPP or 3GPP2. There are other industry consortiums developing broadband wireless access technology, besides 3GPP or 3GPP2. WiMAX (Worldwide Interoperability for Microwave Access) is an IEEE standard for broadband wireless connectivity with at least equivalent access speed as cable modems. The IEEE standard is called IEEE 802.16 (its commercial version is referred as the WiMAX), officially known as WirelessMAN. The earlier WiMAX version is IEEE 802.16e in 2005 to enable high speed and differential QoS for various services. IEEE 802.16j then adds the relaying capability to IEEE 802.16e in which the Relaying Stations can be placed to extend the BS radio coverage. In the PHY layer, IEEE 802.16e uses scalable OFDMA (Orthogonal Frequency-Division Multiple Access) to carry data, supporting channel bandwidths of between 1.25 MHz and 20 MHz, with up to 2048 sub-carriers. The adaptive modulation and coding consider the signal conditions: good, poor, or intermediate. In good signal, a highly efficient 64 QAM (Quaternary Amplitude Modulation) coding scheme is used. If the signal is poor, a more robust BPSK (Binary Phase Shift Keying) coding mechanism is used. In intermediate conditions, 16 QAM and QPSK can also be employed. The 802.16e MAC layer specifies the QoS differentiation that allocates each service flow between the Subscriber Station[1] (SS) and the BS with difference QoS mechanisms. In 802.16e, there are five QoS classes: Unsolicited Grant Service (UGS), Extended Real-time Polling Service (ertPS), Real-time Polling Service (rtPS), Non-real-time Polling Service (nrtPS), Best Effort (BE). According to these classes, the BS implements different QoS request and grant protocols with QoS provisioning. The BS and the SS adapts each service flow with an appropriate QoS class to ensure the bandwidth and delay requirements of the service. A BS covers up to 30 miles with which the ubiquitous broadband access. Moreover, the standard of IEEE 802.16e can support the mobility speed of up to 70-80 mph and the asymmetrical link structure that enables the SS to support various terminal devices, e.g., PDAs, cell phones, or laptops. Recently, the IEEE has begun working on a new version of the 802.16 standard, dubbed 802.16m, which could increase the data rate up to 1Gbps while maintaining backwards compatibility with existing WiMAX radios.

As an alternative of WiMAX 4G, LTE evolutes from the UMTS, towards 4G mobile BWA network (Astely et al., 2009). Both of the WiMAX and LTE 4G are based on the OFDMA modulation to achieve high network capacity. However, the UMTS LTE evolves from the UMTS 3G and it is officially known as the evolved UMTS terrestrial radio access (E-UTRA) and evolved UMTS terrestrial radio access network (E-UTRAN). In November 2004, 3GPP began a project to define the long-term evolution of UMTS cellular technology. 3GPP Release 8 is the major progress for 4G to provide the enhanced cellular system capacity, extended coverage, high peak data rates, low latency, less deployment cost, OFDM based multi-antenna, flexible bandwidth operation, and seamless integration with existing systems. 3GPP Release 9 slightly enhances the performance of the Release 8. In 2009, 3GPP Release 10, known as LTE-Advanced, further enhances 3GPP release 8 with much higher peak rate, higher throughput and coverage, and lower latency for 4G user experience (Ghosh, Ratasuk, Mondal, Mangalvedhe, and Thomas, 2010, Mogensen et al. 2009).

The basic LTE network architecture is an evolution of UMTS and consequently most of the UMTS backbone infrastructure can be reused or upgraded. As a result, the UMTS/HSPA service providers will naturally evolve to LTE with the minimum cost. This may not be directly achieved by using the WiMAX 4G since additional cost is needed for integrating WiMAX with UMTS system. The main innovation of the LTE is the E-UTRAN for higher cellular network capacity,

which can be illustrated from three main aspects as below:

- **UE's eUTRAN Connection Capacity**: LTE provides the improved instantaneous peak data rates – 100Mbps to 326.4Mbps in the downlink and 50Mbps to 84.6Mbps in the uplink. The actual data rate depends on the antenna configuration (downlink 4x2, 2x2, 1x2, 1x1) and modulation depth. LTE improves system performance by allocating a specific number of subcarriers to a given user (or set of users) for a predetermined amount of time. One LTE eNodeB[2] cell supports up to 200 active users. It support user mobility in three scales: (i) Optimized for 0 ~ 15 km/h, (ii) 15 ~ 120 km/h supported with high performance, and (iii) Supported up to 350 km/h or even up to 500 km/h. The radio coverage are supported in three scales: (i) Full performance up to 5 km, (ii) Slight degradation 5 km – 30 km, (iii) Operation up to 100 km should not be precluded by standard.

- **UE's eUTRAN Connection Delay**: LTE reduces the latency – less than 100ms transition from camped state to active state, less than 50ms transition from dormant state to active state, and less than 5ms IP packet latency in the user plane in an unloaded system. It offers Enhanced Multimedia Broadcast Multicast Service (E-MBMS) and enhanced support for end-to-end QoS.

- **Spectrum Flexibility**: LTE is able to deploy the system in many different frequency bands, in paired and unpaired spectrum, and with different spectrum allocations (e.g., 1.25, 2.5, 5.0, 10.0, 15.0 and 20MHz).

Network planning and deployment doesn't always result in an eNodeB's coverage area being optimal. This is because the real coverage of an eNodeBs is not an idea circle as theory and the network domains are not ideally flat without

Figure 2. UMTS LTE network architecture

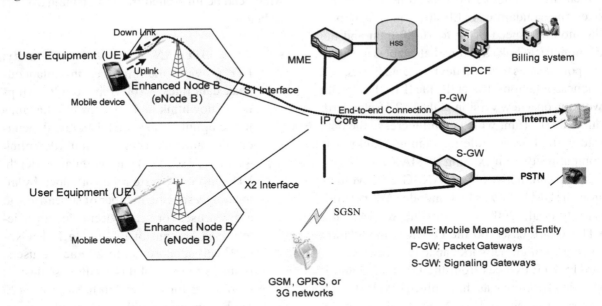

any obstructions. With this consideration, LTE-Advanced development will enable multi-hop relays in such a way that Relays can be deployed for coverage extension and network capacity enhancement. The Relays in the LTE is similar to WiMAX Relaying Stations (e.g. based on IEEE 802.16j/802.16m) to remove the coverage hole in the network as the Relaying Stations can connect to its nearest BSs by multi-hop links.

In this book chapter, we explore the LTE technology and its recent research progress. We structure this chapter as below. In Section 2, we illustrate the basic LTE concept with the illustration of network structure. Section 3 describes LTE PHY (physical) layer design, including the uplink and downlink resource management and user network accessibility. Then, the LTE link layer is discussed in Section 4. Section 5 depicts the handover process for user mobility support and Section 6 describes the LTE security issues. In Section 7, we discuss some open issues for LTE network. Finally, we conclude the chapter in Section 8.

LTE BASIC AND CONCEPT

This section illustrates LTE network architecture and the background of cellular network as well as its evolution. The first LTE version in Release 8 of the 3GPP specifications illustrates the basic LTE network architecture. In this architecture, single hop link is employed for mobile device to access the LTE network. Furthermore, the multi-hop communication is being considered as a part of LTE-Advanced that the mobile device can connect to the LTE base station by multi-hop path with the help of relaying station.

Basic LTE Network Architecture

Figure 2 shows the basic architecture of the UMTS LTE system (3GPP TS 36.300, 3GPP TS 33.401). The UMTS LTE network architecture includes two parts:

- **Evolved UMTS Terrestrial Radio Access Network (E-UTRAN or eUTRAN)**: The LTE E-UTRAN consists of a number of base stations that are stated as the enhanced Bode B (i.e., eNodeB or eNB). Figure 2 shows two eNodeBs which provide the wireless connectivity to mobile users. The user equipment (UE) connects to the eU-TRAN for voice or other services. Specifically, UEs communicate with eNo-deBs through the UE radio interface. The wireless link for the connectivity is based on SC-FDMA (Single-carrier FDMA) for the Uplink and OFDMA (Orthogonal Frequency-Division Multiple Access) for the downlink. Due to mobility of mobile users, the wireless connectivity for eU-TRAN should be provided by eNodeB anywhere and anytime. As GSM and 3G base stations, a number of eNodeBs are hexagonally situated in the network do-mains for full coverage and high radio re-utilization. The full coverage means that there is no coverage gap between to neigh-boring eNodeBs where each eNodeB has six neighboring eNodeBs. The hexagonal eNodeB placement can be repeatable with the extension of network domain, and thus, the radio spectrum can be reutilized if two eNodeBs are outside their interference ranges.

- **UMTS System Architecture Evolution (SAE)**: The UMTS LTE network architec-ture has a modular system design called the system architecture evolution – SAE. SAE consists of different components and the standardized interfaces allows these component to be flexibly added, re-moved, configured, or connected together to evolve or improve the capabilities of an existing UMTS infrastructures. The utili-zation of the existing systems reduces the deployment cost and supports component updates. The main components of the SAE include MME (Mobility Management Entity), S-GW (Serving Gateway), P-GW (Packet Data Network Gateway), and other network components such as HSS (Home Subscriber Server). The MME is the critical signaling node that setups and manage the UE connection. S-GW and P-GW are used for LTE bearer, connecting to the PSTN (Public Switched Telephone Network) or the Internet. As shown in Figure 2, each eNodeB connects to the MME by S1 inter-face via the IP core network. In addition, two eNodeBs can be directly connected with each other using an X2 interface. As shown in Figure 2, the MME connects to eNodeBs through the S1-MME interface and connects to S-GW through the S11 in-terface. In the SAE, multiple MMEs and and S-GWs can be managed as a group (e.g., pool) to meet increasing signaling load in the network. A pool of MMEs and S-GWs allow each eNodeB to be con-nected to multiple MMEs and SGWs in the pool. As a result, the pool could provide network redundancy and load sharing of traffic across network elements in the eNo-deBs, the MME, and the S-GW.

As shown in Figure 2, S-GW can also link to the SGSN (Serving GPRS Support Node). This allows the UMTS LTE system to interoperate with other mobile communication systems, such as GSM, GPRS, and WCDMA. We further illustrate the basic functionalities of these components in Figure 2 by using an example that an UE receives the packets from another network domain. Sup-pose an UE with a mobile device is connecting to an eNodeB and first is in the idle state. The key steps for a LTE service are:

- **UE's eUTRAN Connection**: The connec-tion from the UE to the eNodeB consists of the uplink and the downlink in the Physical layer. The uplink and downlink have dif-ferent network bandwidth availability for user services, both depending on the band-width requirements of the services. In the idle state, the bandwidth for the UE is not physically allocated. The final achievable bandwidth is allocated by the MME that again controls the radio resource of eNodeBs. The significant increase of the link bandwidth for user is the key improvement of LTE, compared to UMTS and other 3G networks. The improvement relies on physical layer technologies such as OFDM, MIMO, and smart antennas. They allow flexible and effective spectrum deployment in existing or new frequency spectrum.

- **Registration and Authentication**: IP-based registration and authentication are performed before a LTE service for the UE is initiated. Similar to the UMTS, a registration process occurs for the UE to visit a local LTE network. The MME is first response for initiating the paging and authentication of the mobile device. The UE will receive a temporary identity for its visitation to a local LTE domain. As the UE moves, the paging procedure allows the MME to track the location of the UE in which the UE continuously updates its current location to its home network (e.g., HSS). The authentication of the UE involves an authentication process by interacting with the visiting HSS and the HSS in the home network. The interactions check the authorization of the UE to camp on the service provider's Public Land Mobile Network (PLMN) and enforces UE roaming restrictions. Security keys are also negotiated during the authentication. LTE maintains interoperability with the existing UMTS system.

- **Service Starts and Terminations**: Due to updating the location at the UE's home network, the traffic (e.g., a voice call or data transmission) can be delivered to the current eNodeBs at the visiting network, and then the traffic is forwarded to the UE via the visiting eNodeB. Once the UE receives the first packet, it turns to active state. The MME is responsible for choosing the right gateway for traffic forwarding. During the service process, the MME assigns necessary resources to provide the required Quality of Service (QoS) for user. The service is also controlled by an S-GW or P-GW. The service session information from the S-GW is reported to a policy control and charging function (PCRF) which translates the information into billing records. Once the service ends, the resource used for the UE will be released and the UE returns to the idle state.

2.2 LTE-Advanced Multi-hop Network Architecture

Multi-hop communication could be an integral part of LTE for UE's eUTRAN connection. LTE-Advanced refers this as Multi-hop Cellular Network (MCN) that combines the benefits of both an ad hoc and cellular network. In the MCN, an UE can access an eNodeB by one or more relaying stations. LTE-advanced states the relaying stations as *relays*. Figure 3 illustrates the LTE-Advanced multi-hop network architecture. Figure 3 illustrates the LTE-Advanced multi-hop network architecture described by Lo and Niemegeers (2009), which illustrates two scenarios for multi-hop eUTRAN connection for coverage extension and capacity enhancement, respectively.

In the first scenario, the UE outside the radio coverage of eNodeB could connect the eNodeB with a multi-hop path. The multi-hop path is constructed by UE, eNobeB, and Relays 1 – 3. Therefore, the downlink and uplink for the UE's eUTRAN connection both travel through these relaying nodes. With the multi-hop eNodeB connectivity, this scenario can be used to extend the reach of the LTE-Advanced terrestrial cellular network to a group of mobile users that are away from the eNodeB. There are a number of applica-

Figure 3. UMTS LE multi-hop network architecture

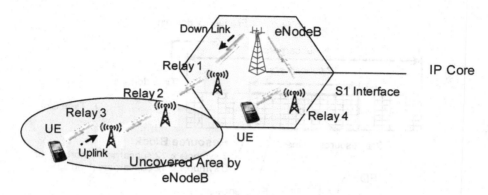

tions that can benefit the coverage extension. The eNodeB coverage can extend to the tunnel (suburban areas, or villages) for many civilian applications. The users in the ocean oil platform could rely on the multi-hop relay for accessing the eUTRAN on the land. For such a purpose, the relays are statically (or minimal movement) situated on the buoys, forming multi-hop paths to the oil platforms. The offshore ships (e.g., Navy consolidated afloat offshore networks) can be connected to the eNodeB by dynamically relaying paths while the relays are placed either at buoys or ships. Otherwise, the users at the oil platform or ships have to solely rely on the satellite communication which is quite expensive.

In the second scenario, two-hop relay can be employed by UE even if it is under the radio coverage of the eNodeB. In Figure 3, Relay 4 is the LTE relay for enhancing the eNodeB capacity. Due to relay, a single transmission between a UE and an eNodeB can be broken into two continuous transmissions. The two-hop connection reduces the transmission distance for each hop, and thus achieves higher data rates as compared to long single-hop transmission. Because of low transmission power employed in each transmission, it can also reduce the co-channel interference. A Relay can enhance the eNodeB capacity by using multi-hop relaying and diverting the traffic from a congested eNodeB to a neighboring eNodeB. The relaying link for Relay could employ the frequency

bands that are different to the accessing links, depending on the access control strategy used at the eNodeB. The relay achieves load balancing among eNodeBs, thereby increasing the effective network system capacity.

LTE PHY LAYER

The LTE PHY is a high efficient means of conveying the data and control information between an eNodeB and UE. The LTE standardization efforts aim for spectral efficiency and coverage. As discussed, the connection between the UE and the eNodeB is divided into downlink (DL) and uplink (UL). The DL is the transmission from the eNodeB to the UE and the UL is the transmission of the opposite direction. In this section, we illustrate the DL and UL transmission technologies.

Resource Block

The entire bandwidth is divided into a number of Physical Resource Blocks (PRBs) (Pokhariyal, Kolding, and Mogensen, 2006). Figure 4 shows the downlink resource grid that is formulated in the frequency and time domains. In the frequency domain, each PRB consists of several (e.g., 12 as shown in Figure 4) resource elements which are called subcarriers. One resource block of 12 subcarriers spans through 180 kHz. Let N be the total

Figure 4. Downlink resource grid and CQI

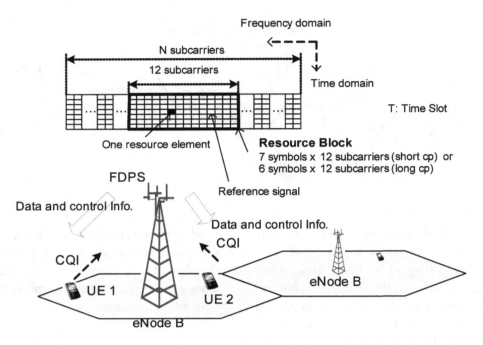

number of subcarriers in the available spectrum. A subcarrier is the minimum scheduling resolution in the time-frequency domain. Depending on the length of the Cyclic Prefix (CP) in the time domain, a time slot can be divided into 6 or 7 symbols. As shown in Figure 4, one resource block forms 6 symbols x 12 subcarriers or 7 symbols x 12 subcarriers, depending on the CP length. Not all subcarriers are used for data transmission since some of them are used to reference signals and control information. The reference signals are transmitted in a fix pattern such as at the first and fifth OFDM symbols of each time slot. Subsequently, in the time domain, not all of the symbol time is used for data transmission. Some of the symbol time, the CP, is used to allow the receiver enough time to wait for multipath to settle and allow for signal propagation.

LTE employ different modulation and multiplexing technologies for supporting scalable LTE bandwidth utilization. In the downlink, OFDMA has been selected as the radio access scheme for facilitating advanced frequency-domain scheduling method. The rational of this is that OFDMA achieves robustness to multipath fading, higher spectral efficiency, and bandwidth scalability. For multiple UEs' downlink connections, the eNodeB assigns different frequency segments (e.g. resource blocks) to individual users, based on the channel conditions. In other words, UEs are allocated a specific number of subcarriers for a predetermined amount of time. The allocation is performed by an eNodeB frequency domain scheduler that manages the available bandwidth such that the allocation avoids subcarrier collision in the time and frequency domains. This is different to contend-based networking schemes (e.g., Carrier-Sense Multiple Access with Collision Avoidance - CSMA/CA). CSMA/CA is distributed medium accessing scheme for ad hoc networks or WLANs. An ad hoc node contends for the shared wireless medium by monitoring the status of the entire carrier (or entire set of subcarriers). If a carrier is sensed as idle, the packet could be sent from it.

If the transmission fails, the node waits for a randomly chosen period of time, and checks again to see if the subcarrier is idle. The contention-based networking schemes exchanges significant signaling control message during negotiating the subcarriers for use and thus results in high signaling overhead. CSMA/CA may utilize 30-40% available bandwidth just for signaling exchanges. Instead, the centralized spectrum allocation reduces the signaling overhead, achieving high efficiency.

Channel Quality Indicator and Downlink Transmission

The interpolation of reference signal is used to estimate the channel response on the remaining subcarriers. In order to optimally schedule resources to the different UEs on the downlink, eNodeB needs channel quality reports from each individual UE by using the reference signal. The feedback from the individual UEs to the eNodeB are sent in the form of a channel quality indicator (CQI), as shown in Figure 4. The CQI is an estimate of the downlink channel at individual UEs. The channel condition is measured by the received signal strength (RSS), the signal-to-noise ratio (SNR), the bit-error-rate (BER) before or after the channel decoder. Homayounfar and Rohani (2009) proposed an approach for efficient CQI reports and a so-called two-sided cumulative sum (cusum) scheme is used for monitoring that the channel quality. For a given channel metric such as BER, this scheme computes the accumulated deviation from a target value (e.g., target BER) over a measurement interval.

The CQI report includes three messages: CQI request, acknowledgement, and negative acknowledgement. Depending on the UE's status, UE acknowledge feedback performs the CQI report by using different channels:

- **PUCCH (Physical Uplink Control Channel)**: CQI can be carried on the PUCCH and periodically reported if the UE is not currently scheduled for transmission. The CQI reports over PUCCH can be decoded by eNodeB instantly.
- **PUSCH (Physical Uplink Shared Channel)**: An UE in active transmission can send its CQI over PUSCH. On-demand, non-periodic, reports are also possible in LTE and are only carried on the PUSCH.

To reduce overhead, the PUCCH must carry much less bits than the PUSCH. On the other hand, the CQI reports over PUSCH must be decoded from several transmissions for less overhead. Consequently, this is the trade-off between how much information can be fed back and how much delay for the eNodeB to retrieve the feedback CQI bits. Hereafter, the packet scheduler at the eBodeB (e.g., FDPS – frequency domain packet scheduling) uses the CQI feedback from individual users to perform resource assignment for every Transmission Time Interval (TTI - 1ms in LTE). This process is called for packet scheduling.

Downlink Frequency Domain Packet Scheduling (FDPS)

OFDMA for DL achieves intra-cell orthogonal multiplexing among physical channels in the time and frequency domains. The downlink defines various physical channels for transmitting broadcast, multicast, unicast, signaling, and control information. These channels are used for maintain the downlink connection and data transmission in an effective way. The synchronization signals, including the primary synchronization signal (PSS) and secondary synchronization signal (SSS) must acquired by the UE to establish the downlink connection. At the same time, physical broadcast channel (PBCH) carries system specific and cell-specific information for downlink establishment. The data traffic is carried over the Physical Downlink Shared Channel (PDSCH).

Before transmitting the data packets, the packet scheduling determines the data rate to be used for each UE in each subframe and perform rate adaptation by using adaptive modulation and coding (AMC) for different subframes.

The time-domain Proportional Fair (PF) algorithm is a packet scheduling mechanism that has been current used in various wireless systems such as cdma2000-based EV-DO (e.g. 1x, Rev A/B). PF algorithm is able to maximize all feasible scheduling rules by a optimizing a utility function. The utility function models the long-term service rate of all UEs to achieve proportional fairness. It achieves high throughput and also maintains proportional fairness amongst all users by giving users with a high-quality channel rates or a low current average service rate.

Based on the PF algorithm, FDPS is a packet scheduling algorithm that considers both the time and frequency domain multiplexing. It works as a scheduling resolution in the order of coherence bandwidth in the frequency domain. Let τ_i be the current scheduling interval. The instantaneous throughput for each UE u on each resource element i is $\eta_{u,i}(\tau_i)$. $\eta_{u,i}(\tau_i)$ for each resource element is computed, according to Shannon's channel capacity, such as:

$$\eta_{u,i}(\tau_i) = B_u(1 + SNR)$$

where B_u is the bandwidth of the resource element (e.g., subcarrier). The other way for $\eta_{u,i}(\tau_i)$ is that the UE directly reports $\eta_{u,i}(\tau_i)$ to the eNodeB in the CQI. Then, FDPS is the problem to pick UE u' for scheduling on resource element i' which maximizes:

$$u' = \arg\max_u \left\{ \frac{\eta_{u,i}(\tau_i)}{\overline{\eta_u}(\tau_i)} \right\},$$

where $\overline{\eta_u}(\tau_i)$ is the average delivered user throughput in the past. The average delivered throughput to UE u is calculated by the traditional recursive method. Recent studies by Lee et al. (2009) of this FDPS model have shown potential gains in system capacity of up to 40-60% over time-domain only PF scheduling.

The above FDPS model has been further extended by Lee et al. (2009) for downlink multiple input multiple output (MIMO) transmissions. MIMO significantly increases the system data rate by employing multiple antennas on both the transmitter and receiver for simultaneous transmissions. The increases in data throughput and link range have no needs of additional bandwidth or transmit power. MIMO can improve the spectral efficiency gain and link diversity by using spatial division multiplexing. In addition, multiple antennas allow for an additional degree of freedom to the channel scheduler.

Different MIMO schemes (Hou, Zhang and Kayama, 2009) are considered in the 3GPP standard, depending on the spatial domain user adaptation over individual resource elements. Single user MIMO restricts each subcarrier to be used only one user in the packet schedule (as either transmission diversity mode or spatial multiplexing mode). In contract, multi-user MIMO allows different users to be scheduled on different spatial streams over the same subcarrier. Multi-user MIMO offers greater spatial-domain flexibility. However, it increases the scheduling complexity and additional overhead.

The simplest way for MIMO-FDPS is to select the best user and corresponding MIMO mode for each individual resource elements independently, without considering the status of other resource elements. However, this strategy occurs high overhead and restricts the downlink transmission of each UE to only one MIMO mode. Lee et al. (2009) focused on the single user MIMO FDPS scheduler and the multi-user MIMO FDPS is still an open issue. The proposed MIMO FDPS maximizes the packet scheduling objective (e.g., proportional fairness) while considering the MIMO constraints. The MIMO constraints are:

- Each resource element can be only assigned to at most one user either using transmit diversity or spatial multiplexing,
- The total number of resource element available, and
- Only one MIMO mode (i.e., diversity or multiplexing) can be selected for a UE across different resource elements fro that UE and for each time instance.

Lee et al. (2009) show that the MIMO FDPS is NP-hard and thus developed two approximation algorithms. The first MIMO FDPS algorithm assumes full CQI feedback while partial feedback is required for the second algorithm. The second MIMO FDPS algorithm could achieve 50% feedback deduction, compared to full feedback.

OFDMA and SC-FDMA in the Uplink

OFDMA and SC-FDMA are both a multiple access scheme based on OFDM where distinguished subcarriers are allocated to different users for data transmissions. As OFDM, they achieve high spectral efficiency and high immunity to multipath fading. The main difference between the OFDMA and OFDM is that the OFDMA eNodeB allocates a subset of carriers to each user in order to accommodate multiple transmissions simultaneously, instead of being allocated all of the available subcarriers. As we illustrated, OFDMA is employed for the downlink where the eNodeB is responsible for managing and allocating the subcarriers resources. The subcarrier resources are organized by resource block. The downlink transmissions are from eNodeB to UEs generally without power constraints since the eNodeB is powered by external power sources. Differently, the uplink transmissions are originated by UEs and directed to the eNodeB while UEs are mobile

devices that are constrained by powers. Therefore, the power consumption should be considered for UEs to wisely allocate the power to subcarriers for the given end user throughput constraint. On the other hand, OFDM and its variation suffer from Peak-to-Average Power Radio (PAPR) problem due to frequency spreading. The PAPR is defined as the ratio of the maximum instantaneous power and the average of the signal, which is:

$$PAPR(x) = \frac{\max\limits_{0 \le t \le T} | x_{enp}(t) |^2}{E\{| x_{enp}(t) |^2\}}, \qquad (1)$$

where $x_{enp}(t)$ is the complex envelope of the signal $s(t)$ at time t and $E\{\bullet\}$ denotes the expectation operation. Amplifiers used in UE circuits have a linear region. To avoid signal distortion, it is ideal for the amplifier to operate with the maximum amplification. On the contrary, for desirable PAPR, the UE should run with a lower amplification such that the peak power does not lie in the non-linear gain region. The farther these amplifiers are operated from the peak power, the less power efficient the UE become. This again leads to increased power consumption. This might not be very important for an eNodeB. However, it will consume UE's batteries quickly while the UE is constrained by power.

SC-FDMA has better performance than that of OFDMA in terms of PAPR (Lin, Xiao, Vucetic and Sellathurai, 2010). Its PAPR achieve lower values on average, mainly due to the fact that they map their input bits to time symbols, as opposed to OFDM and OFDMA which map them directly to frequency symbols. In addition to lower PAPR, SC-FDMA is the less sensitivity to frequency offset because it has at most only two adjacent users. On the other hand, SC-FDMA has almost same link capacity as OFDMA.

Figure 5 illustrates the modulator of the transmitter and receiver for OFDMA and SC-FDMA. As OFDM, OFDMA takes advantage of

Figure 5. OFDMA and SC-FDMA

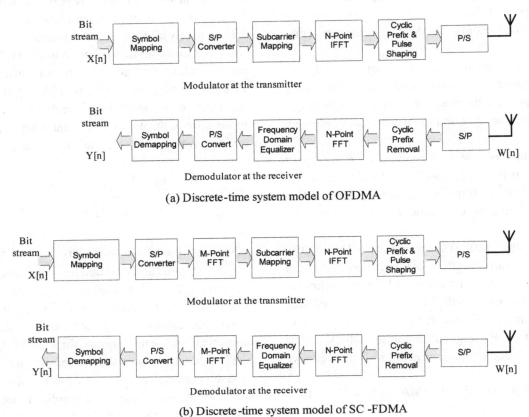

(a) Discrete-time system model of OFDMA

(b) Discrete -time system model of SC -FDMA

frequency diversity to achieve higher data rates. Figure 5(a) shows a discrete-time version of an OFDM system. The input binary data is mapped to constellations in frequency domain by the symbol mapping functional block as shown in Figure 5 (a). The bits can be either modulated into subcarriers by M-ray quadrature amplitude modulation (MQAM) or M-ary phase shift keying (MPSK), depending on the channel condition. The symbols are converted into parallel streams using the serial-to-parallel (S/P) converter. Then, inverse fast Fourier transform (IFFT) is then applied to transfer the modulated subcarrier symbols into the time domain. A guard interval is added to each subcarrier symbol using the cyclic prefix (CP) block, which reduces the effects of the inter-symbol interference (ISI). Before the transmission

on the radio, the symbols are converted to serial stream by the (P/S) converter.

The receiver performs the reverse operations as the transmitter to reconstruct the original bit streams. The reverse operations are shown in the functional blocks in Figure 5 (a) for receivers. The signals are converted into parallel streams using the serial-to-parallel (S/P) converter. It then removes the cyclic prefix (CP) block on the received symbols. The fast Fourier transform (FFT) transfers the time domain data into the frequency domain data. The equalization compensates the distortion introduced by subcarrier.

One important feature of OFDMA is its ability to equalize in frequency domain. There are many different ways such as zero-forcing (ZF) equalizer and the minimum mean square error

Figure 6. Link layer structure

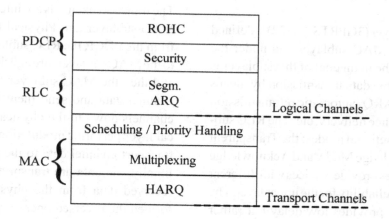

(MMSE) equalizer. They both correctly recover the phase of the signal. The ZF equalizer causes noise enhancement and the MMSE equalizer causes time distortion in the signal. OFDMA is very similar to OFDM in function, with the main difference being that instead of being allocated all of the available subcarriers, the eNodeB allocates a subset of carriers to each user in order to accommodate multiple transmissions simultaneously. As compared to OFDM, OFDMA is its high sensitivity to frequency offset. In OFDM, all the frequencies of the subcarriers were generated by one transmitter, and thus it is relatively easy to maintain the orthogonality of the subcarriers. In OFDMA, eNodeB simultaneously transmits for a number of UEs such that a frequency offset is inevitable and multiple access interference occurs as the power leaks into neighboring subcarriers.

Figure 5 (b) shows the functional blocks of the SC-FDMA. SC-FDMA is the multiple access version of Single-Carrier Frequency-Domain Equalization (SC-FDE). As shown by the functional blocks in Figure 5, SC-FDMA is similar to the OFDMA, having all the functional blocks of OFDMA. As OFDMA, it performs channel estimation and equalization in the frequency domain. Multiple access of SC-FDMA is achieved in frequency domain. For multiple access, SC-FDMA enhances SC-FDE for allowing division

frequency amongst frequencies. This is achieved by an additional functional block of M-point FFT as shown in Figure 5(b). The M points of the signal are mapped to the N subcarriers of the system.

LTE LINK LAYER

The LTE Link Layer is the layer 2 protocol having similar yet improved functions compared to UMTS link layer. The bit stream from the physical layer is delivered to the upper layer of LTE through the link layer, or vice versa. The LTE link layer is to provide better integrity, increased reliability and enhanced security to the upper layers (Larmo et al., 2009). Figure 6 illustrates the structure of the link layer which consists of three sublayers: MAC (Medium Access Control) sublayer, RLC (Radio Link Control) sublayer and PDCP (Packet Data Convergence Protocol) sublayer, from the lower sublayer to higher sublayer (3GPP TS 36.300).

The MAC sublayer (3GPP TS 36.321) is located in the lowest sublayer of link layer for both the eNodeB and UE. In the MAC sublayer, three components, namely, Scheduling/Priority Handling, Multiplexing, and HARQ are designed to receive the multiple services from the lower physical layer, including data transfer services, signaling of HARQ feedback, signaling of scheduling request and measurements of channel quality, etc.

The RLC sublayer (3GPP TS 36.322) is defined on the top of the MAC sublayer and under the PDCP sublayer. The main goal of this sublayer is to guarantee reliable data transmission by means of segmentation, ARQ (automatic retransmission request), in-sequence delivery, etc. The RLC sublayer has three functional modes: the Transparent Mode, Unacknowledge Mode, and Acknowledge Mode. These modes provide services with different speed, delay, and reliability for the upper layer. The transparent mode provides low delay but rather high error rates, depending on the radio condition. The unacknowledged mode adds some additional functions to the transparent mode. However, it does not include the support for retransmissions as the acknowledge mode. The acknowledge mode enables reliable data transmission such as for unicast traffic. It defines segmentation, concatenation, and reassembly by incorporating ARQ functionality. However, it may cause higher delay for the data.

RObust Header Compression (ROHC) is the main component in the PDCP sublayer (3GPP TS 36.323). ROHC defines the packet header compression, which reduces the protocol header overhead. In addition, it improves the link efficiency while maintaining the end-to-end transparency. ROHC is implemented in the UE as well as the eNodeB to specify the compression of IP headers on a per hop basis. The header compression basically includes the generation of IP context while each IP context is given a sequence number which is encoded before sending the information. ROHC results in very high compression ratios and the compressed header size is reduced to around 1-3 bytes. Thus it increase effective link bandwidth and decrease packet processing requirements in power sensitive downstream devices. In addition, ROHC is very robust against bit errors on the link.

As shown in Figure 6, two types of interfaces in the link layers are defined, i.e., logical channels and transport channels. The logical channels

are interfaces between MAC and RLC sublayers. The transport channels are interfaces between the MAC sublayer and Physical layer. For the data from the PDCP, the RLC sublayer forwards them to the MAC sublayer through the logical channels, and then the MAC sublayer formats the logical channel data and send them from the transport channels down to the physical layer. The physical layer performs modulation and transports the transport channel data to the physical channels. Finally, the data are transmitted on the air. The received data from the physical layer are performed the reversed operations before delivered to the upper layer through the transport channels and logical channels. In the following subsection, we describe each of the three sublayers in detail.

MAC Sublayer

Due to OFDM-based physical layer, the LTE employs an OFDM-capable MAC sublayer that supports OFDM and MIMO technology. The OFDM-capable MAC design leads to adaptabilities of OFMD-based modulation, multiple access, and MIMO antenna schemes (3GPP TS 36.300). In this section, we discuss the LTE MAC sublayer design.

The MAC sublayer is responsible for mapping between logical channels and transport channels that are shown in Figure 6. The logic channels interfaced to the RLC sublayer define the types of the information is being transferred. On the other hand, the transport channels interfaced to the physical layer defines how the information is being transferred. Therefore, the MAC sublayer has to map appropriate logical channels to the transport channels.

In the LTE MAC, advanced channel coding schemes are employed for high throughput. As the discussion in the physical layer, a resource scheduler at the eNodeB determines the optimal physical model for each ODFMA subchannel by a resource scheduler. This allows adaptive modulation coding in the physical layer based on the channel state information (i.e., CQI). The MAC layer aggregates data bits as packets and the error is evaluated in terms of probability of a packet error. The probability of a packet error is different to bit error ratio that is defined in the physical layer. In addition to channel conditions viewed from the physical layer, the probability of a packet error is affected by the channel coder used, the coding rate, and the packet length from the MAC layer. Turbo coding is a technology that is used by the MAC to correct bit errors. In LTE, "highly punctured" Turbo codes are used for achieving high throughput such as 150 Mbit/s with 2 X 2 MIMO. Specifically, the turbo code is a systematic parallel concatenated convolutional code with two 8-state constituent encoders and one turbo code internal interleaver. Each constituent encoder is independently terminated by tail bits, which are multiplexed to the end of the streams. The high throughput Turbo code decoder splits a received data block into windows for parallel decoding for very high throughput, low power, and area consumption.

The MAC sublayer performs error correction through HARQ (hybrid automatic-repeat-request). HARQ enhances system throughput by improving SNR and gaining time diversity through retransmissions. In general, HARQ schemes include two types: type-I CC HARQ and type-II IR HARQ. Type-I CC (Chase Combining) HARQ transmits an identical packet in initial transmission and retransmissions. Type-II IR (Incremental Redundancy) HARQ transmits additional redundant bits of FEC (forward error correction) coding in each retransmission. The IR HARQ can be further classified into full IR and partial IR. Full IR HARQ retransmits parity bits of FEC coding only. In addition to the parity bits, partial IR HARQ retransmits the systematic bits, thus each re-transmission is self decodable. Due to high coding gain, IR HARQ could achieve high performance compared to CC HARQ. However, IR HARQ needs additional memory and results in decoding complexity.

The MAC sublayer has some other functions and some of them are illustrated as below.

- **Priority Handling**: It performs the priority handling between data flows of one UE. Also it performs priority handling between different UEs by means of dynamic scheduling.
- **Identification**: When a particular UE is addressed on a common downlink channel, or when a UE is using the RACH, there is a need for in-band identification of the UE. Such identification functionality is performed at the MAC sublayer and is known as identification of UEs on common transport channels.
- **Multiplexing/Demultiplexing**: The MAC sublayer conducts the multiplexing/demultiplexing of upper layer PDUs belong to one or several logic channels into/from transport blocks delivered to/from the physical layer on both common transport channels and dedicated transport channels. By means of this function, several upper layer services (e.g. RLC instances) can be mapped efficiently on the same transport channel, and the identification of multiplexing is contained in the MAC protocol control information.
- **Traffic Measurement**: The MAC sublayer also measures the traffic volume on logical channels. Transport channel switching may occur based on the traffic volume information collected by the RRC. Based on the based on a switching decision made by RRC, MAC sublayer executes the switching between common and dedicated transport channels.
- **Ciphering**: When the RLC is working in the transparent mode, the ciphering function would be used to protect data.

In the following subsection, we discuss more on these functions.

Mapping Between Logic Channels and Transport Channels

Depending on what type of information is transferred, logical channels can be classified into two groups, i.e., five control channels and two traffic channels. Control Channels is only used for the transfer of control plane information, including:

1. **Broadcast Control Channel (BCCH)**: This is a channel used for broadcasting system control information in the downlink.
2. **Paging Control Channel (PCC)**: This channel is used for transferring paging information and system information change notification in the downlink. The network uses paging when it doesn't know the location cell of the UE.
3. **Common Control Channel (CCCH)**: CCCH is employed for transmitting control information between network and UEs which don't have RRC connection with the network.
4. **Multicast Control Channel (MCCH)**: This is a point-to-multipoint channel used to transmit MBMS control information from the network to the UE.
5. **Dedicated Control Channel (DCCH)**. This is a point-to-point bidirectional channel used to transmit control information between the network and UE which has the RRC connection.

Differently, the two Traffic Channels are only used for the transfer of user plane information. The Dedicated Traffic Channel (DTCH) is a point-to-point bidirectional channel for transmitting user information. The Multicast Traffic Channel (MTCH) for multicast data traffic from the network to a number of UEs.

The MAC entity maps the logic channels to the transport channels. The uplink logical channels CCCH, DCCH and DTCH can be mapped to the UL-SCH (Uplink Shared Channel), while for the downlink, the BCCH, CCCH, DCCH and DTCH are mapped to DL-SCH (Downlink Shared Channel), and the MCCH and MTCH are mapped to MCH (Multicast Channel). PCCH is mapped to PCH (Paging Channel), and BCCH is also mapped to BCH (Broadcast Channel).

Random Access Procedure

MAC procedure includes two types of random access procedures. The first is the contention based random access procedure which is used in most of the random access cases. The second is the non-contention based random access procedure that is used only in handover, downlink data arrival or eNodeB triggered uplink re-alignment.

Contention-Based Random Access Procedure

The contention based Random Access (RA) is a four-phase procedure, which is used to establish the uplink-time alignment when uplink timing is not aligned or the alignment is lost. The random access procedure is initialized when a UE receives a PDCCH transmission with matching C-RNTI.

The contention based random access procedure can be explained as four steps illustrated as in Figure 7:

*   **Ransom Access Resource Selection and Transmission:** In this phase, the Random Access Preamble is selected and the next available subframe containing PRACH is determined. The preamble target power is set and the physical layer is asked to transmit the RA preamble using the selected PRACH and subframe.
*   **Random Access Response Reception on PDCCH:** After the random access preamble is transmitted, the UE will wait the Random Access Response until successful

Figure 7. Contention based random access procedure

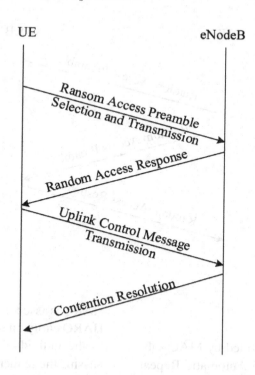

reception of a Random Access Response containing Random Access Preamble identifiers that matches the transmitted Random Access Preamble. If the Random Access Response reception is not successful (i.e., no response is received within the RA response window or not matching response received), UE will proceed to the selection of random access resource again.

- **Uplink RA Control Message Transmission**: In this step, first uplink control message is transmitted on the granted UL resource and a contention resolution timer is started in the meaning time.
- **Contention Resolution**: When there are multiple UEs are contenting for the RA, multiple RA messages may be received by the eNodeB. Upon receive the Uplink Control Messages, the eNodeB will only response to one RA message with the UE identity. The contention resolution timer

will be stopped when the UE receives the acknowledgement with its own identity, which indicates the random access procedure successfully completed.

Differently, non-contention based random access process can be employed as illustrated in the following subsection.

Non-Contention Based Random Access Procedure

Compared with the contention based random access procedure, the non-contention based random access procedure is simpler and only contains three steps. In the first step, the random access preamble is assigned by eNodeB, which will be echoed back in the second step from UE. Then a random access response will confirm the completion of the random access procedure.

Figure 8. Non-contention based random access procedure

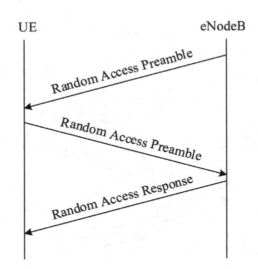

Hybrid ARQ

One important function provided by MAC sublayer is the efficient Hybrid Automatic Repeat Request (HARQ). HARQ used to get fast error detection and correction. In general, HARQ is a combination of forward error-correcting (FEC) coding and automatic repeat request (ARQ). FEC is employed to reduce the frequency of retransmission by correcting some error pattern and ARQ is used to detect uncorrectable errors. Thus, HARQ achieves better performance than ordinary ARQ, especially in poor signal environments.

The HARQ in LTE is an N-process stop-and-wait ARQ based on ACK/NACKs, which is comparable to that of a window-based selective repeat ARQ in the aspects of the functionality while provide better performance. In a stop-and-wait ARQ, during the transmission, only after the sender receives ACK/NACK from the receiver the subsequent transmission can be continued. If the ACK is not received a retransmission is done. To use multiple channels for supporting HARQ service, a module in UE called HARQ entity is used to maintain N parallel HARQ processes to implement N stop-and-wait HARQ protocol. Each

HARQ is associated with a HARQ identifier. The HARQ entity direct HARQ information received to the individual HARQ processes. Instead of passing the sequence number inside the acknowledgement message, a HARQ feedback bit is used to indicate the acknowledgement or negative acknowledgment (ACK/NACK). Since this HARQ feedback bit is mapped to the corresponding transmission attempt by fixed-timing matching, thus it provides exact information of the reception status. In this way, the HARQ functionality ensures delivery between peer entities in lower physical layer. Downlink HARQ transmission is asynchronous and the uplink HARQ transmission is synchronous. The HARQ information about the transmission status of MAC sublayer will be reported to the RLC sublayer, in which another ARQ function will use this knowledge to handle HARQ residual error cases.

RLC Sublayers

The Radio Link Control layer is used to format and transport traffic between the UE and the eNodeB. Functions of RLC sublayer are performed by RLC entities that reside in both the UE and eNodeB. The RLC PDUs are exchanged between these peer RLC entities. The major functions of the RLC syblayer include transfer of upper layer PDUs, error correction through ARQ in AM mode, concatenation, segmentation/reassembly of RLC SDUs in UM and AM date transfer, as well as RLC retransmission.

An RLC entity can work in three data transfer modes, the Acknowledged Mode (AM), Unacknowledged Mode (UM), and Transparent Mode (TM). Correspondingly, the RLC entity is categorized as the AM entity, UM entity and TM entity when it is working in different mode. The AM mode is designed to provide reliable delivery, and is suitable for the non-Real Time (RT) service which can tolerate delay but need high reliability, such as the file download and TCP traffic. The other two modes are used in providing no delivery guarantees services. The UM mode is used for transport delay sensitive Real Time (RT) service such as streaming VoIP traffic which retransmission are avoided. The TM mode is used when the PDU sizes are previously known and there are no segmentation and reassembly of RLC SDUs (Service Data Units).

The fast HARQ protocol in the lower MAC sublayer is further improved by a highly reliable window-based selective repeat-ARQ protocol in the RLC sublayer. The ARQ in the RLC sublayer provide error correction by retransmissions in acknowledges mode (AM). ARQ uses acknowledgement obtained from the HARQ about the transmission / reception status. The ARQ handle residual errors that are not corrected/detected by HARQ by use of a single bit error-feedback mechanism. With the support of the two layer ARQ mechanism, the link layer of LTE is able to provide an efficient and reliable data transfer with low latency and low overhead. Most errors are detected and corrected by the lightweight HARQ protocol in MAC sublayer, and the residual HARQ errors are captured and corrected by the ARQ retransmission in the upper RLC sublayer.

PDCP Sublayers

The PDCP sublayer is the highest level sublayer in the link layer structure. Its major purpose is to provide the hander compression and decompression. In the current version of LTE, only the RObust Header Compression (ROHC) protocol is supported. Every PDCP entity uses at most one ROHC instance. In this ROHC framework, multiple header compression algorithms are defined as profiles. Each profile is defined specially for some particular network layer, transport layer or combination of the upper layer protocol.

Another major function of PDCP is the ciphering function, which provides ciphering and deciphering service. The ciphering algorithm and keys to be used by the PDCP entity are determined by the upper layers. The ciphering function is also activated by upper layer. PDCP sublayer also provides integrity protection and integrity verification of the control plan data. The integrity of the PDU header and the data part of the PDU before ciphering are protected and verified.

MOBILITY SUPPORT

As most mobile wireless systems, one of the main goals of LTE is to provide seamless handover from one cell to another cell, or handover between different networks. To provide pervasive broadband access for users, mobility support is one of the basic requirements for the design of SAE/LTE.

Two areas are defined for handling of mobility in LTE/SAE: Cell and Tracking Area (TA). A cell is the area covered by the eNodeB and a tracking area is a group of cells that are being tracked by a S-GW. Based on the UE information held by the MME, there are two set of states: EPS Mobility Management (EMM) states and EPS Connection Management (ECM) states. EMM states describe the mobility management states that result from the mobility management procedures while the

ECM states describe the signaling connectivity between the UE and EPC. EMM includes two states: EMM-Registered and EMM- Deregistered. In the EMM- Deregistered state, MME hold no valid location information about the UE, while in the EMM-Registered state, the MME has the location information for the UE at least an accuracy of a tracking area. On the other side, the two ECM states are ECM-Idle and ECM-Connected. In the ECM-Idle state, there is no NAS signaling connection between the UE and the network, and the network hold no context for the UE and the location of the UE is known by the MME within the accuracy of a tracking area. In the ECM-Connected state, the signaling connection is built up between the UE and the MME in the form of Radio Resource Control (RRC) connection and S1 connection for the UE is created between the E-UTRAN and the MME. The UE location is known to the MME within the accuracy of a cell. When a UE is connected to the network it switch from EMM-Deregistered state to EMM-Registered state and the ECM state moved from ECM-Idle to ECM-Connected.

Intra-LTE Handover

The intra-LTE handover is a network controlled handover, in which the handover decision is taken by the eNodeB. Handover in LTE requires the connection break before UE take approach, thus it is a hard handover and there is a short interruption during the handover. During the execution phase, the source eNodeB temporarily forwards the buffered and in transit user plane data to the target eNodeB to minimize the packet loss and provide in-order delivery, which are extremely important for TCP-based application. The UE detach from old cell and synchronize to new cell.

In general, the handover contains three phases: preparation phase, execution phase and completion phase. In the preparation phase, the source eNodeB prepares a target eNodeB for handover concurrently with the handover decision. During the preparation phase, the context of the UE's control plane and user plane are transferred from the source eNodeB to the target eNodeB and the resources have been reserved at the target eNodeB when the UE access the target eNodeB. The EPC core network is not involved in the preparation phase, and the preparation messages are directly exchanged between the eNodeBs. The release of the resources at the source side during the HO completion phase is also triggered by the eNodeB.

After the establishment of new connection between UE and target eNodeB, the downlink path is switched at the serving GW (S-GW) in the completion phase. The target eNodeB should first deliver all forwarded packets to the UE before delivering any of the packets received on the new direct path. The source eNodeB will release resource related with the UE to complete the handover.

MME Supported Inter Technology Handover

Inter-technology mobility is the ability to support the user mobility between different wireless access networks. For LTE, the inter-technology mobility includes two types of mobility support (3GPP TR 36.938): mobility support between LTE device and the legacy 3GPP technologies, which is called the intra-RAT (radio access technology) mobility; and mobility support between LTE and non-3GPP technologies such as WiMAX radio technologies, which is called the inter-RAT technologies.

Intra-RAT Mobility Support

The intra-RAT mobility support is designed to support handover procedure between LTE and other 3GPP Technology, such as mobility between E-UTRAN and 3GPP2 networks (3GPP TR 36.938).

The LTE is designed to support the handover from cdma2000 to E-URTAN network. When the E-URTAN is the target network, cdma2000 messages are sent transparently to the target

Figure 9. Architecture for handover between mobile WiMAX and 3GPP access

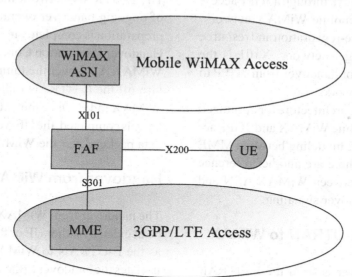

E-ERTAN system with the eNodeB and MME acting as the relay points. The cdma2000 messages are encapsulated in the UL messages over the E-UTRAN air link. The tunneled message is further tunneled to the MME along with a S1 Tunneling Procedure Information within a new S1-MME Information message.

LTE system is also designed to support bi-directional seamless service continuity between cdma2000 HRPD (1xEV-DO). When the HRPD is the target network, the eNodeB initiate the E-UTRAN to HRPD handover based on the measurement reports from the UE. A handover command is received by the UE from the eNodeB which orders it to switch to the target HRPD cell, and then the UE leave the E-UTRAN radio and join the HRPD traffic channel. The HRPD handover signaling is tunneled between the UE and HRPD network. When the E-UTRAN is the target network, it is the UE who will perform an attach procedure and trigger relocation to E-UTRAN. The signaling will be tunneled over the HRPD access and HRPD-MME interface, which include a Handover command from the MME to UE. After the handover is completed, the UE will send a "Handover complete" message over the E-UTRAN radio.

Inter-RAT Mobility Support

As another major 4G technology, WiMAX is a major competing technology with LTE. The LTE is designed to support mobility between E-UTRAN and WiMAX network among all WiMAX frequency bands and E-UTRAN frequency bands (Song et al., 2009, Ng, Lin, Li, and Tatesh, 2009). Figure 9 show the architecture and major reference point for the optimized handover between WiMAX and 3GPP access. A new logic function RAF and a reference point X200 are introduced specially for supporting optimized handover between mobile WiMAX and 3GPP access.

The FAF (Forward Attachment Function) is a logical function which has interfaces to both the target and source systems. The communications between UE and FAF are generic IP access network. The reference point X200 represents a secure communication between UE and the FAF through a generic IP access. The UE can communicate with the FAF through mobile WiMAX IP access before handover to a 3GPP network, or communicate with the FAF through a 3GPP access before handover to a mobile WiMAX network. The X200 is used for pre-registration and resource preparation in the target network. X101 is the reference point used for handover from 3GPP to a mobile WiMAX network.

One other reference architecture for optimized handover between mobile WiMAX and 3GPP access is based on the L2 tunneling between MME and WiMAX ASN. There are another reference point S101 defined between WiMAX ASN and MME to provide handover signaling.

Handover from E-UTRAN to WiMAX

When the UE handover is from the E-UTRAN to WiMAX, some key information of WiMAX network should be transmitted in E-UTRAN, such as DL center carrier frequency, cell bandwidth, preamble index, and BS ID, etc. To support the network controlled handover, the UE should able to make measurement on the WiMAX on the CINR and RSSI quantities of WiMAX. In LTE_ACTIVE mode, the UE identifies the neighboring WiMAX cells and reports their RSSI and/or CINR values when they exceed a certain threshold and can be considered as handover candidates. When the UE make the decision to handover to the WiMAX, UE can pre-register/attach to the WiMAX system in advance of a handover to reduce the time involved in the process of handover.

Before the UE initiates the handover procedure, it will perform handover preparation in the target WiMAX network including setting up a bi-directional tunnel with WiMAX ASN and passing any necessary handover context. Thereafter, based on the measurement reports and network selection criteria, the E-UTRAN network would indicate to the UE to initiate the handover procedure to switch over to the target WiMAX network. The UE would then initiate WiMAX handover signalings which are transparent to the E-UTRAN while continuing to maintain the current connections and send and receive data over the E-UTRAN radio.

The E-UTRAN network may receive the status of ongoing handover operation. Once the target preparation is complete the UE would receive the Handover Preparation Complete indication from WiMAX ASN over the tunnel. Then the UE will turn off the E-UTRAN radio and switch over to WiMAX radio. Once the initial WiMAX network entry is completed, the UE would be able to receive data packets over the WiMAX network.

Handover from WiMAX to E-UTRAN

The handover from WiMAX to E-UTRAN could be decided by either UE or the network. Similarly as the E-UTRAN to WiMAX handover, the UE initiates the handover to the E-UTRAN by tunneling measurement report, including measurement results of the E-UTRAN. After the resources are reserved in the E-UTRAN, the E-UTRAN network will send the handover command to UE. Then, the UE will initiate an attaching procedure to E-UTRAN after leaving WiMAX radio, and a handover confirm message will be sent to E-UTRAN.

LTE security

As the most promising technology to provide high speed mobile communication, to get the successfully deployment and widespread use, the security is one of the important issues that should be carefully considered before deploying the network for practical applications. The security includes many problems such as user authentication, access control, encryption/decryption, billing, and data integrity. As LTE is used as a platform for the commercial applications, for example, LTE has to provide the confidentiality and reliability for financial transactions.

As all other IP networks, LTE needs to address the security challenges at the application and operational levels. In the LTE flat architecture, all radio access protocols terminate at the eNodeB, in which the IP protocols are visible. Thus, the security of eNodeB is more vulnerable to be attacked, compared with legacy 3GPP node, especially in the case that the eNodeB may be deployed in the unsecured domains.

LTE is designed to be able to inter-connect with other wireless networks including legacy 3GPP networks and non-3GPP networks such as WiMAX. The internetworking further imposes new security requirements to the LTE, which makes it more complex other networks are involved in cooperation. Therefore, LTE needs to address these issues for providing authentication and key agreement protocols, with more complex key hierarchy compared with previous wireless technologies (3GPP TS 33.402).

Security Architecture and Functions

In the LTE security architecture, five security feature groups are defined to meet different security objectives (3GPP TS 33.401):

- **Network Access Security**: It is designed to protect the possible attacks on the radio access link, and provide users with secure access to services. This set of security feature group includes the security between ME and AN, ME and SN, USIM and SN.
- **Network Domain Security**: The network domain security is designed to protect attacks on the wireline network, including a set of security features by which node securely exchanges the signaling data, user data between AN and SN, or between SN and HE.
- **User Domain Security**: This represents the security between USIM and ME to provide secure USIM and ME.
- **Application Domain Security**: A set of security features should be enabled for secure communication between user and service provider domain.
- **Visibility and Configurability of Security**: It is used to inform the user whether a security feature is in use and whether the service should rely on the security feature or not.

In the SAE security architecture, the integrity and confidentiality protection terminates in MME for core network (NAS) signaling, while the integrity and confidentiality protection terminates in eNodeB for the radio network (RRC) signaling.

Authentication and Key Management Among UE and EPC Network Elements

EPS (Evolved Packet System) AKA, i.e., the authentication and key agreement procedure used in the E-UTRAN, is based on the UMTS AKA. HSS generates the authentication data (e.g., EPS authentication vectors (AV) including RAND, AUTN, XRES, K_{ASME}) and provides it to MME. In this way, the serving network gets the EPS authentication vector (AV) and uses it for UE authentication. These AVs are specific to the serving network, i.e., AVs that are used in UTRAN/GERAN can not be used in EPS. Initially, there are three keys shared between UE and EP: K, CK an IK. K is the permanent key stored in both the USIM on a UICC and in the Authentication Center AuC. CK, IK are a pair of keys derived from the AuC. After the AKA procedure is successfully completed, an intermediate key K_{ASME} will be shared between UE and MME.

Figure 10 illustrates the EPS AKA procedure. There are three major parties involved in the AKA procedure: ME (Mobile Equipment with USIM), MME and HSS. During the AKA procedure, the MME first sends the User Authentication Request message to the USIM via the ME, which includes random challenge RAND, an authentication token AUTN for network authentication, and a KSI_{ASME} for ME to identity the derived K_{ASME}. When the USIM receives the message, it will verify the freshness of the authentication vector. If it finds that AUTN is acceptable, it will response a User Authentication Response (RES) message back

Figure 10. EPS user authentication (EPS AKA)

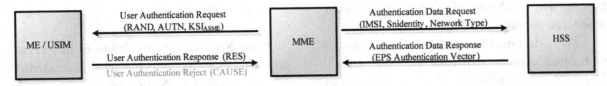

Figure 11. E-UTRAN key hierarchy (3GPP TS 33.401)

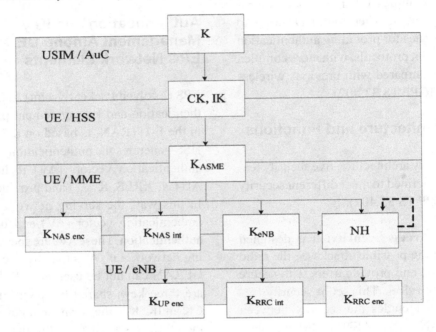

to the MME. Also, the USIM will compute the Cipher Key (CK) and the Integrity Key (IK), and send them to the ME. If the USIM finds the AUTN is not acceptable, it will echo back a User Authentication Reject message with the failure reason indicated by a CAUSE value. When the MME receives the response from the ME, if this is equal to Expected Response (XRES), then the authentication is successful. If MME receives the reject message or the received RES is not equal to XRES, the MME may restart the authentication if required.

The derived K_{SAME} in the AKA procedure will be further used to derive other keys, including K_{eNB}, K_{NASint}, K_{NASenc}, K_{UPenc}, $K_{RRCint\,and}$ K_{RRCenc}. K_{eNB}

is a key derived by ME and MME from K_{ASME} or by ME and target eNodeB. K_{NASint} and K_{NASenc} are used for the protection of NAS traffic in integrity and encryption algorithms respectively. K_{UPenc} is used for UP traffic encryption, while K_{RRCint} and K_{RRCenc} are designed for the RRC traffic. The key hierarchy in E-UTRAN is illustrated as in Figure 11. In the key architecture, Next Hop (NH) is used by UE and eNodeB to derive the new K_{eNB}. When the security context is available, UE and MME derive the Next Hop (NH) from K_{ASME} and K_{eNB}. Otherwise, the NH is derived from K_{ASME} and previous NH.

INTER-NETWORKING SECURITY

Inter-Networking Security with Legacy 3GPP Networks

In the scenarios that the UEs are moving between E-UTRAN and legacy 3GPP networks such as UTRAN/GERAN networks, UE may be registered in both SGSN (Serving GPRS Support Node) in the UTRAN/GERAN and MME in E-UREAN simultaneously. Thus, when the UE is moving from one source system to the target system, both native security context which include the keys created earlier in the target system and the mapped context from the source system will coexist.

In the mobility from E-UTRAN to UTRAN network, the NAS and AS security should always be activated before the handovers really happen. Thus, the source system (i.e., the E-UTRAN) should be able to send a key set to the target UTRAN system during the handover. In the idle mode transition, either mapped or native keys will be used, while for the handover from E-UTRAN to UTRAN, only mapped keys are used. For the mobility from UTRAN to E-UTRAN, native keys are used in most conditions during the idle mode transition. During the handover from UTRAN to E-UTRAN, mapped keys are used while the native keys are still able to be activated and used after the HO competition.

INTER-NETWORKING SECURITY WITH NON-3GPP NETWORKS

According to the 3GPP TS 33.402, three options are available for the mobility between LTE and non-3GPP networks:

- Client MIPv4,
- Dual Stack MIPv4 (DS-MIPv6), and
- Proxy Mobile IP for the network based mobility.

Client MIPv4 and Dual Stack MIPv4 (DS-MIPv6) are used in host based mobility while Proxy Mobile IP is used for the network based mobility. The client MIPv4 security is based on MIP Authentication extensions as defined in RFC 3344, and the MIPv4 signaling messages shall be protected between the UE and HA using MIP authentication extensions and optionally between the UE and FA. The DS-MIPv6 security is based on IPsec IKEv2 as defined in RFC 4877. The IPsec security association is established between the UE and the node acting as HA. To provide the strong access authentication, the proxy mobile IP should only be used in conjunction with AKA-based access authentication.

When the non-3GPP network is not trusted by the EPS network, IPsec tunnel will be used and the tunnel end-point in the network is the ePDG (evolved Packet Data Gateway). The UE and the 3GPP AAA server may implement regular full authentication or fast re-authentication for EAP-AKA, depending on the operator policy. Fast re-authentications for EAP-AKA generates new keys MSK, which may be used for renewing session key used in the non-3GPP access network (e.g., WiMAX network).

HENODEB SECURITY

In E-UTRAN, eNodeB have both wireless radio and backhaul links. In 3GPP Rel 9, there is a specification for a user-installed eNodeB, known as a HeNodeB. The purpose of the HeNodeB is to extend coverage into areas that the eNodeB can't, or isn't able to provide adequate coverage for (in an economical fashion). Installations for HeNodeB's include users own homes, and/or places of business. When using a HeNodeB, the UE is connected to the Home eNodeB (HeNodeB or HeNB) via its radio interface while the backhaul link provides a broadband connection (e.g. cable, DSL, fiber) to the operators 's core network (via SeGW). Due to the importance of eNodeB in the

Figure 12. System architecture of HeNodeB

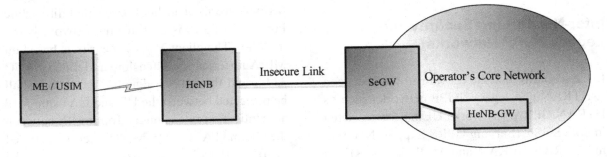

LTE, the security of the eNodeB should be given special treatment.

There are two 3GPP specifications focused on the security of the eNodeB. The technical report TS 32.820 gives an informative study on the eNodeB security. The other is TS 33.320 that is a normative technical specification which specifies the security architecture for the Home (e)NB (HeNodeB) subsystem. As proposed in 3GPP TR 33.820, the system architecture of HeNodeB includes four major components,

- UE,
- HeNodeB,
- Security Gateway (SeGW), and
- an optional Home eNodeB Gateway (HeNodeB-GW or HeNB-GW).

A basic HeNodeB system architecture is illustrated as in Figure 12.

In this HeNodeB system architecture, the air interface between UE and HeNodeB should be backwards compatible with the air interface in UTRAN or E-UTRAN. HeNodeB accesses the operator's core network through the SeGW. Security Gateway represents operator's core network to perform mandatory access control, which is achieved by mutual authentication with HeNodeB. After a successful mutual authentication between the HeNodeB and the SeGW, the HeNodeB will be connected by the SeGW to the operator's core network. Since the communication link between

HeNodeB and SeGW may be insecure, security tunnels may be established between HeNodeB and SeGW to protect information transmitted between them. HNB-GW performs the mandatory access control in case non-CSG capable UE attempt to access the HeNodeB. SeGW may be integrated into HeNodeB-GW when the latter is deployed.

SECURITY ARCHITECTURE OF HENODEB

Based on the system architecture of the HeNodeB, five security feature groups are defined for the HeNodeB security architecture, and each group is targeted to meet some security objectives. These five security feature groups are as below:

- **HeNodeB Access Security**: This is aimed to provide the access control based on the mutual authentication and authorization between HeNodeB and network (via SeGW), and security interactions between SeGW and CN.
- **Network Domain Security**: It includes a set of security features that include security communication between SeGW and CN.
- **HeNodeB Service Domain Security**: This is to provide security communication between HeNodeB and network entities in

the CN, such as the interaction between HeNodeB and OAM server in the CN.

- **UE Access Control Domain Security**: It aims to provide access control mechanisms between UE and CN.
- **UE Access Security Domain**: It is designed to provide UEs secure access to mobile communication system.

Security Requirements and Features of HeNodeB

The security threats to the HeNodeB could be classified into are six categories, which include compromise of HeNodeB credentials; physical/configuration/protocols attacks on HeNodeB; attacks on the core network (including HeNodeB location based attacks); user data and identity privacy attacks, and attacks on radio resources and management. All these threats have been addressed by countermeasures in technical report TR33.820.

These security threats on the HeNodeB imply additional security requirements. For example, the integrity of the HeNodeB should be validated and its identity should be authenticated by the SeGW before the connection to the core network is established. Also, the HeNodeB should authenticate the SeGW. Furthermore, the sensitive data such as cryptographic keys, user information, user plane and control plane data HeNodeB should not be maintained in a secure way such that they are not accessed by any unsecured third party. For the secured connection between HeNodeB and SeGW, the backhaul link is required to protected on the base of IKEv2. This provides integrity, confidentiality and replay protection. In the secured connection based on the IPSec ESP tunnel mode, any all traffic between the HeNodeB and the core network will be tunneled in the secured backhaul link.

To support the enhanced security of HeNodeB, a logical entity called the Trusted Environment (TrE) is introduced to provide a trustworthy environment for the function execution and data storage. All the output of the function inside the TrE will not be visible to the unauthorized external entities. The TrE is designed from a hardware-based root of trust, which is physically bound to the HeNodeB, and takes effect from the beginning of a secure system boot or hard reset. During the secure boot process, the integrity of the TrE is verified by the root of trust, and only after a successful verification it will be able to start to verify other components of the HeNodeB. The device integrity check by the TrE is a mandatory step before components is connecting to the core network.

Security Procedures Between HeNodeB and SeGW

To implement the mutual authentication between HeNodeB and SeGW, both of them should carry device certificates which are issued by some CA trusted by the operator. During the authentication between HeNodeB and SeGW, their certificates will be mutually verified by each other against their unique identity/name, along with a check on the revocation status of the certificates. In the process, the TrE in the HeNodeB are providing several critical security functions supporting the IKEv2 and certificate processes. Both the HeNodeB's identity and private key should be stored in and protected by the TrE. Also the root certificate used to verity the signatures of the SeGW certificate is also stored in the HeNodeB's TrE and only be accessible and modified by the authorized user.

After the mutual authentication is done, the HeNodeB should use the IKEv2 protocol to set up the IPsec tunnel to protect traffic between SeGW. Thus, the signaling, user and management traffic between the HeNodeB and SeGW will be transmitted in a secure IPsec ESP tunnel. During the IPsec tunnel establishment process, the HeNodeB initialize the creation of the IPsec SA, and the SeGW will allocate IP address to the HeNodeB when it receive the request from the HeNodeB.

OPEN CHALLENGE

LTE is a technology that targets to increase revenue, reduce deployment cost, and leverage investment as it cost-effectively provides customers with desirable performance for communication, entertainment, and various business operations over the networks. It leverages the rich heritage of proven and successful technologies as a part of 3GPP family. However, there are still many open issues that are deserved for further research. Some of these issues are power control, spectrum efficiency, interference, network capacity, and LTE applications.

In the mobile network such as LTE, the mobile devices have very limited battery capability. The UE could rapidly consume up its power for accessing rich data services with intensive transmissions. Therefore, how to increase the batter capability and how to save the energy during transmissions are still open for research. Modulation such as SC-FDMA could be further improved with the capability to dynamically adjust the transmission power in such way that the total transmission power is reduced and desirable PAPR is achieved. In addition, the signaling inference due to data transmissions can be reduced which again improve the packet delivery ratio.

LTE could be operated in different spectrum bands and the increase of the spectrum utilization is still an important issue. Compared to traditional voice service, data services demand more radio resources to support the high speed data transmissions as more bandwidth is required, operating in the same range of spectrum band. TLE should be able to properly allocate and effectively use the spectrum resource on the uplink and downlink. A LTE cell with 15KHz maximally supports up to 600 users. However, the link capacity for each user is still limited for high QoS services.

Voice communication is a fundamental application for mobile customers. However, the initial LTE standards development is focused on providing data services. Consequently, the current LTE is highly limited in providing voice services, equivalently to 3G voice. 2G/3G for mobile voice is deployed over the circuit switch network. In LTE, the circuit connection has been dropped and the connection to the user is purely packet-oriented data. Thus, the LTE operators have to implement additional protocols to enhance LTE standards, infrastructure, and user mobile devices for providing voice calling. The voice service over the LTE with QoS guarantee should be carefully addressed in the context of emerging LTE standards to enable end-to-end QoS provision and management. Other issues for LTE voice include voice access control, voice link latency, and voice handover as the voice service is roaming among distinguished networks. Voice safety, on the other hand, has additional requirements beyond the current LTE security solutions. For example, LTE voice security must ensure the voice messages are delivered intended recipient.

CONCLUSION

Over the last few years, mobile users experience the even growing demand for wirelessly accessing the Internet over the mobile device for various services. This motivates the researchers and engineers in the telecommunication industry to define novel air interfaces and system frameworks for high broadband services. The 3GPP LTE is a design to increase the overall system capacity for high speed while reducing the latency. It improves the spectrum efficiency and offer desirable QoS for broadband and high mobile users. The LTE downlink and uplink in PHY define their modulation, multiplexing, and physical channel for improving the LTE network capacity. The spectrum efficiency and latency for the downlink and uplink are improved for supporting scalable LTE bandwidth utilization. LTE Link and MAC layers are designed to establish the wireless links connecting the LTE UE and the eNodeB in such a way to effectively allocate the spectrum subcarriers for packet transmissions. In addition, the LTE security protects the user, infrastructure and application from various malicious attacks.

REFERENCES

Astely, D., Dahlman, E., Furuskar, A., Jading, Y., Lindstrom, M., & Parkvall, S. (2009). LTE: The evolution of mobile broadband. *IEEE Communications Magazine, 47*(4), 44–51. doi:10.1109/MCOM.2009.4907406

Ghosh, A., Ratasuk, R., Mondal, B., Mangalvedhe, N., & Thomas, T. (2010). LTE-advanced: Next-generation wireless broadband technology. *IEEE Wireless Communications, 17*(3), 10–22. doi:10.1109/MWC.2010.5490974

3GPP TR 33.820. (2009). *Security of home node B (HNB) / Home evolved node B (HeNB).*

3GPP TS 33.320. (2009). *Security of home node B (HNB) / Home evolved node B (HeNB).*

3GPP TS 33.401. (2009). *3GPP system architecture evolution (SAE)-Security architecture.*

3GPP TS 33.402. (2009). *3GPP system architecture evolution (SAE)- Security aspects of non-3GPP accesses.*

3GPP TS 36.300. (2008). *Evolved universal terrestrial radio access (E-UTRA) and evolved universal terrestrial radio access network (E-UTRAN)- Overall description, stage 2.*

3GPP TS 36.321. (2008). http://www.3gpp.org/ftp/Specs/html-info/36321.htm *Evolved universal terrestrial radio access (E-UTRA)- Medium access control (MAC) protocol specification.*

3GPP TS 36.322. (2008). *Evolved universal terrestrial radio access (E-UTRA)- Radio link control (RLC) protocol specification.*

3GPP TS 36.323. (2008). *Evolved universal terrestrial radio access (E-UTRA)- Radio link control protocol (PDCP) specification.*

3GPP TS 36.938. (2008). *Evolved universal terrestrial radio access network (E-UTRAN)- Improved network controlled mobility between E-UTRAN and 3GPP2/mobile WiMAX radio technologies.*

Homayounfar, K., & Rohani, B. (2009). *CQI measurement and reporting in LTE: A new framework.* Technical report of IEICE.

Hou, X., Zhang, Z., & Kayama, H. (2009). DMRS design and channel estimation for LTE-advanced MIMO uplink. In *Proceeding of IEEE VTC.*

Larmo, A., Lindström, M., Meyer, M., Pelletier, G., Torsner, J., & Wiemann, H. (2009). The LTE link-layer design. *IEEE Communications Magazine, 47*(4), 52–59. doi:10.1109/MCOM.2009.4907407

Lee, S., Choudhury, S., Khoshnevis, A., Xu, S., & Lu, S. (2009). Downlink MIMO with frequency-domain packet scheduling for 3GPP LTE. In *Proceeding of the INFOCOM.*

Lin, Z., Xiao, P., Vucetic, B., & Sellathurai, M. (2010). Analysis of receiver algorithms for LTE SC-FDMA based uplink MIMO systems. *IEEE Transactions on Wireless Communications, 9*(1), 60–65. doi:10.1109/TWC.2010.01.090199

Lo, A., & Niemegeers, I. (2009). Multi-hop relay architectures for 3GPP LTE-advanced. In *Proceedings of the IEEE 9th Malaysia International Conference on Communications.*

Mogensen, P. E., Koivisto, T., Pedersen, K. I., Kovacs, I. Z., Raaf, B., Pajukoski, K., & Rinne, M. J. (2009). LTE-advanced: The path towards gigabit/s in wireless mobile communications. In *Proceedings of the Wireless VITAE '09.*

Ng, M. H., Lin, S., Li, J., & Tatesh, S. (2009). Coexistence studies for 3GPP LTE with other mobile systems. *IEEE Communications Magazine, 47*(4), 60–65. doi:10.1109/MCOM.2009.4907408

Pokhariyal, A., Kolding, T. E., & Mogensen, P. E. (2006). Performance of downlink frequency domain packet scheduling for the UTRAN long term evolution. In *Proceeding of 17ᵗʰ PIMRC*.

Song, W. J., Chung, J., Lee, D., Lim, C., Choi, S., & Yeoum, T. (2009). Improvements to seamless vertical handover between mobile WiMAX and 3GPP UTRAN through the evolved packet core. *IEEE Communications Magazine, 47*(4), 66–73. doi:10.1109/MCOM.2009.4907409

ENDNOTES

[1] Subscriber Stations are equivalent to terms of mobile device, user equipments, and mobile stations.

[2] In LTE, the Base Station is referred to as eNodeB.

Chapter 17
Service Level Provisioning for Cloud-Based Applications

Valeria Cardellini
University of Roma, Italy

Emiliano Casalicchio
University of Roma, Italy

Luca Silvestri
University of Roma, Italy

ABSTRACT

Cloud computing has recently emerged in the landscape of Information Technology as a compelling paradigm for managing and delivering services over the Internet in a performance- and cost-effective way. However, its development is still at its infancy, with many issues worthy to be investigated. In this chapter, we analyze the problem of service level provisioning and the possible strategies that can be used to tackle it at the various layers of the cloud architecture, focusing on the perspective of cloud-based application providers. We also propose an approach for the dynamic QoS provisioning of cloud-based applications which takes into account that the provider has to fulfill the service level settled with the application users while minimizing the resources outsourced from the cloud infrastructure in such a way to maximize its profits.

DOI: 10.4018/978-1-61350-110-8.ch017

Copyright © 2012, IGI Global. Copying or distributing in print or electronic forms without written permission of IGI Global is prohibited.

INTRODUCTION

Cloud computing has emerged as a new paradigm in IT that lets cloud-service clients deploy their applications in a large-scale environment with an expectation of good scalability, availability, fault tolerance, and reduced administration costs. Cloud computing enables open market service providers and enterprises to outsource computational and storage utilities with the promise to scale up in case of peak load, to rely on high availability, and to drastically reduce the start up and management cost of data centers. Moreover, the "elastic" property of cloud computing, if properly exploited, avoids over provisioning of resources in case of scarce demand that, along with the resource sharing at infrastructure level, contributes to energy saving.

To exploit the opportunities offered by cloud computing, enterprise and service providers need new mechanisms to dynamically and adaptively plan the capacity that can be outsourced from the infrastructures and platforms, thus to provide their end users with the agreed level of service while minimizing the leasing costs they pay to the infrastructures and platforms providers.

The cloud computing architecture consists of three abstract layers: the Infrastructure as a Service (IaaS) layer at the bottom of the stack (*e.g.*, Amazon EC2, Eucaliptus, InterGrid), the Platform as a Service (PaaS) layer collocated in the middle (*e.g.*, Microsoft Azure, Google AppEngine), and the Software/Application as a Service (SaaS) layer at the top that features a complete application offered as a service (*e.g.*, Google Apps, Facebook, YouTube).

The cloud infrastructure owners (that is, the IaaS providers) have to face the problem of virtualized and physical resource management in order to provide the agreed levels of service to their IaaS customers. These problems have been widely addressed in literature, *e.g.*, (Nguyen Van, Dang Tran, & Menaud, 2009), (Song et al., 2009), (Chen, Wo, & Li, 2009) to mention few. In the same way, there is a growing interest in the

provisioning of some Quality of Service (QoS) guarantees at the upper layers (*i.e.*, PaaS and SaaS) of the cloud architecture (Nguyen Van, Dang Tran, & Menaud, 2009), (Fakhouri et al., 2001), (Wang et al., 2007) (Urgaonkar et al., 2008), (Lim et al. 2009), (De Assuncao, Di Costanzo, & Buyya, 2009). QoS provisioning is not a new issue in networked and distributed systems; however, cloud and service computing paradigms increase the system complexity and scale, therefore posing new challenges that are worth to be faced.

In this chapter we discuss the problem of service level provisioning from the perspective of the IaaS customers that provide cloud-based applications to end users (Lim et al., 2009). We first classify the QoS provisioning strategies on the basis of the cloud architecture layer at which they can be applied to and on the basis of the entity that can operate these strategies. Then, we discuss the main issues in dynamic QoS provisioning for IaaS customers and the possible solutions. We next propose some QoS provisioning algorithms for cloud-based applications that we have designed and evaluated through simulation experiments. Cloud-based services are characterized by two key features (i.e., pay-per-use and on-demand resource provisioning) whose economic impact is that consumers only pay for the resources they actually use. Therefore, in the cloud computing environment, the cloud service providers have to minimize the usage of the cloud infrastructure while maximizing the resource utilization in such a way to maximize their profits by fulfilling the obligations settled in a Service Level Agreement (SLA) with their consumers. The approach to dynamic service provisioning we present in this chapter aims to achieve these criteria. Specifically, we propose and evaluate through simulation experiments two algorithms. Both algorithms aim to dimension the pool of resources that the provider offering the cloud-based application has to lease from the cloud infrastructure. The first algorithm reacts to occurred SLA violations, while the second attempts to proactively determine possible future SLA violations.

The chapter is organized as follows. In the second section we present some background on cloud computing, analyzing the resource management and the QoS provisioning problems. We discuss the different layers (i.e., IaaS, PaaS, and SaaS) of the cloud stack at which QoS provisioning strategies can be applied and by whom they can be operated, and how the QoS provisioning strategies interact with the resource management strategies. The third section is devoted to the solutions that the SaaS providers can apply to dynamically manage the QoS provisioning. We do not only analyze solutions that have been proposed for cloud computing, but we also review potential solutions that have been adopted in the last ten years for distributed systems, such as Content Delivery Networks and distributed Web-based systems, and can be successfully applied in the cloud context. In the fourth section, we propose our solution to manage the automated service provisioning for IaaS customers. We formulate this capacity planning problem as an optimization problem and propose both reactive and proactive resource allocation algorithms that approximate the optimal solution by exploiting information about the system performance history. Differently from other approaches that consider service level objectives based on average values of performance metrics, we propose an SLA based on the maximum percentage of SLA violations allowed by the application customers. Finally, we conclude the chapter with some final remarks and discuss the future research directions for the service level provisioning that can be operated by the SaaS providers.

BACKGROUND

Today, cloud computing is often used as general term to indicate any solution that allows the outsourcing of any kind of hosting and computing resources. As discussed in (Vaquero et al., 2009), in less than three years there have been more than 20 definitions of cloud computing, *e.g.*, see (Buyya et al., 2009) and (Armbrust et al., 2009), and recently there has been an attempt to provide a standard definition. Some definitions stress the scalability and "elasticity" properties, other beat on the automation of resource management, other focus on the "pay-per-use" or "pay-as-you-go" business model. Also the National Institute of Standard and Technologies (NIST) (Mell & Grance, 2009) has provided a definition of cloud computing. However, the definition that best fits to our perception of the cloud as a service-oriented, dynamically reconfigurable, and SLA customizable system, has been provided in (Vaquero et al., 2009):

"Clouds are a large pool of easily usable and accessible virtualized resources (such as hardware, development platforms and/or services). These resources can be dynamically reconfigured to adjust to a variable load (scale), allowing also for an optimum resource utilization. This pool of resources is typically exploited by a pay-per-use model in which guarantees are offered by the Infrastructure Provider by means of customized SLAs."

However, neither the cloud computing definition above reported nor the others previously cited, explicitly mention the cloud computing actors and provide details on the cloud computing architecture. Therefore, we will first briefly cover these issues and then move on with the QoS provisioning approaches.

The actors involved in the cloud are essentially three: the *service provider*, the *service user*, and the *infrastructure provider*. The service provider offers services to the users through an Internet-based interface. To this end, the service provider uses resources (virtualized and software) that are furnished and managed by the infrastructure provider, thus to reduce costs and gain in flexibility. It is worth to point out that all the cloud actors take some form of utility from the service exchange and that the latter is regulated by a service contract, the Service Level Agreement (SLA), where the level of service is formally defined (Wu & Buyya, 2011). The SLA may specify the levels of availability, serviceability, performance, operation, and other attributes of the service, such as billing. For each one of these functional and not functional QoS requirements a Service Level Objective (SLO) is defined, that is a threshold on the value assumed by the QoS metrics/attributes (e.g., the minimum availability averaged over a given period, the average response time, or even more stringent requirements such as the 90-percentile of the response time or the tail of the response time distribution). Non-compliance to the agreement may incur in penalties paid by the service providers. To this end, the SLA typically contains an insurance clause offering some form of compensation to the user if the provider fails to provide the SLO according to the minimum levels specified in the contract (e.g., Amazon EC2 or Google App Engine SLA policies). The service contracts in the cloud environment typically differ from traditional SLA contracts in that they provide a more flexible service accounting scheme, typically referred to as "pay-per-use" or "pay-as-you-go". This kind of accounting scheme derives from utility computing (Wilkes, Mogul, & Suermondt, 2004), (Wu & Buyya, 2011).

Cloud computing is architected in a stack composed by three main abstract layers (Zhang, Cheng, & Boutaba, 2010), (Lenk et al., 2009): the infrastructure layer, the platform layer, and the application layer. Each layer offers to the upper layer its resources as a set of services, in the spirit of earlier distributed computing and network architectures. In this new computing paradigm, that allows to access both virtualized and software resources commonly referred to as Anything-as-a-Service (XaaS) (Kim, Beloglazov, & Buyya, 2009), the stack layers are classified on the basis of the service they provide. The three

layers, which are depicted in *Figure* 1 along with the cloud actors, provide the following services:

- Infrastructure-as-a-Service (IaaS) virtualizes the hardware layer and offers computing services such as storage, CPU, memory, and network. The CPU, memory, and local storage are packaged as virtual machines of different sizes, each with a price per hour (or KB in case of memory/storage).

- Platform-as-a-Service (PaaS) offers platform services, such as Web, application, and database servers, and a programming environment associated with it. Programmers can use this environment to develop, test, and deploy their applications. PaaS leases/uses IaaS services by requesting from them virtual machines and storage and deploying application containers on the virtual machines. There can be many platforms running on the same cloud infrastructure.

- Software-as-a-Service (SaaS) consists of simple or composite services (e.g., SOA applications) offered to the end users. Those applications are deployed in PaaS containers on architectures specific for each application. Usually, many applications share the same PaaS. In general, a SaaS user pays a service subscription.

The infrastructure providers manage the IaaS layer and often also the PaaS layer, while the service providers manage the SaaS layer and some time the PaaS layer. The service provider can be also an independent entity that leverages totally or partially cloud computing resources. The service user can be directly a customer of either the IaaS or the PaaS/SaaS. For example, a researcher can lease computational power from Amazon EC2 to run experiments and can use Google Docs to share the experimental results with her colleagues. However, as stated in (Lenk et al., 2009), there are not clear boundaries among IaaS, PaaS, and

Figure 1. Cloud computing stack and its relationship with cloud computing actors

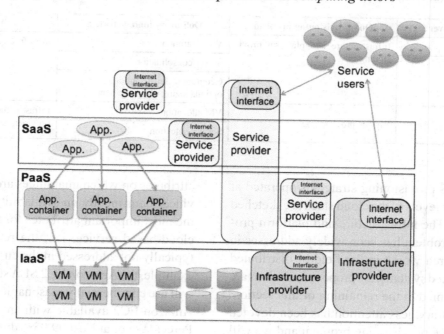

SaaS providers. For example, Google provides solutions at infrastructure level (Google File System and Google BigTable), at platform level (Google App Engine), and at application layer (e.g., Google Docs and Gmail). Similarly, Amazon offers services at the infrastructure (Amazon Elastic Cloud Computing, EC2), platform (Amazon Simple Storage Service, S3, and Amazon SimpleDB), and service levels (e.g., Amazon Alexa Web Information Service, AWIS).

The three cloud computing layers also differ from a quality of service prospective (i.e., performance, dependability, and security). For example, the access to virtualized and software resources results in different dependability and security requirements; a B2B or B2C enterprise user has typically performance, dependability, and security requirements more stringent that the SLO of a consumer (e.g., a researcher); moreover, the revenue/economic model and business goal of the above mentioned users and the cloud computing layers are dissimilar (Litoiu et at., 2010).

This heterogeneity originates diverse and often contrasting challenges that must be addressed at the different layers (Zhang, Cheng, & Boutaba, 2010). In this chapter, we focus on the cloud aspects related to the dynamic QoS provisioning which can be classified according to the layers in the cloud stack:

- the *infrastructure and platform provisioning,* that is related to mapping virtual machines (VMs) on physical resources and application containers on VMs in order to satisfy SLAs agreed with the infrastructure/platform users and to maximize revenues for the infrastructure and platform providers;
- the *service provisioning,* that is related to mapping applications to application containers or applications directly to VMs in order to satisfy SLAs agreed with the users of the cloud-based applications and to maximize revenues of the service providers offering the applications.

Table 1. Cloud computing stack versus QoS strategies

Cloud stack layer	QoS provisioning problem	QoS provisioning strategy	Actuator
IaaS	Infrastructure and platform provisioning	VM migration	Infrastructure provider
PaaS		Server consolidation	
		Geographical distribution, optimal sizing and placement	
SaaS	Service provisioning	VM allocation	Infrastructure provider, service provider, service user
		Service selection	

The QoS provisioning strategies operated at the different levels of the cloud stack are sketched in *Table 1*. The infrastructure and platform provisioning problem has been widely addresses in many research works in the field of distributed and networked systems; the proposed solutions are briefly resumed in the remaining of this section. On the contrary, less attention has been devoted to the service provisioning problem and we will more deeply discuss it in the third section, being also the focus of our proposal.

INFRASTRUCTURE AND PLATFORM PROVISIONING

The infrastructure providers, among all the infrastructure management aspects, deal with the problems related to the mapping of virtual machines on physical resources and of application containers on VMs. At infrastructure and platform levels, the resource management is driven by:

1. the SLA exposed by IaaS (e.g., the minimum availability level that the provider guarantees to its users);
2. the data center policy related to governance costs (e.g., the maximization of resource usage and minimization of power consumption).

With regard to the SLA definition, we observe that most cloud providers define SLAs for the services they offer. However, the non-functional attributes on which guarantees are typically provided focus mostly on availability, while one of the most important attributes for the users of the cloud-based service, i.e., the response time, is typically not addressed in the current SLAs. For example, the Amazon EC2 SLA states that "AWS will use commercially reasonable efforts to make Amazon EC2 available with an Annual Uptime Percentage of at least 99.95% during the Service Year" (Amazon EC2 Service Level Agreement, 2010). The same SLA includes also provider-side penalties to compensate users for downtime periods. The motivation for the lack of the response time guarantee is simple: response times depend on many factors that may be not under the control of the service provider (e.g., the network path to the cloud platform), and the traffic addressed to the cloud-based service may be highly unpredictable (for example, Web-based services are characterized by flash crowds). Therefore, the enforcement of a particular level of the response time is not a trivial task for the cloud provider and requires the ability to dynamically manage the resources assignment to the cloud-based applications in an elastic way in order to face highly variable traffic conditions. For example, cloud providers can allocate additional computational resources on the fly to handle increased demand and can deallocate them when the traffic directed to the application decreases. A well-known example of cloud-based application leveraging the cloud elasticity regards the release of the Animoto web application on Facebook in 2008.

The main strategies adopted to guarantee SLA in *infrastructure and platform provisioning* can be classified as:

- **virtual machine migration**, that provides significant benefits to balance load across the data center and to enable robust and highly responsive provisioning in data centers;
- **server consolidation**, that is a practice to maximize resource utilization while minimizing energy consumption;
- **geographical distribution of data centers**, that along with optimal sizing and placement policies allows to reduce significantly energy, infrastructures, and connectivity costs.

Because of the vastness of the space regarding the solutions for infrastructure and platform provisioning, in this chapter we avoid dealing with them in depth, but we rather provide below only a summary of the main issues and some related references.

Virtual machine migration is an approach introduced in the last decade to improve and automate data centers and clusters administration (fault management, load balancing, and system maintenance) and to isolate performance and resources usage. VM migration is mainly operated intra-cluster or intra-data center, that is VMs are migrated across local area networks. For example, (Clark et al., 2005) suggests operating system live migration as an approach to reduce problems that typically arise during process-level migration. Migrating an entire VM eliminates the problem of residual dependencies management, the original host may be decommissioned, and in-memory state can be transferred in a consistent way. Finally, live VM migration completely decouples the user behavior (e.g., applications running on the VM or OS configuration) from the data center/cluster management. (Wood et al., 2009) presents the Sandpiper system for automatic

monitoring and detection of workload hotspots, that determines when to migrate or resize a VM, and an automatic hotspot migration algorithm, that finds out what and where to migrate and how many resources. This solution allows to respond promptly to sudden changes in the workload conditions. A similar approach to automatic VM migration is in (Andreolini et al., 2009), that presents some management algorithms to decide about reallocations of virtual machines in a cloud context characterized by a large numbers of hosts. The proposed algorithms identify the real critical instances and take decisions without recurring to typical thresholds. Moreover, they consider the load trend behavior of the resources instead of instantaneous or average measures.

While the previous solutions mainly concern intra-cluster/data center migration, WAN extensions have been recently proposed with systems to transfer disk status and to migrate seamlessly network connections. For example, (Hirofuchi et al., 2009) proposes a storage access mechanism that strongly supports live VM migration over WAN. The proposed mechanism is one of the first steps towards the VM migration among service providers, e.g., IaaS providers. However, wide-area live migration still remains expensive to use because of the bandwidth bottleneck, especially when considering migrations of large clusters of virtual machines rather than single instances, and deserves further research work.

Many research proposals that address infrastructure and platform provisioning issues regard VM provisioning and resource allocation. (Nguyen Van, Dang Tran, & Menaud, 2009) proposes a model to provision the appropriate number of physical resources to VMs when application-level SLAs are imposed by the service users. (Padala et al., 2005) uses the classical control theory and the black-box system modeling approach to design an adaptive resource control system that dynamically adjusts the resource shares to individual tiers in order to meet multi-tier application-level QoS goals, while achieving high resource utilization in the data center. (Song et al., 2008) and (Song et al., 2009) propose resource scheduling schemes, including resource flowing algorithms, to optimize resource allocations amongst services.

Service consolidation is an approach to maximize resource utilization while minimizing energy consumption in large scale clusters and data centers. For the readers interested in deepening data center related issues, we suggest the survey in (Kant, 2009). With regard to the server consolidation problem, (Li et al., 2009), (Srikantaiah, Kansal, & Zhao, 2008), and (Jung et al., 2008) propose heuristics to tackle it, being this problem formulated as an NP-hard optimization problem. However, server consolidation may significantly impact on application performances (Jung et al., 2009). For example, the VM footprint may vary over time causing congestion; therefore, the system needs some mechanism to react quickly (Wood et al., 2009).

The geographical distribution of data centers, along with their optimal placement and sizing policies, plays a key role for the QoS provisioning at the infrastructure layer (Greenberg et al., 2009). These issues represent a challenging optimization problem, that involves several factors, and determine interesting research opportunities yet to be explored.

Data servers are usually located close to sources of cheap electricity, water, land, and manpower to reduce their management costs (Kant, 2009); these technical and non-technical factors are used to place mega data centers, which can be composed by 100,000-1,000,000 servers and are typical of large cloud providers (e.g., Amazon, Google, Microsoft). On the other hand, there are fewer restrictions for placing a micro (or even a nano) data center containing a few hundreds or a few thousands of servers. The policies that drive the appropriate sizing of a data center also depend on the kind of the data center, being the difference again between mega and micro data centers (Greenberg et al., 2009). The adoption of small-size data centers is also a trend towards

the greening of the Internet, because it allows to save energy with respect to traditional large-size data centers (Valancius et al., 2009).

Moreover, multiple data centers can be located across multiple sites either within a region or around the world in order to create a geographically distributed data center. The advantages of having geographically dispersed data centers include high availability and disaster recovery (e.g., in case of power outages taking out an entire site), as well as the reduction of the latency between a data center and its end users. However, to achieve these potential advantages many non-trivial issues need to be solved, including data replication (e.g., asynchronous vs. synchronous replication), state replication, monitoring of system components that span multiple system platforms, geographical load redirection, and distribution policies. Although these issues have been largely investigated in the field of distributed systems, to face the ultra-large scale of cloud systems they require new solutions that address jointly the network and data center resources (Greenberg et al., 2009), so that tradeoffs between service performance and network communication costs can be better designed and evaluated.

Table 1 summarizes the main QoS provisioning strategies we have discussed so far and introduce the solutions typically used at the service level that we will analyze in the next section.

SERVICE LEVEL PROVISIONING SOLUTIONS

At application layer, the resource management problem can be formulate as follow: *"To find, in case of unpredictable and suddenly changing workload conditions, the set of VMs that should be allocated, or more in general, the set of services that should be selected to guarantee the SLA fulfillment and to minimize the management cost"*. The resources/services selection is driven by the business-level SLA of the hosted applications, and therefore by the service user needs. It is in charge of the service provider to enforce the SLA agreed with its customers. The SaaS provider should size (by means of allocation or selection) the IaaS/PaaS resources used to provide the cloud-based application in order to satisfy the SLOs of the service users, to scale up the application load, or to meet its own performance, dependability, and/or security requirements while minimizing its operating costs.

For example, a SaaS provider that agrees with its customer an SLA expressed as a response time constraint should use a VM allocation policy that allows to honor the SLAs established with its customers (to avoid penalties and to increase its reputation) and to maximize the VMs utilization (to reduce allocation costs).

There is a variety of mechanisms that a service provider can adopt to guarantee a certain level of QoS, including, besides allocation and selection, admission control and performance isolation. However, when dealing with large scale services subject to suddenly changing workload conditions, all the solutions are based on the concept of autonomic computing (Huebscher & McCann, 2008). The architecture of an autonomic system comprises a set of managed resources and managers. Each manager communicates with the resources through a sensor/actuator mechanism and the decision is elaborated using the so called MAPE (Monitor, Analyze, Plan, Execute) reference model from the IBM's autonomic computing initiative (Kephart & Chess, 2003). This autonomic loop collects information from the system, makes decisions and then organizes the adaptation actions needed to achieve goals and objectives, and controls the execution.

To achieve a high degree of flexibility in allocating the computing resources on one hand and to comply to users' requirements specified in the SLAs on the other, also cloud systems should be organized according to the autonomic loop (Brandic, 2009). In such a way, cloud-based applications could be able to automatically respond to changing components, workload, and environmental conditions while minimizing the operating costs and preventing violations of the agreed SLAs. Up to the time of writing, only few research works have addressed monitoring, SLA management, and self-management issues in cloud systems, while they have received much more attention in related research areas, such as Grid and SOA based systems.

The problem of service level provisioning has been widely investigated in the last thirty years, especially each time a new computing paradigm has been introduced. Several efforts to perform adaptive scaling of applications based on workload monitoring have been proposed in the last ten years. For example, in the context of distributed Web systems, (Guitart et al., 2008) presents an admission control strategy that uses admission control and dynamic resource provisioning to manage application servers running secure web applications. (Urgaonkar et al., 2008) proposes a dynamic provisioning technique for multi-tier Internet applications that employs a flexible queuing model to determine the right amount of resources allocated to each tier of the application, and a combination of predictive and reactive methods that determine when to provision these resources, both at large and small time scales. Also having multi-tier architectures as system target, (Ardagna, Trubian, & Zhang, 2007) proposes a resource allocation scheduler that aims to maximize the profits associated with multiple class SLAs and develops heuristic solutions, being the formulated optimization problem an NP-hard one. (Abrahao et al., 2006) proposes a self-adaptive capacity management framework based on an optimization model. The framework links a cost model based on SLA contracts with an analytical queuing-based performance model in order to adapt in real time the shared platform providing the Internet services to variable capacity needs. The authors of (Irwin et al., 2006) have developed the Shirako system for on-demand leasing of shared networked resources in the

Xen virtualization environment. Shirako allows to allocate virtual resources to guest applications from a pool of available resources across multiple autonomous sites in such a way to adapt to the dynamics of resource competition and changing load. In (Shivam, Babu, & Chase, 2006) NIMO builds a predictive performance model of the application by using active learning techniques and then allocates the resources necessary to the application on the basis of the model.

Now is the momentum of cloud computing and the first solutions for the autonomic service provisioning have appeared in literature. They can be mainly divided in two approaches:

- **service selection** policies;
- **resource allocation** schemes.

(Zeng, Zhao, & Zeng, 2009) proposes a service selection approach to satisfy the user SLO (*e.g.*, minimum cost and maximum gain in term of QoS satisfaction). The authors assume that the services run on a cloud infrastructure and are accessed by the users through a service proxy, which is in charge of the service discovery and selection phases. Another strategy still based on service selection has been proposed in (Nallur & Bashsoon, 2010) that suggests a market-based mechanism, relaying on the concept of service contract bidding in order to allow web applications living in the cloud to self-configure with regard to their quality attributes.

(Lim et al., 2009) suggests a different approach, where the cloud customers are empowered with their own dynamic controller, which is located outside the cloud platform or provided as an extension of the cloud platform. Such controller correlates the VM CPU load levels with the cluster size and automatically adds (or removes) VMs from the cluster when the CPU utilization exceeds (or falls below) a given threshold. Also (Litoiu et al., 2010) proposes that the cloud users (at application level) should be able to access mechanisms and to define policies to automatically size the number of

application container instances, thus to reduce the application cost. Also in this case, the proposed solution is a multi-layer model for adaptive feedback optimization and control. A similar solution available on the market is Amazon Auto Scaling (2010) service, that allows consumers to scale up or down seamlessly and automatically the number of Amazon EC2 instances they are using according to specified conditions, for example when the average CPU utilization of the instances currently used exceeds a given threshold.

Most of the approaches proposed so far for the resource allocation in cloud computing consider as their allocation granularity the whole virtual machine. A fine-grained approach is PRESS (Gong, Gu, & Wilkes, 2010), that proposes an elastic VM resource scaling scheme where the CPU resource limit for the virtual machine is set on the basis of a resource demands prediction. The online prediction is achieved through the usage of lightweight signal processing and statistical learning algorithms.

The recent introduction of EC2 Spot Instances by Amazon (Amazon EC2 Spot Instances, 2010) paves the way to the study of bidding-based solutions in the context of cloud computing. A spot instance is an EC2 instance on which the SaaS provider bids on to allocate it. Whenever the instance price falls below the bid price, the spot instance is allocated to the user, while, in the opposite case, user instances are terminated without warning. It is worth to note that spot instances can be an adequate solution only for non-critical cloud-based applications, because the application should be able to tolerate volatility. In this context, (Andrzejak, Kondo, & Yi, 2010) proposes a market-based probabilistic model for cost and performance optimization using EC2 Spot Instances. To help the user decide how to bid, given some SLA constraints, the authors propose and evaluate through simulation a probabilistic model that allow to optimize cost, performance, and reliability. From this work it emerges that market-based VM allocation can have a strong

Figure 2. System architecture

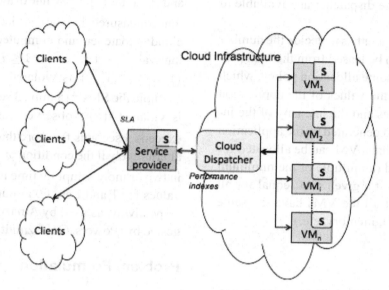

impact on SLA satisfaction. An open challenge is how to apply the market-based probabilistic model to a workload generated by heterogeneous applications.

A service level provisioning policy can be designed to obtain a *short term* or a *medium/long term* performance and cost optimization. A short term solution finds the service selection or resource allocation to guarantee the SLO at the minimum cost for a given service demand and in a given time instant. When a relevant change either in the SLA parameters or in the workload is detected, the provisioning policy computes a new solution, but the decision is taken without considering its effect on the long term. An alternative approach is to take the service level provisioning decision by considering the side effects it can have on the SLA guarantee and on the operating costs over a longer time horizon (medium/long term). For example, de-allocating a pool of VMs to reduce the cost on a short term can result in additional management costs or SLA violations (and therefore on contract penalties) because of the time needed to re-allocate the resources for managing a sudden increase in the workload intensity. All

the above cited approaches are designed for short term service level provisioning. In the next section we propose a solution for medium/long term service level provisioning.

MEDIUM/LONG TERM QOS PROVISIONING

To address the problem of automated medium/long term provisioning for SaaS providers that offer cloud-based applications with SLAs we consider the system architecture illustrated in Figure 2. In this architecture, the provider of a service S, accessible through a web service or a web interface, leases computational power from an IaaS provider. The service provider needs to allocate/deallocate VMs to fulfill the SLA stipulated with the clients (end-users or service brokers) and aims to seek the maximum profit while minimizing the operating costs. The incoming load addressed to the cloud-hosted application is distributed among the active VMs by a cloud dispatcher on the basis of some distribution policy. Performance measures (*e.g.*, response time, requests count, network traffic, etc.) measured at the dispatcher are available to the SaaS provider.

The service provider has to decide the number of VMs that need to be leased from the IaaS provider by means of some allocation policy, which takes into account the values of the application performance indexes and the intensity of the incoming request load generated by the application users. We assume that a VM can be allocated for a given time period (a multiple of the minimum allocation period), at a given cost (equal for all the VMs), and that all the VMs have the same configuration (CPU, memory, etc.).

SLA Definition

We propose a SLA based on the maximum percentage of SLO violations allowed by the clients of the cloud-based application. Hence, the service provider specifies its SLA as a tuple $(\tau, X_{max}, T, V_{max})$, where:

- τ is the SLA observation period used to compute the average response time;
- X_{max} is the maximum value for the average response time during an observation period;
- T is the SLA time span (*i.e.*, window), defined as an integer multiple of τ;
- V_{max} is the maximum fraction of observation periods in T where the observed average response time can exceed X_{max}.

The fraction $V_{T,\tau}$ of observation periods during which X_{max} is exceeded is defined as follows:

$$V_{T,\tau} = \frac{\sum_{i=1}^{N} \Gamma(\hat{x}_{\tau,i}, X_{max})}{N}, \qquad N = \frac{T}{\tau} \qquad (1)$$

where

$$\Gamma(\hat{x}_{\tau,i}, X_{max}) = \begin{cases} 1 & if \ \hat{x}_{\tau,i} > X_{max} \\ 0 & otherwise \end{cases} \qquad (2)$$

and $\hat{x}_{\tau,i}$ is the average value of the service response time, measured by the service provider at the cloud dispatcher, and computed in the i-th time interval $[(i-1)\tau, i\tau]$, $1 \le i \le N$. The SLA $(\tau, X_{max}, T, V_{max})$ is violated if $V_{T,\tau} > V_{max}$. For example the SLA = (5 min., 3 sec., 60 min., 10%) is violated if the observed response time $x_{\tau,i}$ exceeds 3 seconds for more than 9.6 minutes, or alternatively if the condition $\hat{x}_{\tau,i} > 3$ sec. occurs in two or more sampling time intervals. Realistic values for T and τ are 60 minutes and 5 minutes respectively, as used by Amazon EC2 or as suggested by (Powers, Goldszmidt, & Cohen, 2005).

Problem Formulation

Our problem is to find a VM allocation **m** which minimizes the allocation cost in the medium term time horizon $T' = M \cdot T$ and guarantees that the SLA agreed with the application users is not violated.

Let us suppose that the service provider can allocate a virtual machine for a minimum time interval $T_{alloc} = T$ and that the decision to allocate/deallocate a VM is taken every T time unit. Furthermore, we assume that the system is composed by the cloud dispatcher and that the set of VMs can be modeled as a network of k M/M/1 systems (we do not consider the delays introduced by the provider and the dispatcher).

Let us define:

- m_j, the number of virtual machines allocated in the j-th time interval $[(j-1)T, jT], 1 \le j \le M$;
- $\lambda_{i,j}$, the service request arrival rate in the time interval

$$[(i-1)\tau, i\tau] \subset [(j-1)T, jT],$$

- $1 \le i \le N, 1 \le j \le M$, where τ is the SLA observation period previously defined;

- μ, the service rate of each VM (the service time is exponentially distributed). We assume that all the VMs have the same performance characteristics and therefore the same service rate;

- $x_{i,j}$, the average service response time observed at the cloud dispatcher and computed in time interval

$$[(i-1)\tau, i\tau] \subset [(j-1)T, jT], i \in [1, N], j \in [1, M]$$

Assuming that the load is uniformly distributed across the m_j VMs, we have:

$$x_{i,j} = \frac{1}{\mu - \lambda_{i,j} m_j^{-1}} \qquad (3)$$

- c, the cost to use a VM for T time units;
- C, the allocation cost over the medium time horizon T', defined as:

$$C = \sum_{j=1}^{M} m_j \cdot c \qquad (4)$$

Under the assumption that $x_{i,j}$, defined in (3) approximates the observed average service response time $\hat{x}_{i,j}$ of the set of m_j VMs, and that the service provider has to guarantee the fulfillment of an SLA agreed with the users and defined by the tuple $(\tau, X_{max}, T, V_{max})$, we define the optimal VM allocation problem as follows:

OPT: $\min_{T'} C \qquad (5)$

s.t.:

$$V_{T,j} \leq V_{max} \qquad j \in [1, M] \qquad (6)$$

$$x_{i,j} = \frac{1}{\mu - \lambda_{i,j} m_j^{-1}} \qquad i \in [1, N], j \in [1, M]$$

$$(7)$$

$$\lambda_{i,j} m_j^{-1} \leq \mu \qquad i \in [1, N], j \in [1, M] \qquad (8)$$

where, from the SLA definition (Equation 2):

$$V_{T,j} = \frac{\sum_{i=1}^{N} \Gamma(x_{i,j}, X_{max})}{N}$$

and

$$\Gamma(x_{i,j}, X_{max}) = \begin{cases} 1 \ if \ x_{i,j} > X_{max} \\ 0 \quad otherwise \end{cases}$$

The vector $\boldsymbol{m} = (m_1, m_2, ..., m_N)$ is the solution of the optimization problem and represents the number of VMs the service provider should allocate in each time interval to satisfy the SLA $(\tau, X_{max}, T, V_{max})$ while minimizing the cost C it pays to the IaaS provider for using the virtual machines.

Problem Solution

If we assume that the arrival rate $\lambda_{i,j}$ is known for each i and j, the solution of the formulated optimization problem is straightforward: the minimum C over T' is given by the minimum allocation cost in each T that guarantees the SLA fulfillment and can be easily computed. However, the optimal allocation cannot be easily computed in real environments. First, to decide the number of VMs to be allocated, the service provider must know, in advance, the arrival rate of its clients at least for the next time span T. Second, the hypothesis of Poisson arrivals and exponential service times is not realistic (of course, for $x_{i,j}$ we could use a different model from (3)). Moreover, unpredictable workload fluctuations with respect to the average value $x_{i,j}$ are not considered, resulting in over-provisioning of resources or SLA violations.

Therefore, we propose two heuristic algorithms that rely on reactive and proactive decisions and compare their performance, in terms of allocation cost and percentage of SLA violations, with the optimal allocation policy.

Heuristic VM Allocation

The two heuristic algorithms we propose are:

- **Reactive Model-based VM Allocation (RMVA):** a reactive VM allocation policy that computes the optimal solution for the forthcoming SLA time span T on the basis of the arrival rate observed in the previous SLA time span.
- **Proactive Model-based VM Allocation (PMVA):** a proactive VM allocation policy that computes the optimal solution for the forthcoming SLA time span T on the basis of the arrival rate predicted in the next SLA time span.

The RMVA algorithm computes the number of VMs to be allocated in the j-th time span T, assuming that the average arrival rate in T will be equal to the average arrival rate $\hat{\lambda}$ observed in the previous time span. Then, the number m_j of VMs to be allocated is computed by solving the optimization problem for $M=1$ and $\lambda_{i,j} = \hat{\lambda}$.

The PMVA algorithm computes the optimal number of VMs to be allocated in the j-th time span T by predicting, through an autoregressive (AR) model (Box, Jenkins, & Reinsel, 1994), the average arrival rate that will be observed in T. The AR model parameters are estimated offline from the average arrival rate observed in recent historical logs. Then, the number m_j of VMs to be allocated is computed by solving the optimization problem for $M = 1$ and $\lambda_{i,j} = P(\lambda)$, where $P(\lambda)$ are the $\lambda_{i,j}$ values predicted from 1 to N steps ahead. A detailed description of the two algorithms can be found in (Casalicchio & Silvestri, 2010).

Experimental Evaluation

We compare the performance of the RMVA and PMVA heuristic algorithms against the optimal allocation policy by means of the following metrics:

- the cost C (measured in $) defined by (4) and computed over the medium term period T';
- the percentage $V_{T,T'}$ of SLA violations observed over the medium term period T', defined as:

$$V_{T,T'} = \frac{1}{M} \sum_{j=1}^{M} \Gamma(V_{T,j}, V_{\max})$$

where

$$\Gamma(V_{T,j}, V_{\max}) = \begin{cases} 1 & if\ V_{T,j} > V_{\max} \\ 0 & otherwise \end{cases}$$

The average values of the metrics C and $V_{T,T'}$ have been computed over a large set of simulation experiments obtained running a CSIM-based (Mesquite, 2010) discrete event-driven simulation model. The VMs have been modeled as single queue systems. No network delays have been considered and also the service provider delay has been omitted. In all the experiments, we set T = 60 min. and τ = 5 min. (*i.e.,* N = 12). The system workload, reported in Figure 3, has been generated by mixing a portion of the trace of the 1998 FIFA World Cup (logs number 3 and 4 of June 22, 1998) with an exponentially distributed service demand with mean $1/\mu$ = 0.602 sec/req. In particular, for every time unit t in the log, we computed the average arrival rate λ_t and generated requests distributed exponentially with parameter $1/\lambda_t$. To obtain a reasonable trade off between the length of the medium term period T' and the number of requests generated in a time unit, the

Figure 3. Request arrival rate at the cloud-based application

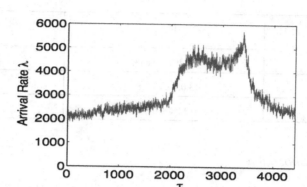

original trace from the 1998 FIFA World Cup log has been stretched changing the time scale from seconds to minutes. This transformation allowed us to simulate a medium term period of about 15 days during which allocation decisions are taken every 60 minutes. We assume that the allocation cost is 0.1$/h for each VM.

The simulation experiments have been organized as follows. First, we computed the optimal allocation $m^{opt} = [m^{opt}_j]$ and the related cost C^{opt}. Afterwards, we calculated offline the parameters of the AR model used in the PMVA algorithm. We considered the average arrival rate (computed every $\tau = 5$ time units) extracted from log number 2 of June 22 of 1998 FIFA World Cup trace file. In this way, we have been able to use a time series of over 4700 observations to estimate the model parameters. By applying time series analysis techniques to these data, we saw that, in the considered case, an AR(2) model allowed to forecast average arrival rates up to 12 steps ahead with a good precision. The parameters estimation has been done through the MATLAB tool using the least-square approach. The predicted values of the average arrival rate λ have been used to compute the PMVA allocation. This allocation corresponds to the optimal one in case of perfect prediction (*i.e.*, the observed average arrival rate is always equal to the predicted one).

Finally, for each allocation algorithm, we ran 50 simulations (with different seeds for random numbers generation) and computed the average values of C and $V_{T,T'}$. Using the same approach, we determined the performance of the Optimal policy, that allocates VMs on the basis of the solution m^{opt}.

The algorithms comparison is summarized in Table 2. An important remark regards the Optimal allocation policy, that exhibits a negligible but not null percentage of SLA violations. This, apparently abnormal, behavior can be explained as follows. The solution m^{opt} is optimal and determines no violation only if the arrival rate $\lambda_{i,j}$ and the request service demand are always lower or at most equal to the average value over T'; however, in the simulation, this hypothesis is not verified.

From the results in Table 2 we can see that the proactive algorithm (PMVA) performs much better than the reactive one (RMVA). RMVA obtains the highest value for $V_{T,T'}$ (13.03%) at the lowest cost (3141.2 $). The allocation obtained through RMVA has almost the same shape of the optimal one (see Figure 4) but the allocation/deallocation choice is operated with a delay T, resulting in a quite high number of SLA violations. PMVA allows to obtain results very close to the optimal case, outperforming the other heuristic both in terms of percentage of violations $V_{T,T'}$ and allocation cost C: the PMVA allocation cost is even a

Table 2. Comparison of VM allocation algorithms

VM Allocation	$V_{T,T'}$	C ($)
Optimal	0.14% ± 0.04%	3204
RMVA	13.03% ± 0.28%	3141.2 ± 1.47
PMVA	0.23% ± 0.06%	3196.8 ± 0.0

Figure 4. Virtual machine allocation

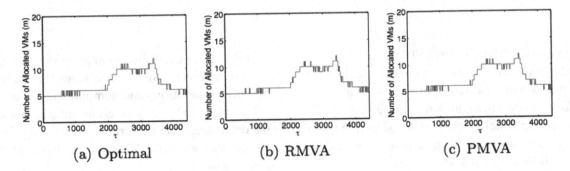

    (a) Optimal   (b) RMVA   (c) PMVA

little bit lower than the optimal case at the price of a few more SLA violations. This happens because the prediction underestimates the number of arrivals and the algorithm allocates a number of VMs that is slightly less than that required by the optimal allocation. Nevertheless, the number of SLA violations observed in the simulation using the PMVA heuristic is still very close to 0 (less than 0.3%).

A first remark is that the prediction performed through AR (or other) models may not work well as in the considered case. Depending on the workload characteristics, in some cases it can be quite hard (or even impossible) to find an appropriate model for time-series prediction and, even if a good model is found, this may become obsolete in a very short time. However, if the workload trend is predictable with a good precision, a model-based proactive algorithm like PMVA allows to obtain results which are very close to the optimal case.

Figures 4, 5 and 6 show the VM allocation, the percentage of SLA violations, and the average response time for the Optimal, RMVA and PMVA allocation algorithms. The figures report the result of a simulation run selected among the 50 runs and show the behavior of the algorithms in the medium period. The horizontal lines in Figures 5 and 6 are respectively the maximum percentage of SLA violations and the maximum value of the average response time agreed by the SaaS provider with the users of the cloud-based application.

From the figures we can see that RMVA and PMVA present an **m** profile (number of allocated VMs) similar to the optimal case (Figure 4), with the difference that the reactive algorithm takes delayed decisions, resulting in a higher average response time (Figure 6) and therefore in a quite high number of SLA violations (Figure 5).

Figure 5. Percentage of SLA violations

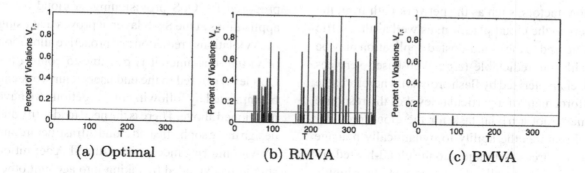

(a) Optimal   (b) RMVA   (c) PMVA

Figure 6. Average response time

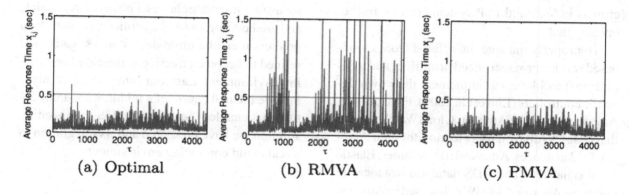

(a) Optimal   (b) RMVA   (c) PMVA

FUTURE RESEARCH DIRECTIONS

The problem of service level provisioning in the cloud computing era presents various research issues that are worthy to be investigated. The open issues we have identified are mainly related to the ability of the SaaS provider to monitor and control not only the application but also the infrastructure on which the application runs. While the application monitoring and control should be under the full control of the service provider in case of "in-house" applications, problems arise when external cloud-based services are used. To address this issue, the SaaS provider can use a third-party cloud monitoring service (e.g., Hyperic's CloudStatus, Nimsoft Monitoring Solution) or a monitoring service provided by the same IaaS provider (e.g., Amazon CloudWatch). However,

methodologies, mechanisms, and tools to monitor the cloud infrastructure are still in their early stage because various issues need to be addressed. For example, the real-time processing and analysis of a huge amount of collected data is an interesting challenge that has been covered only in few works, e.g., (Rabkin & Katz, 2010) and the related Chukwa Hadoop subproject, and surely deserves further investigation.

To be competitive in the cloud market, service providers need to expose a wider set of service level parameters than the "simple" availability, such as SLOs taking into account response times, transaction completions, and security. Such enriched SLAs are very difficult to manage, because they are composed by QoS parameters that depend on a variety of factors that may be not entirely under the control of the IaaS, PaaS, and SaaS providers. For example, response times depend on many factors, such as the network path from the users to the cloud platform, as well as the traffic addressed to the cloud-hosted application may be highly unpredictable (*e.g.*, Web-based services are characterized by flash crowds). Therefore, the enforcement of a particular level of the response time is not a trivial task for the cloud provider and requires the ability to dynamically manage the resources assignment to the cloud-hosted applications in a really elastic way so to face highly variable traffic conditions. To this end, solutions already proposed to detect and manage flash crowds in Web and P2P systems can be further investigated.

To properly manage the offered QoS, cloud-based service providers need primitives and tools (at IaaS/PaaS layer) to implement their own dynamic controllers (Lim et al., 2009). For example, Amazon offers the Amazon CloudWatch service that enables Amazon users to monitor their Amazon EC2 instances, Amazon EBS volumes, Elastic Load Balancers, and RDS database instances in real-time. Amazon CloudWatch is used by Amazon Auto Scaling (2010), that allows consumers to scale up or down seamlessly and automatically the number of Amazon EC2 instances they are using according to specified performance conditions. Google App Engine provides a simpler tool, the System Status Dashboard, that makes it easier for developers to evaluate and monitor the entire App Engine system by enabling them to measure historical uptime, error rates, and latency for each major App Engine component. However, System Status Dashboard does not currently allow to monitor single application performances.

A further open issue is related to the definition of methodologies and languages suitable to describe SLAs at the service layer and map them into corresponding SLAs at the infrastructure layer. For example, there is not a well-known and easy-to-use mechanism to translate efficiently from service-level metrics to resource-level metrics.

With regard to the specific solution we have proposed for QoS provisioning of cloud-based applications at the SaaS layer, it proves that using SLA violations prediction and proactive allocation of virtual machines it is possible to control the QoS level offered to the end users. Our work can be improved by following the directions we have mentioned above. There is the need to identify and design more sophisticated cloud infrastructure and SLA monitoring mechanisms, the SLA definition should be extended by taking into account other metrics related to availability and security, and the virtual machines allocation policy has to account for different service classes. Furthermore, models and methodologies for the applications workload prediction can be more deeply investigated and refined to become effective in the cloud computing environment. Last, our future research plans include the realization of a middleware architecture that enables the dynamic QoS provisioning solution we have presented and its integration in a real cloud computing environment.

CONCLUSION

In this chapter we have provided some background on cloud computing and we have analyzed how the QoS provisioning problem can be tackled at the different layers of the cloud stack. While cloud computing can rely at the infrastructure layer on consolidated (but still rapidly evolving) technologies and quite mature QoS provisioning mechanisms, dynamic QoS provisioning for applications running in the cloud is still an open issue, as demonstrated by the increasing number of ongoing projects and new research results (see the research works cited in this chapter and the program of some recent conferences, such as IEEE CLOUD 2010).

For the QoS provisioning at the SaaS layer, we have identified the actors involved in and presented the state of the art in the field of cloud computing, proposing a classification of the existing solutions according to whether they are based on service selection or resource allocation and take into account short or medium/long term time horizons.

Then, we have proposed our own medium/long term QoS provisioning solution for applications running in a cloud and managed by a SaaS provider that is, in its turn, a cloud infrastructure user. Finally, we have discussed some future research directions that show that there is a large space for future investigation of service level provisioning both on the methodological and practical issues.

REFERENCES

Abrahao, B., Almeida, V., Almeida, J., Zhang, A., Beyer, D., & Safai, F. (2006). Self-adaptive SLA-driven capacity management for Internet services. In *Proceedings of 17th IFIP/IEEE International Workshop on Distributed Systems: Operations and Management* (Dublin, Ireland, Oct. 2006). DSOM 2006.

Amazon Inc. (2010). *Amazon auto scaling*. Retrieved November 2010, from http:// aws.amazon.com/ autoscaling/

Amazon Inc. (2010). *Amazon elastic compute cloud* (EC2). Retrieved November 2010, from http:// aws.amazon.com/ ec2/

Amazon Inc. (2010). *Amazon EC2 spot instances*. Retrieved November 2010, from http:// aws.amazon.com/ ec2/ spot-instances/

Amazon Web Services. (2010). *Amazon EC2 service level agreement*. Retrieved November 2010, from http:// aws.amazon.com/ ec2-sla/

Andreolini, M., Casolari, S., Colajanni, M., & Messori, M. (2009). Dynamic load management of virtual machines in a cloud architectures. In *Proceedings of the 1st ICST International Conference on Cloud Computing* (Munich, Germany, Oct. 2009).

Andrzejak, A., Kondo, D., & Yi, S. (2010). Decision model for cloud computing under SLA constraints. In *Proceedings of the 18th IEEE/ACM International Symposium on Modeling, Analysis and Simulation of Computer and Telecommunication Systems* (Miami, FL, Aug. 2010). MASCOTS 2010.

Ardagna, D., Trubian, M., & Zhang, L. (2007). SLA based resource allocation policies in autonomic environments. *Journal of Parallel and Distributed Computing, 67*(3), 259–270. doi:10.1016/j.jpdc.2006.10.006

Armbrust, M., Fox, A., Griffith, R., Joseph, A. D., Katz, R., & Konwinski, A. … Zaharia, M. (2009). *Above the clouds: A Berkeley view of cloud computing*. In (Technical Report No. UCB/EECS-2009-28), Dept. of Electrical Engineering and Computer Sciences, University of California at Berkeley (Feb. 2009). Retrieved November 2010, from http:// www.eecs.berkeley.edu/ Pubs/ TechRpts/ 2009/ EECS-2009-28.pdf

Box, G. E. P., Jenkins, G. M., & Reinsel, G. C. (1994). *Time series analysis forecasting and control* (3rd ed.). Prentice Hall International.

Brandic, I. (2009) Towards self-manageable cloud services. In *Proceedings of the 2nd IEEE International Workshop on Real-Time Service-Oriented Architecture and Applications* (July 2009, Seattle, WA). RTSOAA 2009.

Buyya, R., Yeo, C. S., Venugopal, S., Broberg, J., & Brandic, I. (2009). Cloud computing and emerging IT platforms: Vision, hype, and reality for delivering computing as the 5th utility. *Future Generation Computer Systems, 25*(6), 599–616. doi:10.1016/j.future.2008.12.001

Casalicchio, E., & Silvestri, L. (2010). Medium/long term SLA provisioning in cloud-based service providers. In *Proceedings of the 2nd International ICST Conference on Cloud Computing* (Barcelona, Spain, Oct. 2010). CloudComp 2010.

Chen, Y., Wo, T., & Li, J. (2009). An efficient resource management system for on-line virtual cluster provision. In *Proceedings of the 2009 IEEE International Conference on Cloud Computing* (Sept. 2009), (pp. 72-79).

Clark, C., Fraser, K., Hand, S., Hansen, J. G., Jul, E., & Limpach, C. ... Warfield, A. (2005). Live migration of virtual machines. In *Proceedings of the 2nd Symposium on Networked Systems Design & Implementation* – vol. 2 (May 2005). USENIX Association, Berkeley, CA, (pp. 273-286).

De Assuncao, M. D., Di Costanzo, A., & Buyya, R. (2009). Evaluating the cost-benefit of using cloud computing to extend the capacity of clusters. In *Proceedings of the 18th ACM international Symposium on High Performance Distributed Computing* (Garching, Germany, June 2009), (pp. 141-150).

Eucalyptus Public Cloud. (2010). *Website*. Retrieved November 2010, from http://open.eucalyptus.com/

Fakhouri, S., Fong, L., Goldszmidt, G., Kalantar, M., Krishnakumar, S., & Pazel, D. P. ... Rochwerger, B. (2001). Oceano - SLA based management of a computing utility. In *Proceedings of the 7th IFIP/IEEE International Symposium on Integrated Network Management* (2001), (pp. 855–868).

Gong, Z., Gu, X., & Wilkes, J. (2010). PRESS: PRedictive Elastic ReSource Scaling for cloud systems. In *Proceedings of the 6th IEEE International Conference on Network and Services Management* (Niagara Falls, Canada, Oct. 2010). CNSM 2010.

Greenberg, A., Hamilton, J., Maltz, D. A., & Patel, P. (2009). The cost of a cloud: Research problems in data center networks. *ACM Computer Communication Review, 39*(1), 68–73. doi:10.1145/1496091.1496103

Guitart, J., Carrera, D., Beltran, V., Torres, J., & Ayguadé, E. (2008). Dynamic CPU provisioning for self-managed secure Web applications in SMP hosting platforms. *Computer Networks, 52*(7), 1390–1409. doi:10.1016/j.comnet.2007.12.009

Hirofuchi, T., Ogawa, H., Nakada, H., Itoh, S., & Sekiguchi, S. (2009). A live storage migration mechanism over WAN for relocatable virtual machine services on clouds. In *Proceedings of the 9th IEEE/ACM International Symposium on Cluster Computing and the Grid* (Shangai, China, May 2009). CCGrid 2009, (pp. 460-465).

Huebscher, M. C., & McCann, J. A. (2008). A survey of autonomic computing—Degrees, models, and applications. *ACM Computing Surveys, 40*(3), 1–28. doi:10.1145/1380584.1380585

Irwin, D., Chase, J., Grit, L., Yumerefendi, A., Becker, D., & Yocum, K. G. (2006). Sharing networked resources with brokered leases. In *Proceedings of the 2006 USENIX Annual Technical Conference* (Boston, MA, May 2006).

Jung, G., Joshi, K. R., Hiltunen, M. A., Schlichting, R. D., & Pu, C. (2008). Generating adaptation policies for multi-tier applications in consolidated server environments. In *Proceedings of the 5th IEEE International Conference on Autonomic Computing* (Chicago, IL, June 2008), (pp. 23-32).

Jung, G., Joshi, K. R., Hiltunen, M. A., Schlichting, R. D., & Pu, C. (2009). A cost-sensitive adaptation engine for server consolidation of multitier applications. In *Proceedings of the 10th ACM/IFIP/USENIX International Conference on Middleware* (Urbana Champaign, IL, Nov. 2009), (pp. 1-20). Springer-Verlag.

Kant, K. (2009). Data center evolution. *Computer Networks, 53*(17), 2939–2965. doi:10.1016/j.comnet.2009.10.004

Kephart, J. O., & Chess, D. M. (2003). The vision of autonomic computing. *IEEE Computer, 36*(1), 41–50.

Kim, K. H., Beloglazov, A., & Buyya, R. (2009). Power-aware provisioning of Cloud resources for real-time services. In *Proceedings of the 7th International Workshop on Middleware For Grids, Clouds and E-Science* (Urbana Champaign, IL, Nov. 2009). MGC 2009, (pp. 1-6). New York, NY: ACM.

Lenk, A., Klems, M., Nimis, J., Tai, S., & Sandholm, T. (2009). What's inside the Cloud? An architectural map of the Cloud landscape. In *Proceedings of the 2009 ICSE Workshop on Software Engineering Challenges of Cloud Computing* (May 2009).

Li, B., Li, J., Huai, J., Wo, T., Li, Q., & Zhong, L. (2009). EnaCloud: An energy-saving application live placement approach for cloud computing environments. In *Proceedings of the 2009 IEEE International Conference on Cloud Computing* (Sept. 2009), (pp. 17-24).

Lim, H. C., Babu, S., Chase, J. S., & Parekh, S. S. (2009). Automated control in cloud computing: Challenges and opportunities. In *Proceedings of the 1st Workshop on Automated Control For Datacenters and Clouds* (Barcelona, Spain, June 2009). ACDC 2009, (pp. 13-18). New York, NY: ACM.

Litoiu, M., Woodside, M., Wong, J., Ng, J., & Iszlai, G. (2010). A business driven cloud optimization architecture. In *Proceedings of the 2010 ACM Symposium on Applied Computing* (Sierre, Switzerland, March 2010). SAC 2010, (pp. 380-385).

Mell, P., & Grance, T. (2009) *The NIST definition of Cloud Computing,* version 15, October 2009. Retrieved November 2010, from http:// csrc.nist.gov/ groups/ SNS/ cloud-computing/

Mesquite Software. (2010). *CSIM simulation engine.* Retrieved November 2010, from http:// www.mesquite.com/

Nallur, V., & Bahsoon, R. (2010). Design of a market-based mechanism for quality attribute tradeoff of services in the cloud. In *Proceedings of the 2010 ACM Symposium on Applied Computing* (Sierre, Switzerland, March 2010). SAC 2010, (pp. 367-371).

Nguyen Van, H., Dang Tran, F., & Menaud, J. (2009). Autonomic virtual resource management for service hosting platforms. In *Proceedings of the 2009 ICSE Workshop on Software Engineering Challenges of Cloud Computing* (May 2009), (pp. 1-8). Washington, DC: IEEE Computer Society.

Padala, P., Shin, K. G., Zhu, X., Uysal, M., Wang, Z., & Singhal, S. … Salem, K. (2007). Adaptive control of virtualized resources in utility computing environments. In *Proceedings of the 2nd ACM SIGOPS/EuroSys European Conference on Computer Systems* 2007 (Lisbon, Portugal, March 2007). EuroSys 2007, (pp. 289-302).

Powers, R., Goldszmidt, M., & Cohen, I. (2005). Short term performance forecasting in enterprise systems. In *Proceedings of the 11th ACM SIGKDD International Conference on Knowledge Discovery in Data Mining* (Chicago, IL, Aug. 2005). KDD 2005, (pp. 801-807).

Rabkin, A., & Katz, R. H. (201p). *Chukwa: A system for reliable large-scale log collection.* In (Technical Report No. UCB/EECS-2010-25), Dept. of Electrical Engineering and Computer Sciences, University of California at Berkeley (March 2010). Retrieved Nov. 2010, from http:// www.eecs.berkeley.edu/ Pubs/ TechRpts/ 2010/ EECS-2010-25.pdf

Shivam, P., Babu, S., & Chase, J. S. (2006). Learning application models for utility resource planning. In *Proceedings of the 2006 IEEE International Conference on Autonomic Computing* (June 2006). ICAC 2006.

Song, Y., Li, Y., Wang, H., Zhang, Y., Feng, B., Zang, H., & Sun, Y. (2008). A service-oriented priority-based resource scheduling scheme for virtualized utility computing. In P. Sadayappan, M. Parashar, R. Badrinath, and V. K. Prasanna (Eds.), *Proceedings of the 15th International Conference on High Performance Computing, LNCS 5374*, (pp. 220-231). Berlin/Heidelberg, Germany: Springer-Verlag.

Song, Y., Wang, H., Li, Y., Feng, B., & Sun, Y. (2009). Multi-tiered on-demand resource scheduling for VM-based data center. In *Proceedings of the 9th IEEE/ACM International Symposium on Cluster Computing and the Grid* (Shangai, China, May 2009). CCGrid 2009, (pp. 148-155).

Srikantaiah, S., Kansal, A., & Zhao, F. (2008). Energy aware consolidation for cloud computing. In *Proceedings of Workshop on Power Aware Computing and Systems* (San Diego, CA, Dec. 2008). USENIX HotPower 2008.

Urgaonkar, B., Shenoy, P., Chandra, A., Goyal, P., & Wood, T. (2008). Agile dynamic provisioning of multi-tier Internet applications. *ACM Transactions on Autonomous and Adaptive Systems, 3*(1), 1–39. doi:10.1145/1342171.1342172

Valancius, V., Laoutaris, N., Massoulié, L., Diot, C., & Rodriguez, P. (2009). Greening the Internet with nano data centers. In *Proceedings of the 5th International Conference on Emerging Networking Experiments and Technologies* (Rome, Italy, Dec. 2009), (pp. 37-48).

Vaquero, L. M., Rodero-Merino, L., Caceres, J., & Lindner, M. (2008). A break in the clouds: Towards a cloud definition. *ACM SIGCOMM Computer Communication Review, 39*(1), 50–55. doi:10.1145/1496091.1496100

Voorsluys, W., Broberg, J., Venugopal, S., & Buyya, R. (2009). Cost of virtual machine live migration in clouds: A performance evaluation. In M. G. Jaatun, G. Zhao, & C. Rong (Eds.), *Proceedings of the 1st International Conference on Cloud Computing* (Beijing, China, Dec. 2009). *LNCS 5931*, (pp. 254-265). Berlin/Heidelberg, Germany: Springer-Verlag.

Wang, X., Lan, D., Wang, G., Fang, X., Ye, M., Chen, Y., & Wang, Q. (2007). Appliance-based autonomic provisioning framework for virtualized outsourcing data center. In *Proceedings of the 4th IEEE International Conference on Autonomic Computing* (June 2007).

Wilkes, J., Mogul, J., & Suermondt, J. (2004). Utilification. In *Proceedings of the 11th ACM SIGOPS European Workshop* (Leuven, Belgium, Sept. 2004).

Wood, T., Shenoy, P., Venkataramani, A., & Yousif, M. (2009). Sandpiper: Black-box and gray-box resource management for virtual machines. *Computer Networks, 53*(17), 2923–2938. doi:10.1016/j.comnet.2009.04.014

Wu, L., & Buyya, R. (2011). Service level agreement (SLA) in utility computing systems . In Cardellini, V., Casalicchio, E., Castelo Branco, K., Estrella, J., & Monaco, F. J. (Eds.), *Performance and dependability in service computing: Concepts, techniques and research directions*. Hershey, PA: IGI Global.

Zeng, W., Zhao, Y., & Zeng, J. (2009). Cloud service and service selection algorithm research. In *Proceedings of the 1st ACM/SIGEVO Summit on Genetic and Evolutionary Computation* (Shanghai, China, June 2009). GEC 2009, (pp. 1045-1048).

Zhang, Q., Cheng, L., & Boutaba, R. (2010). Cloud computing: State-of-the-art and research challenges. *Journal of Internet Services and Applications, 1*(1), 7–18. doi:10.1007/s13174-010-0007-6

Chapter 18

Decentralization in Distributed Systems:
Challenges, Technologies, and Opportunities

Mustafizur Rahman
The University of Melbourne, Australia

Rajiv Ranjan
The University of New South Wales, Australia

Rajkumar Buyya
The University of Melbourne, Australia

ABSTRACT

In recent years, decentralization in distributed computing systems, such as Grids and Clouds has been widely explored in order to improve system performance in terms of scalability and reliability. However, the decentralized nature of the system also raises some serious challenges. This chapter discusses the major challenges of designing and implementing decentralization in Grid and Cloud systems. It also presents a survey of some existing decentralized distributed systems and technologies regarding how these systems have addressed the challenges.

INTRODUCTION

A distributed computing system enables the sharing, selection, and aggregation of distributed heterogeneous computational and storage resources, which are under the control of different sites or domains. The key applications of the

computational distributed systems is to provide solutions to the complex scientific or engineering problems, such as weather forecasting, stock portfolio management, medical diagnoses.

The configuration of a distributed system is considered as decentralized if none of the participants in the system are more important than the others, in case that one of the participants fails, then it is neither more nor less harmful to the

DOI: 10.4018/978-1-61350-110-8.ch018

Copyright © 2012, IGI Global. Copying or distributing in print or electronic forms without written permission of IGI Global is prohibited.

Figure 1. Application runtime environment in centralized and decentralized distributed systems: (a) centralized system, (b) decentralized system

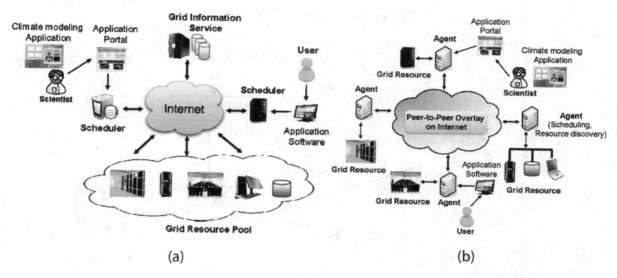

(a)　　　　　　　　　　　　　　　　　(b)

system than caused by the failure of any other participant in the system. Thus, in a Decentralized distributed system, management services, such as application scheduling, resource discovery are distributed over the sites so that if one site is failed, another site can take over its responsibility autonomously. Moreover, decentralized systems are highly scalable as they can seamlessly add or remove the components or resource pool in order to accommodate varying workload. On the other hand, in a centralized distributed system, the central servers play the role of scheduling and resource discovery services. In Figure 1, we present example application runtime scenarios in case of both centralized and decentralized distributed system.

Decentralization of distributed computing systems based on Peer-to-Peer (P2P) network model can certainly overcome the limitations of centralized and hierarchical model in terms of scalability, single point failure, autonomy, and trust-worthiness. However, complete decentralized nature of the system raises other serious challenges in domains of application scheduling, resource allocation, coordination, resource dis-

covery, security, trust, and reputation management between participants.

In this chapter, we aim to identify the basic challenges of decentralized distributed systems and survey some existing decentralized distributed systems and technologies along with a case study. Specifically, we describe the basic functionalities and important features of these systems and technologies, as well as compare them in the context of addressing the challenges. Finally, we outline some opportunities or future directions in this research discipline.

CHALLENGES OF DECENTRALIZED DISTRIBUTED SYSTEMS

Scheduling

In centralized scheduling approach, all the system-wide decision makings are coordinated by a central controller. Centralized scheduler organization is simple to implement, easy to deploy, and presents few management hassles. However, this scheme

Figure 2. Decentralized non-coordinated scheduling in Tycoon

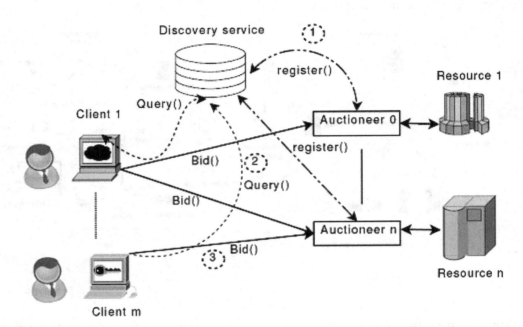

raises serious concerns when subjected to larger system size.

The decentralized scheduler organization negates the limitations of centralized organization with respect to fault-tolerance, scalability, and autonomy (facilitating domain specific resource allocation policies). This approach scales well for both, a small scale resource sharing environment (e.g. resource sharing under same administrative domain) to a large scale environment (e.g. the Internet). However, this approach raises serious challenges in the domain of distributed information management, enforcing system wide coordination, security, resource consumer authenticity, and resource provider's policy heterogeneity. We can classify decentralized scheduling into two categories.

Non-Coordinated Scheduling

In the non-coordinated scheduling scheme, application schedulers perform scheduling related activities independent of the other schedulers in

the system. Condor-G resource brokering system performs non-coordinated or non-cooperative scheduling by directly submitting jobs to the condor pools without taking into account their load and utilization status. This approach exacerbates the load sharing and utilization problems of distributed resources since sub-optimal schedules are likely to occur. Figure 2 shows the decentralized non-coordinated scheduling approach in Tycoon resource sharing system. Auctioneers advertise the resource availability and configuration to the discovery service. Client agents query the discovery service to gather information about available auctioneers in the system. As a result, both Client agents end up bidding to the auctioneer n because of lack of coordination among them.

Coordinated Scheduling

Coordinated scheduling scheme negotiates resource conditions with the local site managers in the system, if not, with the other application level schedulers. Legion-Federation system coordinates scheduling decision with other sites in the distributed environment through job query mechanism. A job query request (containing job type and composition) is sent to k remote sites for bidding. The scheduler of each remote site then contacts its Local Resource Management System LRMS) to obtain job completion time on their local resources and sends this information back to the initiator's site. Finally, the site who bids with the least projected job completion time is selected for job scheduling.

Objective Function

Resources in a distributed system are dynamic in nature and their states can change within small interval of time. Therefore, we need scheduling and resource allocation policies that can adapt to these changing resource conditions. As a result, the participants including resource providers and resource consumers associate various objective functions with respect to resource allocation and scheduling processes. These objective functions are formulated based on the policies and strategies enforced by resource providers and consumers. For example, a resource provider in a decentralized distributed system can enforce pricing policy, admission control policy, and domain specific resource allocation strategy. Similarly, the resource users or consumers can associate QoS-based utility constraints to their applications and expect that the constraints are satisfied within the acceptable limits. We can distinguish the objective functions into two categories.

System Centric

Based on the system centric mechanism, a decentralized distributed system defines relatively simple objective functions. A system centric scheduler focuses on maximizing resource throughput on the provider side, while minimizing overall consumer's application completion time.

User Centric

User centric scheduling mechanisms are market driven and define objective functions based on QoS parameters. From the resource providers' perspective, these QoS parameters include profit, reputation, security or combination of all, whereas QoS parameters for users are cost, budget spent, response time or combination of all.

Exact combination of QoS parameters is determined by the applied economic model. Some of the commonly used economic models in resource allocation include commodity market model, tendering/contract-net model, auction model, bid-based proportional resource sharing model, bartering model, and monopoly model. In cooperative market model, such as bartered economy, there is singleton objective function shared by both consumer and provider, which is maximizing its bartering reputation. On the other hand, in competitive market models, such as commodity market, bid-based proportional sharing, auction, resource consumer and provider usually have different objective functions. Resource providers define objective function with focus on maximizing profit, whereas consumers mainly focus on minimizing cost and response time.

Coordination

The effectiveness of a decentralized distributed system depends on the level of coordination and cooperation among the participants. The participants in a decentralized environment are pools of diverse peers or brokers, which have agreed to co-operate for sharing and controlling resources in order to enhance overall utility of the system. Realizing such a co-operation among these dynamic and selfish participants requires robust mechanism for coordination and negotiation policies. In general, the process of coordinated application scheduling and resource management involves dynamic information exchange between various schedulers and LRMSs in the system.

Negotiation among all the participants can be done based on well-known agent coordination mechanism called contract net protocol (Smith, 1988). Contract net partitions the coordination space into two distinct domains including a manager and a contractor. A resource broker in a decentralized distributed system can adhere to the role of a contractor that negotiates SLAs with resource providers. Effectively, resource provider works as a manager that exports its local resources to the outside contractors and is responsible for decision regarding admission control based on negotiated Service Level Agreements (SLA).

However, distributed negotiation has substantial message overhead and it can worsen as system scales to a large number of participants. For the communication among the participants, we distinguish between three different approaches.

- one-to-all broadcast.
- selective broadcast.
- one-to-one negotiation.

Communication protocols based on one-to-all broadcast is very expensive in terms of number of messages and network bandwidth usage. Similar negotiation protocol has been proposed in the work Legion-Federation for decentralized scheduling. Therefore, Condor-Flock P2P system proposed selective broadcast to the flocks currently indexed by the Pastry routing table (Rowstron et al., 2001). The SLA-based scheduling approach proposed by Ranjan et al. (Ranjan et al., 2006) advocates one-to-one negotiation among contractors and managers.

Some approaches including Bellagio advocate coordinating resource activity among decentralized participants based on centralized coordinators. Figure 3 shows centralized coordination methodology applied by Bellagio system. Resource agents register the resource configuration with the Sword (Oppenheimer et al., 2005) resource discovery service. Client agents query the Sword to locate available resources in the system.

Once the resource lists are obtained, Client agents bid for resources with the centralized auction coordinator. The bid parameters include the sets of resources desired, a time for which application would be deployed on resources, and the amount of virtual money clients are ready to spend.

Security and Trust

The decentralized organization of distributed systems raises serious challenges in the domains of security and trust management. Implementing a secure decentralized distributed system requires solutions that can efficiently address the following security issues:

- preserve the privacy of participants.
- ensure authenticity of the participants.
- provide robust authorization.
- route messages securely between distributed services.

Privacy

The privacy of the participants can be ensured through secret key-based symmetric cryptographic algorithms, such as 3DES, RC4, etc. These secret keys must be securely generated and distributed in the system. Existing key management systems, such as public key algorithms (including DH, RSA, elliptic) and Kerberos (trusted third party) can be utilized for this purpose.

Authentication

Authentication of the participants can be achieved through trust enforcement mechanisms including (i) Public Key Infrastructure (X.509 certificates), (ii) Kerberos (third party authentication), (iii) distributed trust, and (iv) SSH.

Authentication based on X.509 certificates requires a trusted Certifying Authority (CA) in the system. A system can have a single CA, which is trusted by all the participants. However, single CA

Figure 3. Centralized coordination in Bellagio

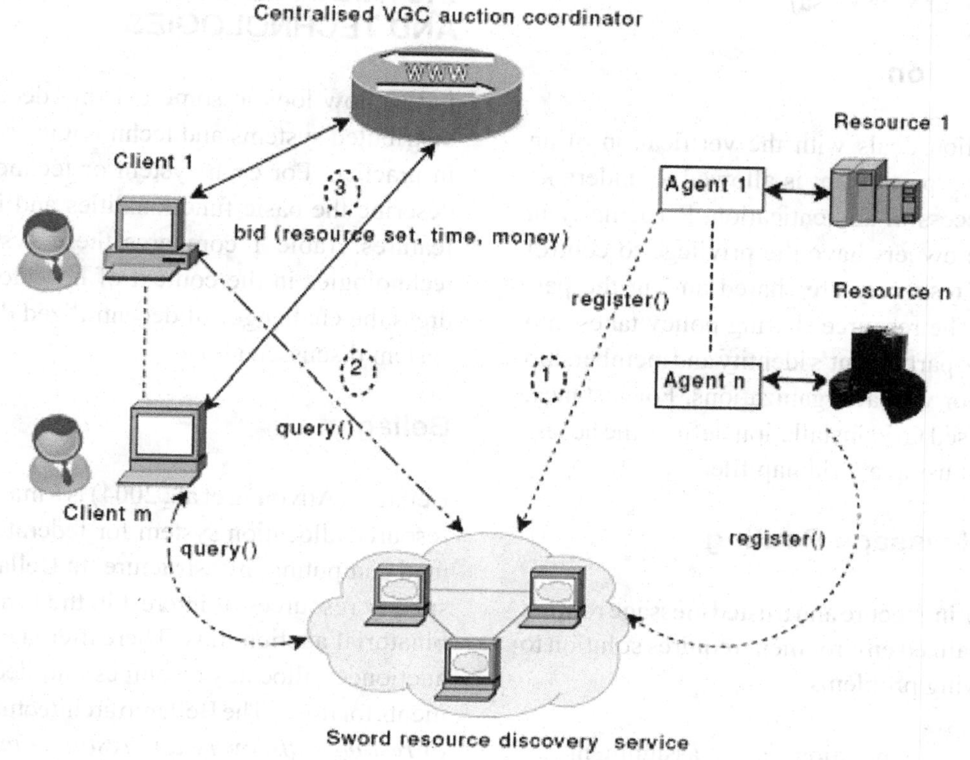

approach has limited scalability. An alternative to this is to have multiple CAs combining together to form a trust chain. In this case, a certificate signed by any CA in the system has global validity.

Kerberos is a network authentication protocol. It is designed to provide strong authentication for client/server applications by using secret-key cryptography. Kerberos based implementation has significant shortcomings as it requires synchronous communication with the ticket granting server in order to setup communication between a client and server. If the ticket granting server goes offline or has a security breach then there is no way the system can operate.

JXTA (Gong, 2001) provides a completely decentralized X.509 based PKI. Each JXTA peer is its own CA and issues a certificate for each service it offers. Each of the CA certificate is verified via the *Poblano: "web of trust"*, a dis-

tributed reputation management system. A similar distributed trust mechanism is PeerReview (Durschel, 2006). These distributed trust management systems determine malicious participants through behavioral auditing. An auditor node A checks if it agrees with the past actions of an auditee node B. In case of disagreement, A broadcasts an accusation of B. Interested third party nodes verify evidence, and take punitive action against the auditor or the auditee.

The SSH based authentication scheme is comparatively easier to implement as it does not require trusted third party certification. However, it does not allow the creation of a dynamic trust chain, and in case a participant's private key is compromised, it requires every public key holder to be informed about this event. Unlike X.509 and Kerberos implementation, SSH does not support certificate translation mechanism (i.e. from X.509 to Kerberos or vice versa).

Authorization

Authorization deals with the verification of an action that a participant is allowed to undertake after a successful authentication. Particularly in Grids, site owners have the privilege to control how their resources are shared among the participants. The resource sharing policy takes into account the participant's identity and membership to groups or virtual organizations. For instance, Globus based Grid installation defines the access control list using a Gridmap file.

Secure Message Routing

Implementing secure and trusted message routing in decentralized environment requires solution to the following problems:

- secure generation and assignment of nodeIds.
- securely maintaining the integrity of routing tables.
- secure message transmission between peers.

Secure nodeId assignment ensures that an attacker or a malicious peer cannot choose the value of nodeIds that can give it membership of the overlay. If the node assignment process is not secure, then an attacker could sniff into the overlay with a chosen nodeId and get control over the local objects, or influence all traffic to and from the victim node. The nodeId assignment process is secured by delegating this capability to a central, trusted authority. Secure message forwarding in the Internet can be achieved through secure transport layer connections, such as TLS and SSL.

RELATED DECENTRALIZED DISTRIBUTED SYSTEMS AND TECHNOLOGIES

Let us now look at some existing decentralized distributed systems and technologies commonly in practice. For each system or technology, we describe the basic functionalities and important features. Table 1 compares these systems and technologies in the context of how do they address the challenges of decentralized distributed system discussed above.

Bellagio

Bellagio (Auyoung et al., 2004) is a market-based resource allocation system for federated distributed computing infrastructure. In Bellagio, users specify resources of interest in the form of combinatorial auction bids. Thereafter, a centralized auctioneer allocates resources and decides payments for users. The Bellagio architecture consists of *resource discovery and resource market*. For resource discovery of heterogeneous resources, Bellagio uses SWORD (Oppenheimer et al., 2005). For resource market, Bellagio uses a centralized auction system, in which users express resource preferences using a bidding language, and a periodic auction allocates resources to users. A bid for resource includes sets of resources desired, processing duration, and the amount of virtual currency which a user is willing to spend. The centralized auctioneer clears the bid every hour.

CondorFlock P2P

Butt et al. (Butt et al., 2003) present a scheme for connecting existing Condor work pools using P2P routing substrate Pastry (Rowstron et al., 2001). Inherently, P2P substrate (overlay network) aids in automating the resource discovery in the Condor Flock Grid. Resource discovery in the flock is facilitated through resource information broadcast to the pools, whose ids appear in the

Table 1. Comparison of different decentralized distributed systems and technologies

System Name	Type	Organization	Scheduling Model	Objective Function	Coordination Model	Security Model
Aneka Federation (Ranjan et al., 2009)	P2P Grid	University of Melbourne	Decentralized coordinated	System centric	Selective broadcast	Distributed trust
Bellagio (Auyoung et al., 2004)	Grid	University of California, San Diego	Centralized	User centric, Bid-based proportional sharing	centralized	SSH
CondorFlock P2P (Butt et al., 2003)	P2P Grid	Purdue University	Decentralized coordinated	System centric	Selective broadcast	PKI / Globus
InterGrid (Assuncao et al., 2008)	Grid	University of Melbourne	Decentralized coordinated	User centric	Selective broadcast	PKI
Legion-Federation (Weissman et al., 1996)	Grid	University of Virginia	Decentralized coordinated	System centric	One-to-All broadcast	Public-key cryptography based on RSAREF 2.0
MOSIX-Fed (Barak et al., 2005)	Grid	Hebrew University of Jerusalem	Centralized	System centric	Centralized	SSH
Sharp (Fu et al., 2003)	P2P	Duke University	Decentralized coordinated	User centric, bartering	One-to-one negotiation	PKI
Trader-Federation (Frerot et al., 2000)	Grid	UFR Science et Techniques	Decentralized coordinated	User centric, Commodity market	One-to-All broadcast	N.A.
Tycoon (Lai et al., 2004)	Grid	HP Labs	Decentralized non-coordinated	User centric, Auction	One-to-All broadcast	PKI
Amazon EC2 (Amazon, 2010)	Cloud	Amazon.com	Centralized	User centric	Centralized	PKI
Azure (Nagy, 2010)	Cloud	Microsoft Corporation	Centralized	User centric	Centralized	TLS/SSL
Eucalyptus (Eucalyptus, 2009)	Cloud	Eucalyptus Systems, Inc.	Centralized	User centric	Centralized	SSH

Pastry node's routing table. The proposed P2P-based overlay network facilitates only resource discovery, while other decisions such as resource sharing policy is controlled by the pool managers. Core Condor LRMS has also been extended to work with Globus (Foster et al., 1997), the new version is called Condor-G resource broker, which enables creation of global Grids and is designed to run jobs across different administrative domains.

InterGrid

InterGrid (Assuncao et al., 2008) provides a software system that allows the creation of collaborative execution environments for various scientific applications on top of the physical infrastructure provided by the participating Grids in the federation. The allocation of resources from multiple Grids to fulfill the requirements of the execution environments is enabled by peering arrangements established between InterGrid Gateways (IGGs). An IGG is aware of the terms of the peering among the Grids connected to it. Thus, it can select the suitable Grids that are able to provide the required resources for a particular application. Moreover, it can also send request to other IGGs for resource provisioning and replies to requests from other IGGs. Request redirection policies determine which peering Grid is selected to process a request and a price at which the processing is performed.

Legion-Federation

Weissman et al. (Weissman et al., 1996) devise a federated model for distributed cooperative resource management. The model proposes federated resource sharing using Legion LRMS. It considers two levels of application schedulers in the system namely, Local Site (LS) Scheduler and Wide-Area (WA) scheduler. Every member site has to instantiate these scheduling services. LSs are responsible for managing and controlling the set of resources assigned to them. WA scheduler has two functional components including a Scheduling Manager (SM), which is an interface to LS, and a Grid Scheduler (GS), which connects to other SMs in the federated system. The connection topology between GSs is a fully connected graph structure.

MOSIX-Fed

MOSIX is a cluster management system that applies process migration to enable a loosely coupled Linux cluster to work like a shared memory parallel computer. Recently, it has been extended to support a Grid of clusters to form a single cooperative system (Barak et al., 2005). Basic feature of this cooperative environment includes automatic load balancing among participant clusters (owned by different owners) while preserving the complete autonomy. Proposed resource coupling scheme can be applied to form a campus or an enterprise Grid. MOSIX federation aims at hierarchical coupling of cluster resources under same administrative domain. Resource discovery in such an arrangement is facilitated by hierarchical information dissemination scheme that enables each node to be aware of the latest system wide state.

Sharp

Sharp (Fu et al., 2003) is a framework for secure distributed resource management. In Sharp, participant sites can trade their resources with peering partners or contribute them to a peer fed-eration according to the local site sharing policies. Sharp framework relies on bartering economy as the basis to exchange resources among various resource domains. A cryptographically signed object called Resource Tickets (RTs) is issued by each participating site. These RTs are exchanged between the participating sites for facilitating coordinated resource management. The fundamental resource management software entities in Sharp include site authority, service manager, and agents. These entities connect to each other based on a peer-to-peer network model.

Trader-Federation

Frerot et al. (Frerot et al., 2000) present a scheme called federation of distributed resource traders, which couples various autonomous resources or resource providers. A resource trader entity acts as an intermediary between consumers and providers. Every trader has local users, clients, and resources who are members of the local resource domain. Federation of traders enables the participants to trade resources at both local and the Internet levels. Various traders cooperate within the federation to maximize a trading function. The trader presents two interfaces, local interface for its local users and resource providers, while remote interface to other traders in the federation. The federation works as a market place where various traders can negotiate for QoS parameter (response time, accuracy) requested by the local users.

Tycoon

Tycoon (Lai et al., 2004) is a distributed market-based resource allocation system. Application scheduling and resource allocation in Tycoon is based on decentralized isolated auction mechanism. Every resource owner in the system runs its own auction for his local resources. In addition, auctions are held independently, thus clearly lacking any coordination. Tycoon system relies on centralized Service Location Services (SLS) for indexing resource auctioneers' information. Application level super-schedulers contact the SLS to gather information about various auctioneers in the system. Once this information is available, the super-schedulers (on behalf of users) issue bids for different resources. In this setting, the super-schedulers might end up bidding for small subset of resources while leaving the rest under-utilized.

Amazon EC2

Amazon Elastic Compute Cloud (EC2) (Amazon, 2010) is a web service that provides resizable compute capacity in the cloud environment. It's simple web service interface that provides the complete control of the leased computing resources to run on Amazon's computing environment. Resource provisioning is achieved in Amazon EC2 by utilizing three web services: Elastic Load Balancer, CloudWatch and Auto Scaling. Elastic Load Balancer is in charge of delivering incoming connections across multiple Amazon EC2 instances automatically. It continuously monitors the health conditions of instances, and re-route traffic from faulty instances to faultless instances within a single availability zone or across multiple zones. Whereas, CloudWatch, is responsible for monitoring cloud resources (i.e. Amazon EC2, Elastic Load Balancer) in real-time and provides information about the performance metrics related to the Amazon EC2 instances, such as resource utilization and network traffic.

Azure

Microsoft Windows Azure Platform (Nagy, 2010) is a cloud platform providing a wide range of Internet services that can be consumed from both on-premises environments and the Internet. It uses a specialized operating system, called Windows Azure, to run its Fabric Layer, which provisions and manages computing and storage resources for the applications running on top of Windows Azure. Azure Fabric Controller is a redundancy tolerance service designed for monitoring and maintaining machines/resources to host the applications that are created and stored in Windows Azure. Besides, it is also in charge of resource provisioning by supporting a declarative service model. Declarative service specifications is appointed in every application and the Fabric Controller looks through Azure Fabric to match resources that meet required demands of CPU, bandwidth, operating system and redundancy tolerance.

Eucalyptus

Eucalyptus Systems (Eucalyptus, 2009) is an open source software infrastructure for implementing public or private clouds on existing Enterprise IT and service provider infrastructure. Enterprise Eucalyptus provides capabilities, such as self-service provisioning, customized SLAs, cloud monitoring, metering, and support for auto-scaling, as a highly available cloud platform. It is composed of four controllers (Cloud Controller, Cluster Controller, Node Controller, and Storage Controller) to control the virtualization environment in a manner of centralized and hierarchical structure. These controllers are used for managing the underlying virtualized resources (servers, network, and storage), monitoring and scheduling Virtual Machine (VM) execution on specific nodes, hosting VMs, and interfacing with various storage systems (i.e. NFS, iSCSI).

CASE STUDY

Aneka Federation

Aneka Federation system logically connects topologically and administratively distributed Aneka Enterprise Grids as part of a single cooperative system. It uses a Distributed Hash Table (DHT), such as Pastry, Chord based Peer-to-Peer (P2P) network model for discovering and coordinating the provisioning of distributed resources in Aneka

Figure 4. Aneka Federation: (a) architecture, (b) layered design

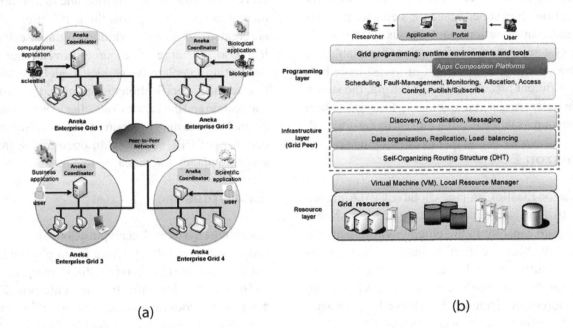

(a)   (b)

Scheduling

Grids. It also employs a novel resource provisioning technique that assigns the best possible resource sets for the execution of applications, based on their current utilization and availability in the system.

Aneka Federation utilizes the Grid-Federation model in regards to distributed resource organization, sharing and Grid networking. Grid-Federation is defined as a large scale resource sharing system that consists of a coordinated federation of distributed Aneka Enterprise Grids. Figure 4 shows the architecture and layered design of Aneka Federation resource sharing environment, consisting of Internet-wide distributed parallel resources in different Aneka Enterprise Grids. Every contributing site or Grid maintains its own Aneka Coordinator service and all these sites are connected through a DHT based P2P network (see Figure 4(a)).

The application scheduling and resource discovery in Aneka-Federation is facilitated by a specialized Grid Resource Management System known as Aneka Coordinator (AC). AC is composed of three software entities: Grid Resource Manager (GRM), LRMS and Grid Peer. The GRM component of AC exports a Grid site to the federation and is responsible for coordinating federation wide application scheduling and resource allocation. GRM is also responsible for scheduling locally submitted jobs in the federation using LRMS. Grid peer implements a DHT based P2P overlay (see Figure 4(b)) for enabling decentralized and distributed resource discovery supporting resources status lookups and updates across the federation. It also enables decentralized inter-AC collaboration for optimizing load-balancing and distributed resource provisioning.

Grid Peer accepts two types of objects from GAM regarding decentralized and coordinated scheduling: Claim and Ticket. A Claim object is sent by GAM to DHT overlay for locating the resources that match with user's application requirements and a Ticket is an update object sent by a Grid site, mentioning about the underlying resource conditions. These objects are also called coordination objects as they encapsulate the coordination logic in Aneka Federation.

Coordination

Aneka Federation uses a DHT (such as Chord, Pastry) based P2P overlay for handling resource discovery and scheduling coordination. The employment of DHT gives the system the ability to perform deterministic discovery of resources and produce controllable number of messages (by using selective broadcast approach) in comparison to using other One-to-All broadcast techniques such as JXTA.

Generally, resources hosted by a Grid site are identified by more than one attribute; thereby a Claim or a Ticket object is always multi-dimensional in nature. In order to support multi-dimensional data indexing (processor type, OS type, CPU speed) over DHT overlay, Aneka Federation leverages a spatial indexing technique, which is a variant of MX-CIF Quad tree. The indexing technique builds a multi-dimensional attribute space based on the Grid resource attributes, where each attribute represents a single dimension.

Objective Function

The main objective function employed in Aneka federation is to increase system's efficiency by balancing the load across the Grid resources in the federation, while minimizing overall user's application completion time by avoiding resource contention.

The load balancing decision is based on the principle that it should not lead to over-provisioning of resources at any Grid site. This mechanism leads to coordinated load-balancing across Aneka Federation and aids in achieving system-wide ob-

jective function, while at the same time preserving the autonomy of the participating Aneka Enterprise Grids. The process of coordinated load balancing is facilitated by implementing the P2P coordination space that takes the scheduling decisions.

Security

Aneka Federation uses distributed trust mechanism to ensure secured resource management across the federation. It utilizes a reputation based scheduling technique implemented by the coordination space in order to prune out the malicious and unwanted users from the system. Furthermore, the Aneka Container component of AC provides the base infrastructure that consists of services for persistence and security (authorization, authentication, and auditing).

CONCLUSION

In recent years, executing various scientific and business workflow applications in distributed systems (Grids and Clouds) has become a common practice. The inherent complexity in workflows requires an execution environment that addresses issues, such as scalability, reliability, user support, and system openness. However, the traditional centralized system for managing these workflows cannot satisfy these requirements. Thus, we can leverage the decentralized systems and technologies to achieve a better solution, given the nature of application environment.

Realizing an efficient, scalable, and robust Relational Database Management System (RDBMS) based on decentralized Grid and Cloud systems is an interesting future research problem. Fundamental to decentralized RDBMS is the development of distributed algorithms for: (i) query processing; (ii) data consistency, integrity; and (iii) transaction atomicity, durability, and isolation. First step in designing a decentralized RDBMS is to partition the relational tuple space across a set of distributed storage resources in the system. The data partition strategy should be such that the query workload is uniformly distributed while efficiently utilizing the resources computational and network bandwidth capability.

Moreover, research in these challenging domains of decentralized workflow management and RDMS is still in early stage. We believe that applying decentralized technologies for efficient and reliable management of workflows and storage will be an area of great interest in the coming years.

REFERENCES

Amazon. (2008). *Elastic compute cloud*. Retrieved November 15, 2010, from http:// www.amazon.com/ ec2

Assuncao, M. D., Venugopal, S., & Buyya, R. (2008, June). Intergrid: A case for internetworking islands of grids. *Concurrency and Computation*, *20*(8), 997–1024. doi:10.1002/cpe.1249

Auyoung, A., Chun, B., Snoeren, A., & Vahdat, A. (2004, October). Resource allocation in federated distributed computing infrastructures. In *Proceedings of the 1ˢᵗ Workshop on Operating System and Architectural Support for the On-demand IT Infrastructure*, Boston, USA.

Barak, A., Shiloh, A., & Amar, L. (2005, May). An organizational grid of federated mosix clusters. In *Proceedings of the 5ᵗʰ IEEE/ACM International Symposium on Cluster Computing and the Grid (CCGRID)*, Cardiff, UK.

Butt, A. R., Zhang, R., & Hu, Y. C. (2003). A self-organizing flock of condors. In *Proceedings of the ACM/IEEE Conference on Supercomputing*, CA, USA.

Durschel, P. (2006, June). *The renaissance of decentralized systems*. Keynote talk at the 15ᵗʰ IEEE International Symposium on High Performance Distributed Computing, Paris, France.

Eucalyptus. (2009, August). *Open-source cloud computing infrastructure - An overview*. Retrieved from http:// www.eucalyptus.com/ whitepapers

Foster, I., & Kesselman, C. (1997). Globus: A metacomputing infrastructure toolkit. *The International Journal of Supercomputer Applications*, *11*(2), 15–128.

Frerot, C. D., Lacroix, M., & Guyennet, H. (2000, August). Federation of resource traders in objects-oriented distributed systems. In *Proceedings of the International Conference on Parallel Computing in Electrical Engineering*, Quebec, Canada.

Fu, Y., Chase, J., Chun, B., Schwab, S., & Vahdat, A. (2003). SHARP: An architecture for secure resource peering. In *Proceedings of the 19ᵗʰ ACM Symposium on Operating Systems Principles*, NY, USA.

Gong, L. (2001). JXTA: A network programming environment. *IEEE Internet Computing*, *5*(3), 88–95. doi:10.1109/4236.935182

Lai, K., Huberman, B. A., & Fine, L. (2004). *Tycoon: A distributed market-based resource allocation system. Technical Report*. USA: HP Labs.

Nagy, S. (2010). *The azure fabric controller*. Retrieved November 15, 2010, from http://azure.snagy.name/blog/?p=89

Oppenheimer, D., Albrecht, J., Vahdat, A., & Patterson, D. (2008). Design and implementation trade-offs for wide-area resource discovery. *ACM Transactions on Internet Technology*, *8*(4), 18.

Ranjan, R., & Buyya, R. (2009, July). Decentralized overlay for federation of enterprise clouds . In Li, K. C. (Eds.), *Handbook of research on scalable computing technologies*. Hershey, PA: IGI Global.

Ranjan, R., Harwood, A., & Buyya, R. (2006). SLA-based coordinated superscheduling scheme for computational grids. In *Proceedings of the 8th IEEE International Conference on Cluster Computing,* Barcelona, Spain.

Rowstron, A., & Druschel, P. (2001). Pastry: Scalable, decentralized object location, and routing for large-scale peer-to-peer systems. In *Proceedings of the IFIP/ACM International Conference on Distributed Systems Platforms,* Heidelberg, Germany.

Smith, R. G. (1988). The contract net protocol: High-level communication and control in a distributed problem solver. In Lenat, D. B. (Ed.), *Distributed artificial intelligence* (pp. 357–366). San Francisco, CA: Morgan Kaufman Publishers.

Weissman, J. B., & Grimshaw, A. (1996). Federated model for scheduling in wide-area systems. In *Proceedings of the 5th IEEE International Symposium on High Performance Distributed Computing,* NY, USA.

KEY TERMS AND DEFINITIONS

Aneka Federation: The Aneka Federation integrates numerous small scale Aneka Enterprise Grid services and nodes that are distributed over multiple control and enterprise domains as parts of a single coordinated resource leasing abstraction.

Cloud Computing: It is a market-oriented distributed computing paradigm consisting of a collection of inter-connected and virtualized computers that are dynamically provisioned and presented as one or more unified computing resources based on service-level agreements established through negotiation between the service provider and consumers.

Coordination: The effectiveness of a distributed computing system often depends on the level of coordination among the distributed components of the system. Lack of coordination among the components may result in communication overhead that eventually degrades the performance of the system.

Decentralization: A distributed system configuration is considered to be decentralized if none of the components in the system are more important than the others, in case that one of the component fails, then it is neither more nor less harmful to the system than caused by the failure of any other component in the system.

Distributed Systems: A distributed system consists of a collection of autonomous computers that are connected and communicated through computer network and distribution middleware, which enable computers to coordinate their activities and share resources in the system, so that users perceive the system as an integrated single computing facility.

Grid Computing: Grid computing enables the sharing, selection, and aggregation of geographically distributed heterogeneous computational and storage resources, which are under the control of different sites or domains.

P2P Computing: Peer-to-Peer (P2P) computing is a distributed application architecture that distributes the tasks or workloads among the available peers/nodes in the network, where each peer is equally privileged and collaborate with others. The term, P2P implies that either peer can initiate a session and has equal responsibility.

Scheduling: In a distributed computing system, scheduling is a process of finding the efficient mapping of tasks in an application to the suitable resources in the system so that the execution can be completed with the satisfaction of objective functions, such as execution time minimization as specified by the users.

About the Contributors

Al-Sakib Khan Pathan received Ph.D. degree in Computer Engineering in 2009 from Kyung Hee University, South Korea. He received B.Sc. degree in Computer Science and Information Technology from Islamic University of Technology (IUT), Bangladesh in 2003. He is currently an Assistant Professor at Computer Science department in International Islamic University Malaysia (IIUM), Malaysia. Till June 2010, he served as an Assistant Professor at Computer Science and Engineering department in BRAC University, Bangladesh. Prior to holding this position, he worked as a Researcher at Networking Lab, Kyung Hee University, South Korea till August 2009. His research interest includes wireless sensor networks, network security, and e-services technologies. He is a recipient of several awards/best paper awards and has several publications in these areas. He has served as a Chair, Organizing Committee Member, and Technical Program Committee member in numerous international conferences/workshops like HPCS, ICA3PP, WiMob, HPCC, IDCS, et cetera. He is currently serving as the Editor-in-Chief of IJIDCS, an Area Editor of IJCNIS, Associate Editor of IASTED/ACTA Press IJCA, Guest Editor of some special issues of Elsevier's and Springer's journals, and Editor of two books. He also serves as a referee of a few renowned journals such as IEEE Transactions on Dependable and Secure Computing (IEEE TDSC), IEEE Transactions on Vehicular Technology (IEEE TVT), IEEE Communications Letters, Journal of Communications and Networks (JCN), Elsevier's Computer Communications, Computer Standards and Interfaces, IOS Press JHSN, EURASIP JWCN, etc. He is a member of Institute of Electrical and Electronics Engineers (IEEE), IEEE Communications Society (IEEE ComSoc), IEEE ComSoc Bangladesh Chapter, and several other international organizations.

Mukaddim Pathan is a Research Scientist at the Commonwealth Scientific and Industrial Research Organization (CSIRO), the national government body of scientific research in Australia. He also holds the position of an Adjunct Lecturer at the Australian National University. Previously, he was a Research Fellow at the Cloud Computing and Distributed Systems (CLOUDS) Lab of the University of Melbourne, Australia. He holds a PhD in Computer Science and Software Engineering from the University of Melbourne. His research interests include data management, resource allocation, load balancing, and coordination policies in wide-area distributed systems such as content delivery networks, cloud computing, and sensor networks. He is one of the developers of MetaCDN that leverages the capabilities of existing storage Clouds for high performance content delivery. He is the editor of the book Content Delivery Networks, Lecture Notes in Electrical Engineering, Vol. 9, Springer-Verlag, Germany. He has authored and co-authored a number of research papers in internationally recognized journals and conferences. He is involved in the organization of the UPGRADE-CN and IDCS workshops and is a PC member of several international conferences. He has edited a few research issues in reputed international journals and also serves as the reviewer of a few renowned journals such as IEEE Transactions on Circuits and Systems for Video Technology (TCSVT), International Journal of Management Science (OMEGA), Journal of Network and Computer Applications (JNCA), Computer Communications, Computer Networks, Journal of Systems and Software, and IEEE Software. He is a member of IEEE, IEEE computer society, and ACM. For further information, please visit: http://www.ict.csiro.au/staff/mukaddim.pathan

Hae Young Lee received his Ph.D. in Computer Engineering and B.S. in Electrical and Computer Engineering from Sungkyunkwan University, South Korea, in 2009 and 2003, respectively. He is currently a Senior Member of Engineering Staff, CPS Research Team, Electronics and Telecommunications Research Institut (ETRI), South Korea. His research interests include wireless sensor networks, cyber-physical systems, modeling & simulation, and intelligent systems. He is a Member of IEEE, SCS, and IEICE.

* * *

Tamer AbuHmed received B.Eng. degree in computer engineering from the University of Gaza, in 2005. He is now a PhD student in the graduate school of Information Technology and Telecommunication at Inha University. His research interests include networks security, data privacy, and cryptography.

Nancy Alonistioti has a B.Sc. degree and a PhD degree in Informatics and Telecommunications (Dept. of Informatics and Telecommunications, University of Athens). She has working experience as senior researcher and project manager in the Dept. of Informatics and Telecommunications at University of Athens. She has participated in several national and European projects, (CTS, SS#7, ACTS RAINBOW, EURESCOM, MOBIVAS, ANWIRE, E²R, LIAISON, E³, SELFNET, SACRA, CONSERN, UNIVER-SELF etc) and has experience as Project and Technical manager of the IST-MOBIVAS, IST-ANWIRE, ICT-SELFNET projects, which had a focus on reconfigurable mobile systems, cognitive mobile networks and FI. She has served as PMT member and WP Leader of the FP6 IST- E²R project. She is co-editor and author in "Software defined radio, Architectures, Systems and Functions," published by John Wiley in May 2003. She has served as lecturer in University of Piraeus and she has recently joined the faculty of Dept. Informatics and Telecommunications of Univ. of Athens. She is TPC member in many conferences in the area of mobile communications and mobile applications for systems and networks beyond 3G. She has over 55 publications in the area of mobile communications, reconfigurable, cognitive and autonomic systems and networks, and Future Internet.

Mohammed Jubaer Arif has focused his research on distributed computing and Internet applications. His main interest is in the development of new algorithms for communications between distributed Internet nodes that are expected to provide better user experiences when compared with traditional algorithms. Arif received his Doctor of Philosophy (PhD) degree in Computer Science from The University of Melbourne. He also has a Bachelor's degree in Computer Science from the Independent University, Bangladesh (IUB). Arif has more than five years of working experience in computing industry as software engineer and consultant. He is the founder of Daily Positive (D+) wiki, a platform to discover and share positive information from all the countries of the world.

Laurent Bobelin is an Associate Professor in Polytech Grenoble at the University Joseph Fourier at Grenoble, France. His research interests include Grid computing, network topology discovery, and network impact on distributed applications. He obtained his M.S. from Université Claude Bernard Lyon 1 in 1999 (Lyon, France). He held an INRIA research engineer position during 2000 at LIP laboratory (ENS Lyon, France), and from 2001 to 2008 held a research and development engineer position in a private company, being involved in Grid projects funded by European Community and France such as DataGrid, EGEE, EGEE II, EleGI, GRaSP, and e-Toile. He obtained his PhD in 2008 from Université de La Méditerranée (Marseille, France), and held a post-doctoral researcher position in LIP in 2009 and a post-doctoral researcher position at CNRS Computing Center of IN2P3 in 2010.

Rajkumar Buyya is a Professor of Computer Science and Software Engineering; and Director of the Cloud Computing and Distributed Systems (CLOUDS) Laboratory at the University of Melbourne, Australia. He received BE and ME in Computer Science and Engineering from Mysore and Bangalore Universities in 1992 and 1995 respectively; and Doctor of Philosophy (PhD) from Monash University, Melbourne, Australia in 2002. He has authored over 220 publications and three books. The books on emerging topics that Dr. Buyya edited include, High Performance Cluster Computing (Prentice Hall, USA, 1999) and Market-Oriented Grid and Utility Computing (Wiley, 2008). Dr. Buyya has contributed to the creation of high-performance computing and communication system software for Indian PARAM supercomputers. He received "Research Excellence Award" from the University of Melbourne for productive and quality research in computer science and software engineering in 2005. The Journal of Information and Software Technology in Jan 2007 issue, based on an analysis of ISI citations, ranked Dr. Buyya's work (published in Software: Practice and Experience Journal in 2002) as one among the "Top 20 cited Software Engineering Articles in 1986-2005". He received the Chris Wallace Award for Outstanding Research Contribution 2008 from the Computing Research and Education Association of Australasia, CORE, which is an association of university departments of computer science in Australia and New Zealand. Dr. Buyya served as the first elected Chair of the IEEE Technical Committee on Scalable Computing (TCSC) during 2005-2007. In recognition of these dedicated services to computing community over a decade, President of the IEEE Computer Society, USA presented Dr. Buyya a "Distinguished Service Award" in 2008.

Carlos T. Calafate graduated with honors in electrical and computer engineering from the University of Oporto, Oporto, Portugal, in 2001. He is currently an Associate Professor at the Technical University of Valencia, where he also received his Ph.D. degree in Computer Engineering in 2006. He is a member of the Computer Networks Group (GRC). His research interests include mobile and pervasive computing, security and QoS on wireless networks, and video coding and streaming.

Juan Carlos Cano obtained the M.Sc. and Ph.D. degrees in Computer Science from the Technical University of Valencia (UPV), Valencia, Spain, in 1994 and 2002, respectively. He is now an Associate Professor with the Department of Computer Engineering, UPV. From 1995 to 1997, he worked as a programming analyst at IBM's manufacturing division in Valencia. His current research interests include power aware routing protocols, quality of service for mobile ad hoc networks, and pervasive computing.

Valeria Cardellini is Assistant Professor in the Department of Computer Science, Systems and Production of the University of Roma "Tor Vergata," Italy. She received her PhD degree in computer science in 2001 and her Laurea degree in computer engineering in 1997, both from the University of Roma "Tor Vergata." She was a visiting researcher at IBM T.J. Watson Research Center in 1999. Her research interests are in the field of distributed computing systems, with special emphasis on large-scale systems and services based on Internet and the Web. On these subjects she has (co)authored more than 50 papers in international journals, book chapters, and conference proceedings. She has been co-chair of AAA-IDEA 2009, has served as a member of program and organizing committees of international conferences on Web and performance analysis areas, and serves as frequent reviewer for various well-known international journals. She is a member of ACM and IEEE.

Emiliano Casalicchio, Ph.D., is a researcher at the University of Roma "Tor Vergata," Italy. Since 1998 his research is mainly focused on large scale distributed systems, with a specific emphasis on performance oriented design of algorithms and mechanisms for resource allocation and management. Domains of interest have been locally distributed Web servers, enterprise, Grid, and mobile systems, Service Oriented Architectures, and Cloud systems. He is author of about 70 publications on international journals and conferences, and serves as reviewer for international journals and conferences (IEEE, ACM, Elsevier, Springer). His research is and has been founded by the Italian Ministry of Research, CNR, ENEA, the European Community, and private companies. Moreover, he is and has been involved in many Italian and EU research projects, among which are PERF, CRESCO, MIA, MOTIA, D-ASAP, MOBI-DEV, AEOLUS, DELIS, and SMS.

Homero Toral Cruz was born in Oaxaca, Mexico, in 1980. He received the B.S. degree in electronic engineering from the "Instituto Tecnologico de la Laguna," Torreon, Coahuila Mexico in 2002, the M.S. and Ph.D. degrees in Electrical Engineering, Telecommunication Section from the "Centro de Investigacion y Estudios Avanzados del I.P.N. (CINVESTAV, I.P.N.)", Guadalajara, Jalisco, Mexico, in 2006 and 2010, respectively. He has been Research Assistant of the Electrical Engineering Department, Telecommunication Section at CINVESTAV, I.P.N. Presently, he is a Professor of the University of Quintana Roo, in Mexico. His research interests include VoIP systems, quality of service in IP networks, and Internet traffic modeling.

Arnoldo Díaz received the B.S. and M.S. degrees in Centro de Enseñanza Técnica y Superior (CETYS University), México. He received his Ph.D. degree in Computer Engineering from the Technical University of Valencia in 2006. He works as Professor in the Department of Computer Engineering at Mexicali Institute of Technology in México since 1992.

Qiang Duan is currently an Assistant Professor of Information Science and Technology at the Pennsylvania State University Abington College. His research interests include data communications, computer networking, network virtualization, next generation Internet, service-oriented architecture, Cloud and Grid computing, and hardware / software design and performance analysis for communications and networking systems. Dr. Duan has more than 40 publications, including book chapters, journal articles, and refereed conference papers. He has served as a TPC member, TPC chair, session chair, and reviewer for numerous international conferences and serves on the editorial boards of several international journals.

Dr. Duan received his Ph.D. in Electrical Engineering from the University of Mississippi in 2003. He holds a M.S. degree in telecommunications and a B.S. degree in Electrical and Computer Engineering.

Giancarlo Fortino is an Associate Professor of Computer Science at the Department of Electronics, Informatics and Systems (DEIS) of the University of Calabria, Italy. He received a PhD in Computer Engineering from the University of Calabria in 2000. He has been a visiting researcher at the International Computer Science Institute (ICSI), Berkeley (CA), USA, in 1997 and 1999. His research interests include distributed computing and networks, agent oriented software engineering, wireless sensor networks, and streaming content distribution networks. He is author of more than 130 papers in international journals, conferences, and books, and currently serves on the editorial board of the Journal of Networks and Computer Applications (Elsevier). He is also co-founder and president of SenSysCal S.r.l., a spin-off of University of Calabria, whose mission is the development of innovative systems and services based on wireless sensor networks for healthcare, energy management and structural health.

Lisandro Zambenedetti Granville is an Associate Professor at the Institute of Informatics of the Federal University of Rio Grande do Sul (UFRGS), Brazil. He received his M.Sc. and Ph.D. degrees, both in Computer Science, from UFRGS in 1998 and 2001, respectively. From September 2007 to August 2008 he was a visiting researcher at the University of Twente, The Netherlands, with the Design and Analysis of Communication Systems group. He has served as a TPC Co-Chair for IFIP/IEEE DSOM 2007, IFIP/IEEE NOMS 2010, and TPC Vice-Chair for CNSM 2010. He is also Technical Program Chair of IEEE Communications Society Committee on Network Operations and Management (CNOM). His areas of interest include policy-based network management, P2P-based services and applications, and management of virtualization for the Future Internet.

Antonio Guerrieri, is a PhD Student in Computer Engineering at the University of Calabria, Italy. He received his Bachelor and Master degrees in Computer Engineering from the University of Calabria in 2003 and 2007, respectively. He has been an intern researcher at Telecom Italia Sparkle of North America (Berkeley, CA, USA) in 2007, and at the University College Dublin, in the Clarity Centre, in 2009 and 2010. His research interests are focused on design methods for high-level programming of wireless sensor networks. He is involved in several research projects on wireless sensor networks such as SPINE, BMF, MAPS, and FP7 CONET. He is a co-founder of SenSysCal S.r.l., a spin-off of University of Calabria, whose mission is the development of innovative systems and services based on wireless sensor networks.

Guangjie Han is currently an Associate Professor of Department of Information & Communication System at the Hohai University, China. He is also the visiting research scholar of Osaka University from Oct. 2010 to Oct. 2011. He finished the work as a Post doctor at the Department of Computer Science at the Chonnam National University, Korea, in February 2008. He received his Ph.D. degree in Department of Computer Science from Northeastern University, Shenyang, China, in 2004. He has published over 80 papers in related international conferences and journals. He has served as editor of ANC and IJIDCS. He has served as Co-Chair for more than 10 various international conferences/workshops and TPC member of more than 30 conferences. He has served as reviewer of more than 20 journals. His current research interests are security and trust management, localization and tracking, and cooperative computing for Wireless Sensor Networks. He is a member of ACM and IEEE.

Takahiro Hara received the B.E, M.E, and Dr.E. degrees in Information Systems Engineering from Osaka University, Osaka, Japan, in 1995, 1997, and 2000, respectively. Currently, he is an Associate Professor of the Department of Multimedia Engineering, Osaka University. He has published more than 100 international journal and conference papers in the areas of databases, mobile computing, peer-to-peer systems, WWW, and wireless networking. He served and is serving as a Program Chair of IEEE International Conference on Mobile Data Management (MDM'06 and 10) and IEEE International Conference on Advanced Information Networking and Applications (AINA'09). He guest edited IEEE Journal on Selected Areas in Communications, Sp. Issues on Peer-to-Peer Communications and Applications. He was a PC Vice-chair of IEEE ICDE'05, IEEE ICPADS'05, IEEE NBiS'09, CSA-09, and IEEE AINA'06, 07, 08, and 10. He served and is serving as PC member of various international conferences such as IEEE ICNP, WWW, DASFAA, ACM MobiHoc, and ACM SAC. His research interests include distributed databases, peer-to-peer systems, mobile networks, and mobile computing systems. He is IEEE Senior Member and a member of four other learned societies including ACM.

Bing He is a Ph.D. candidate in computer science at the Center for Distributed and Mobile Computing in the Department of Computer Science, University of Cincinnati. His current research interests include architecture design, performance optimization and security of wireless mesh networks, and resource allocation in 802.16 WiMAX network. He received his B.S. degree in communication engineering and M.S. degree in signal and information processing from Northern Jiaotong University of China. He has been an engineer with Honeywell Technology Solutions Lab in China.

Lin He graduated as a master student in the department of Computer and Radio Communication Engineering, Korea University, Korea. She received her B.S. degree in College of Science, Jilin Institute of Chemical Technology, China in 2007. Her research field is ubiquitous computing, especially the security aspect of wireless sensor networks, RFID, security, and ad hoc networks. She wrote several papers on these fields.

Tevfik Kosar is an Associate Professor in the Department of Computer Science in the State University of New York at Buffalo. He holds a B.S. degree in Computer Engineering from Bogazici University, Istanbul, Turkey and an M.S. degree in Computer Science from Rensselaer Polytechnic Institute, Troy, NY. Dr. Kosar has received his Ph.D. degree in Computer Science from University of Wisconsin-Madison. He is the primary designer and developer of the Stork distributed data scheduling system and recipient of prestigious NSF CAREER Award for his work in this area.

Apostolos Kousaridas received his B.Sc. degree in Informatics and his M.Sc. degree in Information Systems from the Department of Informatics at Athens University of Economics and Business. He has worked as a software engineer for the "Greek Research and Technology Network" (GRNET) on the "GEANT2 Advance Multi-domain Provisioning System (AMPS) project" as well as for the department of Information Systems Design at the Hellenic Railways Organization. He holds an "Ericsson Award of Excellence in Telecommunications" for his M.Sc. thesis and a performance scholarship from the Greek

National Scholarship Foundation for the academic year 2002-2003. Since mid-2005, he serves as a researcher at the University of Athens, and has worked in the context of E^2R, E^2R II, E^3, Self-NET and UNIVERSELF EU-funded projects. His main areas of interest are complex self-organizing networks, network economics, e-commerce, and mobile services. He serves as a University of Athens delegate at the ETSI Autonomic Future Internet (AFI) Industry Standardization Group (ISG). He is PhD candidate in the Department of Informatics & Telecommunications at the University of Athens and his field of study is cognitive and adaptive communications systems.

Kai Lin is an Assistant Professor at the School of Computer Science and Technology, Dalian University of Technology. He received his B.S. degree in the School of Electronic and Information Engineering, Dalian University of Technology, Dalian, China in 2001, and obtained M.S. and PhD degree from the College of Information Science and Engineering, Northeastern University in 2005 and 2008, respectively. His research interests include wireless networks, ubiquitous computing, and embedded technology. He has published over 40 papers in related conferences, journals, and books.

Carlos Lino received the B.S. and MS degrees in Computer Engineering from Leon Institute of Technology, México, in 1996 and 1999. Since 2008 he has been a Ph.D. student in Computer Engineering at Technical University of Valencia in Spain. He is working on a Ph.D. thesis about applications with wireless personal area networks for low rates. He works as professor in the Departament of Computer Engineering at Leon Institute of Technology since 1996.

Panagis Magdalinos is a researcher in the SCAN group of Lecturer Nancy Alonistioti, in the Department of Informatics and Telecommunications of the University of Athens (UoA). In 2010 he acquired his PhD diploma entitled "Linear and Non Linear Dimensionality Reduction for Distributed Knowledge Discovery" from the Department of Informatics of the Athens University of Economics and Business (AUEB) under the supervision of Associate Professor Michalis Vazirgiannis. He also holds an M.Sc. in Information Systems from AUEB and a B.Sc. degree in Informatics and Telecommunications from UoA. He has been working as a research associate for the SCAN group since 2004 and has participated in a number of European research projects, namely E^2R, E^2R II, E3, and SelfNET. His research interests focus on supervised and unsupervised knowledge extraction from distributed data collections (i.e., learning and mining in distributed environments, parallel data mining, etc.)

Pietro Manzoni (M'96) received the M.S. Degree in computer science from the Universita degli Studi of Milan, Italy, in 1989 and the PhD degree in computer science from the Polytechnic University of Milan in 1995. He is currently an Associate Professor with the Department of Computer Engineering, the Universidad Politécnica de Valencia, Spain. His research activity is related to wireless network protocol design, modeling, and implementation.

Dionatan Teixeira Mattjie is an M.Sc. student in Computer Science at the Graduate Program in Computing (PPGC) of the Federal University of Rio Grande do Sul (UFRGS), Brazil. He received a B.Sc. degree in Information Systems from the Lutheran University of Brazil (ULBRA) in 2006. He currently works in the virtualization management as IT Security & Infrastructure Supervisor. His areas of interest include virtualization, virtualization management, network & systems management, P2P computing, and security management technologies.

Cristina Melchiors is a Ph.D. student in Computer Science at the Graduate Program in Computing (PPGC) of the Federal University of Rio Grande do Sul (UFRGS), Brazil. She currently works on cooperative and distributed network management using P2P technologies. She received a B.Sc. degree in Informatics from the Pontifical Catholic University of Rio Grande do Sul (PUCRS) in 1995, and a M.Sc. degree in Computer Science from Federal University of Rio Grande do Sul (UFRGS) in 1999. Her main areas of interest include cooperative network management, distributed network management, P2P computing, fault management, artificial intelligence applied to network management, and case-based reasoning.

Abedelaziz Mohaisen is a Ph.D. student at the University of Minnesota Twin Cities, where he works on systems security, data privacy, and measurements. He holds a Master's of science in computer science from the University of Minnesota Twin Cities, a Master's of engineering in information and telecommunication engineering from Inha University and a Bachelor's of Engineering in computer engineering from the University of Gaza.

Shojiro Nishio received the B.E., M.E., and Ph.D. degrees from Kyoto University, Kyoto, Japan. Since August 1992, he has been a Full Professor at Osaka University. He served as the Founding Director of the Cybermedia Center of Osaka University from April 2000 to August 2003, and served as the Dean of the Graduate School of Information Science and Technology of this university from August 2003 to August 2007. He has been serving as a Trustee and Vice President of Osaka University since August 2007. He also acted as the Program Director in the Area of Information and Networking, Ministry of Education, Culture, Sports, Science and Technology (MEXT), Japan from April 2001 to March 2008.

DaeHun Nyang received the B.Eng. degree in electronic engineering from Korea Advanced Institute of Science and Technology, M.S. and Ph.D. degrees in computer science from Yonsei University, Korea on 1994, 1996, and 2000 respectively. He has been a senior member of engineering staff of Electronics and Telecommunications Research Institute, Korea from 2000 to 2003. Since 2003, he has been an Assistant Professor of the graduate school of Information Technology and Telecommunication at Inha University, Korea. He is also a consultant for Korean Information Security Agency, member of board of directors and editorial board of Korean Institute of Information Security and Cryptology. Dr. Nyang's research interests include cryptography and information security, privacy, biometrics and their applications to authentication and public key cryptography. Also, he is interested in the security of WLAN, RFID, WSN, and MANET.

Gregory O'Hare was the Head of the Department of Computer Science at University College Dublin (UCD) 2001-2004. Prior to joining UCD he has been on the faculty of the University of Central Lancashire and the University of Manchester. He has published over 300 publications and 6 books. His research interests are in the areas of distributed artificial intelligence and multi-agent systems (MAS), and mobile & ubiquitous computing, autonomic systems and wireless sensor networks. In 2003 he received the prestigious Cooperative Information Agents (CIA) System Innovation Award for ACCESS: An Agent Architecture for Ubiquitous Service Delivery. O'Hare is a member of the ACM, AAAI and a Chartered Engineer. He also held a prestigious Science Foundation Ireland (SFI) Principal Investigator Award 2003-2007. He is one of the Principal Investigators and founders of the Science Foundation Ireland funded Centre for Science and Engineering Technologies (CSET) entitled CLARITY: The Centre for Sensor Web Technologies (2008-2013).

André Panisson received the MSc in Computer Science at the Federal University of Rio Grande do Sul (Brazil) in 2007, under the supervision of Lisandro Granville, and the subject of his thesis was P2P-Based Network Management. He is currently a Ph.D. student at the Informatics Department, University of Turin (Italy). His topics of interest are mobile and complex networks, peer-to-peer systems, information spreading, and recommendation systems. He works in collaboration with the Complex Networks and Systems Group at the Institute for Scientific Interchange in Turin, Italy.

Cuong (Charlie) Pham is a PhD student in the Department of Computer Science at the University of Massachusetts at Boston and a research member of the Network Information Systems Laboratory (NISLab). He received a BS degree in Computer Science from Bowman Technical State University in Moscow, Russia in 2007. His research interests are P2P networks and wireless sensor networks. He was a research intern working on distributed storage networks at EMC (USA) during summer of 2010. He received a Student Travel Award from the NSF and a Research Excellence Award from the Department of Computer Science (UMass Boston), both in 2009.

Akbar Ghaffarpour Rahbar is an Associate Professor in Electrical Engineering department at Sahand University of Technology, Sahand New Town, Tabriz, Iran. Dr. Rahbar received his B.Sc. and M.Sc. degrees in computer hardware and computer architecture both from Iran University of Science and Technology, Tehran, Iran, in 1992 and 1995 respectively. He received his Ph.D. degree in computer science from University of Ottawa, Canada in 2006. He is the director of Computer Networks Research Lab at Sahand University. His main research interests are optical networks, optical packet switching, scheduling, PON, IPTV, VANET, network modeling, analysis and performance evaluation, the results of which can be found in over 60 technical papers (see http://ee.sut.ac.ir/showcvdetail.aspx?id=13).

Mustafizur Rahman is an Endeavour Research Fellow at the Institute of High Performance Computing, A*STAR, Singapore. He received BSc degree in Computer Science and Engineering from Bangladesh University of Engineering and Technology. He has recently completed PhD degree from Department of Computer Science and Software Engineering at the University of Melbourne. His research interests include workflow scheduling and resource management in Grid/Cloud computing systems as well as fault-tolerance and load balancing in P2P and self-managing systems. He has been actively engaged in the research and development projects of CLOUDS Lab at the University of Melbourne. He has authored and co-authored several research papers in internationally recognized journals and conferences. He is a member of IEEE, IEEE computer society, and ACM. He has been involved in the organization of several international workshops and conferences. He also serves as the reviewer of renowned journals such as Future Generation Computer Systems (FGCS) and Concurrency & Computation: Practice & Experience (CCPE).

Rajiv Ranjan is a Senior Research Associate in the School of Computer Science and Engineering, University of New South Wales (UNSW). He has a PhD in Computer Science and Software Engineering from the University of Melbourne, which was awarded in 2009. He also completed Bachelor of Computer Engineering from North Gujarat University, India, in 2002. Dr. Ranjan is broadly interested in the emerging areas of cloud, Grid, and service computing. The main goal of his current research is to advance the fundamental understanding and state of the art of provisioning and delivery of application services in large, heterogeneous, uncertain, and evolving distributed systems. Dr. Ranjan has 26 refereed publications, in journals with high impact factor (according to JCR published by ISI), in proceedings of IEEE's/ACM's premier conferences and in books published by leading publishers. His h-index is 8, with a total citation count of 270. Dr. Ranjan served as Guest Editor for leading distributed systems and software engineering journals and recently joined the Editorial Board of International Journal of Information Technology, Communications and Convergence (Inderscience Publishers). He serves as the editor of IEEE TCSC Newsletter.

Ranga Reddy received his M.S. in Electrical Engineering from Stevens Institute of Technology in 2004. Ranga is involved in wireless communication standardization efforts within IEEE 802. He is a member in the 802.16 working group, and actively participates in the 802.16j and 802.16m task groups. Ranga is also a participant in the 802.22 working group activities. Since 2001 he has been working US Army Communications/Electronics Research & Development Engineering Center (CERDEC) at Fort Monmouth on various projects involving systems engineering, modeling & simulation efforts surrounding development and engineering of several communication technologies MANET, IPv6, & broadband wireless communications.

Joel J.P.C. Rodrigues [SM IEEE] is a Professor at the University of Beira Interior, Covilhã, Portugal, and Researcher at the Instituto de Telecomunicações, Portugal. He is the leader of NetGNA Research Group (http://netgna.it.ubi.pt). He is the Secretary of the IEEE ComSoc TCs on Communications Software and on e-health. He is the Editor-in-Chief of the International Journal of E-Health and Medical Communications. He was the General Chair and TPC Chair of several conferences (including IEEE ICC, IEEE GLOBECOM, IEEE CAMAD, SoftCOM, etc.), member of many TPCs and several editorial review boards. He has authored or co-authored over 130 papers in refereed international journals and conferences, a book, and book chapters. He is a licensed Professional Engineer and he is member of the ACM SIGCOMM, a member of the Internet Society, an IARIA Fellow, and a Senior Member of the IEEE.

Deni Torres Roman was born in Oriente, Cuba, in 1950. He received the Ph.D. degree in Telecommunications from the Technical University, Dresden, Germany in 1986. He is co-author of the book: Data Transmission. He received the Telecommunication Research Prize in 1993 from AHCIET Association. Since 1996 he is Professor and researcher at the Department of Electrical Engineering and Computer Sciences of CINVESTAV, I.P.N. His main research involves Internet traffic measurement and modeling, network quality of service, digital communication of medium and high speed, software and hardware design for telecommunications and modern telephony systems.

Antonio Ruzzelli is a research fellow team leader at the CLARITY centre for Sensor Web technologies at University College Dublin. His research investigates technologies to empower building energy-efficiency, usage prediction, smart energy metering, and wireless networking sensors. In 2010, he has won the Ireland Innovator award for major advances on intelligent energy-monitoring. During his career, Dr. Ruzzelli attracted significant funding which adds up to an excess of €7 Million in total projects cost from national and international funding agencies. He is currently the Principal Investigator on several FP7 projects in the Intelligent Buildings space. In the academic year 2008/09 he lectured COMP40680: Introduction to Sensor Systems at University College Dublin, School of Computer Science and Informatics. He received a 5-year Laurea degree in Electronic Engineering at the University of Ferrara (Italy) and PhD in Computer Science at the University College Dublin (Ireland). Previous work affiliations include University of Twente and Philips Research Eindhoven.

Carlos Raniery Paula dos Santos is a Ph.D. candidate in Computer Science at the Institute of Informatics of the Federal University of Rio Grande do Sul (UFRGS), where he also holds an M.Sc. (2008) degree in Computer Science. In 2005, he received degree in Telematics from the Federal Center of Technological Education of Ceará (CEFET-CE). From October 2004 to January 2006 he was a researcher at the Federal University of Ceará, with the Group of Computer Networks, Software Engineering and Systems (GREat). Currently he is a visiting researcher at the IBM T.J. Watson Research Center, USA, under supervision of Nikos Anerousis, head of the Service Engineering Research group. His main topics of interest include network management, Web services-based management, P2P-based systems, and Web 2.0/3.0 technologies.

Wen Shen is currently perusing his Master's degree from Department of Information & Communication Engineering at the Hohai University, China. He received his B.S. degree in Information & Communication Engineering from Hohai University, China, in 2008. His current research interests are trust management and routing security for Wireless Sensor Networks.

Lei Shu is a currently Specially Assigned Research Fellow in Department of Multimedia Engineering, Graduate School of Information Science and Technology, Osaka University, Japan. He received the B.Sc. degree in Computer Science from South Central University for Nationalities, China, 2002, and the M.Sc. degree in Computer Engineering from Kyung Hee University, Korea, 2005, and the PhD degree in Digital Enterprise Research Institute, NUIG, in 2010. He has published over 80 papers in related conferences, journals, and books. He had been awarded the MASS 2009 IEEE TCs Travel Grant and the Outstanding Leadership Award of EUC 2009 as Publicity Chair, Globecom 2010 Best Paper Award. He has served as Co-Chair for more than 30 various international conferences/workshops, and TPC member for more than 100 conferences. His research interests include semantic sensor networks, wireless sensor network, context awareness, and sensor network middleware. He is a member of IEEE.

Luca Silvestri is a Ph.D. student in Computer Engineering at the University of Roma "Tor Vergata," Italy. He received in 2009 the Laurea degree (Master degree) in Computer Engineering from the University of Roma "Tor Vergata." His research interests are in the field of performance oriented design, focusing particularly on cloud computing, service oriented computing, reactive and proactive monitoring of distributed systems, and service selection algorithms in SOA.

Liane Margarida Rockenbach Tarouco, PhD Electrical Eng. (USP-Brazil), is Full Professor at Federal University of Rio Grande do Sul in Porto Alegre, Brazil. She is Vice-Director at Interdisciplinary Center for Studies on Technology in Education. She is a researcher at Graduate Program in Computer Science at UFRGS, and author of book Computer Networks published by McGraw Hill (in Portuguese).

Duc A. Tran is an Assistant Professor in the Department of Computer Science at the UMass Boston, where he leads the Network Information Systems Laboratory (NISLab). He received a PhD in CS degree from the University of Central Florida (Orlando, Florida). Dr. Tran's interests are focused on data management and networking designs for decentralized networks. His work has resulted in research grants from the National Science Foundation and two Best Papers (ICCCN 2008, DaWak 1999). Dr. Tran has served as a Review Panelist for the NSF, Editor for the Journal on Parallel, Emergent, and Distributed Systems (2010-date), Guest-Editor for the Journal on Pervasive Computing and Communications (2009), TPC Co-Chair for CCNet 2010, GridPeer (2009, 2010, 2011), and IRSN 2009, TPC Vice-Chair for AINA 2007, and TPC member for 40+ international conferences.

Leopoldo Estrada Vargas was born in Jalisco, Mexico, in 1981. He received the B.S. degree in electronic engineering from the "Universidad de Guadalajara" and M.S. degree in electrical engineering from the CINVESTAV, I.P.N., Guadalajara, Jalisco, Mexico, in 2003 and 2007, respectively. He has been Research Assistant of the Electrical Engineering Department, Telecommunication Section at CINVESTAV, I.P.N. He is Ph.D. student at the Department of Electrical Engineering and Computer Sciences of CINVESTAV, I.P.N. His research interests include Internet traffic measurements and long memory stochastic processes.

Lei Wang is currently an Associate Professor with Dalian University of Technology. He received the B.S., M.S., and Ph.D. from Tianjin University, China, in 1995, 1998, and 2001, respectively. He was a Member of Technical Staff with Bell Labs Research China (2001-2004), a senior researcher at Samsung, South Korea (2004-2006), a research scientist in Seoul National University (2006-2007), and a research associate in Washington State University, Vancouver, WA, USA (2007-2008). His research interests include wireless ad hoc networks, sensor network, and embedded systems. He is a member of IEEE, ACM and a senior member of China Computer Federation (CCF).

Bin Xie received his MSc and PhD degrees (with honors) in Computer Science and Computer Engineering from the University of Louisville, Kentucky, USA, 2003 and 2006, respectively. He is currently the President of the InfoBeyond Technology LLC. He is the author of the books titled *Heterogeneous Wireless Networks- Networking Protocol to Security (VDM Publishing House: ISBN: 3836419270)*, and *Handbook/Encyclopedia of Ad Hoc and Ubiquitous Computing (World Scientific: ISBN-10: 981283348X)*. He has published 60+ papers in the IEEE conferences and journals. His research interests are focused on mobile computing, embedded wireless sensor networks, network security, and in particular, on the fundamental aspects of mobility management, performance evaluation, Internet/wireless infrastructure security, and network capacity. He is an IEEE senior member and the vice chair of the IEEE Computer Society Technical committee on Simulation (TCSIM). He serves as the program co-chair of IEEE HPCC-09 and received the Outstanding Leadership Award. He also is the program co-chair of CyberC from 2009 to 2011, QoS-Management 2011 workshop, ICICTA 2009, and CPSC2009. He was the TPC of many international conferences. He delivered keynote speeches for Cyberc 2010 and ICICTA 2008. He also is the editor of International Journal of Information Technology, Communications and Convergence (IJITCC).

Esma Yildirim has received her BS degree from Fatih University and MS degree from Marmara University Computer Engineering Departments in Istanbul, Turkey. She worked for one year in Avrupa Software Company for the Development of ERP Software. She also worked as a Lecturer in Fatih University Vocational School until 2006. She worked at the Center for Computation and Technology as a graduate research assistant until December 2010. She will graduate from Louisiana State University with a Ph.D. degree in Computer Science in December 2010. Her research interests are distributed computing, high-performance computing, and networks.

Sajjad Zare received his M.Sc degree in Information Technology (IT) in the Department of Electrical Engineering at Sahand University of Technology, Sahand New Town, Tabriz, Iran. Mr. Zare received his technician degree in computer software from Imam Khomeini international university, Qazvin, Iran in 2006 and B.Sc degree in computer software from Zanjan University, Zanjan, Iran in 2008. His main research interests are optical networks, scheduling, wireless networks, IPTV, and VOIP.

Yiying Zhang is currently a Vice-Professor in Shenyang Institute of Engineering. He received the B.E degree in Department of Computer Science of Northeast Normal University in China in 1996, and the M.E. degree in the College of Information Science and Engineering of Northeastern University in China in 2003, and the PhD degree in the College of Computer and Radio Communication Engineering of Korea University in Korea, in 2010. He has published over 30 papers in related conferences, journals. His research interests include wireless sensor network, embedded system, ad hoc network, RFID, and ubiquitous computing and security.

David Zhao completed his Bachelor Degree in Electric Engineer in the City College of City University of New York and Master Degree in Electronics Engineer from Stevens Institute of Technology, NJ, USA. He is currently a senior engineer at U.S Army Communications and Electronics Research and Development Center (CERDEC) at Fort Monmouth N.J. His work is to research, examine, and evaluate various commercial wireless technologies and products, and also to determine its adaptability for use in the military tactical environment.

Chuan Zhu is currently a lecturer of Department of Computer at Hohai University, China. He received the B.E., M.E., and Ph.D. degrees from Northeastern University, China, in 2009. His current research interests are coverage and connectivity for Wireless Sensor Networks and smart home.

Index